Management
A Critical Text

Liz Fulop

Associate Professor of Management, University of Wollongong

Stephen Linstead

*Associate Director (Research) and Research Professor of Management,
University of Sunderland*

First published 1999 by
MACMILLAN PRESS LTD
Houndmills, Basingstoke, Hampshire RG21 6XS
and London
Companies and representatives throughout the world

ISBN 0–333–77632–1 paperback

A catalogue record for this book is available from the British
Library.

10   9   8   7   6   5   4   3   2
08   07   06   05   04   03   02   01   00

Printed in Hong Kong

Contents

Preface

In 1992, Liz Fulop, Faye Frith and Harold Hayward collaboratively edited a book called *Management for Australian Business: A Critical Text.* The present book began as an attempt to update the content of that book for students of the next century. In the original preface the editors said:

> It goes without saying that there is nothing simple about management. There never was; nor should there be. Too much is at stake. This book is written with the firm conviction that to become a successful and clever manager involves mastering much more than a few simple 'recipes' or 'easy steps' for performing management functions … the function of a management textbook should be to equip managers with enduring skills and knowledge that will help them cope with the complexity and ambiguity that await them in their daily endeavours. The book places a premium on developing critical thinking and analytical capacities that can be successfully applied to any management situation … an understanding of management is not enhanced by uncritical 'one best way' approaches.

As we looked at the ideas that had animated the first book, what became strikingly obvious was, first, that taking such a critical approach to management was more important than ever and, second, that the market was no better served in this regard than it had been when the first book was written. But things had changed, and changed considerably. A focus on Australian business seemed parochial to the point of absurdity in the context of globalization. What managers of the future would need was an early exposure to ideas and cases from a number of cultures and contexts – the USA, Europe, and the Asia–Pacific in particular. Similarly, learning had moved so much to centre stage in the consideration of how organizations and managers could remain effective that it demanded more extensive and up-front consideration. Diversity as a topic was now more significant than it had ever been, and though all of the material in the book needed to be revisited in this light, the issue of gender could no longer be marginalized but demanded focused treatment. In addition, the growth of a concern with ethics, which was once an optional feature of most programmes, was increasingly being recognized as a foundational element of a critical approach to management.

As we reviewed what needed to be done, we came to realize that the first book, which we had felt was quite radical in its time, was looking more and more conservative – and we more critical than ever! What was needed was a rethinking of many of our assumptions and a reframing of some of the core issues – like power, leadership, motivation – that remain at the heart of studies of management. Some topics, such as interorganizational relations and teams, were so clearly a part of ways of working of the future, and could no longer be dismissed as transitory fashions, that they required proper treatment in their own right, and not as part of a broader and more synoptic consideration.

We had followed the collaborative approach of the original book, with a wider range of specialist international contributors, and as the earliest contributions came in, and we began to edit them, we realized that we had a book which was far more original in its approach than we had perhaps expected. We followed the path opened up – in particular by Robin Snell and Joanna Brewis – and returned to our other authors with a renewed challenge, but with a commitment to work with them to achieve our end of producing a text that was very different from the one they had been asked to write. They took up our offer and readers will note that one or other of us is credited on most of the chapters – and we hope that they will also recognize the benefits of that collaboration in the consistency of approach throughout the book as a whole.

The cases in this book are all substantial, which is connected with the fact that we chose to exemplify our approach to case analysis in the text rather than in an instructor's guide.

Thanks are due to all of our co-authors, for the hard work they put in, for the critical scrutiny they endured, and in some cases for putting up with phone calls that arrived in the middle of the night – one of the perils of collaborating to meet deadlines across time zones! Thanks are also due to our students on the MBA and BCom programmes at the University of Wollongong for their responses to the material in this book as we refined it in classes between 1995 and 1998. Leonie Kirchmajer was responsible for the background biblio-graphical research – which she did with exceptional efficiency and good humour. Barbara McGoldrick of the Department of Management at the University of Wollongong provided us with much needed administrative support throughout numerous drafts and revisions well beyond the call of duty. Lynne Read also pitched in when deadlines were looming. Lea Green typed most of the manuscript, and when disaster in the form of a computer virus struck, retyped most of it too. We can't express our gratitude sufficiently for Lea's unflap-pable support and good humour throughout the production of the book, and particularly during that period when everything seemed to be falling apart. Jennifer Coombs copy edited the book in record time, working late into the night and often taking corrections over the phone. She showed great patience and consideration when we were particularly testy.

We owe thanks to Peter Debus of Macmillan, who initially urged Liz to pursue a second edition of the first book, and then courageously accepted our proposal to produce a quite different one. We also thank Sue McGuinn, who took over the responsibility for the project just around the time the virus epidemic reached Wollongong, and must have wondered for a time whether a manuscript would ever appear, for her patience and diligence, and for her sensitivity in leaving us alone when we needed it.

Finally, it is often the case that when you collaborate on a major project with a colleague you haven't worked with very closely before, the stresses and strains of the process drive you even further apart. Sometimes, if you're fortunate, you come out of it with an enhanced respect for each other's talents and professionalism. And even more rarely, you discover a friendship that makes even the most torrid of labours a pleasure. We were very lucky in this regard, and we hope that some of the enjoyment we got from crafting these ideas together shows through the words on the page – and that you will enjoy reading the book too.

Liz Fulop and Stephen Linstead
Wollongong and Sunderland, June 1998.

Preface

v

Acknowledgements

The authors and publishers would like to acknowledge the valuable contribution of Faye Frith and Harold Hayward in their co-authorship of the precursor to this book, *Management for Australian Business: A Critical Text*. This 1992 publication serves as a foundation on which the current book has been built, and we are grateful for Faye and Harold's excellent work.

The authors would like to thank the following:

Mr Troy Thompson, Director, Business Development, Asia–Pacific Region, Case Corporation Pty Ltd, for his sole contribution on Scenario Planning in Chapter 10; Faye Frith and Harold Hayward for contributions to Chapter 8 from the earlier (1992) text; Dennis Mortimer for contributions to Chapter 7 from the earlier (1992) text; Richard Dunford for contributions to Chapter 5 from the earlier (1992) text.

Robin Snell, author of Chapter 9, would like to thank a number of others for their valuable help. Anthony Wai-kei Cheng, PhD student at City University of Hong Kong (CUHK), provided some useful initial review notes on ethical philosophy and codes of conduct. May Yu, Alice Pang and Richard Wong, former Research Assistants, also at CUHK, helped to compile preliminary case material on Green issues. Almaz Chak, a colleague of the author's at CUHK, conducted the ethical dilemma interview. Faye Frith for some material on whistleblowing based on an article written by her entitled 'Crime and punishment: Whistleblowing and intimidation rituals' in *Employment Relations: Theory and Practice*, 3: 651–2. The interpretations and arguments (and all their faults) are the responsibility of the author.

Liz Fulop is responsible for the theoretical orientation, content, editing and layout of Chapter 11. Ewa and Alan Buttery contributed principally to the sections on the rise of networks, classification of networks (excluding the material on learning network), power dimensions of networks, and some aspects of issues in networking and cross-cultural dimensions. They have drawn on ideas from their previously published book *Business Networks* (Melbourne: Longman Business and Professional).

Richard Dunford has been acknowledged as a co-author of Chapter 5 on the basis of the use of selected material from R. Dunford, 'Leadership and the Manager' in L. Fulop, F. Frith and H. Hayward, (eds), *Management for Australian Business: A Critical Text*, Melbourne: Macmillan, 1992. All new material contained in Chapter 5 has been written by Liz Fulop and Stephen Linstead, who also remain responsible for the content and design of the chapter.

The authors and publishers are grateful to the following for permission to reproduce copyright material:

Academy of Management for Figure 4.3 from 'Diversified Mentoring Relationships in Organizations: A Power Perspective' (diagram), Belle Rose Ragins, *Academy of Management Review*, Vol. 22, No. 2., Exhibit 5.1 from 'Leadership: Do Traits Matter?' (excerpt), Shelley Kirkpatrick & Edwin Locke, *Academy of Management Executive*, Vol. 5, No. 2., Table 5.4 from 'Narcissism, Identity and Legitimacy' (table), Andrew D. Brown, *Academy of Management Review*, Vol. 22, No. 3., reproduced by permission of the publisher via Copyright Clearance Center, Inc; Addison Wesley Longman China Ltd for Table 3.2 and Exhibit 5.6, from *Organizational Behaviour* by R. Westwood © 1992; American Management Association International for Exhibit 10.3 from 'Strategic Management Thought in East Asia' by Rosalie Tung in *Organizational Dynamics*, Winter 1994 © 1994, and Table 5.2 from 'Substitutes for Leadership: Effective Alternatives to Ineffective Leadership' by Jon Howell *et al.* from *Organizational Dynamics* Summer 1990 © 1990, reprinted by permission of American Management Association International, New York, NY, all rights reserved, http://www.amanet.org.; American Sociological Association for Table 7.1 from 'Toward a Sociological Theory of Motivation' by Jonathon H. Turner, from *American Sociological Review,* February 1987 © 1987; Blackwell Publishers for Figure 3.5 from 'Corporate Culture: The Last Frontier of Control' by Carol Axtell Ray in *Journal of Management Studies* ©1986 Blackwell Publishers Ltd; Butterworth Heinemann for Exhibit 3.2 from *Strategies for Cultural Change* by Paul Bate © 1994, and Table 6.3 from *Team Roles at Work* by Meredith Belbin © 1993, reproduced by permission of Butterworth Heinemann; California Management Review for Figure 7.2, copyright © 1975, by The Regents of the University of California, reprinted from the *California Management Review*, Vol. 17, No. 4, by permission of The Regents; Elsevier Science for Figures 10.6, 10.7 from 'Managing Strategic Change' by Gerry Johnson, from *Long Range Planning* 25 (1) © 1992; Financial Times Management for Exhibit 3.1 from *Organizational Culture* by Andrew Brown © 1995; Fortune Magazine for abridged article on pp. 34–5 from Linda Grant, 'First, Get a Weasel Costume' in *Fortune* 1997, reproduced by permission; The Free Press (a division of Simon & Schuster) for Exhibit 10.1 and Figure 10.5 from *Competitive Advantage: Creating and Sustaining Superior Performance* by Michael E. Porter, © 1985 by Michael E. Porter; Gordon & Breach Publishers for extracts on pp. 101, 104–6, adapted from 'Authority and the Pursuit of Order in Organizational Performance' by Heather Höpfl, pp. 252–4 from 'Beyond Goffman' by Iain L. Mangham in *Studies in Cultures, Organizations and Societies* 2(1); Gulf Publishing Company for Figure 5.1 from *Leadership Dilemmas Grid Solutions*, p. 29 by Robert R. Blake and Anne Adams McCanse, copyright 1991 © by Robert R. Blake and the Estate of Jane S. Mouton, used with permission, all rights reserved; Harcourt Brace & Company, Australia for Table 5.1 from *Organizational Behaviour* by Vecchio *et al.* © 1996; HarperCollins Publishers Ltd for Figure 5.4 from *Leadership and the One-Minute Manager* by Blanchard, Zigarmi and Drea Zigarmi © 1985; Harvard Business School Publishing for Figure 3.2 adapted from 'Understanding Your Organization's Character' by Roger Harrison from *Harvard Business Review*, May–June 1972, Exhibit 5.4 adapted from 'The work of leadership' by Ronald Hei Felz and Donald Laurie in *Harvard Business Review*, January–February 1997, extract on p. 241 from 'The

Myth of the Top Management Team' by John R. Katzenbach in *Harvard Business Review*, Nov–Dec 1987, Exhibit 10.2 adapted from 'Strategy as Revolution' by Gary Hamel in *Harvard Business Review* July–August 1996; The Institute of Personnel and Development for Exhibits 2.1, 2.2, taken from *Managing the Mosaic* by Kandola and Fullerton, reproduced by permission of the publishers The IPD, IPD House, 35 Camp Road, London SW19 4UX; JAI Press Inc. for Table 11.1 adapted from *Research in Organizational Behaviour* by Walter Powell ©1990; John Wiley & Sons for Table 5.3 from *Managing for Excellence* by Bradford and Cohen, © 1984 John Wiley & Sons Inc. NY; Jossey Bass Inc. Publishers for Figure 3.1 from *Organizational Culture and Leadership* by Edgar Schein © 1985, and Figures 8.1, 8.2 from *Top Decisions: Strategic Decision Making in Organizations* by Hickson, © 1986 Jossey Bass San Francisco, reprinted with permission; McGraw Hill Book Company for Exhibit 5.3 from *Under New Management: Australian Organizations in Transition* by D. Dunphy and D. Stace © 1990 McGraw Hill Book Company, Sydney; Oxford University Press for extracts on pp. 319–20, 349, from *Moral Mazes, The World of Corporate Managers* by Robert Jackall, 1988; Penguin UK for Exhibit 4.1 from *Understanding Organizations* by Charles Handy ©1985 and Figure 3.3 from *Corporate Culture: The Rites and Rituals of Corporate Life* by Terrence Deal & Allen Kennedy © 1988, reprinted with permission; Plenum Publishing Corporation for Table 11.1 adapted from 'Disciplines of Learning Organization: Contributions & Critiques' by Mark Easterby Smith in *Human Relations,* Vol. 50, No. 9, excerpt on pp. 82–6 adapted from 'The eye of the needle' by Francis Westly in *Human Relations*, Vol. 43. No. 3; Routledge UK for Table 2.3 from *Gender Transformation* by Sylvia Walby, © 1997; Sage Publications Inc. for Table 11.2 from *Organizations Working Together* by C. Alter & H. Hage © Sage Publications Inc. California; Sage Publications London for extract on p. 3, from Chia & Morgan, 'Educating the Philosopher Manager' in *Management Education*, reprinted by permission of Sage Publications; Phil Scott for abridged article 'Jac the Knife' *The Sydney Morning Herald*, 1997.

While every care has been taken to trace and acknowledge copyright, the publishers tender their apologies for any accidental infringement where copyright has proved untraceable. They would be pleased to come to a suitable arrangement with the rightful owner in each case.

Introduction:
A critical approach to management

Liz Fulop and Stephen Linstead

Management is a controversial topic. Airport book stores are bulging with popular management bestsellers, which attests to the level of interest in the subject, and perhaps to the level of anxiety which managers feel about how they go about their task. After all, while the middle levels of management have been shrinking, in what Gibson Burrell (1997) has called 'corporate liposuction' as a result of the downsizing of the 1990s, managers are constantly asked to work both smarter and harder. All employees are being asked to take some managerial responsibility for their work through what is sometimes called empowerment, and the rewards for those at the very top of the managerial tree have been increasing dramatically. In fact, Warren Bennis (cited in Hodgetts 1996), a highly regarded management academic, quotes average salaries of chief executive officers (CEOs) as being 187 times greater than their employees – a trend he describes as obscene. No wonder managers wait anxiously for their flights and thumb the pages of the next panacea with some agitation. The favoured few might become very wealthy, but most managers work long and hard under the shadow of retrenchment or the next performance review, while consultants and top management argue for the dissipation of management functions throughout the organization, in flatter organizations which offer fewer opportunities for advancement. Given this scenario, we might well ask the question: 'Who would want to be a manager?'

This book does not take such a negative view of the future of management. However, neither does it take the 'faddish' approach that there is a new salvation in the latest tools or techniques, or even the latest mantra. We don't think that there are a few basic principles down to which management can be distilled. We do, however, think that managers can manage better by taking a critical approach to their own practice, and the context in which they practise. We also believe that they can learn valuable lessons which they can take into other situations from the learning process. The key skill that managers need to learn is to be able to undertake *critical inquiry*, to learn how to learn, and to be able to do this not just from books, but also from practice. It is the objective of this book therefore, while placing emphasis on the contribution which good critical scholarship can make to the understanding and practice of management, not to neglect the importance of applying knowledge, and even good old commonsense, to managerial problems. But what we do need is the ability to tell the difference between them, and to know when each is necessary and appropriate.

For us, being *critical* does not mean standing outside management and exposing its flaws and weaknesses. It entails an active and passionate commitment to improving managers' abilities to deal with the problems they face, and helping them to discover how to manage better. This involves both sustained investigation at the practical level and equally sustained critical activity at the level of theory and analysis; it also entails a requirement of both managers and academics to be self-critical. A critical capacity then is not something which is outside and opposed to management – on the contrary, it is the very condition for management to be able to learn, adapt and influence the rapidly changing world conditions of the coming century.

The approach of this book

Each of the chapters in this book addresses a core managerial topic, and the content of the chapters is designed to reflect the current state of critical scholarly activity in the field – which of course reflects the state of the practice of management as we approach the next century. The chapters build on existing knowledge in various fields, highlighting some enduring theories and approaches, but then pushing the boundaries of management beyond these ideas. So you will find chapters on *strategy, leadership, culture, power, motivation* and *decision making*, which are familiar topics in most managerial texts. A difference in focus comes in our chapter on *teams* in which traditional approaches to group behaviour in organizations, and some aspects of job design, are reframed in the light of a critical appraisal of the current emphasis, in both academic and popular literature, on teams and team-working. Our approach differs most noticeably, however, when we come to consider *learning, gender, ethics* and *networking*. These topics are no longer marginal notes on the practice of management, but issues which are at the heart of what managers have to address every day, from their own personal development, through their relations with colleagues, and even to the point where organizational boundaries dissolve into networks and virtual organizations. We have brought these topics into the mainstream of this text because we believe that they have already established their intellectual and practical significance in the world of management, and that they represent a realistic agenda for the study of management for the next 10 years.

However, we have also taken an approach in which each chapter, as far as possible and appropriate, addresses a group of key themes related to its content. These themes are:

- sources and uses of knowledge and information;
- learning in organizations;
- reflective practice;
- diversity, including but not limited to race, gender, ethnicity and cross-cultural issues;
- power in its many and varied forms.

We begin each chapter with some questions which you might like to keep in mind when you consider the topic of the chapter… don't jump ahead at this point, but be comforted by the fact that we do attempt to answer those questions at the end of the chapter! Of course, by the time you reach the end of the chapter, you will have your own answers, which might not be quite the same as ours. But there is more than one way to respond to these complex questions and, as we shall see, management is not a simple question of right and wrong, but of using both reasoned judgement and feeling to make sense of complicated situations. Accordingly, we also begin each chapter with a short case study and some questions on it, which we ask you to think about before you read the chapter and reflect on as you progress through the chapter. By the end of the chapter you should be able to make a thorough response to these questions, but to help you along we address them ourselves at the conclusion of the chapter – but not in the sense of us having a final word. We would also expect you to challenge our assumptions, based on your reading of the chapters, and your interpretations of the materials.

Why study management?

There are many sides to management, no simple and clear answers, and no 'one best way' to do it. Management is a complex field of activity and one that requires enormous effort and will to do well. It is not something that comes naturally to many of us, yet it is something that almost all of us might be called upon to do, not only through involvement in formal organizations, but in our private lives as well. Our focus in this book, however, is primarily on formal organizations, but we do consider public, private and voluntary organizations to be within our compass.

There are two main reasons for studying management. The first is to gain knowledge and understanding of management and what it is and, in the process, learn how to be a better and more effective manager. There is no simple way to do this. There is also no guarantee that what will be learnt in the theory of management will be easily translated into the practice of management. This raises the second reason why it is important to study management. When we study management we need a framework that will allow us to develop reflective practice, which is at the heart of critical thinking. In this textbook, the notion of critical thinking remains a core idea considered essential to the development of the manager and, more importantly, to the better practice of management (Fulop 1992; Thomas 1993).

We can develop reflective practice by adopting perspectives that help us see familiar situations in new ways, and by considering things that challenge our perceptions about people, organizations and ourselves. Adopting a questioning, quizzical attitude can help us to recognise and solve problems, identify opportunities and think creatively (Thomas 1993). Robert Chia and Stuart Morgan (1996: 58) state:

> The purpose of management education is not so much knowledge acquisition and accumulation as it is sensitizing students to our own peculiar culturally based (and often idiosyncratic) ways of ordering the world. It is about inculcating an intimate understanding of the way...management knowledge...is organized, produced and legitimized...In other words, the priority of *education* is quintessentially about gaining an understanding of [how we organize and represent knowledge from various sources].

In a nutshell, learning about management requires a critical perspective that is guided by three key processes of inquiry:

1   identifying and challenging assumptions;
2   developing an awareness of the context in which management ideas have evolved historically;
3   always seeking alternative ways of seeing situations, interpreting what is going on, understanding why an organization is configured the way it is, and speculating about the way the organization could be managed differently (Thomas 1993: 11).

Much as these processes sound like work, the essence of managing is learning about managing in a way that keeps '… the connection between *knowledge*, *imagination* and the zest for life' to the fore (Chia and Morgan 1996: 57).

The critical approach

This introduction outlines a *critical approach to management* that enables us to reflect on how we learn about management. It is designed to help us to develop the intellectual rigour and knowledge to deal with the complex and multifaceted issues that arise every day in work situations. Managers need to know how to analyse problems, how to use the knowledge they have acquired in a questioning manner, and how to employ their creative capacities to see things in new ways in order to resolve dilemmas. A vast body of knowledge and research can be drawn upon, for example, to help analyse and respond to what is happening or unfolding in organizational situations.

What *sources of knowledge* about managers and organizations are most useful, and how does a manager use or adapt them in a meaningful and constructive manner? Most of what is found in the management and organizational literature is based on theories, research or studies that have been undertaken in various organizations, sometimes even in laboratories, under different sets of constraints, some more scientific than others, often in different countries, and within different time frames. This means that most ideas or suggestions have to be adapted to take account of the peculiarities and uniqueness of the manager's own situation or context.

In Chapter 1, we discuss some of the complexities and problems associated with learning, both from the vantage point of the individual and the organization. Facilitating individual and organizational learning is perhaps the hardest thing any manager will ever have to learn, and requires the art or skill of *reflective practice*. Reflective practice has been popularized in the organizational learning literature (e.g. Senge 1990), but draws heavily on the work of the late Donald Schön (1977). Some recent commentators argue that this type of learning cannot occur unless organizational members are able to identify new knowledge, transfer and interpret new knowledge, use the knowledge to adjust behaviour or practices and pass on this knowledge (Levinson and Asahi 1995: 59–60).

Others argue that *self-reflexive practice* is a further development of reflective practice. Questions such as 'who am I and who am I becoming?' are ones that self-reflexive practitioners will ask of themselves. Questions such as 'what *really* happened, why, and what can I do about it?' are typically posed by the reflective practitioner. To engage in self-reflexive practice is something akin to trying to rethink and rework one's own identity, values and assumptions, to such an extent that self-reflexive practice has been regarded as being tantamount to trying to '…jump over one's shadow' (Limerick and Cunnington 1993: 221). Our use of the term 'reflective practice' in this book includes the important, more postmodern sense of self-reflexivity. This form of reflective practice adds another dimension to the education of managers. Typically, management has been taught or thought of as something that is achieved by imparting particular forms of knowledge and know-how. Often it is taught as a skills-based activity or set of practices. In contrast, reflective practice emphasizes the need for all managers to develop abilities to critique and to be creative (Chia and Morgan 1996). The very idea of reflective practice also raises the perennial question: what is good management? How do I know when I've done well?

In this book we take the approach that management is the management of relationships and as such is a relational practice, so the answer to these questions will not be fixed and final but will change as the relationships between the elements of management change. However, before we take a look at the nature of these relationships, we need to address our fourth theme, that of diversity.

Diversity is an issue which managers are being forced to confront both in the workplace and increasingly outside it in terms of relationships with, for example, overseas suppliers and overseas manufacturing facilities, investors or joint venture partners. The recognition of the existence of diversity and in some cases the desire to increase or create it have led to a more intense focus on managing relationships in the workplace and managing differences more effectively (see Chapter 2). Differences are based on age, race, gender, ethnicity, beliefs, experience, disability, etc., although often gender and race receive most attention. These differences have to be accommodated, or even celebrated, in managing. For example, whether or not managers are male or female, the fact remains that they have to understand and accommodate better a broader range of differences than in years past. In addition, they need to do their part in providing genuine opportunities for meaningful, equitable and rewarding careers for those whom they manage. By using diversity as a lens through which we examine the content and issues of management, we can begin to become aware of a much broader set of consequences, questions, challenges and potential sources of creative solutions to organizational problems, besides uncovering a few more of these problems to which we were previously oblivious. Certainly the consideration of diversity can change the nature of relationships in the workplace, and can change the nature of what we see as the management task – as we shall see in Chapter 2 in particular it can even change the way we theorize management.

While it is important for managers to learn about and confront issues of diversity, changing the nature of relationships in the workplace will not be achieved unless issues relating to *power* and *control* are also addressed. We explore the complex ways in which power becomes embedded in relationships, both in its more obvious and less obvious forms. Power is integral to explaining how relationships are formed, but also why they often fail or are so difficult to sustain over longer periods.

Management is the management of relationships

Management is often presented as the management of things, which includes resources (and people are treated as *human* resources). This reification (literally, thing-making) reinforces the artificial separation between the component disciplines through which management is defined and taught. However, the separate disciplines of management – accounting, organizational behaviour, information systems, operations management, marketing, etc. – cannot easily be separated in practice as each interlocks with the other. Real-life problems are overlapping and interconnected, rather than self-contained, and even when a management problem is solved successfully, the process is never finished. Relationships are constantly changing and the process of managing, and perhaps improving them, is continuous.

Management is a relational, differential activity, involving criteria which shift and environments which change at different rates. Because management is a relational activity, managers have to deal with multiple realities, roles and identities, and multiple loyalties for individuals. It is the recognition that individuals have multiple realities, roles, identities and loyalties that is so central to managing diversity in organizations. Whether it involves dealing with the natural environment, with other colleagues, with customers and competitors, with communities, networks or alliances, the managing of 'relationships' will be paramount. It is not surprising that the notion of 'relationships' (e.g. employment relations and relational marketing) is a central characteristic of the current shift in thinking and will be at the cutting-edge of such disciplines in the twenty-first century.

Traditional approaches to management tend to emphasize (implicitly and often explicitly) management as the *control of relationships*. Scientific management, as we shall see in Chapter 6, constructs the supervisor – employee relationship as that between the head and the hands, with the head (manager/supervisor) firmly in control, giving the instructions, and the hands carrying them out. Yet studies of business pioneers and entrepreneurs emphasize the role of the entrepreneur in bringing people and things together, the literal meaning of the word 'entrepreneur'. Here the important role of the entrepreneur/manager is the *bringing of relationships into being* for mutual advantage. Some approaches which are more focused on the power of management as a group than on the individual manager, such as labour process theory, emphasize *inequality or asymmetry in relationships*. They focus on relationships where one group becomes powerful and remains dominant over another for long periods of time (see Chapters 4 and 6). Systems thinking, which developed in the 1940s, and has recently enjoyed a resurgence of popularity in the learning literature, takes a particular view of the *process of relationships*, looking for functional and dysfunctional elements and emphasizing the relationship of *fitting in* with the environment in order to survive and grow. Strategic management approaches (which we discuss in Chapter 10) build on this and increasingly view business failure in terms of failure to stay in touch with changes in the competitive environment in terms of *interrupted or distorted relationships*, where something is wrong with the conversion of system inputs into the right sort of system outputs. Developing as far back as the Hawthorne Studies (see Chapter 6), but changing as the field of psychoanalysis changed with each decade, psychodynamic approaches have emphasized *problematic relationships* – organizational pathology as the result of a failure to maintain psychological balance in relations, resulting, for example, in group conflict. In Chapter 5 we discuss the concept of 'narcissism', which is an example of how such distorted relationships can profoundly affect organizational practice. In short, existing studies suggest that at a basic practical level, without building, maintaining and developing relationships a manager cannot manage.

Two things, however, are important to the perspective we are taking here. First, these relationships are in a *dynamic field*, in constant (though not necessarily profound or radical) change, and, second, they embody *flows* of energy and power through the field. The manager then has to be able to monitor how these changes are occurring, and has to be able to channel these flows of energy, interest, knowledge and power in order to get things done in the organization. What becomes of particular interest to studies of these networks or webs of relations is:

- *what* is related, *how*, and how this in turn changes;
- how *changes in one part of the web affect other parts* or are prevented from doing so;
- how managers act in establishing, *maintaining and changing relationships*; and
- how *existing patterns of relationships pose constraints* and how these can be addressed by managers.

What also emerges from these considerations are the skills and qualities which managing these relationships demands:

- sensitivity to a *wide variety of types of information* and forms of knowledge – technical, cultural, emotional, etc. as well as different narrative forms such as stories or workplace myths;
- the ability to visualize and perceive *new patterns* of relationships;
- the ability to tolerate *ambiguity and uncertainty*;
- the ability to be *persuasive;*
- the confidence to *take risks and intervene*, to exercise judgement in the absence of authoritative prescriptions such as rules, policies, procedures etc.; and
- the capacity to be self-critical, to learn from mistakes, and to *develop continuously.*

If we take the individual manager as our focus, these relationships could rather crudely be said to fall into two groups. One group of relationships is those which are related to the job, the organization and *the demands of the manager's formal role* in relation to the organization's 'rational-purposive' dimension: goals like making a profit, meeting production targets, retaining customers, etc. The other group is those which are related to the manager's *personal desires*, ambitions, social demands, familial relations, etc. In the practising manager's world, these fields are in tension and may from time to time be in overt conflict – such as when the managing director calls an 'away day' meeting to discuss changes in the company strategy on your wedding anniversary. Let's look at this division more closely.

Role-focused, goal-oriented relationships

At their simplest, these roles are all about what it is that managers do that differentiates management from any other activity. Lots of writers, for example Henry Mintzberg (1975) and Rosemary Stewart (1988), have focused on this. At this level it is those features of the job and the role in the organization that exert demands and create tensions in the manager's life. Most relevant are practical problems that confront the manager in their formal role, such as how to do the job, how to do it better, how to change it, etc.

Person-focused, self-oriented relationships

This area of concern focuses on managers as individuals, and the impact that the role may have on them. It covers effects on the manager's personality, including emotions and stress (see Chapters 2 and 7). It can also include the consideration of ethical and moral issues that might arise during the course of doing business as personal dilemmas (see Chapter 9), and learning, learning styles, levels and types of learning, self-management and self-development (see Chapter 1). Diversity in the workplace puts emphasis on people, differentiates their perspectives, views and mindsets and stresses that these differences have to be managed to ensure organizations gain the maximum benefit from potential sources of knowledge. Relational management also recognizes that people bring their 'whole self' to work, not just a 'work self', that is, they also bring their sexuality, spirit, emotions and connections to family and friends with them every day. These aspects of people's identity need to be taken into account to enrich the meaning and context of work (Zangari and Cavaleri 1996: 338–9). Commitment and attachment to work and the organization can diminish as people find meaning, identity and the whole self beyond work (Handy, cited in Ettore 1996: 15). It is naive to expect that people will centre their lives entirely around their employment, as we discuss in Chapter 7 (on motivation). The managerial challenge is not to annex and incorporate the personal and social world of their employees, but to allow space for and achieve an appropriate balance between these elements.

Relationships are with constituencies

Relationships are enacted with groups of others as well as with individuals. Where these groups have a strong and recognizable identity we can call them *constituencies*, and these constituencies can be both internal to the organization or outside it and impacting upon it.

Relationships with internal constituencies

Constituencies could be regarded as groups of *stakeholders*. The stakeholder terminology has some rather unfortunate 'representative' and 'bargaining' connotations related to traditional industrial relations approaches. In the sense that we use the term here we are mindful that social reality itself is constructed and negotiated even at the basic level of meaning. Within the organization, this involves consideration of issues like managing other people, vertical and horizontal relationships, internal customers and suppliers, support systems and service suppliers, specialists and professionals, and formal/informal relations, along with some basic principles of organization structure. It is this process of the making and understanding of meaning in which people have their 'stake'.

Relationships with external constituencies

From the organization's point of view, these are the *outside stakeholders* – customers, clients, suppliers, investors, those involved in the micro-legal environment, the public in terms of public image, competitors, collaborators, cooperators, coexistors, collectives, agents/distributors/franchisees, potential recruits/suppliers/customers, etc., and former members of the organization in some cases. This also involves the manager's own community, family, partners and friends who are the core of other networks whose interests and influence may cut across those of the organization and produce tension for the manager. The home, for example, is perhaps the most powerful external constituency for most people.

However, the notion of the outside or external stakeholder has changed in the 1990s and this change has challenged managers' capacities to deal with the relational dimensions of their work. As Warren Bennis (cited by Hodgetts 1996: 75) argues, organizations have responsibilities not only to internal stakeholders (i.e. employees) but to customers and the community. Yet many companies are increasingly focused on serving the needs of shareholders more than their other constituents. Institutional investors (banks, finance companies, etc.) that constitute the most powerful group of shareholders often pursue short-term strategies to maximize shareholder returns. Bennis and others (e.g. Peter Drucker, cited in Caulkin 1993: 42) believe these trends have produced CEOs who benefit from the 'bottom-line', market-driven, hard-nosed, hard-driving image that reaps them millions through stock options. This focus or shareholder-mindset (Bennis 1996: 75, cited in Hodgetts 1996) leaves little room for managing or building long-term relationships, when the personal wealth of CEOs can increase substantially when they downsize or opt for short-term gains. These trends have raised concerns about how organizations can build trust and commitment and create the intellectual capital they need to compete.

Relationships are managed by performance

If we now turn to consider how relationships are managed, it is not too difficult to see that they must be managed by action or performance of some sort. There are three different objects of performance:

1   *The performance of functions, tasks and roles* This involves looking at what managers do in terms of specific tasks, including the functions of marketing, operations management, human resource management (HRM), finance, etc., and how these specialised areas relate to the general properties of management – in other words, what is common or overlapping across these functions. Much work has been done in this area in regard to classical studies of management principles. Colin Hales (1993) in a review of various historical formulations of 'management principles' identified a staggering variety, yet pointed out that this was only a small sample of the existing work.

2   *The performance of interpersonal skills* This is where task performance intersects with the skills of interaction with others – leadership in a personal sense, presentation skills, negotiation skills, group dynamics and facilitation, decision making, competencies, critical thinking, change management. In this mode the manager may come close to the performance artist, employing complex skills, rehearsing and changing roles where necessary. Emotional management is at the heart of this dimension, and all managers need to develop their performance skills to some degree.

3   *The performance of analytical techniques* Managers do need some quantitative or analytic skills, albeit in varying degrees, and at the very least they need to understand enough to know how to use technical specialists in the best ways or interpret quantitative data provided by 'experts' in the course of their work. Quantitative analysis, Just-in-Time (JIT) knowledge, quality measurement and benchmarking, information technology, especially in support of statistical process control, economic analysis, financial and accounting skills, market analysis and research all relate to the general conceptualization of management at this level.

The combination of functional task skills as an accountant, marketer or other specialist, combined with interpersonal skills and the ability to understand and use quantitative data, all enable managers to manage their key relationships flexibly and effectively. But to what ends do they apply these skills?

Relationships are managed through organization

The managers' performance skills are realised through applying them to organize specific arenas of action to their advantage. This means the organization of:

1   *Social processes* In this area the influence of sociological thinking is most clearly felt in studies of management, and particularly in the critical linkage of language, knowledge and power. The performance of tasks and functions takes place through social processes which can constrain or enable different forms of action. Through focusing

on *power*, social processes involving political action such as network and coalition building and establishing and leveraging power bases are emphasized. Critical views also emphasize structural inequality, control, hegemony and domination in relations. They also regard ideology as a mystification which enables power to become the rule of the powerful – to create domination, subordination and hegemony (the perpetuation of one group in domination over another). The labour process perspective is also important here, including issues of exploitation and extraction of surplus value and the manager's role in the process, as are issues of class, race and gender differences and discrimination (see Chapter 4, but also Chapters 2 and 6).

2   *Symbolic representation* An important part of management is what has been called the 'management of meaning'. Thus 'symbolic' management, or the attempt to create corporate cultures, teams, new forms of motivational tools, 'transformational' or visionary leadership (and of course other styles), is significant here (see Chapters 3 and 5). In addition, the dramaturgical view of management as a performance, staged in a theatrical sense, or the acting of scripts and storylines is relevant. The focus here is on verbal and visual *language* used to create meanings that literally define for people the 'rules' of membership in an organization (even down to the appropriate language to use) and the communicative methods by which they are sustained (see Chapters 2 and 3).

3   *Knowledge and information* One of the key influences and drivers of change in organizations is the increasing speed of the flow of information. The ways in which 'knowledge' is formed from information are important to some companies, but are the very reason for being of what are called 'knowledge-intensive firms', a rapidly growing area of commercial activity and study (Microsoft is an example). Networks and virtual organizations all depend on knowledge and information flow, and issues of copyright secrecy, confidentiality, corruption and fraud have assumed new dimensions. Information is at the heart of the 'deal' which produced the spectacular successes on paper and the equally spectacular collapses of the highly leveraged entrepreneurs and corporate raiders of the 1980s. In addition to learning to master information technology, the information superhighway and the range of relevant databases, there is still the pervasive and important traditional form of information flow – the grapevine, the rumour mill, gossip, stories, talks, etc. – which has not diminished in its significance. *Knowledge* and power have a close relationship, and language could be seen as the glue which holds them together (see Chapters 8 and 10).

The manager then exercises performance skills by building relationships based on *managing power*, *managing meaning* and *managing knowledge*. But these processes also have broader social contexts which inform them. Managers do not act in a vacuum – their behaviours are always subject to some constraints due to the complex web of relationships in which they operate.

Relationships are managed in formative contexts

Taking a look at the broader canvas, we could use Brazilian critical legal and social theorist Roberto Unger's idea of 'formative contexts' to express the sense in which action is shaped but not necessarily determined by wider sociocultural influences. These contexts, it should be emphasized here, are historically situated (time, cycles), regionally located (place), and discursively formed and sustained (through specific combinations of customs, languages, cultural knowledge and power relations). In other words, managing is always tailored to considerations of time, place and discourse (see Chapters 8 and 9). These contexts could be divided up into four broad subdivisions which we will call 'environments' which impinge upon and shape the manager's actions:

1   *The regulatory environment* The regulatory context is the formal background of the law, regulations and restrictions against which businesses and managers must operate. The significance of the regulatory environment becomes glaringly obvious to even the most superficial consideration of British economy and society during more than a decade of Thatcherism; as it does, for example, in any consideration of Hong Kong's recent and future development as a capitalist city in a communist country. Political influence, policies and initiatives, economic factors like interest and exchange rates and tariff control, trade agreements and common market agreements all shape the ground on which business is conducted.

    At the organizational level, rules and structures act as frameworks for managerial action, and organizational design options open up choices and facilitate some practices rather than others, although ultimately, like the broader regulatory environment, they are subject to challenge, subversion and change. Alternatives in organizational structures and new forms, global corporations and multinational corporations (MNCs) and strategic alliances, the virtual corporation, and even the question of 'modern' or 'postmodern' organizations affect what management is becoming here. This also articulates with consideration of the competitive environment which is the specific focus of strategy and marketing (see Chapter 10).

2   *The cultural environment* Here the impact of cultural diversity is recognized. Culture can of course be studied at several levels, and here it is that those things which extend beyond organizational boundaries are most significant. While professional, local and industrial subcultures are important, perhaps the most important are national/ethnic and cross-national cultural features. The increasing need to manage across cultures in terms of marketing, procurement and manufacturing combines with the increasing ethnic diversity and mobility of workforces to pose highly significant challenges. Gender issues too are very important at this level (see Chapter 2, and also parts of each chapter).

3   *The physical environment* The rise of 'green management' is one of the best examples of how the physical environment has become central to the study of management. The need to operate in a way which sustains rather than exploits natural resources, limits pollution and cares for the communities in which facilities are located is perhaps the most important new emphasis in global management. An increased concern with risk and reliability as demands for products and services and the speed at which they are delivered increases also raises concerns about managing the physical environment. Recent research and emphases on disaster avoidance and management have led to a very substantial new multidisciplinary field emerging in management and engineering studies. Concerns about the physical environment have spread beyond disciplinary boundaries. This area also covers more traditional issues of climate and geography, and the logistics of infrastructure (see Chapter 10).

4   The ideational environment This is the world of ideas which account for, legitimate, question and make possible certain lines of argument and action, dividing the world up in characteristic ways. This is still shaped by the classic ideas of management, particularly Scientific Management and Fordism, but recently substantial ideas about learning, quality, competence, corporate governance, ethics, restructuring, etc. have come to form a corpus of contemporary ideas about managing which go beyond the superficiality and 'hype' of popular management theory. Nevertheless, it is also important here to consider *why* management seems so peculiarly vulnerable to 'fads and fashions' (see Chapter 1). At this level, too, broader sociological studies of morals and ethics are important beyond the consideration of individual moral dilemmas (see Chapters 9 and 10).

These different levels of consideration can of course be related across their boundaries. For example, if we wanted to consider the management issues relating to the space shuttle Challenger disaster, which occurred in 1986, and in which all lives aboard were lost, we would find that it has been analysed from every possible angle from engineering to psycho-analysis! The US space agency, NASA, was blamed for this accident which became famous because it was the first space mission to carry a civilian. Such cases, incorporating diverse perspectives, oddly enough, are rare. Managers are trained to deal with management problems in a fragmented fashion often with a narrow view. In fact, if you look closely enough and range widely enough, the full range of connections can be made from only a small amount of information. So it is our final argument that the challenge of *relational management* is threefold:

1   to be able to 'surf' the waves of changing relationships and maintain a sense of balance;
2   to be able to sense the immense interconnectedness of things through these relationships, without being overcome by the vertigo of possibilities (a kind of 'analysis paralysis'), and still be able to *act effectively;* and
3   not to look for simplicity where it cannot be found, but rather to see the complexity of managing relationships as a distinct advantage, which is vital to learning about oneself and one's organization.

References

Burrell, G. (1997) *Pandemonium: Towards a Retro-Organization Theory*, London: Sage.
Caulkin, S. (1993) 'The lust for leadership', *Management Today* November, 38: 40–3.
Chia, R. and Morgan, S. (1996) 'Educating the philosopher manager', *Management Learning* 27 (1): 37–64.
Ettore, B. (1996) 'A conversation with Charles Handy on the future of work and an end to the "century of organization"', *Organizational Dynamics* Summer: 15–26.
Fulop, L. (1992) 'Management and critical thinking', in Fulop, L., Frith, F. and Hayward, H. (eds.), *Management for Australian Business: A Critical Text*, Melbourne: Macmillan.
Hales, C. (1993) *Managing Through Organisation*, London: Routledge.
Hodgetts, R.M. (1996) 'A conversation with Warren Bennis on leadership in the midst of downsizing', *Organizational Dynamics* Summer: 72–8.
Levinson, N. and Asahi, M. (1995) 'Cross national alliances and interorganizational learning', *Organizational Dynamics* Autumn: 13–31.
Limerick, D. and Cunnington, B. (1993) *Managing the New Organisation: A Blueprint for Networks and Strategic Alliances*, Sydney: Business and Professional Publishing.

Mintzberg, H. (1975) 'The manager's job: Folklore and fact', *Harvard Business Review* July–August: 49–61.

Schön, D.A. (1983) *The Reflective Practitioner*, New York: Basic Books.

Senge, P. (1990) *The Fifth Discipline: The Art and Practice of the Learning Organization*, New York: Doubleday/Currency.

Stewart, R. (1988) *Managers and Their Jobs*, London: Macmillan.

Thomas, A.B. (1993) *Controversies in Management*, London: Routledge.

Zangari, N.J. and Cavaleri, S.A. (1996) 'Relational management', in Cavaleri, S. and Fearon, D. (eds.), *Managing in Organizations that Learn*, Oxford: Blackwell Business.

1
Management knowledge and learning

Liz Fulop and William D. Rifkin

Questions about management knowledge and learning

1 What sorts of knowledge do managers need?
2 How do managers learn about management?
3 What forms of knowledge are likely to be easier for managers to grasp than others?
4 What role do managers play in helping their organizations to learn?

Chris's dilemma

Silence. No one was volunteering for the project. 'Why not?' thought Chris Stefano.

Five people had gathered in the meeting room. They exchanged pleasantries and a few jokes. Chris had entered the room late, knocking over a chair and spilling the cup of tea perched precariously on top of a pile of computer printouts Chris was carrying. Chris had thanked everyone for coming – it was their lunch break – and outlined the urgency of the situation facing the organization. A detailed description was given of the outstanding work needed to complete the project and meet the project deadline, and Chris finished the presentation by asking for a volunteer. Then there was this silence. No one had come forward. Chris had felt stunned and embarrassed. Chris had a flashback to university days when a team project had been due, and none of the other team members would help on the night before it was to be submitted. The project had been given a fail grade!

Chris was facing a difficult and frustrating situation and was under immense pressure to complete a project of major importance to the organization. The project had been stalled for some weeks, and the deadline for completion was now becoming almost impossible to meet. Critical information had been difficult to extract from the organization's information system, and what data there were, had been presented in a cumbersome form, requiring hours of rework. Whoever volunteered for the project would have a difficult and time-consuming task ahead of him/her. Chris could not

---

employ extra staff to help as there was a freeze on hiring casual staff. The project had to be completed no matter what. Chris had called a meeting of staff to progress the project, specifically to find a volunteer.

Roderick Cage had cleared his throat and mumbled that his workload had doubled since Lou Chan went on paternity leave with no immediate replacement for him. Looking somewhat annoyed, Rebecca Spalding had quickly interjected, saying that since the new accounts system had changed her workload was now the heaviest of all present. Phil Ball, who had recently missed out on promotion, just shrugged his shoulders and said he was understaffed and could not take on any new work. Winjamarra, who had only been in the job for four months, said he believed he was being transferred in the next fortnight. Merilyn Hue simply smirked at Chris, somewhat nonchalantly, and said that she was going on special leave next week.

Chris had looked around the room and had fixed a nervous gaze on Phil and then as pleasantly as possible had said to him: 'I'd appreciate it if you would complete the data for the project and...' Before Chris could finish the sentence, Phil had swung out of his chair, snatched up his papers and stormed out of the room, slamming the door behind him. Chris followed him, but by the time Chris reached the door, Phil had disappeared.

Chris had then rushed down the hall into the Managing Director's office, slammed the door and glared at Dr Cora Harvey. In utter despair and rage, Chris had banged a fist on Cora's table and said: 'None of them would help me! Can you believe it? I had to order Phil to do it.' Cora had stared at Chris with a piercing gaze and had said sternly: 'If I were you Chris...', but just then the phone had rung, cutting her off in mid-sentence. She had beckoned Chris to leave the room, but as Chris walked out she had shouted: 'Sort it out Chris and get the damn project finished. I don't care how you do it! Just do it!'

Chris had shouted back at her: 'If I have to, I will do it myself and then there goes the new defence contract!' Chris thought, just like at university, having to finish the project alone the night before it is due.

Questions about the case

1 What advice would you give to the manager in this incident?
2 What knowledge or experiences have you drawn on to give your advice?
3 How would you judge it to be good advice?

Introduction

The incident selected for this chapter presents a common management dilemma. It might not be judged by many as a spectacular event in the sense that it is not related to a programme of major change, a corporate takeover or the removal of a chief executive officer (CEO). Rather, it concerns the typical struggle of a manager trying to achieve outcomes under intense pressures to perform. Although the individuals in the incident are fictitious, the incident is based on observations and experiences that the authors have had in their own organizations. It is also likely to be an experience that many of us could relate to – trying to get someone to volunteer for an unpleasant, but necessary task. The organization, and the manager in it, might appear to be facing a relatively simple problem, but nothing could be further from the truth. Have a good look at the incident and then try to answer the above questions. As we go through the chapter, the answers to these questions should be revealed.

In this chapter, we examine how managers acquire management knowledge and 'know-how'. Certain forms of knowledge and know-how are easier to come by, and learn from, than others. Ultimately, learning depends on where the manager or the would-be manager searches for knowledge and where that search stops. It is from an understanding of the different forms of knowledge in management that managers gain an appreciation and understanding of the difficulties that confront them as they set out to learn more about management, and in the process help their organizations as a whole to learn.

Many people who want to learn how to manage have unexamined assumptions about the level of practicality or 'hands-on' knowledge and information they need to acquire in order to manage well. Sometimes a manager wants to learn about management so that an immediate problem can be addressed with a successful outcome guaranteed. The consumers of management knowledge and know-how often seek out textbooks and courses on management that will give them 'answers' to their immediate problems and solutions or guides on how to manage certain situations, with promised success. This has been described elsewhere, and by a number of management writers, as the ill-fated quest for the 'one best way' to manage (Fulop 1992: 18; Shapiro 1995: xvi). We say 'ill-fated' because management is neither simple nor subject to definitive answers in many areas of management activity, particularly in managing relationships. Far from it! Management, by its very nature, focuses on many issues and practices that are dynamic, ambiguous, complex, contradictory, often political in nature and involve risking taking and innovation.

Graham Salaman and Jim Butler (1994: 36–9) say that many trainers, management consultants and even business school lecturers have tended to propagate a view that managers learn best through experience and doing and value most practical techniques or methods that have direct or immediate application. Highly theoretical knowledge, for example abstract theory, is believed not to be valued by managers. What is thought to be highly valued are prescriptions or 'one best way' techniques and tools (Fulop 1992: 8–9). We would argue that experience and doing are in fact important, but nonetheless are only a small part of how managers acquire knowledge and know-how.

Management is also a contested or controversial concept. Alan Thomas (1993) points out that all major areas of management – leadership, teamwork, motivation – are subject to disagreement by academics and practitioners and capable of being treated from a number of different perspectives. There is no shortage of declared 'experts' in both the academic and practitioner camps who profess to have 'authoritative' views on managing, and as many opinions on how to do it well. The manager needs to work out from what knowledge base these 'experts' make their claims about management and how these claims impact on the practice of the manager. All managerial practices proceed on the basis of some theoretical assumptions, frames of reference or models of action.

So an important question to ask is: where *should* I start the search for management knowledge or know-how? Should I read a bestseller, emulate the practices of so-called successful CEOs such as Rupert Murdoch (the second-generation media magnate), Richard Branson (the founder of Virgin Airlines and the Virgin Group of companies) or Poppy King (the founder of a cosmetics company)? Should I buy a management textbook, or enrol in a university business course, or is it just as easy to 'fly by the seat of my pants'?

Management knowledge

There are six main sources of management knowledge or know-how. These are outlined in Exhibit 1.1. Some of these sources of knowledge are often not examined in books about management. Their relevance is often trivialized or misunderstood by commentators on management, such as journalists, consultants and managers themselves, who point out that management is mundane, relies heavily on commonsense or is jargon ridden. Other critics, such as academics in non-management areas, would argue management is not theoretical or scientific enough. Managers are thought to deal with many things that are obvious or amount to just plain commonsense. These critics contend that managing a business or organization is obvious to all and sundry (see James 1997: 56). We think our discussion of management knowledge will go some way toward dispelling these images of naive simplicity.

Managers either overvalue commonsense, or seriously undervalue it (Linstead and Harris 1983: 10, citing Burgoyne 1981). Business schools tend to encourage the undervaluing of commonsense, while critics of management draw attention to its overvaluing aspect. Managers often enter business schools looking for 'answers', often valuing the calculative, so-called scientific solutions over simple but effective answers. This has led to business schools (and particularly Master of Business Administration (MBA) degrees) being attacked as irrelevant. Also, even though academic language is jargon laden, so too is commonsense talk – it is often hard for academics to 'learn the language' of some workplace research site and gain access to the meanings and assumptions which are taken for granted by employees. The complexities of these disparate bodies of knowledge about managing are explored in Exhibit 1.1.

- **Learning by doing** Much of managing involves talking to people to get tasks done; much informal learning about managing occurs during these 'first-order' conversations.
- **Hearing local accounts** Ordinary everyday talk or stories about work that has been done; these stories are either first-hand or second-hand accounts of events.
- **Reading popular accounts** Published, electronically transmitted or publically recounted (e.g. at management seminars) accounts of management stories or sagas with 'lessons' or tales of hands-on experiences for other managers to benefit from.
- **Reading the fad approaches or theories and attending workshops** The bestsellers or fads and fashion in management magazines and workshops; dominated by works and training methods that contain recipes or prescriptions for management actions derived from a variety of approaches.
- **Studying 'soft' academic theory or middle-range theories** Textbooks which attempt to link theory and practice, but the manager reading or hearing this material might sense that it has less emphasis on prescription than popular theory and is more demanding analytically.
- **Deciphering 'hard' academic theory** Emphasis on theory building and testing or discovering new principles or fundamentals of organization theory, work, technology, personality, society, etc. This is very analytically demanding and rigorous with a lot less emphasis placed on directly applying knowledge to the day to day practice of the manager. Emphasis is placed on managers extrapolating what they see as important for them.

Exhibit 1.1 Six sources of management knowledge

In the discussion that follows, considerable attention will be paid to the first three methods of acquiring management knowledge. Learning by doing, local accounts and popular accounts need to be addressed as we deal with issues surrounding reflective practice and critical thinking. The popular approaches (the fads and fashions) tend to dominate the consultancy market place. These approaches have direct implications for managers in how they develop critical thinking. The fads and fashion market place is dominated by gurus or would-be gurus who, as David James says, '... command worldwide audiences, often have a more far-reaching effect on industry policy than politicians and have developed one of the most influential dialogues [discourses or ways of talking] in world economics' (James 1997: 53). These gurus, he says, are also '... laying down the law, reshaping institutions, refashioning our language and, above all, reorganizing people's lives' (James 1997: 53). Supporting the fads and fashion market is a vast consultancy market in which many firms trade on selling and repackaging the fads and fashions for individual customers or clients.

Almost all textbooks, and more mainstream management or organizational books, tend to contain or refer to 'soft' or 'hard' academic theory. Complexity, rigour, jargon, the quest for scientific knowledge or principles and the appeal to a select audience typify works in these areas. As Stephen Linstead (1996: 7) has pointed out, the theories that qualify as 'soft' are more concerned with the quest for theoretical understanding of practical problems, and the 'hard' theorists more with the development of knowledge for its own sake – to build new theories and break new ground on how we think about organizations and management. The pursuit of knowledge for its own sake is as important as knowledge that has practical application as its only focus. Through the pursuit of knowledge, we can develop new theories or paradigms, be they based on mathematics, science, philosophy, psychology or sociology. Out of these pursuits come new theories that might help us reorient how we think, feel and act. It is often hard for those outside the academic or scientific community to understand the debates going on about what constitutes knowledge and understanding. The field of theoretical activity, be it of a 'soft' or 'hard' kind, might not seem as attractive or relevant as the others described above, but without knowledge of these areas it is unlikely that a manager can really develop critical thinking and a reflective capacity as mentioned in the Introduction. It is important to have a critical approach to, and a reflective practice of, management because it develops our ability to entertain alternative sources of insight and knowledge, as described in Exhibit 1.1.

Learning by doing

The type of talk that occurs when Chris Stefano rushes into Dr Cora Harvey's office and starts to recount what went on in the meeting goes on in millions of organizations every day. Their conversation represents a first-order account because it is the actual spoken 'text' between two people from which one or both can learn. Much of what goes on in workplaces is in the form of direct conversations, such as that between Chris and Cora, or conversations that recount events such as the incident involving Chris and the others at the meeting. What gets talked about in everyday practice tends to be concerned with survival, getting through the day, determining those things that are important or that demand immediate attention, and identifying those things that can safely be ignored (Linstead 1996: 7). Most of what gets said or done, even in the heat of the moment, is fundamental to how we cope with complexity and uncertainty, and how we deal with things on the basis of their relevance to the task at hand. In one respect, this is why we all tend to operate for a large part of our day in what is anonymously termed 'the mire of immediacy'.

What gets said or often recounted in everyday practice tends to be based on knowledge that draws heavily on *commonsense*. Thus in terms of the dilemma described earlier, it seems to be good commonsense for Chris to call a meeting, outline the task at hand, ask for a volunteer and then expect someone to come forward. There are probably millions like 'Chris Stefano' around the world trying to execute similar management manoeuvres each day. Commonsense operates through determining, in a fairly *ad hoc* fashion, what can be taken for granted, assumed and unquestioned, what is accepted as commonly known, what is left implicit or tacit, and what remains unconsciously 'known' and almost a 'rule of thumb' (Linstead 1996: 7). However, one of the great ironies of organizational life is that commonsense or taken-for-granted knowledge is highly problematic as the basis for getting things done.

Whereas in everyday life we do many things unquestioningly (e.g. answering the phone, taking a coffee break, organizing an outing) in workplaces almost everything we do has to be accounted for, justified and rationalized to someone else and not always to our 'superiors' (Weick 1995: 63, citing Czarniawska-Joerges 1992). When we answer the phone at work, we might be very careful about how we introduce ourselves, the title we give ourselves, the tone of our voice and the information we disclose about the organization. Karl Weick points out that there is a lot of controlled processing and negotiation that has to occur before individuals can begin to address dilemmas and take actions that signal a willingness on their part to take responsibility for those actions (Weick 1995: 63–4). Chris Stefano, like many other managers, was operating on the premise that individuals will attend a meeting if a crisis faces the organization, that because of their status as employees individuals will carry out assigned tasks, and that certain things, such as deadlines, will be met. Commonsense dictates that these assumptions about taking responsibility should be implicitly understood and shared by all, but in fact in the workplace this is not always the case.

Commonsense knowledge (or its application) supports an 'action first' mentality that tends to force individuals to operate through abstractions, simplifications, contractions and abbreviations of events and circumstances (Linstead 1996: 7). These short cuts mean that when it comes to management practice there is a tendency to avoid testing assumptions or taking the time just to rethink how one operates day to day. As a result, we often get annoyed when our assumptions are challenged or we cannot even understand why anyone would want to question our assumptions. The challenge slows things down, causes 'hiccups' in the system, gets in the way of what we might believe is an otherwise smooth-running group, unit or organization. In the interests of 'getting by' and 'getting the job done' or taking action, we tend to resort to commonsense knowledge and expect others to readily see and agree with us over what needs to be done. This 'action first' culture dominates many organizations, and managers often feel that they should be out there doing something rather than taking the time to sit, question and discuss issues and problems (Lawson 1997: 3).

It is often difficult for us to see our commonsense constructs of the world, derived mainly from learning by doing, as mere constructs that need to be tested, modified and challenged. The way we see things is how we think things actually are. We are often afraid to test our commonsense assumptions because we know that these assumptions are not properly formalised and we do not want to appear ignorant or foolish by admitting that we might be in error or have misjudged a situation. Alternatively, we can come to believe so strongly in the 'truth' of our assumptions that we see no reason to question them. The importance of understanding how management knowledge and know-how in particular is acquired is fundamental to our being able to evaluate critically both what we learn formally and our own commonsense assumptions about management. The important thing is not to lose confidence in either form of knowledge acquisition. Managers should have the courage to make assumptions, but they should also have the courage to allow them to be debated, criticized and modified by practice and through discussion (Linstead and Harris 1983: 10). Formal studies of management (i.e. studying 'soft' and 'hard' theories) are essential to challenging commonsense assumptions (Fulop 1992: 8–12).

Commonsense assumptions which remain unquestioned are highly vulnerable to incorporating myths, stereotypes, biases and prejudices that can misguide the manager (Fulop 1992: 12–15). In *Imaginization*, Gareth Morgan (1993) recounts how he asked employees to describe their bosses by using an animal or story book characters. One of the interesting images he recounts is that of a female employee who used Beatrix Potter's *Tale of Jemima Puddle-Duck* to describe the behaviour of her boss; a boss seemingly helpful like the fox in the story, but not to be trusted because he was out for himself alone and was capable of eating you alive. In recounting the story, Morgan's intention was to illustrate how we use metaphors to deal with many intangibles and use images to convey meanings that invoke similarities, such as the one between a manager and a fox. Metaphors are used for dramatic effect and to achieve an impact on the listener. The images they convey are usually biased in that they selectively focus on some behaviour to the exclusion of others. Images are in fact distortions that allow individuals to imagine something as if it were something familiar (Bolman and Deal 1984: 15). However, images, such as metaphors, are powerful constructs that grasp the essentials of how, in the case of the *Tale of Jemima Puddle-Duck*, one individual feels about her boss (Morgan 1993: 24–5; also Fiol 1994: 405). Stereotypes and metaphors narrow and restrict our interpretations of, and responses to, what others do. Yet we all resort to them and use them every day to convey meanings and get our message across to our audience. They are deeply embedded in our commonsense assumptions.

The more we take for granted or operate from commonsense the less anxiety we seem to have in our lives (Downing 1997: 33). Reducing anxiety seems to make it easier for us to get on with the job at hand and to learn other things, and it might even lead to our letting go of or questioning some of our commonsense assumptions. Yet many stereotypes, such as those about foreigners, gender and social class (i.e. based on education, income), are particularly resistant to change or reframing. The stereotypes we carry around with us provide simple guidelines for interactions with diverse groups of people, and we habitually fall back on them to get by, especially when under pressure. Most of our frames of reference also contain rules relating to how we should handle our emotions, and these rules are important in getting by day to day (Downing 1997: 33). Just to get through the day we have to leave a lot of our commonsense, everyday stock of knowledge and frames of reference unchallenged. The problem is that this can breed complacency, ignorance and dogma. Why question or challenge something that appears to give security, ease and, often, even a sense of superiority?

This leads us to another point. Rather than merely focusing on the commonsense, taken-for-granted knowledge that individuals access to make sense of their workplaces, it is also important to ask why individuals do what they do in the first place (Fineman 1993: 23). In other words, what emotions – fear, anxiety, confidence, aggression, jealousy – also contribute to situations arising such as the one described above with Chris? Emotional games or subtexts are played out in every organizational encounter (Fineman 1997; Fulop and Rifkin 1997; Höpfl and Linstead 1997). Perhaps Chris is insecure, feeling threatened by work colleagues or has an annual review coming up and is anxious about it. Chris's anxiety may result in the tension or lack of compliance of the group as a whole. Alternatively, perhaps Phil is just plain upset about his failure to get promoted, and this has coloured his outlook. In other words, Phil might be venting anger and frustration about his non-promotion at Chris, who in Phil's mind represents the authority that denied him his promotion (presuming Chris is Phil's boss). There are two interesting points about emotions: the first is that we are all prisoners of our personal histories (however 'good' or 'bad' these might be), and the second is that most of us are unaware of our most basic motivations and feelings, although we inflict them on others every day (Fineman 1993: 24). In other words, our histories permit events to catalyse a wide array of emotions and, yet, we are often not introspective about them. Nor do many management courses or textbooks deal with these topics, preferring either to put them in the 'too hard basket' or seeing them as irrelevant (see Bedeian 1995).

Stories, which we will address next, result from events at work and the practice of managers. The manager's practices, as we saw above, are most often based on and rationalized in terms of commonsense rather than being the result of a deep questioning of assumptions. Commonsense and rules of thumb save us time and effort and may have a flavour of safe and comforting familiarity. Unfortunately, they can leave us open to decision making misguided by our stereotyping and constrained by the very metaphors that also help us to make sense of, for example, an untrustworthy (fox-like) boss. In addition, each person's emotional history affects their actions and how they respond to and recount the actions of others.

Local accounts

Local accounts abound in organizations and often take the form of stories you hear in corridors, in lunch rooms, in toilets, in car parks, on golf courses and in meeting rooms before meetings start (Fineman and Gabriel 1996: 1). Stephen Fineman (1993: 21) suggests that one of the reasons individuals choose to tell their stories or have conversations in these places is because they are places where emotional control can be relaxed and where they can feel safe to speak away from the scrutiny of those who are their 'superiors' or those likely to be judging their performance. Stories can also be transmitted electronically on the Internet – they need not be face to face. We all participate in telling stories. Gossiping, telling jokes and sharing anecdotes are all examples of the story-like or narrative form. Weick (1995: 127) suggests that individuals think narratively and make sense of organizations in a narrative form. Yet many things that are done or processed in organizations are not based on this easy to digest narrative or story form, but rather are based on argumentation. Diverse ways of recounting events make organizations difficult places for many individuals to negotiate and make sense of. For people from different cultural backgrounds, it is even more difficult; for example, the story of Chris's meeting when told from the perspective of Phil might seem absurd to people from another culture because they are used to a narrative form different from the one that Phil might use. They would tell the story differently with different meanings attached to events. In many South East Asian countries, it would be unacceptable to volunteer for a task – one could lose face by appearing to be inconsiderate of fellow employees. The expectation would be that a senior person would assign the task and would not ask for a volunteer.

The story format is used because it is such an easy format in which to capture the essence of our experiences. So, one might see half of one's life in an organization spent making decisions and acting on commands and orders, and the other half spent trying to make sense of the actions of others. We cram what we perceive into a story's plot but neglect or ignore those aspects that do not fit our preferred version of events. Though these tendencies have their inherent dangers, our words and actions, and the accounts told about them, can be seen as the most accessible and rich reservoir of management knowledge – knowledge we must contend with.

Both accounts in practice and local accounts, and indeed accounts of any kind, depend on the understanding and meanings of those sharing a conversation. When an account is given, there are usually two and often three simultaneous forms of knowledge being imparted to the listener. The first relates to the *content of the communication* (Fiol 1994: 405) which refers to categories or labels (e.g. stereotypes or metaphors) being used. So, in the Chris Stefano story, these might relate to what is said later about other people in the meeting. Chris could be described as behaving like a 'headless chicken'; Roderick Cage criticized for being sexist, Rebecca Spalding for always whingeing, Winjamarra for being lazy or Merilyn Hue for being 'bitchy'. These are all filtered perceptions of reality, and thus are unlikely to be accurate ones. But they might, nonetheless, become a significant part of the content of the communication about the meeting or subsequent local accounts.

Meaning also resides in a second form of knowledge, in *frameworks* or *ways of framing communication.* '"Framing" refers to the way people construct their arguments or viewpoint, regardless of its content' (Fiol 1994: 405). Thus for some the meeting might be a monumental disaster, for others a typical event in a typical day, and for others a great opportunity to improve something in the organization. A third form of knowledge that conveys meaning is a *relationship component* (Austin 1962; Watzlawick, Beavin and Jackson 1967; Bateson 1975; Garko 1994; Rifkin 1994). The importance given to a story may depend on who tells it and what that person's relationship is to a listener. If Winjamarra tells the story of the meeting to a colleague who works for him, the colleague might try to remember the events for future reference in order to impress Winjamarra. If Rebecca Spalding tells the story to a co-worker, it may sound to the co-worker like more whingeing from Rebecca. Given these different dimensions of meaning or forms of knowledge – content, framing and relationships – individuals can be understood to need to agree on a broad frame of reference about events and with the people they might be listening to in order to solve a problem collectively or come up with a brilliant new innovation that many are willing to adopt (Fiol 1994: 406).

One of the greatest paradoxes facing any group, and those trying to manage it, is to work out how members of the group can learn collectively and develop a broad frame of reference they can all share. For collective learning to occur, there has to be some consensus or unity of interpretations about certain things or events and there has to be public confirmation of the interpretations for the sharing of knowledge (Fiol 1994: 404). Then there also has to be diversity of interpretations for new knowledge to develop and for progress to occur in organizations (Fiol 1994: 404). Progress embraces more than just innovations because not all innovations spell improvements for an organization or society (Abrahamson 1996a: 5). Thus both consensus and diversity have to coexist, and neither can be subordinated to the other. This means that collective learning is built upon the sharing of common understandings, but also the development of new understandings, and this often entails exploring and finding new frames of reference. Managers need to understand the ways in which knowledge is shaped and shared in everyday practice, in learning by doing and through local accounts, that create and sustain the frames of reference individuals draw upon to make sense of their organizations and the actions of those in them.

Managers will have to learn more than just how meanings are communicated. All social practices, such as communicating, also involve two other elements: power and the use of normative sanctions (Coopey 1995: 198; Salaman and Butler 1994: 39). All forms of communication are situated within structures (e.g. a hierarchy) and organizational processes (e.g. bargaining and negotiating) of power and underscored by potential normative sanctions such as rewards and punishments. Members of organizations usually seek to control their work lives and conditions, that is, to maximise their opportunities and rewards. Yet organizations create dependency relations in which many tasks and jobs can only be done through collective effort. Collective effort is constrained by unequal personal access to resources, such as finances, promotions, information, opportunities to occupy positions of authority (i.e. give orders to others) and so on that affect how tasks or work are accomplished (Coopey 1995: 197; see also Chapter 4). Having to depend on others involves a risk because failure or success at completing tasks usually carries negative and positive sanctions respectively; the former referring to coercion (punishment) and the latter to inducements (rewards) that are endorsed by top managers and broadly accepted by others in the organization (Coopey 1995: 198). Controlling one's work life or conditions is very much a political process fraught with risks that sometimes are worth it and that at other times can cause chaos and havoc that can seriously harm one's career.

As Salaman and Butler also point out, since managers exist in structures of power, reward and evaluation (i.e. sanctions), they will often learn only what is seen as legitimate (i.e. involves positive inducements or rewards) and helps them get ahead. To do otherwise would be considered mad and managers who did so would likely be made redundant or dismissed (1994: 38–9). In other words, managers often have a vested interest or priorities in *not* learning or adopting new frames of reference, the very source of creativity, innovation and learning. These vested interests can come in the form of, say, departmental loyalty, professional affiliations, different levels of skills, knowledge, expertise and even gender. All these can breed differences in perspectives that can get in the way of cooperation and collective action (Salaman 1994: 39; also Chapter 4).

Popular accounts

Stories that attract or hold our attention tend to be about remarkable experiences that often relate to something unexpected or out of the ordinary (Weick 1995: 127–8). A remarkable enough story gets published – it becomes a popular account. Stories also have particular forms or genres that are derived from quite surprising sources. To explain what we mean by these forms or genres, we need to look beyond learning by doing and local accounts, to what we have termed 'popular accounts'.

A popular account is usually a noteworthy story that is circulated outside the organization. It can be a newsletter story of a boost in production; a newspaper profile of a manager receiving a promotion, a revelation on electronic mail about new products, a manager's report in a magazine of 20 percent growth in productivity due to re-engineering, an in-depth television documentary on reductions in the workforce at a local factory or a 'leak' from an internal policy meeting about changes. It has usually been reproduced in the media in some form or another as a second- or third-order account of an organizational event or state of affairs, and usually in sensationalised form.

Both the person who recounts a story about an exceptional event, person or experience, and the person about whom it is told, are involved in and affected by a particular storyline. The storylines of popular accounts are likely to revolve around six main plots that can be interwoven into one storyline, or one plot might dominate a storyline. Storylines, particularly those that draw on legends and fairytales, function as powerful frames of reference by which individuals come to rationalize or legitimize what goes on in their organizations, including their successes and failures. These storylines become the lessons that others might learn from someone else's experiences. The six dominant plots that are most likely to be represented in popular accounts are ones that we (at least in Anglo-Saxon cultures) have grown up with and learnt about in fairytales and stories. Following Stephen Downing (1997: 37–9), but with the inclusion of the 'disaster' and 'conquest' plots, and some other modifications, the six dominant plots are shown in Exhibit 1.2.

- **The quest** A progressive ('nice') hero or heroine adventurer who challenges the status quo or conventional wisdom, experiences setbacks, but ultimately succeeds and becomes rich and famous. The 'quest' plot is linked to the high adventure novel or the romance genre of the great love affair or story.
- **The contest** A polarised struggle between two heroes or heroines characterised as representing the forces of good and evil in which there is a climactic battle, and good prevails over evil. The plot is melodramatic.
- **The conquest** A hero or heroine who succeeds by way of force, plunder or bullying, but achieves his/her ultimate goal and succeeds in the face of opposition and attack. Unlike the contest, the conqueror comes to be seen as good once he/she has 'saved the day' or achieved fame and fortune. This type of storyline can invite loathsome or begrudging admiration of the feats of the hero or heroine.
- **The downfall** A hero or heroine slips from success and must face danger and humiliation primarily as a result of wrong-doing or some weakness of personality. They usually have to confront fear and suffering and are likely not to prevail or survive. Fear and pity are strong emotions evoked by this plot, which is essentially the modern-day tragedy in which we keep asking: '...if only...'.
- **The disaster** A hero or heroine falls from success and must face danger, humiliation and great loss. Unlike the 'downfall', this loss is likely to be the result of events outside the control of the hero or heroine. They suffer a great deal, but always hold out the hope of a 'comeback'! Pity and disbelief are strong emotions associated with this plot, which is essentially a drama of epic proportions.
- **The scam** A hero or heroine is exposed as incompetent, corrupt or foolish; what were past heroic actions are reinterpreted to reveal a scam to defraud or fool others. This type of plot is riddled with irony as people and events turn out to be not what they seem, and there is a sense of being cheated or let down.

Exhibit 1.2 Dominant plots

Some examples of popular accounts are reproduced in the three inserts below. Try to make out why these accounts have appeal, and then see if you can identify the main plots in each storyline.

Richard Branson

Let's examine a hypothetical situation, a sort of elaborate role-playing fantasy. Prepare to assume the mindset of a character. To begin with, you're a self-made billionaire. You have a parkside mansion in one of the world's great cities and a manor in the country-side and island paradise in the Caribbean – your own island – where you've installed a first-rate chef. You own a record label, an airline that flies to four continents, a national radio station, a pan-European train service, a worldwide chain of music stores, a blue-jeans and casual-clothing company, a string of hotels and a message service. You even own the brand of vodka you drink. You have hundreds of millions of dollars of capital readily available, and yet you don't really need it because other people are willing to put up all the money for your daring business ventures, taking all the risk while you hold majority ownership in the new companies and retain control – such is your track record and professional reputation and your intangible aura of X-factor.

…You're still young (46), handsome, slender and leonine; your hair is thick as a mane. You're a symbol of the baby boomers who came of age in the '60s and later brought their progressive values to their entrepreneurial ventures. You're happily married to the beautiful woman you've lived with for 21 years, and together you're raising two adorable kids. Your wife, a former hippie, apparently doesn't mind when you stay out until 3 am on week nights at your nightclub, flirting shamelessly with the prowling temptresses who surround you wherever you go.

…The entire scenario has been taken from the life of Richard Branson, the chair-man of the Virgin Group of companies – that sweater wearing icon of British business – a man who makes a bizarre hobby out of courting and cheating his own death.

Branson explains…that he likes to finance new companies as a way of helping other people pursue their dreams. Virgin Bride was the brainchild of Virgin Atlantic flight attendant, Alisa Percy, who is now the top executive at the start-up.

…The launch event for the first Virgin Bride store was held on-site, in a grand lime-stone building near London's Trafalgar Square. A legion of impossibly cheerful waitresses buzzed about, pouring champagne. They wore the spiffy scarlet of suits and pumps of Virgin Atlantic flight attendants because that's what they were: cabin crew on a layover. Branson never bandies pretentious jargon like synergy, but that's exactly what he was creating with this endeavour, and it wasn't just that employees were handling other jobs. The new store will help brides book their honeymoons, pushing Virgin flights and Virgin hotels. Synergy!

But wait: that's just the beginning of cross-pollination. Next there was a fashion show, and a procession of models strutted out to show off some of the wedding dresses the store would carry…The catwalkers came from Branson's modelling agency, Storm, which represents the likes of Elle McPherson and Kate Moss.

For the show's finale, Branson himself appeared, the Virgin king pretending to be the Virgin bride. He wore a white gown with white fishnet stockings and big white bow in the back atop a long, fluffy train. Branson had even shaved off the rakish beard he had sported since his teenage years. He threw red roses to the frenzied crowd as the paparazzi shouted, 'Show us your garter!'

There's almost always some kind of big stunt when Branson opens a new store or inaugurates an airline route or launches a company.

Branson is being sued for sexual harassment by one of his American employees, who claims he fondled her breasts at a company party. He denies the allegations, though it's not hard to see how his style of good-natured partying would be treated with less tolerance in the US. He's unabashedly flirtatious, but his lasciviousness goes only so far. The British tabloids have never accused him of marital infidelity.

Branson makes a habit of lavishing his people with recognition and hospitality. Every summer he invites all of Virgin Atlantic's 3,500 employees and their kids to his country house near Oxford for a five-day party...Virgin Atlantic workers aren't paid as much as their counterparts in airlines such as British Airways, but Branson has other, more creative approaches to motivation.

...[Branson hosts] an award dinner for Virgin Atlantic's flight attendants-of-the-month from the previous year, crew members who were mentioned by passengers on survey forms or singled out by their bosses for exceptional work...For the finale, Branson picks one name out of a hat: the chosen crewmate wins a vacation to Neckar, Branson's own Virgin Island. The winner is a woman in a black cocktail dress, and she's exuberant. All of a sudden, Branson picks her up by the waist and turns her upside down, exposing her black underwear. The audience cheers wildly, the woman laughs with them. It's Branson's favourite party stunt...

At 16, [Branson] dropped out of school to go into business. He started a magazine called, ironically, Student, and fearlessly solicited articles from such counterculture icons as Jean-Paul Sartre and James Baldwin. The venture was short-lived and morphed into a discount mail-order record business and then a record label. Branson didn't have much sense about trends in music, but his colleagues did. His own contributions were vital though: charismatic leadership, prodigious energy, unbounded and reckless ambition, shrewd deal-making and negotiating, and a knack for charming bankers and eluding creditors.

Source: Abridged from Alan Deutschman (1997), 'Heavens above', Good Weekend, The Sydney Morning Herald, 23 August, pp. 16–19.

The main storyline involving Richard Branson is the quest, but some parts that have been omitted, such as his battle with British Airways, also reveal the contest plot. The excerpt does not describe his daredevil stunts, but it does allude to the fact that he courts death with his adventures, such as hot air ballooning. He flaunts tradition, rejects the status quo with his dress, is flamboyant, fun, wealthy, powerful, sought after, breaks the rules of business protocol, has temptresses chasing him and has the so-called 'X factor'. He is the modern corporate hero and provides a 'rags to riches' story. The image of the hero is so strong that many of Branson's faults or shortcomings are overlooked or 'forgiven'. For example, the sexual harassment case against him is represented by the male writer as a clear misinterpretation of the antics of a 'harmless' prankster. Branson is the arch non-conformist.

The quest plot influences the ways in which people talk and think about management. For example, leadership theories have been dominated for years by an heroic masculine image (Huey 1994) based on the pursuit of the quest, particularly of self-made entrepreneurs such as the likes of Branson. The dream for many managers might be represented by the Branson-type storyline – quest and contest. Many senior managers, when they talk about such things as strategic planning and creating a mission, purpose and vision, also try to engage others in a type of quest or bold adventure with a promise of a better, wealthier and happier workplace (Downing 1997: 29). The storyline, and its plots, are a way of trying to get others to share a particular frame of reference to legitimise what is being done and how it is being done, and in the process also helping to build commitment and understanding. These storylines become a part of the corporate myth or a way of reinforcing that this is how 'things work around here' (Schwartz 1996: 41). Thus the fact that Branson might do a lot of peculiar things is legitimated through the storyline that becomes the representation of Branson's quest. Branson would hope that all in Virgin subscribe to his storyline and adopt it as their own. It fuels or satisfies the employees' dreams of a 'fairy tale' land, where the dashing and cavalier 'Prince Charming', that is, Branson, wants to make everyone's dreams come true. He wants everyone to have common behaviours, beliefs and perceptions or share common myths about being a Virgin employee (Schwartz 1996: 41).

Liz Fulop and Fran Laneyrie (1995), reviewing a study by Amanda Sinclair (1994) of top male CEOs in Australia, noted that the public tales told by these CEOs centred on heroic images of the sort described above in the Branson story. These heroic images were invariably cast in a narrow, masculine mould. The CEOs' quests described in Sinclair's study drew on mythical images, such as that of Ulysses, the hero who must overcome obstacle after obstacle in a journey that some CEOs might say would inevitably lead them to the top. Along the way, the story of Ulysses depicts temptresses trying to avert the hero from the path to success. Such temptress images reflect what the authors contend is a problematic aspect of success stories, and stories in general in our culture. Almost all mythical images of powerful women, except for the 'mother figure', generally represent evil. Fulop and Laneyrie contend that such constraints in the mythical imagery, from which public tales of success are told, reinforce the stereotypes and biases that work against women climbing to the top of organizations. They support a movement of 'remythologizing' whereby, for example, Ulysses can be recast as 'a sadistic bully, whose joy in plundering and raping and pillaging others is far from heroic' (Fulop and Laneyrie 1995: 64; also Laneyrie 1995). This would be akin to adopting the conquest plot. The Australian CEOs in Sinclair's study also represented women with some positive images, though, portraying some in their organizations as 'good mothers' (the proverbial 'Oedipal myth', the story of Oedipus who loved his mother) or 'good virgins' who were focused, knowledgeable and direct. The women's main virtue is portrayed as being that they are not out solely for their own gain. Such virtue or goodness is even captured in company names, such as Branson's own use of the 'Virgin' company name.

Elvira Ruiz

[The place]: Playas de Tijuana: When Elvira Ruiz took charge of this seaside district's municipal police, she faced a legion of drug punks and street criminals determined to show her who was boss. She was shot at, run off the highway and threatened with death.

Inside the dusty precinct, a different war was being waged. Ruiz's subordinate officers, all male, bristled at the idea of a woman in command. They withheld information. They emptied petrol tanks of patrol cars and disconnected their starter cables. They employed time-honoured gender warfare tactics, smearing her with unsavoury locker room lies. They spearheaded a lobby to oust her.

How Ruiz won her battle on both fronts is a testimony to character over circumstances, Ruiz's image as a clean cop and sheer stubbornness. Her honest reputation, if merited, remains a risky distinction in a city where authorities are forced to choose between *plata o plom*o – bribes or bullets – by the Tijuana drug cartel, an empire backed by an array of well-connected gunmen and millions of dollars in cash. Eight ranking Baja law enforcement officers have been killed in the past year. Some victims, according to US court documents, were corrupt collaborators who got bribes *and* bullets.

US anti-drug experts say it is only a matter of time before reform-minded officers are transferred, intimidated, demoted, bought off – or worse. The most pessimistic believe institutional corruption is so pervasive it is extremely difficult for any honest officers to rise to command.

'Elvira does not steal,' said Baja California Superior Court Magistrate Victor Manuel Vasquez. 'She works night and day. She cannot be intimidated because she knows she is doing the right thing. If there were more Elviras in the police force, we would be much better off.' Ruiz commands an 80-officer division within the 1,200-strong city police force. She is one of five district chiefs who report to Tijuana's police commander. Said Ricardo Arenas, spokesman for the municipal police: 'If there's an emergency call, she answers it herself. If there's a gunfight, she's first at the scene. Our only complaint is she should stop working when she's sick.'

Just shy of 1.5m tall, Ruiz is a soft-spoken, articulate, divorced workaholic who looks younger than her 38 years. When not in uniform, she prefers black designer jeans, blue eye shadow, fuchsia lipstick and maroon nail polish. She does not hide her disregard for *machismo*, the masculine expression of the Mexican gender balance of power, or shrink from the 'F' word. Ruiz is an unabashed *feminista*.

…Ruiz's new command, Playas de Tijuana, was a one-time beach resort that had once been virtually crime-free. But by the time Ruiz arrived, the district was becoming a battleground for control of the local trade in methamphetamines and other drugs…When Ruiz arrived on the scene, street punks who thought of themselves as untouchable were startled to find themselves being photographed for the arrest scrapbook she keeps on her desk. Even car thieves, small-time drug dealers, burglars and drunk drivers began to insinuate that if she didn't leave them alone, she was playing with fire…The death threats began not long after she arrived, and in August 1994 a car sped alongside her and forced her to skid off the road…Like many law enforcers, Ruiz preaches a fatalistic stoicism…'If I were afraid, I wouldn't do this.'

Source: Abridged from Anne-Marie O'Connor (1997), 'Woman shakes up Tijuana police brass', The Sydney Morning Herald, 1 March, p. 24 (report from The Los Angeles Times).

The Ruiz story, by contrast, with its feminine 'hero', is a representation of the contest. Her ethics and *feminista* ideals, her willingness to face danger head on, and being the first at any shoot out, cast her as 'the good' challenging 'the bad'. All decent or honest people would want to see her win and beat the 'baddies'. This makes her a particular type of heroine in the management domain in which she operates.

The contest plot is often the one used to make sense of organizational power and politics, both of which are prevalent in the Ruiz story. The interesting thing to note in this storyline is that the so-called 'baddies' in the story – the drug dealers and cartel members – would probably prefer to present the Ruiz story from the conquest storyline, pointing to her unreasonable aggression and harassment of them as being out of step with the spirit of the law.

Storylines, and their plots, are in one form or another 'vocabularies of motives' in which the descriptions of human conduct, such as those of Ruiz or Branson, are not normally derived from the individuals being described, but are imputed to them by the media or those producing the accounts. Ruiz might or might not be pleased with being described as an 'unabashed *feminista*'. What is also often missing from the stories or popular accounts are '...the diverse objects, resources, events, and social relations...' (Silverman 1985: 10) that are part and parcel of the representations being made. In other words, the stories are always incomplete and often one-sided, particularly when they are abridged as they have been for this chapter. Moreover, as David Silverman argues, '...social relations specify who is obliged to describe whom and the form and consequences of these descriptions...' (1985: 10). Storylines or plots are also 'vocabularies of power'. This means that the description of Ruiz, for example, given by Magistrate Vasquez is one that is legitimately given in a public domain and, as would be expected, is cast in terms of law and order issues. For Ruiz, this description has enormous personal and professional consequences as it has to do with her honesty, accountability and performance. In other words, considerable power is accorded to those who are seen as being legitimately obliged to give descriptions of people – their opinions and views get listened to and are far harder to dismiss than those of others. Their descriptions become a discursive resource or capability that helps to ensure that managers, such as Ruiz, perform as expected, or risk a potentially less flattering storyline being told about them.

Jacques Nasser

Meet Jac the Knife, executive vice-president of the Ford Motor Company, a man hell-bent on reinventing the world's wheels. In the quiet of the cellar, Jacques Albert Nasser sounds not at all like a Jacques. When he responds to a good natured interjection, the accent is more ... Bruce [means a real Australian bloke].

'Don't take the piss too much,' he grins, the delivery as broad and flat as a mulga wood ashtray. The Lebanese-born kid from Melbourne's suburban Northcote, the one they called a wog at school, is running Ford's global operations in Detroit. In his spare time, he's also mounting a rescue of the company's European theatre, amid strikes and saturation media coverage.

Wall Street says Jac Nasser, 49, shapes as the heir apparent to the chairman's office at Ford Motor. Tonight, he's doing one of the many things he does well: laying on the personal charm. Deftly he moves from Grange Hermitage fine wine to computer technology, a rust belt revival and, finally, to Detroit's fondness for overstatement.

Jacques Nasser is less a trimmer of corporate fat than a one-man guillotine. His blade removes arms and legs, but his surgery has returned many Ford businesses to robust health. The word 'ruthless' is often used. 'You can't ask a customer in the marketplace to pay for waste, inefficiency and a lack of focus,' he counters.

Wall Street has IOUs from Nasser amounting to $US11 billion, the promised savings from a dramatic restructuring of the way Ford develops and builds its new cars and trucks – his version of reinventing the wheel. Under a plan called Ford 2000, he has promised to freeze the company's huge new model costs, delivering more profits for the company's Dearborn headquarters and cheaper cars and trucks for customers.

He has shown Wall Street the minutiae: how reducing the variety of cigarette lighters in Ford vehicles from 14 to just one will save a million dollars a year. And the big picture: that 6,000 fewer engineers will be needed when he cuts by a quarter the number of Ford's vehicle 'platforms', the building blocks for every new model, while doubling the number of parts they share.

A shrinker of head counts and a slasher of costs, Nasser also has the flair to create successful, exciting new models which just happen to be very profitable. He is an enthusiast, more than comfortable coaxing young designers into creating his current pet project, a 21st-century version of the 1955 Ford Thunderbird.

For grimy, time-worn Detroit, he is a one-man culture shock. A graduate in business studies from Royal Melbourne Institute of Technology, where he returned this week to collect an honorary doctorate, he is a rare blend of hard-nosed human abacus, astute politician and old-fashioned petrolhead.

He speaks five languages and often eschews a chauffeur, driving a giant red pick-up truck. He's the antithesis of the insular, Detroit WASP high-roller, and his relentless, sometimes colourful, approach has Ivy League colleagues sniffily suggesting he lacks a certain ... polish. 'The old Detroit had a narrow focus on the US,' says Nasser dismissively. 'What we're seeing with the new Detroit is a focus on what's right globally and that's right down my alley.'

As president of Ford Automotive Operations (FAO), Nasser has huge worldwide clout. With more than a tinge of sarcasm, FAO has become known in Detroit as Foreign Accents Only as Nasser strives to break an all-American culture, with wave after wave of offshore executives, enough from his homeland to give rise to another testy label: For Australians Only.

As a Ford executive, you either believed in the Nasser doctrine or you were out of a job. 'He was a bit like that Monty Python sketch with the black knight,' a close colleague remembers. 'He'd cut off an arm, then a leg, but fully expect the knight to continue giving its best.'

Now Nasser is but one step removed from the chairman's office and the ultimate power to steer that 'world beater' vision into reality. His rise has been meteoric since taking the chairman's role at Ford of Europe in 1993. He'd wagered his career by turning down the lesser role of president.

'There's satisfaction in knowing you are ultimately responsible for the livelihoods of thousands of people,' he explains. 'They blame you or they praise you, no one else. That has a certain energising value for me.'

In Europe, as in Australia, Nasser's hands were deep in the clay of new model development...championing among other designs a new small car, the groundbreaking Ka, introduced last year to rapturous response.

'The standard Jac line,' says a former close colleague, 'is always the same. How can we do better? How can we take this and improve it?' Nasser is a talker, a great persuader with infectious enthusiasm and a direct style the media love. Hard as nails but smooth as oiled glass when there's something he wants, he is totally without side when the business is done. Nasser's social skills are extraordinary. He never seems to forget a name or a face and has the happy knack of making those around him comfortable.

'To me, almost everything you do has to be people-related. You can't get away from it. Relationships matter. Emotions are important. Friendships are important. If you start to lose a feeling of loyalty and trust and confidence in your own friends and community you're gone. What's left for you to fight for?'

That legendary patience is sorely tested by the inevitable question. So how do you feel about sacking your mates, Jac? He doesn't miss a beat, but is clearly displeased.

'Yes, I've done that. I've done it when I've really felt that the loyalty wasn't there, that they didn't share common views. When that happens you've really got to separate. I like people who are passionate about what they are doing and I don't suffer fools.'

Source: Abridged from Phil Scott (1997), 'Jac the Knife', The Sydney Morning Herald, The Spectrum Features, 8 March, p. 3.

In the 'Jac the Knife' storyline we see the dominant plot being that of the conquest. This is the classic American 'captain of industry' Rockefeller story who, incidentally, wrote his storyline through autobiography. Such 'captains of industry' were notorious for being hard on employees, often unpopular, but highly focused commercially. It is difficult to see how the quest or contest plots would apply to this story. There is no visible high adventure or romance being depicted or, for that matter, good prevailing over bad. The image that prevails is that of the ruthless manager who conquers all in his path and 'takes no prisoners'. In the end, the success of the individual and their organization invokes admiration for their achievements. The conquest plot has been prevalent in the 1990s with the spread of downsizing and re-engineering of many large organizations, both in the private and public sectors. Those who have masterminded huge labour shedding and cost-cutting exercises became the corporate heroes of the 1990s, and they were identified with and revered for their extreme toughness and grit. It is the ultimate macho storyline. The 'Jac the Knife' storyline has had many similar counterparts across the world. 'The Axe Man Cometh' by Jodie Brough and Michael Millett (1997: 6,6s,7s), for example, describes a very successful senior public servant in Australia whose style of management was described as being '... like fingernails drawn across a blackboard, designed to attract attention' (p. 6).

The business world is dominated by the above three plots. Three others – the downfall, the disaster and the scam – provide counter-stories or lessons about those who fail to make the corporate grade or make it and then 'fail'. They provide powerful imagery and stereotypes of the fall from grace and the loss of power.

A disaster storyline could be depicted for Compass Airlines in Australia, which was established to increase competition and pressure the deregulation of the airline industry. Compass provided cheap, cut-price airfares and was highly successful. Eventually the airline went into receivership due to the pressures from airline regulators and the failure of the two major domestic airlines to cooperate and provide facilities for Compass. A number of unsuccessful re-launches were attempted.

A downfall storyline can be exemplified by businesswoman, Prue Acton, who for 30 years dominated Australian fashion. She was a true entrepreneur, innovating in her field with different fashion designs, accessories and cosmetics. She also designed outfits for five Olympic teams and was awarded an OBE (Order of the British Empire) (Neales 1997: 32). Ms Acton presided over an $11 million a year business, was astute at PR (public relations) and was a high-profile personality who often received as much media coverage as a prime minister. She was: '...wooed by the rich and famous, and a swag of powerful and influential men were linked to her name' (Neales 1997: 33). After her divorce in 1984 from fashion designer Mike Treloar, gossip and innuendo, especially about Ms Acton's private life, hit the press regularly and in very controversial ways. In the end, worn out by the 'bad' publicity and pressures of her business, which were affecting her personal life, Ms Acton sold her business interests and dropped out of public life. Prue Acton had been described, almost in a goddess mould, as '...fashion's darling; ...[having] a bright, butter-wouldn't-melt smile, halo of golden locks, girlish giggle...' (Neales 1997: 32–3).

The corporate collapses of the late 1980s provided excellent material for the scam storyline. In Australia, legends in the scam storyline were abundant. Alan Bond, who was once the toast of the nation after winning the America's Cup yacht race, was convicted of the largest corporate theft in Australia and sentenced to a prison term. Many countries had similar scam storylines about the corporate 'cowboys' and entrepreneurs of the 1980s.

Other typical storylines are the more mundane ones, such as the bureaucratic blunder storyline; the boss who always messes up; the union versus management (or the 'them versus us' approach); the crisis where everything is so badly managed that only a crisis creates action; or the reorganization story where every new manager has to reorganize. The Chris Stefano story, being more mundane and certainly not qualifying as an extraordinary story, could nevertheless be typified as one of these storylines. The issue of storylines and archetype will be revisited in Chapter 5 where we discuss leadership.

The six dominant plots, and their associated storylines, become particularly appealing in periods of rapid change and turbulence in organizations, such as Ford with the 'Jac the Knife' storyline. Each of the three success storylines – quest, contest and conquest – is particularly effective for managers trying to enrol others' support for management's values and beliefs. Each of these plots offers a way of explaining collective experience, and as such has emergent elements of an organizational ideology (Coopey 1995: 209). Authors of the ideology, or its text, can often exert enormous control over the ways in which frames of reference either are allowed to be challenged or become sacrosanct. This sacrosanctness is particularly evident in the 'Jac the Knife' tale, where it is so important to Nasser, and to the future security of employees, that employees share his view. The need for adherence to a public storyline is less obvious in Branson's case because his antics and 'games' tend to distract attention from how he might deal with recalcitrance or those who do not go along with the Virgin storyline. Ideology is essentially captured in the ethos and language of an organization and linked to stories and plots with which we are often familiar and comfortable.

The fads and fashions

We are told that the management consultancy market is one of the fastest growing in the world and, as an industry, the top 25 firms in the market earn between them around $US25.9 billion annually (James 1997: 53; Macken 1997: 46). The world's top management gurus, and they are mainly from the USA and male, earn at the top end of the scale about $US90 000 per day and at the lower end about $US20 000 per day (James 1997: 56). We are also told that book sales in the popular management market are worth around $US930.4 million annually, '...despite 70 per cent of managers saying management tools don't deliver and four out of five failing to finish the books' (Macken 1997: 46). We are not told who or where the 70 percent of managers come from, but this comment reflects the power and influence of management gurus and fads and the industry that they have helped to shape. In Exhibit 1.3 we have reproduced some of the fads and fashions that have been popular in the 1990s. Exhibit 1.3 contains some of the 'buzz-words' that have been generated in the bestselling books often, though not always, written by management gurus. Highly successful managers, such as Ricardo Semler in Brazil, whose book, *Maverick* (1993), became a bestseller, also enjoy guru status.

The fad and fashion market place is divided into several segments, but the two main ones are the consultancy market, which is dominated by management techniques and tools, and the guru market place dominated by the trend-setting books and ideas on management. Both markets tap into an important area of management knowledge, that is, professional practice where managers or would-be managers are usually preoccupied with improving the running of their units or operations and trying to learn quickly from others who have succeeded at management. It seems commonsense for managers to look to successful corporations, other successful managers and their successful advisers/consultants for advice or help.

In contrast to the consultancy market, management gurus invent new ways of talking about management and heavily influence what become the new buzz-words in management (e.g. Exhibit 1.3). These gurus are very adept at making surprising and accurate observations of future trends in management. Their buzz-words become part of the management discourse, and their ideas are used by businesses around the world to gain a competitive edge or to claim they are trying to gain an edge (James 1997: 53–4, 57). The gurus do not make their reputations from solving individual organizational problems, but from being seen to be at the leading edge of organizational and management developments and 'revolutions'.

- **Virtual corporation** Usually high-tech firms inhabited by 'wiz kids' or 'superminds' working in very flexible, creative environments – often with team members interacting mainly via phone and the Internet – that respond to rapid change.
- **Learning organization** Euphemism for a new culture of 'brainwork' or 'not parking your brains at the door' – means being a team player, continuously innovative, creative, and problem solving but also having a mindset that the corporation approves of. (Replaces 'excellence' culture of the 1980s.) Denotes a particular type of organization.
- **Strategic alliances** Usually refers to external relationships with customers, suppliers, distributors and competitors. Part of the trend to globalise firms and reduce costs by outsourcing, re-engineering and becoming more focused on core competence.
- **Value-adding** Anything that is done to improve or refine a process, product, service or people! A string of such activities is known as a 'value-chain'.
- **Empowerment** Associated with the trend to make organizational politics and power struggles things of the past, and make power 'respectable' and something under management's mandate and control. Connected with the idea of post-heroic leadership. Used to label efforts to make managers look as though they are giving power to employees.

- **Re-engineering** Replaces rationalizing and restructuring. Suggests you can start from scratch, make big changes to your processes (via technology/management information systems enhancements). Reinventing the organization by shedding labour.
- **Core competence** Anything you do better than anyone else and is hard to copy or substitute. In other words, you actually know what you're doing well and why you are succeeding.
- **Best practice** Means benchmarking and comparing your firm to others. The difficulty is finding the measures that make sense to your firm in comparing itself with the best.
- **Followership/Stewardship** (or post-heroic leadership) This equates to 'taking the leader out of leadership'. Means everyone is a potential leader and the hero-male image of the 1980s (entrepreneurial cowboy) is no longer fashionable.
- **Teams** Lots of new terms – teamnets, virtual teams, high-performance teams – these days are associated with collaborative learning and replacing supervision with team-based controls.
- **Diversity** About managing differences (gender, age, race, ethnicity, culture, etc.).
- **'Post-'** Implies a break with many of the ideas that were popular in the 1980s. A plethora of 'post-' terms are in currency: post-total quality management (TQM) organization, post-heroic leadership, post-entrepreneurial organization and postmodern organization.

Exhibit 1.3 'Buzz-words'

Management consultants, by contrast, generally make their living from inventing, packaging, interpreting, translating or tailoring the fads and fashions to suit a client's management and organizational problems. Some consultants make their living from helping organizations to solve their problems once the organization has failed to achieve results based on the fads and fashions (Lawson 1997: 3).

From the point of view of the manager, the appeal of fads and fashions is understandable. They have strong rhetorical (persuasive) appeal. As Eric Abrahamson says, 'Rhetorics must not only create the belief that the techniques they champion are rational, but also that they are at the forefront of management progress' (1996a: 10). This belief is achieved in several ways. Examples are cited of companies that have had success using the technique or method, and it is implied that the same performance outcomes can be achieved in all companies. Various quasi-theories are produced in order to support claims for improved performance, or scientific studies are produced in order to support claims of success (Abrahamson 1996a: 10). Fads and fashions hold out the promise to managers that they will be at the leading edge and are doing something to get there. Managers are given an 'assurance' that they are not being left behind and are up there with the best companies in the world (The Editors, *World Executive's Digest* 1997: 19; Shapiro 1995: xv–xvi). They promise significant improvements or results. The following is an example of the types of fads or techniques that are likely to attract managers, the prime rhetorical appeal being the uptake by top companies of the 'bizarre activities' described below, based on pseudo-theories of child development.

There was the time 200 employees were told to dress up like animals – lions, dogs, weasels, you name it – and run through the city streets. Another group was told to ask every limo driver in town for a bottle of Grey Poupon [a brand of mustard whose TV advertisements involved limousines]. The brave souls...[are] employees of Thomson Investment Software in Boston...

All this wackiness emanates from a Boston-based consulting firm called Urban Outing Club for Business, founded by former Proctor & Gamble exec [*sic*] Dick Eaton. His notion is that corporations cannot conquer today's competitive challenges unless creative juices are flowing freely. To get there, he contends, you've got to get people to loosen up and engage in activities that 'bring out the kid in them'.

The idea is that these bizarre activities will break down barriers – fear, shyness, etc. – that keep groups from working closely together. Clients as varied as Hewlett-Packard, Price Waterhouse, and Pfizer have bought into Eaton's theories, sending employees on weird scavenger hunts or bounding through streets dressed like orangoutans…

Source: Abridged from Linda Grant (1997), 'First, get a weasel costume – do people work together better after wearing diapers on their heads and dressing up like animals?', Fortune, 17 March, p. 90.

The fads and fashions fulfil other apparent purposes as well. The language and jargon they extol can be used to establish expertise, to impress, to influence, to exclude, to baffle, to establish ('expert') status or to cover up ignorance or fear (Rifkin 1994; Rifkin and Martin 1997). Managers can use fads and fashions recognized by employees and shareholders to make change seem inevitable and foolish to avoid – to make management look highly competent and rational (Abrahamson 1996a: 3–4). When urgent and pressing problems need quick and tried solutions, when the problem seems insurmountable, the temptation is to reach for one of these panaceas. These panaceas are usually presented as a universal solution to any organization's problems (Huczynski 1996; Fulop 1992: 15–17).

Importantly, the gurus in particular have a way of giving the manager a 'manifesto' or 'message' of self-improvement and organizational renewal – a 'born again' credo (James 1997: 57). The gurus have also helped glamorize the manager and transform him into a hero stereotype (rarely are they women). The gurus provide an identity for the manager, a masculine one almost akin to a mega-star or at least a super sports star. The material that the gurus draw on to illustrate their theories or ideas usually comes from the wealthiest companies in the world, such as the *Fortune 500* companies. And the success stories, which are usually memorable ones, are told from the vantage point of top managers or CEOs who command salaries in the millions of dollars per annum. The gurus also use these CEO voices to articulate what are often very appealing 'theories of action' that seem simple for other managers to follow or learn from.

Theories of action describe how people in organizations respond to challenges and problems, often through trial and error, as they try to operate both defensively and offensively to deal with changes in their organizations (Weick 1995: 121). Theories of action are used to guide behaviour and make sense of it in ways that appear to make problems more manageable and that allow for new rules to be developed to guide future behaviours. Thus many theories of action are based on 'if – then' types of arguments: 'If' you find yourself in this situation, 'then' do this next time or try this (Weick 1995: 122, citing Argyris 1976; see also Argyris and Schön 1978).

One important observation to make about the managers who become the gurus' models is that often the theories of action these managers espouse are inconsistent with the theories they actually use in practice (Weick 1995: 123, citing Argyris 1976 and Silverman 1970; see also Argyris and Schön 1978). For example, Rupert Murdoch is quoted as saying about management: 'Most of it is fairly obvious, you know' (Macken 1997: 46). It is likely Mr

Murdoch would qualify this with a number of very complex 'if – then' type statements about how he, and his large team of highly competent managers, run Newscorp. Mr Murdoch's empire would not be run on a theory of action that works from the principle that most of management is fairly obvious. Thus gurus and their CEO informants often present crude maps of what goes on in organizations (Weick 1995: 123), and these maps are not easy to copy or follow in practice. Yet, these theories of action are sold widely as a commodified (i.e. marketed and sold) version of what some would claim is merely hyped up commonsense, which is what Mr Murdoch is trying to say, that he manages based on commonsense.

With possibly a few exceptions, the fads and fashions in management have come predominantly from the US and rely heavily on US business experiences. There are problems with this trend. One problem is that cultural bias inevitably creeps into the models contained in these works. As the following extract reveals, for managers in countries outside the USA, the fads and fashions have their limitations. Even though some of the fads and fashions mentioned in the article might not be adopted everywhere, it shows that cultural differences make it hard to adopt universally the management fads and fashions without some careful tailoring (see also Chapter 3).

Asia's antidotes

Why fads are doubly dangerous for the region's managers, and how to make them less so

In fashionable boutiques across the region, Asian consumers are snapping up ready-to-wear designer clothes. By flexing their increasing purchasing power, they can instantly acquire a global sense of style.

In many of the region's boardrooms, managers are treating management fashions in the same way. They take the latest fads, apply the generic models that come with them, and expect instant competitiveness. Management approaches, however, are much too complicated for the formula to work.

For one, the impetus [for change] is different. Re-engineering, for instance, was born in a slow-growth U.S. economic environment. Its appeal there came from the promise of realizing higher profits without large increases in sales. In high-growth Asia [up to mid-1997], the cost-cutting aspect isn't as important as the need to raise customer service and operational efficiency to world-class levels. Dr Michael Loh, *World Executive's Digest* contributing editor in Singapore, says Asian CEOs 'despair they cannot change their organizations fast enough to cope with high growth,' and hence, become interested in re-engineering.

The cultures are also different. Dr John Romanga, managing director of QSA Mortiboys in Hong Kong, says that many family-controlled groups quickly spin off new companies to deal with different sets of customers. 'They don't need to create a new commercial culture to replace a bureaucratic outlook,' he says. These cultural differences with the West create inherent problems. Concepts like self-managed teams, total quality management and re-engineering [see Exhibit 1.3] require a high level of participative management. That is not easy to expect from generations of Asian workers used

But managers around the world are attracted to books written by the gurus. That is why these books become bestsellers. The books aimed at the fads and fashion market tend to be easy to read, entertaining and even fun! They are written to be as engaging as a novel and with the aim of simplifying the complex. The knowledge they impart, and how they impart it, are affected by the need for mass marketing and commercial appeal (Abrahamson 1996a: 7). Humour, wit, good storylines and the latest technology are the hallmarks of these best-sellers. And even being against the fads and fashions can give someone a guru status. One of these gurus, Scott Adams, who also has a web site, created the cartoon character Dilbert to actually ridicule management fads and quick fixes. He had two targets – the inept boss (who oversees Dilbert, an electrical engineer working in an aimless company that is forever adopting new management fads), and the abused employees, Dilbert's co-workers. Through Dilbert, humour is used to reveal what Adams sees as the perennial lies of management. The irony though is that the *targets* of the humour, the managers, are also the ones who embrace Dilbert as an icon (Ackroyd and Thompson, 1999).

A number of anti-fads-and-fashion books are in the market place (e.g. Hilmer and Donaldson 1996; Micklethwait and Wooldridge 1996; Spitzer and Evans 1997). Along with academics who spend considerable time critiquing the fads and fashions, these books seek to reveal the enduring problems of management, which the fads and fashions might also address. These enduring problems have been represented as, for example: putting economic performance first; having direction or some shared view of what the problems are of the organization; organizing so that the organization does not impede effective action; and leadership involving developing direction, having people trust you, and delivering on results (The Editors, *World Executive's Digest* 1997: 20). Some writers proffer other perennial problems, such as Roger Allen, who in his book *Winnie-the-Pooh on Management* (1995) suggests the following: establishing objectives, organizing, motivating, developing people, communicating, and measurement and analysis. One can readily see that even these so-called enduring problems are not easily defined or agreed to (see Pfeffer 1993).

Academics raise a number of major concerns about fads and fashions, beside the fact that the gurus, who are often academics themselves, earn a lot more money than do most of their counterparts in academia:

- Management fads or fashions that are truly innovative and progressive (i.e. critique, supplant or refine what has come before) deserve to be popularised, but not all of them fit this category.
- Sometimes fads and fashions do revive what are discredited ideas or those that are incorrect.
- Fads and fashions are often packaged as new ideas, but in fact are often old ideas that have been revamped with the same flaws in them as they had in the past (Abrahamson 1996b: 618; Abrahamson 1996a; Fulop 1992: 15–17, 23; Shapiro 1995).

- The fads and fashions have encouraged the view that a multi-perspective approach is desirable in management (Bolman and Deal 1991; Fulop 1992: 17–23). Multi-perspective approaches imply that managers can borrow from various approaches or theories paradigms to develop management interventions.

We would argue that managers can only operate within a multiple perspective if they are equipped to evaluate critically the paradigmatic and disciplinary issues in management and organization theory. Were managers, for example, to read a book such as *The Fifth Discipline* written by Peter Senge (1990), and then use it as a basis for trying to introduce or experiment with organization learning, they might be well advised, by an academic, to think about the paradigm or paradigms that Senge used in his work. A paradigm is like a frame of reference with implicit assumptions or beliefs about '...what sorts of things make up the world, how they act, how they hang together, and how they may be known' (Weick 1995: 118). It represents a big set of theories or assumptions that are clustered around some central idea, such as the realization that the earth circles the sun and not the other way around. Around these paradigms have been built particular disciplines.

Over the last 10 years the idea of *the learning organization* has gained much prominence in the management and organizational literature. The learning organization is today's label for an organization that improves somehow – it delivers packages more quickly, its hamburgers taste better, the staff at the customer service counter seem more helpful, and profits are healthy if not increasing. Somebody, or some bodies, figured out something to make things work 'better', and the organization continues to innovate. Senge, along with several other academics (e.g. Pedler, Boydell and Burgoyne 1988) have popularized the idea of the learning organization (LO). *The Fifth Discipline* became the blueprint for many different versions of the LO.

From the point of view of disciplines, a number have been particularly influential in the learning in organization literature. Table 1.1 gives a brief summary of these disciplinary approaches.

The point of this summary is to illustrate the fields of knowledge that exist in soft and hard academic theory from which fads and fashions draw. Within each of the groupings there would also be subdisciplines. There is a distinct body of knowledge that explores the process of learning in organizations, while the fad market has been dominated by attempts to build models of the product of such learning – the LO.

In developing his approach to the LO, Senge adopted principally what is termed a 'systems paradigm', and favoured a highly integrated (holistic) view of the organization in which he extolled the virtues of harmony, stability and consensus as the prime logic of the system. The book devotes a lot of space to developing tools and techniques that are also influenced by the author's incorporation of Organization Development (OD) strategies (see Table 1.1). His treatment of issues such as teamwork, power and leadership are influenced by these perspectives and as such are limited. Some of these limitations are quite serious for the manager trying to work with Senge's ideas. For example, the idea of power and politics presented in *The Fifth Discipline* is one that favours the eradication of organizational politics, portraying it as aberrant or deviant and a source of unnecessary distraction and dysfunction. It does not see politics as an inevitable feature of organizations (see earlier discussion and Table 1.1), as endemic to social practice and structures within organizations. Nor does it view power and politics as a likely source of creative tension and innovation (see Chapter 4).

Table 1.1 *Disciplinary approaches in organization learning*

Discipline	Main focus	Key ideas, contributions	Key problems it addresses
Psychology and organization development (OD)	Human development	Importance of context, cognitive maps, underlying values, learning styles, dialogue, hierarchies of learning and experiential learning	Why and how people learn, and how to transfer individual to collective learning
Management science (systems approach)	Information processing	Building knowledge, memory, error correction, holism (understanding how a whole system works), informating (how technology can free up people and help with tasks, but also control people and tasks), creating feedback systems – simple to complex	Non-rational behaviour, information overload, long- versus short-term views, and how to unlearn from mistakes or discard old knowledge
Sociology and organization theory	Social structures and interaction	Effects of power structures and hierarchy, conflict as normal, ideology and rhetoric, interests of actors, meanings and understandings	Conflicts of interests, organizational politics, influence, and discourses of power
Strategy	Competitiveness and core competence	Organization–environment interface, levels of learning, networks and strategic alliances, learning in, across and between groups and nations, exploiting tacit knowledge	Environmental alignment and turbulence, competitive pressures (e.g. globalisation) and general versus technical learning
Production management	Efficiency/productivity	Productivity, learning curves (e.g. cost reduction trends), internal and external sources of learning, links of learning to production design and analysis	Limits of measurement, especially single-dimension measures (e.g. output), uncertainty about outcomes
Cultural anthropology	Meaning systems	Culture as cause and effect of organizational learning, beliefs and values, norms, customs, ritual, problems with cultural superiority views	Culture as a barrier to transferring or learning new ideas, whose ideas dominate?

Source: Adapted from Mark Easterby-Smith (1997), 'Disciplines of organization learning: Contributions and critiques', *Human Relations*, 50 (9), p. 1087.

Teamwork is also presented as a strong tool for homogenizing experiences. According to Senge it can be used to create unity in vision, purpose and direction and help overcome impediments to group behaviour with conformity of members being the ultimate aim. Teams are not seen by Senge as potentially problematic or even unnecessary because issues of diversity and power are not included in his analysis, or in those of other organization-learning theorists (Rifkin and Fulop 1997: 140; Coopey 1995; Easterby-Smith 1997: 1095). Senge's view of leadership suffers similar limitations. While he is not in favour of propagating the heroic leader model (see earlier discussion) of the lone CEO or head of the organization such as Branson and Nasser, and instead favours the idea of followership and a sharing of the leadership role, his analysis does not address leadership in terms of power and control. Thus his recommendations for developing leaders among different layers of management seems unrealistic when examined against the common trend that many in power seem to want to hold onto it and amass it rather than give it up (Coopey 1995: 207). Senge's discussion of leadership leaves the reader unable to examine it in the context of managing diversity, which we mentioned as being a key issue for managers. Senge's approach pays little attention to the differences in the workplace based on gender, ethnicity or race (see Rifkin and Fulop 1997: 139–42).

The consequences for management practice of adopting a particular approach to learning in organizations and the learning organization can be illustrated by describing four different ways to approach the topic (see Rifkin and Fulop 1997):

1   *Learning organization* (LO) – a prescriptive model using predominantly systems theory as popularized in the fads and fashions by Peter Senge.
2   *Organizational learning methods* (OLM) – emphasizing training strategies, tools and techniques to promote learning and knowledge sharing also popularised in fads and fashions and drawing mainly from OD strategies.
3   *Learning environment* (LE) – emphasizing the importance of meanings, understandings and actions and the managerial policies and practices that are directed at creating more disruptive and unorthodox opportunities for learning. The LE is derived mainly from sociology and organization theory.
4   *Learning space* (LS) – focusing on micro practices, such as framing ideas, understanding relationships and interactions, and how these shape or produce effects such as an organization, power relations and agency (i.e. the ability to think, choose, question and act). These ideas are derived mainly from sociology, social anthropology and organization theory.

These approaches represent the views of various 'communities' of scholars or practitioners who strongly identify with their particular approach, often to the exclusion of others as shown in Table 1.1. Thus as mentioned, the LO/OLM approaches tend to originate from popular theory and popular accounts; the LE approaches are characteristic of soft academic theory the orientations of which are critical and interpretive; and insights into LS are found in what the manager would view as being hard academic theory, drawing from postmodernist ideas. Each presents a different role for the manager and each develops a specific approach for what an organization, or its learning processes, should look like. Each also differs in respect of the mode of learning being championed by its proponents. These modes of learning range from specific prescriptions such as do X and achieve Y, as in the popular accounts, to consideration of the extent to which learning reflects processes that a manager should not, or cannot, control, as in the LS.

The LO approach or theme reflects a type of organization to be created, that is a 'learning organization'. LO can also refer to an example which is used as a model by managers in redesigning their own organizations. Chris Stefano, for example, might have heard that Toyota has stimulating team meetings where everyone attends. Chris may see Toyota as a 'learning organization', one to be emulated. Chris may also be enamoured of LO concepts, such as 'team learning', which Senge (1990) promoted as one of his five 'disciplines' for the LO. In the management and organization literature, LO tends to refer both to organizations designed to enable learning (i.e. have the capabilities to learn) and organizations within which learning is already occurring. Typically, LO focuses on such things as managing chaos and indeterminacy, flattening hierarchies, decentralization, empowerment of people, teamwork and cross-functional teams, network relationships, adoption of elaborate technologies and new forms of leadership and mentoring (Mirvis 1996; Steingard and Fitzgibbons 1993: 37).

The OLM theme overlaps conceptually with the LO theme. The OLM theme, as discussed in Table 1.1, usually encompasses measures or methods that a manager can implement to create 'organizational learning', and work toward having a 'learning organization'. OLM popularly refers to a set of processes that result from management practices and training and that will help to create the LO (Addleson 1996: 34; Jones and Hendry 1994). This dual use of the terms LO and OLM has created confusion, and a number of authors have stated that there is no consensus on what OLM is, how organizations learn and what a LO might look like (Crossan, Henry and Hildebrand 1993: 229; Mirvis 1996: 21).

Specific OLM measures that Chris Stefano may be implementing could be team-based projects and the weekly team meeting itself. When one examines how OLM is written about in academic and popular literature, one sees that references to OLM often imply that managers like Chris have some set of tools in their minds to stimulate individual or organizational learning processes. Such measures to stimulate learning make learning seem 'manageable' in that managers feel they can invoke or at least steer learning by individuals and the organization.

However, not all views of learning in organizations are based on tools or models. The LE departs from this view and instead focuses on learning that does not occur in direct response to particular measures that a manager undertakes. The term LE is used here to refer to an approach where primary importance is placed on meanings, actions and understanding or the interpretive capacities of individuals as the building blocks for learning (e.g. Addleson 1996; Mirvis 1996). Attention is focused on conditions that might enable and support what have been variously termed 'communities of understanding', 'organizational renaissance', 'systems of self correction and creativity', or 'self-organizing systems' (Addleson 1996: 38; McWhinney 1992; Mirvis 1996: 25; Stacey 1993, respectively). Associated with these are such ideas as 'liminal learning' or learning from mistakes or trying to anticipate the unintended effects of policies and actions (Turner 1992).

In the LE approach, Chris can contribute to a set of conditions that foster learning by implementing particular processes and policies. What Chris might have done is simply to begin each meeting informally enough so that someone like Winjamarra feels relatively free to interject or, indeed, Chris might just call a meeting that has no agenda and remain silent during most of the deliberations. In taking specific actions such as these, Chris might contribute to an atmosphere that supports learning, but does not necessarily drive learning in any particular direction. Within the LE, individual interpretations of managerial actions differ, but there is a chance that synergistic learning to the benefit of the organization can occur. There is less managerial control inherent in the LE than occurs in the LO or OLM strategies. For this to occur, there would also have to be more open questioning of power and control in the organization.

There is even less managerial control of learning in the LS than in the LE. The LS is a 'space' opened by a conscious and/or unconscious release of control by management. This 'space' is transitory – an opportunity to learn occurs as a kind of momentary and creative collusion of employees and managers. In the LS, people have freedom to think and explore and to engage in uninhibited questioning of such things as managerial control. For example, the question of why Chris Stefano, the team leader, and not someone else, should call a meeting should be open to debate and discussion – perhaps even asking why a team leader is needed at all. Something could come out of such questioning – perhaps a moment of new and inspiring insight – that Chris could not have produced intentionally. Chris might think this is a good idea, but as we mentioned earlier, the politics of the situation might mean that Chris feels negative sanctions will be applied if meetings are conducted in such an unorthodox manner. In other words, there are strong normative and political reasons why the LS remains untapped in many organizations.

To entertain the idea of the LS, the manager would have to engage in considerable reflective practice and critical thinking. The manager would have to be open to examining how, for example, diversity is handled or mishandled through subtle practices that create or are used to 'silence' the voices of those who are different or dissenting voices of those wanting to raise grievances or complaints about the organization. The manager would have to think seriously about how these voices are marginalized by the creation and enforcement of certain rules of inclusion and exclusion; for example, how does Chris's organization work against the spirit of equity and paternity leave by forcing employees, such as Roderick Cage, to work overtime to cover for his colleague on leave and in the process perhaps limiting his and others' abilities to be effective co-workers? Why isn't this an issue in the meeting? If managers were serious about trying to look at the deeper sources of power and control, and at the more subtle subtexts or discourses in their organizations, they would seriously question ideas such as 'teamwork' and 'organizational culture', which are both recognised from the LS perspective as potentially promoting conformity. As already mentioned, this conformity can limit learning by repressing diversity. In the LS, difference and diversity, multiple meanings and multiple realities are the central ideas associated with how people construct their identities and use them to enact their daily lives in the organization (Boje and Rosile 1994; Chia 1995; Heterick and Boje 1992: 54; Watson 1995).

In the LS, managers are meant to reflect on, and engage in, practices that are not controlling or 'managing' *per se*. The uncertainty in outcomes and the difficulty of surrendering control makes the LS, for many, the most difficult approach ever to imagine working in organizations. The fundamental issue in the LS is who sets directions for learning in organizations and whose knowledge should be privileged in the process – is it a particular level or group of managers or is it widespread? (See Fulop and Rifkin 1997: 59; Easterby-Smith 1997: 1095, citing Coopey 1995.) The LS reflects a far more disorganized, disaggregated concept of learning than the LO, OLM and LE approaches. These approaches are characterized by prescriptions for things to do and patterns of practices to engage in rather than by cautions to refrain from interfering and imposing, although this is less the case with the LE approach. Thus each mode of learning, or managing to induce learning, reflects different approaches that are often irreconcilable, particularly on fundamental issues, such as power and control. However, when viewed together each learning approach can be seen to have something to offer, but the manager will need to be able to understand them fully and evaluate them critically and reflectively.

As this discussion reveals, as a source of learning for managers popularly published approaches to managing have their attractions but also their pitfalls, as is the case with local accounts – the stories and conversations in the workplace. The popular and fad approaches promise success. They are conveyed in an engaging way and they are easy to understand. They contain enough jargon to give devotees a sense of belonging – devotees recognise one another by their use of the same jargon. Use of the jargon is also a way to legitimate choices by referring to ideas whose wide acceptance is signalled by its popularity. The adherent to a fad such as this can also envisage becoming a top CEO-type hero. Popular and fad approaches, because of these attractions, can be traps, too. They can address issues that are only transitory or local, which can make such an approach susceptible to being applied unreflectively in inappropriate situations. Even in those instances where such approaches are meant to be applied, a manager needs to know whether they actually work. Important factors, such as diversity or power, are not addressed at all by many of the popular and fad approaches, which is why academics warn against adopting fashions without an understanding of their paradigm-based biases and assumptions.

Conclusion

When managers start to look at knowledge as residing in the six general areas described in this chapter, they are probably moving away from a purely 'foundational' approach to management knowledge and practice (Morgan 1993: 286). A foundational approach to knowledge is one that is dominated by a search for a one best way of doing things or for authoritative approaches that tell the manager 'this is the way it is', or 'this is how you should do it'. By contrast, making sense of such things as local and popular accounts forces the manager to recognise that any situation might have multiple dimensions and meanings. It challenges the manager to try to see situations or problems from a number of perspectives or be able to reframe problems and issues so that they can be tackled from a number of different directions (Morgan 1993: 286; Bolman and Deal 1984, 1991). Being able to reframe problems and see them in novel ways is an important part of developing reflective practice (Morgan 1993: 286).

What is implicit in this sentiment is that we need to come to terms with the six sources of management knowledge and how knowledge is represented in theories, fads, popular stories, myths, metaphors, etc. Consider again the stories of the corporate hero Branson and police maverick Ruiz. They engage. As Robert Chia and Stuart Morgan contend, 'Education entails not just information acquisition but an "awakening" of the senses' (1996: 57). The education of the manager cannot advance with exposure to only a select few ways of gaining knowledge. Although it might seem odd, there will be times when in the interests of practice managers will need to develop some useful formulae or theories of action at the commonsense level. There will be times when managers will need to delve into theory to enhance their understanding of complex issues, and at times these learning experiences might not seem very closely related to day to day practice (Linstead 1995: 9). This suggests that if managers are to develop understanding and the potential to act and change their circumstances, then they have to have a perspective from which to judge such knowledge claims as that 'the LO is the only way for an organization to learn'.

The questions asked at the beginning of the chapter have answers.

1   *What sorts of knowledge are needed by the manager to manage?* There are at least six forms of management knowledge and know-how.
2   *How do managers learn about management?* Managers learn by doing, as well as from local and popular accounts told by colleagues and management gurus. They can also study soft and hard theory in universities or on their own.
3   *What forms of knowledge are likely to be easier for managers to grasp than others?* This whole chapter indicates that things that are most familiar and most organizationally legitimate are easiest to learn but are not necessarily the most insightful or most effective.
4   *What role(s) do managers play in helping their organizations learn?* Managers help the organization to learn by surveying varied sources of knowledge and reflectively questioning assumptions and biases that might be contained in stories, theories and paradigms. This reflection is done with colleagues and other organizational stakeholders.

Based on these conclusions, which constitute soft theory that undoubtedly contains its own biases, you now need to address Chris Stefano's situation. To what degree can the advice you give stand up to scrutiny involving critical thinking and reflective practice? Were myths, stereotypes or metaphors invoked and if so what were the consequences of this? Was there an underlying dominant storyline being pushed? More importantly, was account taken of the politics of the situation and the issues of diversity, and was some attempt made to offer advice from a number of perspectives, with some clarity of the underlying assumptions upon which the various perspectives operate? To get to the point:

1   What advice would you give to Chris Stefano, or to Dr Cora Harvey? How does that advice differ from what you might have said initially, before reading this chapter?
2   What knowledge or experiences have you drawn on? Which types of knowledge do you rely on more and which types do you rely on less?
3   How might you use our analysis here of sources of managerial knowledge to evaluate the potential effectiveness of your advice? Are your recommendations just tips, or are they what has proven to be a reliable approach to difficult situations?

The message of this chapter, and of this book as a whole, is that you need to reframe what you observe and hear from others. People with a variety of different roles, experiences and value sets are looking at exactly the same problem that you are. You need to understand their perspectives in order to manage your relationships with them. A good way to gain this insight is to engage in more formal study of management.

References

Abrahamson, E. (1996a) 'Management fashion', *Academy of Management Review* 21(1): 254–85.

Abrahamson, E. (1996b) 'Management fashion, academic fashion, and enduring truths', *Academy of Management Review* 21(3): 616–18 (Abrahamson responds to critiques of his 1996 article).

Ackroyd, S. and Thompson, P. (1999) *Organizational Misbehaviour*, London: Sage.

Addleson, M. (1996) 'Resolving the spirit and substance of organizational learning', *Journal of Organizational Change Management* 9(1): 32–41.

Allen, R.E. (1995) *Winnie-the-Pooh on Management*, New York: Methuen.

Argyris, C. (1976) *Increasing Leadership Effectiveness*, New York: John Wiley.

Argyris, C. and Schön, D.A. (1978) *Organizational Learning: A Theory of Action Perspective*, Reading, Mass.: Addison-Wesley.

Austin, J.L. (1962) *How To Do Things with Words*, Oxford: Clarendon Press.

Bateson, G. (1975) *Steps to an Ecology of Mind*, New York: Ballaatine.

Bedeian, A.G. (1995) 'Workplace envy', *Organizational Dynamics* 23(4): 49–56.

Boje, D. and Rosile, G. (1994) 'Diversities, differences and authors' voices', *Journal of Organizational Change Management* 7(16): 8–17.

Bolman, L.G. and Deal, T.E. (1984) *Modern Approaches to Understanding and Managing Organizations*, San Francisco: Jossey-Bass.

Bolman, L.G. and Deal, T.E. (1991) *Reframing Organizations: Artistry, Choice and Leadership*, San Francisco: Jossey-Bass.

Brough, J. and Millett, M. (1997) 'The Axeman Cometh', *The Sydney Morning Herald, Spectrum Features* 1 November: 6, 6s, 7.

Burgoyne, J.G. (1981) 'Approaches to integration in management education', in Cooper, C.L. (ed.), *Developing Managers for the 1980s*, London and Basingstoke: Macmillan.

Chia, R. (1995) 'From modern to postmodern organizational analysis', *Organization Studies* 16(4): 508–604.

Chia, R. and Morgan, S. (1996) 'Educating the philosopher manager', *Management Learning* 27(1): 37–64.

Coopey, J. (1995) 'The learning organization, power, politics and ideology', *Management Learning* 26(2): 193–213.

Crossan, M.M., Lane, H.W. and Hildebrand, T. (1993) 'Organization learning: Theory to practice', in Hendry, J., Johnson, G. and Newton, J. (eds), *Strategic Thinking: Leadership and the Management of Change*, Chichester, New York.

Czarniawska-Joerges, B. (1992) *Exploring Complex Organizations: A Cultural Perspective*, Newbury Park, Ca: Sage.

Deutschman, A. (1997) 'Heavens above', *Good Weekend, The Sydney Morning Herald* 23 August: 16–19.

Downing, S.J. (1997) 'Learning the plot: Emotional momentum in search of dramatic logic', *Management Learning* 28(1): 27–44.

Easterby-Smith, M. (1997) 'Disciplines of organizational learning: Contributions and critiques', *Human Relations* 50(9): 1085–113.

Fineman, S. (ed.) (1993) *Emotion in Organizations*, London: Sage.

Fineman, S. (1997) 'Emotion and Management Learning', *Management Learning* 28 (1): 13–26.

Fineman, S. and Gabriel, Y. (1996) *Experiencing Organizations*, London: Sage.

Fiol, M. (1994) 'Consensus, diversity, and learning in organizations', *Organization Science* 5(3): 403–20.

Fulop, L. (1992) 'Management and critical thinking', in Fulop, L., Frith, F. and Hayward, H. (eds), *Management for Australian Business: A Critical Text*, Melbourne: Macmillan.

Fulop, L. and Laneyrie, F. (1995) *Commentary: 'Trials at the top: Chief executives talk about men, women and the Australian executive culture, by Amanda Sinclair'*, *International Review of Women and Leadership* 1(2): 61–7.

Fulop, L. and Rifkin, W.P. (1997) 'Representing fear in learning in organizations', *Management Learning* 28(1): 45–64.

Garko, D.M. (1994) 'Communicator styles of powerful physician-executives in upward-influence situations', *Health Communication* 6(2): 159–72.

Grant, L. (1997) 'First get a weasel costume – Do people get together better after wearing diapers on their heads and dressing up like animals?', *Fortune* 17 March: 90.

Heterick, W.P. and Boje, D.M. (1992) 'Organization and the body: Post-Fordist dimensions', *Journal of Organizational Change Management* 5(1): 48–57.

Hilmer, F. and Donaldson, L. (1996) *Management Redeemed: Debunking the Fads that Undermine our Corporate Performance*, Sydney: The Free Press.

Höpfl, H. and Linstead, S. (1997) 'Introduction: Learning to feel and feeling to learn: Emotion and learning in organizations', *Management Learning* 28(1): 5–12.

Huczynski, A. (1996) *Management Gurus: What Makes Them and How to Become One*, London: Thomas.

Huey, J. (1994) 'The new post-heroic leadership', *Fortune* 21 February: 24–38.

James, D. (1997) 'High priests of the corporate world', *Business Review Weekly* 23 June: 52–7.

Jones, A.M. and Hendry, C. (1994) 'The learning organization: Adult learning and organizational transformation', *British Journal of Management* 5: 153–62.

Laneyrie, F. (1995) 'Images of women in management: Archetypes – a new dimension?', paper presented to Australian and New Zealand Academy of Management Conference, 3–6 December, Townsville, Australia.

Lawson, M. (1997) 'The fad busters', *The Australian Financial Review* 11 April: 3.

Linstead, S. (1996) 'An introduction to management – week 1', in *Page Distance Education Package for Management 906*, Wollongong: Department of Management, University of Wollongong.

Linstead, S. and Harris, B. (1983) 'Reality and role of playing: The use of a "living case study" in management education', *Personnel Review* 12(1): 9–16.

McWhinney, W. (1992) *Paths of Change: Strategic Choices for Organizations and Society*, London: Sage.

Macken, D. (1997) 'How did we ever manage?', *Good Weekend, The Sydney Morning Herald Magazine* 5 April: 46.

Micklethwait, J. and Wooldridge, A. (1996) *The Witch Doctors, What Management Gurus Are Saying, Why It Matters, and How to Make Sense of It*, London: William Heinemann.

Mirvis, P. (1996) 'Historical foundations of organization learning', *Journal of Organizational Change Management* 9(1): 13–31.

Morgan, G. (1993) *Imaginization: The Art of Creative Management*, Los Angeles: Sage.

Neales, S. (1997) 'The lady vanishes', *Good Weekend, The Sydney Morning Herald Magazine* 13 September: 32–9.

O'Connor, A.-M. (1997) 'Woman shakes up Tijuana police brass', *The Sydney Morning Herald* 1 March: 24 (report from *The Los Angeles Times*).

Pedler, M., Boydell, T. and Burgoyne, J. (1988) *Learning Company Project: A Report on Work Undertaken – October 1987 to April 1988*, Sheffield: The Training Agency.

Pfeffer, J. (1993) 'Barriers to the advance of organizational science: Paradigm development as a dependent variable', *Academy of Management Review* 18(4): 599–620.

Rifkin, W.D. (1994) 'Who need not be heard: Deciding who is not an expert', *Technology Studies* 1(1): 60–96.

Rifkin, W. and Fulop, L. (1997) 'A review and case study on learning organizations', *The Learning Organization* 4(4): 135–48.

Rifkin, W.D. and Martin, B. (1997) 'Negotiating expert status: Who gets taken seriously', *IEEE Technology and Society Magazine* Spring 15(1): 30–9.

Salaman, G. and Butler, J. (1994) 'Why managers won't learn', in Mabey, C. and Iles, P. (eds), *Managing Learning*, London: Routledge.

Schön, D.A. (1983) *The Reflective Practitioner*, New York: Basic Books.

Schwartz, P. (1996) *The Art of the Long View*, NSW: Australian Business Network (First published in 1991, New York: Doubleday Currency).

Scott, P. (1997) 'Jac the Knife', *The Sydney Morning Herald, Spectrum Features* 8 March: 3s.

Semler, R. (1993) *Maverick! The Success Behind the World's Most Unusual Workplace*, London: Century.

Senge, P. (1990) *The Fifth Discipline: The Art and Practice of the Learning Organization*, New York: Doubleday/Currency.

Shapiro, E.C. (1995) *Fad Surfing in the Boardroom*, Reading, Mass.: Addison-Wesley.

Silverman, D. (1970) *The Theory of Organizations*, New York: Basic Books.

Silverman, D. (1985) 'Telling convincing stories: a plea for cautious positivism in case studies', revised version of a talk given to the plenary session of the BSA Sociology of Medicine Conference, University of York, September.

Sinclair, A. (1994) *Trials at the Top: Chief Executives Talk about Men, Women and Australian Executive Culture*, Melbourne: The Australian Centre at the University of Melbourne.

Spitzer, Q. and Evans, R. (1997) *Heads You Win – How the Best Companies Think*, New York: Simon and Schuster.

Stacey, R.D. (1993) *Strategic Management and Organizational Dynamics*, London: Pitman.

Steingard, D.S. and Fitzgibbons, D.E. (1993) 'A postmodern deconstruction of total quality management (TQM)', *Journal of Organizational Change Management* 6(5): 27–42.

The Editor (1997) 'The Threat of Fads', *World Executive's Digest* July: 19–21.

Thomas, A.B. (1993) *Controversies in Management*, London: Routledge.

Turner, B.A. (1992) 'Organizational learning and the management of risk', paper presented to the British Academy of Management Conference, 14–16 September, Bradford Management School, Bradford, UK.

Watson, T.J. (1995) 'Rhetoric, discourse and argument in organizational sense making: A reflexive tale', *Organization Studies* 16(5): 805–21.

Watzlawick, P., Beavin, J.H. and Jackson, D.D. (1967) *Pragmatics of Human Communication: A Study of Interactional Patterns, Pathologies, and Paradoxes*, New York: Norton.

Weick, K.E. (1995) *Sensemaking in Organizations*, Los Angeles: Sage.

2

Gender and management

Joanna Brewis and Stephen Linstead

Questions about gender

1 Is gender a biological or a social issue; a profit issue or a moral issue?
2 Does being male or female make a difference to the way you manage?
3 Are women concentrated in certain occupations?
4 Are you more likely to succeed as a manager if you are male?
5 What is meant by the 'glass ceiling'?
6 What is positive discrimination?
7 Are men more motivated than women?
8 Do men experience gender-related problems too?
9 Is globalization creating more opportunities for women or perpetuating their subordination?
10 How can gender be managed?

TransCorp

Matthew looked at his watch as he locked his car and began to hurry across the car park. '7.45 am,' he thought, 'I really should have got in earlier today.' Slightly breathless, he pushed open the doors of TransCorp, pausing only briefly to nod to the caretaker, and ran up the stairs to his office two steps at a time. The office looked less than welcoming – desk positioned strategically to face the door, filing cabinets gleaming, the only personal touch a small cactus on his windowsill – as he removed his jacket and sat down at his PC. It seemed only minutes later when there was a knock at the door and his boss David entered. He began immediately:

'Matt, there's a problem on the floor. Some of the morning shift haven't arrived yet and you know we've got a rush on with that order for InterMotor. Can you go down there and wait for the latecomers? They need talking to. We really need to get this sorted out today – they've been goofing off down there recently and it's not good enough.'

Without further ado, David left. Matthew stared at his screen, willing himself to descend to the shopfloor and reprimand the stragglers. Matthew did not enjoy this particular aspect of his work, but in his position as Deputy Production Manager he knew it was his responsibility. Sighing, he donned his jacket once again and made his way down to the floor.

An hour later, Matthew returned to the office, feeling wrung out and upset. There had been the predictable angry scenes on the floor, with staff complaining that the revised shift start times were inconvenient for them and that it was not fair to expect them to come to work an hour earlier than usual. He had had to reiterate over and over that it was only a temporary measure, that the order was important and that the staff had to arrive on time so as to be able to meet their targets. However, secretly he sympathized with them. He himself was growing increasingly tired of the long hours expected of him, the way he had to behave towards his staff, a style set by David and his other seniors, and the continual effort he had to make to suppress his own emotions, which surfaced particularly when he was feeling tired – as he certainly was today. It was now 9 am and Matthew reflected that people working for other companies, in other positions, were only now arriving at work, knowing that they could leave at 5 pm, or 6 at the latest. He himself faced at least another 10 hours, and that was only if the remainder of the day's production went according to TransCorp's carefully laid plans.

Matthew spent the rest of the morning, in between dealing with constant calls from the floor and interruptions at the door, drafting a plan for the plant's summer shutdown. This year was going to be especially difficult, as machinery needed to be replaced and moved around the floor as well as the usual repairs and maintenance being carried out, but budgets had been cut to the extent that only a very limited number of personnel could be retained during the two weeks that the plant was officially shut. He was only relieved that the responsibility for deciding who these staff were to be belonged to Human Resources and not to his own department. David had made it clear to Matthew that his plan needed to be as radical as possible – the minimum possible number of staff working the maximum possible number of hours. It was 2.30 pm before he looked at his watch and realized that he had not eaten or drunk anything that day. At this point, his phone shrilled again – his partner Sarah wanting to know if he could get home earlier that evening to look after the children, as she wanted to attend her evening class. He told her that he could not, they began to argue and he eventually hung up the phone cursing her. 'She just doesn't understand,' he told himself. 'Here I am struggling to keep it all together at work, in a crucial period for the company, and all she can do is complain about how I'm never at home.'

Later that day, some time towards 7 pm, Matthew walked down to the snack machine at the end of his corridor and began to punch in his request, when Julie, a Production colleague, appeared from her own office, looking furious. She began to reel off her own list of complaints:

You'll never guess what that git of a boss of yours has just said to me. 'Nice legs, Jules!' Can you believe it? God knows, they look at me like I've just landed from Mars if I turn up in trousers and then I have to put up with that kind of rubbish when I wear a skirt. And even then they expect me to walk, talk and behave like a man. I hate this place sometimes.

Matthew remembered Julie's outburst when he was driving home, some two hours later. He thought to himself that while he found his job exciting and challenging on the whole, while it gave him immense satisfaction when an order was completed to the correct standards and went out by the deadline, there were times when he too resented having to be 'one of the boys' and join in with the sexist jokes and chat. This realization really hit him when he arrived home and found Sarah in bed, lights extinguished all over the house and a note on the kitchen table telling him how furious she was. He wearily walked upstairs, undressed and got gingerly into bed beside her, only managing to set the alarm for 6 am before falling into an exhausted sleep.

Questions about the case

1 What are your impressions of TransCorp as an organization?
2 What does the description of Matthew's day tell you about what it means and how it feels to manage in TransCorp? What do you think is expected of managers in this organization?
3 Given Matthew's feelings about his work, does it seem to suit his preferred managerial style?
4 What does this suggest about Matthew's view of himself as a manager? Or as a man?
5 What are the consequences of Matthew's behaviour as a manager:
   (a) for him as an individual?
   (b) for his staff?
   (c) for Sarah and his children?
6 Julie tells Matthew that she is disgusted by the comment that David makes about her legs. What other kinds of problems might you expect a female manager in TransCorp to encounter ?

Introduction

Gender is a powerful principle in the organization of our lives. An individual's identity as either male or female, with masculine or feminine qualities, makes a difference to the way in which they experience their social world. It is therefore significant to consider the influence of gender when examining what managers do, and how they do it.

Although this was not historically the case, there is now a large body of organizational literature which insists that gender be taken into account when examining managerial work. A good part of this is the literature which concentrates on how gender is, and should be, 'managed' in the organization. There are, however, several possible perspectives to take on gender. In this chapter, we begin with an overview of the five major perspectives – *liberal feminist, radical feminist, diversity, gender-in-management* and the *gendering management* approaches. The key characteristics of each are summarized in Table 2.1.

Where the first three approaches place different emphases on the impact of gender on management *practice*, the gendering management approach insists on introducing the concept of gender into management *theory*. This reveals the extremely significant neglect of gender in the foundational theories of management. We then go on to take a look at how some of the main theories about management and organization have failed to take gender issues into account – especially classical management theory, human relations theory and the work of Abraham Maslow on motivation. In fact, in contrast to commentators such as Fiona Wilson (1995), we find that these theories were not gender *blind*, but very gender aware, and actively sought to *suppress difference*. Later theories, which built on them accordingly, failed to take gender into account. We then look at some attempts to bring gender and

Table 2.1 *Perspectives on gender*

Perspective	Key concepts	Typical writers
Liberal feminism	• Women not naturally inferior to men • Importance of social justice/ equality • Vertical segregation (glass ceiling) • Horizontal segregation • Short/ long agendas of equality of opportunity	*Historical:* Mary Astell Mary Wollstonecraft Hannah Woolley *Contemporary:* Charles Cox and Cary Cooper Marilyn Davidson and Cary Cooper Betty Friedan Rosabeth Moss Kanter Barbara White
Radical feminism	• Women naturally superior to men • Importance of social emancipation/change • Radical reversal/inversion of contemporary social structures • Separatism	Mary Daly Shulamith Firestone Marilyn French Germaine Greer Kate Millett Valerie Solonas
Diversity	• Diversity, including gender difference, should be recognized in organizations • Individualist focus • Enhance productivity through widening organizational access and participation • Strong business case • MOSAIC	Rajvinder Kandola and Johanna Fullerton Stella Nkomo R. Roosevelt Thomas
Gender *in* management	• Management relational • Women and men socialized differently, manage differently • Male transactional v. female transformational leadership • Transformational leadership most effective in current socioeconomic climate • Globalization of gender	Beverly Alimo-Metcalfe Helen Brown Marta Calás and Linda Smircich Alice Hendrickson Eagly and Blair T. Johnson Silvia Gherardi Judy Rosener
Gender*ing* Management	• Interaction of gender and management • Foucauldian – gender identity produced by discourse • Masculinist discourse sustains masculine behaviour • Successful managers (male or female) treated as masculine • Problems of this emphasis on masculinity	David Collinson and Margaret Collinson Deborah Kerfoot and David Knights Jeff Hearn and Wendy Parkin Albert Mills and Peta Tancred

management together – the 'feminine-in-management' approach, the globalization approach, which undervalues context, and the gender socialization approach, which over-values context. Finally, we further outline the characteristics of an alternative building on the 'gendering management' approach focusing on management *processes*, that is, regarding gender as fluid, and carefully examining the ways in which gender and management interact and mutually shape each other.

Liberal feminism

Liberal feminism can be traced back to eighteenth century writers such as Mary Wollstonecraft (1970) and further. It argues in the main that men and women are equal in all important respects and, more specifically, that women are as capable as men of reasoned behaviour, such as is seen to be required in the workplace. One strand of the *liberal feminist* literature identifies the existence of a 'glass ceiling' in modern organizations. This refers to an invisible, implicit but impenetrable barrier which prevents women from reaching senior positions within organizations. Marilyn Davidson and Cary Cooper (1992) among others claim that women, because of the ways in which they are viewed, and view themselves, in both wider society and individual organizations, find it difficult to break through this ceiling. Such work argues that the historically influential definition of women as somehow irrevocably feminine, congenitally subordinate, emotional and irrational, and therefore ill-equipped for work at the top of the 'organizational tree', results in *vertical segregation* – the situation in organizations where men dominate the senior positions. In fact, the phenomenon of vertical segregation is easily demonstrated by statistics such as the University of Southern California survey data which revealed that women make up only 4.3 percent of senior management in major US service companies (see Reynolds 1992).

The situation in the UK is similar, with Keith Grint (1991) claiming that, during the twentieth century, women have never made up more than 10 percent of senior management. In July 1990, *Fortune* magazine noted without critical comment that of 4012 people listed as the highest paid officers and directors of their companies, only 19 (less than 1 percent) were women, and the situation in Australia was arguably worse (cited in Cahoon 1994: 304). Furthermore, other findings show that the numbers of women at senior management level are *falling* both in the USA and the UK (Wilson 1995: 17–18). It is also the case that women are underrepresented in management anyway – it seems, for example, that only some 20 percent of all managers in the UK are female. However, things are clearly changing if *all* levels of management are considered. Table 2.2 shows that women in the UK increased their presence in professional and managerial jobs from 5 percent of the total workforce to 13 percent from 1975–94, but men increased their presence from 20 percent to 28 percent (Walby 1997: 35; Office of Population and Census Surveys (UK) 1996: Table 7.4). However, Table 2.3 illustrates that calculations based on comparative census data for 1981–91 show that while men increased their absolute presence in professional and managerial positions in national and local government (33 percent) education, welfare and health (3 percent), science and engineering (4 percent), literature and the arts (12 percent) and general management (9 percent), the numbers of women in these categories increased respectively by 155 percent, 22 percent, 72 percent, 54 percent and 61 percent (Walby 1997: 37). Walby notes that 'the massive changes which are taking place in women's employment and education are transforming gender relations' (Walby 1997: 64).

Table 2.2 *Socioeconomic group by sex, 1975–94*

Socioeconomic group	1975	1985	1994
Men			
Professional	5	6	7
Employer/manager	15	19	21
Intermediate and junior non-manual	17	17	17
Skilled manual, own a/c non-prof*	41	37	35
Semi-skilled manual, personal service	17	16	14
Unskilled manual	5	5	5
Base = 100 percent	10 902	8787	7948
Women			
Professional	1	1	2
Employer/manager	4	7	11
Intermediate and junior non-manual	46	48	48
Skilled manual, own a/c non-prof*	9	9	8
Semi-skilled manual, personal service	31	27	22
Unskilled manual	9	7	9
Base	11 799	9439	8698

Source: Office of Population and Census Surveys (UK) (1996), *Labour Force Trends*, London: HMSO, Table 7.4, presented in Sylvia Walby (1997) *Gender Transformations*, London: Routledge, Table 2.7, p. 35.

* Skilled manual and from their own account non-professional.
All persons aged 16 and over.

Table 2.3 *Gender changes in occupational orders, 1981–91*

		% increase in men	% increase in women
1	Professional and related supporting management; senior national and local government managers	33	155
2	Professional and related in education, welfare and health	3	22
3	Literary, artistic and sports	12	54
4	Professional and related in science, engineering, technology and similar fields	4	72
5	Managerial	9	61
6	Clerical and related	−19	2
7	Selling	−9	6
8	Security and protective services	−12	6
9	Catering, cleaning, hair-dressing and other personal services	0	−1
10	Farming, fishing and related	−24	4
11	Materials processing; making and repairing (excluding metal and electrical)	−20	−27
12	Processing, making, repairing and related (metal and electrical)	−31	−31
13	Painting, repetitive assembling, product inspecting, packaging and related	−25	−26
14	Construction, mining and related not identified elsewhere	−20	43
15	Transport operating, materials moving and storing and related	−23	−9
16	Miscellaneous (general labourers and foremen)	−61	−45
17	Inadequately described and not stated	−74	−79
	Total	−15	5

Source: Data calculated from 1981 census and 1991 census, 10 percent sample, coded using 1980 occupational classification by Sylvia Walby (1997), *Gender Transformations*, London: Routledge, Table 2.9, p. 37.

Liberal feminism also highlights the multiplicity of evidence that suggests that women, because they are perceived to be more or less suited to particular occupations, work for the most part in certain defined sectors of the economy. In the UK, for example, women have been found to be working in education, health-related professions such as midwifery, personal services, hospitality and tourism, library and information work, clerical positions, secretarial positions and the like (see Wilson 1995: 16–17). In Australia, 75 percent of all working women are concentrated in four main industries – community services, wholesale and retail trade, manufacturing, and finance, property and business services (Still 1988; Cahoon 1994: 303). There is also evidence that assumptions about 'women's skills' underpin recruitment patterns in UK service industries (see Brewis and Kerfoot 1994, for example). That is to say, it seems that women are often preferred over men for customer liaison positions in the various service industries (e.g. the financial services) on the basis that women are assumed to be more socially adept, more welcoming and less threatening than men. Indeed, and unusually in comparison to other industries, it is *older* women in particular who employers appear to favour for front-desk positions such as these, the assumption being that they are maternal, sympathetic characters to whom the public can relate easily and with whom they can communicate.

This *horizontal segregation* also occurs at managerial levels – evidence suggests that women tend to work within particular areas of management. Examples are personnel or public relations, those areas which, one might suggest, are again assumed to require a specific kind of people-related skills base, to demand sensitivity, intuition and a certain gentleness. It is this evidence of horizontal and vertical segregation which impels liberal feminists to demand that steps be taken to address gendered inequality of opportunity in the workplace. They demand that gender be managed in organizations in such a way as to minimize any differences between the employment chances available to men and those available to women. One could suggest that the main impetus behind liberal feminist arguments of this kind is *social justice*, the moral case for equality of organizational opportunity. Ironically, the *moral* supremacy of this argument has been uncontested since the late eighteenth century. At this time other political and ideological stratagems became necessary in order to preserve the social subordination of women, which was *practically* necessary to prevent the collapse of the existing social order in the revolutionary decades which followed. Women had to be kept at home looking after the hearth while the men were fighting Napoleon, for example, as the size and permanence of disciplined standing (male) armies became huge (see Laqueur 1990).

Radical feminism

This can be compared to the particular *radical* feminist position taken by Mary Daly (1984), for example, which suggests that women are in fact naturally *different* from men – that they possess certain characteristics which render them closer to nature, closer to their passions and emotions, less rational, and therefore *superior* to men (see also Jaggar 1983). Radical feminism of this kind may advocate that women be deliberately introduced into the higher echelons of management so as to counterbalance the rationality of senior male managers (see, for example, discussion in McNeil 1987). Some even suggest that women-only organizations be set up so as to allow women to work alongside and deal with other women alone (for a fictional account of such organizations, see French 1986).

Feminist writers commonly discuss the short and long agendas which may characterize organizational efforts to manage gender, and consistent with a radical feminist approach may include active *positive discrimination* in favour of women to redress disadvantage. A *short* agenda, as defined by David Goss (1994: 158), is that which seeks only to comply with anti-discrimination legislation. A *long* agenda, on the other hand, seeks to bring about representation for *both* men and women at every level of the organization – its goal being that of equal share. Therefore, the long agenda implies a much more concerted attack on gendered inequality of opportunity, including measures such as an equal opportunities policy, efforts to alter prejudiced behaviour and attitudes at work, skills training for women in particular and provisions such as flexi-time or job share to minimize the problem of the so-called home–work interface for women. Both Cynthia Cockburn (1991) and Goss imply that the long agenda is much more likely to bring about genuine equality of opportunity. This rather radical aim is one of which Cockburn is, in any case, somewhat critical. She prefers to stress what she refers to as parity – a recognition that men and women are equal but different.

Diversity

Further, and in contrast to the equal opportunities stance of which organizational liberal feminism forms an important strand, there is also a growing body of work around the need to manage what has become known as *diversity* in the workplace – to be responsible for and sensitive to the different types of individuals who make up an organization. Gender is an important topic in diversity, as are race, ethnicity, class, (dis)ability and HIV status, as well as other issues less prominent in the equal opportunities literature, such as personality, value systems, work style, religion, lifestyle, education level and so on. Leading US diversity consultant R. Roosevelt Thomas states that:

> … managing diversity begins with these fundamental questions: Given the competitive environment we face and the diverse workforce we have, are we getting the highest productivity possible? Does our system work as smoothly as it could? Is morale as high as we would wish? And are those things as strong as they would be if all the people who worked here were the same sex and race and nationality and had the same lifestyle and value system and way of working? If the answers are no, then the solution is to substitute positive for negative aspects. That means *changing the system* and *modifying the root culture* (Thomas 1991: 26, emphasis in the original).

Thomas (1991: 16–17) is particularly keen to emphasize that managing diversity is *not* about protecting or affirming civil rights or women's rights; that it is not about humanitarianism (acting for the good of the whole human race); that it is not about a moral responsibility to do the right thing; and, furthermore, that it is not about social responsibility (acting for the good of society). Instead, Thomas emphasizes *the business case* as the driving force behind his conceptualization of managing diversity. Thomas (1991: 4–5) stresses that managing diversity is vital in the face of what he refers to as the tough realities of the 1990s:

- intense global competition;
- predicted future labour shortages in the USA;

- the fact that the make-up of the US workforce is becoming more diverse;
- the fact that the celebration of difference is growing, with much less inclination on the part of individuals to go along with what they see society and organizations demanding of them.

Several parts of this analysis have been challenged, especially with regard to its neglect of the impact of global recession, and we could add the current economic crises in Asia (see Hollinshead and Leat 1995: 38–9). Nevertheless, UK commentators Rajvinder Kandola and Johanna Fullerton offer a very similar definition of managing diversity, which also emphasizes the business case, as follows:

> The basic concept of managing diversity accepts that the workforce consists of a diverse population of people. The diversity consists of visible and non-visible differences which will include factors such as sex, age, background, race, disability, personality, work-style. It is founded on the premise that harnessing these differences will create a productive environment in which everybody feels valued, *where their talents are being fully utilised and in which organisational goals are met* (Kandola and Fullerton 1994a: 47, emphasis added).

The main issue for these proponents of diversity management is that the way in which managers manage their staff should empower *everyone* to 'realize their full potential' – with everyone explicitly including white men, as both Thomas and Kandola and Fullerton point out. These commentators argue that equal opportunity approaches such as organizational liberal feminism are aimed only at the disadvantaged and therefore potentially create problems. Exhibit 2.1 outlines some of the key problems associated with equal employment opportunity approaches.

- A stigma being attached to those who are the recipients of supposedly preferential treatment.
- The development of a culture of tokenism, within which getting the numbers right – that is to say, achieving a target number of disadvantaged employees – is the main issue.
- An assimilation or melting pot culture being established where differences are minimized and not developed to their full potential, where individuals are expected to fit in to a predetermined mould, the consequences of which are seen to be a play it safe approach to work and a reluctance to be creative or to take the initiative.
- Targeting the disadvantaged on a permanent basis rather than making efforts to ensure that an organization naturally encourages equality of opportunity for *all*.
- The outdated idea that organizations still need to focus on recruiting the disadvantaged, rather than ensuring that they are present at all levels of the organization.
- The incorrect assumption that overt and blatant prejudice is still an issue in organizations.
- The creation of poor role models for aspiring members of disadvantaged groups; and so on.

Exhibit 2.1 Problems of equal opportunities approaches

Source: Based on Rajvinder Kandola and Johanna Fullerton (1994b), Managing the Mosaic: Diversity in Action, *London: Institute of Personnel and Development and R. Roosevelt Thomas, Jr (1991),* Beyond Race and Gender: Unleashing the Power of Your Workforce by Managing Diversity, *New York: AMACOM.*

As a result of these identified deficiencies of equal opportunity approaches, the managing diversity camp suggest that an alternative is to focus on individual development needs, to allow all members of the organization the opportunity to develop as they need to do in order to become fully productive employees. Kandola and Fullerton (1994b: 49) suggest MOSAIC as a paradigm for managing diversity. Exhibit 2.2 outlines key components of the MOSAIC approach.

Mission	A set of values which supports and justifies diversity management and encourages the expression of differences.
Objective	All organizational processes (for example, recruitment) must be regularly audited in order to ensure that they are fair to *all*.
Skilled	Managers and workforce must be skilled in 'fairness and awareness' – that is, they must understand the principles of diversity management, know why it is important and work to ensure that diversity is respected. Managers should adopt an approach of continuous development of self and others, asking for feedback on their own performance and working to improve that performance continually, and ensuring that others' progress is not left to chance.
Active	Active flexibility also needs to be implemented, not only in the organization of work (for example, flexi-time), but also in benefits. A 'cafeteria' of benefits can enable each employee to choose the benefits that most suit them. For example, if an individual does not have children, they will not have need of an organizational crèche, but may be keen to own company shares.
Individual	Individual employees are the focus of diversity management, *not* groups of employees such as women.
Culture	Must be empowering, encouraging employees to experiment with ways of respecting and managing diversity themselves.

Exhibit 2.2 Managing diversity

Source: Based on Rajvinder Kandola and Johanna Fullerton (1994b), Managing the Mosaic: Diversity in Action, London: Institute of Personnel and Development, pp. 49–50.

The following case study gives an example of how the managing diversity approach can work in practice. Yet because the main objective is to improve performance, there really is no moral or social strength to these initiatives as such benefits are incidental. A company pragmatically following gender-sensitive policies as a result of diversity initiatives to increase productivity on the shopfloor might find itself following research and development or marketing practices which ignore and ultimately damage the interests of women – as Dow Corning did with the breast implant scandal.

Managing diversity in the workplace: Corning USA

When James Houghton took over as Chief Executive Officer of Corning in 1983, Thomas claims that he made diversity management a key principle. This was primarily because Houghton had identified that turnover rates for women and blacks were higher than for white men, with the consequence that Corning's investment in these groups in terms of recruitment and selection costs, and training and development, was being wasted. He also felt that the make-up of Corning's workforce should become more reflective of its customer base, so as to ensure better consumer relations. To address these issues, Houghton firstly implemented two quality improvement teams – one for blacks and one for women. Awareness training was made mandatory throughout the organization so as to identify which unconscious organizational values were working against these groups. One issue identified as a result of this training was the importance that the Corning culture placed on working late and the way in which it disadvantaged women, who were more likely than men to have pressing domestic responsibilities. There was also a general improvement in communication about diversity – for example, the publication of stories in the company newspaper about Corning's diverse workforce and about successful organizational projects involving diverse groups of people. Further, career planning was introduced for everyone. Corning also began to offer educational grants in exchange for working summers at a plant within the corporation. Many of the students on this programme then came to work for the organization upon graduating. Corning's summer internship programme also expanded, with a particular emphasis on offering places to women and blacks, and, finally, contacts with university groups such as the Society of Women Engineers were instigated. Significantly, given the overall thrust of the managing diversity argument, while James Houghton acknowledges the social and moral benefits of the approach that he has implemented, he also states that: 'It simply makes good business sense' (Houghton, cited in Thomas 1990: 10).

Source: Based on R. Roosevelt Thomas (1990), 'From affirmative action to affirming diversity', Harvard Business Review, March–April: 10.

Authors' note: Ironically, a Corning subsidiary, Dow Corning, was in 1997 forced to pay several millions in damages to thousands of women – damaged by its faulty silicone breast implants. The alleged cause was that the product was insufficiently tested, that is, women did not have sufficient voice in its development and their needs were not properly monitored.

Gender *in* management

This approach argues that management is relational, and that as men and women are socialized differently, they manage differently. The search has been conducted by several researchers to identify the key characteristics of a feminine managerial style. Especially with regard to leadership, masculine characteristics have been associated with 'transactional' or administrative styles, while feminine characteristics have been associated with change-oriented styles. Beverly Alimo-Metcalfe (1995), among others, argues for an assertion of the *feminine-in-management* as transformational leadership styles are most effective in the current socioeconomic climate. Critics of this school, however, adopt a *gender globalization* approach, which insists that specific styles are relatively insignificant except that they facilitate the globalization of masculinized organization (Calás and Smircich 1995). Women are introduced into the domestic workforce as having the most appropriate managerial styles because this allows males to strut the international stage and be more globally mobile. The *gender socialization* approach takes a cautionary view about the potential overvaluation of context, whether global or local, and argues that socialization takes place both inside and outside the workplace and needs to be taken into account (Gherardi 1995). We discuss these three approaches in detail later in the chapter. The third position, as represented by Gherardi (1995), naturally leads into the fifth school, whose work we are developing in this chapter.

Gender*ing* management

A more recently developing section of the literature on gender and management places the emphasis on *managing* gender, on introducing what might be dubbed 'gender awareness' into management *practice*. An alternative approach is to insist on *gendering management*, introducing the concept of gender into management *theory*, and understanding how gender affects the way managers think and act. To this end, we will look at the theory of managerial work, the theory which attempts to conceptualize what management is, with particular attention to the presence and positioning of gender within that analysis. Management and organization theory has generally either completely neglected gender or has used relatively simple descriptive models of frameworks that treat gender as no more than a variable of which account should be taken (Mills and Tancred 1992: 13).

Nevertheless, as Chris Grey (1995) points out, we should not overstate the gendering of management and organizational analysis. The 'gender' lens is not the only way to look at management, any more than the 'structure' lens, the 'functions' lens or the 'culture' lens. It does not reveal any ultimate or privileged truth about management, but is an important, and practically useful, means of understanding how management gets 'done' in modern organizations. But is not gender something we are born with, that determines our later behaviour? Why should we be so interested in what we cannot change?

Natural Born Women ... and Men ?

Despite its apparent biological basis, it is often argued that gender is not a natural division (see Parsons and Zales 1956; Tiger and Fox 1972), and that therefore men and women are *not* automatically suited to particular and different kinds of work in any predetermined sense, except in a few cases. Men and women are not naturally and exclusively different, save biologically, and it is often suggested that all other differences are socially attributed. This argument can be evidenced in many ways, but perhaps one of the most interesting is Katherine O'Donovan's (1985) discussion of babies born with indeterminate genitalia (also see Brewis, Hampton and Linstead 1997: 1279). O'Donovan tells the story of a child born with what appeared to be a misshapen penis, but no testicles. This child was identified and subsequently raised as a male. However, when he reached puberty, he began to develop breasts. As a result, surgery was performed and this intervention revealed that this boy actually possessed a uterus, ovaries and a vagina – but he refused, nonetheless, to identify as anything else except as male. Consequently, hormones were administered to this individual to allow him to develop external male characteristics such as facial hair. As O'Donovan points out, accounts such as this indicate both how error can occur in the assignment of sexual identity, but also how much the later social construction and development of gender identity creates difference between human beings who may not be biologically different (O'Donovan 1985: 62).

Just as gender is constructed in organizations, it is also constructed in what we write about organizations. In the next section we will take a look at how gender has been constructed in management and organization theory. As we shall see, much of this construction has taken place by implication in the absence of explicit discussions of gender.

Gender and management theory

It has been widely suggested that mainstream management theory is actually more accurately labelled 'malestream'. It fails to recognize the relationship between management and gender: first, because it makes little or no room for any analysis of those actual individuals who occupy the management role, treating management as an abstract set of functions, principles or processes (see Chapter 6 on managing teams); and, second, because it fails to recognize gender as being a significant variable even in the face of overwhelming empirical evidence. Management in this kind of theory is presented as gender neutral, either as a mere collection of functions (classical management theory) or as a more or less appropriate relationship to one's workforce (theories of human relations or management 'style'). However, management is an inescapably *embodied* and, therefore, gendered *experience*, an experience which is different for men and women whether they are the managers or the managed. The omission of gender by mainstream/malestream theories of management means that such theories cannot account for the complexity of the management experience – that they cannot capture *how it feels* and *what it means* to manage in a modern organization – so they either ignore or deny certain significant aspects.

Classical management theory

For classical management theory, as exemplified in the work of Col. Lyndall Urwick (1937), Frederick Winslow Taylor (1947) and Henri Fayol (1949) in the early twentieth century, and later by Mooney (1947) and Brech (1965), management consists simply of the execution of a series of *functions*. It is these functions, suggest these theorists, which assure the smooth and effective running of the organization. Management here is presented as a depersonalized activity – it is manage*ment* that is the focus for these theories rather than the real-life *process* of manag*ing* (Huczynski and Buchanan 1991: 432; Hayward 1992: 186–8). A similar view dominates the organizational theory literature in which, in classical theories, the *organization* refers to an enterprise or social entity and formal roles while *organizing* emphasizes the enacted and sense-making processes of those being organized (Hayward 1992: 157–8).

As Urwick puts it, the study of human experience of organizing can yield up principles which can govern *any form* of human organization. For him, regardless of the organization's purpose (a local church, a hospital, a government agency, an army regiment, a supermarket or a newspaper, for example), its people (manuals, intellectuals, men or women, for example) or the political and social theory behind its creation (capitalism or socialism), these principles were technical and universal. They applied to *all* managerial situations (Urwick 1937: 431). In Communist Russia, for example, Lenin was keen to apply F.W. Taylor's capitalist scientific management methods! Taylor's other principles are outlined in Chapter 6, but unfortunately other commentators could not agree with his 'universal' principles, and management theorists generated lists of principles which varied from four to 14 – all supposedly universal (Hales 1993). Nevertheless, the belief in universality held firm for several decades.

There is an overall emphasis within classical management theory on the application of science to the study of management in order, through observation, hypothesis development and experimentation, to arrive at the 'one best way' to manage. Fayol (1949), for example, on the basis of his observations from his own management experience, suggested that management (which he referred to as administration) consisted of :

- *organizing* (that is to say, dividing labour and ensuring that this division is efficient and effective);
- *coordinating* (overseeing this division of labour in terms of ensuring that the parts support each other);
- *controlling* (monitoring the activities of workers within this division of labour, including disciplining them if necessary); and
- '*purveyance*' (forecasting and planning future workforce activity).

In a similar vein, Taylor's (1947) thesis of Scientific Management addressed itself to the most efficient way to manage. His key ideas were, for example, that every individual's labour should be designed using a scientific analysis of that work. He also placed a good deal of emphasis on rigorous selection of, and training and development for, all workers. Furthermore, Taylor stated that managers must also cooperate with their workers in order to ensure that those workers are following the procedures laid down for them. Finally, he believed in a strict separation of conception and execution. That is to say, Taylor stated that managers should manage and workers work; he counselled that workers should not themselves have any control over the way in which they work or over what they do.

Scientific Management does not ignore the fact that individuals have different abilities – far from it. Taylor was at pains to point out that not everyone was capable of working in a scientifically determined 'one best way'. He stated that individuals needed to be selected carefully according to their abilities to work hard and in accordance with instructions. In his earlier work, he was emphatic that rates were to be negotiated with individuals only and not with the collective or group, although, as Chris Nyland (1989) has pointed out, Taylor came to embrace the necessity, and arguably the positive features, of collective bargaining with trade unions in his later years. Similarly, he was aware that there were women in the workforce. Nyland (forthcoming) republishes a contemporary review of the role of women in Scientific Management by Sue Ainslie Clark and Edith Wyatt, which Taylor welcomed, and a correspondence with Taylor by Wyatt, who later gave very supportive evidence to a US Congressional Committee addressing Scientific Management. Yet, despite his awareness of and interest in the effects of Scientific Management on women (including his suggestion that women should be given two days a month off with no questions asked, the implication being that this was to accommodate the menstrual cycle), individual or gender characteristics were not the *defining* features of either work or management. Defining features remained other underlying, objectively observable principles that determined what work and management were and that could be measured.

Within this approach, the gender of the individuals who are managing has no relationship to the way that they *should* manage. However, Taylor implicitly acknowledged that in reality, and in most circumstances, it will have some relationship to the way they *do* manage, which is precisely *why* he argued that the principles of Scientific Management need to be enunciated and understood. Scientific Management would enable women and men to overcome any differences in 'innate' style of managing and both to manage in the most efficient way.

Here, then, the main emphasis is on the manager as a functionary, as an individual who works for the benefit of the whole organization – and therefore of all of those within it (the last assumption is especially apparent in Taylor's work) – but who has no especial identity or contribution which is unique to them *as an individual* as far as the organization is concerned. Management for Taylor and the classical management theorists is *normative*, whereas the argument of this text is that management is fundamentally *relational*. For the classical management theorists, as argued in Chapter 6, any work on relationships was just a matter of aligning people with the correct abstract principles, which was the function of management. Difference and diversity were not just to be ignored, they were to be *suppressed*. Rationality, traditionally a male trait, was to dominate in the workplace.

Max Weber, whose theory of bureaucracy was as theoretically influential as was Taylor's method for practice, similarly had a clear view of the association between women and emotion and the need to banish emotion (and consequently women) from the public organizational stage in favour of objective institutional rationality (Burrell 1997: 244; Bologh 1990: 28–9). Yet it was in the reform of office work, and particularly through the efforts of Frank and Lilian Gilbreth (1911), that the labour process became most obviously gendered, where men managed women – as immortalized in the film *Cheaper by the Dozen*. The routinization of the workplace was extended into the home, and even the womb (the Gilbreths had 12 children), and turned into an ironic romp about the way they reputedly lived their lives together according to work study principles. The 'one best way' to do things was gently 'sent up'. But gender is not allowed to be directly addressed as an issue in classical management theories.

Human relations theory

What is sometimes viewed as a 'softer' turn in management and organization theory, away from the measurement and timing of classical management, was primarily associated with the Hawthorne Studies, and their development under the influence of Elton Mayo. It is also associated with the later theoretical influence of Abraham Maslow and his theory of the hierarchy of human needs. Both Mayo and Maslow conducted work in which women (or females) were a significant part, yet produced theories which ignored gender as a factor. The reasons for this are different in each case, but had a considerable effect on later studies.

The Hawthorne Studies were initiated in 1924 by managers of the Hawthorne Plant of the Western Electric Company in Chicago. They had originally been ergonomic studies of the effects of the physical surroundings of work on productivity, particularly that of lighting. As an electricity producer, Western had an obvious interest in demonstrating that using more electricity could increase other companies' profits – an approach which is currently being rediscovered in the 1990s as managing your customers' value-added. Since the First World War there had been clinical studies of fatigue and monotony, and the methodologies used by Hawthorne were an extension of these. It is often suggested that the managers involved in the early phases of the studies had no idea how to interpret the data and asked

Mayo, an Australian philosopher/psychologist working at Harvard University, to help them analyze the data because of similar workplace studies he had conducted and his connections with the prestigious Rockefeller Foundation. The managers, on the contrary, had plenty of ideas – what they wanted was for an expert to help *mediate* their interpretations. Mayo, however, had ideas of his own and when he eventually did come to write on the studies he treated the data rather selectively and as a platform for his own theories (Gillespie 1991; Mayo 1945, 1933/1960; Trahair 1984).

One of these theories was based on the fact that as a young man he had had bad experiences of political demagogues in Adelaide who had swayed the local unions and caused considerable industrial and social unrest and political damage. He was, as a result, deeply mistrustful of collective sentiment. Second, he had failed twice, in Adelaide and Edinburgh, to become a doctor of medicine, and had channelled his energies into clinical psychology, particularly counselling and psychiatry. Mayo's approach to organizations was to treat their problems as symptoms of a malaise which might be collective, but was probably individual. The source, he felt, was the disruption of traditional community occasioned by urban concentration, and he felt that work organizations had to fulfil some of the functions of community for the workers to prevent tensions manifesting themselves in lowered output, absenteeism, fatigue, boredom, sickness and what he called 'pessimistic reveries'. A third factor might be added, which was that Mayo had never fitted neatly into academic disciplinary categories himself, and read widely if not always wisely in many genres and brought this into his methodology as multidisciplinarity. One of the most distinctive features of the Hawthorne Studies was the inclusion of psychologists, social anthropologists, statisticians and others in the programme.

Mayo liked to build 'big picture' social arguments, and his perspective was not too dissimilar from that of Taylor, as critical commentators like Harry Braverman (1974) have pointed out. Yet it is still remarkable that although the empirical phase of the Hawthorne experiments was conducted on two groups, one of which was entirely male and the other entirely female, this gender segregation was not treated as an object of analysis. The female group was initially coerced into taking part in the experiments and was separated from the main body of the shopfloor by being put in a separate room, with a male supervisor. They were closely supervised and monitored, involved in the distribution of activities and the organization of work, given incentives and manipulated in other ways, and were also medically monitored for changes in their condition which might lead to fatigue. Such was the intrusiveness of the management that two of the workers who had become difficult and vocal in their argumentation for improvements in conditions, etc. were removed from the group against their will.

In discussing the accounts of the experiments, Richard Gillespie (1991: 204) points out that both Mayo (1933/1960, 1945) and later Fritz Roethlisberger and William Dickson (1939) ignored the possibility of collective action by workers. The only dimension that mattered was the individual, and any economic arguments – even where, as with the male group in the Bank Wiring Room, these seemed to have considerable merit – were regarded as 'simply an unconvincing rationalization of behaviour actually driven by sentiments' (Gillespie 1991: 204). This is despite the fact that output by the women increased and output by the men decreased! As Jeff Hearn and Wendy Parkin (1994) point out, the absence of gender and sexuality from the consideration of human relations, interpersonal relations and emotional relations calls into question what these terms can possibly mean.

They argue that these are attempts by men not just to reorganize social relations, but to incorporate gendered and sexual relations into organizational analysis in an agendered and asexual way (Wilson 1996: 829). This, however, was not 'gender *blindness*' as Wilson argues, but an aware and *active suppression* of gender difference arising from an intellectual commitment to abstract generalizations, disembodied reasoning and a basically Freudian view which saw women, despite their surface differences, essentially as men without a penis.

Maslow's Hierarchy of Needs

Another theorist whose work, though not directly related to organizations, was incorporated into the Human Relations approach was the psychologist Abraham Maslow. Maslow had similar views about the fundamental nature of human beings to those of Mayo, and his theory of motivation is said to treat men and women as if gender were inconsequential. Maslow argued that human beings are 'driven' by needs which can be classified according to a hierarchy ranging from survival at the bottom, through safety/security, social/affiliative and esteem/recognition to self-actualization. For Maslow, self-actualization was the ultimate need, but critics have argued that although his studies of self-actualizing people included women, his definition of it reflects stereotypical *male* experiences and traits (Cullen 1994; Kasten 1972; Wilson 1996). Thus, self-actualization becomes an expression of the male self which *denies* relatedness rather than the female self which *defines* itself in relation to others (Chodorow 1989). Mayo privileged the notion of a hierarchy rather than seeing these needs as webs of interrelated emotional and physical needs (Gilligan 1982; Wilson 1996).

Maslow's hierarchy was founded on his research on captive primates, with regard to dominance behaviour. Human behaviour was in the 1930s widely held to be predominantly determined by sex (Freud) or dominance/power (Adler). Maslow's interest was in exploring this issue, and he began by working with primates in order to develop a basic understanding of dominance behaviour. As Dallas Cullen (1997) points out, his research was deeply flawed, particularly by the fact that, as later field studies demonstrated, apes behave differently in their wild communities where social skills rather than physiological traits were more important in the emergence of certain apes in dominant roles. Indeed, the most recent studies have indicated that the reproductive strategies of females are far more complex than was hitherto assumed. Females will deliberately mate during their most fertile period with males outside their community, thus adding variety to the gene pool, while continuing to mate with males from the tribe during infertile periods. Hidden subversive behaviour, then, seems to have greater consequence than more obvious dominance behaviour (Weiss 1997).

Maslow felt that the apes that were less aggressive and most relaxed about their dominance (and consequently most *worthy* of their position) had greater confidence in themselves. He carried this idea through in his research on sexuality, which focused on women and what he called 'dominance-feeling' and later 'self-esteem', which was an essential underpinning for self-actualization. Maslow, when giving examples of self-actualizers, came up with a sample which was predominantly male, which has been variously held to be a result of restricted opportunities for women in society (Friedan 1963: 310), or a consequence of the fact that ways in which Maslow believed women self-actualized (e.g. motherhood) are not publicly recognized (Maslow 1954: 92; Cullen 1994: 130). However, the gender bias in the hierarchy came from the conflation of dominance behaviour with self-esteem, which led Maslow to conclude that high-dominance women, who displayed more masculine traits, had more in common with high-dominance men than low-dominance women, and he suggested that the gender distinction could be *dropped altogether* as it was so misleading (Maslow 1939: 18; Cullen 1994: 134).

This is not gender *blindness*, but the deliberate suppression of observable difference for theoretical reasons. As Cullen points out, the low-dominance women had many qualities which were indicative of high self-esteem if viewed from a more relational perspective, but for Maslow they could not be self-actualizers. The high-dominance women, we would add, conversely display many behaviours which could be regarded as narcissistic or self-centred. Cullen (1994: 134–5) points out many methodological flaws in Maslow's study, but perhaps the most disturbing aspect of it is that on the basis of his knowledge of high-dominance women he observed in 1963 that in contrast to men 'women generally were not destroyed by being raped because fear makes women more feminine and rape represents a woman's desirability and power since the rapist has an erection' (Lowry 1982: 90, cited in Cullen 1994: 136). Yet the hierarchy built on flawed primate research and even more flawed sexuality research, and displaying very significant gender bias, has been so influential in management and organization theory as to have been regarded as a 'classic among classics' (Matteson and Ivancevich 1989: 369, in Cullen 1994: 127).

Later theories

Later management theories do become more sophisticated in their greater recognition of the fundamentally relational nature of the management task (Wilson 1996). These theories pay greater attention to the fact that managing not only involves the persuasion and cooption of others, but also itself evolves as an activity in response to the outcomes of these negotiations. The developing relationship between workforce and management, leaders and followers, emerges as important. Such theories also recognize that management is a process rather than a function, that it involves undertaking the task of managing, that there are various different alternative ways to manage, and that some of these are more appropriate or effective in certain circumstances than others. So these later theories retain the emphasis on the organizational efficiency and effectiveness characteristic of classical management theory, but also emphasize that management is relational, stylistic and processual. Much of this work has concentrated on leadership styles, and often crosses the boundary between leadership and management, which is discussed in Chapter 5.

All of these more relational theories can also be criticized for their continued gender blindness and perhaps here it is a blindness rather than a suppression, because none of the theorists here seems to be following such a grand social mission or theoretical plan as Taylor, Mayo or Maslow and, indeed, are mere technicians when considered alongside the influence of these giants. Managing here is more modestly acknowledged to be temporally located, but there is more emphasis on the relationship between the manager and the workers than on the specific characteristics, background and extrinsic factors which affect the individual who is involved in managing. Yet the individual manager is a shadowy figure, someone who remains anonymous, a non-reflective practitioner who simply needs to choose or be assigned to manage in suitable ways in appropriate situations. There is no discussion of the embodied experience of managing, of how it feels and what it means to be a manager – and therefore no discussion of the individual manager's gender. In particular, even more recent theories of management, leadership and motivation have not introduced discussion of the considerable number of non-mainstream studies, which have addressed the issues of women as leaders, women's motivation to work and as managers, and women's personality features at work (Wilson 1995, 1996).

Gender *in* management

Despite the absence of gender from mainstream/malestream management theory, some organizational analysts have sought to establish the interrelation between gender and management practice. That is to say, they consider the *embodied* nature of managerial work, management as performed by gendered subjects, by individuals who identify as male or female, masculine or feminine, and the consequences that this may have for organizational and managerial practice. In other words, how male and female managers *actually* manage becomes the focus. This work tends to retain the emphasis on management as process and the differences between managerial styles, which the relational theorists emphasize, as well as relying (perhaps surprisingly) on the classical management theory notion of a 'one best way' to manage as regards organizational effectiveness, if perhaps seeking to reverse it. However, the real contribution of this more contemporary theory is arguably its acknowledgement that it *matters* what kind of person is doing the managing.

However, again there are different approaches which we discuss in turn below:

- The *feminine-in-management* approach takes the position that men and women have different natural styles, and that contemporary management is changing in ways that require the more feminine styles in order for businesses to be successful.
- *Undervaluing context* – the *gender and globalization* approach which critically engages with the ways in which globalization is gendered and ignores the 'reserve army' role of women in the local context.
- *Over valuing context and differences* – this approach argues that the differences between locally specific forms of socialization in work and outside work should not be ignored and it is unwise to overplay gender differences.

Let us look more closely at these approaches.

The feminine-in-management approach

Judy Rosener's (1990) research asked male and female managers to describe their preferred managerial style. She discovered that male managers, by their own account at least, adopted what she refers to as a 'transactional' leadership style. This style uses the principle of exchange in managing – offering rewards or punishment for work done well or badly. Rosener's male respondents also said that they relied a good deal on their positional authority, that is to say, the status conferred upon them by the organization, in order to manage. Women, on the other hand, reportedly used a style that Rosener calls 'transformational' leadership with a small 't'. This places the emphasis on motivating staff through persuading them to commit to group/organizational goals, on regular interaction with staff and on encouraging them to participate in decision making, on managing through personal qualities rather than by using organizational status, and on trying to make staff feel good about themselves. Rosener attributes these differences to gender socialization in early childhood.

She is also fairly emphatic that the female style of leadership is likely to be more apposite and more successful in the turbulence of the current economic climate than the command-and-control style used by her male respondents. Monique Siegel (in *Harvard Business Review* 1991: 154) agrees, stating that she is particularly impressed with Rosener's conclusion that women managers have been successful *because* they are women and not because they have adapted to a masculine, directive and authoritarian style of managing. Siegel states explicitly that women should be proud of themselves for these achievements and that they should *not* try to adapt to the more masculine transactional style.

There is evidence from a review of the literature on management styles and gender (a total of 162 studies using varying methods) that in *laboratory studies* women do adopt a more democratic and people-centred approach than men to managing, although *organizational studies* do not indicate a difference (Eagly and Johnson 1990). Male managers tend to be more autocratic and more task/production oriented. Gender differences, apart from the issue of democracy versus autocracy, were found to be strongest in artificial environments such as laboratories or assessment centres. Reviews of the research on gender and leadership both indicate the importance of perception in the process. Subordinates had a tendency to perceive men and women leaders differently, while men and women leaders also tended to present themselves differently across studies (Wilson 1995: 172–6; Chemers and Murphy 1995; see also Chapter 5).

Taking a different approach, the British researcher Beverley Alimo-Metcalfe begins from the incontrovertible premise (Adler 1993) that there are relatively few women in managerial positions. It is her aim to ascertain why this might be, although she does acknowledge that a multiplicity of different reasons – cultural, legal, educational and social – have been put forward as explanations. She prefers, however, to focus on organizational processes and, more specifically, assessment in the form of the selection and promotion of managers. Alimo-Metcalfe (1995: 4) makes reference to the body of research on whether women and men manage differently and states, in fact, that this research as a whole is largely *inconclusive* in its findings. For example, Jeffrey Powell (cited by Sonnenfeld in *Harvard Business Review* 1991: 159) concluded that there were *no* gender differences present in managers' predilection to task-oriented behaviour and/or people-oriented behaviour. This, of course, flatly contradicts Rosener's and some of Alice Hendrickson Eagly and Blair T. Johnson's findings which we discussed above. Rather than continue to ask the same questions and get the same inconclusive results, Alimo-Metcalfe asks 'What do women and men perceive as qualities and behaviours of leadership?' She sees this issue to be significant in explaining why there are so few women in management. The reason is that men constitute the majority of those who make selection and promotion decisions regarding management positions in organizations (also see Alimo-Metcalfe 1993, 1994). However, even given this rather different spin on gendering management, it is significant that her findings, which were gathered by asking the question cited above, mirror Rosener's findings about differences in management style according to gender.

From Alimo-Metcalfe's (1995: 6) research, it seems that male and female managers certainly *do* define effective management differently. For example, her female managers perceived an effective manager to be someone who relates to others as equals and who is sensitive and aware of the effects of what they do on others. Alimo-Metcalfe's male managers, on the other hand, valued influence and self-confidence as being particularly important among managerial interpersonal skills. Her female managers, furthermore, valued a working style which allows for creativity to be developed in others, which allows for love at work, which empowers and builds teams. Alimo-Metcalfe's male managers, by way of contrast, placed the emphasis on drive, direction, organization and the transmission of a clear purpose to staff. Alimo-Metcalfe also borrows from Rosener in designating these differences of style as transformational and transactional. The important issue for Alimo-Metcalfe is that of a particular kind of *empowerment* being a key component of transformational management. This kind of empowerment rests on interdependence and cooperation between the *managed* and the *manager*. However, it is Alimo-Metcalfe's concern that a much more masculine version of empowerment is currently valued – that of giving power and, therefore, of also giving accountability for mistakes and failures. This latter kind of empowerment, as she puts it, underplays connectedness, the relations between the managed and the manager: instead it emphasizes individuality and separation. Even where transformational empowerment is valued generally in subordinates by managers, she finds that it is *not* valued when displayed by women (Alimo-Metcalfe 1995: 7).

Therefore, she asserts that these kinds of qualities are undervalued when management selection and promotion is taking place, primarily because such decision-making processes are dominated by men, as established above. The need to understand leadership and transformational leadership in particular has heightened on a global scale, she argues, and all the research emphasizes the importance and relevance of the transformational leadership approach in a complex and diverse world (Rosenbach and Taylor, cited in Alimo-Metcalfe 1995: 8; see also Chapter 5).

In sum, then, Alimo-Metcalfe's conclusions – that men and women managers value different kinds of managerial style, and that the style valued by women may be more apposite in today's organizational world, whatever the stance taken by those who select for and promote to managerial positions – are actually very similar to those from Rosener's research. Finally, it is significant to consider Helen Brown's suggestion that women-*only* organizations demonstrate a flat structure with diffused leadership (Brown 1992). It is also argued that women have the necessary social skills and are better suited for the creation and management of democratic and non-hierarchical organizations (Brown 1992, cited in Gherardi 1995: 91).

Undervaluing context – gender and globalization

A radical critique of the feminine-in-management approach comes from Marta Calás and Linda Smircich (1995). They argue that this approach combines with the emphasis on globalization to perpetuate the second-class status of women in the workforce. At the risk of oversimplifying their subtle argument, they point out, in the context of the USA, that as globalization increases and male managers are forced to become the 'global manager' and spend long periods of time overseas, there is a need for them to be replaced. Couple this to the argument that new flexible workforces, which employ team-based work and expect high commitment from their members, need softer, more relational, more 'feminine' caring skills rather than the controlling hard-driving style of traditional management. The result? A greater 'domestication' of US home industry while the global scene becomes more of a battlefield. Women are brought into the workforce and increasingly into management positions to care for the workforce while the promotable males are sent overseas to grow and develop the business – to do battle with the competition in the global market place, or to develop strategy in the rarefied air of the boardroom. Others also argue that the building blocks of the international order are gendered and the personal is not only political but international (Enloe 1989; Walby 1997: 185–7). The changing role that women are playing in the economy is therefore deeply connected to global developments which the feminine-in-management approach tends to ignore.

Overvaluing context and difference – gender socialization

However, to suggest, as do Rosener and others, (1) that women are socialized to manage in certain ways and/or to value a particular kind of managerial approach and (2) that this supposedly more feminine approach is particularly appropriate in the current economic circumstances is arguably problematic. This is because this work seems to take much less account of important processes *within* the organization. One could criticize this kind of thinking for placing too much emphasis on life outside the factory gates. In other words, there is an implication here that men and women arrive at work fully socialized, that the workplace itself has little effect on the ways in which these individuals behave. Thus, while these studies recognize the importance of introducing gender into the analysis of management work, they perhaps fail to recognize the interplay of gender and management, the ways in which gender works to shape managerial work *and vice versa.* Rather, they seem to represent an add gender and stir approach.

In criticizing theorists such as Rosener, Cynthia Fuchs Epstein (in *Harvard Business Review* 1991: 151), for example, places much more emphasis on work context than pre-work gender socialization as shaping individuals' behaviour at work. For example, Epstein cites her own research among lawyers as demonstrating that women managers frequently engage in what she describes as combative, punitive and authoritarian behaviour. Gender is perhaps perceived as being too 'sexy' in contemporary management theorizing, attracting so much analytical attention that the exploration of other important factors, which influence the way management is done, are neglected (Mansbridge, in *Harvard Business Review* 1991: 154–6). It has also been argued that *in*-work variables such as the size and age of the organization should not be underplayed as influencing and in turn being influenced by managerial style. Additionally, age, class and cultural differences as *non*-work variables, aside from gender, may also shape/interact with managerial behaviour. In the same vein, women managers' preference for the transformational style of leadership may actually be a function of *those that they manage* (Cohen, in *Harvard Business Review* 1991: 158). Allan Cohen argues that Rosener, for example, overlooks the fact that many of her female managers were responsible for professionals who may well have not taken kindly to a highly directive managerial approach. Cohen in fact states that Rosener overestimates the influence of pre-work gender socialization.

We should not, however, over-state the *differences* between men and women's socialization. The socializing of women to work outside the home does not occur in a context separate to that of men. Neither does their socialization into the essentially private world of caring and nurturing. Women do not learn to be women in isolation from men and then bring these values into the workplace – they are socialized in interaction with men (Gherardi 1995: 91).

If we overplay gender differences in management theorizing, Silvia Gherardi asks, how can we account for those men who prefer to work within a more democratic organizational framework and to manage in more democratic ways? She therefore suggests that some accounts of gender and managerial work tend to over-valorize the 'either/or' of the gender framework. Gherardi (1995: 94–5) points instead to the concept of dual presence, as identified by 1970s Italian feminists, such as Balbo and Zanuso, which represents the mindset of women at this time who identified with themselves in a 'cross-wise' manner. These women saw themselves as subverting but not abandoning conventional feminine role models by operating in many arenas across the social spectrum. They did not allow the world to be symbolically divided up into 'men's business' and 'women's business' – they continually transgressed, did things they were not supposed to do, caused men's and women's activities to merge until the gender divide, at the level of action at least, became more fluid (Gherardi 1995: 95).

However, it is not simply this theoretical 'gap' which is the critical weakness of the feminine-in-management approach. One might suggest that the kind of conclusions reached by this work will only reinforce the kinds of stereotypical recruitment patterns which are already apparent in management *practice*. Management functions such as personnel and public relations can be seen to be female ghettos. That is to say, they are dominated by women. Furthermore, such functions have also, historically at least, been undervalued in terms of their importance to the organization. The recruitment of women to these particular management functions can be argued to be founded upon understandings of women as having particularly well-developed people skills, as being more intuitive, more sympathetic, more effective communicators and more easy to communicate with than men. By way of contrast, Epstein argues that:

> Women ought to be in management because they are intelligent, adaptable, practical, and efficient – *and* because they are capable of compassion, as are other human beings ... men also can (and do) express [humanitarian values] if they are not made to feel embarrassed about showing them. And those categories of toughness and drive that many men are made to feel comfortable with should be prized in women who wish to express them when they are appropriate. The category is 'people', not 'men and women' (Epstein, in *Harvard Business Review* 1991: 151, emphasis added).

The Japanese model of management (which many commentators identify as being the same as so-called transformational leadership) has derived from organizations dominated by *men* (Goldberg, in *Harvard Business Review* 1991: 160). It thus seems then that it is a mistake to embed men and women within a fixed and dualistic gender framework, where men are men and women are women and their characteristics are both different and unchanging. To suggest that socialization makes us *either* masculine *or* feminine at all times according to our sex is not only theoretically but also practically problematic. This kind of approach can lead to the channelling of women into a restricted range of management functions. This kind of segregation at work limits women's opportunities in management, as well as those of their male counterparts, who may be considered insufficiently masculine if they undertake positions which are seen to constitute women's work, or indeed may experience difficulties in gaining access to this kind of work *per se*. Any analysis of gender and managerial work must take into account not only the orientation to work that gender socialization outside of work might produce, but also how the experience of work *in itself* is instrumental in producing, reproducing and sustaining particular forms of gender identity. These identities are a good deal more fluid and non-sex-specific than the analyses provided by Rosener, Alice Eagly and Blair Johnson and Alimo-Metcalfe might imply. The process of becoming gendered continues *and changes* through life. How does this process happen in the workplace?

Gendering management: A critical analysis

In contrast to the traditional sociological approaches to gender and work, not only is one's identity as male or female, masculine or feminine, something separate from one's biological sex, but the development of one's sense of oneself as gendered is a result of the operations of power and knowledge. Masculinity and femininity are clusters of textual roles created by the operations of contemporary discourse around gender difference, roles up to which individuals must strive to live. The discourse of gender difference tells us who we are, and shapes and delimits the possibilities open to us (Brewis *et al.* 1997: 1277). Most men never reach the fantasized ideal of masculinity, the kind of image film heroes like Arnold Schwarzenegger project, just as few women look like Cindy Crawford or Elle Macpherson. But these images, and the degree to which they are valued, cause ordinary people to strive towards them, and as a result may oppress their lives, through anorexia, bulimia or simply discontent. The fact that film stars are rarely anything much like their images does not matter – the images may not be real, but they have real-world effects.

This suggests that we as human individuals are constituted by the powerful operations of discourse. We come to know who we are through being exposed to particular interpretations of what it is to be human – in this case, either male or female, masculine or feminine. Consequently, women may work to be masculine as well as men. Masculinity is *not* what men do and what they are without thinking much about it – men have problems being men, and they do not have exclusive property rights on masculinity (Kerfoot and Knights 1993: 660). Neither is being male definitive or exhaustive of all that men are or can be (Kerfoot and Knights 1996: 85).

Masculine values

Equally, those women who crave workplace success or who already belong to the ranks of management may be *particularly* driven to identify with masculinity, or at least to achieve an acceptable balance between masculine and feminine attributes (Sheppard 1989; McDowell and Court 1994; Collinson and Collinson 1995; Collinson and Hearn 1996; Brewis *et al.* 1997). One of the prevailing forms of contemporary masculinity revolves around being rational, objective, sure of oneself, logical, decisive, aggressive and competitive. This form of masculinity revolves around control. Some of the other features of this form of masculinity involve (in Western cultures) being hard, tough, unemotional, impersonal and objective. It means being explicit, saying what you think and speaking your mind plainly; being outer-focused, possibly aggressive; valuing work, sports and organized activities; being action oriented, liking to get things done, a doer; being analytic, or calculating about situations, rather than intuitive, relying on hunches or gut-feel; being dualistic, or tending to see things as black or white, either or, which can lead to competitiveness; preferring quantitative solutions which involve numbers to qualitative ones which involve opinion; linear thinking (e.g. this causes that, making predictable connections, administrative) rather than lateral thinking (this is associated with making unusual connections, creative thinking); being rationalist, or valuing reason more than emotion or playfulness; being reductionist, or liking to reduce things to their simplest terms and principles, rather than relishing subtle differences; and being materialist, with a constant eye on resources, costs and benefits (Hines 1992: 328). Not all men will be all these things, as this is a stereotype, but it is one which still operates powerfully in Western society even at the level of myth.

Traditional Western masculinity focuses then on dominating and being dominant in situations, and on independence from others (this might not be the same in Asia, for example, where collectivity is important), and even when in a successful team Western males usually worry about not being the 'weak link'. In fact, there is a hidden fear at the heart of this masculinity. In taking a position to the world which emphasizes being active and assertive over others rather than yielding, listening and being gentle, men reject intimate relations with others and achieve social status and esteem by means which glorify force – in war, in sport – or force expressed as power in business and politics. Men then have difficulty handling their feelings because feelings make them vulnerable and womanly. Emotion is dangerous not only because it implies independence – that you are governed by personal rather than organizational objectives – or that it is impossible to fully control, but also because it is alien, representative of all that masculinity rejects (Glaser and Frosh 1994: 24). Only certain feelings, such as anger, which may be channelled towards competitive organizational goals, may be legitimately expressed (Reynolds 1992).

Striving to identify with this form of masculinity then makes the individual a successful organizational subject (as in the subject of a monarch), someone who is suitable to join the ranks of management, because of the requirement to remain in control by virtue of rational and objective decision making without anger or bias. Managerial prerogative – the exercise of the 'right to manage' and command others in contemporary organizations – depends on instrumental control, on sustaining output through imposing targets that are quantifiable and often highly abstract, but which can carry penalties if not achieved and are coercively policed (through the threat of discipline and dismissal, for example) (Kerfoot and Knights 1996: 90). Managers need to demonstrate their ability to take command of the organizational world and its context. Accordingly, being allowed the 'right to manage', to become a manager, in most modern organizations depends on displaying masculine forms of behaviour. Those who reject this form of masculine identity, those who identify with the *feminine* (women in the main but this can include men), may find themselves disenfranchized by the world of work because prevailing organizational values are so alien to these feminine subjects.

Many women reject competitiveness, the impersonality of bureaucracy, the rejection of intimacy, and they often refuse to allow the demands and objectives of work to dominate their lives. This can result in them distancing themselves from the content and the context of their work, appearing detached and uncommitted, valuing home, friends and family above their job (Kerfoot and Knights 1995: 19). There is empirical evidence to the effect that even women who have reached the organizational peak may opt out (Marshall 1995). Judi Marshall concluded that several of the women whom she studied, all of whom had held senior management positions, had left the organizations in which they were working because they could no longer tolerate the masculine style required within those workplaces. Some of these women became unemployed, others set up their own businesses and managed them according to *their* preferred style.

The modern work environment creates, sustains and reinforces masculine ways of relating to self and of behaving, that is to say, seeking to control one's environment, one's colleagues and oneself. However, even this form of masculinity is not static. A recent study in the financial services industry noted a shift from traditional paternalistic, protectionist forms of masculine management to modern, strategically led, macho, aggressive and competitive masculine management (Kerfoot and Knights 1993). This supports our view taken here that masculinity is historical *in itself*, existing in different forms in different times, in different cultures and in different locations within the same culture (Brittan 1989). For a good example of this latter point, see the John Ford film *The Man Who Shot Liberty Valance* (1962), where the efforts of both the two-fisted Western hero (John Wayne) and the Eastern-trained peace-loving lawyer are needed to civilize a town.

What is clear is that the requirement to do masculine behaviour is a social challenge, not a natural expression of the essence of being male – and it is a struggle (Connell 1995). In the workplace, behaving in this way in order to succeed as a 'manager' is *problematic* – the masculine ways in which organizational subjects are required to relate to themselves and each other in order to reach the ranks of management and remain there is never without a personal cost and is potentially damaging. The privileging of masculine behaviour in organizations is therefore something to be questioned, not celebrated or preserved. Our argument here is that the workplace helps produce, reproduce or secure masculine identities. In contrast to some earlier arguments discussed above, our emphasis is much less on gender management as a route to business efficiency. We are interested in the fact that in the quest to become a real manager, people come to depersonalize others, to turn them into objects and resources rather than see them as people. At the same time, sacrificing a whole range of one's own experience causes managers to become desensitized, further diminishing their capacities to empathize and care about others and even themselves (Sinclair 1995: 6). Macho managers who are hard on their employees are often even harder on themselves, and this self-sacrifice is another important element of masculine experience (Donaldson 1993). At the end of this process of stifling emotion, thwarting impulses, suppressing spontaneity for control, concealing true feelings and intentions – the process of *self*-discipline – managers come to regard their self as just another resource, just another commodity to be 'downsized' if necessary (Jackall 1988, cited in Sinclair 1995: 4).

The effort to sustain a sense of oneself as a managerial subject can even prove too much given the difficulties it generates regarding personal intimacy (Kerfoot and Whitehead 1995: 5). Masculine identity work is said to result in an unhealthy denial of one's emotions and a feeling of self-alienation or disengagement because of the high level of self-control required (Kerfoot and Knights 1993, 1995, 1996). Managers do things, but they do not feel that it was them*selves* who acted – they were playing a role. Deborah Kerfoot and David Knights also suggest that this project of masculine identity is a demanding exercise *in itself*. Masculinity/management involves the quest for control of the environment, of colleagues and of self, and this is a fundamentally anxious way to be, a way of being in which one must seek constant reassurance that one is actually in control. It is also a way of being in which it becomes impossible to trust others. Those who seek to manage successfully find their identities continually threatened. The masculine values which prevail in modern organizations are actually damaging to the health of the individual members of those organizations, whether they are (would-be) managers themselves, are on the receiving end of managerial attentions (employees) or are involved with managers in the realm of personal relationships (family and friends). This also suggests that the masculine, far from being a seat of contentment and complacency, is a particularly worrisome place; an identity on which one must work continually to gain and assert control.

Feminine values

The question we now must ask is: *Would feminine values provide a better alternative to the dominance of masculine identities in workplaces?* Some writers argue that feminine values should be reintroduced into organizations, to balance out the values of controlling, competitive, aggressive masculinity. They argue that the existing imbalance is damaging to personal survival, growth and wholeness, psychologically, physically and spiritually. This argument says that what is at stake is not just the suppression of *women*, individually or as a group, but the suppression of ways of thinking (feeling, acting) that are considered *feminine*. These possibilities for thinking and doing become unavailable to either men *or* women (Hines 1992: 314–15).

The values of the feminine are, Ruth Hines argues, not sufficiently valued in modern organizations. A better balance of organizational values would ensure a healthier workplace. The wide-ranging taboo on the feminine at work is problematic because organizational subjects come to relate to themselves and to others in highly restricted and restrictive ways. They can neither be fully themselves nor fully *human*. This kind of *analysis* does not necessarily privilege the feminine *over* the masculine but, rather, catalogues the problems which an *im*balance of values can generate in the organization. It presents some *argument* that organizations should be informed by a consideration of what is at present unwelcome in the workplace, that is, the values of the feminine, or at least by a critical examination of the masculine character of modern organizational values/managerial practice and its consequences.

The problem with this analysis in some of its forms is that it remains attached to its liberal feminist origins. It tends to be written in a paradoxical combination of demands for political action and gentle new age spirituality with its idea of 'balance' implying inertia. This, as a view of gender, is as we have argued above too *static*. Gender emerges and changes in a *dynamic* between a variety of features and forms of masculinity and femininity, which grow alongside each other. This argument may take new forms here, but in itself it is not new. In the 1850s Frederick Engels remarked that within the working class the men were the bourgeoisie and the women the proletariat, in an internal relation of domination in which the oppressed *supported* the oppressors (Campbell 1984). Beatrix Campbell provides a detailed discussion, if not an analysis, of how this relationship worked in the north of England during the depression of the early 1980s. As she points out, in establishing these relations detail is everything. Ongoing studies of the organizational micropractices by which gendered subjectivity is shaped, the actual relations of power, knowledge and gender in talk, myth, image and action, need to be produced as a matter of course if we are to understand better how gendered identity emerges, changes and affects management practice over time.

In sum, then, 'gendering management' identifies the ways in which gender and management actually *interact*. It does not focus on management as a process which needs to result in organizational effectiveness and measures its value in accordance with its contribution to that process. Rather, it suggests that the most interesting and socially valuable material that can be gained from a study of management is a focus on how and why it happens in the way that it does.

Conclusion

So, having discussed gender in theory at some length, let us try to apply some of our ideas in practice, and return to look at the case study with which we began. The case is fictionalized, but is drawn from our research – the problems of Matthew and Julie are real ones.

- To begin with, it seems from the case that TransCorp is an organization which expects its employees to work *long hours* – Matthew, as Deputy Production Manager, works a 12 hour day, on average, and his staff are also expected to work beyond the confines of 9 am to 5 pm, if the organization requires it. TransCorp's culture also appears to emphasize a very *impersonal mode of interaction* – staff are expected to leave their personal feelings and effects at home. This is evident in the symbolism of Matthew's office, a shrine to efficiency and lack of distraction. TransCorp is also an organization which values *hardheadedness, logic and the bottom line* in decision making. Matthew is relieved that he does not have to make the difficult choice as to who will work during the summer shutdown, but he is expected to come up with a staffing plan to cover that period which focuses on minimum cost and maximum output, but seemingly pays little *attention to the effects* on those staff involved (and indeed those staff not involved). Finally, it seems that TransCorp does not value its staff sufficiently to *listen* carefully to their opinions and needs. The layout of Matthew's office, with its desk positioned carefully to provide both a physical vantage point (they can't sneak up on him) and a symbolic barrier between himself and visitors, is testimony to this. As is, perhaps more evocatively, David's insistence that the production staff are simply goofing off when they fail to turn up on time for an early shift start.

- TransCorp can be seen as a very masculine organization, conforming to Hines's description of the prevailing form of masculinity as '…hard, dry, impersonal, objective, explicit, outer-focused, action-oriented, analytic, dualistic, quantitative, linear, rationalist, reductionist and materialist' (Hines 1992: 328). Its culture emphasizes *formal rationality* at the expense of substantive rationality. This is reflected, as we might anticipate, in what TransCorp requires from its managers. Matthew is expected to keep his staff *in line*, to *control* them (David's insistence that he talks to the latecomers on the early shift); to appear *formally* dressed at all times (having to put his jacket back on to visit the shopfloor); to put *organizational targets* above the needs of his team (reiterating the requirement for them to start their shift early to meet a particular deadline); and to approach his managerial work with the *bottom line* always in mind (the 'radical' plan required for the shutdown).

- It is clear that Matthew *resents* having to be one of the boys, or at least having to align himself with the prevailing definition of masculinity/management at TransCorp. One might surmize from his objection to having to work long hours, behave in a dictatorial manner with his staff, and suppress emotion in dealing with others that his personal preference might lean more towards what Rosener (1990) and others call a *transformational leadership* style – encouraging staff *participation* in goal setting; *relating* to staff as equals; *interacting* with and leading staff by virtue of his personal qualities rather than his managerial position; having some measure of *personal intimacy* with his staff; and being *sensitive* to the effect what he does has on his staff and others in the organization. So we might suggest that Matthew's image of himself as a manager is in conflict with what TransCorp actually requires of him, and, furthermore, that he perhaps resists the discourse of masculinity which prevails in the wider society. It seems that he does not necessarily conceive of himself as masculine in terms of being rational, objective, sure of himself, logical, decisive, aggressive and competitive, nor yet does he fear the expression of emotion. Thus to some extent Matthew is the kind of man that Gherardi (1995) acknowledges as (ideally) preferring to work within a more democratic organizational framework and to manage in a more democratic way – the kind of man who *subverts either/or assumptions about the gender framework*.

- What is interesting is that Matthew also *identifies with the prevailing managerial discourse* at TransCorp because, it is implied, he will not be considered successful in his managerial work if he does not. He has not, therefore, rejected the masculine identity that life in TransCorp creates, sustains and reinforces to the extent that he finds himself having to opt out, as Kerfoot and Knights (1995) suggest might happen to those who find such values entirely alien. He does find his work exciting and challenging, and also satisfying (although at the same time he resents it for what it forces him to do). Thus Matthew has not reached the stage where he totally: '…resist[s] the bureaucratic displacement of intimacy and refuse[s] to allow organisational goals and career aspirations to dominate [his life]' (Kerfoot and Knights 1995: 19). It is arguably this *ambiguity* in his life as a manager and as a man which creates specific problems for him as an individual. He obviously finds his work stressful and entirely too demanding at times. He does not eat properly during the day, he wakes up tired and goes to bed exhausted. He anticipates with anxiety any confrontation during the day, and any negative consequences of the decisions he makes. However, he is not sufficiently disaffected to withdraw from TransCorp – as is made clear when he reacts angrily to Sarah's request for him to come home early and look after the children. This in itself reveals an enduring *commitment* to TransCorp on Matthew's part – he mutters to himself that he is struggling to keep it all together at work, *in a crucial period for the company*.

- Second, Matthew's approach to management, conforming as it does to the prevailing culture at TransCorp, clearly has ramifications for his staff, as he is rendered *unable to listen* to their complaints or suggestions, and instead exercises managerial prerogative in any situation of conflict. He is *disengaged* from their concerns and only occasionally permits himself to 'empathize and care' (Sinclair 1995: 6) about them in his more depressed moments. Finally, Matthew *spends very little time at home with his family*, which his partner clearly resents, and which he himself is dimly aware of. However, one might surmise that he also has a nagging sense that he is doing the right thing by his family by acting as the breadwinner (which might be argued to be a component of the prevailing form of masculinity, as David Collinson (1988) has pointed out), and therefore perhaps fails to realize the damage that he may be doing to them by allowing work to take over his life.

- What does managing mean for Matthew, working within an organization which values a particular kind of masculinity as being the most appropriate way to interact with others and to relate to oneself and one's managerial work? This form of masculinity is not necessarily one to which Matthew himself fully aspires, which causes him some inconsiderable difficulty, but, at the same time, he is also able to lose himself in it to the extent that he does not always acknowledge the impact that this identification has on him as an individual, on his staff and on his family life. Managing is partly a trap, yet a rewarding and frequently exciting one – a paradox.

- Expectations of managers at TransCorp mean that women within the organization are subject to the same demands if they aspire to success, as Kerfoot and Knights (1993, 1996) claim is frequently the case. Julie complains to Matthew that she is expected to walk, talk and behave like a man by TransCorp in order to *prove herself* as a manager. However, Julie's other complaint is that TransCorp also expects her to retain some measure of femininity – for example, she says that her colleagues 'look at me like I've just landed from Mars if I turn up in trousers ...'. This bears testimony to the particular problems experienced by women managers, or by those women who aspire to managerial positions, in organizations like TransCorp. On the one hand, they have to *relate to themselves* and to behave in a very masculine way, which may be alien because of the particular way that women are socialized to be feminine within modern Western cultures. On the other hand, they must not appear to be too masculine, as they will be punished in equal measure if they step too far *beyond their prescribed societal gender role* (which Kerfoot and Knights (1996: 87) describe as: '...not instrumentally attached to securing itself through projects and goals, and ... more engaged with, rather than detached from, the world'). The balance can be difficult to achieve, as researchers such as Deborah Sheppard, Linda McDowell and Gill Court, David Collinson and Margaret Collinson, and Jo Brewis *et al.* have suggested, and Julie's disgust at David's sexism is evocative of this. The *advantage* that men like Matthew have over women like Julie, then, is that the strong cultural link between biology and gender behaviour makes it more *acceptable* for male managers to identify totally with the masculine discourse of management than it is for women.

In short, then, we can see from the case that management is a process and a set of practices which can be usefully understood by reference to discourses of gender difference. Any exploration and analysis of gender, as we have discussed earlier, provides examples of the ways in which gender intersects and informs managerial behaviour. In particular, it suggests that the predominance of masculinist discourses of management in organizations bears examination and study in terms of the particular challenges and demands that this presents for real managerial subjects. It would, however, be foolish, not to say inaccurate, to *over*estimate the power of gender as an organizing principle of management work. It is crucial also to acknowledge that, as Susan Bordo suggests:

> Gender never exhibits itself in pure form, but in the context of lives that are shaped by a multiplicity of influences which cannot be neatly sorted out (Bordo 1990: 114).

While a consideration of the interaction between gender and management is a fruitful one through which to arrive at an understanding of what it means and how it feels to manage, there is also room for applying a similar analysis to issues of race, class, (dis)ability and the limitless other differences of *diversity* which form important components of our relationship with ourselves as individuals and as managers. Recalling one of the major objectives of this book, what is important is that these things about which we tend to make assumptions are subjected to *critical thinking*. This is the only way in which we can guard against *blindness* – gender blindness, race blindness, disability blindness – in all its forms. We can then challenge *suppression* where it is found, and as a result we can *learn*, personally and organizationally. We can then manage with our eyes fully open.

Finally, to return to our set of opening questions. By now you should be able to come up with some answers to these for yourself, so rather than answer them for you, we will finish with a guide to where we discuss the issues in the text.

- *Is gender a biological or a social issue?*
  Introduction: pages 51–2; Natural born women … and men?: pages 59–60.
- *Does being male or female make a difference to the way you manage?*
  The feminine-in-management approach: pages 66–8; Gendering management: A critical analysis: pages 71, 74.
- *Is gender a profit issue or a moral issue?*
  Diversity: pages 55–8.
- *Are women concentrated in certain occupations?*
  Liberal feminism: page 53.
- *Are you more likely to succeed as a manager if you are male?*
  Liberal feminism: page 52.
- *What is meant by the 'glass ceiling'?*
  Liberal feminism: page 52.
- *What is positive discrimination?*
  Liberal feminism: page 55.
- *Are men more motivated than women?*
  The feminine-in-management approach: pages 66–8; Overvaluing context and difference?: pages 69–71.
- *Do men experience gender-related problems too?*
  Masculine values: pages 71–3.
- *Is globalization creating more opportunities for women or perpetuating their subordination?*
  Undervaluing context – the impact of globalization: pages 68–9.
- *How can gender be managed?*
  Gender and management – the whole chapter. But you will need to think and reflect carefully about what *you* can do about it!

And one final question. Thinking back to the case of Chris Stefano in Chapter 1, what gender is Chris? We deliberately did not give any clues, but you probably gave Chris a gender anyway. Thinking about *how* you came to ascribe to Chris the gender you did might give some clues as to your own potential gender bias.

References

Adler, N. (1993) 'An international perspective on the barriers to the advancement of women managers' *Applied Psychology: An International Review* 42(4): 289–300.

Alimo-Metcalfe, B. (1993) 'Women in management: Organisational socialisation and assessment practices that prevent career advancement', *International Journal of Selection and Assessment* 1(2): 68–83.

Alimo-Metcalfe, B. (1994) 'Gender bias in the selection and assessment of women in management', in Davidson, M.J. and Burke, R. (eds), *Women in Management: Current Research Issues*, London: Paul Chapman.

Alimo-Metcalfe, B. (1995) 'An investigation of female and male constructs of leadership and empowerment', *Women in Management Review* 10(2): 3–8.

Bologh, R. (1990) *Love or Greatness*, London: Unwin Hyman.

Bordo, S. (1990) 'Feminism, postmodernism and gender-scepticism', in Nicholson, L.J. (ed.), *Feminism/Postmodernism*, New York: Routledge.

Braverman, H. (1974) *Labour and Monopoly Capital: The Degradation of Work in the Twentieth Century*, New York: Monthly Review Press.

Brech, E.F.L. (1965) *Organisation: The Framework of Management* (second edition), London: Longman.

Brewis, J., Hampton, M. and Linstead, S. (1997) 'Unpacking Priscilla: Subjectivity and identity in the organisation of gendered appearance', *Human Relations* 50(10): 1275–304.

Brewis, J. and Kerfoot, D. (1994) 'Selling our "selves"? Sexual harassment and the intimate violations of the workplace', paper presented to the British Sociological Association Annual Conference, 'Sexualities in Social Context', 28–31 March, University of Central Lancashire, Preston, UK.

Brittan, A. (1989) *Masculinity and Power*, Oxford: Blackwell.

Brown, H. (1992) *Women Organising*, London: Routledge.

Burrell, G. (1997) *Pandemonium: Towards a Retro-Organisation Theory*, London: Sage.

Cahoon, A. (1994) 'Gender differences in management', in Stone, R.J. (ed.), *Readings in Human Resource Management*, Vol. 2, Brisbane: John Wiley.

Calás, M. and Smircich, L. (1995) 'Dangerous liaisons: The "feminine-in-management" meets "Globalization"', in Frost, P., Mitchell, V. and Nord, W. (eds), *Managerial Reality*, New York: HarperCollins.

Campbell, B. (1984) *Wigan Pier Revisited: Poverty and Politics in the Eighties*, London: Virago.

Chemers, M.M. and Murphy, S.E. (1995) 'Leadership and diversity in groups and organizations', in Chemers, M., Oskamp, S. and Costanzo, M.A. (eds), *Diversity in Organizations: New Perspectives for a Changing Workplace*, Thousand Oaks: Sage.

Chodorow, N. (1989) *Feminism and Psychoanalytic Theory*, New Haven, CT: Yale University Press.

Cockburn, C. (1991) *In the Way of Women: Men's Resistance to Sex Equality in Organisations*, Basingstoke: Macmillan.

Collinson, D.L. (1988) '"Engineering humour": Masculinity, joking and conflict in shopfloor relations', *Organisation Studies* 9 (2): 181–99.

Collinson, D.L. and Collinson, M. (1995) 'Corporate liposuction and the re-masculinization of management in the UK financial services', paper presented to the Gender and Life in Organisations Conference, 9 September, University of Portsmouth Business School, Portsmouth, UK.

Collinson, D.L. and Hearn, J. (eds) (1996) *Men as Managers, Managers as Men: Critical Perspectives on Men, Masculinities and Management*, London: Sage.

Connell, R.W. (1995) *Masculinities*, Sydney: Allen & Unwin.

Cullen, D. (1994) 'Feminism, Management and Self-Actualization', *Gender Work and Organisation* 1(3): 123–37.

Cullen, D. (1997) 'Maslow, monkeys and motivation theory', *Organisation* 4(3): 355–73.

Daly, M. (1984) *Gyn/Ecology: The Metaethics of Radical Feminism*, London: The Women's Press.

Davidson, M.J. and Cooper, C.L. (1992) *Shattering the Glass Ceiling: The Woman Manager*, London: Paul Chapman.

Donaldson, M. (1993) *Time of Our Lives: Labour and Love in the Working Class*, Sydney: Allen & Unwin.

Eagly, A.H. and Johnson, B.T. (1990) 'Gender and leadership style: A meta-analysis', *Psychological Bulletin* 108(2): 233–56.

Enloe, C. (1989) *Bananas, Beaches and Bases: Making Feminist Sense of International Relations*, London: Pandora.

Fayol, H. (1949) *General and Industrial Administration* (translated by C. Storrs), London: Sir Isaac Pitman.

French, M. (1986) *The Women's Room*, New York: Abacus.

Friedan, B. (1963) *The Feminine Mystique*, New York: Dell.

Gherardi, S. (1995) *Gender, Symbolism and Organisational Cultures*, London: Sage.

Gilbreth, F.B. (1911) *Motion Study*, New York: Van Nostrand.

Gillespie, R. (1991) *Manufacturing Knowledge: A History of the Hawthorne Experiments*, Cambridge: Cambridge University Press.

Gilligan, C. (1982) *In a Different Voice*, Cambridge, Mass.: Harvard University Press.

Glaser, D. and Frosh, S. (1994) *Child Sexual Abuse*, London: Macmillan.

Goldthorpe, J.H., Lockwood, D., Bechhofer, F. and Platt, J. (1969) *The Affluent Worker in the Class Structure*, Cambridge: Cambridge University Press.

Goss, D. (1994) *Principles of Human Resource Management*, London: Routledge.

Grey, C. (1995) 'Review article: Gender as a grid of intelligibility', *Gender, Work and Organisation* 2(1): 46–50.

Grint, K. (1991) *The Sociology of Work: An Introduction*, Oxford: Polity Press.

Hales, C. (1993) *Managing Through Organization*, London: Routledge.

Harvard Business Review (1991) 'Debate: ways men and women lead', January–February: 151–60. It incorporates: Cohen, A.R. (p. 158); Epstein, C.F. (pp. 150–1); Goldberg, C.R. (p. 160); Graham, P. (pp. 153–4); Mansbridge, J. (pp. 154–6); Siegel, M.R. (p. 152); Sonnenfeld, J.A. (pp. 159–60).

Hayward, H. (1992) 'Management: Theory and practice', in Fulop, L. with Frith, F. and Hayward, H., *Management for Australian Business: A Critical Text*, Melbourne: Macmillan.

Hearn, J. and Parkin, W. (1994) 'Sexuality gender and organisations: acknowledging complex contentions', British Sociological Association Annual Conference, 'Sexualities in Social Context', 28–31 March, University of Central Lancashire Preston, UK.

Hines, R. (1992) 'Accounting: Filling the negative space', *Accounting, Organisations and Society* 17(3): 314–41.

Hollinshead, G. and Leat, M. (1995) *Human Resource Management: An International and Comparative Perspective on the Employment Relationship*, London: Pitman.

Huczynski, A.A. and Buchanan, D.A. (1991) *Organisational Behaviour: An Introductory Text* (second edition), Hemel Hempstead, Hertfordshire: Prentice-Hall International.

Jackall, R. (1988) *Moral Mazes*, Oxford: Oxford University Press.

Jaggar, A. (1983) *Feminist Politics and Human Nature*, Brighton, Sussex: Harvester Press.

Kandola, R. and Fullerton, J. (1994a) 'Diversity: More than just an empty slogan', *Personnel Management* November: 46–9.

Kandola, R. And Fullerton, J. (1994b) *Managing the Mosaic: Diversity in Action*, London: Institute of Personnel and Development.

Kasten, K. (1972) 'Toward a psychology of being: A masculine mystique', *Journal of Humanistic Psychology* 12(2): 23–4.

Kerfoot, D. and Knights, D. (1993) 'Management, masculinity and manipulation: From paternalism to corporate strategy in financial services', *Journal of Management Studies* 30(4): 659–77.

Kerfoot, D. and Knights, D. (1995) 'The organisation(s) of social division: Constructing identities in managerial work', paper presented to the European Group on Organisation Studies Colloquium, 6–8 July, University of Bosphorus Istanbul, Turkey.

Kerfoot, D. and Knights, D. (1996) '"The best is yet to come?": The quest for embodiment in managerial work', in Collinson, D.L. and Hearn, J. (eds), *Men as Managers, Managers as Men: Critical Perspectives on Men, Masculinities and Managements*, London: Sage.

Kerfoot, D. and Whitehead, S. (1995) '"And so say all of us?": The problematics of masculinity and managerial work', paper presented to the Gender and Life in Organisations Conference, 9 September, University of Portsmouth Business School, Portsmouth, UK.

Laqueur, T. (1990) *Making Sex: Body and Gender from the Greeks to Freud*, Cambridge, Mass.: Harvard University Press.

Likert, R. (1967) *The Human Organization*, New York: McGraw-Hill.

Lowry, R. (ed.) (1982) *The Journals of Abraham Maslow*, Brattleboro, VT: Lewis Publishing.

Marshall, J. (1995) *Women Managers Moving On: Exploring Career and Life Choices*, London: Routledge.

Maslow, A. (1939) 'Dominance personality and social behaviour in women', *Journal of Social Psychology* 10(1): 3–39.

Maslow, A. (1954) *Motivation and Personality*, New York: Harper.

Mayo, E. (1945) *The Social Problems of an Industrial Civilization*, Boston, Mass.: Division of Research, Graduate School of Business Administration, Harvard University.

Mayo, E. (1960) *The Human Problems of an Industrial Civilization*, New York: Viking Press (original 1933, New York: Macmillan).

Matteson, M.T. and Ivancevich, J.M. (eds) (1989) *Management and Organizational Behavior Classics*, Homewood, Ill.: BPI, Irwin.

McDowell, L. and Court, G. (1994) 'Performing work: Bodily representations in merchant banks', *Environment and Planning D: Society and Space* 12: 727–50.

McNeil, M. (1987) 'Being reasonable feminists', in McNeil, M. (ed.), *Gender and Expertise*, London: Free Association Books.

Mills, A.J. and Tancred, P. (1992) 'Organizational analysis: A critique', in Mills, A.J. and Tancred, P. (eds), *Gendering Organizational Analysis*, Newbury Park, California: Sage.

Mooney, J.D. (1947) *The Principles of Organization*, New York: Harper and Row.

Nyland, C. (1989) *Reduced Worktime and the Management of Production*, Cambridge: Cambridge University Press.

Nyland, C. (forthcoming) 'A contemporary account of Scientific Management as applied to women's work with a comment by Frederick W. Taylor', *Journal of Management History 5*.

O'Donovan, K. (1985) *Sexual Divisions in Law*, London: Weidenfeld and Nicolson.

Office of Population and Census Surveys (UK) (1996) *Labour Force Trends*, London, HMSO.

Parsons, T. and Zales, R.F. (1956) *Family, Socialization and Interaction Process,* London: Routledge and Kegan Paul.

Reynolds, L. (1992) 'Translate fury into action', *Management Review* 81(3): 36–8.

Roethlisberger, F.J. and Dickson, W. (1939) *Management and the Worker: An Account of a Research Program, Conducted by the Western Electric Company, Hawthorne Works, Chicago,* Cambridge, Mass.: Harvard University Press.

Rosener, J. (1990) 'Ways women lead', *Harvard Business Review* November–December: 119–25.

Sheppard, D.L. (1989) 'Organisations, power and sexuality: The image and self-image of women managers', in Hearn, J., Sheppard, D.L., Tancred-Sheriff, P. and Burrell, G. (eds), *The Sexuality of Organisation*, London: Sage.

Sinclair, J. (1995) 'Morality, emotions and the new work ethic', paper presented to the European Group on Organisation Studies Colloquium, 6–8 July, University of the Bosphorus, Istanbul, Turkey.

Still, L. (1988) *Becoming a Top Woman Manager*, Sydney: Allen & Unwin.

Storey, J. (1992) *Developments in the Management of Human Resources: An Analytical Review*, Oxford: Blackwell.

Storey, J. (ed.) (1995) *Human Resource Management: A Critical Text*, London: Routledge.

Taylor, F.W. (1947) *Scientific Management*, New York: Harper and Row. (Original 1912)

Thomas, R.R., Jr (1990) 'From affirmative action to affirming diversity', *Harvard Business Review* March–April: 107–17.

Thomas, R.R., Jr (1991) *Beyond Race and Gender: Unleashing the Power of Your Workforce By Managing Diversity*, New York: AMACOM.

Tiger, L. and Fox, R. (1972) *The Imperial Animal*, London: Secker and Warburg.

Trahair, R.C.S. (1984) *The Humanist Temper: The Life and Work of Elton Mayo,* New Brunswick, NJ: Transaction Books.

Urwick, L. (1937) 'Organization as a technical problem', in Gulick, L. and Urwick, L. (eds), *Papers on the Science of Administration*, New York: Columbia University Press.

Walby, S. (1997) *Gender Transformations*, London: Routledge.

Weiss, R. (1997) 'Evolving view of chimp communities: Dominant females' reproductive success suggests new hierarchy model', *The Washington Post*, 8 August: A03.

Wilson, F.M. (1995) *Organisational Behaviour and Gender*, London: McGraw-Hill.

Wilson, F.M. (1996) 'Research note: Organisation theory: Blind and deaf to gender?', *Organisation Studies* 17(5): 825–42.

Wollstonecraft, M. (1970) *A Vindication of the Rights of Woman* (second edition), Farnborough, UK: Gregg.

3
Managing culture

Stephen Linstead

Questions about culture

1 What is organizational culture? What is it good for?
2 Are companies with strong cultures always successful?
3 What are the dysfunctions of culture?
4 What are subcultures, and are they healthy?
5 How is organizational culture related to national culture?

Culture at Company T

The organization (upon which this particular case is based) is a Canadian automobile assembly plant employing some 1300 people. In response to increased foreign competition, the corporation decided to implement a participative management program focused on quality. In 1980, the plant hired consultants to help implement a Quality of Working Life program. The union refused to participate, but approved a participative management program and the plant management decided to go ahead.

The plant was functionally organized. There were a plant manager, assistant plant manager and six department managers, including industrial relations, controller, quality, operations, manufacturing engineering and materials. The plant ran two shifts a day and in addition to the operations manager there were two production managers (one responsible for each shift), eight superintendents, 22 general supervisors, seven utility supervisors and 66 foremen, each of whom supervised up to 50 hourly workers.

As a result of problems encountered in the implementation of the QWL program after two years, it soon became clear that while both consultants and managers had originally engaged in a process with social and technical redesign goals, the real challenge was one of cultural change and personal transformation. They were up against a distinctive and extremely strong company culture, whose assumptions were working a kind of sea change with their interventions, distorting their purpose and twisting their outcomes.

Aggression: 2 × 4 management

The culture of Company T was distinctive even by the estimation of company members. It positively sanctioned an aggressive 'macho' management style, termed 2 × 4 management, which consisted of reprimands in the form of intensive verbal abuse ('yelling and screaming'), dramatic confrontations, and generally, figuratively, 'beating up' on offenders. Extreme examples of this behavior had become myth in the organization and perpetrators were spoken of as something of folk heroes.

In the old days here, there used to be a lot of grandstanding, but a lot of it was for show. I can remember one day, 'X' came out onto the floor and he saw a piece that he did not like, and he started jumping up and down on it and he bashed it all in and yelling and screaming and then he said, 'Now throw it out, because it is not good for anything' and when he turned around, he winked at me. It was a show, it was fun, it was a game. It was just like a John Wayne movie, as soon as the movie was over with, they became human again.

The perception was that those who were good at 2 × 4 management got promoted at Company T.

If your boss catches you out, catches something wrong with the product in your area, you can respond in one of two ways. You can say, 'O.K., I'll find out what's wrong,' or you can say, 'God dammit, it's John Smith. I'm going to call him in here and chew him out.' The second way looks much better, more glory in it.

This macho style was seen by many as being quite anachronistic, as representing a culture very distinct from the 'larger' culture in which managers spent their family, civic and recreational lives. Some experienced embarrassment when describing their work environment to their friends and families.

My brother, who is an accountant, says he cannot believe this place, that it is like a game instead of a workplace, but he thinks everything about this place is ridiculous.

And even the worst 2 × 4 managers were recognized as being quite different away from work.

Mind you, he was a fine fellow outside. He used to tell me that he kept his leopard skin suit in the guard house and would put it on when he came in. In the past, if you wanted to get ahead, you had to do a little more of the 2 × 4. The idea was, if you did not beat, you got beaten.

Managers referred to the company culture as a jungle, the workers as 'animals', the extreme 2 × 4 type managers as 'monsters', and yet, while many expressed aversion to the harsh style, others found it tough, 'honest', and, hence, appealing.

I prefer the straightforward approach. I don't like the foul language. But I do not think people listen to you if you are a nice guy. I don't think people listen to (the assistant plant manager) as much as they used to. People are scared of someone who chews them out.

Competitiveness: 'Shiftitus' and empire building

If the tough macho management style can be seen as one of the salient values underlying the Company T culture, the other was an intense competitiveness which manifested itself in two forms of behavior: competition between shifts ('shiftitus') and lack of cooperation between functions ('empire building'). Both these forms of competition were highly valued. 'Shiftitus', with its disease-like connotations, was defined by one manager as 'we do not like to see the other shift run as well as we do'. It was intense in Company T. As mentioned earlier, there were two shifts designated, A and B. The two shifts were constantly compared and invited to compete in order to encourage people to work hard. At times, however, it got out of hand.

It is a big game, to get the other guy. There is a lot of resentment and competition. We base everything on results and so people will resort to things like counting back on the line [including items made on the production line but not packed or despatched as shift output], to get a better count for their shift. Sometimes the foreman will lock up his tools so that the other people on the next shift will not get them. We have to do process books, to make sure things like tools and materials are exchanged, otherwise people start breaking into each others lockers. Rivalry is good but you have to keep the lid on.

Despite the recognized damage and waste incurred by the competition, it had some defenders. These fell into two categories. There were those who felt that, in general, it was healthy because it fostered 'good, clean competition'. Others felt that it was part of the fun of working at Company T. It was a macho, competitive, street fighting world:

I knew everything about the machines in my area and I used to turn up the speed on the line for brief periods of time so that my boys could produce more units than the other shift. Sometimes the foreman from the other shift would sneak in early to make sure I was not going on overtime. But I just knew to regulate the line and get things done faster and I had everyone behind me, my boys loved to do it that way. They loved to shove it in their (the other shift's) face.

Similarly, functional loyalty was very strong in Company T. This was sometimes referred to as 'empire building' and permeated all levels of the organization from the operating committee down.

It is really incredible how one unit pits itself against another in this place. It is as if there is a wall at the end of each unit, and anything that passes through that wall is no longer a problem for that unit. People pass things along because there is always pressure, there is always pressure to deliver the numbers. Despite all the lip service about quality being most important, if you do not get the numbers, you get nothing.

Lying, cheating and stealing culture

While the two values of 2×4 management and competitiveness formed the basis of the company culture, pursuit of these values on the individual level was commonly recognized as resulting in a set of interconnected assumptions about behavior which were widely recognized as dysfunctional. On an individual level, the 2×4 management led to considerable fear of being exposed and humiliated and forced people into a secretive, self-defensive mode termed 'covering ass'.

I've had it solid, with that 2×4 style, it nullifies you. You just start covering ass and playing your cards close to the vest. You collect a lot of excuses and you are ready to hand them out if anything comes up. So the problems never get solved.

The competitiveness, on the other hand, meant that functions and shifts worked actively to pass the buck, passing poor quality products from one department to another, failing to take responsibility for product defects, and rushing faulty products out the door in an effort to 'beat' the other production shift in a race for numbers. This activity was known in the culture as 'shipping shit'.

The biggest problem around here is that there is no trust, no one wants to get blamed for anything. So say the sealer goes bad and you know how to fix it, but you do not fix it, what you do is to call maintenance or to call industrial engineering. That way they get stuck with the problem and you do not get chewed up for it. It could be that it was your fault, that your guys screwed up the gun, but you try to cover that up and get it pinned on maintenance and engineering. For example, if you had a big hole, it might be something you could fix, but if you fixed it too many times, then it would become your responsibility, you would pick up the job and you can't hold that job.

The combined need to hide personal and functional problems and failures, fuelled by the desire to be competitive and to win, combined with the fear of retaliation, resulted in tacit acceptance of all kinds of rule breaking which managers in Company T called 'lying, cheating, and stealing'. Essentially, these terms referred to the concealing of information, parts and personnel and was viewed as a 'survival tactic'.

This culture (lying, cheating, and stealing) is still important, this is how they survive. If someone gets on their back, they say 'we know how to fix that: lie, cheat, and steal'. There is not real progress there. There is a recognition that it is a problem, but to tell you the truth I think (the assistant plant manager) does it as well. He lies, cheats, and steals to get the plant manager off his ass.

'Lying, cheating and stealing' also involved concealing (stockpiling) parts, hiding personnel and falsifying reports concerning injuries, defects and manpower.

The book records say that we have a million dollars of obsolete material. But before the last launch, we shipped it out and it turned out to be 2 million dollars worth. There are kitties all over the place. Foremen squirrel things away that they think they need. Foremen get hit over the head all the time for scrap, so it is better to hide it away and call it lost stock. I think I would do the same thing. But it makes for a lot of waste in the system.

Another example is, if you are running rough on certain parts of the line and defects come up, someone will stamp it off so that it does not show up as a loss for our department. That is dangerous, it is just bad for the company. We are more concerned about covering ass than quality or quantity. We would rather run with one man less than we need to do the job properly. We expect the repairmen to pick up the slack. If the repair does not get it, it goes out and the warranty gets it.

Again, as with competition and the macho style, lying, cheating and stealing, while felt by some to be dysfunctional, were seen by others as simple flexibility, with the goal of getting the job done. This perspective is not unusual and often forms an important aspect of the informal value system of organizations.

Another example are budget costs. We all fight to keep down costs, but maybe we are not fighting hard enough, because costs are still way out of control. But you know, it is mostly the new supervisors whose budgets are way over. If they understood the old system better, they maybe would lie, cheat, and steal a little and would be better off. Old supervisors who know the ropes, his budget will always be under. The words make it sound bad, but lying, cheating, and stealing is a system which has worked. Everyone watched what they spend and they stayed on their toes. I do not see that the issue has to be changed unless it is hurting the plant. Most seasoned supervisors can keep it within limits.

Finally, of course, there were those who perceived the lying, cheating and stealing as part of the fun of Company T culture. It represented a kind of freedom to wheel and deal, to live by your wits. It was perceived as a game with its own challenges and satisfactions, a healthy environment for those that survived. Part of the difficulty in introducing change was that many managers liked the excitement and the subterfuge. They had survived in Company T because they were good at playing a game and holding a job which required considerable skill, knowledge and personal toughness.

Source: Adapted from Frances Westley (1990) 'The eye of the needle: Cultural and personal transformation in a traditional organization', Human Relations 43(3), pp. 273–93.

Questions about the case

1 Does company T have a shared culture?
2 Is company T a 'strong' culture?
3 What are the problems of the culture?
4 Do you think the company can be changed?

Introduction

Organizational culture has become an essential element in our understanding of organizations. There is an interrelatedness between this concept and other concepts such as leadership, organizational structure, motivation, power and strategy. The rise of the popularity of the organizational culture concept in the 1970s and 1980s, offering as it did to secure employee commitment, coincided with the relative decline in both the popularity of and research interest in the field of motivation. Although culture was often presented as the 'answer' to the problems of failing companies, Peter Anthony (1994: 6) in discussing one of the few longitudinal studies of organizational change notes that 'the attempt to change corporate culture was accompanied by complex political processes and structural adjustment' and later comments 'the case for culture cannot win; if change is confined to culture it will not work, if accompanied by structural change it cannot be isolated as crucial to success' (Anthony 1994: 15). There has more recently been a growing recognition that it is impossible to extricate culture as a 'variable' from other elements of the organizational context. Nevertheless, one of the main reasons for the rise in interest in organizational culture was to understand how it impacts on organizational change; for a time it was seen as the hidden obstacle to success.

The growing concern with the economic ascendancy of Japanese companies and the need to dismantle the crumbling industrial bureaucracies of the West at the end of the 1970s fuelled the dramatic rise of the organizational culture or 'excellence' literature (see Pascale and Athos 1980; Peters and Waterman 1982; Deal and Kennedy 1982). Old structures and the old-fashioned values associated with them needed to be replaced, but with what? Thomas Peters and Robert Waterman and Terrence Deal and Allen Kennedy were in no doubt that 'strong' cultures were the key to prosperity. The suggestion was simple, timely, flattering and inspiring in its concern with success, and comforting in its implication that for a company to become successful it simply had to change its core values (Guest 1992; Anthony 1994: 16).

Unfortunately, most of the major culture changes of the 1980s were accompanied by major downsizing or divestment and depended significantly on size and growth strategies (see Chapter 10). This is not to deny that culture is an important dimension of organization, although it does seem to be easier to argue for culture as a barrier to change (Johnson 1992) than as a guarantor of success. Steven Feldman (1996) argues that culture is neither one thing nor the other, and is simultaneously both an obstacle to change and a ground for creative development – it forms the *context* for action. Frances Westley (1990), as we have seen above, provides an example of a culture with which no one was happy but to which almost everyone subscribed, in an organization that was committed to conflict, violent and abusive management and internal competition. Company T, as Westley calls it, was proud of its 'two-by-four' management, which dealt with people verbally as though they were hitting them with a '2 × 4' inch plank of wood; 'shiftitus' where shifts doing the same job would strive to better each other to the extent of damaging overall performance; and 'lying, cheating and stealing', which was basically do or say anything to make yourself and your group look good and everyone else look bad. The people who worked in this system did not like it, but it was nevertheless powerful and they felt unable to change it – as a culture it was just as 'strong' and pervasive as McDonald's or IBM but worked against organizational effectiveness.

The origins of organizational culture

The idea of culture in relation to organizations has a long, but tortuous history. From the 1920s, at least, it was recognized that the social dimensions of work are important elements of effectiveness through the Hawthorne Studies, which also identified the critical function of the supervisor or shopfloor leadership (see Chapter 5). Elliott Jaques (1952) perhaps first coined the term 'culture' in relation to work organization in *The Changing Culture of a Factory*, which was part of a series of accounts of participatory management in the Glacier metal company, although structure (i.e. size and design of the organization), reward systems and the use of hierarchy (i.e. different layers of authority from top management to shopfloor supervisors) were also important to the success of the project.

During the following years, organizational psychologists such as Chris Argyris (1964) were beginning to note the importance of the subconscious dimensions of organization and its psychological health. In the 1950s Alvin Gouldner (1954, 1955), a sociologist, also identified the importance of implicit dimensions of working life that were taken for granted, in two books, *Wildcat Strike* (1955) and *Patterns of Industrial Bureaucracy* (1954). In the first he tells the story of a gypsum mine in which the local managers had been accustomed to letting the men have little favours – borrowing equipment, leaving early, taking breaks, etc. – in return for working committedly when necessary. The mine was taken over by new management from outside the area – 'cosmopolitans' – who did not understand the implicit system of concessions and obligations (which Gouldner called the *indulgency pattern*) and who immediately tightened up discipline and rules. The workforce did not like this and performance dropped, culminating in a 'wildcat strike' when one of the workforce was dismissed for an infringement which had been normal practice under the old regime (see also Chapter 4).

Another related development in the 1960s was the discovery of 'negotiated order theory', which was based on work done in psychiatric hospitals by Anselm Strauss and his colleagues (1963). What Strauss argued was that hospitals are composed of different groups or 'congeries' of professionals and non-professionals. Each of these groups has an interest in how, for example, a patient is managed, treated by drugs, given occupational therapy or cared for on the ward, and each has an influence over how the actual treatment happens in practice (think of a time you may have spent in hospital: Did you prefer it when one doctor saw you rather than another? When one shift of nursing staff was working rather than another? How about the cleaners or voluntary workers? How did the presence and behaviour of the other patients affect your treatment? Did you ever notice any tensions between groups of staff?). Strauss argued that each of these groups had a view about what made their job easier, what should be their responsibility and into what decisions they should have an input; each also had a view about what was morally and ethically desirable behaviour. In addition, individuals within groups developed relationships with particular patients and shared these perceptions over time, individuals have careers and even patients can have 'sick careers', and there were always issues of power and resource allocation in the background. Strauss argued that the way things were done was constantly shifting and realigned from time to time, that there were implicit rules as well as explicit ones, and that groups customarily *negotiated the order* of how things happened, consciously and unconsciously. A good film to watch, which relates to negotiated order, power and culture, is *One Flew Over the Cuckoo's Nest* (1973) starring Jack Nicholson and directed by Milos Forman (see also Chapter 4).

Around the same time, Harold Garfinkel (1967/1984) was developing *ethnomethodology*, a form of sociology which concentrated on the ways in which people make sense of their social situations, that stressed the importance of unspoken rules, talk, commonsense and the taken-for granted aspects of social life. The idea of *membership* was also important to Garfinkel, and particularly the things people had to learn to become a 'member' of a social group. Much of Garfinkel's work overlapped with the work of anthropologists, who customarily studied exotic societies, and in 1971 Barry Turner (who was influenced by the work of Garfinkel and the philosopher Alfred Schutz, on whose work Garfinkel based many of his ideas) published the first book to bring the two disciplines together in looking at the way stories, rites, rituals and humour shaped behaviour in organizations in his book *Exploring the Industrial Sub-Culture.* Turner's book did not have immediate impact but is recognized as having been pioneering some 25 years later.

Related to the emphasis of this work on the non-obvious, and the importance of the implicit and taken-for-granted in forming our experience of organizations, some social psychologists involved in organizational change, who called themselves Organizational Development (OD) specialists, began to recognize the significance of the unsaid as a barrier to transformation. They often argued that their work was to bring out the unconscious obstacles to organizational change, as a form of cultural intervention. So ideas of culture, in relation to organization and organizational change, had been around for quite a while before the 'excellence' literature picked them up, but in contrast to that literature they emphasized *the implicit and unconscious* elements of experience and *the processes of sense making and meaning making* rather than the content of communication and the explicitly expressed values (see Chapter 1).

Jim Olila (1995) argues that in the tradition of the study of the non-obvious, anthropologists who study organizations are interested in the tensions that people experience as a series of 'gaps' in their organizational experience. Not exactly creating a definition of culture, he suggests that in practical terms cultural tension as the object of investigation can be seen as 'gaps'. These gaps are described as:

- the *ideal/real* culture gap (the tension between what ought to be done and what in actuality takes place);
- the *formal/informal* culture gap (the tension between the official, often written description of who, what, why and when in an organization versus the unofficial, unwritten, yet frequently, the most comfortable, traditional or successful ways of getting things done with those who are deemed best, most fun or most compatible for the job or task regardless of their official position or title or duties);
- the *overt/covert* culture gap (the tension between known and publicly acknowledged ways of thinking, feeling and doing and those known ways which are never spoken about, the shadowed or occluded areas of the culture); and
- the *conscious/unconscious* gap (the tension between ways of thinking, feeling and doing in which we are aware we participate and those in which we engage but are not aware are taking place).

He also argues that this approach recognizes the complexity of everyday life: that rather than having *single* identities, loyalties and experiencing the same reality, we all have *multiple* identities, loyalties and experiences of reality, and the exciting thing about investigating organizational cultures is teasing out this tissue of differences and seeing how it works or can work better. In a management sense, we are talking about the *management of diversity*.

Charles Hampden-Turner (1990) also draws on anthropological sources and argues similarly that culture is a response to human *dilemmas*, a means of problem solving. Human beings are faced with alternatives in living their lives in a very fundamental way: how to develop communities; how or whether to cultivate the land; whether to be dominating or cooperative as a society; how to arrange for procreation and succession of the race; how to manage time and adapt to climate; whether to be individualistic or group oriented. Some of these things, through mutual interaction over time become shared and common; others become more elaborated and differentiated, a result of the difference that Olila identifies. In organizational terms, these dilemmas become formulated in such terms as 'the need to adapt the organization to a changing environment' versus 'the need to integrate members of the organization internally'; or 'the need for periodic change' versus 'the need to preserve key continuities'. Culture is what evolves to bridge these gaps.

Defining culture

A myriad of attempts has been made to define culture, but this does not necessarily mean that the concept is elusive – on the contrary, the manifestations of culture are often very concrete in building behaviours. Andrew Brown (1995) gives a list of what he calls definitions of culture, but in actuality, taken out of the context of the pieces they were originally part of, most of them are just partial descriptions of culture, and all of them make some sense (see

Exhibit 3.1). Brown also attempts to classify these into a rather crude structured hierarchy, but this is a confused and confusing exercise, as is his account of the development of theories of culture.

- The culture of the factory is its customary and traditional way of thinking and of doing things, which is shared to a greater or lesser degree by all its members, and which new members must learn, and at least partially accept, in order to be accepted into service in the firm. Culture in this sense covers a wide range of behaviour: the methods of production; job skills and technical knowledge; attitudes towards discipline and punishment; the customs and habits of managerial behaviour; the objectives of the concern; its way of doing business; the methods of payment; the values placed on different types of work; beliefs in democratic living and joint consultation; and the less conscious conventions and taboos (Jaques 1952: 251).
- The culture of an organization refers to the unique configuration of norms, values, beliefs, ways of behaving and so on that characterize the manner in which groups and individuals combine to get things done. The distinctiveness of a particular organization is intimately bound up with its history and the character-building effects of past decisions and past leaders. It is manifested in the folkways, mores, and the ideology to which members defer, as well as in the strategic choices made by the organization as a whole (Eldridge and Crombie 1974: 89).
- A set of understandings or meanings shared by a group of people. The meanings are largely tacit among members, are clearly relevant to the particular group, and are distinctive to the group. Meanings are passed on to new group members (Louis 1980).
- Culture is a pattern of beliefs and expectations shared by the organization's members. These beliefs and expectations produce norms that powerfully shape the behaviour of individuals and groups in the organization (Schwartz and Davis 1981: 33).
- Organizational culture is not just another piece of the puzzle, it is the puzzle. From our point of view, a culture is not something an organization has; a culture is something an organization is (Pacanowsky and O'Donnell-Trujillo 1982: 126).
- A pattern of basic assumptions – invented, discovered or developed by a given group as it learns to cope with its problems of external adaptation and internal integration – that has worked well enough to be considered valid and, therefore, to be taught to new members as the correct way to perceive, think and feel in relation to those problems (Schein 1985: 9).
- The shared beliefs top managers in a company have about how they should manage themselves and other employees, and how they should conduct their business(es). These beliefs are often invisible to the top managers but have a major impact on their thoughts and actions (Lorsch 1986: 95).
- Culture is 'how things are done around here'. It is what is typical of the organization, the habits, the prevailing attitudes, the grown-up pattern of accepted and expected behaviour (Drennan 1992: 3).

Exhibit 3.1 Definitions of organizational culture

Source: Adapted from Andrew Brown (1995), Organizational Culture, *London: Pitman, p. 6.*

Paul Bate (1994) also seeks to examine what other writers have tried to define culture *as*, and also comes up with a wide variety of types of definition (see Exhibit 3.2). But his approach is both more subtle and more alert than is Brown's. What Bate argues is that culture and strategy are not just related, or similar, but that strategy is a cultural phenomenon (an outcome of cultural processes) and that culture is strategy (a way of dealing

- Directions for performance ('Directives')
- Guiding beliefs and philosophies
- Recipes
- A design for living
- Coded instructions
- 'This is the way things are; and this is why they ought to be as they are'
- A set of means for achieving designated ends
- A system of meanings
- 'It shapes the way we organize our experiences and choose our actions' (dispositions to action)
- A collective orientation/positioning
- A set of limits – prescriptions and proscriptions of conduct
- Propositional knowledge
- A set of interpretations and propositions
- Signposts
- Conventionalizing signals
- An historically emergent set of ideas
- A prevailing logic
- A framework governing behaviour
- A framework giving order and coherence to our lives
- A way of thinking
- A way of proceeding

Exhibit 3.2 Paul Bate's inventory of definitions of culture

Source: Paul Bate (1994), Strategies for Cultural Change, *London: Butterworth Heinemann, p. 20.*

with problems so that living becomes easier). This does not mean that the culture of a company and its strategy will be seamless and supportive, but that work needs to take place in both areas simultaneously if either is to change. The issue of culture and strategy is explored further in Chapter 10. However, given Peter Anthony's argument that every culture change process has taken place at the same time as a structural change, so its effects are hard to measure, there is little wonder that the many attempts to isolate and measure 'culture' as a variable (from the early and ill-conceived 'climate' studies onward) have tended to founder. Is culture a factor for success? Despite the views of managers and consultants, research has been unable to demonstrate it, although there does seem to be some evidence that it has impact in particular combinations of factors, including economic climate, and that it can be a *barrier* to success (Barney 1986).

Culture is a means of finding a way to resolve differences, of helping people work together, often through symbols which work effectively without our having to think about them (see also Johnson 1992). We 'know' what things mean, without having to be too specific – in other words, symbols work best as an umbrella which is sufficiently general to contain a diversity of orientations (like the national flag of a country; the Union Jack of the UK actually contains the national flags of England, Scotland and Wales within it) rather than having a great deal of specificity. Ed Young (1989) and Stephen Linstead and Robert Grafton Small (1992) also argue that rather than culture being an exclusive expression of shared values, where it is most strongly expressed it is an attempt to contain potentially divisive difference and conflict. In short, if we all think the same we do not need to express it, we tend to accept it. In fact, we are not even aware that we do all think the same, because we accept our views as reality and don't positively choose to accept or reject alternatives. The historian Edward Gibbon once observed that the one feature that indicates that the Koran was written by an Arab is the complete absence of camels in the text. A Westerner trying to write a Middle Eastern document would think that camels were an important symbol of authenticity and would remark on them repeatedly; an Arab who saw them constantly, however, would take them for granted and think them not worthy of remark. This raises a major question about 'strong' visible cultures – to what unspoken problems are they a response, and what conflicts are being avoided or suppressed? Paradoxically, perhaps where cultures are most visible is where we should expect the deepest conflict and divergence of opinions.

Of course, *organizational culture* still relates in many ways to a system of shared meaning held by members that distinguishes the organization from other organizations, but this may not always be easy to articulate for the members. In fact, the concept of 'culture' relates to something that most of us can recognize from our experience of organizations, but is rather elusive when we attempt to define it. For Deal and Kennedy (1982) and Peters and Waterman (1982), culture is 'the way we do things around here' or 'the rules of the game for getting along in the organization'. For Linda Smircich (1983), culture is 'not something an organisation *has*, but something an organisation *is*'. In other words, an organization is a place where cultural processes happen, but it is also an outcome of those processes working in society. The organization itself is both a product and a producer of culture. This dual dimension is often missed by the more managerialist of commentators who seem to see culture as an object. But we can go further to suggest that cultural processes do not operate in a unified way – they are fragmentary, incomplete, contradictory, disrupted and neither stop nor start when we want them to. Although culture cannot be completely controlled, it can still be open to some manipulation.

Edgar Schein (1985) defines culture as 'the deeper level of basic assumptions and beliefs that are shared by members of an organisation, that operate unconsciously, and that define in a basic, "taken-for-granted" fashion, an organisation's view of itself and its environment'. Schein has a model which identifies three levels of culture (as described in Figure 3.1). The three levels comprise: *artefacts* and *creations* (objects, buildings, uniforms, technology, etc.); underpinned by *values* which are not visible, but of which we are or can be made aware; and *basic assumptions*, which are taken for granted, invisible and preconscious and hard to access. Furthermore, he argues that the culture reveals itself when it is most stressed, when presented with problems, rather than in its routine, which is similar to Hampden-Turner's dilemma-centred view of culture. This has an important consequence: to observe what a culture does when faced by problems, you have to be there, you cannot rely on questionnaires. Further, if culture is unconscious, it cannot be easily articulated – questionnaires can therefore only access the known, visible and pretty unremarkable aspects of culture. Nevertheless, many 'culture investigations', both academic and commercial, rely on such instruments. Whatever it is that these instruments elicit, Schein and others (especially social anthropologists) would argue, it is not culture.

Linstead and Grafton Small (1992) argue that a distinction can be made between 'corporate culture' and 'organizational culture'. The former is 'devised by management and transmitted, marketed, sold or imposed on the rest of the organisation, with both internal

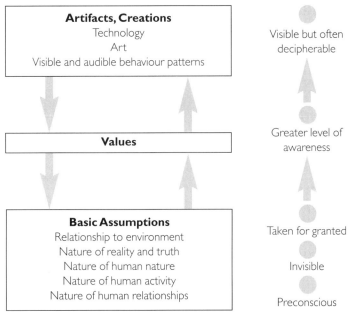

Figure 3.1 Schein's three levels of culture

Source: Edgar Schein (1985), Organizational Culture and Leadership, San Francisco: Jossey-Bass, p. 14.

and external images yet also including action and belief – the rites, rituals, stories and values which are *offered* to organizational members as part of the seductive process of achieving membership and gaining commitment'. The latter, however, is that which 'grows or emerges within the organization and which emphasises the creativity of organizational members as culture-makers, perhaps resisting the dominant culture'. In other words, the organizational culture may consist of subcultures, it may be fragmented, but it will be the outcome of cultural processes which take place wherever human beings attempt to achieve a collective understanding of their everyday world by making it meaningful.

Strong cultures

Nevertheless, the literature has not been obsessed with cultural processes but with 'strong cultures' and how they can be created. Traditional control processes in organizations tend to operate through direct orders or programmes and procedures. Cultural control strategies tend, however, to operate by generating the consent of the workforce through the diffusion and popularization of either the culture of the senior management, or a culture which senior management popularize without actually sharing (Bate 1994: 39). The values and norms are first disseminated; then there may be some denial and censorship of alternate or oppositional views; finally there will be some attempt to define and limit the parameters of what is able to be discussed, and eventually people will internalize this and just avoid certain topics and lines of critique (Kirkbride 1983: 238). Interestingly, people tend to leave organizations when this happens! However, control is increasingly being exercised over sensory, aesthetic and emotional responses – people are being told what to feel as well as what to think, and these feelings are played on by culture manipulators. Omar Aktouf (1996), in Exhibit 3.3, outlines some of the characteristics which managers seek to disseminate among the brewery workers he studied.

The **'good employee'** (who has the potential to become a foreman) is:

- *submissive*: ever consenting, obedient and disciplined;
- *punctual*: doesn't lose a half-minute of production time;
- *serious*: 'doesn't talk', totally absorbed in his task;
- *malleable*: lets himself be 'formed', acquires the 'right' bent;
- *ambitious*: 'wants it', 'works his guts out' to succeed, gives 'his maximum'.

Foremen should (in order of importance):

- *achieve their assigned objectives*: quotas are first and foremost, everything else comes 'after';
- *set an example*: particularly concerning the points listed above;
- *be 'firm'*: never yield on any issue, do not be 'soft', output before all else;
- *be a policeman with 'velvet gloves'*: supervise and obtain productivity without problems;
- *'have a grip'*: able to boss the men, the inflexible and uncompromising;
- *not 'try to please'*: 'to please' the employees is 'playing their game';
- *know how to be tough*: 'deal severely with', 'sanction' and 'make an example of offenders to avoid shirking' on the part of the employees;
- *be 'able to solve his own problem'*: 'to show initiative';
- but all the same, know how to 'communicate' while 'maintaining discipline' and 'not going further than he's asked'.

Formal criteria for the evaluation of foremen in Montreal:

Production per line

Production per machine

Production per job

Number of breakdowns

Number of conflicts.

Exhibit 3.3 Supervisory culture in Algiers and Montreal: managers' views

Source: Omar Aktouf (1996), 'Competence, Symbolic Activity and Profitability', in Stephen Linstead, Robert Grafton Small and Paul Jeffcutt (eds), Understanding Management, London: Sage, pp. 66–77.

Strong cultures are intended to engender commitment, dedication and devotion, enthusiasm, passion and even love in employees. And they can work – at least they can have great impact. If employees 'feel' for the company – if it touches them in some way – they will follow its leaders anywhere because they value – even idolize – everything it stands for. Or so the argument runs. Arlie Hochschild's book *The Managed Heart* (1983) looks at the issue of emotional labour, where employees are required to manage their selves sufficient to generate a display of emotion for the benefit of the company. Flight attendants are required to 'smile from the inside'; debt collectors have to project the sort of self-image that would make debtors pay their bills. Hochschild argues that human feeling has been commercialized, manipulated for competitive advantage. Companies expect their employees artificially to generate sincere feelings. The job of the leader then is not just the management of meaning

(Smircich and Morgan 1982), but also the management of feeling (Bate 1994).

Employees, as Deal and Kennedy (1982) argue, are uncertain not only about what to think in the modern world, but also about what to feel – and whether they are worthy to be in that world. Companies with strong cultures offer to fill these mental and emotional gaps – 'think this', 'feel this' and act accordingly and you will be worthy, they say (Schwartz 1990). Dedicate yourself to the company, constantly go the extra mile, love its products and services – Ray Kroc of McDonald's constantly urged his employees to love the beauty of a burger, an aesthetic which still escapes many of us – and success is virtually assured.

Bate (1994) goes on to look at how order is maintained in strong cultures. He identifies six processes:

- *Taking care of people* – making them feel safe, valued, comfortable and secure, fully employed and protected. But it also means, as Deal and Kennedy (1982: 56) put it, 'not permitting them to fail'. This is sometimes known as 'tough love'.
- *Giving people their head* – people are given freedom, responsibility and considerable autonomy in how the task is achieved. But this freedom depends entirely on whether they 'deliver'. It requires the employee to take the corporate mission personally, to take it literally *to heart*. This is referred to as 'loose–tight' control (Peters and Waterman 1982: 318).
- *Having fun* – criticism and resistance to control can be disarmed by encouraging an atmosphere of playfulness and a sense of fun. In many companies with strong cultures joking is common, parties frequent, fancy dress, pranks and humorous gifts and spoof awards habitual. Everyone joins in; affection, loyalty and community are developed; having a good time and laughing at oneself are encouraged while questioning the point of the event is discouraged. Not that employees do not see through the hokum – they acknowledge it *and* value it for its playfulness, its non-seriousness. In this way, criticism is neutralized (Willmott 1991: 10). A good example of this is given in Chapter 1, with the 'First, get a weasel costume' strategy.
- *Giving personal gifts* – companies can reward employees with personal gifts direct from the CEO after good performance. Scandinavian Airline Systems in Sweden (SAS) did this in 1982 with Jan Carlzon, the Managing Director, himself sending each employee a gold watch after a year in which the company returned to profitability (Carlzon 1987: 113). The range of gifts, being direct and personal, is supposed to have more impact than a mere monetary bonus. Bate argues that this affects the individual *cognitively* – that is, accepting the gift from the leader is tantamount to accepting the leader's definition of the corporate mission – and *emotionally* – as such a gift can physically trigger positive emotions about the company which can be recalled for a long period.
- *Spelling it out* – the vagueness of feelings is always grounded in specific rules which define standards. Even if these rules are informal and implicit, violation of them can be serious to the point of termination.
- *Getting heavy* – strong cultures, in short, need their 'bastards' to make them stick (Deal and Kennedy 1982: 56). Making visible public examples of people – one executive at National Cash Register (NCR) in the USA returned from lunch to find

Finally, strong cultures do not only have to manage the positive, softer emotions like love and affection – fear, anger and jealousy can be powerfully manipulated too. These issues are explored further in Chapter 7. They might not produce the apparent degree of unity behind the corporate mission or the sense of dedication and loyalty that the celebratory cultures do, but they are deeply ingrained and hard to dislodge. Both types of culture 'trap' people. Company T is an example of such a culture, as were many of the big engineering-based industrial bureaucracies that dominated Western smokestack industry for most of this century. Some of these companies have become dramatically smaller since the 1980s, but little seems to have changed in their cultures. Organizations with strong cultures not only seek complete loyalty and compliance from members but also try to become the dominant basis for a member's identity. Some regard these organizations as 'greedy institutions' that make extraordinary demands on individuals (Flam 1993: 62).

Cultural heterogeneity

Organizational cultures, even when they do represent a common perception held by the organization's members, or a system of shared meaning, are not uniform cultures. Large organizations, like British Airways, might have one *dominant culture* expressing the core values of the corporation, which in a very general way are shared by most of the organization's members. They also have sets of *subcultures* typically, but not exclusively, defined by department designations and geographical separation. However, as Hampden-Turner (1990) argues, the corporate response to tension between subcultures, as in that between the service elements and the operational elements in British Airways, is what shapes the culture itself. His approach to culture seeks to identify key dilemmas. In British Airways, despite the undoubted success of the airline in turning itself round from public loss-maker to private profit-maker, there were divergences between the rhetoric of the corporate culture and its professed values, and what people reported as the reality. Aktouf (1996), in his ethnographic study of breweries in Algiers and Montreal, noted the same thing at an empirical level. There was a strongly articulated idealized view by the managers as to what their criteria for promoting supervisors were, as we saw in Exhibit 3.3, yet the workers' more realistic view of what it was necessary to actually do in order to get promoted diverged strongly from this, as we see in Exhibit 3.4.

The worker's profile of an ideal foreman
- *'competent'*, firstly;
- *has confidence in us*, doesn't feel obliged to be incessantly on the workers' backs;
- *we can trust him*, isn't 'two-faced';
- *a man of his word*, dignified, a 'true example';
- *talks to the employees*, listens, 'has a heart';
- *'respects' the employees*, treats them like 'people';

- *is fair;*
- *is not 'tense'* (obsessed with output, and who transfers obsession to everybody).

The profile of the typical real foreman

- 'Most of the guys are chosen (to become foremen) not because they're competent hard workers, but because they're "two-faced" or "hard-headed"; these are guys who climb over the backs of their colleagues, I don't like that'.
- 'They don't know anything, don't do anything except try to catch you out just to shame you! Those are the types that are encouraged'.
- 'Good or bad, they're all the same. A dog doesn't eat dog, so they close ranks against us'.
- 'There are some here who only want to crush you, crush you with work and filth'.
- 'They never stop pushing. One might think they're only here to make trouble'.
- 'One time I injured my hand, blood was pissing out of me, and all the boss was interested in was that I fill out a report before going to the hospital! And they come around every year to shake your hand!'.

Exhibit 3.4 Supervisory culture in Algiers and Montreal: the workers' view

Source: Omar Aktouf (1996), 'Competence, Symbolic Activity and Profitability', in Stephen Linstead, Robert Grafton Small and Paul Jeffcutt (eds), Understanding Management, *London: Sage, pp. 66–77.*

Basic cultural types

Some commentators have attempted to identify basic types of culture found in organizations. These typologies are necessarily crude and general, but may nevertheless have value in broadly characterizing organizations. Perhaps the earliest such attempt was by Roger Harrison (1972) and later developed by Charles Handy (1993: Chapter 7). Harrison uses dimensions of centralization and formalization to identify four cultures – role culture, task culture, power culture and atomistic culture (which Handy calls a person culture) as shown in Figure 3.2. Formalization refers to the extent to which rules, policies and procedures dominate organizational activities, while centralization refers to how much power and authority is concentrated at the top levels of an organization. Centralization is most evident in terms of what types of decisions are allowed at various levels of an organization, particularly in authorizing and giving rewards to employees.

Ironically, Harrison's dimensions are in fact *structural* dimensions rather than cognitive or behavioural ones – and are certainly not symbolic ones! However, what he is saying is that there are typical sets of behaviours, and associated mindsets, that tend to go along with particular structures, examples being project teams, big bureaucracies, small entrepreneurial companies or chambers of lawyers. Andrew Kakabadse, Ron Ludlow and Susan Vinnicombe (1988: 225–37) took the same framework but looked at what they called *power levers,* that is, the characteristic and different types of influence which work best in each culture. Again, in this example culture is difficult to separate from power and structure (see also Chapter 4). Their framework is described in Table 3.1.

Another typology was also attempted by Deal and Kennedy (1982) as shown in Figure 3.3. They related the amount of *risk* involved in the core activities of the company to the speed of *feedback on performance* to assess the organization's culture, which enabled them to categorize four main cultural types, described in more detail under Figure 3.3.

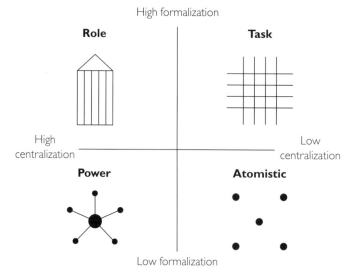

Figure 3.2 Culture quadrant by Roger Harrison

Source: Modified from Desmond Graves (1986), Corporate Culture: Diagrams and Change, *New York: St Martin's Press; adapted from: 'Understanding your organization's character',* Harvard Business Review, *May–June 1972, pp. 119–28.*

Bet-your-company *High risk* *Slow feedback* e.g. Oil company	**Tough-guy macho** *High risk* *Fast feedback* e.g. Film company
Process *Low risk* *Slow feedback* e.g. Insurance company	**Work hard, play hard** *Low risk* *Fast feedback* e.g. Restaurant

Amount of risk

Speed of feedback

Figure 3.3 Simple quadrant by Deal and Kennedy

Source: Derived from Terrence Deal and Allen Kennedy (1988), Corporate Culture: The Rites and Rituals of Corporate Life, *London: Penguin, pp. 107–27.*

- *The tough-guy macho culture* A world of individualists who regularly take high risks and get quick feedback on whether their actions were right or wrong.
- *The work hard, play hard culture* Fun and action are the rule here, and employees take few risks, all with quick feedback; to succeed the culture encourages them to maintain a high level of low-risk activity.
- *The bet-your-company culture* Cultures with big-stakes decisions, where years pass before employees know whether decisions have paid off. A high-risk, slow-feedback environment.
- *The process culture* A world of little or no feedback where employees find it hard to measure what they do; instead they concentrate on how it's done. We have another name for this culture when the processes get out of control – bureaucracy!

Table 3.1 Relationships between power-related behaviours and cultures

Type of power levers	Power culture	Role culture	Task culture	Person culture
Reward levers	Rewards offered for supporting key power figures	Rewards offered for following existing rules, regulations and procedures	Rewards for high task performance, project leadership, etc.	Acceptance by peers
Coercive levers	Mistakes, misdemeanours and actions punished if they threaten key power figures	Punishment for working outside role requirements or breaking rules, procedures or communication patterns	Focuses on low task performances or differences of expert opinion. Rejection from elite group or cancellation of project possible	Threatened by/with group expulsion
Legitimate levers	Rules and regulations can be broken by key power figures	Behaviour in keeping with defined authority, relationships, rules, procedures, job outlines and descriptions	Problem-solving ability through technical expertise. Senior management can be challenged on technical grounds	Behaviour according to needs of individuals in situation. Loyalty to those with whom one interacts, with allegiance to organization as a whole
Personal levers	Strong, decisive, uncompromising, charismatic behaviour. Manipulation by leaders. Low support for those who are not key power figures	Personal power from perceived rightful issuing, observance and interpretation of rules, procedures and allocation of work. Personal support offered only to fulfil role requirements	Status and charisma derived from problem-solving skills	Personal power through sharing and partnership. Personal growth, developing supportive environment
Expert levers	Knowledge and performance standards based not on professional criteria but on influence over others – political	Working solely within one's specialist role – not crossing boundaries or disturbing existing role structure	Constant skills development to solve new and more complex problems. Driving standards higher	Behaviour and work standards developed by group members at any one time. Individuals expected to adhere to current informal standards
Information levers	Information valued only if it helps achieve personal ends	Information flows according to role prescriptives and established patterns and procedures	Driving to acquire and share new information for better problem solving	Any relevant information to be shared among the group
Connection levers	Making numerous contacts and connections is vital, within and without the organisation. Generates a closed shop culture	Contacts and connections only required to fulfil role demands according to regulations – e.g. health and safety advisers	Extensive network of experts inside and outside the organization. Loyalty to experts (profession, discipline) rather than organization	A personal sympathetic/emotional link with others. Satisfy a need to be with people one likes

Source: Adapted from Andrew Kakabadse, Ron Ludlow and Susan Vinnicombe (1988), *Working in Organizations*, London: Penguin, pp. 228, 229, 232, 234.

Managing culture

In Deal and Kennedy's scheme, the major influencing factor on the culture seems to be the *task* of the organization, coupled with the financial consequences of its operations. But feedback about task performance also affects the identity of employees, their sense of who they are in these companies. Collectively, groups develop patterns of behaviour which may become ritualistic; symbols and symbolic behaviours (or meanings associated with particular behaviours) which are peculiar to them; their own language and jargon; and stories, legends and traditions. These features help to establish meanings and beliefs and they are transmitted – as culture is a communicative phenomenon – through formal and informal socialization processes. The formal processes emphasized in much of the culture literature include:

- education and training;
- selection and appraisal;
- role modelling by superiors and peers; and
- leadership.

Culture and leadership

In particular, leaders can exert a powerful influence on the culture of their organization, especially if they are the founder. Organizations are replete with stories and myths about founders, and significant leaders who came after the founder. Leaders can shape the culture of their organizations by:

- what they pay attention to and notice;
- their reactions to problems and crises;
- role modelling, coaching, mentoring and teaching;
- their criteria for selection, reward, promotion and punishment/sanction; and
- their influence on organizational structure and policy.

This is in general reinforced, or may be undermined, by its consistency of fit with:

- mechanisms of control in the organization (e.g. meetings, budgets, peer surveillance);
- organizational structure (e.g. size of subunits, levels of hierarchy, number of sites, distance of divisions from headquarters);
- organizational systems (e.g. types of production technology, operating procedures); and
- formal statements (e.g. policies, reports, manuals, press releases).

We might think of the leader's actions (the first list) as the reality and the more formal arrangements (the second list) as the rhetoric or the difference between doing and saying. Sometimes bringing policy and practice into alignment is referred to as the need to 'walk the talk', which is not always easy to achieve. The study by Aktouf cited earlier revealed a glaring dichotomy, as he says:

the organization (i.e., its members) does the utmost to maintain an official discourse, and then acts in direct opposition to that discourse. When asked about the reasons for the systematic promotions of foremen whose behaviour and attitude are a blatant contradiction with the organization's official position, managers inevitably answer that it was 'because the workers did not want to be promoted'!

When companies are small and leaders can be visible and lead by example, the influence they can have over the development of the company can be much more directly felt than when they are CEOs of a large multidivisional company. Communication then becomes critical, but it is often seen as being one way, the problem being defined as spreading the CEO's word to get people to follow, rather than increasing upward and lateral flows of communication to improve sharing, if shared meaning is really what culture is about. Two examples of this are illustrated in the short text that follows.

In 1988, at a management development seminar held at the Basingstoke Hilton in the UK, the arrival of the company's Human Resources Director was preceded by a flurry of activity to present a well-ordered reception. He had masterminded the company's much vaunted and very successful culture change over the previous three years. The Great Man arrived, his acolytes running before him to announce his coming. The conference room was hushed. 'Now,' he began, 'the first thing I'd like to see is you all holding up your mission cards!' A forest of small cards rustled across the room as hands were raised in the apparent expression of a common faith. Within a year, the company and the Great Man parted abruptly at the Chief Executive's instigation.

On another occasion, at the end of a management development course, managers gathered at the company's country house management development centre. The Chief Executive was to arrive en route to the airport to take a flight to the Far East. He would interrupt his progress to present awards to the assembled managers. The morning was spent in preparation, scripting, the preparation of the ceremonials, the formal dressing, the arrangement of the setting, the rehearsal of the presentations, the preparation of the appropriate frame of mind. The Chairman arrived. His limousine pulled up outside the centre and mentally course participants, tutors and staff of the centre alike, came to attention. His hand was raised, the signal given and the ceremony began. The course participants went forward one at a time to shake hands with the incarnate author of their corporate performance. It was a dignified and solemn moment. He exchanged a few words with each of the managers in turn and many commented afterwards that he seemed 'quite human'. The performance completed, he gestured his valediction. A chauffeur ushered him to his waiting car, to the airport and to other incarnations, other performances.

Source: Adapted from Heather Höpfl (1996), 'Authority and the pursuit of order in organizational performance', in Paul Jeffcutt, Robert Grafton Small and Stephen Linstead (eds), Organization and Theatre, special issue of Studies in Cultures, Organizations, and Societies 2(1), pp. 73–4.

The above quite empty incidents demonstrate how difficult it is for the CEO to change anything so 'deep' as culture with the customary methods in use. Much of the culture literature recognizes that meaning and commonsense understanding are the bedrock of culture, and that they are transmitted in some circumstances by stories, myths, rites and rituals (see Chapter 1). But primarily they are imparted by experience, especially shared experience, and the everyday occurrence of events which may be weakly and metaphorically described as rites, or as story-telling. These rites have the advantage of being living and organic, changing and developing, rather than having the dead quality of the contrived stories which most companies now construct or stage-manage about their senior managers. For example, Michael Levin, the consultant who helped British Airways to change their culture in the 1980s, tells this story of the first day of the relaunched Super Shuttle service from London to Manchester, which provided hot breakfasts and newspapers for the first time:

> We then had 96 people lined up in front of the BA desks. I was frantic. We were not clearing them fast enough. I tried to get some four-stripers [supervisors] to help but they said 'We are four-stripers, we can't do that'. But then I happened to see out of the corner of my eye that one of the managers was helping. Guess who it was – Marshall [the CEO]. They were in horror, they were aghast (Young, D. 1989: 3).

While one might wonder what the CEO was doing at the check-in desks, and who on earth had trained him to use the computer system, it makes a good story. British Airways modelled their changes on the changes in Scandinavian Airline Systems, which had been described in the bestselling book *Moments of Truth* by Jan Carlzon (1987), their Managing Director. In the book, Carlzon tells an almost identical story of himself helping with the baggage on a flight, saying that he did it to emphasize to the workers that everyone at every level is responsible to the customer and if necessary should help out. British Airways and Marshall had to have not only copied this example, with the slight change to check-in desks, but to have contrived it – Marshall had no skills, and he had no experience in the airline industry, so if he was not to make things worse he had to have been trained beforehand. If the incident ever happened, of course (other than Levin, neither the author nor his colleagues in several years of working and researching in British Airways was ever able to find anyone who actually witnessed the incident). Ironically, in June 1997, while British Airways were negotiating with the unions on a pay cuts and redundancy package it was revealed that they were training their managers to operate flights and check-in procedures in preparation for a strike. It was widely felt that British Airways engineered the strike to break the union, and it completely backfired on management and the high-profile CEO Robert (Bob) Ayling, who no doubt was planning a similar publicity stunt himself. However, by the time of the strike he was so unpopular with the customers he would have found it difficult to show his face in the check-in area. British Airways is now trying strenuously to rebuild both its public image and its culture – by reaffirming the importance of people (Walsh 1997).

Additionally, no matter how hard the CEO might try to motivate with corporate symbolism and ritual, and the issuing of mission statement cards to everyone, and even if the message is successfully bought by the shopfloor, the level where culture hits a problem is the level where organizational politics is most keenly felt. Sometimes this is in senior management, sometimes at supervisory level as in this short example.

> Sometimes, workers find that managerial politics get in the way of their motivation to perform well in accordance with the 'mission' of the organization. Meeting production targets and delivering a quality product or service often conflict – and 'culture' is supposed to resolve these kinds of dilemmas. In a bakery in the north of England, where the workers in question were making fruit mince pies for the early Christmas market, the

work force frequently showed considerable concern for their product's quality. They would often fail to pack pies which they considered to be substandard. Once a pie was made, the policy according to supervision was 'pack as much as we can get away with', although quality control had other ideas. When confused about what to pack and what not to pack, and finding the criterion of whether they would like to purchase the goods themselves in such a condition of no help, (and) caught between supervision and quality control, they resorted to the management for arbitration. 'Who pays your wages?' said Jack (the Production Manager), 'me or Quality?' The workers, in some puzzlement, replied that they thought it was the company.

It was very difficult for workers in this organization, with an understanding of the organization's mission and an understanding of what the customer (who could easily be themselves) would want, to find that these considerations were overridden by internecine warfare between the plant manager and quality control. This is also difficult for CEOs to understand and hear about – people generally will not tell them, it will not appear as a response in a survey, and generally employees will be reluctant to reveal it to inquirers. Middle managers also experience difficulties with corporate culture initiatives, according to Peter Anthony (1994: 64–77), because top management often engineers its culture change with staged performances, such as we have discussed, with the only real objective being to improve financial performance, not to change values. But they sell it to middle management as the great new initiative, and expect them to sell it to supervision and the shopfloor. Supervision and the shopfloor workers have, of course, seen it all before, and are typically cynical – they go along with change for a while but expect that top management will eventually show its 'true colours' with dismissals, redundancies, savage cuts, disciplinary measures or just plain heartlessness. Eventually this might happen, especially if top management never believed in the 'new order', but got their efficiency gains; the shopfloor expected to be sold out and they were; and the middle managers who believed in and worked for the new cultural changes often feel deeply betrayed and cheated. It is now quite common to find managers still working long hours effectively, but who claim to have lower morale than ever. They work because of their professionalism, they say, not because of their 'commitment'.

Symbolic action

Jeffrey Pfeffer (1981) introduced the distinction between 'symbolic management' and 'substantive management' in the early 1980s, to distinguish between those acts of a manager which were done deliberately to carry extra meaning, and those which were part of the normal run of things. This distinction has been widely propagated, mostly by writers who have little understanding of the symbolic process. The corollary of this is that managers often believe that anything can become symbolic, but just because they think it *ought* to be does not make it symbolic. Neither does it make it inevitable that if it does become symbolic, the manager's preferred meaning will be the one that is taken (Feldman 1996). Of course, if you are the CEO and have the power, you are more likely to be able to make your meaning stick, at least in public. The stories of Marshall and Carlzon above were of 'symbolic' management, yet there is little *evidence* as to how these stories were received, although they were widely retold. But they were powerful images, and as such would be likely to circulate and have impact. Jack's rebuttal of the workers on the quality issue was no less symbolic, and delivered a powerful message to those involved, but it was not a memorable image.

Sometimes humour will be used to undermine the intended symbolic message. Acting symbolically is more a matter of acting publicly in ways that give off powerful images which can be easily associated with the other more content laden messages that are being given out. Ralph Halpern, for example, Chairman of the UK Burton Group, a menswear manufacturer and retailer, always wore the group's clothes and insisted from his first days in changing the strategy that the companies' employees would 'wear the strategy' – actually wear the clothes they were selling to the public. This gave a powerful message to the employees. Some years later, when the fifty-something Halpern, now Sir Ralph, was exposed for having an affair with an 18-year-old topless model, she revealed that he still insisted that she wear the group's products during their erotic assignations (luckily the group had by that time diversified into sexy lingerie!). The shareholders found this consistency symbolically reassuring, perhaps additionally consoled by his reported demands for sex 'up to five times a night'. Four days after his exposure they voted him Britain's best CEO remuneration package of £2 million p.a. and called him 'the greatest Englishman since Churchill'. Halpern was clearly no novice in the art of symbolic management as Gerry Johnson (1989: 547) points out. Back in 1977 when the Burton Group was in crisis, he obtained a reduction in capacity, which could have just as easily been obtained by closing several small plants, by closing the main headquarters plant in Leeds. He did this because the headquarters 'castle' symbolized the stability and complacency he wanted to challenge, and closing it down signalled that manufacturing was not the heart of the company, giving a much-needed boost to the retail section. The Burton turnaround was spectacular, with it becoming Britain's most profitable retailing group less than 10 years after posting a £13 million loss.

So although the idea of symbolic management is theoretically flawed, and is practically very difficult to control, acts with strong symbolic associations and high image quality do seem to have impact upon and help to change people's minds about a company, often without them knowing it, because symbols are effective to the extent that they mean something without the 'reader' having to think about it. Some companies then fall into the trap of contriving images and events and symbolic performances, while others do not. The example below illustrates one extended metaphor that in the end had the opposite effect of what was intended.

What were you doing the day the war ended?

The British Airways UK Sales Conference: September 1989

The following account of a piece of organisational theatre was provided by a participant. It demonstrates how meanings are invested in performance and what happens when the performance becomes insupportable.

'That Autumn the airline business was buoyant. The company was achieving most of its revenue targets and people in the Sales Department were charged with anticipation. Every September, all members of the Sales Department, some three hundred people, are invited to participate in the Annual Sales Conference and this particular year everyone felt they really had something to celebrate.

The location and theme of the conference is always a fairly well kept secret. This adds to the general air of expectancy. Stories and anecdotes concerning previous conferences were rife. Rumours, predictions and theories about who, where and what were put forward by just about everybody in the weeks before the event.

The suspense was eased yet stimulated by the arrival of "The Invitation". The location was Gatwick or rather a four star hotel very close to it. The theme was announced as, "What were you doing the day the War ended?" The Invitation itself came from the Allied HQ and was printed in a 1940s style. All those attending the conference were requested to dress in the attire which they felt best fitted in with the theme of the conference.

The conference itself started on a warm Saturday afternoon in September. It was to run through to Monday morning. A large majority of the participants had requested a day off for the Monday aware that alcohol and sheer exhaustion would necessitate at least 18 hours sleep after a "good sales conference".

The next thing to do was to hire a costume. This turned out to be quite costly despite sales teams using the same fancy dress hire shop and getting a bulk order discount. The cost of hiring the costumes, £35 for the weekend (washing, if necessary, was extra) promised to be well worth it. The first opportunity to "dress up" came on Sunday morning. The scene at breakfast was extraordinary. Italian generals ate cornflakes with women from the French Resistance. An American five star general with foot long epaulettes on each shoulder politely ordered bacon, sausage and tomato. The Field Sales Manager, Adolf Hitler, swapped jokes with two young London evacuees who were fully kitted out with gas masks and name labels. The feeling of excitement continued as everyone boarded coaches taking them to the venue for the main conference seminar. Here an introduction to the proceedings was given by the Field Marshall, General Manager UK Sales. His role was to explain the campaign strategy, to identify the location of enemy action. He prowled up and down, pointing with his swagger stick to the battle lines drawn up on a wall chart.

And so the day went on. All the presentations contained innumerable references to war. The evacuees, French Resistance, Gestapo, American Generals, The Home Guard and the Medical Corps all listened dutifully. Lunchtime continued with the war-time theme. Wooden trestle tables, benches, masking tape crosses on the windows and a catering company's idea of what 1940s army rations might have been kept "the troops" in the mood. Indeed, all the days events were planned to keep people "in the mood" but by 4.30 in the afternoon the proceedings began to drag. The novelty of being dressed as a Japanese Admiral or a Desert Rat began to wear off. The team from Northern England Sales who were all dressed as clowns began to have trouble with their face make-up. The Japanese Admiral finally discarded his heavy overcoat with a sigh of relief.

The presentations ran on. The event should have finished by 6.00pm but it was 6.30pm when the Field Marshall rose to give his final address. It was too late. He was confronted by a weary and lack-lustre assembly of ridiculously over-dressed, tired and irritated individuals who had enough of the "performance". As their leader tried to rouse them with exhortations to future performance targets their own performance and participation had become unbearable. They had thrown off their roles and the props which supported them.'

Source: Heather Höpfl (1996), 'Authority and the pursuit of order in organizational performance', in Paul Jeffcutt, Robert Grafton Small and Stephen Linstead (eds), Organization and Theatre, *special issue of* Studies in Cultures, Organizations, and Societies 2(1), pp. 74–5.

Culture and control

One of the surprisingly few writers to publish theoretical critiques of organizational culture, Carol Axtell Ray (1986), argues that in the early years of the twentieth century, Scientific Management and associated techniques established what Max Weber (1964) termed *bureaucratic control.* In essence, the *manipulation of rewards* established, or rather bought, the workers' *loyalty*, which led to the organization's ultimate objective, *increased productivity.* After the impact of the Hawthorne Studies (see Chapter 2), the recognition of the social needs of the workforce was increasingly taken into account. In this model of *humanistic control*, it was the provision of a *satisfying task or workgroup life* that produced worker *loyalty*, which in turn led to *increased productivity.* In more recent times, *culture control* has been achieved. By a *manipulation of culture,* including myth and ritual, the workforce comes to *love the firm and its goals* and as a result, we find *increased productivity.* Of course, the actuality is rather more complex than this, but the critique does have substance. For some commentators, cultural management is just the latest control strategy, a direct descendant of Taylorism, except that human control replaces technical control (see Boje and Winsor 1993: 66–7; see also Chapters 2 and 6).

Figure 3.5 From bureaucratic to symbolic control

Source: Adapted from Carol Axtell Ray (1986) 'Corporate culture: The last frontier of control?' Journal of Management Studies *23(3), pp. 287–98.*

In a similar vein, Steve Smith and Barry Wilkinson (1996) offer an unusual account of what they call a *totalitarian* culture. The company they studied, Sherwoods, is a progressive, non-hierarchical company, a very successful part of a hugely successful multinational. Pursuing 'furious interaction' and 'knocking the corners off politics' with a religious fervour that places everyone, even top management, in an open-plan office, they produce a self-policing conformity. Managers can be demoted by their subordinates if they are not performing, and they are paid well in excess of the industry norms in order to keep them – the 'golden handcuffs'. Smith and Wilkinson raise some disturbing questions about how conflict is apparently obliterated in this company, arguing that 'Sherwoods takes on a nightmarish quality because tight control co-exists with a high degree of autonomy and an almost citizen status for members. If there is an analogy with penal institutions, it is the open prison.'

Sherwoods

The central feature of this organisation is that it is both an open system and yet achieves unusually complete control. There is little scope for privacy. Managers have been active in bringing this about *qua*. 'We are our *own* policemen.' They are not passive 'cogs in a machine'. The Family who own the company would not want them to behave mechanically. Anti-bureaucratic, relatively undifferentiated, this organisation is *not an organisation*. Yet its reach is very complete. This degree of control is exceptional: the institutionalisation of cooperation; the exorcism of politics through the 'cleansing' effect of 'free speech', job rotation between functions for managers – 'safer promotions', and through keeping the characteristics of new recruits within known, and agreed parameters – the 'sheep dip'. Sherwoods is a somewhat *total*-itarian system not in a fascist, violent sense, but strictly because, research scientists excepted, who work in a separate building, it is *total*. It is full of methods for creating consent. Several of its officers reported that when they first came, they thought Sherwoods 'a bit funny', but they can 'see it as natural now'.

This lack of privacy precludes serious dissent. Criticism is encouraged, but only within bounds. Excepting the unchallenged, strategic rules of ROTA (the accounting system – Return on Total Assets), Open Management and FAN (social responsibility, lobbying and supplier control policy – Friends and Neighbours), day-to-day restrictions are set by the evolving collective conscience of the organisation itself. Control is not imposed by *officers*. Control does not have a specific location. 'Everybody is at the heart of things', but everybody also has several others within their gaze, and everybody is clearly observed by others. Everybody is *central* both as a necessary agent and in terms of the encircling attention of co-agents.

Attentiveness is probably the best approximation of the way Sherwoods works. In any organisation there are dividing lines and points of censure. But few would devote the attention that Sherwoods gives to happy 'separations', nor the obsessive degree of quality control, for which Sherwoods is well known. In this attentive organisation, members are also held to attention. They are their own policemen.

Source: Adapted from Steve Smith and Barry Wilkinson (1996), 'No doors on offices, no secrets: We are our own policemen: Capitalism without conflict?', in Stephen Linstead, Robert Grafton Small and Paul Jeffcutt (eds), Understanding Management, London: Sage, pp. 130–44.

Drawing on these critiques and examples, we can pick up two lines of critique which are essentially postmodern, that culture can be seen either in terms of *surveillance*, where control is exercised through peer observation and self-discipline, a view which will be explored further in Chapter 6 in relation to teams, or *seduction*, where people 'buy into' a version of their organization, which is in fact a fantasy, a blueprint copy of a supposedly successful original that never existed. In fact, many companies nowadays maintain control through a combination of both these strategies, as can be illustrated in Disneyland or McDonald's, where fantasy images of the company are used to sell the product, where surface pleasantry is vital, but where behind the smile are two very Tayloristic and disciplinarian corporations (see Ritzer 1990; Van Maanen 1991).

The move from bureaucratic to symbolic control is in fact difficult for many organizations, particularly those in which there are concentrations of professionals, such as in hospitals and universities and other areas of public service. A number of studies have drawn attention to how public sector employees tend to have stronger union affiliations, strong client-based relations, weak identification with the employing organization, stronger identification with professional bodies and peers, considerable expert power (see Chapter 4), and are more likely to be oriented to ethical as opposed to commercial values (Sinclair 1991: 326–7). Research from which these observations are made supports the view that professional public sector employees, such as clinicians, nurses, academics, welfare workers and engineers, are less likely to tolerate management-imposed constraints, will treat the organization as a means to an end, and as a place to do the work they have chosen as a vocation or career. These professionals tend to strive for high levels of autonomy or freedom and have generally high expectations of achieving intrinsic self-fulfilment without strong identification with the organizations in which they work. Strong beliefs about public service, dedication or almost a 'calling' to the job, especially where there are heavily client-based relations, such as with clinicians, strengthens the view that strong subcultures or multicultures flourish in these types of organizations (Eastman and Fulop 1997, citing Bovens 1992 and Sinclair 1991). As Amanda Sinclair comments, control through a dominant culture, especially one based on private sector models, such as McDonald's, might not be an appropriate management approach to integrate, accommodate or exploit the differences in organizations with strong multicultures (1991: 328–9). Moreover, many public sector organizations are recognized as having a range of governance or control structures, including collegial, bureaucratic and professional ones that defy one all-embracing culture (Sinclair 1991: 328, citing Benveniste 1987).

In many organizations there might also be different operational demands that encourage a 'culture' that is not easily brought under any group or individual's control. Members of the University of California, Berkeley, in the USA have been studying organizations that they describe as 'high-reliability organizations'. They have studied aircraft carriers, nuclear power plants, air traffic control systems and the operation of large electric power grids – organizations all likely to be involved in major crises, needing rapid response capacities and even having to deal with major catastrophes (Pool 1997: 44). In high-reliability organizations there is no one permanent structure or pattern of activity, in the sense that some groups operate bureaucratically and in a hierarchical manner, others in a professional and collegial way (as described above), while others operate in an emergency mode. The high-reliability organization, or the ones that seem to outperform others in their industry, has the capacity to have *everyone* switch between these modes of operating, depending on the situation. At any one time, all members might be operating in an emergency or crisis mode for a period of time. Communication in these organizations is intense, frequent and encouraged, as is the practice of challenging rules and procedures or looking for what can go wrong before it happens. Mistakes are not punished when someone is trying to do the 'right' thing. An inbuilt tolerance or expectation of ambiguity and uncertainty in management practices is the norm, which the researchers noted was one of the most unsettling aspects of these organizations. Often managers and employees alike struggle with this ambiguity because they believe that a well-functioning organization always knows what it is doing next and how (Pool 1997: 44–5). To sustain 'high reliability' literally means working with and encouraging multicultures as the basis of encouraging a 'culture' of learning (see also Pauchant and Mitroff 1988).

The cultural relativity of management

Another reason why values might be difficult to change could be the extent to which they are connected to wider cultural values which support them. Workforce diversity is increasingly a worldwide phenomenon. Many cultures still hold or have held parochial attitudes and ethnocentric views, even when their society is multicultural in its composition. Whether these biases translate into a predominantly monolingual society or an intolerance towards other cultural norms, it does prevent a country or organization from taking full advantage of new global opportunities in faster growing regions like China and the Asia–Pacific. That companies need to 'Think Global: Act Local', or practise globalization in the new world markets, has now become something of a cliché (see Torrington 1994). However, some writers have examined the consequences of the developing global–local dilemma (Humes 1993) and found that despite the visionary rhetoric, the practice is anything but simple. Hari Bedi (1991) provides an insightful analysis of globalization from the practising Asian manager's point of view, critiquing the extension of Western practices (Ersatz capitalism) into other cultures, which themselves have long histories of civilization and their own complex social arrangements and values.

However, as Edward Hall (1959) argues, cultures are communicated by more languages than simply the verbal. Consider the following questions:

> *1* You arrive for a meeting with a business client at the scheduled time of 10:00. By 10:45 the client is still not ready to see you. What do you think?
>
> *2* You arrive for a meeting with an agent whose performance is likely to be very important to your operations. The agent's office is small, crowded and cluttered and in a seedy part of town. How is your confidence affected?
>
> *3* You arrive at the offices of a major supplier who has told you how well the business is doing. However, the Managing Director's office is almost bare, with simple furniture and little decoration. Do you still believe the company is doing well?
>
> *4* Your company asks you to review the restaurant of a friend as a venue for entertaining clients. The food is awful. Your friend tells you he really needs the business and is relying on you for a good review. What do you do?
>
> *5* You have clinched the deal and shaken hands on it, but when you try to set a date to meet and sign formal contracts, the other party is reluctant to commit. What do you do?

Each of these questions would normally be interpreted as a warning signal in Australia, the UK or the USA. But they would be answered quite differently in other cultures, such as South America, East Africa or Japan (where the Western haste to do business is often a disadvantage); the Middle East (where a crowded office is a good sign that the agent is busy and in touch with the action); Japan (where minimalist furnishing is a sign of great discernment and can even be more expensive than opulence); various parts of South East Asia, the Middle East and South America where personal relationships incur obligations (that is, you would give the good public review but tell the friend in private the food required improvement); and parts of Asia and Africa where a 'Gentleman's Agreement' is considered more binding than a written contract. Hall identifies five non-verbal languages which communicate information to us without anyone speaking, and they correspond to each of the five questions above:

- the language of *time;*
- the language of *space;*
- the language of *things;*
- the language of *relationships;* and
- the language of *agreements.*

Hall's point is that we all have a characteristic way of 'reading' these things according to our cultural background, and we do this without thinking. When we go into other cultures, however, we may be making the wrong reading, and we need to be on our guard against this.

Two other major frameworks have also been developed to help identify the differences in cross-cultural understanding. Robert Westwood (1992) gives a useful outline of the theory behind the concept of culture, including the framework developed by Kluckhohn and Strodtbeck (1961; see also Adler 1991). These two frameworks identify five basic orientations or core dimensions of culture as responses to questions which all societies must answer:

- What is the essence of *human nature?*
- How do/should people relate to their *environment?*
- What is the basic *time orientation* of people?
- What state of *being and action* are people basically predisposed to?
- What is the basis for a *relationship* between people?

The frameworks then identify three states of possible cultural responses – positive, negative and neutral – which are tabulated horizontally against the five vertical dimensions, as shown in Table 3.2. Although the columns in Table 3.2 may be vertically related, the orientations may also vary horizontally between questions. In other words, because you believe that people are basically evil does not *necessarily* mean that you think they are subservient to nature – a negative response to one item does not automatically entail a negative response to all. So, any culture may not necessarily have all its scores in one column, and may have items of value in all three as part of its basic cultural matrix. Understanding this cultural underpinning can often help to make inexplicable actions – like the Arab car mechanic who refuses to commit to a time for having your car repaired – explicable (Arab cultures would score in column 1 in Table 3.2 across the dimensions of 'time', 'being' and 'relationships', a

Table 3.2 *Dimensions of basic cultural assumptions*

Core dimensions	Cultural Assumptions 1	2	3
What is the essence of human nature?	People are basically evil	People are a mixture of good and evil	People are basically good
How do/should people relate to the environment?	People are subservient to nature	People are in harmony with nature	People should be masters of nature
What is the basic time orientation of people?	To the past	To the present	To the future
What state of being and action are people basically predisposed to?	The desirable state is simply to 'be'; to act spontaneously and without long-term expectations	People should act and strive towards their own self-development and actualisation	People should act so as to achieve measurable accomplishments
What is the basis for a relationship between people?	Lineal – orientation is towards the group – is based on family ties; continuance of family line is a prime goal	Collateral – orientation towards a group – less emphasis on blood-ties. Continuance through time	Individual – the individual person is the focus. Individual interests take precedence over group interests

Source: Adapted by Robert Westwood (1992), *Organizational Behaviour,* Hong Kong: Addison Wesley Longman China, p. 43 (from Kluckhohn and Strodtbeck 1961).

common phrase being *'En sha'Allah'* or 'if God wills it'). Given respect for the past, they value traditional obligations highly, and lineal obligations can at any time take precedence over work-related ones. This also poses problems for the introduction of quality initiatives which require the statement in advance of performance standards, service standards and benchmarks (see Chapter 6). In Chapter 1, we also gave the example where many management fads were difficult to copy in Asia and one reason for this was the strong basis of family ties in businesses (i.e. scoring in column 1 on 'relationships').

The oft-quoted studies by Geert Hofstede (1980) saw the development of a framework of cultural differentiation along four continuums, and Hofstede and Michael Bond (1988) recently added a fifth:

- *Individualism–Collectivism* (that is, is it more important to stand out as an individual, or to be established as a member of a group?);
- *Power distance* (that is, tall societies with the very poor and very rich, and authority structures in which those in authority do not respond to the wishes of those below, are distinct from those egalitarian societies in which many voices are heard and taken into account);
- *Uncertainty avoidance* (that is, need for certainty, risk avoidance, caution);
- *Masculinity–Femininity* (or quantity, measurement, regulation and order as against quality of life, caring, concern with feelings and expression);
- *Long-term–Short-term orientation* (or Confucian dynamism – the ability to pursue long-term and general goals as against short-term gain and advantage).

Managing culture

These dimensions, when related to each other, produced cultural maps of the world which enabled countries to be located relative to each other. This classification has not been without its critics and controversies. Cultural assumptions are very deep, and are expressed in a variety of ways, of which verbal language is just one. Learning to read the other non-verbal languages of culture is an important skill, which international managers of the future must acquire.

These five continuums, for Hofstede, are the assumptions, shared meanings and relativities which underpin social and organizational life in different national cultures and inevitably shape behaviour. In terms of the power distance dimension, we would appreciate power differently, for example, according to whether we lived in a society in which a few people had wealth and influence and many people had little wealth and no influence, or whether we lived in a society in which most people had a good standard of living and a chance to participate in decision making. Our view of knowledge, in terms of what we may know and how we may know it, could vary similarly: high power distance societies often restrict the flow of information from the few to the many, regarding most people as not worthy of knowledge; while low power distance societies are more open and communicative about a variety of matters, regarding most people as having great ability to learn and improve themselves. So the concepts of organizational learning and the learning organization are likely to be highly culturally relative: in Hong Kong, for example, it has been very difficult for researchers to gain access to companies and gather evidence. Cultural differences, as argued especially by Hofstede (1980, 1991), are associated with these forms of power and knowledge and traditional justifications such as membership of certain clans or castes, religious rituals, veneration of ancestors, etc. and are often used to maintain the exclusion of the many from access to knowledge and power. Patriarchs in societies who encourage headship not leadership (see Chapter 5) do not want their employees to learn too much. Similarly, in certain collective cultures with high power distance, where members of certain family groups or tribes have job security, such as parts of the Middle East, there is often little incentive for managers to develop themselves, and initiatives such as total quality management (TQM) have had great difficulty in getting a foothold. Many of the concepts Western businesses use to talk about 'competitiveness', 'efficiency' and 'profitability' are technique driven and ignore the harder aspects of culture, both national and organizational (Negandhi 1986).

These cultural substructures have *expressive forms* in social and organizational institutions like the education system, the property system or the tax system, and are represented in language and symbol. Thinking again of *institutions* in terms of the power distance idea, high power distance societies would tend to have an elitist education system for the children of the wealthy, whereas more egalitarian societies would tend to provide education for all those who were able to benefit. Political systems would usually offer at best a restricted participation in high power distance societies and would more often be dictatorships, even if paternal ones. Low power distance societies would tend to have more participatory, democratic systems. In terms of specific *practices* and behaviours, high power distance societies would have more rules of exclusion restricting individual freedom, more initiation rituals and more taboos, while low power distance societies would have rules conferring individual rights and guaranteeing access to information. Privately, individuals in high power distance societies would tend to have more topics which they would discuss in open conversation, such as religion or politics, whereas in low power distance societies these would often be the subject of popular debate and satirical humour.

Non-verbal artefacts (things, objects, social and organizational arrangements) can carry cultural meaning as well as verbal ones. Hierarchy, as a structure, is a highly significant symbol of life in high power distance societies, and in some societies such as Japan it is necessary for a person to know the exact social level of another one before they can determine the correct way to address them. Position in the hierarchy here carries privilege and respect and requires others to act in a deferential way. In low power distance societies, such as the USA and the UK, hierarchy is regarded more loosely, and in terms of function in the organization not in terms of personal worth, and is less meaningful. To be the managing director of a company in Hong Kong is far more socially significant than being the managing director of a similar company in Huddersfield, Houston, Helsinki or Hyderabad. Societies where place, time, body language, buildings, dress, property and other non-verbal symbols are regarded as important are known as *high-context* societies, where the primary focus is on *who* is speaking rather than the content, and many Asian and Middle Eastern societies fit this description. Western societies, where what people say tends to be taken at face value, are known as *low-context* societies, and here the focus is on *what* is being said rather than on who said it. In a high-context culture, criticism of a speech is seen as criticism of the speaker and as disrespectful; in a low-context culture it is seen as criticism of the words only, and no disrespect is implied. It is very difficult for low-status managers from a low-context culture, where they may have been used to speaking freely in front of the managing director and having their opinions listened to, to move into a high-context culture where they will find themselves ignored and will run the risk of giving great offence to the senior managers there.

Nonetheless, the notion that a unified, homogeneous national culture can adequately explain all patterns of behaviour at the organizational level is subject to questioning. Many studies do not differentiate between national and organizational culture and often treat organizational culture as homogeneous because it exists in a particular country (Tayeb 1988: 41). Even though perceptions of power are heavily influenced by wider cultural influences, Monir Tayeb (1988) suggests that such things as education, age and the seniority of a manager are also likely to affect perceptions of power and these demographics might explain differences found in organizations in similar cultures. National culture does impact strongly at the organizational level in areas such as autonomy and freedom, economic rewards, job expectations and management approaches (Tayeb 1988: Chapters 8 and 9). Attitudes, values and norms relating to autonomy and freedom influence expectations about delegation and hence authority within organizations as well as devolution or the decentralization of such things as decision making. Thus, as previously stated, the extent to which participatory and democratic practices are possible in organizations is largely culture specific. As a result, many management approaches are, according to Tayeb, also strongly related to the national culture. Thus, whether or not egalitarian and democratic management approaches, as opposed to inegalitarian, paternalistic and autocratic ones, are considered appropriate in an organization is largely a by-product of national culture and extremely difficult to change. Formalization, or the degree to which people accept rules, policies and procedures, is also determined to a large extent by national culture and thus impacts more directly on organizational culture. Values relating to privacy and independence of the individual over the group are the key determinants of how much formalization is tolerated in workplaces.

A range of other *societal factors*, such as the labour market composition (e.g. level of skills, levels of employment, degree of unionization, extent of casual versus full-time employees), the industrial relations system (laws covering employment and work conditions, conciliation and arbitration of disputes and union and employer rights) and the class system of a country (e.g. how wealth and opportunities for social mobility are distributed) also affect how organizations operate and the cultures in them. These are often referred to as *institutional factors*. Commitment and trust of employees by management, for example, are two particularly important aspects of organizations that can also be heavily influenced by such things as the labour market and industrial relations systems within countries (Tayeb 1988: Chapters 8 and 9). Other *national factors*, such as the economic system (e.g. capitalist, socialist, mixed economy, closed economy), systems of government (e.g. elected, dictatorship) and the legal system (e.g. nature of civil and commercial law) also affect certain work practices and the cultures of organizations. Both the social and national factors are embedded in national cultures, but they are often more easily changed or manipulated than widely held attitudes and values (see Fulop 1992: 361–9). For many years Japanese companies offered such things as life-time employment, which many observers attributed to something paternal or clan-like in the culture of Japan, and hence its organizations. Yet when hard economic times arose these practices were quickly questioned and ceased in many large companies (Fulop 1992: 367).

At the organizational level, a number of other factors called *contingency variables* also influence the type of organizational structure and culture that might emerge. Thus the size of an organization might mean that larger organizations tend to be more bureaucratic and therefore centralized, no matter where they might be located. The markets organizations enter are likely to influence how they practise management; for example, many Japanese 'transplant' companies in the car industry have had to modify their management practices to operate in countries such as Australia, the USA and the UK. Technologies can also influence how organizations develop their management practices, for example, certain computer technologies, mass production and assembly methods produce similar problems across a range of countries irrespective of national culture. It is no surprise to realize that core aspects of Scientific Management were adopted in many parts of the world. The ownership of the company or business (e.g. shareholders versus owner managers) can affect the degree of centralization and hierarchy in organizations, probably more than national culture (Tayeb 1988: Chapters 8 and 9).

The culture of one organization may be a weave of subcultures or multicultures, over-crossed by a variety of external cultural, social, national and contingency factors. Culture, structure and strategy are not separate 'variables', as some theorists might wish to argue, but rather need to be seen as inseparable and treated holistically as suggested by Bate and Anthony. Because culture is not an 'independent' variable, you cannot change structure or strategy without affecting culture.

Gender and culture

Talk is an important part of culture. Therefore, if men and women communicate differently we might anticipate differences in the kinds of cultures which develop where one or the other is dominant. We might also expect that the way people are customarily required to communicate will make it easier for one or the other gender to become successful in that culture. Men and women have never been viewed as, or treated as, equals in the workplace. Jobs have been differentiated and even whole occupations, especially those in service industries, have been designated 'women's work'. As we saw in Chapter 2, fewer than 20 percent of all managerial posts are held by women, and at more senior levels this falls to 10 percent. Men are often seen to be rational, calculating and resilient whereas women are seen as being emotional, changeable and lacking resolution. This forms the background to what men and women do in any real organization, but Deborah Tannen (1990) indicates that men and women actually talk differently and thus communicate different things when they speak. As Tannen (1990) argues, women tend to learn styles of speaking which make them appear less confident and self-assured than they really are, and as a result they lose out on those organizational issues – like promotion – that depend on appearing confident. Women tend to say 'we' rather than 'I' when discussing work, and as a result get less credit for what they do. They tend to boast less, and ask more questions which can often make them seem less sure of themselves. Women downplay their certainty while men minimize their doubts. Men are more likely to save their own face in a problem situation. Above all, powerful people, which usually means men, are more likely to reward people with similar language styles to their own.

To give another example, a New York psychiatrist in the mid-1980s joined one of the earliest Internet chat groups in order to try to develop a new way of counselling and helping people. He chose as his name 'Doctor', which he had not fully realized was gender neutral. One day he was chatting in a side room with a woman and he realized that she had thought that he too was female. He was astonished by the richness and openness of the communication that he was receiving and assumed that this was the way women talked to each other. As a result, he created a false identity for himself, an easy thing to do on the Internet, as a woman. He was able to build some very loyal friendships in this way and helped many people, but he wearied of the strain of constantly having to be someone else, and so he joined the group under his own identity, his female alter ego introducing him as a great guy and a lovely person, a fine doctor, etc. He hoped that he would build relationships with all his friends and the female alter ego could disappear from the picture. Unfortunately, none of his friends from his other identity could get along with him when he was being himself, and they found him stiff and a bit cold! As a man, he could not communicate in the same way – they did not expect it and were unreceptive to it – and they did not communicate with him in the same manner either (Stone 1995: 63–87).

So what you say and how you say it are different depending on your gender, and this may both open and close doors to you depending on your gender's position within the organization's culture. Of course an organization which only rewards one communicative style is losing its ability to hear a wide range of information and increase the flexibility of its actions, but it does not stop there. As Silvia Gherardi (1995) notes, organizations tend to write stories for their participants, with gendered roles for women to play. She identifies six discursive positions that were offered to or imposed on women in her studies, in which men were basically either friendly or hostile, when women's position was either accepted, contested or imposed (see Table 3.3).

Women could be accepted in a friendly manner, as a guest, treated pleasantly, but politely circumscribed and not allowed to be a 'real' member of the culture like the men were. Gherardi's respondent, Giovanna, tells us:

Table 3.3 *Gherardi's classification of women's cultural positioning*

| | Women's reciprocal positioning | | |
Male positioning	Accepted	Contested	Imposed
Friendly	*The guest* A cooperative position	*The holidaymaker* A mismatched position	*The newcomer* An open-ended position
Hostile	*The marginal* A stigmatized position	*The snake in the grass* A contested position	*The intruder* A unilaterally imposed position

Source: Silvia Gherardi (1995), *Gender, Symbolism and Organizational Cultures*, London: Sage, p. 109.

I felt as if I was a guest. Just as a guest is placed at the head of a table, treated politely, and never allowed to wash the dishes, so I was surrounded by a web of polite but invisible restraints. I began to suspect something when I saw the other women when they arrived and were, so to speak, 'integrated'. For example, I almost never go into the production department to talk with the workers. My older male colleagues go because they like it. They go and see their friends, and then they pretend that they are protecting me from the 'uncouthness of the working class'. So I find myself constantly on the phone dealing with the editorial office, the commercial office, the administration. I'm almost always in the office. *It's as if I'm at home and they're always out.* It's true that they are better at what they do, and I'm better at what I do, or we women are, but constantly being their guest is getting me down (Gherardi 1995: 110–11, emphasis added).

We might recall the argument of Marta Calás and Linda Smircich in the last chapter on how women are being used to domesticate the workforce and free-up males for international assignments, apparently because of women's greater interpersonal and caring skills. It is part of the permanent guest role that women are being asked to play. However, things could be more unpleasant if the males were hostile. Gherardi's respondent, Fiorella, tells of her experience of being marginalized:

I felt I'd become invisible, I thought I was transparent. There's no point in recounting individual episodes or blaming things on hostility. Formally, everything was as it should be, and they treated me politely, like gentlemen, but I counted for nothing. I discovered this little by little and it was tough admitting it to myself. What had I got to complain about? The situations were quite clear, the solutions were reasonable, indeed they were the only ones feasible. Everything was already decided and all I had to do was agree and implement. There was no need to open my mouth at meetings. I realised I had been pushed to one side even though my expertise was publicly praised (Gherardi 1995: 112).

These kinds of examples show how limited by organizational culture the equal opportunities and positive discrimination approaches can be. Nothing was done wrong in either of these situations, and the men were reasonable, polite and even gentlemanly. However, the women were 'second-class citizens', and powerless.

In Gherardi's other examples, the positions are more uncomfortable. If the woman is in the *holidaymaker* position, then everyone else is just waiting for her to move on, nothing really changes, and they all make contingency plans behind her back; if seen as a *snake in the grass* then they plot to get rid of her and make her fail; if seen as a *newcomer* then they reserve judgement, for long periods of time, are anxious and make it hard to get commitments to projects and participation in processes; and if seen as an *intruder*, she will be constantly openly challenged. Many of these categories could apply to men in some situations, but the question is clearly one of degree – women start off by being *other* whereas men at the very least receive the benefit of the doubt, and the 'testing' of a new male appointee is not likely to last for years but to be resolved fairly quickly. The feeling of being trapped by invisible nets is a typical indicator that the problem is cultural, and making these invisible nets visible is difficult particularly when the 'nets' are often constructed and enacted by those with the power to change the situation.

Conclusion

Let us take a look at the questions we raised on the case study in the light of our discussion.

First, does company T have a *shared culture*? The answer here is broadly 'yes'. Although many people declare themselves unhappy with it, because of the 'sink or swim' nature of the culture, they go along with it and play the game. One feature of culture is that if a culture is shared this does not mean it is shared *equally* – not everyone will believe in it to the same extent, some may be enthusiastic, some may hate it, some just comply. The culture, however, is not one which unites them behind a collective objective – the shared culture is a divisive one of every shift/department for itself.

Second, is company T a *'strong' culture*? The answer here is again 'yes'. It is not a positive one in the sense that the literature talks about companies like McDonald's, Hewlett-Packard, Marks and Spencer, Ben and Jerry's, of which commitment, dedication and love of the company are hallmarks, and few people seem to be having fun, but it is one which quickly sanctions those who are not part of it. You suffer if you do not play the game. It is also very explicit and dramatic, but the performances are not formally staged on occasions – people do the 'staging' on an everyday basis, which suggests that the behaviour is habitual and ingrained and will consequently be hard to shift.

What are the *problems of the culture*? Well first of all, it is divisive and defensive. It sets sections up against each other and produces senseless internal competition. Managers try to look good and cover up problems, and no one is working towards a mutual goal or goals. The lying, cheating and stealing means that the organization has systems and procedures that do not work and those new managers who try to follow them end up failing. The organization is not getting the information it needs passed up the hierarchy, and as a result it cannot be a learning organization. Development will be difficult, if not impossible. At an individual level, the 2×4 culture makes people anxious, perhaps bitter, but certainly risk averse. Fear is the worst climate for creativity and problem solving. In addition, although there is no evidence on the gender balance of the company, it would appear to have a masculinist culture, which would affect the potential benefits to be gained from a greater diversity of approaches.

Finally, *can the company be changed*? Well, any culture can be changed given time. The consultants in this case worked with key managers at an interpersonal level, exploring with them the problems they were facing and the effects of the culture, and tried to get them to change their behaviour. This was not always easy for them – people who have been 'beaten up' every day have a tendency to miss the beatings when they stop and crave the structure that the old ways gave them. Additionally, any change produces a period of mourning for the old way before the new behaviour is internalized, and so plenty of support and reinforcement is necessary. However, managers involved in this type of individual change can provide mutual support for each other. It is also essential in opening up channels of communication. At the right time, top-down support will also be an important reinforcement, especially if changes in structure and procedure are complementary to and require changes in behaviour. So change will be difficult, but it is possible given effort across a range of mutually supporting areas.

Let us now revisit our questions on culture at the beginning of the chapter.

1 What is organizational culture? What is it good for?

Organizational culture is a complex phenomenon, usually related to shared values and shared meanings in an organization, but also related to common ways of dealing with, or ignoring, commonly experienced problems. It is a form of commonsense, an outcome of cultural processes at work in a particular setting. The benefits of paying attention to culture are that it focuses on people but in particular on the symbolic significance of almost every aspect of organizational life. It emphasizes shared meanings, even if implicit, and alerts us to the influencing potential of values, beliefs, ideology, language, norms, ceremonies, rituals, myths and stories. It constructs leaders as shapers of meaning. It also emphasizes the importance of communication and learning; it emphasizes the importance of how others perceive us; and it alerts us to the fact that organizational environments are also socially constructed.

2 Are companies with strong cultures always successful?

No! Strong cultures can be a barrier to change if they are negative cultures, but, even so, with the happiest, most creative culture there are still other factors that can frustrate performance, such as the economic climate and competitive situation, that are out of the organization's control.

3 What are the dysfunctions of culture?

Culture tends to select and socialize people who are alike, and so often there is a lack of diversity and critical thinking in strong cultures, and the tendency to stick to old recipes even when things change. There can be a focus on the emotional and non-rational to the extent that simple but important technicalities – like structural arrangements, inventory control or quantitative analysis of the market – can be neglected.

4 What are subcultures, and are they healthy?

Subcultures are groups of people who are part of a wider group, subscribing to the overall culture but with some distinctly different values of their own. Large companies will certainly have many of these; sometimes they will be associated with functions – marketing, maintenance, etc. – or with professions – engineering, legal, accounting. But they can occur in companies even of small size and may not be related to any company features. They can be a source of creativity or a source of division and destructive conflict, depending on the nature of their values and how they differ from those of the rest of the company.

5 How is organizational culture related to national culture?

Organizational culture is often influenced by the background culture in which it is located, sometimes explicitly. Indeed, British Airways has recently removed the British flag from the tailplanes of its jets and replaced it with a variety of different ethnic tailplane designs to reflect the diversity of its business and its increasingly global culture – or at least, to give that impression. There are several deep-lying assumptions about the world, which are characteristic of different national cultures and affect the ways in which people habitually think, and orient them towards particular organizational preferences. However, these assumptions are not intractable, although it should not be assumed that they can be easily changed or set aside. Culture is a complex concept and other variables such as national and contingency ones need to be considered when trying to make sense of organizational cultures and subcultures.

References

Adler, N. (1991) *International Dimensions of Organizational Behavior*, Boston: PWS-Kent.

Aktouf, O. (1996) 'Competence, symbolic activity and promotability', in Linstead, S., Grafton Small, R. and Jeffcutt, P. (eds), *Understanding Management*, London: Sage.

Anthony, P. (1994) *Managing Culture*, Buckingham: Open University Press.

Argyris, C. (1964) *Integrating the Individual and the Organization*, New York: John Wiley.

Barney, J. (1986) 'Organizational culture: Can it be a source of sustained competitive advantage?', *Academy of Management Review* 2(3): 656–65.

Bate, S.P. (1994) *Strategies for Cultural Change*, London: Butterworth Heinemann.

Bedi, H. (1991) *Understanding the Asian Manager*, Sydney: Allen & Unwin.

Benveniste, G. (1987) *Professionalizing the Organization*, San Francisco: Jossey-Bass.

Boje, D.M. and Winsor, R.D. (1993) 'The resurrection of Taylorism: Total quality management's hidden agenda', *Journal of Organizational Change Management* 6(4): 57–70.

Bovens, M. (1992) 'Conflicting loyalties: Ethical pluralism in administrative life', paper presented at the First International Productivity Network Conference, 21–24 July, Canberra, Australia.

Brown, A. (1995) *Organizational Culture*, London: Pitman.

Carlzon, J. (1987) *Moments of Truth*, New York: Harper and Row.

Deal, T.E. and Kennedy, A.A. (1982) *Corporate Cultures: The Rites and Rituals of Corporate Life*, New York: Addison-Wesley.

Deal, T.E. and Kennedy, A.A. (1988) *Corporate Cultures: The Rites and Rituals of Corporate Life*, London: Penguin.

Drennan, D. (1992) *Transforming Company Culture*, London: McGraw-Hill.

Eastman, C. and Fulop, L. (1997) 'Management for clinicians or the case of "bringing the mountain to Mohammed"', *International Journal of Production Economics* 52: 15–30.

Eldridge, J.E.T. and Crombie, A.D. (1974) *A Sociology of Organizations*, London: Allen & Unwin.

Feldman, S. (1996) 'Management in context: Culture and organizational change', in Linstead, S., Grafton Small, R. and Jeffcutt, P. (eds), *Understanding Management*, London: Sage.

Flam, H. (1993) 'Fear, loyalty and greedy organizations', in Fineman, S. (ed.), *Emotion in Organizations*, London: Sage.

Fulop, L. (1992) 'Management in the international context', in Fulop, L., Frith, F. and Hayward, H. (eds), *Management for Australian Business: A Critical Text*, Melbourne: Macmillan.

Garfinkel, H. (1984) *Studies in Ethnomethodology*, Cambridge: Polity Press (original 1967).

Gherardi, S. (1995) *Gender, Symbolism and Organizational Cultures*, London: Sage.

Gouldner, A. (1954) *Patterns of Industrial Bureaucracy*, New York: The Free Press.

Gouldner, A. (1955) *Wildcat Strike*, London: Routledge and Kegan Paul.

Graves, D. (1986) *Corporate Culture: Diagrams and Change*, New York: St Martins Press.

Guest, D. (1992) 'Right enough to be dangerously wrong: An analysis of the "In Search of Excellence" phenomenon', in Salaman, G. (ed.), *Human Resource Strategies*, London: Sage.

Hall, E. (1959) *The Silent Language*, New York: Doubleday.

Hampden-Turner, C. (1990) *Corporate Culture: From Vicious to Virtuous Circles,* London: Economist Books/Hutchinson.

Handy, C. (1993) *Understanding Organizations,* London: Penguin.

Harrison, R. (1972) 'How to describe your organization', *Harvard Business Review* 50(3): 119–28.

Hochschild, A.R. (1983) *The Managed Heart,* Berkeley: University of California Press.

Hofstede, G. (1980) *Culture's Consequences: International Differences in Work-Related Values,* London: Sage.

Hofstede, G. (1991) *Cultures and Organizations,* London: HarperCollins.

Hofstede, G. and Bond, M.H. (1988) 'The Confucian connection: From cultural roots to economic growth', *Organizational Dynamics* 16(4): 4–21.

Höpfl, H. (1996) 'Authority and the pursuit of order in organizational performance', in Jeffcutt, P., Grafton Small, R. and Linstead, S. (eds), *Organization and Theatre,* special issue of *Studies in Cultures, Organizations, and Societies* 2(1): 67–80.

Humes, S. (1993) *Managing the Multinational: Confronting the Global–Local Dilemma,* New York: Prentice Hall.

Jaques, E. (1952) *The Changing Culture of a Factory,* New York: Dryden Press.

Johnson, G. (1989) 'The Burton Group (B)', in Johnson, G. and Scholes, K. (eds), *Exploring Corporate Strategy,* London: Prentice Hall.

Johnson, G. (1992) 'Managing strategic change – strategy, culture and action', *Long Range Planning* 25(1): 28–36.

Kakabadse, A., Ludlow, R. and Vinnicombe, S. (1988) *Working in Organizations,* London: Penguin.

Kirkbride, P.S. (1983) 'Power in the workplace', unpublished PhD thesis, University of Bath, UK.

Kluckhohn, F.R. and Strodtbeck, F.L. (1961) *Variations in Value Orientations,* Evanston, Illinois: Row, Peterson and Co.

Linstead, S.A. and Grafton Small, R. (1992) 'On reading organizational culture', *Organization Studies* 13(3): 331–55.

Lorsch, J. (1986) 'Managing culture: The invisible barrier to strategic change', *California Management Review* 28(2): 95–109.

Louis, M.R. (1980) 'Organizations as culture-bearing milieux', in Pondy, L.R., Frost, P.J., Morgan, G. and Dandridge, T.C. (eds), *Organizational Symbolism,* Greenwich, Conn.: JAI Press.

Negandhi, A.R. (1986) 'Three decades of cross-cultural management research', in Clegg, S.R., Dunphy, D.C. and Redding, S.G. (eds), *The Enterprise and Management in South-East Asia,* Hong Kong: Centre for Asian Studies, University of Hong Kong.

Olila, J. (1995) 'Corporate anthropology and organizational change', unpublished working paper, Erasmus University, Rotterdam.

Pacanowsky, M.E. and O'Donnell-Trujillo, N. (1982) 'Communication and organizational culture', *The Western Journal of Speech and Communication* 46 (Spring): 115–30.

Pascale, R.T. and Athos, A.G. (1980) *The Art of Japanese Management,* London: Penguin.

Pauchant, T. and Mitroff, I. (1988) 'Crisis prone versus crisis avoiding organizations: Is your company's culture its own worst enemy in creating crisis?', *Industrial Crisis Quarterly* 2: 53–63.

Peters, T. and Waterman, R.H. (1982) *In Search of Excellence,* New York: Harper and Row.

Pfeffer, J. (1981) 'Management as symbolic action: The creation and maintenance of organizational paradigms', in Cummings, L.L. and Staw, B. (eds), *Research in Organizational Behaviour* 3(1): 1–52.

Pool, R. (1997) 'When failure is not an option', *Technology Review* July: 38–45.

Ray, C.A. (1986) 'Corporate culture: The last frontier of control?', *Journal of Management Studies* 23(3): 287–98.

Ritzer, G. (1990) *The McDonaldization of Society,* Thousand Oaks: Pine Forge Press.

Schein, E. (1985) *Organizational Culture and Leadership,* San Francisco: Jossey-Bass.

Schwartz, H. (1990) *Narcissistic Process and Corporate Decay,* New York: NYU Press.

Schwartz, H. and Davis, S.M. (1981) 'Matching corporate culture and business strategy', *Organizational Dynamics* 10: 30–48.

Sinclair, A. (1991) 'After excellence: Models of organisational culture for the public sector', *Australian Journal of Public Administration* 50(3): 321–32.

Smircich, L. (1983) 'Concepts of culture and organizational analysis', *Administrative Science Quarterly* 28(3): 339–58.

Smircich, L. and Morgan, G. (1982) 'Leadership: the management of meaning', *Journal of Applied Behavioural Science* 18(2): 257–73.

Smith, S. and Wilkinson, B. (1996) ' No doors on offices, no secrets: We are our own policemen: Capitalism without conflict?', in Linstead, S., Grafton Small, R. and Jeffcutt, P. (eds), *Understanding Management,* London: Sage.

Stone, A.R. (1995) *The War of Desire and Technology at the Close of the Mechanical Age,* Boston: MIT Press.

Strauss, A., Schatzman, L., Ehrlich, D., Bucher, R. and Sabshin, M. (1963) 'The hospital and its negotiated order', in Friedson, E. (ed.), *The Hospital in Modern Society,* New York: Macmillan.

Tannen, D. (1990) *You Just Don't Understand: Men and Women in Conversation,* New York: William Morrow.

Tayeb, M.H. (1988) *Organisations and National Culture,* London: Sage.

Torrington, D. (1994) *International Human Resource Management,* New York: Prentice Hall.

Turner, B.A. (1971) *Exploring the Industrial Sub-Culture,* London: Macmillan.

Van Maanen, J. (1991) 'The Smile Factory: Work at Disneyland', in Frost, P., Moore, L.F., Louis, M.R., Lundberg, C.C. and Martin, J. (eds), *Reframing Organizational Culture,* Newbury Park, CA: Sage.

Walsh, J. (1997) ' BA hopes to clear air with top-flight moves', *People Management* 23 (October): 11.

Weber, M. (1964) *The Theory of Social Economic Organizations,* London: Heinemann.

Westley, F.R. (1990) 'The eye of the needle: Cultural and personal transformation in a traditional organization', *Human Relations* 43(3): 273–93.

Westwood, R. (1992) *Organizational Behaviour,* Hong Kong: Longmans.

Willmott, H. (1991) 'Strength is ignorance; slavery is freedom: Managing culture in modern organizations', *Journal of Management Studies* 30(4): 515–52.

Young, D. (1989) 'British Airways: Putting the customer first', unpublished paper, Ashridge Strategic Management Centre, Ashridge Management College, UK.

Young, E. (1989) 'On the Naming of the Rose: Interests and multiple meanings as elements of organizational culture', *Organization Studies* 10(2): 187–206.

4

Power and politics in organizations

Liz Fulop, Stephen Linstead and Faye Frith

Questions about organizational power and politics

1 Are power and politics generic to all organizations?
2 Do some circumstances, more than others, give rise to power struggles and politics in organizations?
3 Why is power such a difficult thing to deal with in organizations?
4 Is everyone able to gain or exercise power in organizations?

As with the previous chapters, we begin with a case study that sets the scene for discussing power and politics in organizations. The case study in this chapter is presented in two parts.

Fawley Ridge

In the UK in the late 1980s, many polytechnics were about to become universities, of which Fairisle Polytechnic was one. At this time, however, they were still under the control of local authorities and they still provided non-advanced further education (NAFE) course – work of sub-degree standard. It was becoming clear that this level of work was regarded by the government as the province of the local authority institutions. It would only be left in the hands of the new universities if there was no alternative local provider, and in Fairisle there were several competent others. It followed that any site which was designated a NAFE site by the Asset Commission would revert to the local authority when they decided on the terms of separation, i.e. 'divorce and alimony'. Fairisle currently occupied as one of its many sites a campus at Fawley Ridge, an area of prime residential land, rapidly appreciating in value and conservatively estimated to be worth at contemporary prices around £1.5 million as a piece of land alone. The new university would need such an asset given its desperate need for building space – but the site was almost exclusively NAFE, being devoted to evening classes in a huge range of languages and providing daytime courses for local business people. Only the highest level of linguistic qualification offered was regarded officially as being 'advanced' for funding purposes – and this was only 5 percent of the total workload.

In that period, a new Director, Paul Kost, had taken over the reins of the polytechnic, which held some very specific challenges. Kost was considered an outstanding candidate for the directorship: he had contacts in government on all sides, had a thorough understanding of parliamentary procedure and committee work, and he had an almost uncanny ability to pre-empt ministers and government policy. Personally, he was a brilliant public speaker, an erudite and charming host and chairman, but was also blunt and ruthless once he made a decision. Kost inherited a structure of what was basically 16 baronial fiefdoms or empires with several scandalous situations – financial and academic – ready to explode.

Fairisle Polytechnic, on Kost's accession, was an inappropriate organizational structure with inadequate financial accountability, inadequate monitoring of quality, inappropriate physical accommodation, underperformance in research, and staff who were highly unionized and politicized and who had tried to resist the squeezing of resources.

Kost set about structural change by grouping departments into faculties, combined some of them, removed many of the 16 heads and forced others to reapply for their posts. Deans were created by external and internal appointments. The new heads were charged with two missions – to scour out the corruption of the old guard, and to identify any slack or underperformance in teaching commitments, supervision, research or quality monitoring. They were required to suspect everything and trust no one. Kost removed some deputy directors, created new heads who were his political affiliates and, with no constituency in the academic community, were entirely accountable to the Director.

Derek Elliott was appointed as Head of the Department of Continental Management. He was relatively young at 35 to be a head, but he was experienced in course administration and also had a good publications record. The department was a product of Kost's restructuring efforts. Elliott was politically astute, but also had a personal commitment to managing in an open way, with a 'light hand on the tiller'.

Early in his tenure at Fawley Ridge, the Director told Derek that the site was out of financial control with earnings not being properly accounted for to the centre, and the only way to get on top of this was to remove Cyril Lancashire, the lecturer-in-charge, to whom many of the staff felt a strong allegiance. Cyril was close to retirement age and it was not difficult for Derek to persuade him to accept the Director's offer of leaving early, but Derek felt uneasy about the rationale. He had found the affairs of the centre to be entirely proper; Cyril to be honest and well intentioned and staff to be dedicated. The Director did not see it that way and needed to be clearly in control of Fawley Ridge and therefore Cyril Lancashire had to be removed. The staff were, however, devoted to Cyril and were hurt by the way they perceived him being treated.

Despite his feelings about this incident, Derek intended to try to manage according to his principles. As part of his policy of openness and involvement in strategic planning, Derek had begun to discuss possible futures and priorities with his staff on all the three sites on which the department operated. After talking to his six full-time staff at Fawley Ridge, however, a disaster occurred. Derek had asked them to consider several 'what if' scenarios, including possible closure of some courses; by the time this leaked 'along the grapevine', it became a story that the polytechnic was to close the site. One of the students, a newspaper reporter, published this story and Derek found himself sitting facing an angry public meeting with the Dean, the Director and 300 irate students.

Kost was brilliant in his handling of an explosive situation and chose not to deny that closure was a possibility and suggested that it was a threat because of government policy. He suggested that the students should organize a political lobby, and the polytechnic would support them. He was cheered to the echo at the end of the meeting.

However, there was a ground swell of resentment building up. Shortly after this incident, Kost attempted to acquire a building from the Textile Industry Association (TIA), which would mean students would have to move to a different site for classes. The students, who had not been consulted, mounted a very effective campaign of demonstrations and slogans and leaflets – eventually the TIA pulled out of the deal.

At this point, Derek, the Head of the Department which occupied the site as one of its three subdivisions, was called in to the Director's office with William Fisher, the Deputy Director. The position was outlined. Space in the polytechnic was at a premium. Fawley Ridge was a valuable property which under present usage the new university would lose after vesting day. It was imperative that the property be safeguarded by bringing its usage for advanced (degree or equivalent level) work up to over 60 percent. The only viable proposition would be to transfer the Languages and Business degree (for which Derek's department was responsible), library holdings, support staff and language labs over to the Fawley site. Students would have to be bused six miles for their classes, after a three-mile journey for most of them to reach the present departmental HQ site, Shaw's Park, from which they would have to leave, Fawley being so inaccessible. Derek looked glum. The Director reassured him somewhat hollowly, 'We haven't made the decision yet. If anything emerges that clearly indicates that this will damage the quality of education of the students we won't – we daren't – do it. The whole situation is very delicate as I'm sure you appreciate. But everything else is negotiable. Work closely with William and see what you can do – at this point it's our only option.'

Source: Adapted from Stephen Linstead (1997), 'Resistance and return: Power, command and change management', Studies in Cultures, Organizations and Societies 3(1), pp. 67–89.

Questions about the case

1   Who has power in this situation?
2   What are the sources of their power?
3   What kind of power is it?
4   What are the conflicts of interest, and how would you expect people to behave as a result?

Attempt to answer these questions before you read the chapter.

Introduction

Power is an indisputable part of everyday life, a feature of every type of social relationship imaginable, and probably one of the most widely discussed phenomena in organizations. Nothing is more certain than that every individual will experience various aspects of it in their work life. By virtue of participating in an organization, individuals are automatically placed in potential power struggles. There are many examples of such situations: strikes over redundancy payments; equal employment opportunity policies; noisy or dirty facilities; size of offices; titles given to positions; patronage and preferential treatment; nepotism and favouritism; closures and relocations, etc. Power is experienced, interpreted and dealt with differently by each individual or group.

Power is an extremely complex and important phenomenon for managers to understand. Power and influence are sought-after 'prizes', even though managers may be reluctant to admit that they operate politically, and thus fail to understand fully the importance of managing this relational aspect of organizations.

Organizations in their various forms, and particularly in hierarchies such as universities and large corporations, tend to reproduce a structure of command, although not absolute command, that creates many sources of discontent and resistance. Hierarchical organizations are structures of difference in which those at the top speak both *for* and *to* those below. Organizations are also structures of desire or aspirations, as those below seek to rise in the hierarchy in order to receive deference themselves in some small way. All too often, those who rise in the hierarchy pass on the unpleasantnesses associated with being exclusively subjected to command without having anyone to whom they can give command. Indeed it is the deference relationships that produce the key relational problems in organizations and give rise to power struggles and organizational politicking.

The chapter reviews four main approaches to power: the unitary, pluralist, radical and relational approaches. Diverse ideas and perspectives are apparent in each approach, but by far the most popular approaches in management discourse have been the unitary and pluralist views.

Approaches to power

The dominant approaches to power have all emphasized behaviour and its outcomes. Steven Lukes's (1974) work is a classic in the field. He identified three 'dimensions' of power, to which recent commentators (e.g. Burrell 1988, Clegg 1989 and Knights and Vurdubakis 1994) have added, *de facto*, a fourth. Cynthia Hardy (1994) was one of the first theorists to explicitly develop a fourth dimension. Lukes integrated three dominant views of power and he termed these the one-, two- and three-dimensional views of power. Table 4.1 provides a summary of the four views of power.

Following Lukes, a *one-dimensional* view of power, the behavioural view (exemplified by Robert Dahl 1957), takes a focus on behaviour in the making of decisions over which there is overt conflict of interests. In other words, A has the power to get B to do something B would not otherwise do. A *two-dimensional* perspective, incorporating the non-decision-making view as taken by Peter Bacharach and Morton Baratz (1962), involves the consideration of ways in which decisions are prevented from being taken on potential issues over which there is observable conflict of interests. In other words, A prevents B from realizing that B has a problem, through deception, trickery and other illegitimate tactics, and thus B continues or begins to do what they would not otherwise do. If B had been given the information or the opportunity to raise issues and be party to discussions, instead of being duped, B might act differently. The second dimension of power is considered more fully in Chapter 8, which is on decision making.

Table 4.1 Four views of power

	Description	Focus	Critique	Theorists	Image
One dimensional	The behavioural view	Decision-making behaviour. Overt conflict (observable). Subjective (perceived) *interests* seen as policy preferences revealed in political *participation*.	Of 'grand theories' of power in political economy – focuses on overt *action*. Power is *exercised*.	Dahl	Power is like a *hammer* hitting a nail.
Two dimensional	The political view	Includes *non-decision making*. How potential issues are avoided. How conflict is avoided. Interests manifest as policy preferences or grievances.	Qualified critique of behaviour adds focus on *inaction*. Negative behaviour and resistance are the focus. Power can be felt though *not exercised*.	Bacharach and Baratz	It is possible to hide the nails or the hammer and still 'hit' the nail.
Three dimensional	The radical structural view	The *dominant* are in control of socialization processes and political agendas. They control how issues are defined because of common *ideology* and *beliefs*. Conflict can be *latent* because unconscious *real* interests differ from *subjective* ones – manipulation and influence used to control and suppress interests of certain groups.	Of behavioural focus, insists on importance of *social structure* and *ideology*. False consciousness, management of meaning, unobtrusive control.	Lukes	Power is like a dark *building* through which we must move.
Four dimensional	The relational view	*Power* is involved in everything we do – always implies *resistance*. Not only the dominant are powerful, it is *relational*. Conflict is *relative*. Issues are defined by *discourses* which shape knowledge. 'Discourse' includes *locally* variable contexts, practices, institutions, techniques, etc.	Of *structure* – looks at how *power* depends on *knowledge*, but also influences how *knowledge* is formed. Power is a capillary *force*, moving *everywhere* and not the property of so-called dominant groups.	Foucault	Power is everywhere, moving through a *crowd* – sometimes chaotic, like a carnival, sometimes coordinated, like a 'Mexican Wave' at the sports ground.

The third of these dimensions, the *radical structural view* of Lukes himself, is that power includes the power to determine decisive socialization processes, and therefore the power to produce reality. In other words, A educates and persuades B to accept their role in the order of things, and not to perceive any conflict of interest. In organizations, and in a much reduced form, this is close to the 'management of meaning' approach to leadership and organizational culture (Anthony 1994) mentioned in Chapter 3. In criticizing the behavioural and political approaches in general, the radical or third-dimensional view of power draws attention to the unobtrusive, but nonetheless insidious methods of control used in organizations to ensure that power, authority and control remain in the hands of managerial groups who represent dominant interests such as capital (Clegg and Dunkerley 1980: 197–8).

Extending Lukes's analysis, the fourth view of power could be called the *relational view*. Power in this view exists not as a property of A or B, but as a quality of the relationship between them. Each is empowered in certain ways, each limited in others, by the relationship. Both master and slave, for example, are constrained to behave in particular ways by the roles assigned to them and neither can escape these encumbrances without difficulty nor afford to take them lightly. Thus rather than seeing power as held by the powerful and exercised to enforce conformity among the powerless, it is more instructive to attend to 'those contextually specific practices, techniques, procedures, forms of knowledge routinely developed in attempts to shape the conduct of others' (Knights and Vurdubakis 1994: 174; Hardy 1994; Buchanan and Badham 1998: 173–5). In this chapter we focus on the relational aspects of power but leave the more detailed analysis of discourse until Chapter 8.

While the above present very specific sociological views of power, other perspectives have been put forward in management theory, such as the unitary and pluralist views of power, empowerment, and the political organization. Both the unitary and pluralist views of power have dominated the management literature. Lukes's work became a benchmark for critiquing both these views of power, especially his radical view of power. Unitary and pluralist views of power are usually covered by Lukes's first dimension of power (Hardy and Leiba-O'Sullivan 1998: 461). Considering the fourth dimension of power introduces a more reflexive view of power that focuses on its relational aspects.

Unitary approaches to power and authority

A unitary framework presents management's authority as being relatively automatic, its legitimacy sanctioned through hierarchical relations, rules and procedures within an organization. In the unitary approach, the exercise of power is seen negatively and is associated with force, coercion and threats. The unitary (or rational) organization is one in which managers emphasize the importance of common goals and purposes. It is presumed that those at the top of the hierarchy have the right to make all the critical decisions and that the authority to do this is vested in the position and office of senior management. Contractual agreements bind everyone to the principle of 'a fair day's work for a fair day's pay'. The goals of profitability and efficiency are the same for all, and the contract of employment binds subordinates to a common managerial purpose. Titles, formal lines of communication, organizational charts, contracts, rules and policies all vest authority in management and its prerogative flows from this. Power has no place in the unitary or rational organization.

Authority prevails. Overt power struggles are symptoms of a breakdown of authority relationships and the stability that the organization is designed to achieve (Velasquez 1988: 303–5). They signal a potential challenge to management's authority and their right to exercise absolute control in the interest of maintaining concerted action(s) to achieve organizational goals (Forster and Browne 1996: 139).

Even Max Weber, whose theory of bureaucracy contained a very complex view of authority, left no doubt that power was a pervasive force in any organization. Weber's notion of rational–legal authority stated that authority was not automatically accepted by individuals but had to be legitimated (Weber 1964: 124, 152–3, 324–9). By legitimation, he meant the execution of rules or orders in such a way that those in organizations believed that orders or commands issued were binding on them and desirable to imitate or follow. Nevertheless, Weber was not advocating that those in command had automatic authority, but rather that there were conditions and rules that had to be adhered to in order to maintain authority. Once a leader legitimated his or her authority, Weber believed this would be mirrored in the followers' willingness to carry out the leader's orders or commands with compliance. Weber clearly recognized the potential for power struggles in his own theory of bureaucracy, especially in the role of professional experts and seasoned bureaucrats. Weber's focus was principally on how public sector organizations created and maintained the authority relations between politicians and bureaucrats. So while Weber dealt with authority, it was not within a unitary approach (see Fulop 1992: Chapter 6).

The concept of authority, as subscribed to in the unitary approach, is strongly bound up with notions of obedience, trust, mutual respect, paternalism, discipline, command and control. Many approaches to leadership have unitary assumptions. For example, Douglas McGregor's (1960) famous Theory X model of leadership (described in Chapter 5) captures one dimension of the unitary view of authority: its coercive, disciplinary, forcing, policing and punishment aspects. His Theory Y model, by contrast, focuses on the manipulative and cajoling approach to leadership. Even though McGregor advocated participatory practices under Theory Y, the use of more subtle forms of control, and a more 'velvet glove' approach to authority, he still maintained that the exercise of authority was the absolute prerogative of management. The simple fact is that McGregor never really elaborated or discussed the issue of power. Other leadership theorists (e.g. Blake and Mouton 1978; also see Chapter 5) also share a unitary perspective because they advocate supportive and participative leadership styles in which authority must be accepted by subordinates and imbalances in power or power issues will not arise. Unitary views of authority focus on power being dysfunctional because power is usually associated with conflict and is thus defined as being divergent from good management practice (Forster and Browne 1996: 139).

Having now looked at the unitary perspective, how might the questions raised at the beginning of the chapter be answered from this point of view?

Pluralist views of power

Pluralist approaches to power have attempted to shift the focus away from authority. Instead, these approaches emphasize the study of power and influence in social interactions. According to one view of pluralism, any partner to an exchange (i.e. where someone does something for another person) enters into a *dependency relationship*. All interactions are considered to involve exchange, and hence dependency. Thus to gain acceptance into any group usually involves giving up some freedom or rights in order to belong. According to some pluralists, exchange involves questions about the types of influence that will be tolerated or rejected, and how dependencies might be created or neutralized. For some pluralists, *influence* means the use of power, which is associated with acquiring certain resources that help create dependencies. Dependency is the obverse of power: dependency can weaken or strengthen power (Dawson 1986: 159; Handy 1985: 118–19; Pfeffer 1981: 99–115). There are many versions of the exchange model of power but it assumes people are conscious of the power plays going on around them. It usually involves individuals (as per Dahl's one-dimensional view of power, often referred to as A and B) or groups (e.g. departments or subunits) doing something they would not otherwise have done had influence been absent. Pluralists generally concentrate on explaining overt forms of influence (i.e. influence that most parties are aware of) and the power resources used to create unequal dependency relationships. The approach presumes individuals are generally aware of influence being exerted over them because it is usually associated with some form of overt conflict.

Power of lower participants

Early pluralist studies focused attention on the exercise of power among groups who were described as lower participants. David Mechanic's (1962) famous study described how lower participants in various organizations gained influence over their superiors by using power resources such as information, persons and instrumentalities to build up dependency relationships. Mechanic defined these resources as follows: *information* refers to knowledge of organizational procedures, rules and resources; *persons* means having access to experts or important individuals; *instrumentalities* relates to control over physical resources such as equipment, machines or facilities. He argued that the access to these resources was not solely dependent on a person's position in the hierarchy and that lower participants could, through such things as *effort* and *interest*, increase their access to these resources, thereby making others dependent upon them. These 'others' can and did include senior staff (Mechanic 1962).

Mechanic's study showed how hospital attendants were able to create a dependency relationship between themselves and doctors through resolving problems associated with the administration of wards. Attendants assumed the administrative responsibilities of the ward in exchange for having an increased say in decisions affecting patients, for example scheduling of the operating theatre. Doctors disliked doing administrative work and gladly 'traded' these duties with the attendants, but in so doing helped build a dependency relationship. This was a *quid pro quo* arrangement in which attendants gained some influence through their efforts and interest in routine administration. This also increased their *access to information* (power) resources and made them indispensable to the doctors, who came to defer to the attendants on matters of routine ward administration. The price of limiting the influence of attendants (lower participants) would have meant extra work and effort on the part of doctors in an area of hospital administration that did not interest them. Doctors had discretionary control over these tasks and were able to unofficially delegate these responsibilities. Had hospital rules and procedures prevented this, then attendants might not have been able to create the dependency relationship. If a wards person, for instance, had objected to these informal practices, then power struggles and conflicts would inevitably have arisen.

Pluralists argue that lower participants in any organization can gain some control over power resources and thus exert some influence over their superiors. Mechanic gives the example of prison guards bending rules or allowing violations of regulations (e.g. possession of certain illegal items) in order to extract cooperation from inmates. Logically, guards should try to enforce sanctions and punishment against inmates who break rules and regulations – but at the risk of appearing to lack authority and the ability to command obedience should prisoners riot or simply refuse to comply. So informal practices avoid the types of confrontation and conflict associated with the win–lose situations warders might be anxious to circumvent. The study of the power of lower participants highlights the generic nature of dependency and exchange relationships in organizations. Translated into everyday practice, pluralists suggest that managers or supervisors who have nothing of relevance or value to trade with their employees or subordinates might encounter resistance and be unable to extract cooperation or satisfactory performance from lower participants. Supervisors who have no input, for example, into the promotion or salary review of their staff will probably lack influence and be heavily dependent upon subordinates to get things done (Dawson 1986: 161).

Subunit power

Pluralists have also sought to identify the types of influence used by departments or subunits in organizations. This type of collective influence is considered to be different in many respects from individual methods of influence. Michel Crozier's famous study, *The Bureaucratic Phenomenon* (1964), examined a group of maintenance men in the French tobacco industry and the study provided important insights into subunit power and paved the way for a *strategic contingencies view of power*. The strategic contingency theorists argued that the maintenance men controlled and authorized the repair and maintenance of machines. Speedy repair of breakdowns and proper maintenance helped reduce uncertainties for management and other workers, thus creating dependencies. Strategic contingency theorists suggested that the reason the maintenance men were powerful was because of a number of interrelated factors. The plant used technologies and work processes which were interdependent, so that if a machine broke down the whole plant would grind to a halt. Maintenance men resisted attempts to routinize their work through planned or preventative maintenance and used their union to forestall the introduction of alternative or substitute methods to carry out maintenance. Thus they were very influential because they remained central to workflows, coped with uncertainties and were able to prevent substitute methods or activities being introduced. Their jobs were non-routine and the dependence on them was very strong. All levels within the plant had to defer to their decisions and demands while they remained strategically important or were able to cope with critical uncertainties (Hickson *et al.* 1971; also see below).

Subsequent studies have supported the argument that for subunits the important power resources are *centrality*, *coping with uncertainty* and *non-substitutability* (Hickson and McCullough 1980). However, as David Hickson *et al.* (1971) suggest, these power resources or strategic contingencies are always susceptible to erosion, especially through routinization and technology. A sales department, for example, which attracts a high volume of orders during an economic recession is likely to have increased influence and power. It acts to reduce uncertainty in the organization by guaranteeing future growth and profits. By the same token, if the department secures a number of long-term orders, then it might become strategically less important. Subunit power is variable (contingent) and managers will always have to deal with subunits or departments which have strategic importance to the organization. The strategic contingency approach to power gives ample clues as to how subunit members foster dependencies and the strategies managers can use to deal with these dependency or power relationships.

Power resources and strategies among managers

None of the studies mentioned so far has directly examined the methods of influence used by supervisory or managerial groups. Table 4.2 describes some of the pluralist theorists who have dealt with this aspect of power. John French and Bertram Raven's (1959) typology of power attempted to explain how subordinates react to managers' power (they did not differentiate power from influence). Thus *coercive power* is reflected in a subordinate's fear of punishment or negative consequences of his or her actions. *Reward power* is associated with a belief that benefits will flow from complying with management's orders. *Referent power* is similar to charisma, invoking strong identification with a manager; it is one of the most effective ways of gaining compliance. *Expert power* means that a subordinate accepts the superior knowledge of a manager. *Legitimate power* is probably similar to authority or the acceptance of a manager's position and the rights and responsibilities associated with it. This typology of power identifies the individual power resources of managers and their effects on subordinates. It is quite a simple typology and does not explain how or when these resources can be used.

A more complex model emerged in Charles Handy's typology of power. It still concentrated, however, on explaining individual sources of power, adding the dimension of influence (Handy 1985: 118–36). Handy's typology advanced the pluralist argument by separating power resources from methods of influence. He also pointed out that power is not an absolute factor in a social relationship, but can vary depending on its salience or relevance to another individual, the balance of power between two individuals (remember even prisoners have power), and the limits placed on power (e.g. managers can most affect their direct subordinates, but not others) (Handy 1985: 121). Exhibit 4.1 outlines Handy's typology. All the resources can be used positively (i.e. to gain promotions, support peers, achieve results) or negatively (i.e. to obstruct, hinder or disrupt). Not every manager will succeed in acquiring all power resources (hence methods of influence). The most common ones are resource and position power although in Chapter 5 on leadership it is argued that expert and personal power are becoming more important.

The choice of various methods of influence will also depend on the type of environment in which a manager works. For example, in a consultancy firm expert power and persuasive influence are thought to be the most potent. In fact, Handy believes these are the preferred or most effective combinations in many modern organizations (Handy 1985: 152). He has a number of other dimensions to his typology dealing with how subordinates react and cope with influence.

John Kotter (1977) and Henry Mintzberg (1989) have also presented interpretations of the more overt forms of power and influence available to managers. Mintzberg's 'political games' model contains a number of common tactics or strategies that are considered effective in protecting one's position while simultaneously coping with potential threats and

Table 4.2 *Development of power perspectives in management*

French and Raven (1959)	*Handy (1976–85)*	*Kotter (1977)*	*Mintzberg (1983)*
All managers	**All managers**	**Middle managers**	**Middle managers**
	Power resources	*Influence*	
Reward power	Physical	Creation of sense of	Games to resist authority
Coercive power	Resource	obligation	Games to counter resistance
Legitimate power	Position	Building of reputation as	Games to build power base
Referent power	Expert	expert; fostering	Games to change the
Expert power	Negative	identification	organization
	Personal	Creating dependence by	
		acquiring resources or	
	Influence	making others believe the	
	Force	manager has resources	
	Rules	Using formal authority	
	Procedures	(i.e. position)	
	Exchange		
	Persuasion		
	Ecology		
	Magnetism		

Source: Modified from Faye Frith and Liz Fulop (1992), 'Conflict and power in organisations', in Fulop, L. with Frith, F. and Hayward, H., *Management for Australian Business: A Critical Text*, Melbourne: Macmillan, p. 225.

1. **Power resources**   Physical, resource, position, expert, personal
2. **Method of influence**   Force, rules and procedures, exchange, persuasion, ecology, magnetism
   Match of power and influence

Power	Physical	Resource	Position	Expert	Personal
Influence	Force	Exchange	Rules	Persuasion	
		Ecology		Magnetism	

1. Power resources

Physical force	Bullying, stand-over person, shouting
Resource power	Benefits others, usually contained in job contracts, etc. Need not be material, e.g. giving status or recognition or invited to exclusive clubs
Position	Entitlements and rights of one's position, affects resource power, e.g. control over information, right of access, right to organize
Expert power	Knowledge, specialist training or education, very sought-after resource
Personal power	Charisma as described by Weber

2. Method of influence

Force	Threats, bullying, physical punishment, boss who loses his or her temper
Rule and procedures	Institute rules and procedures, and most likely to be used by those with position power
Exchange	Bargaining and negotiating or even cajoling or bribing, e.g. incentive systems or motivation schemes
Persuasion	Logic, power of argument and evidence of facts
Ecology	Environmental constraints, noise, size, organizational structure, climate, etc.
Magnetism	Attraction, popularity, charm (personal or expert power is usual source)

Exhibit 4.1   Handy's typology of power

Source: Modified from Charles Handy (1985), Understanding Organizations (third edition), Harmondsworth, UK: Penguin, pp. 129, 151.

uncertainty. *Games to build power bases* involve such things as: securing a powerful sponsor or 'star'; building an 'empire' with subordinates; securing control of resources; and flaunting one's expertise or authority. Mintzberg advocates that, played in moderation, these games are healthy; in excess they are considered destructive to the survival of the organization (Keys and Case 1990; Kotter 1977: 128–43; Mintzberg 1983: 188–217; Mintzberg 1989: 238).

Empowerment

One of the most comprehensive attempts to develop the concept of *empowerment* emerged in the writings of Rosabeth Moss Kanter (1977a, b, 1979, 1982, 1983, 1989a, b). Kanter has made the term power synonymous with entrepreneurship and innovation, and later with 'empowerment'. In her early definition of entrepreneurs or 'change masters', she refers to those middle managers who successfully used power resources to change and innovate, so that new strategies, products, work methods and structures could be created. There was no doubt in Kanter's mind that organizations can only survive if they empower their middle managers. For Kanter, managers who occupy positions that do not give them access to vital power resources, hence making them highly visible and successful, are more likely to become 'stuckers' who are unable to innovate or promote change. Many bureaucratically structured positions, she says, breed powerlessness because they provide few opportunities to act or work other than in a routine way.

Kanter saw the important power resources consisting of three 'lines' or methods of access:

- *Lines of supply* Managers have the capacity to bring in the things that their own departments need, for example materials, money or resources, to distribute as rewards.
- *Lines of information* To be effective, managers need to be 'in the know' in both the informal and the formal sense.
- *Lines of support* In a formal framework, a manager's job parameters need to allow for non-ordinary action, for a show of discretion or exercise of judgement. And, informally, managers need the backing of other important figures in the organization whose tacit approval becomes another resource they bring to their own work unit (Kanter 1983: 134).

These power resources were very similar to those identified by Mechanic. Kanter's empowering strategies were also more or less a hybrid of those mentioned in Table 4.2. She identifies four key empowering strategies available to middle managers. The first of these is 'ride the right coattails' which means working with someone who has clout and is successful. This also relates to gaining sponsorship (or mentoring) and succeeding by being associated with other successful managers in the organization. 'Monument building' is about creating or rearranging departments or divisions to promote uncertainties and provide new rewards for loyal subordinates (e.g. a new position). 'High visibility' is associated with risk taking and solving critical problems or coping with uncertainties. 'Peer alliances' relates to building networks and establishing supportive relationships with those moving up the ladder. Most of these strategies were identified by Kanter as masculine ones, not readily available to women (Kanter 1977b). Kanter was one of the first theorists to consider and analyse diversity as a dimension of power relations. We will return to this point shortly.

Kanter's approach was also different from other pluralists because she recognized structure as an important factor in empowering managers. She acknowledged that empowering was not solely dependent on individual initiatives or actions, but was limited or hampered by inappropriate structures that have to be changed by senior management. As already stated, powerlessness was identified by her with bureaucratic structures and values. Kanter maintained that power resources must circulate and if they did not then the more negative and destructive aspects of conflict and powerlessness would engulf the organization.

In an attempt to enlarge on the empowerment concept, and give people a method of assessing their own or their employees' level of empowerment, John Jones and William Bearley (1988) developed an *empowerment profile*. The profile identifies eight dimensions along which empowerment can be measured and these are described in Figure 4.1. The dimensions are interdependent and overlap, with an absence of one or more potentially affecting a person's overall profile. Again, the use of the empowerment profile focuses on visible sources of power and sources of power the individual is conscious of and able to recognize. *Strength* refers to one's own sense of strength; *climate* refers to how power is used in the organization; *autonomy, centrality* and *involvement* refer to someone's role and functions, while *control, influence* and *resources* determine one's potential impact in the organization (Jones and Bearley 1988: 11).

The dimensions in Figure 4.1 are described in Exhibit 4.2.

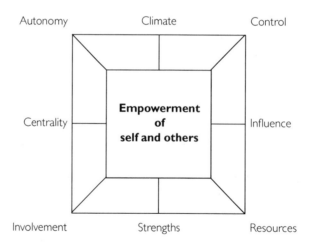

Figure 4.1 The dimensional empowerment model

Source: John E. Jones and William L. Bearley (1988), Empowerment Profile, *King of Prussia, PA: Organization Design and Development, p. 10.*

- **Strengths** – people high on strengths are risk takers, cope with uncertainty, have relatively sound political skills and understand how power is distributed in their organizations. This is almost similar to Kanter's idea of 'high visibility'.
- **Autonomy** – how much freedom you have to do your job and this is affected by the level of approval or authority needed to perform tasks, the freedom to set your own standards, not being

rule bound and having resources to do your job. Again, this is similar to Kanter's idea of 'high visibility'.

- **Centrality** – how central your work or leadership is for the organization. How expendable your job is and how central your unit is in the organization's overall operations (this also relates to the ideas that are similar to strategic contingency theorists such as Crozier and Hickson *et al.*).
- **Involvement** – is related to how involved you, your team, group or department is in such things as problem solving, setting policy and being able to veto the decisions of others.
- **Influence** – the ability to get others to follow your lead and the effective use of power skills and strategies identified by Kanter, others in Table 4.2, and by Handy in Exhibit 4.1.
- **Resources** – relates to the ability to access resources of all kinds, for example, access to information, decision makers, discretionary funds, ability to reward. This is very much connected to Kanter's ideas and indirectly to Mechanic's approach to the power of lower participants (see earlier discussion).
- **Climate** – is related to the conditions under which a manager exercises power and, for example, would relate to such things as not having to compromise personal values, spend a lot of time competing with others, working under lots of rules (i.e. having few 'non-negotiables' in one's job) or having to slavishly comply with a boss's wish(es). Again, this follows Kanter's ideas of having jobs with discretion.
- **Control** – is concerned with such things as veto powers, being able to determine the pace of work, having control of budgets and rewards, controlling scarce resources, being able to set work priorities, etc., being able to determine the training others receive, and having influence over who succeeds the manager in their position.

Exhibit 4.2   Empowerment profile

Source: Modified from John E. Jones and William L. Bearley (1988), Empowerment Profile, *King of Prussia, PA: Organization Design and Development, p. 10.*

One of the problems with the empowerment profile, and indeed with pluralists' views of power, is that it fails to address issues of diversity. Kanter (1989c, cited in Ragins 1997: 487) pointed out that mentoring relationships help protégés to develop power resources in and across the organization and provide 'training' for protégés in developing their political skills and influence. As Kanter noted, mentors can also provide challenging assignments and place their protégés in highly visible positions where they can develop expert power and be noticed by those who count in terms of career development. Moreover, mentors provide 'reflected power' to protégés and the mentor's influence can augment those of protégés both in terms of the resources they get and the protection they receive from adverse organizational events or forces. Mentors provide career development and advancement opportunities (Kanter 1977b, 1989c, cited in Ragins 1997: 487).

Belle Rose Ragins (1997) has reviewed extensively studies and research on mentoring to discover what impact diversity has on mentoring, and hence on power in organizations. Ragins has drawn mainly on pluralist perspectives to examine the issue of diversified mentoring relationships. Her findings expose some real biases in the pluralist approaches to power. All the approaches mentioned in Table 4.2 are essentially blind or neutral to diversity issues, as is the material in Exhibit 4.2 on empowerment.

Informal mentoring relationships are the main types found in organizations although some organizations do establish formal mentoring programmes. Ragins argues that informal mentoring relationships are not easy to form among people from diverse backgrounds. Diversified mentoring relationships are those involving people from different power and status-related groups (based on gender, sexuality, race, disability or ethnicity) (Ragins 1997: 499). People in these relationships usually find it more difficult to identify and relate to each other. Mentoring relationships with people of similar characteristics or social status (i.e. more homogeneous relationships), create potentially greater comfort and ease for those involved. Ragins points to research which has found that cross-gender or cross-race mentoring relationships face particular problems. In one US study cited by Ragins (1997: 499), women reported being reluctant to form mentoring relationships with men for fear that this approach by them could be construed as a sexual advance by the male mentor or others in the organization. Similarly, social activities outside work (e.g. playing golf) are far more limited in diversified mentoring relations than those involving persons of the same gender.

A 1996 study of 461 women executives in the USA (Ragins 1997: 497, citing Catalyst 1996) found that even women who attributed their success to having a mentor also claimed that they had to consistently exceed performance expectations and present themselves in ways that made male co-workers feel comfortable with them. Joan Margretta (1997: 19) has coined the term 'comfort syndrome' to describe a range of implicit, often subtle codes of feeling that are likely to affect mentoring between men and women. The comfort syndrome covers feelings and emotions and gender stereotypes such as fear, prejudice, envy, greed and aggressiveness in women.

Ragins (1997: 492) also indicates that diversity for any individual or group usually comprises multiple identities (e.g. an ethnic male, a woman who is also a lesbian, a male who also has a disability) and therefore the split into homogeneous and diversified mentoring relationships is in some ways an artificial construct which simplifies what are often extremely complex relationships. Another major complicating factor is whether or not the diverse mentoring relationship involves minority or majority participants. Ragins identifies several ways in which minority or majority status can also affect mentoring relationships. A male, for example, who has minority status in an organization (i.e. is not numerically represented) and is therefore in an organization dominated by women can still be treated as though he has majority status because in the wider social context (at least in the USA and most countries) men dominate positions of power and influence. Conversely, Ragins argues that people who have a minority status in society (not well represented numerically in positions or offices associated with power and influence) and have a minority status in organizations (i.e. are not numerically represented) face difficulties in being mentored or being someone's protégé or in becoming a mentor. Ragins cites research in the USA (Ely 1995), for example, which found that organizations (i.e. private sector ones) having few women in positions of power were more likely to support and foster stereotypical gender roles as opposed to firms with more balanced representation.

Ruth Simpson (1997: S122) lends support to Ragins's findings by citing research in the UK which found that women who typically form a minority (20 percent or less of the total workforce for any minority makes them token members) find themselves being marginalized and excluded through stereotypes. Stereotypes can be polarized or exaggerated to create boundaries between groups, assimilated into a group's subculture or even more widely adopted in the organization. Women tend to be isolated in these cultures, but are nonetheless still highly visible (Simpson, citing Kanter 1977b). Some of the stereotypical 'role traps' can include: 'mother role (comfortable and caring), the seductress (sexy and dangerous), the pet (sweet but incompetent)', and for those who do not conform to these the 'iron maiden (asexual and strident)' (Simpson 1997: S122). Simpson cites research by Marshall (1995) confirming evidence of role traps being used in corporations to marginalize and exclude women from power and influence through these informal processes. In her study of 100 women managers who were MBA graduates Simpson found no evidence of role traps but rather strenuous efforts being made by women to avoid these role traps by overperforming or performing well above expectations (see below).

Mentoring that involves minority relationships, let alone diverse mentoring relationships, carries risks associated with the increased visibility of these people (who are often token members). These risks include performance pressures (usually having to outperform on many criteria or not having one's competency recognized appropriately) and behavioural expectations (deference, submissiveness, etc.) (Ragins 1997: 497, citing Kanter 1977b). Ragins notes that diversified mentoring relationships more so than others also elicit unique work-group reactions such as charges of favouritism, perceptions of inequity and co-worker jealousy (Ragins 1997: 500, citing Myers and Humphreys 1985).

Figure 4.2 summarizes the key findings emerging from Ragins's paper and principally suggests that the most successful mentoring relationships are those that involve homogeneous majority mentors and protégés. Sometimes diversified mentoring relationships with a majority mentor and minority protégé can also succeed. According to research by Kram (1985, cited in Ragins 1997: 505), career development is the most important mentoring function likely to benefit a protégé. Ragins cites a wide range of studies that show protégés generally receive more promotions, have higher incomes, report more career satisfaction and mobility than non-protégés. Psychosocial support from mentors can also alleviate both the negative and positive protégé outcomes listed in Figure 4.2.

Moderators (mentioned in Figure 4.2) can affect how diverse mentoring relationships develop in different contexts and between different individuals; for example, high-ranking mentors with extensive experience can usually achieve more for a protégé than a less experienced, more junior mentor (Ragins 1997: 506). Demographic variables refer to such things as age, career stage, socioeconomic class and education and these can potentially affect mentoring relationships across all categories. People from higher socioeconomic status or backgrounds, for example, receive more career development support from mentors than do people from lower socioeconomic backgrounds (Ragins 1997: 507, citing Whitley, Dougherty and Dreher 1991). This is covered by the old adage 'it's not what you know but who you know'. As Ragins (1997: 507) also points out, even groups that have similar demographic characteristics can experience differences in values, attitudes and beliefs among their members.

Ragins's work illustrates that there is a 'vicious cycle' in diverse mentoring relationships that adversely affects groups such as women in a special way. Paul Gollam (1997: 25–6), writing on staff selection in Australia, noted how the apparent undervaluing of women in Australian businesses means that it would probably take another 170 years to achieve equal representation between the sexes in management. He quotes research showing that between 1995 and 1996 the proportion of women in management positions had declined. For this same period women only occupied 11 percent of top management positions and had a very dismal representation on executive boards. He also cited research showing that 73 percent of Australian women managers leave their jobs because of limited career opportunities. In other words, not only is the pool of mentors available to other women not expanding, but

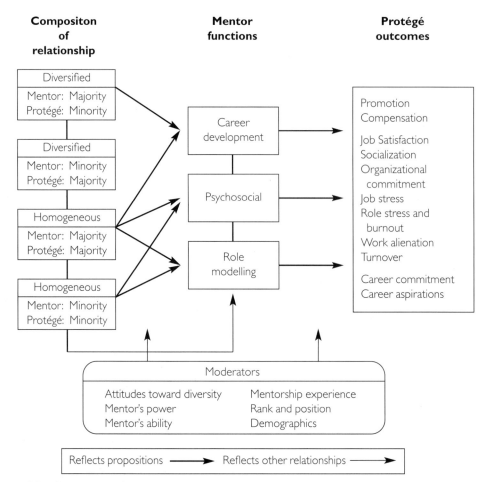

Figure 4.2 Composition of relationship, mentor functions and protégé outcomes

Source: Belle Rose Ragins (1997), 'Diversified mentoring relationships in organizations: A power perspective', Academy of Management Review 22(2), p. 505.

the problems with diverse mentoring relationships are probably also taking their toll. Gollam (1997: 25) suggests that when one looks at management in Australia, one is still confronted with an image of the 'old boy network'. It is likely that this image manifests across many countries.

Similar trends are apparent in the UK (see also Chapter 2) where a national study in 1995 found only 5 percent of women were at the senior levels and only 3 percent directors of boards (Simpson 1997: S121). In Simpson's study (mentioned earlier) the single greatest barrier women experienced in their careers was the presence of the 'Men's Club'. In her study, token women (i.e. women in the minority) recorded a much higher incidence of having experienced the 'Men's Club' as a barrier to career advancement than did those women who were in organizations that had a greater gender balance (i.e. non-token women). Simpson (1997: S122, citing Coe 1992; Maddock and Parkin 1994) says the 'Men's Club' can operate to separate and exclude women through sexual innuendo (sexist jokes) and conversations dominated by such things as sport. These tactics, which are often ritualized, act to exclude women from informal encounters where important information is exchanged often affecting decisions and, ultimately, careers (Simpson 1997: S127).

Empowerment became one of the 'buzz-words' of the 1990s in many areas of management and business. Yet Cynthia Hardy and Sharon Leiba-O'Sullivan (1998: 463) suggest that management rarely introduces empowerment strategies in order to share power or to create a more democratic workplace. Rather, empowerment programmes are usually associated with management's goals of improving productivity, lowering costs or increasing customer satisfaction. In fact they argue that there are two main approaches to empowerment adopted in business. The first entails delegating power and authority to those employees who thrive on stress and challenges and can be trusted to use power for the benefit of the organization.

Empowerment can also be used by management as a motivational strategy. This entails using open communication, inspirational goal setting and leadership to increase the commitment and involvement of people to their organization's success (Hardy and Leiba-O'Sullivan 1998: 464). Instead of focusing on the delegation and sharing of power this motivational approach to empowerment seeks to give people encouragement and feedback, help them to learn, provide them with emotional support to alleviate stress and anxiety, and create positive emotional responses to organizational goals. This is a very unitary view of power because its main aim is to address the feelings of powerlessness among people and not the imbalances in power.

The political organization

The political perspective views organizations as coalitions of individuals or groups who are by and large pursuing their own agendas and interpretations of what constitute appropriate or valid goals (Bailey 1970: 19–22; Child 1973: 192; Burrell and Morgan 1979: 202–5). Conflicts of interest arise in predictable ways because of the interdependencies and power differentials that are structured or built into organizations through such things as the division of labour and task specialization. These help to create horizontal and vertical dependencies. Interdependence is also fostered by the technologies adopted in organizations, particularly the extent to which they can be either substituted or routinized or used to skill or deskill organizational members.

Organizations also have limited resources or operate under conditions of scarcity. This means that rewards and opportunities are never adequate to meet everyone's expectations, thus conflict and power struggles remain endemic. Through centralization or decentralization, power resources can be either concentrated at the top of the organization or allowed to flow down the hierarchy. Organizational members will react to either situation, with the probability of conflict being greater in decentralized structures. Figure 4.3 summarizes some of the common sources of conflict and power struggles in political organizations. As Figure 4.3 shows, conflict derives from both internal and external influences on organizational members.

The concept of the seminal political organization was also evident in Alvin Gouldner's (1954) and Crozier's (1964) works. Both of these works emphasize the ways in which structures (e.g. division of labour, rules, technology) both constrain and enable certain strategies or tactics of organizational members.

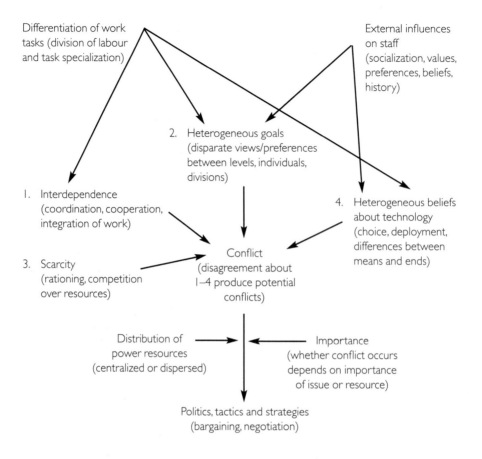

Figure 4.3 Conditions for the use of power

Source: Adapted from Jeffrey Pfeffer (1981), Power in Organisations, *London: Pitman, p. 69, developed by Graeme Sheather, University of Technology, Kuring-gai, New South Wales.*

Gouldner conducted research into the effects of rules and his work identified three different types of bureaucratic patterns which can exist in the workplace, depending on how rules are established in the first place: *punishment-centred, mock* and *representative rules*. In the mock pattern, rules exist but are ignored by both staff and management (e.g. no smoking rules were breached). In the representative pattern, rules are mutually agreed to and are accepted as fair by all (e.g. using safety clothing in a toxic industry). In the punishment-centred pattern, one party imposes rules against the others' wishes, generating conflict and power struggles (e.g. abolishing tea breaks to save money). Gouldner's research in a gypsum mine in the USA highlighted how difficult it was for management to eliminate perks and privileges and change mock rules. Changing rules against pilfering eventually led to bitter industrial conflicts and the final closure of the mine. According to Gouldner, bureaucracy is man-made and 'is a function of human striving; it is the outcome of a contest between those who want it and those who do not' (quoted in Salaman 1979: 147). To simply presume that all rules could be agreed to and exercised by those at the top of the hierarchy ignores manipulation, dissent and rejection of them (Byrt 1973: 49; Gouldner 1954: 20; Pugh, Hickson and Hinings 1983: 20–4; Lansbury and Spillane 1983: 105–6).

Gouldner's study was a descriptive piece of research that attempted to draw attention to the manner in which rules could be interpreted and acted upon differently by all within organizations. It was a study which did not adopt a managerial perspective and tried to show that rules had significantly different meanings for workers and for managers. The more management tried to institute more bureaucratic procedures (i.e. stricter rules, regulations and disciplinary measures), the more workers resented the abolition of practices that were based on nepotism and favouritism, even though these were detrimental to improving productivity. Gouldner's study was one of the first to approach the problem of control and authority from an action approach, by focusing on the importance of meaning systems, as also pointed out by Weber (Silverman 1970).

While Gouldner's work highlighted the problem of rules and authority, the study by Crozier (1964) created even more doubts about the unitary view of authority. Crozier set out to study how authority was actually exercised in large organizations, especially in areas in which it was not always easy to replace people or eliminate their tasks. He did not start from the premise that people's actions were oriented to rule following or complying with authority, but rather from the assumption that through the organization's effort to eliminate the discretion of employees, some area of uncertainty will remain, and such uncertainty is the breeding ground for efforts to achieve some, however slight, self-control. It supported the view that '[The] final structure of an organization…is the result of these negotiations, interpretations in which organizational members actively strive to resist some directions and control' (Salaman 1979: 146).

In the case of Crozier's maintenance men, their expertise and ability to repair machines enabled them to avoid the otherwise tight regulatory system that applied to other areas of production and, through their union, resist routinization of maintenance procedures. Power struggles ensued between the maintenance men and management, with the latter attempting to regain control through increasing the rules and regulations affecting the work of the maintenance men. However, Crozier noted that even these actions of senior management were partially constrained by cultural norms in French society, which frowned upon such things as open exercise of authority or face-to-face conflict (Reed 1985: 159–61).

In the political organization, human agency or actions give shape and meaning to structure. The interests of organizational participants are implicated in some way in the social relations and structures that they experience as either enabling or constraining them. In such an organization, the rules of the game, the 'prizes' and conduct expected of participants are very much a negotiated process in which the struggle for power — to limit, resist or escape it – is an endemic feature (Clegg 1989: 207; Reed 1985: 141–6). The political organization, as described by pluralists, is very different from the unitarist's description. Whether an organization is labelled as 'innovative', 'entrepreneurial' or 'divisionalized', pluralists believe they all signal political organizations.

Mintzberg has argued that politicized organizations must include both internal and external coalitions such as shareholders, unions, governments, bank suppliers and customers. To be a politicized organization, in Mintzberg's view, means enduring or experiencing conflicts between internal and external coalitions. He says a 'complete political arena' exists when an organization experiences severe and uncontrollable conflicts between internal and external coalitions. He argues that conflicts have predictable forms, depending on their intensity (i.e. level of hostilities), pervasiveness (i.e. how widespread) and duration (i.e. brief or lasting). According to Mintzberg, few organizations can survive very intense, highly pervasive and lasting conflicts: they self-destruct. Political arenas (or politicized organizations) are enduring configurations and emerge wherever organizations are wholly or partially captured or invaded by obvious and visible conflicts. By this definition, every organization is a political arena (Mintzberg 1983: 420–66, 497–502; Pfeffer 1981: 154–76).

Theorists, such as Kanter, have proposed that the successful political organization must institutionalize power by developing empowering strategies and structures (Kanter 1983, 1989a, b; Mintzberg 1989: 237–302). Kanter says that in the post-entrepreneurial organization traditional concepts of hierarchy, task specialization and even departments are giving way to more complex and fluid structures in which interdependence is taking on new forms. Power is becoming more decentralized in these organizations. Trends Kanter sees as pointing to the emergence of the new political organization are listed below under four main arguments.

First, relationships of influence or power are shifting from the traditional hierarchies to such fluid structures as peer networks, cross-functional projects, business units, joint ventures with other companies, labour management forums and strategic partnerships with suppliers or customers. These are creating new centres of power which cut across the chain of command in quite diverse ways. Information flows in all directions and expertise and traditional positions of authority are being changed by these new centres of power. Middle managers and supervisors become involved in many more cross-boundary relationships, that is, across departments, companies, suppliers, etc. (see also Chapters 6 and 8 for discussion of the virtual organization concept).

Second, the developments mentioned in point one create a greater variety of channels for taking action and exerting influence through agenda setting. Cross-functional relationships place managers in more diverse coalitions and the scope to redefine assignments, tasks, jobs and interdependencies increases. Delegation and responsibility for more strategically important decisions are dispersed since senior management is unable to maintain tight control over these more complex, messy and fluid arrangements. Reputations inside and outside organizations become an important source of power and influence.

Third, political skills associated with networking, bargaining, negotiating and building alliances become as important for success as technical expertise or qualifications (see Bolman and Deal 1991: 207–19).

Fourth, external relationships become as important and vital to success as internal ones for developing a career and gaining power and influence. Informal networks and coalitions are essential to the empowered manager.

Kanter's model of the political organization proposes the institutionalization of power and interests so that politics become a normal part of management strategies and daily practices. The post-entrepreneurial organization is also a learning organization or a more democratic organizational form. In the post-entrepreneurial organization, the employability of managers is determined by their relative value in both internal and external labour markets, which in turn largely depends on their political skills. It is top management's responsibility to empower managers by providing power resources and support, freeing up information and devolving decision making (Bolman and Deal 1991: 433). Kanter moves across a number of perspectives to explain how the post-entrepreneurial organization works. However, she is just one of a number of theorists who see empowerment as a central issue in the design and management of organizations of the future (see also Clegg 1990: 190–5).

Pluralists, in a sense, acknowledge that conflict and power struggles are inevitable 'facts' of organizational life and a part of any manager's role. However, they are inclined to view power and political behaviour as benefiting individuals or subunits at the expense of the organization (Forster and Browne 1996: 139). Thus empowerment is seen as a key set of strategies for managers to consider to minimize the dysfunctions of political behaviour.

Having now read the material on pluralist views of power, how might some of the questions at the beginning of the chapter be answered from this point of view?

The radical view of power

Pluralists have been criticized on a number of counts, but primarily for their assumptions that power is widely dispersed and not concentrated in the hands of an élite group because there are diverse spheres of influence (e.g. networks or coalitions) that are generally accessible to all who wish to participate in power games (Burrell and Morgan 1979: 216). In this respect, although the pluralist approach is an improvement on the unitary perspective it still does not adequately deal with power disparities between groups. For example, in the pluralist model the bargaining or negotiating processes are seen as 'tools' for restoring equality in the power bases between various stakeholders, including management. It is argued that having balanced power bases between the various groups creates checks and counter-checks that lead to the stability of the power system within organizations.

The pluralist model, however, though moving further than a unitary one, still does not focus adequately on the fact that in organizations disparities exist between the power of the managed and those who manage them. Because the pluralist approach defined the dominant group, owners/managers, as just another power group, the model is said to become an ideological tool of subordination and legitimation, used semi-purposely to condition subordinates into accepting the status quo (Kirkbride 1985: 277).

The issue of domination is a critical one because it raises the problem of the relationship between authority and power and the different types of influence that flow from each. Pluralists are weak in their analysis of authority and hence fail to address the deeper and more complex aspects of domination and control in organizations. Stewart Clegg and David Dunkerley suggest that all organizations have hegemonic systems or identifiable power groups that are strategically positioned not only to play power games, but define the very rules of the power game (Clegg and Dunkerley 1980: 444). To put this into context, Clegg argues that in any game of chess, the queen is more powerful by virtue of the rules of the game – the queen has more moves and options than does a pawn or a castle. Anyone positioned this way has more power to interpret the rules by which to play the game or make more strategic moves (Clegg 1989: 210). From this view, every organization represents a system (or systems) of domination. Domination is another way of describing the basis of legitimacy and acceptance of authority within organizations. It is argued that any system of domination is sustained by often unobtrusive or unquestioned methods of control that are accepted as legitimate. 'Legitimacy derives from internalised norms which provide a broad base for compliance' (Dawson 1986: 150). These internalized norms can lead to unquestioning compliance with such things as recruitment procedures and job descriptions, even though these may be discriminatory in nature and consistently disadvantage particular groups. They can be parts of the storylines used in organizations, especially by senior management.

Pluralists make no reference to systems of domination. In fact, because they treat power and authority as two different things, collapse them or ignore authority altogether, they create the impression that bargaining, negotiating and developing dependency relationships afford ambitious and astute individuals some real gains and advantages. In the case of lower participants, for example, effort and interest are said to increase power resources (i.e. control over information, persons and instrumentalities) and hence influence. The question has to be asked, however: influence to do what? Lower participants, such as ward attendants, may indeed gain discretionary control over ward administration but doctors continue to have the authority to change the rules, procedures, policies and technologies (e.g. computerize jobs) and to control appointment and review procedures. Doctors can circumvent the influence of the ward attendants if they choose. If a dependency relationship becomes a problematical one, then authority and power can crush the endeavours of lower participants. Mechanic in fact presented his theory to show how managers could enhance their control over aspiring lower participants. The same could be said of the subunit power perspective. In this vein, pluralists reinforce power differentials in organizations often keeping lower participants in their places (Clegg and Dunkerley 1980: 438–44; Ryan 1984: 37).

Following on from the previous point, pluralists emphasize overt methods of influence (i.e. strategies and resources) while ignoring covert forms of influence. They suggest that power struggles usually follow from the efforts of individuals or groups to secure scarce resources and maximize their advantage against other groups. Organizations are continually subject to conflicts, upheavals and change. However, organizations, and their members, are subject to constraints which are often so entrenched that they are taken for granted and not questioned. From the radical point of view, constraints act to reinforce the status quo and maintain systems of domination. Constraints come mainly in the form of technology, administrative rules and procedures, structure (e.g. hierarchy, division of labour) and ideologies (Clegg and Dunkerley 1980: 444–51; Dawson 1986: 145–65; Pfeffer 1981: 179–225; Ryan 1984: 29–40; Hickson and McCullough 1980: 27–55).

Take the example of rules. For many years rules and policies relating to recruitment based on seniority were accepted and unchallenged in many organizations, even though these policies discouraged the merit principle and rapid promotion among young and talented employees. The individuals most likely to change these rules were usually those in senior positions who most benefited from them. In other words, actions can be constrained by seemingly entrenched policies. Many structures, procedures and rules reflect the interests of those who have a stake in maintaining the status quo.

Similarly, according to the radical view, ideological constraints can act to preserve the status quo and maintain the balance of power and authority within an organization. Ideological constraints partly refer to the critical forms of meaning that are sanctioned or legitimated in the language, symbols, rituals and practices of an organization. Kanter alludes to this when she refers to the 'rites of passage' to senior management being essentially a masculine ritual (i.e. sponsorship, patronage) from which women are generally excluded. Similarly, from a radical perspective sexist categorizations in the workplace also act as an ideological constraint ensuring gender relationships mirror female subordination. It is now generally accepted that labelling jobs as masculine and using male standards for job descriptions have kept women from participating in certain occupations and, devaluing the work they perform (Burton 1987, 1991). As Erving Goffman says of female subordination:

> The expression of subordination and domination through this swarm of institutional means is more than a mere tracing or symbol or ritualistic affirmation of the hierarchy. These expressions considerably constitute the hierarchy; they are [its] shadow and substance (Goffman 1979: 6).

Lastly, pluralists have argued that power and influence are associated with overt forms of conflict. The extent of such conflict or knowledge of the critical issues affecting an individual varies. However, pluralists would contend that if there is no visible conflict between parties, then power is not normally involved or being exercised. In the case of Crozier's maintenance men, conflict and power occurred in tandem; the men knew the critical issues and the actions that were in their best interests. They sought and used influence and power to secure a strategic advantage however, without their collective power (union strength) they may have had to accept the decisions of managers and defer to their authority.

According to the radical view, pluralists cannot explain how more covert forms of influence are used to manipulate individuals, so they are unable to identify the critical issues that may gravely affect them. Suppose employees at a chemical plant are offered higher salaries and bonuses in exchange for increased productivity so that backlogs on new orders and contracts can be met. These orders and contracts require handling and processing highly toxic substances. To increase productivity and profitability, the company decides to continue with its current safety standards even though more toxic substances are being handled. The company advises workers that current safety standards are adequate and appropriate even though some information available to management raises some serious doubts about one of the substances. In this case, the best interest of workers (health, etc.) does not become an issue – it has been suppressed. The best interests that are put forward in these situations are management's. Power has been exercised but conflict is unlikely to arise. The decision of the managers is not likely to be challenged. They have used influence to minimize conflict and potential disruptions to work. This form of influence (i.e. manipulation) has depended on both the exercise of authority and power (Lukes 1974).

It is sometimes difficult to establish what is in the best interest of workers or managers. However, Clegg (1989) points out that in most power situations there is likely to occur 'organizational outflanking'. This means the outflanked (usually those with limited power) either have an absence of knowledge (i.e. they are ignorant) or they have sufficient knowledge of sorts that consistently discourages resistance, allowing systems of domination to prevail. In terms of ignorance or absence of knowledge, this can extend to the outflanked not even knowing that a power game is in play. By contrast, sufficient knowledge of the outcome of courses of action (i.e. its probable outcome and benefits) can ensure that power games are 'won' without the game even being played (Clegg 1989: 221–3). When whistle-blowers are publicly condemned and sacked for their purported disloyalty and clandestine actions, this provides sufficient knowledge for other would-be whistle-blowers of the costs of resistance and the limited likelihood of success (Glazer and Glazer 1989 and Chapter 9).

How would the questions raised at the beginning of the chapter be answered from the radical perspective?

The fourth or relational view

At this point it is important to address the distinction between conscious and unconscious resistance as, following from the radical view, it appears that subjective circumstances themselves prove resistant to certain types of change in ways which are not fully understood by the subjects themselves. Clegg (1994: 295) observes that 'organizational outflanking' (the sort of moves which occur in the second and particularly the third dimensions of power to prevent resistance arising) is something that occurs prior to resistance because resistance requires consciousness. This is only partially true, as Clegg implicitly acknowledges. He observes that 'people can exercise power without knowing that they are doing so', but fails to link this with the Foucauldian view of power and resistance as a continuity or force ever present in social situations (Clegg 1994: 308; Barbalet 1986: 531).

The fourth view of power distinguishes 'frictional' resistance (imposing limits on power through an absence of positive interest in the goals of power) from intended or direct resistance (noted by Clegg 1994: 286). This at least leaves the door ajar for the conceptualization of an unawareness that one's actions are affecting the interests of power in any way. Indeed, often the interests of power are thwarted precisely because the powerless would need more information in order to perform more effectively, which would entail the revelation of motives the powerful would rather suppress. If power is a relational flow, then the medium through which it flows may be more or less conductive, and that medium is subjective consciousness shaped by the history of past actions and past decisions, patterned practices and previous instances of making sense of how things fit together. Power in this view does not exist as a property of A or B, but is a quality of the relationship between them. Each person is empowered in certain ways, each limited in others by the relationship (Linstead 1997: 69). Thus the fourth view of power can be called the relational view, which attempts to explain sites of differences and sites of resistance, for example, and steps outside the hegemonic view of power. Although conscious resistance is perhaps the most important category of types of resistance, change agents, for example, every day face the reality of unconscious resistance in assessing readiness for change by all sorts of individuals in organizations. Even when the subject (be this a manager or someone else) is consciously resisting, they themselves may not be aware of the motivational sources of that resistance. Often the discussions which take place during the planning and negotiation of change are ambiguous – questions which are apparently commonplace are interpreted as resistant, managers' routine activities are interpreted as power plays. Change itself is often messy, confused and paradoxical to the extent that members do not really know whether they are resisting it or not, and find it difficult to articulate their positions. Part of this is reflected in the diverse local accounts that people have of a change situation, and the storylines they adopt (see Chapter 1).

How individual resistance becomes collective resistance is a perennial problem. However, the work of Elias Canetti, the Nobel Prizewinner, on crowds and revolutions offers a breakthrough in understanding. Power can be defined, Canetti urges, *as the expression of order through command*. A command consists of two dimensions, *momentum* and *sting*. The momentum forces the recipient to act, in accordance with the command. The sting remains behind, mute, invisible, unsuspected 'and may only reveal its existence by some faint scarcely perceptible recalcitrance before the command is obeyed' (Canetti 1987: 354). The sting sinks deeper into the person who has carried out the command, and even though they might feel uneasy or unhappy about the command no immediate action is taken to avenge it. The effect of the sting might remain hidden for years before it comes to light, waiting for the chance to be avenged. Freedom from control, in this sense, is not being able to rid oneself of commands by carrying them out then passing them on, but of avoiding them altogether in the first place (in Clegg's organizational sense, outflanking rather than resistance). The longer it takes to rid oneself of the command, if at all, the less free that person is (Canetti 1987: 355). This drive to reproduce previous situations, but in reverse, 'is one of the chief sources of energy' in human activity, Canetti argues. Robert Cooper (1990: 49) notes that this desire for reversal can play an explanatory role in human motivation, which transforms it from an individual characteristic to a social product, such as avenging a command.

The reversal of the sting is in most cases deferred, often for years or decades – even, Canetti argues, generations. The sting is the objection to an *obeyed* command or occasioned *act of deference*, but organizations are *structures* of deference. Often a command is experienced without having a clear source, it is dispersed among several people, a group appears to give the command, or the command is not crisply defined. Even when a clear command from a single commander is discernible, it may be possible for the recipient to avoid carrying it out, or to carry it out in such a way as to subvert it (Collinson 1994). If the recipient is forced to carry out the command against their will, and feels this 'sting', the drive to reversal of the sting is inevitably deferred though not indefinitely – sometimes it can even be immediate.

Organizations are a particularly effective way of domesticating commands (Canetti 1987: 355–7) and perpetuating deference over time. In a sense, organizations operate on the basis that instead of killing the faithful dog, the master feeds it – as he or she also does with the faithful servant or worker. Nevertheless, even when this return in kind becomes transformed into salaries, rewards and pension schemes, even membership of exclusive clubs, 'every command contains the same threat. It is a modified threat, but there are stated penalties for non-compliance and these can be very heavy' (Canetti 1987: 357). Of course, the fact that the command is given and the sting invoked, and the 'victim' remains alive, means that there can be recoil or pain to the giver of the command, which Canetti calls 'the anxiety of command'. This is an interesting dimension to the understanding of stress (and leader burnout), which goes beyond seeing it as a by-product of unhealthy practices, to be remedied by counselling or therapy. It is an inevitable condition of one's position in the deference structure, of the tension produced by the chronically deferred sting and the giving of commands.

If we look at the ways in which corporate cultures are allegedly established and transmitted, a great deal of the success of these 'cultures' is not cultured behaviour in the sense of shared understanding and problem solving established over time, but *crowd* behaviour associated with the alleviation of the fear of the sting. In fact, the cultural dimensions of organizations are importantly shaped by the myriad of acts that invoke the deferred return of a sting. Every organization's culture is implanted and dispersed with deferred stings that can be released as collective grievance if circumstances permit. Sites of resistance might not emerge for some time, hidden in the corporate memory of many people's different experiences of a deferred sting.

Finally, we should also consider the dimension of *reciprocation* implicit in the sting, because reciprocation implies a *relationship*, giving each participant some kind of power over the other. Reciprocation also defines acts of deference. Marcel Mauss (1990) argues that there are three aspects to gift giving that create reciprocation – (1) *the obligation to give*, (2) *the obligation to receive*, and (3) *the obligation to reciprocate*. Thus on gift giving occasions, one is not able to refuse to give, and, depending on the particular society or setting, gift giving is often a necessary way to explore and build relationships. If a gift is offered, it must be received in the appropriate manner, and the recipient cannot refuse it without giving great offence both socially and personally. Then, having received the gift, the recipient is placed in debt, and is thus in *a state of deference* created by the apparent kindness of the other. But as Mauss emphasizes, this ritualized giving is not a kindly or voluntary act but obligatory one and hence there must be reciprocation on the part of the recipient. This obligatory form of reciprocation is intended to restore the imbalance created by the asymmetrical situation between the giver and recipient, and reverses the *sting of the deferential burden* placed on the recipient. It could be logically inferred that if the gift is not received appropriately the potential recipient escapes deference and the sting of a deferential burden. They escape indebtedness to another and the need to deal with a potentially asymmetrical power relation.

The notion of reciprocation is a very complex one and is revisited in Chapter 7 when we discuss commitment and trust. However, an illustration will help explain how reciprocation can become a source of a deferred sting. In many organizations people often feel that they not only contribute their labour, as defined in job contracts, agreements and various packages, but also give a 'gift' to the organization in the form of such things as loyalty, trust, commitment, dedication, long hours (above what is paid for or expected), personal sacrifices (such as time away from family or other valued relationships) and so on. If there is no adequate recompense for these 'gifts of labour' this can cause people over time to feel the *sting of an improperly reciprocated deference* relationship. Persons who are not being adequately recompensed (appreciated, rewarded or given some recognition they seek) can develop an unconscious desire for reversal (as mentioned earlier), and this might motivate them or others to avenge the situation, even if this occurs some years down the track. This can happen in many ways, but the end result is an act of resistance or retaliation by an individual or group who seeks to bring the asymmetrical power relationship into some temporary or permanent balance – to return the sting.

The failure on the part of the employer, in this example, to recognize that they have this added debt to the employee – that the employer is being perceived by the employee to be in a state of deference to them – sows the seeds of future resistance. The sting of the deferential burden is not being accepted or even recognized by the employer who might fall back on the employment contract, awards and agreements to define the basis of their reciprocal relationship or obligation to their employees. The employee, on the other hand, might struggle many years with an unconscious sense that they are not receiving adequate or just recompense for the gift they have offered in the workplace. Subconsciously they want reciprocation for the gift, but the relationship might well be defined by one party (the employer) as not being a gift giving situation at all. The problem is that organizations operate both formally and informally with the idea of reciprocation which underpins such things as trust and commitment.

In the fourth dimension, many instances of political behaviour on the part of individuals and groups occur either in retaliation to the sting associated with an 'unwelcome' command or to imbalances arising from the reciprocation of the deferred sting. The case study below goes on to explain how Derek and the Deputy Director, William Fisher, sought to handle the transfer of students and courses to Fawley Ridge. It raises issues particularly sensitive to the fourth dimension of power.

Fawley Ridge – the move

Derek, with William's approval, immediately called the President of the Students' Union, Ed Grimley. Ed agreed to come with representatives of the committee to an open meeting to be held with William and Derek, and David Burland, the Dean. Ed warned them that this move would be unpopular and the union would fight it. 'All we ask you to do is come along and keep an open mind' he said, 'and unless you agree to it we won't do anything.' The staff were also invited, as were students likely to be affected. The understanding was that Students' Union representatives and staff (academic and non-academic) had priority of admission, then any available space could be taken up by students. In the three days before the meeting the students mounted a virulent campaign. Anti-move stickers were printed and appeared all over the campus. On the day of the meeting there was a large demonstration outside the meeting room with banners and chants of over 200 students. The meeting room was packed, and William and Derek faced the crowd, resolving to relax despite the dryness of their throats. William outlined the pressure on the Shaw's Park site where the meeting took place and the problems of finding alternative accommodation. He also pointed out that Fawley had lots of daytime space and plenty of complementary resources. He added that the purpose was to help to support the move but not to push it through regardless, and that it could not go through without the support of everyone – technicians, secretaries, academics, and students.

What they needed to know was: How would people be affected by such a move? What did they need to overcome the difficulties such a move would impose? What would absolutely stop such a move being viable? Derek took over to propose that the meeting determine a working party from within each of the groups. Each group would look at its own position and requirements, staff relocations, resources, transport, equipment, etc. and decide on its criteria for evaluation of the move. Then the group representatives would meet together and gain an overview of the move as a whole. At this point, if the group could say that educational quality would be affected badly, the move would not take place. Otherwise, the group was left to its own professional judgement to decide what things were required to make the move a success and William and Derek would negotiate the resources with the institution.

Questions followed. The working party went away, came up with recommendations and William and Derek followed up what they could. They then held another question and answer session. Individual staff were encouraged to come to see Derek if they had concerns. Derek visited the site frequently to talk to staff there. Gradually the opposition to the change, despite continuing demonstrations, evaporated – no one group, not even the students, would say that it could not go ahead. Then Derek set up a change planning group to manage the change. A site head was appointed, being one of the members of staff who had been most opposed to the move, and other parts of the move down to scheduling the buses and negotiating the contracts with the bus company were all delegated and weekly question and answer sessions continued.

Requests for resources and follow-up plans were constantly refined, until the physical move took place over the summer recess. Derek claimed he had done very little, but such was the commitment of the staff that one Saturday when the language labs were to be relocated, the academic staff started to dismantle and remove the equipment when the removal men were late, despite the fact that they were on holiday. The move went smoothly, and Derek's job became to respond to and relay requests from the site head and others to deal with any problems arising connected with the move. Follow-up meetings were held and were institutionalized as part of the course review and evaluation procedures. The site was secured as an asset, and Ed Grimley, the Students' Union President, called Derek to congratulate him on his handling of the move. 'That's how it should have been done' he said 'with consultation right from the word go.' The Dean, David Burland, remarked on how impressive he had found the hands off approach to change, and how difficult he felt it must have been for Derek and William not to be directive. Nevertheless, despite the success, Derek still felt some uneasiness – and within six months he had left the institution for another job.

Source: Adapted from Stephen Linstead (1997), 'Resistance and return: Power, command and change management', Studies in Cultures, Organizations and Societies 3(1), pp. 67–89.

More questions about the case

1   How well do you think the change was managed?
2   How was conflict anticipated and dealt with?
3   What forms of power were at work here, and who used them?
4   Why was Derek uneasy?

Analyses

Let us take a look at how each of the views of power we have discussed would make sense of the Fawley Ridge case and the questions asked about the case at the beginning of the chapter. The questions would be answered differently depending on the approach one adopts.

Unitary view

From a unitary view it could be concluded from the case study that as communication was widely used in open meetings, interpersonal problems were overcome and unions were included, all was well, as there was a common strategic focus, with all members working in a coherent and coordinated fashion to reach a common objective, and consensus over those common objectives prevails because of the notion of a common set of norms and values. Kost's earlier actions were entirely justifiable as the exercise of management's right to manage, bringing the organization back under control in *everyone's* interest. Politics and power struggles would be seen as dysfunctional, detracting from achieving the goals of management – the move to Fawley Ridge.

Pluralist view

In a pluralist view, power is seen to be diffused throughout the organization and all groups or coalitions have power and no one group is wholly sovereign. In the case study a pluralist analysis would contend that all the key parties were known, the issues were clear and visible and all groups were potentially able to influence the decision-making processes. Conflict was overt as interest groups bargained over the decision-making processes, *vis à vis* scarce resources. In the case study we can see how organizational politics involves effort by various actors to mobilize interest groups and coalitions. The case study also highlights how organizational change can threaten the existing power bases and resource allocation and thus political action will occur. Kost demonstrated the importance of using *external* pressure groups.

The pluralist view would also incorporate Lukes's two-dimensional view of power, which would emphasize such things as non-decision making. An example of this in the case is where Kost does not bring into the public arena the reasons why he intends to move students to the Fawley Ridge site. Once Kost has 'made' this decision, everything else becomes 'academic', so to speak, to justify the decision.

Kanter would focus on how Kost does or does not provide adequate power resources (e.g. lines of information) to his heads of department. She would focus on how managers at Fawley Ridge might develop strategies to get ahead such as gaining high visibility and being seen to be solving problems for the organization. This is clearly what Derek is doing in trying to solve problems for Kost, such as 'removing' Cyril. Kanter would also focus on the structures at Fawley Ridge and she would see the bureaucratic structure, with its hierarchy and command structure (Kost's new direct reports who were political appointees), as problematical and bound to create powerlessness for some of the 'old guard' managers. Kanter says this sort of 'monument building' – creating or rearranging departments – ensures uncertainty and builds loyalty (and fear) amongst subordinates.

Radical view

In this view, Lukes would argue invisible power is used and exercised in such a way that the best interests of a group or groups are not being served, in that they are unable to form conscious preferences or choices around issues, and thus they are never consciously able to formulate or understand their real interests.

In the case study, a radical view would argue that Kost was able to hide the 'real' issues by using arguments apparently based on uncontestable educational principles and not allowing them to come to the surface; consequently the *real* interests of the groups were never discussed. Choices were made and accepted as a result of the use of invisible power and the domination and control of outcomes orchestrated by Kost. Kost, by setting up a system of domination, was able to create a set of values to advantage some individuals or groups over others. Derek and the new heads of department are 'co-opted' in Kost's new system, and are asked repeatedly to accept his rationalizations and the government's to save Fairisle Polytechnic. Kost does not encourage open debate but creates a 'climate' for all to mistrust each other and accept no one from the 'old guard' as an ally.

The relational view

This view would argue that there is resistance present, and Fairisle Polytechnic shows examples of the sting working at different levels. The deference relationship, underscored emphatically by the government's approach to academic staff, being seen as the source of commands, which led to depressed salaries, larger classes, fewer resources and deteriorating buildings, was the source of the stings experienced by individuals. Academic staff had been complying with specific commands with which they were not in agreement for some time, but Kost's accession and his hard-line approach to dealing with perceived problems was seen to be qualitatively much more severe. A sense of injustice and unrest was prevalent, coupled with a sense of dislocation as the hierarchy seemed to engineer a split between Deans and the Directorate – influence was not moving upwards, only command was moving downwards. In this situation, a specific command does not have to be directly given as long as the recipient perceives what is said to be a command, or to rest on a command which is veiled behind rhetoric. Kost's policies were turning the staff into a *crowd*.

The Director, in apparently asking Derek to talk to Cyril about early retirement, was giving a command. Derek felt it, did not want to carry it out, but nevertheless complied with the deference order and performed persuasively. Cyril, for his part, could see that he was being made an offer he could not refuse, that he would be removed from his position in some other way if he stayed and his present situation was untenable. Cyril was, in effect, being given the command 'Go!' and he knew it. So did the rest of his staff, and Derek, through the hierarchy, was seen as the commander. The episode involving Cyril and his staff would not be lost from the corporate memory – it would be remembered by many others who over time might feel the same sting of an improperly reciprocated deference relationship. Cyril and his staff's gift of labour (long service, loyalty, dedication) were not being seen by Kost as valuable or worthwhile. Derek's position in talking to and trying to incorporate the staff into his strategic thinking was something that was difficult for them to appreciate, given their history and the particular past actions, past decisions and patterns of practices that had characterized their response to being managed. They almost instinctively interpreted this intervention as yet another piece of command hiding behind fine words, and some of them at least decided to lash back – they would not mildly carry out this perceived command to plan for their own demise. The stings of recent events would be returned in a demand for accountability – not of them to their managers, but of the managers to the body public.

Kost handled this perfectly in two ways. One was that he deflected the returned sting onto a wider body. Just as sting can be passed on down the hierarchy, so return, in some circumstances, can be deflected up the hierarchy. This restored the balance of constraints under which he was labouring. Second, as Canetti emphasizes, he perceived the large gathering's need to become a crowd, and by skilful use of rhetoric he made them one. The perceived sting was thus generalized and dispersed, its specificity and focus and hence its returnability dissipated.

Unfortunately, for reasons which certainly included the need to try to come to a quick decision, Kost was unable to avoid this in the TIA episode. The sting of his recent commands was being felt by the students, the atmosphere of suspicion was rife, and the apparent command to move to the TIA building, which was presented as non-negotiable, produced a challenge which built on the cumulated stings (many of them reaching back beyond the time) and produced the drive to become a crowd. The students formed themselves into a crowd through slogans, and were able to focus on a closely defined issue, which resulted in their success.

Kost wisely chose to stay out of the Fawley Ridge negotiations. He realized that he had been seen to be the architect of the TIA defeat and that the students, flushed with success, would relish another confrontation. He also intuitively knew that it was wise to seek consensus before a decision was presented or perceived to have been made. Although there was opposition, the consistent refusal of Derek and William to commit themselves to a decision until the participants had thought through all the aspects and gathered the relevant information was successful in removing the sting – *without command there can be no sting*, and without a focus for reversal, sting cannot be returned. The decision was removed from the command structure which was reversed – the criteria, once jointly set, became the authority, and as the working group translated the criteria into imperatives the 'commanders' facilitated those imperatives by taking upward or horizontal action.

Why then was Derek uneasy? Was this not a successful example of avoiding the sting and return? Substantially yes, but Derek knew that the situation was more complex. No one knew that the site was likely to be a valuable asset. That possibility had never been put forward as one of the criteria at issue as, if it had become public knowledge, the local council would have cried 'foul' on the move as a subterfuge. Once the move was established and the process seen to be thorough, it could be defended along with the site. Derek knew that despite the fact that there was a real need for space at Shaw's Park, the real estate value of Fawley was the main reason. If it ever became apparent that this had been the case, and that in fact there had been a veiled command behind the process, it would be seen as nothing more than a piece of successful brinkmanship. If any attempt was made to decommission and dispose of the site soon after Vesting Day, or other deals were done with the same effect, this would retrospectively evoke the sting and possibly its immediate return. The consequences for staff relations, given especially the way in which morale had been positively affected by the move, could have been disastrous. So Derek really reserved his judgement to see if the follow-up procedures were maintained, the promised resources materialized, and the style of change management was embedded as a characteristic feature of the institution rather than a happy bit of expediency.

One interesting question to ponder is: Why are all the key players in the case male? Fawley Ridge is a real case study although pseudonyms have been used. What do you think for example, would have happened if Derek had been a woman manager?

Conclusion

It is generally true that pluralists offer a more comprehensive way of dealing with organizational problems than do unitary approaches. Through adopting such an approach to power, managers have a wider range of understandings and techniques by which to deal with the diverse problems confronting them. Clearly, a pluralist manager is still better equipped to deal with conflict and power than is a unitary one. The unitary approach belonged to an era of management in which conformity and authority were seen as mutually self-reinforcing and unchallengeable. That era no longer exists, although managers may act as though it does.

Even though the political perspective allows for a deeper understanding of interests, and power, it is still only a partial account of organizational politics. The pluralist view of power tends to blur or conceal practices of domination found in organizations, thereby often distorting sources of real power. Issues of domination and control are not readily dealt with in a pluralist framework. The pluralist presentation of the political organization, in its various forms, rests on the premise that there is relatively equal access by all to the power resources and strategies that ultimately account for who succeeds, wins or gets ahead. The discussion on mentoring and diversity suggests the latter view is subject to criticism. The more deeply entrenched and pervasive systems of domination that are structured into many organizational systems and processes are denied or neglected by pluralists.

The radical view of power attempts to redress the naïve pluralist assumption that organizations are 'level playing fields' in which power struggles are contested on relatively equal footings. Instead, the radical view argues that much of what happens in organizations is about sustaining managerial dominance and control over the workforce. Thus many of the techniques and methods of conflict resolution offered by pluralists are considered to be manipulative strategies used by management to weaken the collective power of labour (i.e. unions). Radical theorists would be looking to push for significant changes in power relationships between management and workers through the creation of more democratic work organizations.

The fourth dimension argues that power is dispersed, that everyone has some power, that resistance is born alongside power, and that power is relational. Although the 'playing field' is not level, and the advantage is to the powerful, this is not a static and unchanging situation of domination. What is necessary is to understand how discourse and argument come together with power to define *knowledge*, and on the basis of knowledge people act. So rather than looking at how action is controlled, this view looks at how knowledge is produced, how the powerful are advantaged in shaping knowledge through discourse, and how resistance can begin from insignificant origins – even to topple the Berlin Wall. Of course, the critical analysis of discourse, and the production of knowledge, also lead to more open and democratic organizations, but also emphasize how *learning* needs to occur in an awareness of the relationship between knowledge and power.

We will now go back to the questions raised at the beginning of the chapter.

1 Are power and politics generic to all organizations?

The answer is 'yes', at least in the pluralist, radical and relational views of power and politics. Each of these approaches offers different accounts of why this might be the case, and all of them suggest different strategies or ways of addressing power issues. Only the unitary approach implies that the 'normal' state of events is to have no politics or power struggles. The pluralist view is somewhat ambivalent on this point, preferring to see the power and politics managed for the good of the organization. Notwithstanding the insights drawn from the radical and relational views of power and politics, most management strategies are dominated by the unitary approach – even more so than the pluralist one. The latter is often the rhetoric managers use when they talk of power and politics, while their theories in use are often unitary. Both the unitary and pluralist views provide a 'comfort zone' for dealing with power and politics, suggesting that there are practices or activities that managers can ultimately control and remedy. This is not the case with the radical view, which implies that management is an agent of capital (or capitalism) and as a collective group is responsible for the power imbalances and exploitations that give rise to power struggles and organizational politics. Organizations are deeply embedded structures of domination. The relational view presents power and resistance as generic to social relations within command structures and never totally controllable or solvable by management alone. Managers would need to be highly skilled in reflective practice and critical thinking (see the Introduction) if they wish to understand the relational view of power and act from its assumptions. People engage in various discursive practices (e.g. local and popular accounts) that can become the basis for questioning assumptions and ways of thinking that often appear entrenched and highly resistant to change.

2 Do some circumstances more than others give rise to power struggles and politics in organizations?

The answer again is a qualified 'yes'. The case study analysis under each perspective addresses this question. The circumstances that are identified are based on value assumptions and particular frames of reference peculiar to each approach. However, the relational view of power presents the most complex and subtle perspective on the circumstances that might give rise to power and the resistance to it, particularly the notions of the command, the sting and reciprocation.

3 Why is power such a difficult thing to deal with in organizations?

This derives from the fact that managers often favour the unitary or pluralist views of power as their preferred 'stock of knowledge' on the topic. As Kanter says, many managers also treat 'power' as a 'dirty word' – something to be denied, decried and discarded (Kanter 1979: 65). Furthermore, managers are often reluctant to analyze or deal with the more complex sources of power and resistance identified in the radical and relational views of power. Many are unable to create a learning environment (LE) or learning space (LS) (see Chapter 1) that would help them to raise debate, discussion and dialogue relating to power issues. Ultimately, managers who believe they have power (and authority) do not often feel compelled to question it, share it or surrender the prestige and status often used to embellish their positions, particularly at the senior levels (see Chapter 5).

4 Is everyone able to gain or exercise power in organizations?

Three of the approaches are circumspect on this point. Only the unitary approach is clearly against this idea, seeing it as deviant or aberrant for individuals to pursue their interests through power and politics. The pluralists are likely to present the organization as a level playing field with checks and balances in place to ensure that smart or clever managers can advance themselves or their careers through power and politics. The radical view does not see a level playing field at all and fears that the less powerful are always outflanked or out-manoeuvred by dominant groups and interests. The relational view does not suggest that there is necessarily a level playing field, but that there are opportunities to enter power relations that can effect certain wins to groups that the radical view would normally view as powerless. The radical or third-dimensional view is more concerned with aggregated or collective power of groups, such as management, organizations, government, the state and unions to whom it attributes a form of collective consciousness or ideology. The fourth view is more focused on the pressure points within these relations and does not accept a monolithic or aggregated view of power. It does acknowledge that people can act collectively to avenge a grievance (or deferred sting) if circumstances permit. One such circumstance can be the imbalance in reciprocation.

It would be a very unwise manager who did not seriously contemplate the answers to these questions, and who did not, as a result, start to reflect on their own assumptions and practices in relation to organizational power and politics.

References

Anthony, P. (1994) *Managing Culture*, Buckingham: Open University Press.

Bacharach, S. and Baratz, M.S. (1962) 'Two faces of power', *American Political Science Review* 56(4), November 947–52.

Bailey, F.G. (1970) *Strategems and Spoils*, Oxford: Blackwell.

Barbalet, J.M. (1986) 'Power and resistance', *British Journal of Sociology* 36(1): 521–48.

Blake, R. and Mouton, J. (1978) *The New Managerial Grid*, Houston: Gulf.

Bolman, L.G. and Deal, T.E. (1991) *Reframing Organizations: Artistry, Choice and Leadership*, San Francisco: Jossey-Bass.

Buchanan, D. and Badham, R. (1998) *Winning the Game: Power, Politics, and Organizational Change*, London: Paul Chapman.

Burrell, G. and Morgan, G. (1979) *Sociological Paradigms and Organisational Analysis*, London: Gower.

Burrell, G. (1988) 'Modernism, postmodernism and organization studies 2: The contribution of Michel Foucault', *Organization Studies* 9(2): 221–35.

Burton, C. (1987) 'Merit and gender: Organisations and mobilisations of masculine bias', *Australian Journal of Social Issues* 22(2): 424–49.

Burton, C. (1991) *The Promise and the Price: The Struggle for Equal Opportunity in Women's Employment*, Sydney: Allen & Unwin.

Byrt, W.J. (1973) *Theories of Organisation*, Sydney: McGraw-Hill.

Canetti, E. (1987) *Crowds and Power*, Harmondsworth, UK: Penguin.

Catalyst (1996) *Women in Corporate Leadership: Progress and Prospects*, New York: Catalyst.

Child, J. (ed.) (1973) *Man and Organizations: The Search for Explanation and Social Relevance*, London: Allen & Unwin.

Clegg, S.R. and Dunkerley, D. (1980) *Organizations, Class and Control*, London: Routledge and Kegan Paul.

Clegg, S.R. (1989) *Frameworks of Power*, London: Sage.

Clegg, S.R. (1990) *Modern Organizations: Organization Studies in the Postmodern World*, London: Sage.

Clegg, S.R. (1994) 'Power relations and the constitution of the resistant subject' in Jermier, J., Nord, W. and Knights, D. (eds), *Resistance and Power in Organizations: Agency, Subjectivity and the Labour Process*, London: Routledge.

Coe, T. (1992) *The Key to the Men's Club*, London: Institute of Management.

Collinson, D. (1994) 'Strategies of resistance: Power, knowledge and subjectivity in the workplace', in Jermier, J., Nord, W. Knights, D. (eds), *Resistance and Power in Organizations: Agency, Subjectivity and the Labour Process*, London: Routledge.

Cooper, R.C. (1990) 'Canetti's sting', *SCOS Notework* 9(2/3): 45–53.

Crozier, M. (1964) *The Bureaucratic Phenomenon*, Chicago: University of Chicago Press.

Dahl, R. (1957) 'The concept of power', *Behavioural Science* 2 July: 201–15.

Dawson, S. (1986) *Analysing Organisations*, London: Macmillan.

Ely, R.J. (1995) 'The power in demography: Women's social construction of gender identity at work', *Academy of Management Journal* 38: 589–634.

Forster, J. and Browne, M. (1996) *Principles of Strategic Management*, Melbourne: Macmillan.

French, J.R.P. and Raven, B. (1959) 'The bases of social power', in Cartwright, L. and Zander, A. (eds), *Group Dynamics, Research and Theory*, London: Tavistock.

Frith, F. and Fulop, L. (1992) 'Conflict and power in organisations', in Fulop, L. with Frith, F. and Hayward, H., *Management for Australian Business: A Critical Text*, Melbourne: Macmillan.

Fulop, L. (1992) 'Bureaucracy and the Modern Manager', in Fulop, L. with Frith, F. and Hayward, H., *Management for Australian Business: A Critical Text*, Melbourne: Macmillan.

Glazer, M.P. and Glazer, P.M. (1989) *Whistle-Blowers: Exposing Corruption in Government and Industry*, New York: Basic Books.

Goffman, E. (1979) *Gender Advertisements*, New York: Harper and Row.

Gollam, P. (1997) 'Successful staff selection: The value of acknowledging women', *Management* October: 25–6.

Gouldner, A.W. (1954) *Patterns of Industrial Bureaucracy*, New York: The Free Press.

Handy, C. (1985) *Understanding Organizations* (third edition), Harmondsworth, UK: Penguin.

Hardy, C. (1994) 'Power and politics in organisations', in Hardy, C. (ed.), *Managing Strategic Action: Mobilizing Change*, London: Sage.

Hardy, C. and Leiba-O'Sullivan, S. (1998) 'The power behind empowerment: implications for research and practice', *Human Relations* 15(4): 451–83.

Hickson, D.J. and McCullough, A.F. (1980) 'Power in organizations' in Salaman, G. and Thompson, K. (eds), *Control and Ideology in Organizations*, Milton Keynes: Open University Press.

Hickson, D.J., Hinings, C.R., Lee, C.A., Schneck, R.E. and Pennings, J.M. (1971) 'The strategic contingencies theory of intraorganisational power', *Administrative Science Quarterly* 16(2): 216–29.

Jones, J.E. and Bearley, W.L. (1988) *Empowerment Profile*, King of Prussia, PA: Organization Design and Development.

Kanter, R.M. (1977a) 'Power games in the corporation', *Psychology Today* July: 48–53.

Kanter, R.M. (1977b) *Men and Women of the Corporation*, New York: Basic Books.

Kanter, R.M. (1979) 'Power failure in management circuits', *Harvard Business Review* 57(4): 65–75.

Kanter, R.M. (1982) 'The middle manager as innovator', *Harvard Business Review* 60(4): 95–105.

Kanter, R.M. (1983) *The Change Masters: Innovation and Entrepreneurship in the American Corporation*, New York: Simon and Schuster.

Kanter, R.M. (1989a) 'Swimming in newstreams: Mastering innovation dilemmas', *California Management Review* 31(4): 45–69.

Kanter, R.M. (1989b) 'The new managerial work', *Harvard Business Review* 67(6): 85–92.

Kanter, R.M. (1989c) *When Giants Learn to Dance: Mastering the Challenge of Strategy, Management and Careers in the 1990s*, New York: Simon and Schuster.

Keys, B. and Case, T. (1990) 'How to become an influential manager', *Academy of Management Executive* 4: 38–51.

Kirkbride, P.S. (1985) 'The concept of power: A lacuna in industrial relations theory?', *Journal of Industrial Relations* 27(3): 265–82.

Kotter, J. (1977) 'Power, dependence, and effective management', *Harvard Business Review* 55(4): 125–36.

Knights, D. and Vurdubakis, T. (1994) 'Power, resistance and all that', in Jermier, J.M., Nord, W.R. and Knights, D. (eds), *Resistance and Power in Organizations: Agency, Subjectivity and the Labour Process*, London: Routledge.

Kram, K.E. (1985) *Mentoring at Work*, Glenview, Ill.: Scott, Foresman.

Lansbury, R.K. and Spillane, R. (1983) *Organisational Behaviour in the Australian Context*, Melbourne: Longman Cheshire.

Linstead, S. (1997) 'Resistance and return: Power, command and change management', *Studies in Cultures Organizations and Societies* 3(1): 67–89.

Lukes, S. (1974) *Power: A Radical View*, London: Macmillan.

Maddock, S. and Parkin, D. (1994) 'Gender cultures: How they affect men and women at work', in Davidson, M. and Burke, R. (eds), *Women in Management: Current Research Issues*, London: Paul Chapman.

Margretta, J. (1997) 'Will She Fit In?', *Harvard Business Review* March–April: 18–32.

Marshall, J. (1995) *Women Managers Moving On: Exploring Career and Life Choices*, London: Routledge.

Mauss, M. (1990) *The Gift*, London: Routledge.

McGregor, D. (1960) *The Human Side of Enterprise*, New York: McGraw-Hill.

Mechanic, D. (1962) 'Sources of power of lower participants in complex organisations', *Administrative Science Quarterly* 7: 349–64.

Mintzberg, H. (1983) *Power In and Around Organisations*, Englewood Cliffs, NJ: Prentice Hall.

Mintzberg, H. (1989) *Mintzberg on Management: Inside Our Strange World of Organisations*, New York and London: The Free Press.

Myers, D.W. and Humphreys, N.J. (1985) 'The caveats in mentorship', *Business Horizons* 28(4): 9–14.

Pfeffer, J. (1981) *Power in Organisations*, London: Pitman.

Pugh, D.S., Hickson, D.J. and Hinings, C.R. (1983) *Writers on Organizations*, Harmondsworth, UK: Penguin.

Ragins, B.R. (1997) 'Diversified mentoring relationships in organizations: A power perspective', *Academy of Management Review* 22(2): 482–521.

Reed, M. (1985) *Redirections in Organisational Analysis*, New York: Tavistock.

Ryan, M. (1984) 'Theories of power', in Kababadse, A. and Parker, C. (eds), *Power, Politics, and Organisations: A Behavioural Science View*, London: John Wiley.

Salaman, G. (1979) *Work Organisations, Resistance and Control*, London: Heinemann.

Silverman, D. (1970) *The Theory of Organisations*, London: The Open University.

Simpson, R. (1997) 'Have times changed? Career barriers and the token woman manager', *British Journal of Management* (Special Issue) 8: 5121–30.

Velasquez, M. (1988) *Business Ethics*, Englewood Cliffs, NJ: Prentice Hall.

Weber, M. (1964) *The Theory of Social Economic Organization*, London: Heinemann.

Whitley, W., Dougherty, T.W. and Dreher, G.F. (1991) 'Relationship of career mentoring and socioeconomic origins to managers' and professionals' early career progress', *Academy of Management Journal* 34: 331–51.

5

Leading and managing

Liz Fulop, Stephen Linstead and Richard Dunford

Questions about leadership

1 What is a leader?
2 Are all managers leaders?
3 Are women and men different as leaders?
4 Can leaders change their styles or behaviours?
5 Do we need leaders?

BHP installs holy trinity at top of tree

When those masters of business redesign, McKinsey and Co., went to see John Prescott about shuffling the management structure of BHP, Australia's largest company, they took with them models of the way the best in the world run shows. But the McKinsey team never got to strut its stuff. Instead, Prescott showed them what he wanted to do and the McKinsey team left knowing they might have a radical new model to show prospective clients. Yesterday Prescott lifted the curtain on BHP's new shape, unveiling structural change of an unprecedented dimension, at the same time anointing a new generation of senior managers, giving them the opportunity to stake their claims on his office. From today, BHP will take on what is, in Australian business at least, a unique configuration, with the greatest oddity being the holy trinity which now tops the management tree.

BHP has swept aside its management hierarchy in a fundamental restructure which unambiguously concentrates power in the hands of an executive triumvirate led by the managing director. The comprehensive organizational changes breathe life into Mr Prescott's 'One Company' vision for BHP. The shakeup transforms BHP's five existing divisions into eight – effectively carving BHP minerals into three new businesses and splitting BHP Steel into two. Eight key divisions – petroleum, copper, integrated steel, steel products, ferrous minerals, world minerals, coal and services – now make up BHP's $35 billion global asset portfolio. The restructure flows from the resignation of three key executives last month. BHP Minerals executive general manager, Dick Carter, and BHP Iron Ore group general manager, Geoff Wedlock, both resigned in stunning circumstances after a $1 billion cost blowout at BHP's $2.45 billion hot briquetted iron (HBI) project in Western Australia. BHP Petroleum chief executive, John O'Connor, resigned in the same week after falling out with the board over his desire to spin off the division as a separate entity. The executive bloodletting, HBI plant problems and disappointing earnings combined to slash the BHP share price, provoking severe criticism of the company's management.

Mr. Prescott said the changes would result in 'simpler management structures with fewer layers that (would) allow the operating systems to be more focused on their business… While BHP's decentralised management structure has served it well for the past two decades, enabling the company to become a successful global business, it has also allowed patterns of behaviour to evolve which have undermined that success' he said.

Prescott has added very senior executive muscle to an institution of long standing at BHP, the office of the managing director. Prescott will be joined in the renamed Office of the Chief Executive by Ron McNeilly and Graham McGregor. Prescott said yesterday his office would operate as a seamless triumvirate. When quizzed yesterday about whom the new steel operations will report to, Prescott was unequivocal: 'They report to me,' he said. In the same breath though, Prescott, with equal assurance, suggested McNeilly and McGregor had been promoted. In BHP speak, McNeilly has been given the task of 'capturing the company's cross-group strengths'. In reality, he has been charged with the job of proving that BHP is worth more than the sum of its parts. To do that McNeilly will become chairman of three 'BHP Business Councils': steel, minerals and energy. They have been told to develop formal links across BHP to draw tangible, bottom-line benefits from a far slicker flow of information across the business. Prescott said he drew his most senior men closer to his side to ensure he had the manpower to reassert the power of BHP's head office over its operations. The result will be greater accountability, the ambition to make BHP a faster, safer machine.

'Why do cars have brakes?' Prescott asks. 'Simple. So they can go faster.'

City reactions were varied. 'It strengthens Prescott's position at the very top' said one analyst. 'I think you are going to end up with a fairly bureaucratic management structure out of all this' said another. 'You are paying people a lot of money to make decisions but what seems to be happening is that their decision-making autonomy is being taken away from them. I don't think those guys are going to be happy having a business council look into their decision-making process.' On bringing in Philip Aiken as executive general manager of BHP Petroleum, Prescott said 'If Philip is to proceed further in the company he has to take responsibility for businesses of which he has relatively little knowledge. After all, that is the test of a chief executive.'

Another analyst called it 'a very silly move'.

BHP last changed its management structure in December 1995 when 'sweeping leadership changes' were said to have ushered in 'a new generation of leadership'.

Source: Adapted from articles by Richard Sproull and Matthew Stevens (1997), The Australian, 1 October, pp. 25–6, and B. Pheasant (1995), The Australian Financial Review, 11 December, p. 21.

Questions about the case

1 How would you characterize John Prescott's leadership style?
2 What considerations seem to be most important to Prescott?
3 What kind of relationships would you expect Prescott to have with (a) his triumvirate, (b) his eight divisional heads and (c) the BHP shopfloor workers?
4 How does Prescott think it is appropriate to develop future leaders?
5 How would you characterize the leadership approach at BHP?

Introduction

Leadership can be associated with both negative and positive behaviour. 'Good' or 'bad' leadership means different things to different people. Cruel and despotic behaviour can characterize the leadership style of one individual while another leader may develop a style based on kindness and benevolence. In either case, the leader is able to influence and persuade others to follow him or her. Often, leadership is associated with great political figures who inspire others because of their extraordinary vision or commitment to high ideals. These leaders seem to embody the most desirable and sought-after characteristics: they are people who are able to command loyalty, commitment, trust, dedication, respect, obedience, love or even worship from their followers. In the extreme, some followers are prepared to lay down their lives for their leaders or the leader's cause.

This type of leadership seems far removed from many workplaces. Yet one of the most significant claims of the Human Relations Movement was that leadership was the single most important factor in motivating employees and improving productivity. Early leadership studies focused attention on finding a 'one best way' style of leadership appropriate for shopfloor or supervisory conditions. A major aim of these studies was the development of training programmes to assist managers to become good or effective leaders. However, once leadership studies moved beyond supervisory levels, a more complex picture emerged, one in which leadership became associated with influence and visionary qualities. In fact, leadership is a fundamental component of many theories of organization and management.

This chapter presents an overview of the way leadership has been analyzed and assesses its relevance to claims about managerial performance, beginning with some very early, though nonetheless influential theories, and moving to studies questioning the role of leadership in organizations. The 'dark' side of leadership – a topic often omitted from management texts – is also examined in the context of the narcissistic leader. We also include gender and cross-cultural considerations of leadership, carrying on themes developed in our earlier chapters.

The trait approach

The most basic approach to understanding leadership focused on the notion of traits, that is, the assumption that good leadership resides in the innate abilities of certain individuals who are considered to be born leaders – usually 'great men' of history such as Churchill, Gandhi, etc. This approach has attractions in that it promises good leadership will be achieved by selecting individuals with the appropriate traits. However, the negative side is that it also involves the assumption that it is not possible to develop leaders through training. The interest in leadership traits developed as part of the personnel testing movement in the period immediately following the First World War. Wartime use of psychological testing for the selection of military personnel was followed by industrial applications of similar techniques. Leadership research developed as part of this (Stogdill 1974a). However, there is a notable lack of evidence for a certain trait or set of traits being universally appropriate in all situations (Stogdill 1974b; Spillane 1984). Even if it was accepted, for example, that Gandhi, the charismatic leader from India who in the 1940s led the independence movement, was a born leader, it is impossible to establish that his qualities would create effective leadership in another culture or society.

However, Shelley Kirkpatrick and Edwin Locke (1991), in reviewing recent research on traits, found that certain traits do appear to have a consistent impact on leader effectiveness. These traits include those listed in Exhibit 5.1.

• **Drive**	• high desire for achievement
	• ambition to get ahead in work and career
	• high level of energy
	• tenacity or persistence in the right things
	• initiative to change things and make things happen
• **Leadership motivation**	• the desire to lead
	• the willingness to assume responsibility
	• the seeking of power as a means to achieve desired goals (*socialised power motive*) rather than as an end in itself (*personalised power motive*)
• **Honesty and integrity**	• the correspondence between word and deed
	• being trustworthy
	• the foundation to attract and retain followers through gaining their trust
• **Self-confidence**	• needed to withstand setbacks, persevere through hard times and lead others in new directions
	• the ability to take hard decisions and stand by them
	• managing the perceptions of others on self-confidence, and commanding their respect
	• emotionally stable
• **Cognitive ability**	• above average intelligence to analyse situations accurately, solve problems effectively, and make suitable decisions
	• not necessarily a genius, usually not
	• managing the perceptions of others on intelligence
• **Knowledge of the business**	• able to gather and assimilate extensive information about the company and industry
	• necessary for developing suitable visions, strategies and business plans

Exhibit 5.1   Common leader traits

Source: Shelley Kirkpatrick and Edwin A. Locke (1991), 'Leadership: Do traits matter?', Academy of Management Executive 5(2), pp. 48–60.

Nevertheless, there is no fixed set of traits that constitutes good leadership. The traits above can be found in a variety of mixes in effective leaders in practice – and it is difficult to distinguish between some of the above traits and acquired skills or behaviours. Are we born with all the above traits or are some of them attained through learning, experience and relationships?

Charles Manz and Henry Sims (1992: 310–11) suggested that a variation on the 'great man' model of leadership was the 'strong man' one. Deliberately masculine in its assumptions, this form of leadership was reserved for males. It glorified the tough, head-kicking image of authority in which the leader had superior strengths, skills and the courage to size up the situation, take decisive action and command the troops. Reprimands (head-kicking or 'kick-ass') and punishment followed non-compliance by subordinates. The authors suggested that while this leadership approach might seem out of favour, there was still evidence of it in corporate America (and no doubt elsewhere).

The focus on leadership style

The inability of researchers to identify a fixed set of leadership traits led to a growing focus on leadership behaviour, that is, on how leaders act, not what they in some innate sense supposedly 'are'. Much of the discussion on this matter has revolved around the concepts of *autocratic* and *democratic* styles, the former associated with various interpretations of Taylorism and the latter with the Human Relations Movement (see Chapters 2 and 6). The superiority of the democratic style in terms of worker satisfaction and performance became accepted wisdom permeating the human relations approach.

Theory X and Theory Y

The argument that there is a superior leadership style, suitable for all situations, was formalized in the work of Douglas McGregor (1960), a practising manager turned academic. His work was a development of the motivation theory of Abraham Maslow (1987), who argued that human behaviour flowed from the effects of certain innate needs: physiological (e.g. food), safety (security), social (e.g. a sense of belonging), esteem (being valued) and self-actualization (fulfilling one's potential) (see also Chapters 2 and 7). Central to Maslow's model is the notion that these needs constitute a hierarchy: that is, physiological needs must be largely met before safety needs, then safety needs before social ones, and so on. McGregor argued that it was the higher-level needs that were the most relevant to 'modern' employees, but that leadership practices often failed to reflect this. Rather, the leadership practices are often a product of the following set of assumptions:

- The average human being has an inherent dislike of work and will avoid it if possible.
- Because of this most people must be coerced, controlled, directed and threatened with punishment to put adequate effort into the achievement of organizational objectives.
- The average human being prefers to be directed, wishes to avoid responsibility, has relatively little ambition and wants security above all (McGregor 1960: 33–4).

This set of assumptions he labelled 'Theory X'. As well as believing that Theory X was based on an inadequate understanding of motivation, McGregor believed that it was self-fulfilling, in that if workers were treated in accordance with such assumptions their behaviour might well come to reflect these assumptions. For example, workers treated as if they lacked initiative might well believe that initiative was neither encouraged nor rewarded, and consequently feel that there was little point in showing it. McGregor was also highly critical of the American management style, which he saw as largely reflecting Theory X assumptions. He believed that managers felt threatened by the idea that workers might have needs for such things as social association, recognition and responsibility.

Wage incentives, fringe benefits or even job security could not redress apathy and hostility in the workplace: rather, opportunities had to be created for satisfying higher-order needs. McGregor did not propose specific strategies for achieving this, but he did identify the type of management or leadership style that would have to be adopted to satisfy such needs. While McGregor dubbed this approach a 'Theory Y' style of management, he did not propose that Theory X management had no place in business. He concluded that in times of economic recession, for example, when people were concerned with struggling to keep their jobs and wages at a decent level, Theory X might be an acceptable leadership style. In ordinary circumstances, however, it could never be an appropriate style (McGregor 1960: 40). There was always a 'one best way' to manage.

As an alternative to a style of leadership based on Theory X assumptions, McGregor argues for the virtues of Theory Y, consisting of the following assumptions:

- Work is as natural as rest or play.
- External control and threat of punishment are not the only means for bringing about effort towards organizational objectives. People will exercise self-direction and self-control in the service of objectives to which they are committed.
- Commitment to objectives is a function of the rewards associated with their achievement.
- The average human being learns under proper conditions not only to accept but to seek responsibility.
- The capacity to exercise a relatively high degree of imagination, ingenuity and creativity in the solution of organizational problems is widely, not narrowly, distributed in the population.
- In most work organizations, the abilities of most employees are only partially utilized (McGregor 1960: 47–8).

McGregor was adamant that if employees were lazy, indifferent or unwilling to take responsibilities, uncreative and uncooperative, then Theory Y implies that the causes lie with management. Under the Theory Y approach, management and organizational members' goals had to be arrived at through consultation and joint decision making. Participatory management encouraged the development of different forms of management control other than those more commonly associated with Theory X. In Theory Y, the emphasis was placed on developing indirect controls such as self-direction and self-control among individuals and groups and this is still a strong theme in many approaches to teamwork (see Chapter 6). If management and organizational goals were determined through mutual consultation and joint decision making, McGregor believed this would ensure that employees identified with such goals and were committed to achieving them. Theory Y encourages employees to abandon negative behaviours (e.g. apathy and laziness) and exercise greater individual self-control and direction in achieving agreed goals. The leadership style for effective management is thus deemed by McGregor to be one which is democratic, consultative and participative.

The validity of McGregor's approach is rather difficult to assess, however, because it is more a philosophical stance than a coherent set of conclusions drawn from specific research data. Stephen Robbins (1988) claims that there is a lack of evidence that actions consistent with Theory Y assumptions lead to more motivated workers, a view shared by Tony Watson (1986), although the latter does argue that McGregor's work is beneficial to the extent that it invites managers to think about the behavioural assumptions they make in their dealings with subordinates. Still, many managers easily identify with the Theory X and Y distinction and its normative view of 'good' and 'bad' leadership.

Concern for task and concern for people

McGregor's dilemma is reflected in the fact that many studies in the style tradition are centrally concerned with the notion that a leader's style can be analysed in terms of its focus on *task accomplishment* and *concern for subordinates,* rather than purely motivational assumptions.

A widely referenced study was begun by researchers at Ohio State University in the USA in the late 1940s. Data on subordinates' assessments of their leaders' behaviour were analyzed and deemed to be reducible to two core dimensions. The first, *consideration*, refers to the extent to which an individual is likely to have job relationships characterized by mutual trust, respect for subordinates' ideas and concern for their feelings. The second, *initiating structure*, refers to the extent to which leaders are likely to define and structure their role and those of subordinates towards attainment of formal organizational goals (Fleishman and Peters 1962; Stogdill 1974b: 128–41).

The Ohio State researchers argued that:

- High 'consideration' was associated with higher subordinate satisfaction.
- High 'initiating structure' was associated with greater effectiveness, higher grievance levels and higher absenteeism.
- Leaders could be rated high or low on both dimensions. When a leader was rated high on both, the high grievance levels did not occur.

The results were interpreted as indicating that the ideal leader would be high on both dimensions. However, critics of these studies have been much less prepared to accept this interpretation (Korman 1966).

A complementary set of studies based around research at the University of Michigan in the USA differentiated *production-centred* and *employee-centred* managers. The former were characterized by rigid work standards, detailed task organization and close supervision; the latter involved the encouragement of participation in workplace practices, trust and respect (Likert 1961). Its findings were much the same as those of the Ohio studies, with a high ranking on both criteria being seen as ideal.

Other studies tended to confirm the conclusions of the Ohio State and Michigan University studies, though with slight variations on themes and variables examined (Vecchio, Hearn and Southey 1996: 481–6).

The leadership grid

A widely used approach that focuses on style (using an extended version of the production–employee-centred theme) is the leadership grid approach developed initially by Robert Blake and Jane Mouton (1978) and then refined by Blake and Anne McCanse (1991). Popular in management training, this grid identified one particular style as the most effective.

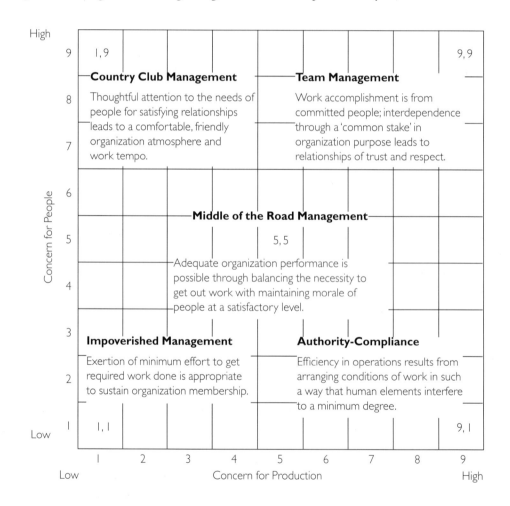

Figure 5.1   The leadership grid

Source: The Leadership Grid Figure from Robert R. Blake and Anne Adams McCanse (1991), Leadership Dilemmas – Grid Solutions, Houston: Gulf, p. 29. Copyright © 1991, by Scientific Methods, Inc. Reproduced by permission of the owners.

Management: A Critical Text

166

This style (9, 9 in Figure 5.1), involves maximum concern for both production and people, with these two factors being seen as interdependent, rather than being treated as independent (or as separate dimensions), as in the Ohio studies and Theory X and Theory Y.

Blake and Mouton's management grid, developed in the 1960s, identified four factors, while the Blake and McCanse one identifies five basic combinations of concern for people and concern for production, using a scale of 1–9 for each factor. These five factors are described in Figure 5.1.

The leadership grid approach, with its arguments in favour of the team management style, fitted in well with the human relations notion that productivity and satisfaction could be mutually optimized. However, empirical support for the universal application of their model is at best mixed (see, for example, Larson, Hunt and Osborn 1976; Bryman 1986). Furthermore, Blake and Mouton, in advocating a preferred leadership style in all situations, also espoused 'one best way' to manage or lead.

The System 4 approach

The System 4 approach developed by Rensis Likert (1961, 1967, 1979) is based on four kinds of management systems, as described below:

- *System 1* **Exploitative authoritative:** where leadership is autocratic, incorporating punishment-centred motivation, minimal delegation, minimal information provision to subordinates and decision making by edict.
- *System 2* **Benevolent authoritative:** use of rewards to motivate but no less centralization of decision making than in System 1.
- *System 3* **Consultative:** subordinates are consulted over decisions; some trust and teamwork exist.
- *System 4* **Participative group:** high level of trust and confidence; decision making through participation; communication/information flows upwards, downwards and laterally.

Likert developed the fourfold management systems model by surveying over 200 organizations in an attempt to isolate their performance characteristics. Later he used the management systems classification to look at a broad range of organizational activities, including leadership, motivation, communication, interaction and influence, decision making, goal setting and control processes. Likert surveyed several hundred managers and found that the least productive departments or units equated with Systems 1 and 2, and the more productive with Systems 3 and 4. A participative style of leadership (i.e. System 4) was found to be superior in terms of high productivity and quality and fostering loyalty and cooperation among subordinates (Mullins 1985: 149). System 4 is another version of the 'one best way' approach to leadership and is very similar in concept to Theory Y. Systems 1 and 2 leadership bear some relationship to Theory X.

Contingency approaches (or it all depends on the situation)

A central problem with the style approach is that it gives no place to the significance of the *situation* or *context* in which the leader is operating. Contingency approaches to leadership seek to systematize the relationship between situation and leadership style. That is, they attempt to identify particular contextual situations and to determine the style of leadership most appropriate in that situation. Contingency theory is based on the assumption that for a given situation there will be one identifiably best leadership style.

Matching leader and situation

The classic contingency study is that of Fred Fiedler (1967, 1974). His contingency theory involves the identification of leaders as either *relationship-centred* or *task-centred*, thus continuing the duality of styles present in the previous style studies. An individual's leadership style is assessed on the basis of the Least-Preferred Co-worker (LPC) scale or coefficient. This involves the individual thinking of the person that he or she least enjoyed working with and then characterizing him or her in terms of a set of bipolar adjectives, for example 'pleasant–unpleasant', 'friendly–unfriendly'. On the basis of an individual's answers on the LPC scale, he or she is characterized as relationship or task oriented. An individual who has a high score (64 and above) is strongly relationship oriented while a person with a low score (57 or below) will be task oriented.

Fiedler argued that a low LPC score, for example, indicated that the person, when given the choice, would opt for getting the job done rather than worrying about developing good interpersonal relations. A relationship-motivated or high LPC leader accomplishes tasks through good interpersonal relations and in situations that involve a whole group performing tasks. The relationship-motivated leader may perform poorly under pressure or stress because of his or her propensity to pay attention to interpersonal relations rather than the task. Alternatively, the task-motivated or low LPC leader is strongly committed to completing the task through adopting clear, standardized procedures and a no-nonsense attitude to getting the job done. Under pressure or when the situation is out of control, the task-motivated leader will put the task ahead of the group's feelings and pursue its accomplishment at all costs (Fiedler, Chemers and Mahar 1976: 6–11).

The situation determining leadership style is analyzed in terms of three aspects: *leader–member relations, task structure* and *leader's position power*. Leader–member relations refers to how well leaders get on with their subordinates, how well they are respected or trusted. Task structure is a measure of how clearly the task is specified (e.g. highly structured and detailed). Leader's position power is a measure of the formal authority of leaders and their capacity to exercise authority through rewards or punishments. Collectively, these three factors are known as the 'favourability of the situation'. In favourable situations there is little need for relationship-focused activities, since relationships are already good. In this situation, the task-centred leader performs best. On the other hand, in an unfavourable situation, the relationship-centred leader may give insufficient attention to task-related problems. In this situation, the task-motivated leader comes to the fore. The task-oriented leader operates best at these extremes. In the 'middle', that is, where the situation is moderately favourable, the skills of the relationship-centred leader come into their own (see Figure 5.2).

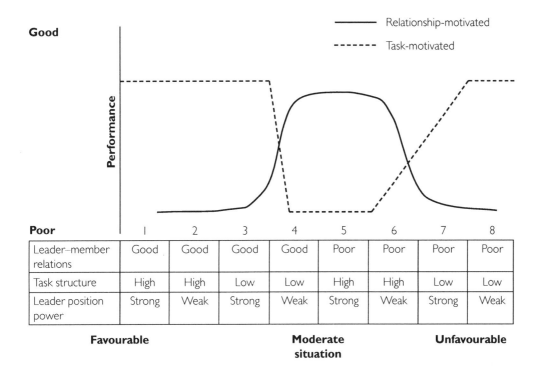

	1	2	3	4	5	6	7	8
Leader–member relations	Good	Good	Good	Good	Poor	Poor	Poor	Poor
Task structure	High	High	Low	Low	High	High	Low	Low
Leader position power	Strong	Weak	Strong	Weak	Strong	Weak	Strong	Weak

Favourable **Moderate situation** **Unfavourable**

Figure 5.2 The performance of relationship and task-motivated leaders in different situational-favourable conditions

Source: Fred E. Fiedler (1974), 'The contingency model – new directions for leadership utilisation', Journal of Comtemporary Business 3, Autumn, p. 71.

An example of Situation 1 leadership in Figure 5.2 would be a popular squad leader in the army. The member–leader relations are good, especially because expertise and experience are highly regarded, the task is structured and position power is very strong. In this situation, Fiedler's model suggests that a task-oriented leader would be most effective. Situation 5 leadership is where a person occupies an unpopular position, such as a shopfloor supervisor, and while authority can be wielded it will not often succeed in gaining cooperation. In this situation, the relationship-oriented leader is likely to achieve continuous support and compliance (Duncan 1978: 232–3).

Unlike the stance taken by theorists such as Likert or Blake and Mouton, Fiedler is not confident that a person's leadership style can be changed by training. Instead, he argues that it is likely to be more effective to try to change the situational conditions (Fiedler *et al.* 1976). Leader–member relations might, for example, be changed through such things as increasing informal or social interaction with subordinates or showing greater appreciation for their efforts. Task structure might be modified by such things as delegating more (or less) decision making to subordinates. Position power can be altered by such strategies as giving more (or less) authority to subordinates or by increasing (or decreasing) subordinates' access to information.

Despite its classic status, Fiedler's study has been subject to considerable criticism. This includes the claims that the LPC measure corresponds poorly with subordinates' accounts of leader behaviour; that the LPC score for an individual often varies over time; and that there has been a failure to replicate results (Bryman 1985, 1986). However, Fielder disputes these criticisms, arguing that the LPC score is 'a highly reliable and surprisingly stable measure' (Fiedler and Garcia 1987: 79) and that the weight of evidence clearly attests to the validity of the model (Fiedler and Garcia 1987: 86–93). Some organizational behaviour texts do note that there has been some dispute over the validity of Fiedler's approach (Hellreigel, Slocum and Woodman 1986; Stoner, Collins and Yetton 1985), but others simply treat it as an uncontested classic study (Hunsaker and Cook 1986).

Path–goal theory

Path–goal theory, developed by Robert House (1971) and others (Evans 1970), proposes that leaders can affect the job satisfaction, motivation and performance of group members by their actions. One way is to make rewards dependent on the meeting of performance goals, but the leader can also help the subordinates to achieve these goals by outlining the paths toward the goals and by removing obstacles in their way. This may entail the leader adopting different styles of leadership according to the situation. The theory identifies four different types of behaviour:

1   *Directive leadership* – giving specific guidance to subordinates and asking them to follow standard rules and regulations. Shows low consideration for people, but high regard for task and structure.
2   *Supportive leadership* – includes being friendly to subordinates and sensitive to their needs. Shows high consideration for people, low regard for task and structure.
3   *Participative leadership* – involves sharing information with subordinates and consulting with them before making decisions. Shows high concern for both structure and consideration.
4   *Achievement-oriented leadership* – entails setting challenging goals and emphasizing excellence while simultaneously showing confidence that subordinates will perform well. It does not really involve subordinates, so it is not that high on consideration in that sense – in fact, it has some similarities with the more positive features of Scientific Management.

House argues that all four styles can be, and often are, used by a leader in varying situations, or as a situation unfolds, and among his research subjects have been US presidents, who have to influence a wide variety of people. The theory has put forward a number of propositions on what behaviours suit what type of situation; for example:

- *Ambiguous situations* benefit from *directive behaviour*. Subordinates appreciate their superior's help in increasing the probability that they will be able to attain the desired reward. Where situations have greater clarity in the nature of the task or the goal this will be less necessary.
- *Stressful situations* benefit from *supportive leader behaviour* which alleviates subordinate tension and dissatisfaction.

The existing research on path–goal theory tends to support these propositions, which are clearly consistent with earlier theories and, one might add, with commonsense. One of the strengths of this theory has been argued to be its attempt to link leader behaviour with theories of motivation. Yet much of what is implicit in the theory relies on assumptions about power and organizational politics that are taken for granted. For example sharing information under participative leadership might not occur for political reasons rather than because of a style issue.

Leader–member exchange theory

Originally called the *vertical dyad linkage model of leadership*, this theory was developed by George Graen and his colleagues (Dansereau, Graen and Haga 1975; Graen and Schiemann 1978; Liden and Graen 1980). Graen questions the conventional view that leaders display the same style and behaviours towards all their subordinates. On the contrary, he argues, there is no 'average' leadership style. Just take your own experience of work or school – can you think of one boss or teacher that everyone liked, or by whom everyone felt that they were treated the same? Such equitable treatment is hard to achieve, and leaders are only human – the nature of their tasks and their own personal preferences will mean that they interact with some people more than others. Graen argues that leaders behave somewhat differently towards *each* subordinate, and the resulting linkages or relationships between the leader and a subordinate (the *dyad*) are likely to differ in quality. The same superior might have poor interpersonal relations with some subordinates but fairly open and trusting relations with others. Graen argues that these patterns of relations fall into two groups, being dependent on whether the subordinate is 'in' or 'out'. Members of the *in-group* are invited to share in decision making and are given added responsibility, and are often taken into the manager's confidence. Members of the *out-group*, however, are supervised within the narrow terms of their formal employment contract, and managed on a 'need-to-know' basis. The trusted 'right hands' in the in-group tend to find their jobs enriched and their personal development accelerated, while the 'hired hands' in the out-group have limited opportunities and display low satisfaction and higher turnover.

Leaders and in-group members tend to believe that competence is the major reason why they are members of that group, but out-group members argue that it is ingratiation, favouritism and politics (Aktouf 1996). Interpersonal attraction certainly must be important, and research has demonstrated that in-group members tend to see problems in the same way as their leader. This may be an indication that leaders prefer people to be like them, which has its own dangers of 'groupthink' and the 'yes-man' (*sic*) mentality. As initially indicated by the Hawthorne Studies, once people are separated into high-performing and low-performing groups, this tends to become a self-fulfilling prophecy, and people become high or low performing accordingly, but favouritism can also lead to people being promoted beyond their competence. Omar Aktouf (1996), in a study conducted on both capitalist and communist workplace relations, argues that although supervisors report *competence* as a criterion for promotion and preferment, it is impression-management that seems to be most important in practice.

Graen has undertaken research on the model in Confucian cultures, where society is based on concentric circles of intimacy and favouritism from the family outwards. Despite the social background of several circles, in practice the in-group/out-group dualism is common where the patriarchal leadership style prevails. Research has not yet been done on the gender dimensions of this theory, but one would expect it to display close links to the 'glass-ceiling' concept of limits to women's progress in organizations (see Chapter 2).

Leaders and followers: Hersey and Blanchard's situational leadership

One characteristic of an effective leader is, according to Warren Bennis (1985), the ability to *manage* and *communicate meaning* to ensure that those leading can capture the imaginations of others and align these behind the organizational goals and priorities. Paul Hersey and Kenneth Blanchard (1996; Hersey 1985) develop their situational leadership model to enable better understanding of how to achieve this, focusing on the 'actual behaviour' of leaders rather than their 'values or orientations', as in other approaches. Their approach to leadership has two basic assumptions:

1   *what leaders do to people is more important than what they intend to do*, that is, leaders are judged and assessed by others on their behaviours not their attitudes (for this reason, it is important to explore the various behaviours that leaders can adopt); and
2   *what leaders do to others must be task specific*, that is, leadership effectiveness depends on the ability to influence individuals and what they are doing.

Let us consider the implications of both of these assumptions for leadership effectiveness.

The first part of the discussion relates to the behaviours leaders can adopt when attempting to influence the performance of others. Hersey and Blanchard suggest that there are two distinctive sets of behaviours which you use when leading others – directive and supportive behaviour.

Directive behaviour

This behaviour relates to the extent to which leaders show or tell people what to do, how to do it and where and when to do it, and then closely supervise those people's performance. A leader has a choice, in any given situation, to use a lot or very little of this behaviour (e.g. *highly directive*: 'I want you to take the hammer in the right hand, hold the nail with the left hand, and when I nod my head, hit it with the hammer with all your might' – in which case the instructions must be clear and non-ambiguous! – or *low directive*: 'You decide what will work best in this situation to achieve the given objective').

Supportive behaviour

This represents the extent to which you encourage and praise people and facilitate involvement in problem solving and decision making by seeking their ideas and opinions and listening actively to their responses. A leader, again, has a choice as to how much support is offered (e.g., *highly supportive*: 'What do you need to tackle this problem – how can I help you get the best result?', or *low supportive*: 'Just get it right, or else').

Hersey and Blanchard subsequently defined four leadership styles which are the combinations of high and low directive and supportive behaviours. Figure 5.3 describes the four leadership styles proposed by Hersey and Blanchard.

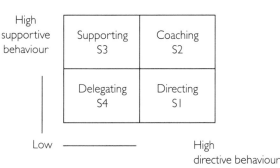

High supportive behaviour	Supporting S3
	Coaching S2
	Delegating S4
	Directing S1

Low ———————— High directive behaviour

Figure 5.3 Hersey and Blanchard's leadership styles

Source: Adapted from Kenneth Blanchard, Patricia Zigarmi and Drea Zigarmi (1985), Leadership and the One-Minute Manager, *London: Harper Collins, p. 47.*

They labelled these styles S1 to S4 and suggested that whenever leaders encountered situations where it was necessary to influence another's performance, they always had four possible approaches (Blanchard, Zigarmi and Zigarmi 1985: 56). These approaches are:

- S1 – *directing* – providing structure and control
- S2 – *coaching* – providing direction and support
- S3 – *supporting* – praising, listening and facilitating
- S4 – *delegating* – turning over responsibility for day to day decision making

Task specificity

The skill of effective leadership is to know the characteristics of the situation wherein the various styles are likely to work most effectively. The authors also concluded that two critical aspects of the follower (the person being influenced) are important determinants of leadership effectiveness – and that for all followers, these characteristics are task specific. They coined the term *development level* and suggested that it has two elements:

1. *competence* – the extent to which the person, for a particular task, possesses the knowledge and skills which could be gained from education, training and/or experience; and
2. *commitment* – the extent to which the person possesses the confidence and motivation to do the task.

Hersey and Blanchard suggested that the four leadership styles relate to four different development levels, being various combinations of competence and commitment. They defined these development levels in the following way.

- D1 *Enthusiastic beginners* Characteristic of people who lack competence, but are enthusiastic and committed. The authors suggested that such people need direction and supervision to get them going (S1).

173

- D2 *Disillusioned learners* Characteristic of people who have some competence but lack commitment (having become disillusioned about their ability to achieve outcomes). The authors suggested that such people need direction for their lack of total competence but also support to rebuild their enthusiasm and self-esteem (S2).
- D3 *Reluctant contributors* Characteristic of people who actually have the competence to do a task but lack confidence and/or motivation actually to attempt the task. It is suggested that rather than needing to be told how to perform, these people need support and encouragement to raise their flagging commitment (S3).
- D4 *Peak performer* Characteristic of people who are both competent and committed to achieving a particular task. Such people need only the opportunity to perform (S4).

The resulting model (SLII) is illustrated in Figure 5.4, which comes from Blanchard *et al.* (1985). It suggests several important thing, as outlined on p. 175:

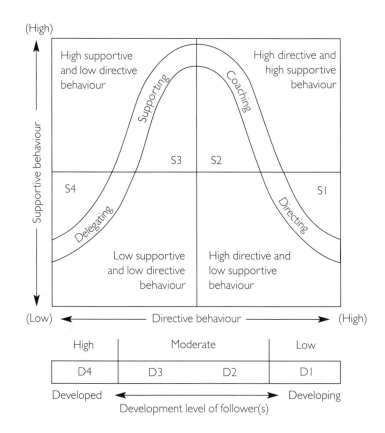

Figure 5.4 The four leadership styles

Source: Kenneth Blanchard, Patricia Zigarmi and Drea Zigarmi (1985), Leadership and the One-Minute Manager, *London: Harper Collins, p. 69.*

- individuals' development levels change in a more or less 'typical' pattern which follows the increase in levels of competence;
- for different tasks people may or will have different levels of development;
- effective leaders match their leadership, for each task, to the development level of their followers; and
- effective leaders recognize the 'development cycle of individuals learning a task' and therefore vary their leadership style to meet the followers' need.

The management of meaning for the leader becomes a task of understanding:
- what goal is to be achieved;
- what tasks must be undertaken to achieve this goal;
- who will be undertaking these tasks;
- what their development level is for each task; and
- what leadership style is thus appropriate.

The main features of the contingency approaches we have discussed are summarized in Table 5.1. The importance of these theories was to show the variability and complexity of leadership situations and the problems of adopting a 'one best way' to lead or manage.

Contingency theorists have been criticized on a number of points, there being two main criticisms. First, the theories do not present a cumulative set of ideas, with each one seeming to choose different variables (or contingency factors) to explain or build the theory. Often the choice of the variables, such as 'supportive' and 'directive' behaviour, as in the case of Hersey and Blanchard, is not sufficiently well explained or justified. Contingency theorists seem to amass a range of factors that can leave the manager overwhelmed and unclear about

Table 5.1 *Comparison of major contingency leadership models*

Model	Leader behaviour	Situational variables	Outcomes/criteria
Fiedler's contingency model	Task-oriented (low LPC) Relationship-oriented (high LPC)	Leader–member relations Task structure Position power	Performance
Path–goal theory	Directive Supportive Participative Achievement oriented	Task structure Subordinate characteristics	Satisfaction Motivation Performance
Vertical dyad linkage	Differential treatment of subordinates (in-group or out-group)	Subordinate competence Subordinate loyalty	Satisfaction Performance Turnover
Hersey–Blanchard	Concern for people (directive or supportive) Concern for task (competence and commitment)	Developmental levels of subordinates (D1, D2, D3, D4)	Effectiveness

Source: Modified from Robert Vecchio, Greg Hearn and Greg Southey (1996), *Organizational Behaviour*, Sydney: Harcourt Brace, p. 497.

which factors are the important ones to consider (Barrett and Sutcliffe 1992: 12). Second, the contingency factors are not related to or explained in terms of such things as organization structure, technology, size or other dimensions that are also likely to impact on leadership processes (Barrett and Sutcliffe 1992: 12).

Leadership substitutes

Contingency approaches assume that there is no one right style for all situations, but they also assume that there is a right one for a particular situation: it is assumed that leadership style is important. This is questioned by Steven Kerr and John Jermier (1978), who argue that leadership is sometimes not important because of the existence of *leadership substitutes* or *leadership neutralizers*. Table 5.2 summarizes the Kerr and Jermier model based on subsequent research by Jon Howell *et al.* (1990) whose model included the concept of *enhancers*.

A *leadership substitute* is something which by its presence makes the behaviour unnecessary, for example, employees with a strong attachment to a profession are likely to develop horizontal relationships inside and/or outside their organization, thereby making any leadership style less relevant. Highly trained and educated individuals are more likely to be self-directed and seek autonomy, minimizing the importance of leadership. Experience on the job can also reduce the need for leadership. To the extent that professional peer assessment is important, such as in professions like medicine, the significance of the organizational leader's role is reduced, if not removed in some circumstances.

A *leadership neutralizer* is something that by its absence prevents the leadership behaviour from being important; for example, to the extent that the employee is indifferent towards the rewards that the organization is able to provide, any type of leader loses significance. On the other hand, organizations might look for leadership substitutes if they believe leaders are not performing well and cannot be retrained, removed, transferred or their position redefined. This could be the situation, for example, facing organizations in which a family member has been appointed to management. Leadership neutralizers include such things as removing rewards from the control of leaders or managers so that promotion, etc. is not influenced by them. Others are listed in Table 5.2.

Leadership *enhancers* amplify the impact a leader has on employees, such as altering reward systems. Leadership enhancers increase the influence of leaders, while neutralizers are deliberate strategies used to create 'power vacuums' (Howell *et al.* 1990: 30–4). Leadership substitutes are difficult to overcome and often lie outside the control of management yet are recognized as important influences on the changing role of leadership in organizations.

Kerr and Jermier see their approach as 'a true situational theory of leadership' (1978: 401), in that it is based on the argument that in some situations the role of the leader is replaced by alternative mechanisms. Effective leadership is correspondingly treated as 'the ability to supply subordinates with needed guidance and good feelings which are not being supplied by other sources' (Kerr and Jermier 1978: 400). One of the criticisms made against Kerr and Jermier's approach is that rather than acting as substitutes or neutralizers, such factors are supplements to leadership, that is, they coexist, 'filling in for one another as the situation dictates' (Howell and Dorfman 1981: 728). Thus the point is made that leadership is merely one factor at play in the determination of organizational outcomes.

Table 5.2 *Leadership substitutes, neutralizers and enhancers: Eleven managerial leadership problems and effective coping strategies**

Leadership problems	Enhancer/Neutralizer	Substitutes
Leader doesn't keep on top of details in the department; coordination among subordinates is difficult	Not useful	Develop self-managed work teams; encourage team members to interact within and across departments
Competent leadership is resisted through non-compliance or passive resistance	*Enhancers*: increase employees' dependence on leader through greater leader control of rewards/ resources; increase their perception of leader's influence outside of work group	Develop collegial systems of guidance for decision making
Leader doesn't provide support or recognition for jobs well done	Not useful	Develop a reward system that operates independently of the leader. Enrich jobs to make them inherently satisfying
Leader doesn't set targets or goals, or clarify roles for employees	Not useful	Emphasize experience and ability in selecting subordinates. Establish group goal-setting. Develop an organizational culture that stresses high performance expectations
A leader behaves inconsistently over time	*Enhancers*: these are dysfunctional *Neutralizer:* remove rewards from leader's control	Develop group goal-setting and group rewards
An upper-level manager regularly bypasses a leader in dealing with employees, or countermands the leader's directions	*Enhancers:* increase leader's control over rewards and resources; build leader's image via in-house champion or visible 'important' responsibilities. *Neutralizer*: physically distance subordinates from upper-level manager	Increase the professionalization of employees
A unit is in disarray or out of control	Not useful	Develop highly formalized plans, goals, routines and areas of responsibility
Leadership is brutal, autocratic	*Enhancers:* these are dysfunctional. *Neutralizers*: physically distance subordinates; remove rewards from leader's control	Establish group goal-setting and peer performance appraisal

Leadership problems	Enhancer/Neutralizer	Substitutes
There is inconsistency across different organizational units	Not useful	Increase formalization. Set up a behaviourally focused reward system
Leadership is unstable over time, leaders are rotated and/or leave office frequently	Not useful	Establish competent advisory staff units. Increase professionalism of employees
Incumbent management is poor; there's no heir apparent	*Enhancers*: these are dysfunctional. *Neutralizer*: assign non-leader duties to problem managers	Emphasize experience and ability in selecting employees. Give employees more training

Source: Howell *et al.* (1990), 'Substitutes for leadership: Effective alternatives to ineffective leadership', *Organizational Dynamics* Summer, pp. 28–9.

* The suggested solutions are examples of many possibilities for each problem.

Leadership as political influence

One of the main limitations of leadership studies is the predominant focus on supervisory style. Whether it be in terms of democratic versus autocratic or task-oriented versus people-oriented, leadership studies have primarily focused on the way in which leaders have treated their subordinates in a supervisory sense. This has led to a relative lack of attention to the actions of those in designated leadership positions as 'organizational networkers'. In the late 1940s, Donald Pelz (1952) attempted to identify the attitudes and behaviours that lead to greater employee satisfaction. To his surprise, he discovered that there was no significant difference in this regard between the leaders of 'high-satisfaction' and 'low-satisfaction' groups. The key explanatory factor seemed not to be the leader's style, but rather the extent to which he or she had influence outside the group, in the broader organizational milieu. Pelz found that:

> If a supervisor (or any group leader) has considerable influence within his organization, then when he behaves so as to help employees towards their goals, he will achieve concrete benefits for them… Not his good intentions, but his actual accomplishments are what pay dividends in employee satisfaction (Pelz 1952: 213).

In fact, well-meaning, democratic leaders without influence may actually reduce satisfaction because they might arouse expectations they are subsequently unable to meet (Pelz 1952). This 'lost tradition' in leadership research was resurrected by theorists such as Rosabeth Moss Kanter (1977, 1979, 1983) who argued that what was important was the leader's ability to get a good share of available resources, opportunities (for promotion, etc.) and rewards for his or her subordinates. Leadership thus had more to do with developing lateral and vertical contacts (or connections) than with the supervisory style of the leader. The role of leader is likely to be predominantly one of acting strategically within an established network of connections. This is what the employees in Pelz's study were referring to when they asserted the importance of the leader having 'influence'. It was not influence over them that concerned them; it was the ability of leaders successfully – in terms of their sub-ordinates' expectations of what they can do for them – to operate in or be influential in the broader organizational networks (Bolman and Deal 1991: 437–9). Exhibit 5.2 identifies some indicators of a manager's influence within an organization. The political and power implications of this approach were discussed in Chapter 4, but are also discussed below.

> **To what extent a manager can intercede favourably on behalf of someone in trouble with top management**
>
> - Get a good placement for a talented subordinate
> - Get approval for expenditures beyond the budget
> - Get above-average salary increases for subordinates
> - Get important items on the agenda at various meetings
> - Get fast access to top management
> - Get regular, frequent access to top management
> - Get early information about important decisions and major changes to policy

Exhibit 5.2   Some common symbols of a manager's organizational power (influence upward, influence outward)

Reprinted by permission of Harvard Business Review. An excerpt from 'Power failure in management circuits' by Rosabeth Moss Kanter, July–August 1979, p. 67. Copyright © 1979 by the President and Fellows of Harvard College; all rights reserved.

Leadership as strategic influence

The view of leadership that emerges from the recognition of the limitations of the style per-spective is centred on the strategic influence of particular individuals. When we talk of leadership what we are referring to is the notion that in any collectivity it is likely that spe-cific individuals play a dominant role in structuring activities and creating interpretations for others that come to hold sway or influence. Linda Smircich and Gareth Morgan (1982: 255) express this perspective on leadership when they claim that individuals:

> emerge as leaders because of their role in framing experience in a way that provides a viable basis for action, e.g., by mobilising meaning, articulating and defining what has previously remained implicit and unsaid, by inventing images and meanings that provide a focus for new attention and by consolidating or changing prevailing wisdom.

From this perspective leadership is fundamentally a matter of providing a clear sense of purpose, of 'what are we doing and why are we doing it' (Pondy 1978). Sometimes this is referred to as providing a clear 'vision'. In particular, the management literature of the 1980s and early 1990s argued for the virtues of *transformational leadership*, which gives a high pri-ority to this aspect of visionary leadership (Bass 1985; Tichy and Devanna 1986; Kouzes and Posner 1989). Transformational leadership involves a focus on change and on the importance of developing a sense of direction and commitment. Exhibit 5.3 presents a summary of the characteristics of a transformational leader.

1. **Visioning a new corporate future**
    - creating the new vision
    - breaking the old frame
    - demonstrating personal commitment to the vision

2. **Communicating the vision**
    - communicating and dramatizing the vision
    - focusing on people
    - seizing the moment

3. **Implementing the vision**
    - building an effective top team
    - reorganizing
    - building a new culture

Exhibit 5.3   Transformational leadership

Source: Dexter Dunphy and Doug Stace (1990), Under New Management: Australian Organisations in Transition, *Sydney: McGraw-Hill, p. 155.*

Transformational leadership is typically contrasted with *transactional leadership*, which focuses on leadership being essentially a matter of supporting, directing and coordinating work or effort towards a known goal or purpose. Transactional leadership is not focused on initiating radical or dramatic change but rather fine-tuning what goes on in the organization. In an effort to evangelize the virtues of the transformational leader, the transformation/transaction difference tends to suggest that only transformational leaders create meanings that organizations should value. It can be argued, however, that all leadership activity involves the establishment of meaning, even if it is unconscious and possibly negative, as can even be the case with transformational leadership (Smircich and Morgan 1982, Pondy 1978). Transformational leadership is most closely related at its roots, however, to the image of great political leaders, and heroic leadership, and thus focuses on visionary leadership, creating a vision, communicating it and finding the symbols and experiences to support it (Bolman and Deal 1991: 439–45).

Noel Tichy and David Ulrich (1987: 299) in Figure 5.5 illustrate how transactional leadership can stop short of what an organization needs in attempting to change. Moving along from the trigger events on the diagram, the bottom half represents the emotional reactions to what is happening in the top half. Once there is a perceived need for change, which could be a marked decline in sales, for example, key leaders will try to initiate change and will encounter resistant forces – technical obstacles, political obstacles from powerful pressure groups within the organization, and cultural obstacles where people cannot think differently. Emotionally, they are disengaged and disenchanted because the old ways have to end. When they move into the transition state, transactional leaders tend to stick with technical solutions to problems or incremental change because they have no alternative vision. However, what the organization needs is not just death and disintegration, but a way of seeing endings as new beginnings, a vision to enable rebirth. Transformational leaders are able to create a new technical, political and cultural vision, mobilize commitment to the vision on these levels, and institutionalize the changes on these levels so that there is no

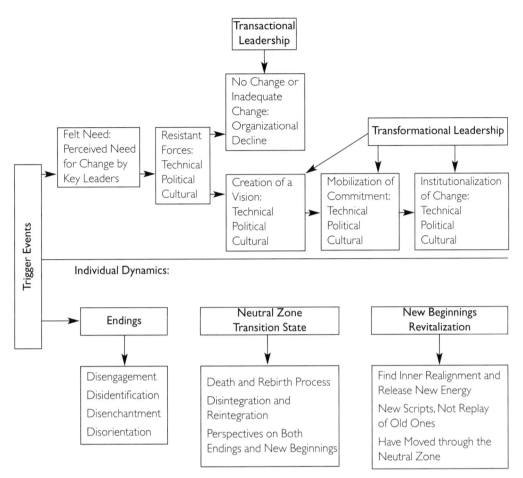

Figure 5.5 Transformational leadership

Source: Noel Tichy and David Ulrich (1987), 'The leadership challenge: A call for the transformational leader', in A.D. Timpe (ed.), Leadership, *New York: Facts on File Publications, p. 29.*

turning back. The revitalized organization finds new energy, stops replaying old scripts and embraces new ones. Thus the key skills of transformational leaders are not just in visioning, but in making things happen at all levels, and it can require at times close hands-on involvement to drive through. The transformational leadership approach is often said to be needed in situations of organizational crisis.

Criticisms of the transformational leadership approach have focused on such things as the excessive, almost evangelical role accorded the transformational leader, who almost single handedly has the vision to steer (as a captain would) the organization through turbulent change and crisis. Transformational leadership theorists have also propagated the view, or at least reinforced it, that leadership and management are separate activities. They have thus indirectly reaffirmed the trait theory of leadership. To 'qualify' as a transformational leader is to be equivalent to the 'great man' model that was edified by the early trait theorists. Whereas the leadership-style theorists subscribed to a view that managers could be trained as leaders, and contingency theorists argued that situations determined appropriate leadership approaches, the transformational leadership approach has presented an elitist view of leadership. This heroic form of leadership can only be the attribute of a few dynamic, charismatic and no doubt highly remunerated individuals (Barrett and Sutcliffe 1993: 22).

The transformational leadership approach has principally drawn support for its claims from data collected through the interview method based on the perceptions followers have of the attributes of the leader. Research has found that the ratings transformational leaders give of their attributes tend to correlate with those given by their subordinates or followers (e.g. Hater and Bass 1988). John Coopey says that if we substitute the words 'transformational leadership' with 'a drive or need for power' then these findings on transformational leadership can be seen in a very different light. He says that research using projective tests (special tests to determine dimensions of personality) suggests that people in leadership positions crave power or have a higher need for power than do others (Coopey 1995: 207, citing Shackleton and Fletcher 1984). Those who have a strong, life-long desire for power, which is reinforced through their socialization (i.e. how they learn and behave in school, the family and the wider community), usually also have a strong life-long hunger for acceptance and confirmation (Coopey 1995: 207, citing Kets de Vries 1991). Whatever other skills, attributes or abilities these people have, it is their high need for power that sets them apart. Conversely, followers oblige this type of leader by a process of 'idealized transference', in which the followers make every effort to please the leader to compensate for their own sense of helplessness and vulnerability. Coopey adds that unless leaders of this type are sufficiently self-reflexive and able to distance themselves from this adulation, they are likely to mirror the adulation and come to believe in their own 'greatness' (Coopey 1995: 207). It is not surprising then that there are strong correlations between the perceptions of followers and transformational leaders about the latters' attributes and qualities.

Post-heroic leadership

Post-heroic leadership became popular in the 1990s as a reaction to a number of noticeable trends (discussed below). However, its origins date back to the work of David Bradford and Allan Cohen (1984). Bradford and Cohen identified a new form of leadership, which is associated with transformational leadership but has a much greater emphasis on the *manager developing their subordinates*. There is a tendency for transformational leaders still to display, and be expected to display, heroic characteristics, to be either the super *technician* who can do everything in the organization as well as or better than the next person, or the super *conductor* who sits on top of the organization directing the players with a 'wave of the baton'. In neither of these situations is responsibility shared; nor are employees empowered, and they do not develop into new and emerging roles. Bradford and Cohen argue that the *post-heroic* leader is the manager as *developer*, who approaches every situation as an opportunity for themselves, their employees or the organization to develop their capabilities and capacities – in effect to become a learning organization. They believe that the technician and conductor models have their uses, but that the circumstances for which they were most fitted are not the characteristics of most post modern organizations. Table 5.3 summarizes the three leadership styles proposed by Bradford and Cohen.

Post-heroic leadership, or the questioning of the image of the transformational leader, intensified during the 1990s. Three key factors contributed to this development: rapid and often turbulent changes in the business environment, a general feeling of malaise or

Table 5.3 *Appropriate leadership styles*

	Technician	Conductor	Post-heroic
1. Subordinates work independently	×		
2. Subordinates do simple tasks	×		
3. Environment is stable	×	×	
4. Subordinates have low technical knowledge compared to boss	×	×	
5. Subordinate commitment not needed	×	×	
6. Subordinates do complex tasks		×	×
7. Subordinates require considerable coordination		×	×
8. Environment is changing			×
9. Subordinates have high technical knowledge			×
10. Subordinate commitment necessary for excellence			×

Source: David Bradford and Allan Cohen (1984), *Managing for Excellence*, New York: John Wiley, p. 56.

discontent with the image of managers and by extension leaders, and the problem of managing diversity in the workplace, particularly accommodating women managers *cum* leaders.

Rapidly changing and turbulent business environments refers to a complex set of factors, of which the following were particularly important in debunking notions of heroic leadership:

- Downsizing and flattening of businesses led to many layers of management being removed, forcing or allocating responsibility for managing change to all levels of the organization. As John Kotter says, 'More change always demands more leadership' and leadership is focused on initiating change (Kotter 1990: 104).
- Internationalization and globalization of businesses, and the burgeoning of regional offices throughout the world, have made it increasingly difficult to centralize power, hence leadership, in the head office of the organization.
- Rapidly changing, highly sophisticated, integrated networked technologies have allowed for more information dissemination and exchange and the involvement of many more managers and employees in decision-making and strategic activities.
- The increasing number of executive and employee share option programmes, profit sharing and other performance-based remuneration has encouraged more people to want to have a say in strategic decision making.
- Deregulation of markets has increased competition and brought into stark relief inefficient business practices that often necessitate organization-wide change and commitment, not just at the senior levels.

A number of the above factors, and some mentioned below, are similar to the *leadership substitutes* (e.g. creating teams of highly trained individuals, using computer technology to aid decision making) or *neutralizers* (e.g. physical distance) mentioned earlier (Howell *et al.* 1990).

The general *feeling of malaise and discontent* with leadership emerged again from a complex set of factors:

- The failed corporate entrepreneurs of the late 1980s, who became associated with greed and ruthlessness, did much to damage the image of the lone, heroic (male) leader. Alistair Mant (1994, cited in Caulkin 1993: 40) made the observation that most leaders who fit this image are male authoritarians, of stunted intellect with another abnormal qualification – greed.
- Associated with corporate failures was a general questioning of how leadership actually contributed to wealth creation in organizations.
- The general trend of running companies through committees and boards tended to diminish the idea that a single leader was setting the direction and vision for the organization.
- The rise to chief executive officer (CEO) positions of functional specialists in accounting and finance, who were less concerned with, and often less skilled in, leadership (e.g. visioning, motivating, communicating, building cultures for change), and who placed a greater focus on 'bottom-line' issues such as cost cutting, shedding labour and return on investment, led to the downgrading of the leadership factor in management (Caulkin 1993: 41; Haigh 1994: 14).
- Research has found, not surprisingly, that leaders have followers, and sometimes the followers are just as capable as the leaders of providing leadership (Nutt 1995: 68, citing Kelley 1992). This trend might be expected whenever you have a professional and highly educated workforce often being managed by an older generation of less qualified and educated managers.
- Research in the USA also found that at least 50 percent of followers surveyed, or people being lead, expressed deep dissatisfaction with their leaders (often managers), citing the fact that few of their leaders provided positive role models and even fewer instilled *trust* (Nutt 1995: 68, citing Kelley 1992). This has been supported by observations made by Andrew Campbell, who argues that leaders '… can equally well be saints or complete bastards, simple and sane or rampant schizophrenics' (quoted in Caulkin 1993: 40). (Also see discussion on the narcissistic leader below.)
- The recognition that the time has long gone when a company could rely on a single leader to do the thinking (strategic or otherwise), while the followers 'parked their brains at the door', added to discontent with leadership theories (Caulkin 1993: 40).
- It was also thought that followers, especially if empowered, which presumes post-heroic leadership, were more likely to be able to provide checks and balances in an organization. Powerless employees have little opportunity, other than through, say, whistle-blowing, of keeping those at the 'top' accountable for their actions (Caulkin 1993: 41).
- As John Huey (1994: 26) states, post-heroic leadership works where organizations are trying to gain competitive advantage from creating intellectual capital and attracting knowledge workers (see Chapter 8) who do not readily respond to the highly controlled mode of leadership found under the transformational approach or the heroic activities of a single leader (see also Crawford 1991).
- Pressures for life-long learning (see Kotter 1995), and the need to promote radical innovations and change, are increasingly seen to be dependent on employees' willingness to change – forceful and remote leadership is seen as counterproductive to this.
- The pressure for ordinary managers to invent, push and implement radical change, and to encourage more teamwork, has also brought into question the relevance of heroic leadership (Sherman 1994: 73; also Chapters 6 and 7).

- Organizations are always experimenting with new ways of gaining competitive advantage, and one of these is to tap the 'spiritual' or deeper emotional sides of people's personalities. The 'macho' transformational hero *cum* leader image does not sit well with efforts to tap the tacit (or personal) knowledge of employees for sources of creativity and innovation (Sherman 1994: 74; Cavaleri and Fearon 1996: 363–74; and Chapter 7).
- As organizations also become more involved in networks and interorganizational relations (IOR) with suppliers, customers and competitors, different styles of leadership will be required. We pursue these issues further in Chapter 11, but suffice it to say, the leadership skills a manager might use effectively within the organization are not always likely to translate to successful leadership practices outside the organization.

The problems of *managing diversity* were discussed in Chapter 2. Leadership, particularly in relation to women managers, remains an area of considerable debate and controversy.

- Managing diversity has raised concerns about how men and women manage and has again brought into question the gender stereotyping associated with heroic leadership. A growing body of literature (e.g. Rosener 1990; Denmark 1993) has suggested that women do lead differently, even in terms of the transformational variables, that is, women are more likely to adopt empowering strategies and develop followers. Even though some of these gender assumptions have been questioned in Chapter 2, the issue of women in management, and women achieving senior or top management positions, have helped raise concerns about gender stereotyping and the dominance of heroic images of leadership (see discussion on pp. 195–7 of this chapter).

Research by Robert Kelley (cited in Nutt 1995: 69 and Caulkin 1993: 41) suggests that many organizations do not need heroic leaders because they are already well endowed with 'exemplary followers'. These exemplary followers challenge the very idea of leadership. He states that many leaders feel threatened by their subordinates, yet exemplary followers are crucial to the success of an organization because they are vital to designing and carrying out plans. Exemplary followers are active, independent and critical thinkers. They also tend to have strong values and are what Kelley calls the 'courageous conscience' of the organization (Nutt 1995: 69, citing Kelley 1992). However, according to Kelley, leaders cannot 'create' exemplary followers. They can, however, use a number of strategies to ensure that exemplary followers and leaders form partnerships and that the CEO (strategic leader) ensures that exemplary followers succeed and are productive. This can be achieved in several ways:

- Information sharing with exemplary followers.
- Involving exemplary followers in the co-determination of major strategies.
- Sharing the risks and rewards with exemplary followers – including the 'glory' of success.
- Making sure these people have the resources to do their jobs.
- Letting them shine – allowing exemplary followers to lead teams and share the limelight when there is success.

To quote:

> To be a post-heroic leader requires very different qualities to that of the heroic leader, post-heroic leaders do not expect to solve all the problems themselves. They realise no one person can deal with the emerging colliding tyrannies of speed, quality, customer satisfaction, innovation, diversity and technology. Virtual leaders just say no to their egos (Huey 1994: 26).

Power has been omitted from many theories of leadership, including consideration of the legal and proprietorial rights CEOs and top managers enjoy, and against which they are judged, and which also help them to gain wealth within companies. The 'heroic image' goes with this power (Coopey 1995: 195). Many CEOs or senior managers might not wish to embrace the idea of post-heroic leadership (as described in the quote above), as they might perceive it as threatening their status, power, prestige and public standing. Take, for example, one of the key elements of providing support for exemplary followers mentioned earlier, that is, sharing in risks and rewards. According to Kelley (cited in Nutt 1995: 69), this means that leaders must, when times get tough, such as when there is downsizing or layoffs, demonstrate that they are willing to share the loss with their followers. Kelley gives an example of the CEO of Firestone (a large multinational based in the USA) who accepted a huge bonus at a time when his company was halving its workforce. He also describes how, by contrast, Perot, a vice-president on the board of General Motors, resigned from the board in the 1980s in protest of increased executive bonuses at a time when plants were being closed. Another example comes from the UK, where, in 1998, the Chief Executive of Goodyear sacrificed his annual salary in an attempt to impress on employees the need to think carefully about the company's position before demanding a wage rise.

A number of different versions of the post-heroic leadership approach have emerged in the management literature (see, for example, Manz and Sims 1992 on self-leadership). One approach developed by Ronald Heifetz and Donald Laurie (1997) encapsulates many elements of the post-heroic agenda. The authors argue that changes in societies; markets being more open; customers being more demanding, diverse and international; increased competition and collaboration through networks and alliances; and technological advances require a serious rethinking of what leadership might mean in many organizations. They believe that *the leader's work* is focused now more than ever on coping with a multiplicity of adaptive challenges rather than on one major crisis. Instead of focusing on styles or contingencies they argue that leadership is now the work of many people in an organization. They believe (as do many other theorists) that organizations have to rethink their values, develop new strategies and learn new ways of operating to meet adaptive challenges. Leaders have to be able to mobilize (i.e. influence) people to adopt new behaviours and in the process, the leaders have to change their own behaviours, especially the tendency to provide solutions, solve problems and take responsibility for driving change (i.e. transformational leader with the 'vision' in hand).

Heifetz and Laurie identify subtle changes in leadership and followership as a result of having to face adaptive challenges. Adaptive challenges mean leaders must figure out how to harness the collective intelligence of the organization through building new relationships within, across and outside the organization. This, they say, requires: 'Leaders from above or below, with or without authority – [engaging] people in confronting the [adaptive] challenges, adjusting their values, changing perspectives, and learning new habits' (Heifetz and Laurie 1997: 134). Solutions are discovered or learned and are no longer 'handed down' or 'given out' by leaders, as envisaged in heroic approaches to leadership.

The authors note that the adaptive challenges are also distressing because they make demands on people to take on new roles, relationships, values, work practices and behaviours (Heifetz and Laurie 1997: 124). All of these changes can involve pain, a sense of loss and fears about the future, and leaders need the sensitivity, skills and knowledge to manage the emotional labour involved in such change (see Chapter 7).

Heifetz and Laurie propose six principles as guides to the work of leading to meet adaptive challenges:

1   *Getting on the balcony*
    • Leaders (or leadership teams) need to be able to stand back and reflect on the need for change. They no longer 'helicopter' over the organization seeing the 'big picture' as in the transformational leadership approaches. Rather, the leader (or leaders) needs to be able to create or see the context for change, and then impart this need for change in a compelling story or narrative that allows others to let go of the past, to embrace the need for change, and to accept responsibility for shaping a new future. There is no all-embracing vision but rather a direction for change that is negotiated through confronting issues and challenges. An example of how this might work is discussed in Exhibit 5.4. Richard Hackman (1992: 156–9) notes that the voluminous literature on leadership and management includes little on the direction-setting activities of managers. He notes that in trying to create a self-managing unit, leaders walk a very fine line between being too directive and not being directive enough. Hackman uses the metaphor of climbing a mountain to make his point. He says that in many circumstances the choice of the mountain to climb (direction) might be non-negotiable, but how to climb it might be left open to negotiation and choice. Hackman believes a direction has to be set to orient members toward common objectives, to energize them by giving new purpose and meaning, and to provide some tangible criterion for working out alternatives to follow.
    • Although leaders metaphorically speaking stand on a balcony to take a broader view of what is happening in the organization, they must come down to the field of action or the minutiae of the change process to see where power struggles and resistance to change are occurring or amassing. Leaders must be able to devise strategies with others to deal with the 'normal' resistance to change.

2   *Identifying adaptive challenge*
    • Leaders must develop trust among colleagues so that people learn to collaborate and develop a collective sense of responsibility for change (Heifetz and Laurie 1997: 126). We return to the issue of trust in Chapter 7, but point out here that creating trust is far more complex than is suggested by Heifetz and Laurie, and it is extremely difficult to develop trust across a whole organization, yet trust is a key factor in many aspects of knowledge work and building intellectual capital in an organization.
    • Leaders need to be able to differentiate between technical challenges (identified as basic routines) and adaptive challenges – as distinct from the former, the latter requires learning new ways of doing business, developing new competencies and the need to work collectively (Heifetz and Laurie 1997: 126).

- Conflicts are clues for adaptive challenges and leaders must dig deep to unearth root causes of conflicts. Often conflicts appear to be over technical issues (e.g. procedures, schedules) but usually go deeper to values, norms and politics, and leaders must push to have these deeper issues addressed.
- Leaders must hold up a 'mirror' to see how they, as leaders of change, are also a part of the adaptive challenge. They need to ask in what ways is the executive team dysfunctional (see Chapter 6) and how might its members develop insights to help them better understand their roles in confronting adaptive challenges (Heifetz and Laurie 1997: 126) (i.e. how can they develop reflective practice as mentioned in Chapter 1).

3   *Regulating distress*
- Leaders need to strike a delicate balance between having people feel the need for change and at the same time not allowing them to get overwhelmed by it, yet all the while keeping up the momentum for change (Heifetz and Laurie 1997: 127).
- Leaders take responsibility for the direction of change: they articulate key adaptive challenges by framing key questions and issues; they offer protection so that the pressure for change does not become intolerable for people; they have to challenge those roles that need to change, but resist the pressure to define new roles too quickly; they expose conflict and see it as important to creativity and learning; they help challenge norms that need to change and protect those that must endure (Heifetz and Laurie 1997: 127–8).
- Leaders have to have the emotional capacity to endure uncertainty, frustration and pain and understand fears, stresses and sacrifices yet the poise and steadiness to instil confidence.

4   *Disciplining attention*
- Leaders build on diversity, multiple views, realities and perspectives in order to encourage innovation and learning. To do this leaders (or managers) must deal with, and bring out into the open, all forms of work avoidance, such as scapegoating, denial, stereotyping, focusing on technical issues, blaming others, attacking individual perspectives and so on. Leaders need strategies that enable them to get people to refocus on building dialogue, problem solving and creativity (see Chapter 1).

5   *Giving work back to people*
- Leaders share the responsibility, pain and need for change by learning to support rather than control employees, who will often need to learn how to take responsibility for success and failures (Heifetz and Laurie 1997: 129). 'Give work back to people' is a short-cut term for 'empowerment'. Empowering can involve such things as sharing information (extensively), including opening up the company's books to employees and exposing sensitive information (Quinn and Spreitzer 1997: 39). This was also mentioned by Kelley (1992) in followership strategies. Robert Quinn and Gretchen Spreitzer point out that empowerment is not a set of specific management practices but rather a reflection of a person's beliefs or feelings about their work. Empowered people have a strong sense of

self-determination, that is, they feel relatively free to choose how they do their work; they care about their work, or it means something important to them; they feel competent, or confident about their ability to perform; and they have a sense of impact (i.e. they feel they have influence and others listen to their ideas (Quinn and Spreitzer 1997: 41; also Chapter 4). These views echo the sentiments of Peter F. Drucker who has said: 'It is not a great step forward to take power out at the top and put it at the bottom. It's still power. To build achieving organizations, you must replace power with responsibility' (Drucker, quoted in Harris 1993: 122).

- Ironically rewards (monetary or others) are not mentioned by Heifetz and Laurie, but are considered important by others as compensation for people taking more risks and responsibilities, and being held more accountable for outcomes (Quinn and Spreitzer 1997: 40). This is certainly a criticism of many approaches to leadership that have ignored monetary reward, almost as an excessive reaction to Taylorism.

6   *Projecting voices of leadership from below*
- Heifetz and Laurie (1997: 729) say that it is important to give a 'voice' to all people in the organization and that this giving of voice is key to encouraging experimentation and learning (see also Chapter 1). Yet they note that whistle-blowers, creative deviants and other original thinkers often have their voices smashed or routinely silenced because organizations and their managers (leaders) want equilibrium, harmony and consensus, and often seek affirmation of their views and support for their pet projects. Teamwork or being a team player, and other 'unifying' or 'conforming' strategies, are often used to bring dissenting voices into check (see Chapter 6). The reasons why leaders often do not listen to the 'voices of leadership from below' are much more complex than Heifetz and Laurie suggest. They believe people who speak beyond their authority are apt to be self-conscious and generate too much passion about their cause, and are likely to pick the wrong place, time and person to open up to. They exhort leaders to see these people as valuable sources of information, insight and leadership and not persons to be silenced (Heifetz and Laurie 1997: 129–30).

In Chapter 9 we discuss in greater detail the ethical reasons why managers *cum* leaders are likely to silence and victimize the very actions Heifetz and Laurie want to 'normalize' as a part of post-heroic leadership. In the next section of this chapter we also explore why some managers, described as narcissistic leaders, could never undertake the work of leadership associated with post-heroic leadership or the leadership approach outlined by Heifetz and Laurie. But the question inevitably arises: how does the post-heroic agenda, outlined above, work in practice?

Exhibit 5.4 describes how one organization studied by Heifetz and Laurie encapsulates what they see as the work of leadership within the context of meeting adaptive challenges. Huey (1994: 28) summarizes in a nutshell what adaptive challenges constitute for managers: getting people from diverse backgrounds to pull in the same direction when they have to.

KPMG Netherlands
(Leaders in auditing, consulting and tax-preparation partnership)

The chairperson of the company, Ruud Koedijk, recognized in 1994 that although the KPMG partnership was the industry leader in the Netherlands and was highly profitable, the growth potential for their services was limited. New opportunities for growth had to be found. The chair and his board had the strategic skills to reposition the organization but they were less certain they could gain commitment to strategic change from the firm's partners. The partners had a history of resisting change, having been successful for so many years and also having built the organization of 300 around small fiefdoms of power and control. Profitability of individual units was the sole criterion of success. Independence, unit autonomy and minimizing conflict was the norm. Change was not overtly resisted, partners would just work on the idea of 'say yes, do no'. Directors and partners rewarded other professionals for not making mistakes and for delivering a high number of billable hours per week. Innovation and creativity were not rewarded. Koedijk's approach to leadership was to do the following:

1. He called a meeting of 300 partners to review KPMG's history, current business position and future issues. He asked questions about how to go about changing the firm rather than offering a direction. Beginning a dialogue rather than pronouncing 'edicts' (as leaders often do in the media, etc.) was Koedijk's only real strategy.

2. One hundred partners and non-partners were released for 60 percent of their time for four months to work on strategic challenges. Twelve senior partners formed a strategic integration team to work with the 100 professionals. Four task forces were set up covering three areas: gauging future trends and discontinuities, defining core competence and grappling with adaptive challenges. 'The 100' (as they were called) were housed on a separate floor, unencumbered by the rules and protocols of the rest of the organization. They had a project manager, KPMG's director of marketing and communications. Many non-partner members who had never been involved in strategy processes were included.

3. Inertia and dysfunctions emerged as 'the 100' tried to do strategy work confined by a 'culture' perceived of as fostering opposing views (i.e. individualism and unit loyalty), demand for perfection and conflict avoidance. Producing an alternative view of a desired culture became the focus of the teams. This also became a part of individual adaptive challenges – everyone had to examine attitudes, behaviours and habits that needed change and actions had to be devised to make the change happen. The alternative new culture that was identified subsequently had three key characteristics: opportunity for self-fulfilment, developing a caring environment and maintaining trusting relations with colleagues.

4. Stress levels in 'the 100' were often high, and various forums with the board, including theatrics (e.g. a board member standing on a table during a breakfast meeting) were used to push for more creativity and change, yet allowing for venting of frustrations, fears and even anger.

5. Dress rules were relaxed, new symbols were created, games were used to encourage fun at work and rules were developed to encourage listening and understanding other people's perspectives.

6. KPMG identified $50–$60 million worth of new business opportunities and in the process changed the services it offered to clients – one being to teach others how to use adaptive challenges to change and to use leadership as a learning strategy.

Exhibit 5.4 Leading as adaptive challenge

Source: Adapted from Ronald Heifetz and Donald Laurie (1997), 'The work of leadership', Harvard Business Review January–February, pp. 130–3.

The case in Exhibit 5.4 represents only one possible approach to post-heroic leadership. Other organizations, such as SEMCO in Brazil (Semler 1993) and W.L. Gore and Associates in the USA (Huey 1994; Skipper and Manz 1994), are regularly cited as examples of post-heroic leadership in practice. Both these organizations have developed a post-heroic, or even craft-style approach to leadership (Mintzberg 1997: 14) by working on the principles of trust and commitment to spread the work of leadership to as many people as possible. In the case of SEMCO, this has involved shopfloor employees or relatively unskilled workers taking on leadership roles and rotating leadership positions at the executive level. W.L. Gore and Associates is a high-tech company employing highly professional people whereas SEMCO is principally a manufacturer of pumps, mixer valves and other industrial equipment. Neither firms' owners portray themselves as leaders (Ricardo Semler of SEMCO sees himself as a 'counsellor') and both shirk titles and many symbols of status in the workplace, such as a large office. SEMCO has built its system of trust to include a package of monetary rewards, including profit sharing and incentives.

The narcissistic leader

The most powerful critical responses to the rhetoric of the transformational leaders recognize the tendency toward superficiality in the advocacy of 'visionary' leadership. Indeed, despite the advocacy of the 'post-heroic' leadership style, heroic behaviours, images and virtual cult followings seem still to be very much in evidence. But the vision which many managers have is not of the organization, or the future, but of *themselves*, and they seek to remake the world in their image (see Fineman 1993: 25–7). Many are suffering from what has been defined as the most common behavioural disease of the late twentieth century – *narcissism* (Callaghan 1997).

Narcissism was first identified by Freud, but its extent and social impact was not mapped until Christopher Lasch's 1979 book, *The Culture of Narcissism*. Coming as it did at the end of the 'me' decade, it was at first interpreted as a review of the 1970s, but Lasch insisted that it was a warning, and was as prophetic as it was documentary. In 1980 narcissism was officially given a diagnosis and set of symptoms in the *Diagnostic and Statistical Manual of Mental Disorders* and several books have since developed the subject (e.g. Symington 1993). Howard Schwartz (1990) applied the concept to organizational cultures, as we discussed in Chapter 3; Adrian Carr (1994, 1998) has applied the concept to individuals establishing identity within organizational relationships; Andrew Brown (1997) has considered its impact at individual, group and organizational levels; and Alan Downs (1997) has applied the concept specifically to managers.

The narcissist, as a result of experiences in childhood, is driven by an anxiety, an inner feeling of lack of self-worth. This anxiety develops as a form of self-absorption or self-obsession which can appear as the opposite of this – as arrogance, over-confidence, disdain or contempt for others, and a ruthless determination to stop at nothing to get what they want. The narcissist learns three basic lessons:

1 They must be something more than they are.
2 Their value as a person is dependent upon the image they project.
3 Other people are objects who must be manipulated to get the validation the narcissist needs.

As Downs (1997) argues, narcissistic behaviour produces a dearth of values, careful image management, an absence of empathy, loyalty or any deep emotion, and an obsession with personal gain. The narcissist, as leader, creates problems for organizations. For them, organizations should word their value statements carefully so that they can be easily discarded or twisted. Wrong-doing is sanctioned not by ethics but by such things as the legal liability faced by the company. Loyalty to employees, caring for customers or altruistic philanthropy (i.e. anything not geared to making more money) is considered weakness.

The problem is that as one or two ruthless managers start to be successful, the message spreads and the behaviour develops into a situation of epidemic proportions. Eventually, corporate cultures succumb, and everyone must play by the narcissist's rules – 'kill or be killed'. Downs sees this as a major sickness of corporate America but Lasch sees it as one of American society as a whole, and according to Callaghan it is not confined to the borders of the USA. If this is true, the malaise is deeper than Downs thinks. We can think of several examples of narcissistic leaders we have worked for – our only hope is to recognize them for what they are and try to handle them appropriately.

Brown (1997) has attempted to specify both the basic features of narcissism and how they impact at different levels of the organization, on individual behaviour, group process and organizational culture. The traits are *denial* (of unacceptable facts about the narcissist or their situation); *rationalization* (which means where action or fact has to be acknowledged it is explained away); *self-aggrandizement* (self-flattery, fantasies of omnipotence and control); *attributional egotism* (blaming others for the narcissist's own personal problems); *self-entitlement* (exploiting others for personal gain) and *basic anxiety* (a constant striving for certainty and struggling for self-worth). These dimensions are explained in Table 5.4.

Downs points out that narcissistic behaviour and cultures are difficult to change. Once a manager has reached a position of authority, they have probably had a couple of decades or more of reinforcement of their narcissism. The underlying problem cannot be fixed easily, and it requires the narcissist to want to change. Cultures in which narcissistic behaviour is widespread and has become the norm need top management commitment to change – and that commitment has to be towards openness, trust and a respect for the truth (see Chapter 7). However, Downs tends to take the approach that cultures are basically a collection of individuals, and underemphasizes the extent to which structures – of power, political groupings, coalitions of interests, resource control and flow of information – may severely restrict what individuals can achieve. Downs does acknowledge that change in reality may not be possible, and suggests ways of living with a narcissistic colleague or manager.

The first step is always to know your own motivation and what you need from the narcissist. None of us is immune to narcissistic behaviour and sometimes we can contribute to the problem. Problems most often occur with narcissist leaders when we are trying to serve the same needs, primarily for power and recognition, as they are. The three most common difficulties arising from this are competition, conflict and incompatibility. The latter occurs when one party is focused on internal motivations like personal satisfaction and the other on external ones like monetary reward. Table 5.5 shows the methods suggested by Downs for coping with these difficulties.

Table 5.4 *Narcissism in organizations*

Narcissistic traits	Level of analysis		
	Individual	*Group*	*Organization*
Denial	Individuals deny the reality of market demands and resource constraints, facts about themselves and features of past occurrences	Groups deny facts under the influence of groupthink and through denial myths	Organizations deny facts about themselves through spokespeople, propaganda campaigns, annual reports and myths
Rationalization	Individuals rationalize action, inaction, policies and decisions	Groups offer collective rationalizations for their activities, their structures and behaviour, their decisions and their status	Organizations provide rationalizations that structure thought and *post hoc* justify their actions, inaction, and responsibility
Self-aggrandizement	Individuals engage in fantasies of omnipotence and control, exhibit grandiosity and exhibitionism, create cultures in their own image, narrate stories that flatter themselves, make nonsensical acquisitions, engage in ego-boosting rituals, and write immodest autobiographies	Groups use myth and humour to exaggerate their sense of worth, fantasize of unlimited ability when under stress, and engage in exhibitionistic social cohesion ceremonies	Organizations endow themselves with rightness, make claims to uniqueness, commission corporate histories, and deploy their office layouts and architecture as expressions of status, prestige and vanity
Attributional egotism	Individuals blame external authority for their personal plight and narrate stories that contain self-enhancing explanations	Collectivities attribute the failure of their decisions to external factors	Organizations (or management groups) use annual reports to blame unfavourable results on external factors and attribute positive outcomes to themselves
Sense of entitlement	Individuals are exploitive, lack empathy, engage in social relationships that lack depth and favour their interests over shareholders	Groups use songs and humour and ceremonies to express a sense of entitlement	Organizations are structured according to a principle of entitlement to exploit. Organizations assume entitlement to continued successful existence
Anxiety	Individuals suffer internally, need stability and certainty, experience deprivation and emptiness, are paralyzed by personal anxiety and tension, and struggle to maintain a sense of their self-worth	Management groups are prone to anxiety. Groups such as nurses and social care workers suffer from particularly high levels of anxiety	Organizations suffer from anomie and alienation, requiring shared culture, moral order, a common sense of purpose; leadership attempts to secure commitment, and the broader distribution of work responsibilities

Source: Adapted from Andrew D. Brown (1997), 'Narcissism, identity and legitimacy', *Academy of Management Review* 22(3), pp. 643–6, 652–3.

Table 5.5 *Suggestions for handling narcissist leaders*

Competition	Conflict	Incompatibility
1. Create a clear division of *labour* without overlap	1. Create a clear division of *responsibilities* without 'turf' overlap	1. Recognize that their *motivations* may be different from yours, but you can *coexist*
2. Show them how your *success* will *support* them	2. Keep talking at the *highest* level of *agreement*. Do not get bogged down in conflict over details	2. Scan each situation for what will motivate *them* (i.e. extrinsic rewards)
3. Do not be *greedy*. Share the spotlight	3. Assure the leader of your agreement over *larger* objectives; request control over small areas within this	3. Make decisions based on what will bring *them* the *extrinsic* satisfaction they need, while meeting your *intrinsic* needs

Source: Adapted from Alan Downs (1997), *Beyond the Looking Glass,* New York: Amacom, pp. 168–74.

However, it would be a mistake to think that narcissism does not affect other approaches to leadership. Daniel Sankowsky (1995) has examined how narcissism can also be found in those who are identified as being charismatic or transformational leaders. He says that these types of leaders possess great symbolic power because their followers often come to idolize them and perceive them as someone they can profoundly trust. In turn narcissistic charismatic leaders expect to be idolized by their loyal followers. Followers tend to idolize charismatic leaders because of all or one of the following: (1) omnipotent archetype (the leader will nurture and guide them); (2) leader as mystic (knows the way and has the answers); (3) heroic stereotype (can move mountains); and (4) the value-driven virtuous leader (looks after the collective good and is empowering) (Sankowsky 1995: 64).

Sankowsky suggests that when charisma and the pathology of narcissism are combined, leaders often promote visions that reflect their own sense of grandiosity, sweeping others up in their grand plans. They often approach ventures based on their own sureness of self rather than their command of information or clarity of insight (Sankowsky 1995: 65). They expect people to defer to them, expecting others to accept blindly their view of reality. Sankowsky (1995: 67) gives examples of a number of leaders who might qualify as narcissistic charismatic leaders, for example, Steve Jobs (creator of Apple and NeXT), whose followers often spoke of him in terms of his perfection and high expectations, and of how they, as followers, could never be as good as him. One important aspect of charismatic/narcissistic leaders' influence is their ability to diminish the self-worth of others or make them totally dependent on the leaders' approval.

Finally, Carr (1998: 86) points out that to see narcissism as a disorder with *only* negative effects is to neglect its 'Janus-like nature'. He reminds us that Freud considered that narcissism was ubiquitous and a necessary element in loving relationships, and cites Alford's observation that 'narcissism may serve as a stimulus for the achievement of the highest ideals' (Alford 1988: 27 in Carr 1998: 86). The source of the narcissist's anxiety and feeling of inferiority is the demands of an image of an ideal self that they find impossible to satisfy, but the pursuit of this ideal may lead to socially valued activities and goals as well as undesirable ones. Although Downs is probably correct in saying that the negative aspects of narcissism have reached epidemic proportions, we should not neglect its positive possibilities. Nor should we neglect the fact that narcissism is a quality or behaviour that not only plagues managers and leaders but can manifest in subordinates and peers as well, resulting in distinct problems for handling this behaviour in the workplace (Diamond and Allcorn 1990).

Gender and leadership

The existing research on women and leadership has been aptly summarized by Fiona Wilson (1995: 172–8). She points out that the study of leadership (or power) has rarely included sex or sex roles as organizationally significant variables. Leaders seem not only to be male, but quite masculine with it, and where women and leadership is a topic in texts on leadership, it is usually treated as a separate chapter. In other words, women are not integrated into the mainstream theorizing of leadership. This is hardly surprising given the fact that most theories of leadership have ignored gender (see the discussion in Chapter 2).

Judy Rosener, in researching prominent women leaders and men across a number of countries, found men tend to describe themselves in ways consistent with 'transactional' leadership. They viewed their performance as a series of transactions with subordinates involving rewards and punishment or what are really exchange relationships. Women in the study described themselves in ways consistent with transformational leadership (Rosener 1990: 120) although with different emphases from the masculine heroic image. Among the transformational qualities women favoured were: interactive leadership or participation, making people feel important and energized, sharing information and power and placing less emphasis on formal authority (i.e. status, position). A similar study in the UK found that women reported themselves as catalyst or visionary leaders, while the men were traditionalist leaders (see Wilson 1995). Florence Denmark (1993) in a US study also found women were perceived to be more democratic than men, that is, they encouraged more participation in decision making. Denmark also found that when women behaved autocratically (or like many male managers might) they were viewed more negatively by both men and women. Women who occupied leadership positions traditionally held by men were more devalued by male evaluators. Yet men rated women superiors higher in leadership qualities than did women (Denmark 1993: 353–5).

But the differences are less clear when we look at how subordinates perceive men and women leaders. Wilson noted that other women subordinates responded differently to the same behaviour depending on whether it was displayed by a man or a woman. Wilson also noted that consideration behaviours displayed by a woman leader tended to be more favourably evaluated, and women subordinates preferred a more democratic style of leadership and sought greater involvement in decision making (Wilson 1995:173). Exhibit 5.5 summarizes some findings on research on female leaders.

Research has found female leaders to be:
- accommodative or affiliative (close to those people they interact with);
- less self-enhancing;
- more self-disclosing;
- more vulnerable;
- willing to admit to lack of self-confidence;

- willing to express emotions;
- more positive in giving encouragement, support and information;
- less assertive;
- better communicators;
- better at reading non-verbal behaviour;
- more sensitive and socially objective;
- more cooperative and democratic;
- better group facilitators and consultants.

Exhibit 5.5 Characteristics of female leaders

Source: Adapted from Fiona Wilson (1995), Organizational Behaviour and Gender, *London: McGraw-Hill, pp. 173–6.*

Interestingly, women appear to perceive power (hence influence) differently from men, seeing it as a liberating force in the community (i.e. capacity, competence and energy) rather than as a means of controlling and dominating others, and they tend to be therefore non-aggressive and more concerned for the welfare of others (Huxham 1996: 22, citing Hartsock 1985). Men, on the other hand, are more likely to seek to maintain distance from their subordinates in order to maintain status, to be instrumental and task orientated, and to be more dominant, self-assured, directive, precise and quick to challenge others. These views are echoed by Judith Pringle (1994: 136–7) who cites research from the USA (Astin and Leland 1991 and Helgesen 1990) which supports the view that women do interpret and represent their leadership styles as being different from those often portrayed as being masculine, particularly in terms of power. Women, she says, describe a leader as someone who plays a catalytic empowering role, and who works to create a collective effort to improve the quality of life of those who work for them. There are also men who would identify with this more 'feminine' version of leadership.

Much of the research, however, does appear to indicate that there may be considerable pressure on both men and women to conform to stereotypes held by subordinates. Richard Scase and Robert Goffee (1990) also argued that the reportedly preferred managerial styles of both men and women are influenced by prevailing fads and fashions about effective management. In a study carried out in the 1980s, when assertiveness became popularly valued, 88 percent of women managers surveyed claimed to be tough, aggressive, firm and assertive, while less than 50 percent mentioned being open, cooperative and consultative. Additionally, how people look and their appearance is important to the way in which people respond to them as leaders and it is an advantage to look mature rather than glamorous or even 'sexy'. This may have affected the power-dressing fashion of the 1980s (Brewis, Hampton and Linstead 1997).

It seems clear, though, that however difficult it may be to determine a feminine or a definitively masculine managerial style of leadership, women do display skills and behaviours which complement, and sometimes challenge, those traditionally displayed by men. It is quite possible that as organizations change in style and structure, even the concept of 'leader' may change. But before this happens there will need to be more serious critical anlaysis of the masculinist domination of the discourse about leadership, as Marta Calás and Linda Smircich (1995) reveal (see also Chapter 2). We might well ask: why have leadership studies neglected gender issues or sought to represent the differences between men and women as a 'negative difference' for women in management (Sinclair 1998)?

Cross-cultural dimensions of leadership

Another neglected dimension of leadership – and most other dimensions of organization theory – is its culture boundedness. As argued in the chapter on gender (Chapter 2), the knowledge project in which early management theorists were engaged was about the identification of universal principles which were context free – thus gender was suppressed and so was culture. At a technical level, at which much of scientific management was involved, some of these principles were readily adaptable to other countries including the USSR and Japan. In fact, the former president of Sony Corporation, Akio Morita, said 'US and Japanese management are 95% the same, and differ in all important respects'. What he meant was that culture was the 5 percent difference, the rest was methods, technology and structure.

Leadership then falls into the 5 percent, and as Geert Hofstede (1980/1992) argues, the very theories which purport to be universalistic are in fact shaped significantly by the fact that they were developed by US theorists in the USA. He also argues that if we want to know whether US theories apply abroad, there is no need to test them before we can reach a view – looking at the key characteristics of different cultures according to his model will predict whether there will be difficulties and what those difficulties are likely to be.

As mentioned in Chapter 3, Hofstede developed a measure of culture on four dimensions and, later, with Michael Bond, added a fifth. These were *power distance, uncertainty avoidance, masculinity* (or quality of life), *individualism/collectivism,* and *long-term/short-term orientation.* Differences in these dimensions will affect the way leaders see their role and also the way subordinates perceive it – in fact, the differences in subordinate perception are most significant because it is these assumptions that will make it difficult for a manager from a different culture to operate in a new one.

Most of the US leadership theories tend to advocate, implicitly or explicitly, participation by subordinates in decision making, but the initiative in extending participation is the manager's (Hofstede 1980/1992). This is consistent with a medium power distance culture such as the USA. In a high power distance culture, such as Hong Kong, the manager's authority would not be shared, and in a low power distance culture, such as Scandinavia, participation would be seen as the norm, not a managerial option (see Chapter 6). Another dimension that affects this is uncertainty avoidance – in a low uncertainty avoidance country, such as Sweden, local experiments in democracy are encouraged and if successful become regulation, but in a high uncertainty avoidance country, such as Germany, the regulatory framework (laws, etc.) has to come first.

Hofstede (1980/1992: 113–18) discusses the problems in imposing management techniques associated with leadership styles which have an implicit cultural bias. An example might be the case of self-managed work teams (see Chapter 7), which assumes medium power distance (negotiations are meaningful, employees not too weak), weak uncertainty avoidance (i.e. willing to take risks) and high masculinity (performance orientation). Hofstede also notes the difficulties of operating with subordinates with differing cultural biases from the manager, pointing out that often subordinates from high power distance cultures, such as those in Asia, prefer autocratic Theory X leadership. David McClelland (1961) found variations on the need for achievement, an important factor in leadership style, between Turkey (3.62) and Belgium (0.43) (see Chapter 7). Such a wide variation across cultures questions whether we can meaningfully use the same term for 'leadership' in

Turkey and Belgium. The more complex combinations of cultural factors may require that the concept of leadership be replaced altogether with a different concept, such as 'influence'. However, we need to keep in mind that there will always be variations within nations regarding these cultural dimensions and as stated in Chapter 3 a whole range of experiences might predispose a manager to act or behave outside cultural expectations and norms (see Triandis 1995).

Robert Westwood (1992) identifies one particularly common alternative model to the Western leadership model in the East. This is the model of headship or paternalism. The paternalistic leadership style characteristic of South East Asia, especially in small businesses, is derived from cultures with a high level of power distance, and hence tends to be more directive and autocratic. It has the combination of characteristics shown in Exhibit 5.6.

- **Dependence orientation of subordinates** The acceptance of hierarchy and the concept of filial piety lead to the cultural norm of conforming to headship and dependence on the patriarch.
- **Personalism** Personal relationships play a more important role in governing behaviour than formal systems and rules.
- **Moral leadership** The leader is assumed to possess virtues such as humanity and integrity as a requirement in his role. He must act as a model and must be worthy of respect.
- **Harmony building** Part of the leadership role is to build and maintain harmony. He should be sensitive to feelings of the subordinates.
- **Conflict diffusion** The leader needs to make sure that conflicts are prevented from happening.
- **Social distance** The leader tends to stay at a social distance from the subordinates to preserve his father-like authority.
- **Didactic leadership** The leader is assumed to be the master who possesses the necessary knowledge and information and is expected to act like a teacher.
- **Dialogue ideal** A subtle and informal communication is expected so that the leader can signal his intentions and be aware of the sentiments and views of the subordinate.

Exhibit 5.6 Paternal leadership style

Source: Robert Westwood (1992), Organizational Behaviour, Hong Kong: Addison Wesley Longman China, pp. 121–41

The adoption of this style also leads to the use of some very specific behaviours and tactics which keep the father figure leader – and you will notice that we deliberately use the pronoun 'he' throughout this section when referring to the leader – in unchallenged authority as described in Exhibit 5.7.

- **Centralisation** The leader, as part of the autocratic elements of his leadership, will not allow much involvement of subordinates in the decision-making process.
- **Non-specific intentions** The leader will not be explicit in revealing his intentions and expectations.
- **Secrecy** The leader will always keep certain information or knowledge to himself.
- **Avoidance of formality** The leader will avoid turning the way of doing things through relations into formal procedures.
- **Protection of dominance** The leader will seek to protect his authority position through playing down the importance of the subordinates, altering the responsibility requirements at will, making subjective evaluation of subordinate performance, etc.

- **Patronage and nepotism** The leader will use his position power and the resources at his disposal to do selective favours to the subordinates. Family members or those linked to the leader are often appointed to key positions.
- **Non-emotional ties** The leader will avoid emotional bonds with the subordinates to shield his dignity and to evade obligations.
- **Political manipulation** The leader controls the group through differential treatment of the individuals.
- **Reputation building** The leader will be very concerned about building and protecting his reputation, especially in t external ties with business associates.

Exhibit 5.7 Paternal leadership tactics

Source: Robert Westwood (1992), Organizational Behaviour, *Hong Kong: Longmans Group (FE), pp. 121–41.*

Now, it might be useful to pause a moment to consider this question: In what ways is the 'paternalistic style of leadership' commonly demonstrated by small business owners in South-East Asia different from the 'autocratic' style discussed in the Western world? You should be able to answer this question by reviewing the above material.

Conclusion

Leadership is widely regarded as a central determinant of organizational performance but it is a difficult concept to tie down. Trait and style approaches have proven limited in utility, while the contingency perspective threatens to become paralysed by the volume of possible contingent factors, although the latter approach has value in establishing that there is no 'one best way' to lead in all situations. These approaches tend to focus on leadership as supervisory style. An alternative approach is to see leadership as political and strategic *influence* centred on such activities as building and maintaining networks, and creating and perpetuating a sense of purpose enabling and empowering followers and basically sharing the power and glory of leadership. Post-heroic leadership questions the importance of leadership as something that belongs to a lone hero manager.

Nonetheless, most leadership training still focuses on the concept of style within a contingency/situational framework. As such it is subject to an extremely basic criticism: that style is simply one aspect of leadership. Perhaps such training is relatively harmless, but the focus on styles as manifest in leadership training may have its darker side. Underlying the style perspective is a perspective on organizations which assumes that once the most appropriate styles of leadership are known, first, selections will take place guided by this knowledge and, second, leadership styles will be changed as a result of training. This ignores some fundamental aspects of organizational life.

The selection of leaders is embedded in the complex politics of organizational life and the qualification of having an appropriate leadership style as designated by current theory constitutes merely one claim for selection. Embedded commitments and established images of the 'right sort' are likely to be more formidable bases for selection. The rules of the organizational world, as presumed in leadership training, are often at odds with the reality of organizational practice. Second, leaders are not merely free agents who can choose to change their leadership style as a result of training-based 'enlightenment'. Enmeshed in the organization, the individual leader is constrained both positively and negatively. Pressures to conform to the expectations of peers, subordinates and superiors are likely to affect the actual behaviour of leaders (Pfeffer 1978: 20). This applies equally to men and women.

One implication of this chapter for leadership training would seem to be the utility of reorientating it so that it focuses on the activity of leaders as networkers, as strategic actors, as influencers in the organizational network. A central part of this should involve an ability to analyze the leadership implications of the organizational culture, since this can be a significant influence on how a leader is received. Steven Feldman (1986) notes the response of senior managers to a new CEO who had a quite different style of leadership from his predecessors. The executives were used to non-ambiguous, directive CEOs. They complained of a 'lack of direction' and an absence of 'presence of command'. The established organizational culture revolved around a 'strong' CEO. In view of this kind of finding, perhaps it is the organization which needs training not the leader. But certainly explicit attention needs to be given to issues like follower maturity related to gender and diversity issues if women and other minorities are to break through the glass ceiling into leadership positions – it is not enough simply to regard this as a problem for training individuals.

We have also identified a post-heroic leadership agenda for organizations and their managers. There is a tendency in the popular literature to suggest that post-heroic leadership is 'one best way' for managing or leading in the new age of the knowledge or brain worker. However, we would argue that key elements of the approach, such as the role of trust in organizations, have not been examined in sufficient depth for us to have confidence in the broad applicability of the approach. Our discussion of the narcissistic leader also illustrates the point that managers *cum* leaders do not 'park their emotions at the door' when they come to work, including their egos. As Huey reminds us, much of the post-heroic leadership agenda requires that many managers say 'no' to their egos. A narcissistic leader could never do this.

The case study

To answer the questions on the BHP case, we can begin by trying to characterize John Prescott's leadership style. He seems to be very task and structure oriented so, in Blake and Mouton's terms, he would rate high on this factor and probably low to medium on people, given that three of the top managers recently left, making it an *authority-compliance* basic style. In Likert's terms, he would be somewhere between S1 and S2, but Fiedler would suggest that this style was appropriate for the 'crisis' which BHP was arguably facing. Of course, whether this style is appropriate for a CEO every day is questionable. Hersey and Blanchard would categorize the behaviour as S1 or S2, but the followers in this case are highly skilled and experienced managers. The way in which Prescott talks about Aiken suggests that his approach, though delegating, is more of a test than a coaching opportunity.

What is most important to Prescott? Clearly, bringing things under control seems to be at the centre of his plan. His own personal authority also seems to be an issue, and to that extent his approach seems to be narcissistic. Those theories which suggest that leaders need to change styles imply that leadership is a performance, but they tend to underestimate the wider audience for that performance – in this case the shareholders. Prescott may be doing what he thinks the 'City' wants rather than exactly what he himself wants. Yet his rebuttal of the McKinsey consultants suggests that he owns the changes, and that it is indeed his solution.

Prescott's relationships with his triumvirate would need to be cordial and close, despite the fact that they may each see themselves as his potential successor. In terms of leader–member exchange theory, they are a very small in-group, and would probably see the world in a very similar way to Prescott and be mutually supportive. The wider group of heads would be less cohesive as Prescott seems to be encouraging them to compete among themselves for the possibility of succeeding him. Here path–goal theory might be relevant if Prescott were clearer about rewards and goals for these people. However, Prescott seems to apply what is sometimes called 'Theory F' – appear to trust people, keep rewards a vague promise, but make it clear that failure of any kind will not be tolerated. The 'F' is for fear (see Linstead and Chan 1994).

Prescott's relations with the shopfloor are likely to be even more remote after the restructure, which increases power distance.

Prescott seems to take something of a sink or swim attitude to the future leaders of the company – challenging them rather than coaching them, and testing them rather than supporting them, requiring them to compete rather than collaborate. They are certainly likely to feel under stress.

Is Prescott a transactional or transformational leader? Clearly he sees himself as driving change, even being radical, but his solutions are conservative and, as some commentators suggest, are rolling back the dimensions of trust and delegation. However, he is more than transactional as he is breaking up the routines. Perhaps Prescott falls into a third category, the *conservative transformational* or the *radical transactional*, where change is an extreme reassertion of older, perhaps forgotten principles. Certainly he seems neither heroic nor post-heroic.

Ironically, in March 1998 Prescott rather unwittingly provided another example of the perceived importance of leadership. After continued poor performance by BHP he was placed under pressure to resign, which he did. It would seem that Prescott's structural approach to radical change had ultimately been seen as too transactional, and the company announced that it was seeking an external, international and more visionary leader than the long-serving Prescott to drive deeper cultural change. Despite the fact that there was no immediately obvious successor to his post, his removal caused the value of BHP shares on the market to leap dramatically. The value of Prescott's own shareholding rose by $2 million as a result of him losing his job! It appears that where leadership at the highest level is concerned, both success and failure reap considerable rewards; and also that structural change divorced from cultural change only masks the problem rather than solving it.

Questions at the beginning of chapter

We will now go back to the questions at the beginning of the chapter.

1 What is a leader?

This has changed over the years, particularly as leadership ideas have been adapted to changes in organizations. One of the dominant themes in the leadership research has been the role played by heredity and traits in the shaping of leadership qualities, particularly the drive or need for power. Views tend to polarize around the 'born leader' versus the trained or 'made leader'. Certainly, the popularity of the transformational leadership image of the 1980s lent support to the trait theory. Conversely, as organizations change – and not necessarily in uniform ways – the idea of post-heroic leadership has become ever more popular. The post-heroic leadership idea supports leadership teams, rotating leadership positions, and generally sharing power and spreading it around. Yet many large companies, such as the one in the BHP case study, seem less able to embrace the idea of post-heroic leadership. These very large companies, with major shareholders, boards and committees, have governance structures that still seem to favour 'the captain of industry' model of leadership – 'the great man' of the trait theorists and the absolute power of the leader this entails.

The essence of leadership is not something that can be agreed to, especially as issues of diversity no longer make it sensible to subscribe to one dominant model of leadership. Many leadership approaches have also been gender or culture blind. Leadership is very much a product of the society in which organizations operate, and these are now becoming international or global societies (see Chapter 3). Cultural variables will affect how managers from different cultural backgrounds manage in expatriate or foreign cultures and with culturally diverse groups. Leadership is also a product or is defined in terms of the problems or circumstances facing an organization. We suggest that leadership, or the role of the leader, is most appropriately thought of as predominantly concerned *with influence* and the form of influence that is used has to be seen as legitimate by a wide group of interests within any organization. The particular form of leadership influence chosen or practised by leaders or leadership teams should relate to, and be judged as part of, enhancing the performance of any organization.

2 Are all managers leaders?

The answer to the question of whether or not all managers are leaders depends on which school of leadership thought one subscribes to. Early theories of leadership were definitely focused on selecting the born leader and nurturing him to greatness. Then again, the style and contingency theorists had strong views on the malleability or adaptability of leadership styles. In their views, all managers had leadership potential, even if in some cases it was, say, Theory X leadership. The post-heroic leadership literature has tried to dispel the notion of a single heroic leader running the organization and has proposed instead more broad leadership development across the organization. The performance of organizations adopting a post-heroic style or approach to leadership needs to be evaluated further as the number of post-heroic leadership organizations grow.

3 Are women and men different as leaders?

When it comes to the question of gender and leadership, research lends support to the idea that men and women are different as leaders. However, on close examination of this evidence there is no clear indication as to *why* this should be, and the idea of there being a masculine style versus a feminine style is very difficult to support. Even the idea of the androgynous leader who has both male and female characteristics is rather superficial, and further problems occur when we recognize that perceived behaviour reported by managers varies from that reported by subordinates, and female managers are just as influenced by fads and the need to appear to be doing the right thing as anyone else. What this means is that there are differences, and we need more studies of actual women leaders at work, in context, rather than more surveys, in order to understand better the field of interacting forces in which they operate.

4 Can leaders change their styles or behaviours?

One of the most vexing questions in leadership is can a leader change his or her style of leadership? It is unlikely that narcissistic leaders can change their style, and the reality is that organizations can promote this form of leadership. Cultural aspects of leadership are also likely to be highly resistant to change. However, crises or major upheavals have been known to precipitate change in leadership approaches. This might involve altering or attenuating aspects of leadership style or bringing in a new leader or leadership team. Organizations reward certain styles of leadership and politically it is often these styles that ensure career success. Our view is that adopting post-heroic leadership styles for many managers, or even Theory Y for the narcissistic leader, is very difficult. Politics, power and certain predispositions suggest that training of managers to adopt particular leadership styles only works to a degree, and only if their organizations genuinely reward or encourage a particular approach.

5 Do we need leaders?

This is perhaps the hardest question to answer. Leadership substitute theories seem to suggest there are ways and circumstances in which leadership is not necessary. Post-heroic leadership theories do not subscribe to the abolition of leadership, but to a radical rethinking of it often using leadership substitutes and neutralizers or ideas drawn from the organization learning literature. Others propose that leadership is the work of every one if adaptive challenges become the focus of this work. We are also reminded that many of the qualities of post-heroic leadership are often nothing more than the qualities needed to do everyday work (Sashkin 1992: 155). In organizations of all kinds the question of whether leadership is important or needed, and the type of leadership that is championed, is determined by those who wield power and who have vested political and personal interests in favouring a particular rhetoric and approach to leadership. To change the leadership practices in an organization usually requires leadership from somewhere at the top levels. On this point alone, it is clear that there will always be organizations that claim they need strong, visionary leaders, heroic or otherwise, and will not subscribe in practice to any post-heroic agenda. There will also be those organizations that will adopt the 'post-heroic' discourse, but their leadership practices might stay relatively heroic.

References

Aktouf, O. (1996) 'Competence, symbolic activity and promotability', in Linstead, S., Grafton Small, R. and Jeffcutt, P. (eds), *Understanding Management*, London: Sage.

Alford, C. (1988) *Narcissism: Socrates, the Frankfurt School, and Psychoanalytic Theory*, New Haven, CT: Yale University Press.

Astin, H. and Leland, C. (1991) *Women of Influence, Women of Vision: A Cross-Generational Study of Leaders of Change*, San Francisco: Jossey-Bass.

Barrett, M. and Sutcliffe, P. (1992) 'Incorporating a critical perspective into management: The case of leadership models', paper presented to 1992 ANZAM Conference Penrith, 6–9 December, University of Western Sydney: 1–29.

Barrett, M. and Sutcliffe, P. (1993) 'Leadership theories: A critique and its implications for management education', *Queensland University of Technology, Faculty of Business, Key Centre in Strategic Management, Working Paper Series, No. 24*, Brisbane: Queensland University of Technology.

Bass, B. (1985) *Leadership and Performance Beyond Expectations*, New York: The Free Press.

Bennis, W.G. (1985) *Leaders: Strategies for Taking Charge*, New York: Harper and Row.

Blake, R. and McCanse, A.A. (1991) *Leadership Dilemmas – Grid Solutions*, Houston: Gulf.

Blake, R. and Mouton, J. (1978) *The New Managerial Grid*, Houston: Gulf.

Blanchard, K., Zigarmi, P. and Zigarmi, D. (1985) *Leadership and the One-Minute Manager*, London: Harper Collins.

Bolman, L.G. and Deal, T.E. (1991) *Reframing Organizations: Artistry, Choice and Leadership*, San Francisco and Oxford: Jossey-Bass.

Bradford, D. and Cohen, A. (1984) *Managing for Excellence*, New York: John Wiley.

Brewis, J., Hampton, M. and Linstead, S. (1997) 'Unpacking Priscilla: Subjectivity and identity in the organization of gendered appearance', *Human Relations* 50(10): 1275–304.

Brown, A.D. (1997) 'Narcissism, identity and legitimacy', *Academy of Management Review* 22(3): 643–86.

Bryman, A. (1985) 'Leadership' in Elliot, K. and Lawrence, P. (eds), *Introducing Management*, Harmondsworth, UK: Penguin.

Bryman, A. (1986) *Leadership and Organizations*, London: Routledge and Kegan Paul.

Calás, M.B. and Smircich L. (1995), 'Dangerous liaisons: The "feminine-in management" meets "Globalization"', in P. Frost, V. Mitchell and W. Nord (eds), *Managerial Reality*, New York: Haper Collins.

Callaghan, G. (1997) 'Here's Looking at Me, Kid', *The Australian Magazine* 25–26 October: 12–17.

Carr, A. (1994) 'For self or others? The quest for narcissism and the ego-ideal in work organizations', *Administrative Theory and Praxis* 16(2): 208–22.

Carr, A. (1998) 'Identity, compliance and dissent in organizations: A psychoanalytic perspective', *Organization* 5(1): 81–99.

Caulkin, S. (1993) 'The lust for leadership', *Management Today* November, 38: 40–3.

Cavaleri, S. and Fearon, D. (eds) (1996) *Managing in Organizations that Learn*, Cambridge, Mass.: Blackwell Business.

Coopey, J. (1995) 'The learning organization: Power, politics and ideology', *Management Learning* 26(2): 193–213.

Crawford, R. (1991) *In the Era of Human Capital: The Emergence of Talent, Intelligence, and Knowledge as a Worldwide Economic Force and What It Means to Managers and Investors*, New York: Harper Business.

Dansereau, F., Graen, G. and Haga, W.J. (1975) 'A vertical dyad linkage approach to leadership within formal organizations: A longitudinal investigation of the role-making process', *Organizational Behaviour and Human Performance* 15: 46–78.

Denmark, F.L. (1993) 'Women, leadership, and empowerment', *Psychology of Women Quarterly* 17: 343–56.

Diamond, M.A. and Allcorn, S. (1990) 'The Freudian factor', *Personnel Journal* March: 54–65.

Downs, A. (1997) *Beyond the Looking Glass*, New York: Amacom.

Duncan, W.J. (1978) *Organizational Behavior*, Boston, Mass.: Houghton Mifflin.

Dunphy, D. and Stace, D. (1990) *Under New Management: Australian Organizations in Transition*, Sydney: McGraw-Hill.

Evans, M.G. (1970) 'The effects of supervisory behaviour on the path-goal relationship', *Organizational Behaviour and Human Performance* 5: 277–98.

Feldman, S.P. (1986) 'Culture, charisma – and the CEO: An essay on the meaning of high office', *Human Relations* 39: 211–28.

Fiedler, F.E. (1967) *A Theory of Leadership Effectiveness*, New York: McGraw-Hill.

Fiedler, F.E. (1974) 'The contingency model – New directions for leadership utilization', *Journal of Contemporary Business* 3: 65–79.

Fiedler, F.E., Chemers, M.M. and Mahar, L. (1976) *Improving Leadership Effectiveness*, New York: John Wiley.

Fiedler, F.E. and Garcia, J.E. (1987) *New Approaches to Effective Leadership*, New York: John Wiley.

Fineman, S. (1993) 'Organizations as emotional arenas', in Fineman, S. (ed.), *Emotion in Organizations*, London: Sage.

Fleishman, E.A. and Peters, D.R. (1962) 'International values, leadership attitudes and managerial success', *Personnel Psychology* 15: 127–43.

Graen, G. and Schiemann, W. (1978) 'Leader–member agreement: A vertical dyad linkage approach', *Journal of Applied Psychology* 63: 206–12.

Hackman, R.J. (1992) 'The psychology of self-management in organizations', in Glaser, R. (ed.), *Classic Readings in Self-Managing Teamwork*, King of Prussia, PA: Organization Design and Development Inc.

Haigh, G. (1994) 'Power without glory', *The Australian Magazine* 25–26 June: 13–16, 20.

Harris, T.G. (1993) 'The post-capitalist executive: An interview with Peter F. Drucker', *Harvard Business Review*

May–June: 115–22.

Hartsock, N.C.M. (1985) *Money, Sex and Power: Toward a Feminist Historical Materialism*, New York: Simon and Schuster.

Hater, J.J. and Bass, B.M. (1988) 'Superiors' evaluations and subordinates' perceptions of transformational and transactional leadership', *Journal of Applied Psychology* 37(4): 695–702.

Heifetz, R.A. and Laurie, D.L. (1997) 'The work of leadership', *Harvard Business Review* January–February: 124–34.

Helgesen, S. (1990) *The Female Advantage: Women's Ways of Leadership*, New York: Doubleday.

Hellreigel, D.J., Slocum, W. and Woodman, W. (1986) *Organizational Behaviour*, St Paul: West Publishing.

Hersey, P. (1985) *The Situational Leader*, New York: Warner Books.

Hersey, P. and Blanchard, K. (1996) *Management of Organizational Behavior: Utilizing Human Resources*, Englewood Cliffs, NJ: Prentice Hall.

Hofstede, G. (1980/1992) 'Motivation, leadership and organization; Do American theories apply abroad', in Lane, H.W. and DiStefano, J.J. (eds), *International Management Behavior*, Boston: PWS/Kent.

House, R. (1971) 'A path–goal theory of leader effectiveness', *Administrative Science Quarterly* 16:321–38.

Howell, J.P., Bowen, D.E., Dorfman, P.W., Kerr, S. and Podsakoff, P.M. (1990) 'Substitutes for leadership: Effective alternatives to ineffective leadership', *Organizational Dynamics* Summer: 20–38.

Howell, J.P. and Dorfman, P.W. (1981) 'Substitutes for leadership: Test of a construct', *Academy of Management Journal* 24: 714–28.

Huey, J. (1994) 'The new post-heroic leadership', *Fortune*, 21 February: 24–8.

Hunsaker, P.L. and Cook, C.W. (1986) *Managing Organizational Behavior*, Reading, Mass.: Addison-Wesley.

Huxham, C. (ed.) (1996) *Creating Collaborative Advantage*, London: Sage.

Kanter, R.M. (1977) *Men and Women of the Corporation*, New York: Basic Books.

Kanter, R.M. (1979) 'Power failure in management circuits', *Harvard Business Review* 57(4): 65–75.

Kanter, R.M. (1983) The *Change Masters: Innovations for Productivity in American Corporations*, New York: Simon and Schuster.

Kelley, R. (1992) *The Power of Followership*, New York: Doubleday.

Kerr, S. and Jermier, J.M. (1978) 'Substitutes for leadership: Their meaning and measurement', *Organizational Behaviour and Human Performance* 22: 375–403.

Kets de Vries, M. (1991) 'Whatever happened to the philosopher king? The leader's addiction to power', *Journal of Management Studies* 28(4): 339–51.

Kirkpatrick, S. and Locke, E.A. (1991) 'Leadership: Do traits matter?', *Academy of Management Executive* 5(2): 48–60.

Korman, A.K. (1966) '"Consideration", "Initiating Structure" and organizational criteria – a review', *Personnel Psychology* 19: 349–61.

Kotter, J. (1990) 'What leaders really do', *Harvard Business Review* May–June: 103–11.

Kotter, J. (1995) *The New Rules: How to Succeed in Today's Post-Corporate World*, New York: The Free Press.

Kouzes, J.M. and Posner, B.Z. (1989) *The Leadership Challenge*, San Francisco: Jossey-Bass.

Larson, L., Hunt, J.G. and Osborn, R.N. (1976) 'The great hi-hi leader behaviour myth: A lesson from Occam's Razor', *Academy of Management Journal* 19: 628–41.

Liden, R.C. and Graen, G. (1980) 'Generalizability of the vertical dyad model of leadership', *Academy of Management Journal* 23: 451–65.

Likert, R. (1961) *New Patterns of Management*, New York: McGraw-Hill.

Likert, R. (1967) *The Human Organization: Its Management and Value*, New York: McGraw-Hill.

Likert, R. (1979) 'From production and employee-centredness to systems 1–4', *Journal of Management* 5: 147–56.

Linstead, S. and Chan, A. (1994) 'The sting of organization: Command, reciprocity and change management', *Journal of Organizational Change Management* 7(5): 4–19.

McClelland, D. (1961) *The Achieving Society*, Princeton, NJ: Van Nostrand.

McGregor, D. (1960) *The Human Side of Enterprise*, New York: McGraw-Hill.

Mant, A. (1994) *Leaders We Deserve* (second edition), Melbourne: Currency Production.

Manz, C.C. and Sims, H.P., Jr (1992) 'Becoming a super leader', in Glaser, R. (ed.), *Classic Readings in Self-Managing Teamwork*, King of Prussia, Pa: Organization Design and Development Inc.

Maslow, A.H. (1987) *Motivation and Personality*, New York: Harper and Row.

Mintzberg, H. (1997) 'Toward healthier hospitals', *Health Care Management Review* 22(4): 9–18.

Mullins, L.J. (1985) *Management and Organizational Behaviour*, London: Pitman.

Nutt, P.C. (1995) 'Transforming public organizations with strategic leadership', in Halachmi, A. and Bouckaert, G. (eds), *Public Productivity Through Quality and Strategic Management*, Amsterdam: IOS Press.

Pelz, D. (1952) 'Influence: A key to effective leadership in the first line supervisor', *Personnel* 29: 209–17.

Pfeffer, J. (1978) 'The ambiguity of leadership', in McCall, M.W., Jr and Lombardo, M.M. (eds), *Leadership: Where Else Can We Go?* Durham: Duke University Press.

Pheasant, B. (1995) *The Australian Financial Review* 11 December: 21.

Pondy, R. (1978) 'Leadership is a language game', in McCall, M.W., Jr and Lombardo, M.M. (eds), *Leadership: Where Else Can We Go?*, Durham: Duke University Press.

Pringle, J. (1994) 'Feminism and management: Critique and contribution', in Kouzmin, A., Still, L.V. and Clarke, R. (eds), *New Directions in Management*, Sydney: McGraw-Hill.

Quinn, R.E. and Spreitzer, G.M. (1997) 'The road to empowerment: Seven questions every leader should consider', *Organizational Dynamics* Autumn: 37–44.

Robbins, S. (1988) Essentials of Organizational Behavior, Englewood Cliffs, NJ: Prentice Hall.

Rosener, J. (1990) 'Ways women lead', *Harvard Business Review* November–December: 119–25.

Sankowsky, D. (1995) 'The charismatic leader as narcissist: Understanding the abuse of power', *Organizational Dynamics* Spring: 57–72.

Sashkin, M. (1992) 'Strategic leadership competencies', in Phillips, R.L. and Hunt, J.G. (eds) *Strategic Leadership: A Multiorganizational-Level Perspective*, Wesport, CT: Quorum Books.

Scase, R. and Goffee, R. (1990) 'Women in management: Towards a research agenda', *International Journal of Human Resource Management* 1(1): 107–25.

Schwartz, H. (1990) *Narcissistic Process and Corporate Decay*, New York: NYU Press.

Semler, R. (1993) *Maverick: The Success Story Behind the World's Most Unusual Workplace*, London: Century.

Shackleton, V. and Fletcher, C. (1984) *Individual Differences: Theories and Applications*, London: Methuen.

Sherman, S. (1994) 'Leaders learn to heed the voice within', *Fortune* 22 August: 72–8.

Sinclair, A. (1998) *Doing Leadership Differently: Gender, Power and Sexuality in a Changing Business Culture*, Melbourne: Melbourne University Press.

Skipper, F. and Manz, C.C. (1993) 'W.L. Gore & Associates Inc.', in Rowe, A.J., Mason, R.O., Dickel, K.E., Mann, R.B. and Mockler, R.J. (eds), *Strategic Management: A Methodological Approach* (fourth edition), Reading, Mass. Addison-Wesley.

Smircich, L. and Morgan, G. (1982) 'Leadership: The management of meaning', *Journal of Applied Behavioural Science* 18(3): 257–73.

Spillane, R. (1984) *Achieving Peak Performance*, Sydney: Harper and Row.

Sproull, R. and Stevens, M. (1997) *The Australian* 1 October: 25–6.

Stogdill, R.M. (1974a) 'Historical trends in leadership theory and research', *Journal of Contemporary Business* 3: 1–17.

Stogdill, R.M. (1974b) *Handbook of Leadership*, New York: The Free Press.

Stoner, J.A., Collins, R.R. and Yetton, P.W. (1985) *Management in Australia*, Sydney: Prentice Hall.

Symington, N. (1993) *Narcissism*, London: Karnak Books.

Tichy, N.M. and Devanna, M.A. (1986) *The Transformational Leader*, New York: John Wiley.

Tichy, N.M. and Ulrich, D. (1987) 'The leadership challenge: A call for the transformational leader', in Timpe, D.A. (ed.), *Leadership*, New York: Facts on File Publications.

Triandis, H.C. (1995) *Individualism and Collectivism*, Boulder, CO: Westview.

Vecchio, R.P., Hearn, G. and Southey, G. (1996) *Organizational Behaviour*, Sydney: Harcourt Brace.

Watson, T.J. (1986) *Management, Organization and Employment Strategy*, London: Routledge and Kegan Paul.

Westwood, R. (1992) *Organizational Behaviour*, Hong Kong: Longmans Group (FE).

Wilson, F.M. (1995) *Organizational Behaviour and Gender*, London: McGraw-Hill.

6 Managing teams

Graham Sewell, Liz Fulop, Stephen Linstead and William D. Rifkin

Questions about teams

1   What is a team?
2   What needs and whose needs can a team serve?
3   Do managers need to manage differently in a team situation?
4   Are there different ideas of what a team is and does?
5   How do teams develop?

Wombat Manufacturing – Part 1

Wombat Manufacturing, a maker of automotive components, was an organization in which change was being driven by a theoretical framework advanced by one of its managers, Norman Stone. Stone promoted a principle called 'process intent', where the overall objectives of production processes should be understood clearly by everyone concerned. This principle would allow Wombat managers to innovate and change specific work processes as long as the integrity of the intent (that is, the purpose and objectives) of the process was maintained. Such change was to be achieved through: (1) a quality focus on statistical process control (where monitoring the frequency and magnitude of production errors guides improvement); (2) an emphasis on participative management with shopfloor team involvement in the process; and (3) the achievement of productivity gains, which involved taking a look at cost effectiveness throughout the whole production 'value-chain', reaching from suppliers through to delivery to the manufacturers.

    Wombat Manufacturing, as an academic researcher found it, was undergoing an intensive process of participative redesign of their traditional work systems. The plant's personnel were, the academic wrote, '… not only pioneering a new shopfloor-driven approach to productivity and efficiency, but a new theory of organizational change to go with it'. This exciting prospect seemed substantive, for the '… employee involvement programme is not a shop-window programme, all appearance and no substance. It does encourage genuine involvement, and it does lead to some shopfloor improvements,' which were supported by documentation. Taking a look at the process of change, the researcher noted that the company was '… now engaging directly with the establishment of genuine self-managing teams or semi-autonomous work groups', a process involving the 'painstaking reintegration of fragmented shopfloor tasks and devolution of production authority'. The researcher noted 'the dogged determination the groups have shown in identifying problems, and manoeuvring their way around obstacles lying in the path of a solution'.

What then were the key factors contributing to successful change? First of all, the change process was built on the back of an earlier Employee Involvement Programme, under which various cross-functional groups (combining workers with different tasks and specialities) had been established. In addition, a more recent firm-based, quality accreditation programme, which also employed cross-functional teams (but with less shopfloor involvement than the earlier initiative), was established to address production problems. The result of these developments was a major improvement in production quality (as measured by defect rates). Stories circulated about how one of the teams succeeded in solving what had previously been an intractable quality control problem with one of the mountings of a dashboard component. Second, an industrial relations and skill development package had been put in place that involved not only a payment agreement (the usual industrial relations outcome), but also the establishment both of a career development path and competency-based training for unskilled shopfloor employees (an innovation in this arena). Third, process management within Wombat was improved via a greater emphasis on shopfloor responsibility and through the introduction of more effective systems in the areas of production scheduling (with the introduction of a Japanese-type kanban production control system), quality control (through a greater emphasis on inspection by operators backed up by a periodic, quality audit procedure) and performance management (through a focused, performance measurement system administered by the shopfloor work groups). Fourth, teams were introduced throughout the plant with the establishment of work area groups, which were supported at a supervisory level by a team of managers acting as production and team coordinators and 'blockage removers'.

Source: Richard Badham, Paul Couchman and Stephen Linstead (1995) 'Power tools: Narrating the factory of the future', Annual Conference on the Labour Process, Blackpool, University of Central Lancashire, April.

Questions about the case

1 How important is the theory behind the practice in Wombat?
2 What impact have the changes had?
3 How far are teams involved in setting their own performance levels?

Introduction

We trained hard – but it seemed that every time we were beginning to form up into teams, we would be reorganized. I was to learn later in life that we tend to meet any new situation by reorganizing, and a wonderful method it can be for creating the illusion of progress while producing confusion, inefficiency and demoralization (*Attributed to Caius Petronius Arbiter, AD 66*).

It has become fashionable nowadays to introduce discussions of teams and organizational change with this quote, allegedly but probably incorrectly attributed to the writings of the Roman Senator, Petronius, author of the *Satyricon* (Davis 1994: 248). The seeming currency of this quote (or even its invention and continued use) signals that teams and teamwork are now a central feature of many organizational change programmes. The quote's message is, first, that there is nothing new under the sun and that teams are as perennial a feature of organizational life as change itself. Second, teams are fragile, take time to establish themselves and are susceptible to the impact of top managers' desires for organizational change for its own sake. Third, the introduction of teams must be carefully managed in order for them to be a success. Perhaps a fourth point could be added, that only a limited range of choices are available in terms of the types of teams managers can introduce with some hope of success (Harris 1993:12, citing Peter F. Drucker 1993: 121).

Reverting to historical sources to bolster the appeal of teams is a common feature of popular management literature, reflecting a significant theme: that collective organization resembling teams is somehow the natural way to organize human effort, and, since the industrial revolution, the use of production lines has undermined this natural inclination to work in groups. Perhaps the most sophisticated representation of this position is contained in Jon Katzenbach and Douglas Smith's book, *The Wisdom of Teams* (1993). Here, the authors allude to an idealized period of pre-industrial manufacturing where production was undertaken by independent craftworkers operating in loosely governed, cooperative groups. This type of image attracts managers in modern organizations to teams and an ideal of autonomous and collaborative 'empowered' workers. Many other writers on teams seem to hold an implicit and unchallenged assumption that teamwork is a good thing. Is it, in all its forms?

To understand the benefits and pitfalls of various approaches to teams, both as an ideal and as applied in the workplace, it is important to appreciate the history behind current models of teams and team-based production. It is also important to appreciate the impact of teams on productivity and manager–worker relations, including issues of power and control. The rest of this chapter will tackle these two main issues – history and managers' objectives – in the following ways. First, we will examine how, from early in the twentieth century, managers sought the standardization and formalization promised by Frederick Winslow Taylor's scientific management approach, and the isolation from co-workers associated with bureaucracy and assembly-line manufacturing. In this context, managers saw teams as positively dysfunctional and a threat to efficient organization. Second, we will see how the pendulum has swung back to where the standardization and isolation of assembly-line work have come to be considered by managers, workers, unions and academics as dysfunctional and inefficient. Third, we will look at how contemporary prescriptions for teams attempt to overcome these shortcomings in the search for continuous improvement and knowledge sharing. We examine different types of groups and teams, the stages in their development, the roles of team leaders and other team members' potential contributions and the challenges these pose for managers.

The origins of teams

Although contemporary texts may tend to overstate or mythologize the role of teams before the industrial revolution, there are similarities between these earlier approaches to teams and modern ones. For example, historical research by Sidney Pollard (1965) and David

Landes (1969) indicates that craftworkers may indeed have exercised a good deal of group self-determination over the way they performed factory tasks. This position on work-group autonomy is lent further support when we consider that early industrialists and political economists like Richard Arkwright, Andrew Ure, and even the philanthropist Robert Owen, often went into print decrying the inability of factory owners to exercise close direction and control over their workforce. Having little or no experience of factory work themselves, managers would have found it difficult to exercise authority by claiming superior technical knowledge about how to perform a task.

In many organizational situations, groups, rather than individuals, have always provided a basis for coordinating human effort to get work done. Consider for example, the current vogue for cross-functional teams, where specialists come together from many parts of an organization, or even from other organizations, to pool their expertise in order to focus on a particular problem. It is a well-established practice in project management, such as in the construction industry, from the design stage right through to the erection of the building. The advertising industry is similar: account managers, creative staff and client representatives cooperate on a particular campaign. Over 50 years ago, coal mining, which is now highly mechanized, was organized around tightly knit familial groups that today would undoubtedly be called *teams* (Trist and Bamforth 1951).

Factory work in the first half of the twentieth century, especially the assembly of mass-produced consumer products, caused teams to fall out of favour with managers. This move away from teams came about in response to the Scientific Management Movement, mentioned in Chapter 2, which has left a very visible and widespread legacy today.

Taylor's principles of Scientific Management

One of the key developments in management thinking this century both disrupted traditions of teams and has coloured the recent resurgence in popularity of teamwork. This historical development was the general emergence of Scientific Management. Frederick Winslow Taylor (1903, 1911, 1964, 1972) is widely considered to be the founding father of Scientific Management – and indeed he coined the term for his own particular brand of work measurement and control. However, the emergence of 'management', as a new occupation during the industrial revolution, was an important precursor to Taylor's work. Engineers such as Taylor became key people in designing the technical and social structure of organizations (Clegg and Dunkerley 1980: 87). Indeed, Taylor played such a strong role in its development that Scientific Management and Taylorism have become synonymous. Based on his personal observations of the organization and execution of work tasks in the Midvale steel plant in Bethlehem, Pennsylvania, Taylor came up with a systematic approach to the study and design of work. This is captured in his *Principles of Scientific Management* book (1911), and these principles are outlined below in Exhibit 6.1.

- **Principle One** By identifying, through systematic observation, the great mass of traditional knowledge possessed by workers and translating it into laws, rules and mathematical formulae, managers are involved in the creation of a science whereby work activities can first be standardized and formalized to optimize execution of repetitive tasks (such as tightening bolts on an assembly line).
- **Principle Two** Managers must study the character, nature and performance of individual workers so that they can scientifically select those most suitable for performing a particular task.

- **Principle Three** Taylor uses the term 'bringing together' to convey the sense of this third principle. Here, Taylor takes 'bringing together' to mean the coordination of the activities of many individuals in order to execute a number of interrelated tasks.
- **Principle Four** By his own reckoning, Taylor considered this principle to be the most difficult one to explain. When first stated, the principle might sound counter-intuitive – under Scientific Management there would be an almost equal distribution of actual work between managers and workers. Taylor noted that, under previous forms of management, the responsibility for both the conception and execution of work lay with the workers themselves and that managers did very little genuine work at all, simply checking to see when a particular set of general instructions had been completed. Under Taylor's approach, management must take over the responsibility for how work needs to be done down to the most minute level, leaving the workers to execute a series of predetermined tasks laid out for them. It may seem odd that Taylor equated the effort of shopfloor work with the planning activities of professional managers. However, this separation of brain work – to be done by managers – from physical toil – to be done by workers – is one of the defining characteristics of Taylorism, and it seems widely evident today (see also Braverman 1974: 104).

Exhibit 6.1 Principles of Scientific Management

Taylorism had a profound influence on the way work was organized, especially in terms of the practical impact of the principles of Scientific Management. In addition, as we shall see later, its political and ideological impact was also substantial. Whereas previously, even under large-scale factory organization, the responsibility for both the conception and execution of work might have rested with fairly autonomous groups of craftworkers, now there was a scientific rationale for breaking this convention. This shift also threatened the potential power base of skilled workers. Moreover, the formalization and standardization of tasks at the level of the individual eroded any tendency to organize work in teams. Given that work was designed to be repetitive, was synchronized by stopwatches and therefore precisely measured, and also involved high levels of division of labour, it was no surprise that workers had little responsibility and discretion. According to Taylor, it was the scientifically-trained manager's duty to understand the workers' expertise and it was management's prerogative as to how it was used. This was a particularly urgent consideration as Taylor believed that workers would use their expertise to ease their own workload rather than to aim at raising profits.

Giving responsibility to workers would mean that, potentially at least, the best laid plans of management could be subject to disruption as the workforce pursued their own interests – such as a more relaxed pace of work – rather than those of the organization – such as higher production. These two tendencies combined to form the basis of what Taylor called *soldiering* – a process whereby workers used their ingenuity, expertise and intimate knowledge of the work process to achieve marginal improvements in doing their work to improve their own working conditions. However, workers would still hide the benefits, in terms of potential productivity gains, from the company in order to keep an area of discretion over how hard they worked. Taylor thought workers were quite rational in behaving this way while ever managers were acting in arbitrary and non-scientific ways (Taylor 1912: 20–1; Rose 1975: 32–3). If workers only performed tightly monitored tasks determined on a scientific basis by an elite group of highly trained managers, Taylor argued that soldiering could be eliminated and efficiency could be pursued. Collusion within a team to ease work would only undermine the principles of Scientific Management and hide improvements in productivity from management.

The emergence of Taylorism is also one of the key events in the professionalization of management during the twentieth century. First, it did much to create management as a separate activity enacted by trained individuals (mainly engineers), whose status and effectiveness was determined by their access to, and understanding of, a body of management knowledge. Second, it provided the foundation for the elevation of the single worker as the basic unit of industrial organization. Although, as Taylor had noted, workers needed to be 'brought together', the analytical focus of Scientific Management was on the isolated individual performing an endlessly repetitive set of tasks; essentially, the worker was considered to be a piece of technology. Although Scientific Management individualized the work tasks in this way it also portrayed workers as completely interchangeable (like parts in a machine), provided they had received an adequate level of training. This interchangeability was possible because the tasks were not designed for the talents of one particular person, but were based on some notional average level of human performance. So long as new workers could conform to this average level, they were deemed to be acceptable substitutes.

Scientific Management was, if anything, a theory of *knowledge*. It was concerned with developing a rational, scientific basis to management, rather than one of seeking the accommodation of individual differences and embracing a diversity of values. Management, for both Taylor and many contemporary management theorists, means 'getting things done through other people' and involves persuading those other people to contribute, accessing their knowledge and directing their actions toward a specific set of goals, which may well not be ones employees personally espouse. However, for Taylor management was simply the *function* of ensuring that people carried out appropriate tasks in accordance with scientific principles. In this sense, individual characteristics, including *gender* and *ethnicity*, were irrelevant to the function of management, as shown in Chapter 2.

Similarly, although Taylor himself conducted his work in steelworks, where there were relatively few women to be found, the apparent lack of consideration of gender in his work is neither due to this lack of women to observe nor accidental – it is part of a broader and more purposeful attempt to improve control and to suppress *diversity* by constructing it as being irrelevant to organizational purposes. Suppression of some dimensions of diversity caused organized dissent. Unions saw a threat to craft status through deskilling (the simplifying of work by giving some tasks to machines, thereby making the work do-able by less skilled workers) and the threat to jobs of piecework pay rates (paid for output or productivity) (Merkle 1980: 28–9). Management saw a threat to managerial discretion, judgement and patronage systems of reward and promotion from objectively determined standards. Both voiced opposition to Taylor's views. Yet, gender as a dimension, in both Scientific Management and the critique of Scientific Management, remains silenced because diversity in general – in terms of gender, class, ethnicity or race – was silenced. This 'silence' remained prevalent in management thinking, particularly in Western societies, well into the 1980s, and still persists.

It is worth noting that 'Fordism', which is a term used to describe the technological and industrial system based on the classic production line, developed by Henry Ford in the USA, was different in nature from Scientific Management. Fordism refers to a system of mass production and the development of a mass consumption market to support this form of production (Mathews 1989: 31–4). Taylorism did not depend solely on assembly-line concepts or mass production, but rather on the scientific design of work and the creation of what Taylor called a total mental revolution in how management was practised.

Taylor's third principle (bringing together) was most vividly captured in Henry Ford's use of the moving assembly line in his car manufacturing plants. Ford's innovation was, in many ways, independent of Taylor's advocacy of Scientific Management, but it nonetheless benefited greatly from the application of Taylor's principles in its operation.

Problems of Taylorism

The tendency of Taylorism to isolate the worker from workmates (*sic*) – preventing team-work – closely resembles (but is not identical to) the effects of bureaucracy. As such, Taylorism is prone to some of the problems or dysfunctions that research and experience have found are associated with bureaucracy (see also Fulop 1992 and Robbins and Barnwell 1994 for a summary of the problems of bureaucracy). Three key problems were identified by Robert Merton (1940) and are summarized in Exhibit 6.2.

1. **Goal displacement** Merton noted that the advantage of reliability and predictability brought about by the use of standardized and formalized rules and procedures also had a potentially significant disadvantage in that workers may become fixated on fulfilling the minute details of their task with little consideration of the actual outcome of their activities. For example, individuals who struggle to fulfil their work quota in an allotted time may have little regard for the quality of the final product.

2. **The inappropriate application of rules and procedures** A second dysfunction of bureaucracies and Taylorism, closely related to goal displacement, is that of continuing to apply standardized rules and procedures even in situations where they may be considered inappropriate. Taylor himself would have surely hoped that an individual who encountered such a situation would be aware of the problem and seek to use their experience and ingenuity to adapt or innovate to solve the problem. However, the relentless ideological message contained in Scientific Management concerning the separation of 'mental' and manual work was likely to mean that even if they were able to adapt or innovate, workers would be unwilling to attempt anything for which they might be blamed.

3. **Employee alienation** Distance separates workers from the design and assignment of tasks they are performing. The manager designs and assigns tasks, and the worker becomes unable to attach personal significance to the act of working. This loss of potential pride in – and sense of 'ownership' of – one's work eventually leads to powerful forces of demotivation setting in.

Exhibit 6.2 Dysfunctions of bureaucracy

An extension of Merton's problem, this time at a broader organization level, was identified by Philip Selznick (1949). He noted another problem associated with specialization in that, through differentiating between functional activities (e.g. design, manufacturing, accounting, marketing), each of these groupings becomes more concerned with their narrow, day to day operational problems at the expense of the 'bigger picture'. This could also occur within subdivisions. Take, for example, the assembly stage in a car plant where the pressing shop may be producing body panels with little regard for the way in which their finish might affect downstream activities like body assembly or painting.

While still focusing on the problems of standardization and formalization, Alvin Gouldner (1954) identified a third problem related to goal displacement. Alienated workers, caught up in the monotony of following rules and procedures imposed by managers, would come to see these rules as defining not just the minimum but also the maximum level of performance, that is, an individual performing a task would stop once a particular target had been achieved even if they could do more. This point has important implications for modern theories of teamwork, and we will return to discuss it later (also see Chapter 4).

Finally, Victor Thompson (1961) reversed the direction of scrutiny by looking back up the hierarchy at managers themselves. He found that, all the way up the managerial ladder, individuals would often hide behind the protection offered by rules in order to obscure their own culpability, performance limitations or poor decision making (see also Chapter 8).

Taylorism had very definite practical implications in the area of industrial organization and beyond – critical followers of Taylor, Frank and Lillian Gilbreth (1914), applied the principles of Scientific Management to many work settings, including the office. Taylorism's impact in terms of politics and ideology was equally as important. The initial interest in Scientific Management was significant enough to initiate an inquiry by the United States Congress, where Taylor gave famous testimony in 1912 before an investigating committee. The generally favourable outcome of the senate inquiry went a long way to legitimizing Scientific Management as an approach to the organization of work, and it was adopted widely, although not universally, in the USA and elsewhere. Nevertheless, a study of the development of US manufacturing shows that enthusiasm for Taylorism was by no means universal among corporate leaders and the employees, a position echoed by others (Hounshell 1985).

Some authors have argued that Taylorism's real impact was far more political than practical, and its significance in furthering a managerial ideology of domination and control was far greater than its role in instigating a wholesale transformation across manufacturing industry. Harry Braverman (1974), a Marxist critic, has gone as far as identifying the rise of Scientific Management as the key event in the development of capitalist domination. This is because although the herding of workers into factories owned by others that occurred during the industrial revolution led to a subordination of labour, the real subordination of labour did not come about until the separation of mental and manual work advocated by Taylor.

One particular problem associated with Taylorism – the isolating and repetitive nature of work tasks – stands out on both sides of what has become the classical Marxist debate. For workers and their advocates in the trades union movement, it was seen as the ultimate dehumanizing and alienating approach to work. Managers, too, found that the demotivating effect of the endless monotony of the factory was likely to emerge in the long run. This relationship between the quality of working life and motivation is a perennial concern of much management literature, and this is clearly brought out in the work of the Human Relations Movement.

Human Relations Movement

As early as the 1920s, it became evident that the more optimistic claims of increased efficiency associated with Taylorism were more difficult to obtain in practice. So, researchers and managers began to examine other factors that might play a role in productivity (see

Chapter 2). The famous Hawthorne Studies (named after the suburb of Chicago where the plant under study was located) were undertaken between 1924 and 1932 to examine such factors. The Hawthorne Studies were run by the Western Electric Company managers, but with the effective academic direction after 1926 of Elton Mayo, an expatriate Australian who, before moving to the USA, had been the inaugural chair of philosophy at the University of Queensland. The studies were intended to establish the effect of the work environment on productivity, with the initial focus being on lighting levels. It soon became obvious to the researchers that the physical organization of production also had to be compatible with its social organization. Furthermore, alongside the formal social organization of the plant there exists a set of *informal social relationships* – perhaps based on kinship groups, ethnic background, personal friendships, sentiment and emotion (Bendix 1956: 313–17; Rose 1975: 120–2). Although these informal relationships could have a positive impact on productivity, the Hawthorne Studies found that there was an unofficial and, in the eyes of Mayo, a distinctly negative code of behaviour, which exerted a strong influence on members of informal groups. This code of behaviour can be expressed as follows:

- Do not work too hard. If you do you will 'show up' other members, and you will receive the disapproval of your peers by being identified as a 'rate buster'.
- Do not take it too easy. If you do you run the risk of 'letting the side down', and you will receive the disapproval of your peers by being identified as a 'chiseller'.
- Do not tell anybody in a supervisory position anything that might expose your peers to disapproval. If you do, then you are a 'squealer'.

Here, Mayo (1933, 1945) had identified the strong peer group pressure that operates on individuals to conform to certain norms within the workplace. Two main implications emerge from taking this position. First, regardless of whether they have any previous affiliations, no collection of people can be in contact for any length of time at work without informal groupings forming and 'natural leaders' emerging. Second, because of their resilient nature, it would be futile, and even unwise, to try and break up such groupings. Rather, management should seek to establish a convergence of interests between the organization and its employees and design work practices that are compatible with informal associations at work. If this design is effective then, at worst, informal groupings should have a neutral effect on productivity and, at best, they should prove to be positively beneficial. Here, we see a possible confluence between Taylorist drives for efficiency and the potential of teamwork.

Although Mayo's work is, in retrospect, often presented as being quite progressive in its attitudes toward issues such as the quality of work life and the psychological impact of work, he is understood to have been ideologically motivated by a desire to reduce the likelihood of workplace unrest. It must be remembered that, at the time of the Hawthorne Studies, the Russian revolution was a recent and sobering memory, and there were real concerns that it might be repeated in the USA and other liberal democracies. In this sense, Mayo was intent on making minor concessions in terms of marginal reforms in work practices and the work environment rather than bringing about significant change, such as a recombination of mental and manual work, which Taylor had separated. The responsibility for studying work practices and designing new approaches still lay with professional technocrat-managers – rather than the workers themselves. Moreover, work was still to be analyzed and organized on an individualized basis, in a similar way to Taylorism, with the informal groupings identified through the Hawthorne Studies merely being 'taken into account' in any design process. Thus two significant points emerge:

1   Mayo's work did little to reverse the impact of Taylorism in emphasizing the individual as the focus for standardizing and formalizing work tasks.
2   Mayo's work did not undermine the legitimacy of managers – rather than workers – to exercise control over the determination of work tasks. On the contrary, it reinforced the role of the manager, and particularly the supervisor as an expert who employed knowledge not known to the worker to design tasks and to compensate for the effects on production of workers' friendships with work colleagues. The separation between the inception and execution of work was maintained.

Nevertheless, Mayo's work has continued to be influential, not least because it seems to promise a rationale for addressing problems associated with Scientific Management. In addition to the Human Relations Movement, which Mayo's work initiated, it also had an impact, according to Stephen Waring (1991), on a number of subsequent management approaches, including quality of work life (QWL), job enrichment schemes and quality circles (see below and Chapter 7). These approaches all entail extensive prescriptions for workplace reorganization, which include greater involvement of the workforce in task design and general decision making. None of these movements radically challenged the fundamental issues at stake under Scientific Management – the individual remained the basis of the organization of tasks and mental and manual labour continued to be separated. Indeed, Waring rather uncharitably but, nevertheless, tellingly describes them all as an attempt to '… hide the excesses of Taylorism behind chintz curtains'. Given this assertion, is the current championing of teams yet another pair of *chintz curtains*, preserving repressive or alienating aspects of Taylorism, though promising the accommodation of human needs for meaningful work and workplace relationships?

Some of these tensions can be discerned in how Wombat Manufacturing went about trying to introduce new changes into the organization.

Wombat Manufacturing – the project – Part 2

Following the enthusiastic reports of developments in teamwork and participative management at Wombat, another team of researchers were attached to the company to support the introduction of a new production process in part of the plant. The new process was to be designed and put in place to assemble a new version of the main dashboard component (the design of which had been more or less finalized). The project – to introduce a new assembly process employing in some way teams or 'cells' of workers – was initiated with a brainstorming session of all managers, supervisors and engineers (but not shopfloor personnel) at the plant. This session clarified the features of the new component and identified a set of broad objectives (covering both production and people issues) for the design of the assembly process. Following this, a cross-functional design team, with shopfloor representation, was established to implement the objectives. The team, facilitated by the researchers, met regularly over a four-month period and explored various options for cell-based and conventional assembly processes in order to meet the project objectives within the set time frame. There was considerable debate and conflict within the team, as the disparate team members sought to gain a common understanding both of the production design challenges and of the constraints on any solution to it (e.g. two major constraints were, first, the product design was fixed and, second, only limited funds were available for new production facilities). The researchers contributed to this debate with suggestions and specific analyses (e.g. using a computer simulation programme, a study was carried out of how quickly production could resume after a stoppage for two configurations, workers clustered in cells versus workers strung out along assembly-lines).

The cross-functional design team was forged through a difficult process as the group pursued the project's goal of moving beyond what were seen by the 'Fordist' (meaning roughly that they favoured production lines) engineers as conventional solutions to production system design. It was widely agreed that the whole group were all on a very steep learning curve. The researchers also had to deal with a number of crises. These were brought to a head when a meeting was convened between the project's research managers and the senior managers in the plant in order to ensure a clear understanding of the project's goals and to reinforce management commitment toward these goals.

Progress towards an agreed solution was being made, however, until the team design process was brought to a premature conclusion by the plant's engineering manager. He imposed his own solution (which appeared to have been developed separately from the team's activities), much to the consternation of the team members. The imposed solution was a compromise between the team-based cell concept and a conventional assembly-line. Assembly was to be split into three distinct stages: a team would be responsible for each of these stages, which were to be managed as cells, and 'buffer' stocks were to be accumulated between each stage to achieve the desired effect of uncoupling production so as to permit it to work in three segments, versions of the original cell idea.

Shortly after this pronouncement, even that solution was cancelled as a result of an engineering failure in another area of the plant. The existing assembly-line was retained (although a small experimental cell was later set up to assemble a small number of the old-model components, as 'carry-over' products, alongside production of the new models). The engineering manager also selected another team to modify the main production line so that it could be used for the new product, and by excluding the researchers from this, effectively brought the project to a halt.

More questions about the case

1 How effective was the involvement process?
2 What were its problems?
3 How significant was the engineering manager's management style?
4 How would you characterize the plant culture at this stage?
5 How would Taylor and how would Mayo interpret what happened at Wombat?

Recent trends in organizing work

The impact of the Human Relations Movement has been significant and long lasting in countering some of the downside of Taylorism's effects on workers – influencing, for example, the emergence of the 'anthropocentric' (i.e. human-centred) approach to manufacturing pioneered in northern European countries like Sweden and Germany (Berggren 1994: 47). In recent years, however, one of the most noticeable trends in management thought has been toward the creation of teams. Teamwork, though, conflicts with the main thrust of Taylorism and does not address the main tenets of human relations. In the former approach, the implication is that any form of group working – either formal or informal – is likely to undermine the principles of Scientific Management and lead to erosion of the separation between mental and manual labour. In the latter approach, it is acknowledged that informal groups will have a significant impact on efficiency and that any formal organization of work must take this into account. It does not necessarily imply that formal organization itself should be undertaken on a group basis (Mouzelis 1975: 102–3).

Recent writings on teams diverge from these two ideologies of managing in two important respects. First, there is a powerful message that the separation of mental and manual labour ignores the rich resources of expertise, experience and knowledge held by workers, which can be exploited to the benefit of employers. Although Taylor acknowledged that workers possessed these qualities, he was worried that they would rarely be exercised to the benefit of the company. Bearing in mind this risk, he claimed that it was better to pursue a strategy of close scrutiny and control through formalization and standardization, such as in creating standard operating procedures.

An almost complete reversal of this position appears to have taken place. In the total quality management (TQM) movement, for example, this view is particularly evident (see Table 6.1 and Chapter 7). Employees are seen as the most knowledgeable and insightful about how to do their jobs best, a pre-Taylorist assumption, although they will not necessarily exercise their insights in the cause of knowledge, that is, a Taylorist assumption. This belief leads to calls for workers to take responsibility, or 'ownership', of problems on the shopfloor, to exercise their discretion and to participate in problem-solving activities although necessarily policed by formal reporting systems. Above all, workers must be 'empowered' to act on their own initiative, or so the story goes. But how is the expertise, experience and knowledge, in short the ingenuity of the workforce, best captured? The answer recently is, invariably, through teams. As argued by Jon Katzenbach and Douglas Smith:

> … teams – real teams, not just groups that management call 'teams' – should be the basic unit of performance for most organizations, regardless of size. In any situation requiring the real-time combination of multiple skills, experiences, and judgements, a team inevitably gets better results than a collection of individuals operating within confined job roles and responsibilities (Katzenbach and Smith 1993: 15).

Just examine the popular approaches to management described in Table 6.1. Not only are teams a central pillar of each one, but each is also seen as a radical departure from ways of organizing that have dominated the twentieth century. This leads to a second major implication of modern visions of teams – that it is absolutely imperative for the formal organization of work to revolve around a *collective* form, unlike the extreme individualism of Taylorism or even its more moderated version found in Human Relations. Rather than

Table 6.1 Summary of recent perspectives on organizational restructuring

Nominal approach	Exemplary texts	Diagnosis of existing forms	Prescription	Organisational implications
Total quality management	Deming (1986)	Orthodox mass production creates a consciousness where the responsibility for quality does not reside at the point of production. Problems are the fault of poor management rather than a defective or recalcitrant work force	Deming's 'fourteen points' focusing on training, quality assurance techniques, continuous improvement, communication between management and hourly-paid workers, and the 'ownership' of quality problems. Acknowledges the contribution workers can make to continuous improvement. Workers must be 'trusted' to take responsibility for quality problems and devise solutions themselves	Dismantle the traditional division of labour and reorganize using teams as the fundamental unit of production. Teams provide the main forum for identifying and resolving quality problems
The 'network' firm	Lipnack and Stamps (1994)	Traditional hierarchical approaches to organization are not responsive enough to cope with today's dynamic business environment	Dismantle hierarchy and facilitate intra- and inter-organizational communication through information technology	Dismantle 'hierarchy/bureaucracy' and install 'team-networks' – i.e. cross-functional groupings which incorporate individuals within and between organizations
Organisational learning	Senge (1990)	Organizations are 'prisoners' of outmoded approaches to environmental adaptation	Senge's five disciplines of 'Systems Thinking'; 'Personal Mastery'; 'Mental Models'; 'Building a Shared Vision'; and 'Team Learning'	Reduce the complexity of organizations to encourage flexibility and openness. 'Localize' authority by investing 'real' decision-making power in devolved teams
Lean production	Womack *et al.* (1990)	Taylorized/Fordist mass production perpetuates sub-optimal use of productive resources to protect against the uncertainty of demand, labour supply, etc. Problems are the fault of poor management rather than a defective or recalcitrant work force	Institute Just-in-Time production, shorten time to market of new products through 'concurrent' engineering, utilize flexible productive technology	Radical restructuring of the physical layout of manufacturing plants. Augment dedicated product and continuous-flow (i.e. Fordist) production lines with flexible and multiskilled teams
Business process re-engineering (BPR)	Hammer and Champy (1993)	Hierarchy and the minute division of labour cannot respond to the demands of fragmented markets. Problems are the fault of poor management rather than a defective or recalcitrant work force	Reject '200 years' of orthodox organizational thinking and adopt 'discontinuous thinking' to embrace BPR in a series of incremental steps. However, BPR must break from the past in being a fundamental, radical, and dramatic change in business processes. Use information technology to facilitate change to achieve flexibility in responsiveness. Visionary leadership essential	Wholesale dismantling of discrete functions of an organization and a reintegration to eliminate waste. Interesting tension between team-oriented restructuring and the desire to rationalize in order to reduce duplication and unnecessary complexity

Source: Graham Sewell (1998), 'How the giraffe got its neck: An organisational 'Just-So' story', in S. Clegg, E. Ibarra, and L. Bueno (eds), *Theories of the Management Process: Making Sense Through Difference*, London: Sage.

Managing teams

breaking down tasks to their most minute elements, as Taylor suggested, tasks should only be broadly specified. The team is then able to exercise its collective wisdom in order to establish how a particular task should be executed. The team should be 'empowered' to undertake this task along the lines that it has itself devised. Management and supervisory roles are invariably seen as centring on 'coaching' or 'facilitating' rather than 'directing' activities. There is much discussion in the team literature about how effective leaders might be identified and trained. The appealing message is that managers are no longer encumbered by the need to exercise close control and are liberated to get on with developing the 'strategic vision' so prized by contemporary management gurus.

Teams and organizational knowledge

The shift away from individualism and towards collective organization is frequently presented as a way of 'working smarter, not harder'. Some of the apparent benefits of teams, for organizations and their employees alike, can be summarized as shown in Exhibit 6.3 (see also Eunson 1994: 14–15).

- Teams work better where mass production technology and standardization are not important, such as in more craft-based industries or where highly customized goods and services are produced.
- Invoking the principle of 'two heads are better than one', it improves the effectiveness of problem solving in the workplace. One of the key areas where this principle has been pursued is in the area of quality management. Teams come together to identify and solve quality problems at the point where they occur. They are claimed to improve productivity.
- Teams can result in fewer levels of official hierarchy, in part by dissolving Taylor's separation of planning and doing. It allows for a flatter organizational structure to be instituted. This is compatible with many contemporary management approaches that advocate the restructuring of organizations away from the traditional tall and inflexible bureaucratic form. It can also mean reducing middle management (supervisory) functions and devolving these to teams.
- By bringing together people from a wide range of functional areas it allows an organization to structure its activities around core, value-adding 'processes' rather than arbitrarily drawn departmental boundaries. Cross-functional teams can also speed up innovation by sharing knowledge more widely, exposing people to new forms of knowledge or different ways of thinking, creating more flexibility in solving problems and developing creativity through people having to integrate new knowledge.
- Multiskilling (i.e. the ability of people to undertake a wide range of activities across their team's area of responsibility) gives an organization a great deal of flexibility in changing all sorts of processes. It also reduces the likelihood of bottlenecks forming in the absence of particular individuals. It can also lead to shedding jobs as workers become interchangeable.
- Generally speaking, the increase in autonomy and empowerment that is commonly seen as an essential component of teamwork significantly contributes to a greater quality of work life for those involved.
- Teams are claimed to encourage democratization in the workplace by increasing participation in decision making.
- Knowledge workers (i.e. better educated, skilled and professional workers) are less likely to accept traditional, authoritarian styles of management, leadership and supervision. Teams can substitute for more indirect forms of integration and supervision.

Exhibit 6.3 Benefits of teamwork

But how do teams actually enable organizations to work 'smarter'? A way of looking at this is to examine how teams derive and use organizational 'knowledge'. If we return to Taylor's First Principle of Scientific Management, it is evident that he was interested in revealing and organizing workers' knowledge of the work process and pressing that into the service of the organization. Prefiguring contemporary management thinking by many decades, this was a tacit acknowledgment by Taylor that, in many instances, workers know more about their work than their managers. The only trouble was that the workers could not always be trusted to pass on this knowledge to their manager. They were more likely to use it to their own ends in the form of soldiering. Taylor's fear of soldiering meant that his controlling instincts won out over any inclination to allow workers the autonomy and discretion to exercise this knowledge. Thus Taylorism has meant initially gathering and analyzing the knowledge of workers on a once-and-for-all basis to design procedures to use as the benchmark for subsequent work behaviour. Any transgression of these rules, even if it might lead to improvements in productivity, would be seen as a threat to managers' prerogative to determine work tasks. This threat might eventually undermine a manager's authority to impose control on the work process. Of course, this attitude would effectively preclude ideas from workers that could contribute to what today we would call *continuous improvement*. The key departure that many recent management texts, academic and popular, take from Taylor is just this point, that workers possess intimate and detailed knowledge about their jobs, but also that they should be 'trusted' or 'empowered' to use it in the search for continuous improvement.

A link between this search for continuous improvement and the need to reveal organizational knowledge is explained by Sidney Winter (1994). He identifies three interdependent elements of this relationship: (1) *corporate knowledge* in an organization, which is embedded in (2) *organizational routines*, and needs to be revealed through a process of (3) *organizational learning*.

Firms improve when managers and workers scrutinize existing routines and identify and select new routines, such as new assembly methods. These new routines do not come from some universal technical handbook. Rather, they derive from examining the idiosyncrasies of processes that grew from unique aspects of an individual firm's history (for example, a particular assembly-line could be oriented along a north–south axis due to the prevailing natural light in the building). For Winter, the crucial element in this process of learning is the elicitation and representation of the knowledge embedded in these organizational routines and patterns of work.

Knowledge embedded in routines is commonly unearthed via the use of teams. In the recent, post-Taylor resurgence of interest in teams, an early example of this use of teams as a source of knowledge for continuous improvement was the popularity of quality circles in the 1980s. Quality circles provided a means of focusing the workforce's problem-solving capabilities on specific issues within the workplace (for a review of the effectiveness of quality circles see the extensive literature on TQM and quality circles in Japanese-style management and see Chapter 7). Quality circles are, however, a far cry from reorganizing work around teams on a systematic and wholesale basis – they are only an adjunct to pre-existing methods of production organization. Like the teams of the Human Relations Movement before them, quality circles represent provisional committees which are meant to reflect on procedures rather than teams used as the basic unit of industrial organization. Nevertheless, quality circles are often presented as a staging post on the way to the creation of 'true' teamworking conditions, and they do represent an attempt to reveal organizational knowledge in pursuit of continuous improvement. Let us consider two examples of how teamwork can either coexist under Taylorism or can be used to transform Taylorist practices, and the implications each has for the control or sharing of knowledge.

Teams under conditions of Taylorism

Teamwork under the conditions of Taylorism has proven benefits to management in terms of continuous improvement. This potential can be seen in one of the richest discussions of the transformation of the modern factory setting, the work of Paul Adler, especially his conception of the *Learning Bureaucracy* (Adler 1993b; see also Adler 1993a) or the *Enabling Bureaucracy* (Adler and Borys 1996). Adler's depiction of NUMMI – the General Motors–Toyota joint venture assembly plant in Fremont, California, called New United Motor Manufacturing Inc. – provides the reader with a vivid representation of problems and possibilities posed by teamwork. Adler's discussion of NUMMI shows how a plant can combine many of the features of orthodox, Taylorist and Fordist organization (i.e. the assembly-line) with the use of teams in order to pursue continuous improvement.

The General Motors (GM) assembly plant, which predated NUMMI, was described by one of its managers as 'the worst plant in the world' (Adler 1993a: 98). Originally organized along Taylorist and Fordist principles, the plant had the lowest productivity of any GM plant, quality was abysmal, drug and alcohol abuse were rampant, absenteeism was high, the union was militant, and between 1963 and 1982 wild cat strikes and lock outs occurred on several occasions. The plant was closed in 1982 at about the same time that Toyota and GM had begun discussions on a joint venture operation on the site. NUMMI, the new plant's name, resulted from the joint venture agreement which saw GM take responsibility for marketing and sales and Toyota for product design, engineering and daily operations. The new production system was based on Toyota's methods.

The new 2220-strong shopfloor workforce comprised 85 percent of previously employed workers from the old plant. By contrast, few of the salaried (clerical, office, etc.) employees from the old plant were re-employed. Wages and benefits were secured by the unions on condition that they accept the new Toyota-based production system. A diverse workforce was recruited with 61 percent comprising women, Hispanics and African-Americans. Shopfloor team leaders and team members were jointly interviewed and selected by management and the union. The union played a role in selecting many of the management staff (Adler 1993a: 99). NUMMI's first 450 team leaders, and the entire management group, were trained in Japan for three weeks at Toyota's Takaoka plant. Adler points out that the NUMMI workforce had to be able to perform their work for 57 seconds out of every 60 seconds of worktime, while previously this had been 45 seconds out of 60 seconds.

Adler's conclusion from his research on NUMMI was that time-and-motion study – a key element of Taylorism – brings with it a discipline and formal structure that is necessary for efficiency and quality in routine operations. Toyota's approach did just that. NUMMI's performance, even compared to Toyota's Takaoka plant, was impressive given that the workforce at NUMMI was on average ten years older than their Japanese counterparts (Adler 1993a: 108, 99). By 1986, productivity was nearly as high at NUMMI as in Takaoka, as was quality, absenteeism had dropped to 3–4 percent (at the old plant it was as high as 20–25 percent), and suggestions by employees for improvements had risen from 26 percent in 1986 to 92 percent by 1991 (Adler 1993a: 99). In fact, NUMMI became one of the most productive and harmonious plants within the GM group.

Despite their extensive use of teams, Adler uses terms like 'regimentation' and 'standardization' to characterize NUMMI's principles of organization. Adler suggests that, in this case at least, teams under conditions of routinization are not a paradox. Management at the plant insisted that teams should seek to improve upon standardized work on the basis that standards set minimum performance criteria. The role of the team was seen as a vehicle for establishing new standards on the basis of improvements made on the shopfloor, which is just what Winter argued (see above). This approach reflects an acknowledgement of the inability of managers to come up with a perfectly standardized and continuously improving programme of work. Planning is no longer left solely to the manager, as Taylor had originally conceived. The team assists in work planning but in a restricted way. The team concentrates its problem-solving energies very tightly around existing routines and standards set primarily by managers. The team provides a means by which crucial operational issues are prioritized.

The continuous improvement programme (or the gathering up of the knowledge of workers) at NUMMI is described by Adler (1993a: 102–3) as including: a very aggressive suggestion system, with special teams designated to examine individual suggestions and carry out improvements; continual refinement of procedures; the design of every machine and process to detect malfunctions, missing parts or incorrect assembly; careful analysis and design of jobs; rotating workers; cross-training workers in all team assignments; tight scheduling of production, including quotas, etc. As Adler (1993a: 103) states, 'team members themselves hold the stopwatch' and must learn the techniques of work analysis, description and improvement – part of the 'brain work' Taylor sought to remove from the worker's discretion or decision making. Adler summarizes the key element of knowledge transfer at NUMMI that ensures continuous improvement:

> Using learned analytical tools, their own experience, and the expertise of leaders and engineers, workers create a consensual [agreed to] standard that they 'teach' (sic) to the system by writing job descriptions. The system then teaches these standards back to workers, who, then, by further analysis, consultation, and consensus, make additional improvements. Continual reiteration of this disciplined process of analysis, standardization, re-analysis, refinement, and re-standardization creates an intensely structured system of continuous improvement (Adler 1993a: 104).

This continuous improvement is used to increase standardization in the ways jobs are performed in teams and thus help to reduce variability – a goal of Taylorism. Thus team members at NUMMI time one another using stopwatches; establish the most efficient pace of work; break down tasks to explore how they can improve performance; compare and analyze results from other teams on various shifts doing the same task and then write detailed specifications for how team members doing that job will carry out the task. As Adler states – all workers are 'industrial engineers' (Adler 1993a: 103).

Although the amount of autonomy afforded to workers in teams at NUMMI is limited, management must still ensure that any innovations made in the production process are both revealed (made explicit) and then operationalized positively. This is the 'double-bind of discretion' (Sewell 1998) – teams need to be managed to concentrate their efforts on solving problems that benefit the organization as a whole yet given enough autonomy that they freely exercise their learning capabilities to the extent that such problems are actually solved. Adler's position on how this double-bind is overcome in the case of NUMMI is not very clear, although he seems to suggest that the team's discretion in being able to make changes to its work process is sufficient to motivate members to seek continuous improvement. It is as if discretion is its own reward. Adler identifies three distinct drivers stemming from this discretion that motivate employees to work toward company goals:

1   The desire for *excellence*, the instinct of craftsmanship and the desire to do a job well.
2   An understanding by psychologically mature workers (i.e. a mature sense of realism) of the need to *protect jobs* and the plant's competitive position by constantly *improving its performance*. Adler says (1993a: 106) that along with this mature realism is an acceptance by shopfloor workers that work in the automobile industry for unskilled people is basically devoid of intrinsic motivation so they have a choice whether to take a negative or positive view about their fate.
3   The *respect and trust* that management show towards workers can be reciprocated through the *commitment* shown in return by those workers. Associated with this was NUMMI's policy of no layoffs (redundancies). This was negotiated with unions and compels the company only to lay off employees under severe economic downturns. Management salaries, for example, must be reduced before layoffs (Adler 1993a: 102).

Thus we see an attempt to retain the standardizing benefits of Taylorism while incorporating the knowledge-finding and motivating possibilities of teamwork (see Chapter 7). According to Adler, NUMMI's successful implementation of teams stemmed directly from the democratic slant of management practices. He argues that empowerment at NUMMI has several elements, one of the most important being the checks and balances that have emerged because unions and workers still have enormous negative power to disrupt work and undermine continuous improvement (1993a: 107–8). Adler argues that unions are (via contracts) able to voice many concerns and have been able to gain concessions from NUMMI's management particularly in areas of team improvement.

The experience of NUMMI can be seen as a partial reversal of some of the tendencies of Taylorism – especially the separation of the planning and execution of work. The workers are now also responsible for gathering up the knowledge of craftspeople and workers under the banner of continuous improvement. Yet irrespective of such continuous improvement, the NUMMI plant is also typified by intense machine pacing (e.g. 60 seconds to complete tasks on the assembly line), rigid production quotas, close surveillance, regimentation, the sacrificing of safety standards (Berggren 1994), and hard-driving management practices.

Teams going beyond Taylorism

Paul Thompson and Terry Wallace (1995, 1996) came to their own conclusions about what makes teams work as a result of a study of Volvo truck plants in Sweden, Belgium and the UK. Volvo has had a long tradition of progressive job design and work-group autonomy at its Kalmar car plant since the 1970s, which was a completely new factory, or green field site, similar to NUMMI. Specifically, Thompson and Wallace focused on manufacturing, where a team structure would contrast with a production line of individual workers. They found that Volvo generally used teams not as a policy – such as a move toward shopfloor democratization – but as a response to production requirements, especially at its Kalmar plant (see also Fincham and Rhodes 1992: 212).

At Kalmar, workers were responsible for clusters of tasks with variations on the production line concept. Christian Berggren (1989, cited in Fincham and Rhodes 1992: 212) argues that Kalmar still involved centralized control, and teams or semi-autonomous work groups were limited (see Chapter 7). Uddevalla, Volvo's most team oriented plant, represented a more socialized form of production with the plant having a massive automated materials handling centre around which operated 51 independent assembly workshops. Even at Kalmar, the technology was later changed back to machine-paced production (Fincham and Rhodes 1992: 212–13).

Paul Bernstein (1992: 355–6) also details the complexity of Volvo's team experiments that began in 1966 with what was termed the 'Spontaneous Trial Period' to overcome absenteeism, high turnover, recruitment costs, ergonomic problems and changed work expectations. In all, they cite seven plants, and a range of team based approaches that culminated in the radical approach used at Uddevalla, where the emphasis was on building a learning environment through team work. In 1985, when Uddevalla was being planned, Volvo had already introduced its *Dialog* program to encourage and support change and learning. *Dialog* embraced the Volvo culture: '…quality, care, competence, communication, development and involvement…' (Bernstein 1992: 368). Uddevalla was closed in 1993 as a result of a drop in sales, excess capacity and cash-flow problems (Carmona and Grönlund 1998: 22), and the production moved to a plant that was not designed around teams. This suggests that teams are something Swedish firms (including management and unions), such as Volvo embraced when it was economically viable to do so, and are not so deeply embedded in the culture and institutions of Swedish society as some theorists suggest (Carmona and Grönlund 1998: 22).

Based on their Volvo studies, Thompson and Wallace suggest that the essential factors affecting the success of teams can be grouped into three categories – technical, governance, and normative (Thompson and Wallace 1995; Marks *et al.* 1997). The *technical* dimension has to do with the team's ability to offer degrees of 'flexibility and self-regulation' that one could not get from a production line of individuals. That is, the team members' collective abilities to accomplish a range of tasks and to guide their own work are greater than those of separate individuals. Two important *support systems* that help develop these team-based competencies are the type of industrial relations system in the organization and the selection methods, reward and performance appraisal systems used. In terms of *governance*, direct supervision can shift from one manager overseeing a hundred employees on a production line to a team leader with six team members. Governance also includes the role of managers and experts in the team process. Even with a team structure, though, the question remains of where decisions get made – by the team, the team leader, the leader's supervisor, or by higher-ups. A critical support system here is how organizational decision making processes work – are they hierarchical or decentralized or bits of both? The *normative* dimension involves aligning individuals' goals with the goals of the organization to boost productivity via a more coherent focus. The main support system helping this happen is training and staff development. Figure 6.1 describes teamwork competencies as described by Marks *et al.* (1997). These dimensions make it possible to compare team competencies across different work sites.

Governance

Key competencies

- Are effective communicators, are prepared to listen to others, give feedback and exchange information
- Take part in and promote the devolved decision-making process
- Can exercise leadership, directing and motivating others, facilitating the coordination and planning of team activities

Normative

Key competencies

- Promote the cohesiveness of the group, demonstrating collective responsibility among team members
- Have a willingness to undertake informal communication and are prepared to initiate and innovate
- Accept personal responsibility for own tasks and are ready to support and receive assistance from others

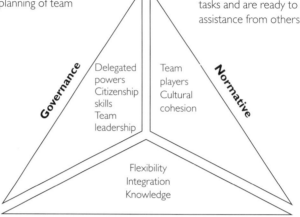

Technical

Key competencies

- Demonstrate flexibility in the job; can alter working arrangements and move between a range of tasks within the team
- Possess a willingness and capacity to acquire task-based knowledge
- Are able to use knowledge as an aid to problem solving and the development of continuous improvement

Figure 6.1 Dimensions of teamwork competencies

Source: Adapted from Abigail Marks, Patricia Findlay, James Hine, Alan McKinlay and Paul Thompson (1997), 'Whisky galore: Teamworking and workplace transformation in the Scottish spirits industry', 15th Annual Labour Process Conference, March, Edinburgh (Appendices 1 and 2).

As noted above, the technical dimension persuaded management at various Volvo sites to engage teams. In terms of governance, Thompson and Wallace suggest that the team structure seemed to take hold more readily in Volvo's Swedish plants, where the history of industrial relations had a more cooperative flavour than in the UK and Belgium. According to Robin Fincham and Peter Rhodes, Volvo admits that hard economic motives had driven its job reforms mainly because '… you cannot get Swedes to work on assembly lines…' (1992: 213), especially given that unions and the Swedish employers' federation have both actively pursued job redesign. Because of this cross-cultural difference, Thompson and Wallace argue that a stronger normative effort is likely to be required in the UK and

Belgium to build the concept of a 'team player' than was evident at Uddevalla. Other contextual factors, beyond industrial relations harmony, also affect the success of teamwork. These factors include the local history of the plant in question, business market concerns (i.e. what products are required at what rate), the type of leadership in the plant, and the role of specialists (engineers, etc.) in teams. The result of this mix of factors means that the approach and responses to teamwork at each site have differed even for Volvo. Different ways of organizing production, of selecting employees and of payment and promotion have taken root (Thompson and Wallace 1995, 1996).

Thompson and Wallace's assessment of the Volvo 'experiment' also exemplifies the importance of *knowledge gathering*. At Uddevalla, for example, Volvo's management used two interrelated concepts to encourage learning: the *holistic principle* and the *reflective principle* (Berggren 1994). In the case of the former, this meant that employees had to understand the whole process of car assembly and the interdependence of all tasks. With respect to the latter, workers in the plant were not only asked to perform complex tasks, they had to have detailed and articulated (i.e. they could talk about it) intellectual understanding of the processes of car assembly. These two principles resulted in, for example, cost and time reductions in the introduction of new models of cars. Assembly teams implemented changes for new car models, including redesigning their work patterns. They were skilled at analyzing the requirements for new product design, including anticipated faults and problems, and were able also to incorporate continuous improvements without the 'lean production' system at NUMMI.

One of the very early problems faced at Uddevalla with implementing a team or holistic approach was that many manufacturing and industrial engineers did not know how to fit into this new team approach, preferring instead to keep the old, hierarchical ways and deliberately shunning cooperation with assembly teams (Berggren 1994). Engineers did not want to surrender the status and power that they enjoyed in the old system. For a time the assembly teams on the shopfloor had a decentralized structure, while the management structure remained hierarchical and management was located in a separate building from the main plant. Later a new plant manager changed all this by creating two hierarchies – shopfloor and plant management. Managers and engineers had to work in assembly teams and were relocated closer to the shopfloor (Berggren 1994).

Uddevalla also had a diverse workforce, employing nearly as many women as men (40 percent were women), and this also encouraged more innovative work practices relating to such things as leave, work hours, etc. (Berggren 1994). The design of tools and work methods also reflected the high percentage of women in the workforce. Unions were included in decision making and planning and treated as independent partners with legitimate claims and interests (Berggren 1994).

Thompson and Wallace, somewhat echoing the findings from NUMMI, note that management benefits from profitability by using team insight and knowledge to boost production, and workers benefit from potential avenues for collective input into the nature of their work. On the other hand, management suffers from potential collective action on the part of workers, and workers suffer from potentially closer scrutiny of their work by the team members.

Teams and innovation

Teams, in their contemporary sense, need to effect the move from 'people management' (and control) to 'knowledge management' (and dissemination). Teams are a critical element in ensuring that individual learning is transmitted to organizational activities, and are also a source of innovation if they are able to achieve a fluid collective process (Bell, Blackler and Crump 1997). If this is to happen, teams must not be drawn or forced into competing with each other, and structural arrangements need to facilitate cross-functional communications. Liz Bell, Frank Blackler and Norman Crump argue that there are four types of innovation as shown in Exhibit 6.4, and that these types affect the nature and form of teams required.

- **Normal innovation** includes the kind of incremental developments that are part of everyday working and is a sort of base camp for more complex innovation.
- **Domain innovation** is significant development within a specialism or subspecialism, such as image engineering, and requires its expert or group of experts.
- **Boundary innovation** is significant development that arises from cooperation and coordination across specialisms. Here open mindedness and dialogue, and cultures and working practices that support this, are necessary.
- **Radical innovation** is development that is both significant scientifically – that is, an important advancement in knowledge – and across disciplines. Yet while some 'super-scientists' or 'hero innovators' may work in this area, it is equally important that these innovations are diffused and the general capacity of the organization to innovate is increased (Bell *et al.* 1997: 59).

Exhibit 6.4   *Types of innovation*

Teams involved in innovation are important in providing the right amount of support in conditions of uncertainty and change, and enable this chaos to stimulate creativity rather than collapse. Teams can improve the capacity and ability of staff in learning skills, questioning, considering, communicating, modelling, improvising and reconstructing ideas. Pilkington developed 'virtual teams' (see below) to work across sites and disciplines using video conferencing and intranet technology (Bell *et al.* 1997). Percy Barnevik, head of ABB (Asea Brown Boveri), spends $US800 million a year on ABB's global network technology linking 70000 people – which he argues makes it 'possible to design a piece of equipment in the US, manufacture it in Brazil and sell it in Kazakhstan' (McLachlan 1997: 12). Teams can also prove significant in facilitating the type of restructuring they require to be effective, developing a sense of community, empowerment and collective problem solving (Bell *et al.* 1997: 59).

Jessica Lipnack and Jeffrey Stamps (1994; see also Lipnack and Lipnack 1997) describe what they call 'teamnets' as including clusters of organizations connected in a kind of social network which collaborate as team members to serve specific customers better than any one company could. Lipnack and Stamps point to the VISA credit card corporation with 23 000 collaborating financial institutions and 11 million merchants in 250 countries and territories as a successful teamnet (1994: 90).

Lipnack and Stamps focus on a spirit of – and conditions for – collaboration that should infuse interactions between any two or more team members. In addition, they extend the notion of team member to include whole organizations and beyond, though one senses that the effective member is most likely a key *individual* within the organization.

Table 6.2 describes some of the teamnets identified by Lipnack and Stamps (1994). The teamnet type attracting most interest, both now and probably into the next millennium, is the virtual team (Lipnack and Stamps 1997). A number of the teamnets described in Table 6.2 (e.g. cross-functional teams, sociotechnical systems) would be considered by many theorists to be teams, not teamnets. The term 'teamnet' is confusing because many of the examples given under 'enterprises', 'alliances' and 'economic megagroups' are more appropriately seen as examples of networks or interorganizational relations (IORs) rather than any sort of team-based organizational form (see Chapter 11).

Table 6.2 Teamnets along the organizational scale

Scale	Type	Example	Explanation
Economic megagroup	Regional clusters	Silicon Valley	Network of business groups in geographical areas (see Chapter 11)
	Keiretsu	Toshiba	Linking of large number of firms in diverse industries governed by a major bank or manufacturer
Alliance	Flexible business nets	IBM/Apple/ Motorola	Network of small firms, often developed through government funding or by companies (see Chapter 11)
	Strategic alliance	Corning Inc.	Cooperation and competition between large-scale organizations. Members are independent, can even be competitors. These are voluntary relationships with cooperation based on joint purpose (see Chapter 11)
	Joint ventures		Traditional forms of partnership, minimal network (see Chapter 11). Two or more companies form a separate entity. Corning is one of the most successful joint venture companies in the world
Enterprise	Core firms	EBC Industries	Vendor and customer partnerships can operate outside the core firm. Creates a form of virtual suppliers
	Service webs	Hyatt Hotels	Hyatt manages 100 hotels with separate owners and expectations of semi-autonomous units. Sometimes involve partnership structures in firms such as accountancy
	Virtual corporations	Chiat/Day	Leading advertising firm links its officers around the world using computers. Aim of Chiat is to no longer have large offices but people working from home and client sites
	Internal markets	ABB	Any unit in the organization is free to buy services or products internally or externally and develop their own supplier relationships
	Kaizen/TQM	Eastman	Kaizen or continuous improvement (see below) using quality improvement teams to implement company-wide change
Large organization	Sociotechnical systems	Digital Equipment	Digital Equipment used sociotechnical systems to build its state-of-the-art midrange computer. Refers to efforts to merge organizational change with technological change that takes account of individual (social) needs

Scale	Type	Example	Explanation
	Clusters/profit centres	W.L. Gore & Assoc.	Organizations such as W.L. Gore & Associates (ABB, British Petroleum, Microsoft) limit the size of their 'units'. In the case of W.L. Gore & Associates it is to 150–200 employees. Sometimes the units are large enough to have their own administrative arrangements
	Cross-functional teams	Hewlett-Packard	Departments, functional groups (e.g. service) send representatives who set up a charter, elect a leader and work on projects or problems. Hewlett-Packard has company-wide 'councils' that operate through a Product Generation Council
Small group	Top teams	ABB	ABB in Switzerland is organized into 'Target Oriented Teams' (TOTs) (not functional departments). TOTs operate as profit centres that form companies. The Executive Top Team has only 13 people
	Virtual teams	Starmer's 'lab without walls'	Span the globe through electronic online, worldwide web systems, and other interactive technology. People can instantly interact, chat, exchange information irrespective of place or time (see Chapter 8)
	High-performance teams	AT & T Universal Card Services	Combines innovative management with information technologies. AT&T has empowered its teams to be free to take actions, yet remain focused on goals/results
	Self-directed teams	Eastman	Uses self-directed teams at senior levels to carry out manufacturing functions

Source: Extracted and modified from Jessica Lipnack and Jeffrey Stamps (1994), *The Age of the Network: Organizing Principles for the 21st Century*, Essex Junction, VT: Oliver Wight Publications Inc. pp. 98–104.

Teams are far more important than just a means of improving workplace practice as shown in NUMMI and Uddevalla. They have the innovatory potential to change a business. But does the idea of the 'virtual team' destroy the critique of teams as modern Taylorism based on control and surveillance? Not necessarily. Earlier we argued that even Taylorism was a knowledge project; what is important to remember here is that the nature of knowledge and information has changed radically over the past two decades and continues to do so. Virtual teams can still practise surveillance, and are certainly controlled, but exactly how this happens and the associated changes in knowledge are important topics for further research.

Teams as surveillance

Despite the best intentions by managers, teams can descend into various exploitative practices where the teams themselves take on many of the disciplinary and controlling roles previously associated with managerial supervision (Barker 1993). Teams may be viewed as an unobtrusive or 'invisible' form of control, one that enables managers to give workers a sense of autonomy without the manager actually surrendering much, if any, control. Rather, the avenue for control has changed. From this perspective it is the group dynamics of the team itself that create the disciplinary force that keeps its objectives and actions in line with those of the organization (Barker 1993; Sewell and Wilkinson 1992a, b; Sewell 1998; also see Heterick and Boje 1992; Steingard and Fitzgibbons 1993). Traditionally, surveillance has been associated with establishing obedience and maintaining order which is fine if individual workers are expected to follow management instructions – surveillance, in the form of workplace performance monitoring, can always identify those who are not up to it. This is particularly suited to Taylorized work roles, where obedience involves following carefully work procedures planned by managers. However, such restriction, as shown in the NUMMI case, does not fit in well with expectations of 'continuous improvement' via the extraction and use of workers' knowledge, hence the use of teams. The same systems of surveillance that identify workers who fail to reach management targets, however, can also reveal those who exceed them. This also applies to the team performance – surveillance of a team can identify those members who are outperforming their peers in some way. Here the team takes on a disciplinary role like that identified by James Barker (1993), providing a means whereby expected performance by each member is at, or close to, the standards set by the highest performing individual in the group. In this sense, working 'smarter' by one person is working harder for all. Team members boost their productive capacity, which means that their ingenuity and potential has been used to pursue organizational objectives alone. This process can give rise to all kinds of coercive peer group pressure and petty tyranny that are probably far away from the vision of teams that most management texts contain.

One phenomenon that has been noticed in groups is that as group sizes increase there is a tendency for the effort put in by the group to be less than the average individual effort put in by individuals engaged on the same task separately. This is described by writers influenced by industrial economics as the *free-rider* problem, where the collective nature of the 'contract' obscures the fact of one member failing to honour their part of the contract (Albanese and Van Fleet 1985). Organizational psychologists tend to view this problem as one of *social loafing* and typically define it as one where everyone puts in a little less (Gabrenya, Latane and Wang 1981). Taylor viewed it as 'systematic soldiering', and Mayo as the role of the 'informal group'.

Reasons for social loafing are not conclusive. One possibility is that an individual perceives that others in the group are not pulling their own weight, and so reduces their own effort, but this would hardly explain the widespread nature of the phenomenon and would tend to force itself into a downward spiral that would need to be constantly checked and readjusted by the group, resulting in noticeable perturbations in performance. It is also possible that where the contribution of the individual is not visible or attributable in terms of outputs, and hence of rewards, then they see no benefit in putting in the maximum effort. The relationship between surveillance, peer group pressure, team performance and continuous improvement programmes such as that at NUMMI ensure that, as Adler says, the 'stopwatch' resides with the team.

How teams develop

Teams, in whatever context, will always display some of the basic principles and characteristics of small-group behaviour. These features include distinct stages in group or team evolution; individual attitudes, roles and behaviours in teams; and internal and external forces felt or experienced as pressure by teams. The most common form of representing the basic stages of group development was developed by Bruce Tuckman (1965), and more recently four additional stages are sometimes added to this list as shown in Exhibit 6.5.

- **Forming** Team members getting to know each other and trying to comprehend their task.
- **Conforming** Team members fall into an easy consensus in order to feel as though they are really working together.
- **Storming** Frustration emerges over differences and conflicts that have been suppressed, with arguments about who leads, what goals and procedures should be, etc.; personalities clash.
- **Norming** The group sets standards and agrees on goals; patterns of acceptable behaviour take root.
- **Reforming** The group checks and operates the new norms, reorienting itself to the new standards in practice and correcting problems.
- **Performing** Members get down to work at full effectiveness.
- **Adjourning** The process of signalling completion and deciding that the task is completed. In its positive mode this involves a rational letting go; in its negative mode it involves a reluctance to conclude, with much reminiscing and congratulating or blaming.
- **Mourning** The individual and collective processing of sadness of parting from compatriots can become nostalgic. When group members are involved in new projects, they constantly try to recreate the old project in a new form, often saying things like 'we always did it this way in my old project team, company, etc.'. This prolongs the reluctance to move on and learn new things.

Exhibit 6.5 *Stages of group formation*

Teams do not necessarily progress through all stages in any schema of evolution nor do they progress through all stages in the order specified. In addition, the transition from one stage to the next one often occurs abruptly (Gersick 1988). This notion of abrupt transition between fairly stable states of activity is called 'punctuated equilibrium', a term developed to describe abrupt changes during biological evolution.

Connie Gersick (1988, 1989) noted that teams tend to evolve in a sequence of abrupt stages rather than by making a smooth transition between stages. Gersick observed two teams of students as part of a project to test a team effectiveness model, which was not related to team evolution at all. However, while observing, Gersick became interested in team evolution and observed two additional teams go through a complete project life cycle. She concluded that all four teams had made an abrupt transition midway through their project. She likened the shift to a 'midlife transition', a concept developed by Dan Levinson (1978), as all the teams seemed to experience a crisis at a point half-way between their inception and their delivery deadline, *regardless of the length of time of the project.*

Gersick then observed an additional four teams – at a community agency, a bank, a hospital and a mental health treatment facility – to show how group focus shifted over time. It seemed that up to the half-way point, roughly conforming to the forming, storming and norming stages, after initial direction-setting inertia set in, low-performance ensued and options were only infrequently re-examined. However, the midpoint 'wake-up alarm' plunged the team into a reassessment of its goals, more storming and usually resulted in some sort of a change of direction. It appears that insufficient or even missing storming/conflict in the early stages comes back to haunt the group later on – the suppressed differences will need to be addressed before the group can produce effectively. The final stages then are high performing, pressured activity and adjourning. Gersick explained the pattern of development by borrowing from biology, and social studies of science, the concept of 'punctuated equilibrium' – stable periods of steady progress interrupted by abrupt transitions to new states from which steady progress resumes.

Team roles

Meredith Belbin (1993), developing and modifying a classic work originally published in 1981 identifying eight key team roles, produced a typology of nine significant team roles. He identified key contributions that had to be made by all members, and allowable weaknesses of people filling these group roles, if the team is to perform successfully. These roles are described in Table 6.3. It should be noted that Belbin's model does not preclude overlap in these functions, and more than one role may be performed by a person, especially in a small group, but the important consideration is balance. Additionally, where much of the work on teams emphasizes flexibility and multiskilling, Belbin's work emphasizes interpersonal multiskilling, but still leaves room for technical expertise to be drawn upon by the group in the ninth role of 'specialist', which was not in the original typology.

Table 6.3 Belbin's team roles

Roles and descriptions – team-role contribution		Allowable weaknesses
	Plant: Creative, imaginative, unorthodox. Solves difficult problems.	Ignores details. Too preoccupied to communicate effectively.
	Resource investigator: Extrovert, enthusiastic, communicative. Explores opportunities. Develops contacts.	Overoptimistic. Loses interest once initial enthusiasm has passed.
	Co-ordinator: Mature, confident, a good chairperson. Clarifies goals, promotes decision-making, delegates well.	Can be seen as manipulative. Delegates personal work.
	Shaper: Challenging, dynamic, thrives on pressure. Has the drive and courage to overcome obstacles.	Can provoke others. Hurts people's feelings.
	Monitor evaluator: Sober, strategic and discerning. Sees all options. Judges accurately.	Lacks drive and ability to inspire others. Overly critical.
	Teamworker: Cooperative, mild, perceptive and diplomatic. Listens, builds, averts friction, calms the waters.	Indecisive in crunch situations. Can be easily influenced.
	Implementer: Disciplined, reliable, conservative and efficient. Turns ideas into practical actions.	Somewhat inflexible. Slow to respond to new possibilities.
	Completer: Painstaking, conscientious, anxious. Searches out errors and omissions. Delivers on time.	Inclined to worry unduly. Reluctant to delegate. Can be a nit-picker.
	Specialist: Single-minded, self-starting, dedicated. Provides knowledge and skills in rare supply.	Contributes on only a narrow front. Dwells on technicalities. Overlooks the 'big picture'.

Source: R. Meredith Belbin (1993), *Team Roles at Work*, London: Butterworth/Heinemann, p. 23.
Strength of contribution in any one of the roles is commonly associated with particular weaknesses. These are called allowable weaknesses. Executives are seldom strong in all nine team roles.

An important message in Belbin's (1981) work was that, while balance was important in team roles, successful teams tended to have persons with coordinating strengths, that is, those able to bring people together, being appointed as chairpersons. At least one person who could fill the 'plant role' was also included in winning teams. Belbin did not consider 'shapers' to be generally good team leaders and too many of them in any team was found to cause problems. This imbalance of 'shapers' in team situations is likely to be noticeable among professional groups such as academics, lawyers and doctors.

How teams work

Behaviours in groups, which ultimately affect the behaviours *of* groups, can be classified as task oriented, group-maintenance oriented, and self-oriented. *Task behaviours* involve initiating structure, communicating, establishing consensus and advancing the problem-solving process. *Group maintenance* involves gatekeeping, harmonizing, supporting, setting standards and improving the process of interpersonal interaction. *Self-oriented behaviour* is concerned with the individual's own needs and not those of the group. Whenever people form into groups they have to address questions about their identity in groups – they find that things they would normally be aware of are not necessarily present, especially if the group members are not known to each other or normal hierarchies do not apply. There are four *vacuums* present in leaderless, newly formed groups, but awareness of these vacuums remains as a threat even as groups develop. The four vacuums are:

> *1* the *structure* vacuum (expressed in terms of who has authority, who will play what role, what role will I play, can I be who I want to be);
> *2* the *knowledge* vacuum (who has the key information, knowledge, skills, expertise);
> *3* the *emotional* vacuum (how do I feel about the people in this group, how do they feel about me, will I be liked or feared, accepted or rejected);
> *4* the *power* vacuum (who controls the group, who has most influence, who are potential allies/enemies, what are my interests and those of others, will there be conflict).

Groups and individuals will gradually fill these vacuums as roles are assigned, created or seized, although this will usually not be without its problems. The process may involve attacking or defending, blocking others, withdrawing from interaction, appealing for sympathy from others, or dominating by over-contributing or 'points-scoring'.

One type of self-oriented behaviour that often makes a team task difficult is defensive behaviour. Basic types of defensive behaviour were characterized well by the British psychologist Wilfred Bion before and during the Second World War. Bion (1959) contended from studies of therapy groups of servicemen, that pressure makes members of groups revert to primitive types of defensive behaviour. Pressure is that which threatens the individual's perceived identity – and what counts as 'pressure' depends on the individual – an imminent deadline, possible retrenchment, a domineering colleague, or a potentially positive change that challenges firmly held beliefs, such as switching from 'the boss will always tell us what to do' to ' we need to set our own production goals'.

Humans react to psychological threat in much the same way as animals react to physical threat – by fighting back or running away. Bion identified primitive defences as: *fight-or-flight* behaviour (arguing or withdrawal, where groups may become extremely combative among themselves, or engage in diversions from the task like joking to avoid confrontation); *dependency* on authority replacing individual initiative; and *pairing* among individuals, a move toward strength in numbers (see also Stacey 1993). Josh MacNeish and Tony Richardson (1994), Australian management consultants, have characterized each defence as a step towards group cohesion in response to a threat or learning opportunity. Individual *feuding* is followed by dependency on the manager, possibly counter-dependency as a reaction to the inevitable failure of authority to solve all the problems, then pairing, but eventually group members can achieve productive interdependence.

Of course, all the stages other than interdependence are dysfunctional, and Ralph Stacey (1993: 198, citing Turquet 1974) suggests that this is because of a false sense of *oneness*. Typically a group that forms to create a powerful force or union can allow members to feel there is overwhelming unity when this might not be so. This sense of oneness can render members passive to the actions of the group.

Because self-oriented behaviour is emotional in its origins, the style adopted by self-oriented individuals depends on whether their emotional orientation is affectionate towards others, hostile to others or neutral to others. These three basic orientations were developed into archetypes identified by David Kolb and colleagues (1984) as shown in Table 6.4. They are:

- *friendly helper* – who strives for harmony at all costs;
- *tough battler* – who sees all decisions as a contest or conflict; and
- *logical thinker* – who strives for order and reason.

Archetypes do not refer to individuals in explicit roles but to basic, often unquestioned, emotional dispositions that compel people to behave in a particular way. Archetypes are often unconsciously supported by others and society by the persistence of myths and strong images, such as the dominant aggressive male and the submissive caring female (see Chapter 1). Most people will exhibit a combination of behaviours from each of the archetypes, and some of the most effective group performers are those who know how to behave caringly, confrontingly or logically as the need arises. The difference between them and those who conform to one archetype consistently is that behaviour changes in accordance with what they think is necessary to get the job done, the problem solved or some other task.

It is possible to associate both positive and negative influences with specific types of behavioural concern in groups as shown in Figure 6.2. For example, there is a need to integrate the actions of various members if a group is to function effectively. However, it is possible that instead of organizing action towards a group goal, an individual could use others calculating, manipulating and using actions to further their own interests rather than those of the group. In organizations it is not unknown for a manager to make things happen so that they look good in the short term, perhaps taking credit for the work of others, so as to ensure that they get a promotion and move on – leaving others to tidy up the long-term mess that the manager created. Figure 6.2 summarizes essential actions for group functioning in the inner circle, helpful behaviours related to these actions in the middle circle and unhelpful behaviours in the outer circle.

Table 6.4   *Three bests of all possible worlds*

1. Friendly helper	2. Tough battler	3. Logical thinker
A world of mutual love, affection, tenderness, sympathy	A world of conflict, fight, power, assertiveness	A world of understanding, logic, systems, knowledge
Task-maintenance behaviour		
Harmonising Compromising Gatekeeping by concern Encouraging Expressing warmth	Initiating Coordinating Pressing for results Pressing for consensus Exploring differences Gatekeeping by command	Gathering information Clarifying ideas and words Systematising procedures Evaluating the logic of proposals
Constructs used in evaluating others		
Who is warm and who is hostile? Who helps and who hurts others?	Who is strong and who is weak? Who is winning and who is losing?	Who is bright and who is stupid? Who is accurate and who is inaccurate? Who thinks clearly and who is fuzzy?
Methods of influence		
Appeasing Appealing to pity	Giving orders Offering challenges Threatening	Appealing to rules and regulations Appealing to logic Referring to 'facts' and overwhelming knowledge
Personal threats		
That he or she will not be loved That he or she will be overwhelmed by feelings of hostility	That he or she will lose his or her ability to fight (power) That he or she will become 'soft' and 'sentimental'	That his or her world is not ordered That he or she will be overwhelmed by love or hate

Source: David Kolb, Irwin Rubin and James McIntyre (1984), *Organizational Psychology: An Experiential Approach to Organizational Behaviour*, Englewood Cliffs, NJ: Prentice Hall, p. 133.

How an individual or team performs can be a reflection of external pressures as well. Such factors external to the team include organizational strategy, formal authority structures, informal and political alliances, procedures for selecting new employees, reward systems for existing employees, the physical setting and technology in use, and the organizational culture or cultures. These factors fit with those mentioned earlier by Marks *et al.* (1997) except that they make no mention of political alliances or power. Of these internal and external factors, the most significant barriers to team success were identified by the Wilson Learning Corporation (Kunze 1993: 24) in a survey of 500 firms as:

- reward systems and individual performance schemes that are not team focused;
- team members lacking strategic information; and
- management lacking commitment to teams and goals.

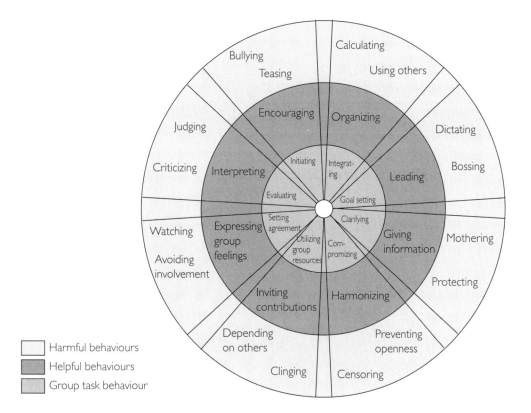

Figure 6.2 Helpful and unhelpful behaviours in groups

Source: Unknown.

Of course, one must remember that the factors that are reported by participants may not be the same ones that an observer blames. In light of this caution, one can conclude that group participants *identify* factors as most important to team failure that are both internal – for example, lack of strategic information – and external – for example, lack of management commitment.

Empowering teams

The warm reception that teams seem to have received in the popular management literature has not been universal. A number of studies of their implementation have begun to challenge the overwhelmingly positive assumptions of approaches like those summarized in Table 6.1. Notable among these have been Mike Parker and Jane Slaughter's *Choosing Sides* (1988) and Guillermo Grenier's *Inhuman Relations* (1989). Both of these books associate teams with a managerial agenda of intensification of effort (getting people to work harder), increased managerial control and anti-trade union industrial relations. These claims suggest that empowering teams is likely to be well nigh impossible.

Power and control within teams, as well as in relation to those who lead them, is an important issue. Many who hold leadership positions are either unable to empower teams because they do not know how or they simply do not want to give up the control that the

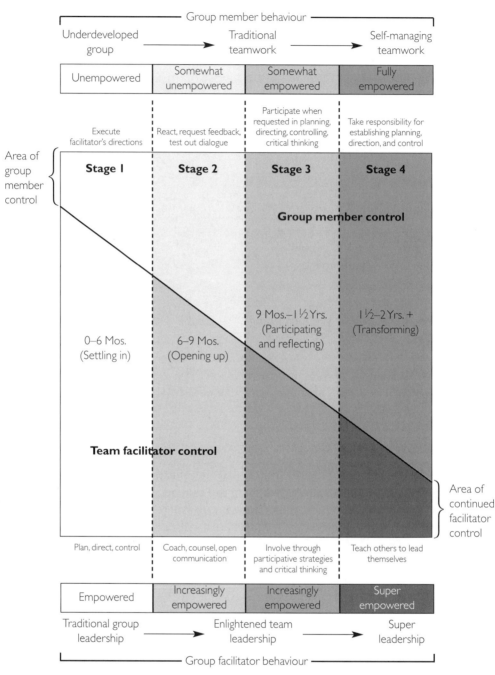

Figure 6.3 Facilitative leadership model

Source: Rollin Glaser (1992), Moving Your Team Toward Self-Management, King of Prussia, PA: Organisation Design and Development Inc., p. 9.

teams threaten to take from them. A critical aspect of empowering is leadership. Rollin Glaser (1992) has proposed a four-stage model of facilitative leadership as shown in Figure 6.3, in which he describes how empowerment switches over time from team facilitators' control to the group members' control'.

Glaser's approach focuses on leadership that helps create self-managing work teams and how this role might change over time. Self-managing work teams usually include elements of the following: they manage themselves (e.g. plan and organize their own work); control and monitor their work; assign jobs to members (e.g. who does what, where and when); control work schedules, pace of work and goals to be achieved; make decisions about inventory, quality, work stoppages, repairs, etc.; and take actions to remedy problems (e.g. customer service/complaints; quality issues, discipline and rewards) (Kirkman and Shapiro 1997: 731). Based on this description, Uddevalla would be considered to have embraced many of the attributes of self-managing work teams. NUMMI would be classified as a less developed example.

In Stage 1, there is no empowerment of the team but the leader consciously uses traditional hierarchical forms of control to try to get the team to direct itself. In Stages 2 and 3, there is increasing evidence of empowerment of group members where in Stage 2 the leader as facilitator tries to open up communications and discussion. In Stage 3 the team becomes involved in meaningful problem solving, decision making and critical reflection. In Stage 4, the group members are substantially empowered, and no longer need a leader or coach but lead themselves. By empowering others, the superleader has theoretically freed himself/herself to allow others to accomplish tasks through self-leadership, meaning that the collective output of *both* the 'leader' and the team improves. This is similar to post-heroic leadership described in Chapter 5.

Glaser develops his idea of superleadership based on the notion of followership (see Manz and Sims 1992; Manz 1992). Superleaders have the capacity to help their followers develop self-leadership so they can all contribute more fully to their organization's efforts. Team facilitators have to be empowered in order to empower teams. Empowerment for Glaser is measured along the dimensions of the power profile described in Chapter 4.

It is interesting to note though that Glaser considers two years plus not an unreasonable time span to develop fully empowered teams. It is quite probable that many teams might never reach Stage 4.

Glaser's notion of stages in team development is supported by Steve Kozlowski, Stanley Gully, Eduardo Salas and Janis Cannon-Bowers (1996) who also suggest some general principles and guidelines for team leaders, focusing on how different leadership skills are needed at different stages of team evolution. The authors contend that training in team leadership is often too simplistic, arguing that the team leader's training role needs to evolve as the team evolves. The authors maintain that during *formation*, a team is often a team in name only and that the leader needs to model appropriate 'team' behaviour or bonding and act as *mentor*. What follows the formation stage is a '*novice*' stage where the leader acts as a technical *instructor* in guiding task development and knowledge. Then comes stage one of the *refinement* stage where the leader acts as a *coach*, blending task work with teamwork in what are now seen as *expert teams*. Stage two of the refinement stage is where the leader is a *facilitator* of what is really supposed to be *reflective practice* for a self-leading team (see Introduction and Chapter 1).

Despite Glaser's optimistic view of empowerment of teams, others argue that teams can, and do, face a number of challenges, which are often played down by the more popular advocates of teamwork. Internal politics (or power struggles) is one of them. Rosabeth Moss Kanter (1983: 260–2) suggests that internal politics in teams arise from a number of factors, common to many teams. This occurs for a number of reasons.

While teams are meant to ensure democracy and participation, it is difficult to eliminate internal competition or jockeying for status within teams. Individuals have self-interest and different outcomes they want from the team, such as impressing those who reward and promote them. Few people completely subordinate their self-interest for the benefit of the team. This self-interest can be more pronounced in teams when the organization is divisive and uncooperative, for example, encouraging departmental rivalry.

Teams which have to compete for scarce resources and rewards outside the team are likely to generate internal conflicts and competition. Teams where members are representing a department, unit or function are likely to be more political in protecting their 'turf' than where team members participate as individuals. It is difficult for 'representative' members to support a team decision that disadvantages their 'constituents' or colleagues. Kanter argues that individual representation is superior to other forms in many team situations.

Teams can become arenas for 'flexing muscles' and politicizing agendas. This can occur if a few members come to dominate the team and behave like 'oligarchies' in the team; for example, Kanter cites a factory in which participative practices were encouraged but team members feared ostracism by a clique in the team. Peer pressure is a strong mechanism of group control upon which management often depends in trying to keep teams performing. Teams can become politicized when there are historical tensions between them. Many management and labour (or union-based) teams simply amplify conflicts and hostilities and members never reach or agree on mutual problem-solving strategies. Kanter says it is naive to expect that in all cases historical combatants will set aside their differences for the good of the team.

Teams are often presented as developing processes that will help to minimize power and eliminate organizational politics. A team is almost meant to be non-political and be representative of consensus and conformity to group norms and expectations. These pressures can force teams towards homogeneity and discourage diversity of views and opinions or stifle open debate and dialogue (also see Rifkin and Fulop 1997: 140). Much of the empowerment literature, and that on team leadership, propagates the view that 'real' teams are somehow non-political and that politics and conflict do not have positive benefits. Kanter says if a team is dominated by the 'best' and most skilled persons, then this is likely to produce better decisions even though not every member is empowered and consensus is far from evident.

Eunson (1994: 58) suggests that teams are also increasingly favoured as ways of harnessing expert power or knowledge. Team leadership, he says, requires more than expert power to build trust and commitment (see Chapter 7). Yet it is often not easy for team members to change roles. Amanda Sinclair (1990) echoes these sentiments, saying that teams need 'champions' who are respected for their expertise, but teams have changing leadership needs that might require shared leadership strategies or power-sharing, which is not mentioned by Glaser (see above). Sinclair also notes that in reality not everyone is suited for teamwork, let alone leadership, and the 'tyranny' of teams created by the fads and fashions leaves no room for legitimate 'avoidance' of teamwork.

Only recently has the management literature focused on the difficulty that top management people have working in teams. Jon Katzenbach (1997: 84) argues that the basic discipline of teams – that is, a small number of people, complementary skills, common purpose, performance goals, and an approach for which the members hold themselves mutually accountable – rarely holds for top management teams. In fact, he suggests that the idea that organizations naturally have a 'top management team' is often a myth. Katzenbach presents a number of arguments as to why teams at the top often do not make sense. He lists six key points that he says are often difficult to reconcile and certainly discourage the view that teams are beneficial in all situations. He notes that not having teams at the top fits well with the power structure in many organizations. He says there is a 'power alley' in organizations consisting of those who have the most clout, make the critical decisions and are responsible for aligning actions and decisions in ways that do, or at least appear to, support corporate priorities (Katzenbach 1997: 86). A single-leader approach fits this sort of structure better than teams. Top management teams face six key challenges that often make them unworkable. These challenges are listed in Exhibit 6.6.

- Top executives are individually accountable for whatever happens on their watch. They enforce such accountability in the organization by rewarding and punishing managers according to how well they meet clear-cut individual objectives. A team learns to hold its members mutually accountable for collective results.
- Top executives are primarily responsible for broad corporate strategy, policy, and objectives. A team's purpose and goals must be tightly focused on specific performance results.
- Top executives must create and maintain a sense of urgency about resolving those issues that are critical to overall company performance. A team mobilizes around a meaningful purpose and a commitment to specific, common goals; a team's purpose and goals may be important without being either urgent or critical.
- Top executives make decisions on their own; they exercise personal judgement about risks, resources, and strategic options. A team makes collective judgements by means of open dialogue, conflict resolution, and collective *real work*.
- Top executives assign people to tasks based largely on their position in the organization. Members of a team are assigned on the basis of the specific skills required by the task at hand, regardless of their formal role in the company.
- Top executives leverage their time and experience by means of efficient organizational and managerial processes; as executives become more efficient and thus more valuable, they are given responsibility for more people and greater assets.

Exhibit 6.6   Key challenges faced by top management teams

Source: John Katzenbach (1997), 'The Myth of the top management team', Harvard Business Review November–December, p. 87.

Katzenbach does not exclude situations in which top management teams might work well, for example at times of mergers or takeovers and major corporate or market collapses. However, top management teams cannot easily share leadership roles, as teams do, because of lines of accountability and responsibilities at the top level, especially individual responsibility. The image that Katzenbach presents of large corporations in the USA also raises questions about how realistic it is to talk about post-heroic leadership, given the 'alley of power' that exists in many corporations.

He also suggests, as does Kanter (above), that the pursuit of consensus (or elimination of conflict) in teams is not necessarily a positive indication of team performance. Teamwork is focused on issues of cooperation, communication and consensus, but team performance is not necessarily dependent on consensus or teamwork and teams can thrive on conflict

(Katzenbach 1997: 85). Katzenbach also suggests that consensus building at the top levels is not the norm and can distract executives from their real work.

Avoiding teams, even for those not in top management, does not automatically mean that someone is not productive or contributing to the organization in some collective manner. Mayo (mentioned earlier) was extremely insightful about how informal groups operate in organizations, although he saw these as being dysfunctional and a serious threat to management control. Creating more formal teams was thought to be an answer to this problem, although Mayo recognized, as have others (e.g. Thompson and McHugh 1995: 269) that informal processes exist in even the most formal group or team. Ralph Stacey (1993: 243, 349–56) suggests that for innovation and learning to occur, organizations and their managers need to think beyond ideas such as self-managing work teams, self-leading teams and to embrace *extraordinary leadership*. He says managers need to encourage more *self-organization* through informal groups. Self-organization, he says, is one of the most important ways managers can create new knowledge through allowing small groups of people to develop spontaneously and who can also determine tasks for themselves. These self-organizing networks need not be democratic but can be highly political, diverse or homogeneous (Stacey 1993: 353).

Self-organization, as a concept, means management does not 'authorize' these networks of informal members to meet or form. Management does not or cannot empower these networks – they empower themselves. Self-organization does not mean that self-managing work teams are dismantled, but that their limitations for innovation, learning and change are acknowledged. Self-organizing networks are not permanent structures, as are self-managing work teams, but Stacey believes organizations need to develop greater flexibility to cope with rapid and turbulent change. One important aspect of self-organization is that it does not presuppose a need for a strong culture (i.e. shared vision and values) and people sharing the same beliefs. Inevitably, self-organization networks are likely to increase tensions and conflicts or at least there are no guarantees this will not happen (Stacey 1993: 371). Self-organizing principles involve dispersing power more haphazardly and taking risks regarding the level of disruption or 'anarchy' these networks can create. The self-organization concept does, however, raise questions about how much innovation, knowledge sharing and learning is possible in self-managed work teams. These more informal groups can provide emotional and intellectual support outside the hierarchy or formal team structures (Ulrich 1998: 23).

Cross-cultural issues and teams

Bradley Kirkman and Debra Shapiro (1997) argue that self-managing work teams produce a number of substantial benefits when they are working successfully, hence the worldwide interest in them. These benefits include some of the following: greater levels of team productivity; higher quality; greater customer satisfaction; greater levels of safety (or fewer accidents); lower levels of team costs to produce goods and services. Individually team members in self-managing work teams report greater job satisfaction and commitment to the organization (Kirkman and Shapiro 1997: 731–2). Kirkman and Shapiro suggest that cross-cultural factors will influence whether or not self-managing work teams – a Western business concept – can be successfully or easily introduced in non-Western cultures and still reap the benefits mentioned above. They suggest that self-managing work teams comprise two critical dynamics or processes that are evident in greater or lesser degrees in those teams: *self-management* and *teamwork*.

1 *Self-management* relates to the degree to which a team has discretionary decisions over such things as hiring and firing co-workers and being able to procure raw materials and services. Resistance to self-management in teams can manifest in overt actions such as sabotage, protests and other forms of disruptive behaviour. Resistance can also impact attitudinally and can include withdrawal from the organization through avoidance of co-workers, refusal to cooperate and a general lack of commitment to the job evident in such things as absenteeism, lateness and substandard work (Kirkman and Shapiro 1997: 732–3).

Borrowing from Geert Hofstede (see Chapter 3) and others, Kirkman and Shapiro argue that self-managing work teams in non-Western countries, which they term globalized self-managed work teams, are affected by three key cultural variables that influence acceptance or resistance to self-management: *power distance* (PD), *doing or being orientation* (DBO) and *determinism* (DE). These three cultural variables are claimed by the authors to vary more across cultures than within them. The authors note that the culture within an organization can moderate the influence of these broader cultural variables, as indeed do a number of others including those mentioned earlier by Marks *et al.* (1997). Nonetheless, the authors believe that these cultural variables, and the ones to be discussed below in relation to teamwork, provide useful predictors of potential success or failure in globalized self-managing work teams. The following summary is drawn from Kirkman and Shapiro (1997: 737–9).

- *Power distance* In countries that have low power distance cultures (see Chapter 3), it is acceptable to bypass one's boss or superior to get work done. Status, formality and titles are not expected to be conformed to and people are generally comfortable with accepting higher levels of responsibility in their jobs than is defined in their titles. Countries such as the USA, Australia and Canada have low power distance cultures. Malaysia, by contrast, provides an example of a high power distance society where individuals do not accept delegated responsibility or authority very easily and are usually poor at developing these skills in others. Bypassing a boss or a superior is considered insubordinate. Autonomy and responsibility are likely to be resisted or not well handled in high power distance cultures, suggesting that globalized self-managing work teams are likely to face resistance. Kirkman and Shapiro suggest that Japanese society's high power distance accounts for the absence of innovation in many of their team approaches (e.g. continuous improvement).

- *Doing versus being orientation* This relates to the extent to which individuals in a society value work ('doing') versus non-work ('being') activities. Dominant doing-oriented cultures stress hard work and accomplishment through work. Dominant being-oriented cultures favour work as second to enjoying life away from work. People from dominant 'doing' cultures are more comfortable and willing to set their own goals and respond to goal-directed behaviour. Both these attributes are important in self-management. The authors cite countries such as Mexico and Malaysia as having dominant being-oriented cultures in which self-management is likely to flounder as part of a team strategy.

- *Determinism versus free will*   Cultures that have a strong element of determinism create a sense or feeling among people that many things are beyond their control and governed by external forces. The Muslim faith has strong elements of this. Dominant 'free-will' cultures such as the USA stress people having control over events and actions and their destinies. Self-management requires making changes within the team that often mean altering strategies, plans and even directions, and establishing new standards of performance or outcomes. A deterministic world view would not easily support these aforementioned aspects of self-management.

2 *Teamwork* focuses on how groups work interdependently to solve problems and accomplish tasks (Kirkman and Shapiro 1997: 739). Others such as Katzenbach (1997) suggest that teamwork depends on such things as communication, collaboration, cooperation and compromise. These processes will help individuals deal with their interdependency. Interdependency varies among teams, and high interdependency means team members can only successfully accomplish their tasks collectively and thus have frequent encounters with each other for such activities as exchanging materials and information. Kirkman and Shapiro (1997: 739–40) suggest that resistance to teamwork is resistance to the interdependence that is necessary for highly effective self-managing work teams. They point out that people might accept greater responsibility for tasks (which is a self-management aspect) but may not want to share that responsibility (which is a teamwork aspect) in self-managing work teams. In some cultures teamwork might be more readily embraced but not self-management and vice versa.

- *Collectivism* versus *individualism*   These variables most affect the success or failure of teamwork across cultures (see Chapter 3). People from collectivist cultures tend to identify with group interests, put aside self-interest and are thus more willing to rely on group decisions. This can also mean that individual performance differences can be disregarded when giving employees rewards. Shame and loss of face can also be associated with behaviour that contravenes group norms. Pursuing individual agendas (usually politically) is publicly frowned upon. By contrast, individualistic cultures promote the interest of the individual over the welfare of the group (Kirkman and Shapiro 1997: 740). This most notably occurs with the phenomenon of 'social loafing' (mentioned earlier).

A study of managerial trainees from the USA and the People's Republic of China found the social loafing effect in the US sample but not in the Chinese sample. The study by Christopher Earley (1989) suggests that people from a highly collectivist culture (such as China) will more readily throw themselves into work for collective goals in a collective manner than will those from a highly individualistic culture (such as the USA). It might also be added that where the individual's sense of self depends very much on the groups of which they are a member, they will not feel themselves to be *fully* themselves unless working in a group situation and may feel uncomfortable working in a very large group where they feel isolated or on their own. Individualistic cultures produce a sense of self which is not realized collectively by immersion in and playing one's part in the group, but rather by differentiating and asserting one's attitudes as an individual. People from individualistic cultures are less likely to accept teamwork in self-managing work teams where interdependence requires members to focus on the welfare of the group and not the individual.

We sound a note of warning, however, that collectivist groups (and those who write about them) tend to romanticize the condition of group harmony and undervalue creative conflict, just as individualist groups may tend to overvalue conflict. It is also important to note that while collectivist cultures may not display the mechanisms of group surveillance and control as visibly as do individualist cultures for the reasons just mentioned, there are often sets of overt and covert forces – social expectations, sanctions and benefits – working outside the group that serve to discipline group members before they enter the group (Kondo 1990; Sewell 1992; Yamamoto 1990).

Kirkman and Shapiro (1997: 741) also note that people from individualistic cultures prefer equity-based rewards where team members are differentially paid based on performance. In collectivist cultures equality-based pay, where each team member is paid the same, is often accepted and serves to reduce status differences. Not surprisingly, these two aspects relate to perceptions of fairness of pay and suggest that team-based pay is very likely to be more acceptable in collectivist cultures.

The authors also argue (Kirkman and Shapiro 1997: 745–6) that among the moderators of all these cultural influences diversity is a very strong one. The diversity of a group affects the level of resistance to, and success of, self-managing work teams. Diversity within a team tends to increase turnover, therefore opportunities for long-term influence are limited. Diverse teams also have less scope for cohesiveness along cultural lines and consensus is also more difficult to achieve. Resisters simply have a more difficult task of influencing others in a diverse group. Minority views (i.e. dissenting voices) usually find it more difficult to influence majority views in diverse teams, so resistance is again more difficult. Team leaders, however, can have undue influence over teams in resisting either element of self-management or teamwork.

Kirkman and Shapiro developed 16 possible scenarios for promoting self-management and teamwork based on the influence of the cultural variables discussed. They concluded that significantly different strategies need to be adopted depending on the combination of cultural variables.

Conclusion

Given the pervasiveness of teams across popular and academic management texts, it should come as no surprise that an emerging critical backlash can be identified. This backlash is evident in the mainstream, to some extent. Take, for example, Stanley M. Herman's *A Force of Ones* (1994) or Lyman Ketchum and Eric Trist's *All Teams Are Not Created Equal* (1992), which are against teamwork. These authors see themselves as reeling in some of the more excessive claims that other, less circumspect books make in support of teams. At the same time, there is a long and well-developed tradition of workplace democratization that emanates from Northern Europe. This movement sees teamwork as an important component of efforts to increase self-determination and genuine democracy at work.

Democracy at work, though, is far removed from the highly normative and instrumental approaches to teamwork that are currently associated with management's fads, fashions and the North American 'management gurus', which simply see teamwork as a means of increasing traditional benchmarks like profitability, competitive advantage, capital utilization or productive efficiency. This is not to say that teamwork, in any of its incarnations, is a necessarily unattractive proposition for organizations and their employees. Rather, we should be sceptical of the claims made for teamwork, subjecting them to critical scrutiny in order to establish whether they create conditions of mutual benefit where top management, middle management, workers, customers and the community all gain or whether they perpetuate or even develop new forms of organizational asymmetry. This critical perspective will enable us to make informed choices about important organizational changes, like the shift toward teamwork, rather than blindly following the exhortations of the latest management guru.

Questions at the beginning of the chapter

We can see that although there are many possible definitions of a team, they apply commonly to a group working towards a defined or shared set of objectives. Where definitions may diverge is around the degree of specificity of the roles played within the team by individuals, the degree of empowerment and autonomy of the members, and the extent of hierarchy if any in particular.

Within some teams, job design considerations may lead to higher motivation and job satisfaction for workers, whose needs may appear to be better satisfied than in other forms of organizing. However, teams can also be stressful places where members are expected to police themselves and become self-controlling, and where they are expected to work both harder and smarter in the service of managerial needs and ends. They might also be used as a means for management to erode trade union influence.

Managers, and particularly those at supervisory level, do need to manage differently in a teamwork situation, but the nature and type of leadership skills they need to exercise will vary according to the type of team they are in and its stage of development and whether they are aiming for 'self-managing' work teams and 'self-leadership' principles.

Furthermore, there are clearly different ideas of what a team is and does, and the success or failure of a team depends both on its relationship with its context as well as its internal characteristics.

Teams develop, and succeed or fail, in context. Teams may work well in one company and not in another. They might be broadly embraced and effective in one national culture and not in another. The shape of teams will therefore be affected by contextual forces which constrain or enable them to develop. Nevertheless, this development is likely to take place following patterns of development, stages, periods of activity and inertia, which have been identified by recent research. Teams might not be the universal panacea which some popular treatments claim, but they do have some common features and properties, knowledge of which can help us both to manage some teams and be a useful member of others.

The case study

The theory behind the practice seems to be very important in this case, and the basic principles have been thoroughly worked out by the manager, Norman Stone. Indeed, these principles seem sound and well understood. They have had considerable impact on performance in the short term, although the process is still in its initial stages, and several significant gains seem to have been experienced. The employees are not heavily involved as yet in setting their own standards and the groups are, at best, at Stage 2 of Glaser's model of facilitative leadership, with operators being used as inspectors rather than anything more creative. But problem solving has occurred and progress seems exceptionally good at the end of the first part of the case.

In the second part of the case some problems emerge. First, the involvement of the teams in the design process was limited, and the resources they were given were rather limited, which meant that they were working under severe constraints. While the researchers were able to help and facilitate the groups, it appears that the engineering managers did not fully understand their role in the team project, and the researchers were not receiving information. The engineering manager's management style here seems very different from that of Norman Stone, and the theory outlined in the first part of the case is not being put into practice. Essentially, the engineers want to develop another production line and are reluctant to design anything jointly with the operators that will give them control over their own work. The plant culture seems to be hierarchical and task and function dominated, with some evidence of a thinly veiled power struggle which the engineers want to win, and by the end of this section the operators would be very dispirited and disillusioned. Taylor would not have seen the project as mistaken, but mishandled – he would not have approved of the efficiency losses or the lack of clarity of procedures, but he would also not have approved of the loss of *esprit de corps*. Mayo would have seen the earlier phases as a necessary part of letting the workers get things out of their system, and would have castigated the managers for not listening to the workers' concerns more closely. However, he would have advocated greater training and support for the supervisory role within the existing structure rather than a new structure.

How could the outcome described earlier have happened, given the first researchers' story about the plant? Contrary to the innovative, participatory change process coordinated by a supportive management team, there was a tense industrial relations climate (exacerbated by broader conflicts within the industry), with little trust between shopfloor workers and management. The management structure at the plant was confusing to workers (and constantly changing), and there was poor coordination across management functions. While there had been some notable team successes in solving production problems (as the earlier study illustrated), there was in fact very little diffusion of effective teamwork throughout the plant. The successes were transitional phenomena restricted to only limited areas. The work area 'teams' existed more in name than in any substantive meaning of the term. The only 'team activity' engaged in by these groups was a weekly problem-solving session when the line was stopped during normal production time to allow for it. Wombat's much-vaunted 'employee involvement' programme proved to be more a token gesture than a form of meaningful participation. Top managers, as described, overruled recommendations of employee teams.

This situation was a result of two main problems. The first was that the *processes for team problem solving were inadequately developed*, and no specific plant-wide training was provided for teamwork (although the company did provide other, widely praised, competency-based training programmes for its shopfloor employees). The second problem was that the *production process at the plant remained dominated by conventional industrial engineering*. Thus the organization of work followed Taylorist/Fordist principles with extensive task fragmentation, short task cycles (of around 60 seconds), machines setting the pace of work, very little shopfloor autonomy and responsibility, and traditional supervision and control mechanisms.

Within this unfavourable climate, three other factors contributed to the team/cell project's outcome. First, most of the plant's management 'team' and engineers had not been involved in the establishment of the project, and so were neither adequately prepared for nor fully committed to it. The project had been developed in negotiation with the original manager (Norman Stone) and his senior manager responsible for new business. Although the other managers had been informed about the project, they had had little other preparation and no chance for consultation on the project's details. Second, and exacerbating the first factor, Norman Stone retired before the project actually began. He was replaced by another manager who was not sympathetic to the project and its aims. As an industrial engineer, the new plant manager was much more technocratic (at one stage he commented 'We have tried the team approach, and as far as I am concerned it has not worked') and so was more committed to introducing technical solutions to solve problems at the plant. Third, the management and engineering teams were excessively 'lean', with relatively small numbers of salaried employees responsible not only for managing existing processes but also for the development and introduction of new products and their manufacturing processes. This lean structure allowed little time for innovative projects and put considerable pressure on the assembly process design team.

There was far less senior management commitment to change than was originally claimed, a far greater climate of distrust and suspicion among the workforce, far less extensive teamwork, and a less innovative organizational culture.

The failure of teams at Wombat arose from the fact that several situational factors were not favourable. The tense climate and lack of trust, the engineers' lack of understanding of the project and lack of commitment to it, the loss of Stone's leadership, which was central to putting the theory into practice, and failure to diffuse successes across the organization all meant that early changes were not sustainable. What seems to be important here are the need to educate on a wide basis all those who need to understand the proposed changes, to persuade them of the value of the changes, to continue to communicate from the top while allowing the teams considerable autonomy, and attention to breaking down existing political obstacles. If teams are to be successful in the future, they need to be linked to the culture of the organization, which may necessitate change on a broad scale, and will necessitate sustained top management support and leadership over a number of years.

References

Adler, P.S. (1993a) 'Time-and-motion regained', *Harvard Business Review* 71 (1): 97–108.

Adler, P.S. (1993b) 'The "learning bureaucracy": New United Motor Manufacturing, Inc', *Research in Organizational Behaviour* 15: 111–94.

Adler, P.S. and Borys, B. (1996) 'Two types of bureaucracy: Enabling and coercive', *Administrative Science Quarterly* 41(1): 61–89.

Albanese, R. and Van Fleet, D.D. (1985) 'Rational behaviour in groups: The free-riding tendency', *Academy of Management Review* 10(2): 244–55.

Badham, R., Couchman, P. and Linstead, S.A. (1995) 'Power tools: Narrating the factory of the future', *Annual Conference on the Labour Process*, Blackpool, University of Central Lancashire, April.

Barker, J.R. (1993) 'Tightening the iron cage: Concertive control in self-managing teams', *Administrative Science Quarterly* 38(3): 408–37.

Belbin, R.M. (1981) *Management Teams: Why They Succeed or Fail*, London: Butterworth-Heinemann.

Belbin , R.M. (1993) *Team Roles at Work*, London: Butterworth-Heinemann.

Bell, L., Blackler, F. and Crump, N. (1997) 'Look smart', *People Management* 23, October: 56–9.

Bendix, R. (1956) *Work and Authority in Industry*, New York: Harper.

Berggren, C. (1989) 'New production concepts in final assembly: The Swedish experience', in Wood, S. (ed.), *The Transformation of Work?*, London: Unwin.

Berggren, C. Adler, P.S. and Cole, Robert E. (1994) 'NUMMI vs Uddevalla; Rejoinder', *Sloan Management Review* 35(2): 37–9.

Bernstein, P. (1992) 'The learning curve at Volvo', in Glaser, R. (ed.), *Classic Readings in Self-Managing Teamwork*, King of Prussia, P.A: Organization Design and Development Inc.

Bion, W. (1959) *Experiences in Groups*, New York: Basic Books.

Braverman, H. (1974) *Labor and Monopoly Capital: The Degradation of Work in the Twentieth Century*, New York: Monthly Review Press.

Carmona, S. and Grönlund, A. (1998) 'Learning from forgetting: An experimental study of two European car manufacturers', *Management Learning* 29(1): 21–38.

Clegg, S.R. and Dunkerley, D. (1980) *Organizations, Class and Control*, London: Routledge.

Davis, G. (1994) 'Research Note: "The stubborn silence of Petronius Arbiter"', *Australian Journal of Public Administration* 53(2): 248–51.

Deming, W. (1986) *Out of the Crisis: Quality, Productivity and the Competitive Position*, Cambridge, Mass.: MIT Press.

Earley, P.C. (1989) 'Social loafing and collectivism: A comparison of the United States and the People's Republic of China', *Administrative Science Quarterly* 34(4): 565–81.

Eunson, B. (1994) *Communicating for Team Building*, Brisbane: John Wiley.

Fincham, R. and Rhodes, P.S. (1992) *The Individual, Work and Organization: Behaviour Studies for Business and Management* (second edition), London: Weidenfeld and Nicolson.

Fulop, L. (1992) 'Bureaucracy and the modern manager', in Fulop, L. with Frith, F. and Hayward, H. *Management for Australian Business: A Critical Text*, Melbourne: Macmillan.

Gabrenya, W.K., Latane, B. and Wang, Y.E. (1981) 'Social loafing in a cross-cultural perspective', *Journal of Cross-Cultural Psychology* 14: 368–84.

Gersick, C. (1988) 'Time and transition in work teams: Toward a new model of group development', *Academy of Management Journal* 31(1): 9–41.

Gersick, C. (1989) 'Marking time: Predictable transitions in task groups', *Academy of Management Journal* 32(2): 274–309.

Gilbreth, L.M. (1914) *Psychology of Management*, New York: Sturgis and Walton.

Glaser, R. (1992) *Moving Your Team Toward Self-management*, King of Prussia, PA: Organisation Design and Development Inc.

Gouldner, A.W. (1954) *Patterns of Industrial Bureaucracy*, New York: The Free Press.

Grenier, G. (1989) *Inhuman Relations: Quality Circles and Anti-Unionism in American Industry*, Philadelphia: Temple University Press.

Hammer, M. and Champy, J. (1993) *Reengineering the Corporation: A Manifesto for Business Revolution*, New York: Harper Business.

Harris, T.G. (1993) 'The post-capitalist executive: An interview with Peter F. Drucker', *Harvard Business Review* May–June: 115–22.

Herman, S.M. (1994) *A Force of Ones: Reclaiming Individual Power in a Time of Teams, Work Groups, and Other Crowds*, San Francisco: Jossey-Bass.

Heterick, W.P. and Boje, D.M. (1992) 'Organization and the body: Post-Fordist dimensions', *Journal of Organizational Change Management* 5(1): 48–57.

Hounshell, D. (1985) *From the American System to Mass Production, 1800–1932: The Development of Manufacturing Technology in the United States*, Baltimore, MD: Johns Hopkins University Press.

Kanter, R.M. (1983) *The Change Masters: Innovations for Productivity in the American Corporation*, New York: Simon and Schuster.

Katzenbach, J.R. (1997) 'The myth of the top management team', *Harvard Business Review* November–December: 83–91.

Katzenbach, J.R. and Smith, D.K. (1993) *The Wisdom of Teams*, Boston, Mass.: Harvard Business School Press.

Ketchum, L.D. and Trist, E. (1992) *All Teams Are Not Created Equal: How Employee Empowerment Really Works*, Newbury Park: Sage.

Kirkman, B.L. and Shapiro, D.L. (1997) 'The impact of cultural values on employee resistance to teams: Toward a model of globalized self-managing work team effectiveness', *Academy of Management Review* 22(3): 730–57.

Kolb, D.A., Rubin, I.M. and McIntyre, J.M. (1984) *Organizational Psychology: An Experiential Approach to Organizational Behavior*, Englewood Cliffs, NJ: Prentice Hall.

Kondo, D.K. (1990) *Crafting Selves*, Chicago: Chicago University Press.

Kozlowski, S.W.J., Gully, S.M., Salas, E. and Cannon-Bowers, J.A. (1996) 'Team leadership and development: Theory, principles, and guidelines for training leaders and teams', *Advances in Interdisciplinary Studies of Work Teams* 3: 253–91 (Greenwich, CT: JAI Press).

Kunze, H. (1993) 'Work teams have their work cut out for them', *HR Focus* January: 14.

Landes, D.S. (1969) *The Unbound Prometheus*, Cambridge: Cambridge University Press.

Levinson, D. (1978) *The Seasons of a Man's Life*, New York: Alfred A. Knopf.

Lipnack, J. and Stamps, J. (1994) *The Age of the Network: Organizing Principles for the 21st Century*, Essex Junction, VT: Oliver Wight Publications Inc.

Lipnack, J. and Stamps, J. (1997) *Virtual Teams: Reaching Across Space, Time and Organizations with Technology*, New York: John Wiley.

McLachlan, R. (1997) 'Harrogate Report, 3: Knowledge management – Porter fails to focus on employees', *People Management* 6 November: 11–12.

MacNeish, J. and Richardson, T. (1994) *The Choice: Either Change the System or Polish the Fruit – A Pictorial Guide to Creating Productive Workplaces*, Sydney: Don't Press.

Manz, C.C. (1992) 'Beyond self-managing work teams: Toward self-leading teams in the workplace', in Glaser, R. (ed.), *Classic Readings in Self-Managing Teamwork*, King of Prussia, P.A: Organization Design and Development Inc.

Manz, C.C. and Sims, H.P. (1992) 'Becoming a superleader', in Glaser, R. (ed.), *Classic Readings in Self-Managing Teamwork*, King of Prussia, P.A: Organization Design and Development Inc.

Marks, A., Findlay, P., Hine, J., McKinlay, A. and Thompson, P. (1997) 'Whisky galore: Teamworking and workplace transformation in the Scottish spirits industry', paper presented to the 15th Annual Labour Process Conference, March 1997, Edinburgh.

Mathews, J. (1989) *Tools of Change: New Technology and the Democratisation of Work*, Sydney: Pluto Press.

Mayo, E. (1933) *The Human Problems of an Industrial Civilization*, New York: Macmillan.

Mayo, E. (1945) *The Social Problems of an Industrial Civilization*, Boston, Mass.: Division of Research, Graduate School of Business Administration, Harvard University.

Merkle, J.A. (1980) *Management and Ideology*, Berkeley: University of California Press.

Merton, R.K. (1940) 'Bureaucratic structure and personality', *Social Forces* 17: 560–8.

Mouzelis, N. (1975) *Organisation and Bureaucracy*, London: Routledge and Kegan Paul.

Parker, M. and Slaughter, J. (1988) *Choosing Sides: Unions and the Team Concept*, Boston: South End Press.

Pollard, S. (1965) *The Genesis of Modern Management*, Harmondsworth, UK: Penguin.

Rifkin, W. and Fulop, L. (1997) 'A review and case study of learning organizations', *The Learning Organization: An International Journal* 4(4): 135–48.

Robbins, S.P. and Barnwell, N. (1994) *Organisation Theory in Australia* (second edition), Sydney: Prentice Hall.

Rose, M. (1975) *Industrial Behaviour* (Second edition), Harmondsworth, UK: Penguin.

Selznick, P. (1949) *TVA and the Grass Roots: A Study in the Sociology of Formal Organisations*, Berkeley: University of California Press.

Senge, P. (1990) *The Fifth Discipline: The Art and Practice of the Learning Organization*, New York: Doubleday/Currency.

Sewell, G. (1992) 'In (In)formation we trust?(?)', paper presented to MERIT 10th Anniversary Conference, 10–12 December, Maastricht, the Netherlands.

Sewell, G. (1998) 'How the giraffe got its neck: An organisational "Just-So" story', in Clegg, S., Ibarra, E. and Bueno, L. (eds), *Theories of the Management Process: Making Sense Through Difference*, London: Sage.

Sewell, G. and Wilkinson, B. (1992a) 'Someone to watch over me: Surveillance, discipline and the Just-in-Time labour process', *Sociology* 26: 271–89.

Sewell, G. and Wilkinson, B. (1992b) 'Empowerment or emasculation: Shopfloor surveillance in a total quality organisation', in Blyton, P. and Turnbull, P. (eds), *Reassessing Human Resource Management*, London: Sage.

Sinclair, A. (1990) 'Myths about teamwork', *The Weekend Australian* 7–8 April: 39.

Stacey, R.D. (1993) *Strategic Management and Organizational Dynamics*, London: Pitman Publishing.

Steingard, D.S. and Fitzgibbons, D.E. (1993) 'A postmodern deconstruction of total quality management (TQM)', *Journal of Organizational Change Management* 6(4): 27–42.

Taylor, F.W. (1903) *Shop Management*, revised 1947 and republished 1964 as *Scientific Management*, New York: Harper and Row.

Taylor, F.W. (1911) *Principles of Scientific Management*, revised 1947 and republished 1964 as *Scientific Management*, New York: Harper and Row.

Taylor, F.W. (1912) 'Testimony before the Special House Committee', revised 1947 and republished 1964 in *Scientific Management*, New York: Harper and Row.

Taylor, F.W. (1964) *Scientific Management*, New York: Harper and Row.

Taylor, F.W. (1972) *Scientific Management*, Westport, CN: Greenwood Press.

Thompson, P. and McHugh, D. (1995) *Work Organisations: A Critical Introduction*, London: Macmillan.

Thompson, P. and Wallace, T. (1995) 'Teamworking: Lean machine or dream machine?', *13th International Labour Process Conference*, University of Central Lancashire: Blackpool.

Thompson, P. and Wallace, T. (1996) 'Redesigning production through teamworking: Case studies from the Volvo Truck Corporation', *International Journal of Operations and Production Management*, special issue on Lean Production and Work Organization, 16(2): 103–18.

Thompson, V. (1961) *Modern Organizations*, New York: Alfred A. Knopf.

Trist, E. and Bamforth, K.W. (1951) 'Some social and psychological consequences of the Long Wall method of coal getting', *Human Relations* 4: 3–38.

Tuckman, B.W. (1965) 'Developmental sequences in small groups', *Psychological Bulletin* 63(6): 384–99.

Turquet, P. (1974) 'Leadership: The individual and the group', in Gibbard, G.S., Hartman, J.J. and Mann, R.D. (eds), *Analysis of Groups*, San Francisco: Jossey-Bass.

Ulrich, D. (1998) 'Intellectual capital = competence × commitment', *Sloan Management Review* Winter: 15–26.

Waring, S.P. (1991) *Taylorism Transformed: Scientific Management Theory Since 1945*, Chapel Hill: University of North Carolina Press.

Winter, S.G. (1994) 'Organizing for continuous improvement: Evolutionary theory meets the quality revolution', in Baum, J.A.C. and Singh, J. (eds), *Evolutionary Dynamics of Organizations*, Oxford: Oxford University Press.

Womack, J.P., Jones, D.T. and Roos, D. (1990) *The Massachusetts Institute of Technology 5 Million Dollar 5 Year Study on the Future of the Automobile Industry*, New York: Rawson Associates.

Yamamoto, K. (1990) 'Japanese style industrial relations and an 'informal' employee organization: A case study of the Ohgi-Kai at T', *Electric Institute of Social Science Occasional Paper* No. 8, Tokyo: University of Tokyo.

Managing motivation

Liz Fulop and Stephen Linstead

Questions about motivation

1 Why do people work?
2 Are people motivated in the same ways?
3 Is how we work affected by how we feel?
4 Can one person motivate another?
5 Is the way a job is designed important for motivation?
6 Does motivation vary from culture to culture?

Commitment in Chester

The scene is a hotel room in Chester, UK. It is a cold February night and ten *senior managers* are gathered around a table having eaten and drunk a great deal. Ostensibly they are here for a strategy meeting scheduled for the next day; occasionally these so-called away days are used to deal with difficulties between members of the group. More often than not, this dealing with consists of joking, scapegoating and other attempts to cut the victims down to size. On this occasion, Graham, the manager of a business unit, has raised some issues about the role that Eric, the managing director, and Steve, the personnel director, are playing in his business [unit]. Several attempts have been made to cut him down to size:

Eric: (to the waiter) And we'll need some more brandy. Bring another bottle. Right. Where were we before we were so rudely interrupted? Ah, yes. The question of commitment, Graham?

Graham: I was not talking about commitment, I was talking about Personnel's right to shift people around without consultation.

Eric: But the rest of us were talking about commitment, Graham.

Colin: My people are committed to plan, Graham, are yours?

Graham: You might have been happy to join in, Colin, for reasons best known to yourself, but I was not talking about commitment, I was talking about poaching my people.

Roger: But your people are not committed, I've heard them say it themselves.

Graham:	Roger, I do not give a toss what you claim to have heard. I am not talking about plans or commitment! I am talking about poaching!
Tony:	(drunkenly) He's right! He's right! That's what we started talking about. That's what the boy started on about. I distinctly remember.
Roger:	You're too pissed to remember anything...
Eric:	Get it off your chest. Tell us what the issue is and then we'll talk about commitment.
Graham:	Eric, I've told you what I think the issue is and I don't want to talk about commitment, as you keep calling it, now or later. Either I am running my unit or I am not. I deeply resent Steve telling me that he is moving one of my better – no, my best man – and giving him to Roger.
Steve:	It wasn't like that, Graham, and you know it. I talked to you about it...
Graham:	You talked to me about it AFTER... AFTER you had decided – with Eric no doubt and probably Roger – what you were going to do. He is my man, in my unit, working for me.
Eric:	And for the good of the team as a whole, we decided that we needed his contribution elsewhere.
Graham:	Cant! Sheer bloody unadulterated cant! 'For the good of the team.' What bloody team? This lot? Us? Look at us! Senior managers in a public company, pissed as newts, debating nonsense – commitment, the good of the team! Working together, contributing to the company. It's all wind! Bloody hypocrisy. Tripe. We make bloody biscuits and crisps, and snacks and pizzas. What's all this crap about commitment and team spirit? It's not life or death, is it? It's no big deal. Biscuits, crisps, toffee bars, stuff everyone can do without. What is all this crap about commitment and team spirit? We are not supposed to be a bloody religious order. We are not on some crusade to save the world! Commitment, for God's sake. Who cares if we make a few more Nut Surprises? Sell a few more Dream Delights? A handful of shareholders, that's who cares? We have to ask ourselves what all this is about. What is the point of pouring huge amounts of energy into making more and more things that are of no use to anyone? Dream Delights, for God's sake! What's it all come down to? What's it all about? We throw ourselves into this nonsense as if it mattered. As if we were working to free the world from cholera or something. We are riding a monster. Production profit, grind it out. Push it on. Where is it all leading? I'll tell you where – bloody nowhere! It is not progress making more and more biscuits, more and more crisps, the biggest pizza in the world. We go on about being committed as though a few thousand quid either way will make a difference. Right, if you want to know, I am not committed, as you put it. I do not spend every waking hour thinking about Nut Surprises or Dream Delights. I do not want to spend my life thinking about Nut Surprises or Dream Delights. I question the sanity of anyone who does. I don't want to be in the office at seven in the morning and leave nine or ten at night. I do not want to spend time here. Now. Listening to this twaddle about commitment. Arguing about who works for whom. You are welcome to my staff, Roger – all of them. I'd rather be

at home. What do you want from me? Blood? I work to live, not the other way round. And so do most of the rest of you – if you don't, you are mad. I work hard not because I am committed. I work to support my wife and family. There is life beyond this company, and I am sick of pretending otherwise. You can have me from nine to five, beyond that I am my own man…

Silence. No one moves. No one catches anyone else's eye. Something has been put asunder, a disjuncture has occurred; one senses a space, a void, a crack opening up, a rush of stale air being expelled; something starkly, rudely present. The door opens and the waiter enters…

Source: Iain Mangham (1996), 'Beyond Goffman', in P. Jeffcutt, R. Grafton Small and S. Linstead (eds), Organization and Theatre, special issue of Studies in Cultures, Organizations, and Societies 2(1): 33–5.

Questions about the case

1   How many different views of commitment are evident in the case?
2   How could Graham's real or apparent 'lack of commitment' be handled? Does it need to be addressed?
3   What has precipitated the 'blow-up' at Chester?

Introduction

Managing motivation has traditionally focused on two dominant perspectives, neither being entirely separable from the other: developing individual performance-based schemes to reward organizational members and redesigning work to increase performance outcomes for the organization and the individual. Redesigning jobs has a long history in management, gaining prominence with the emergence of Taylorism, and is the main focus of this chapter. Since the 1960s job redesign emphasized making jobs more interesting, satisfying and challenging. By the 1970s worker participation and democracy in the workplace had been included. In the 1980s and early 1990s teamwork, culture, empowerment, total quality management (TQM) and business re-engineering (BR) were fashionable. As we begin the 21st century, learning organizations, virtual organizations, intellectual capital and brain work are the fashion.

Job design was initially aimed at reversing the negative effects of Scientific Management, particularly in shopfloor and routine jobs such as clerical work. Management theorists in the 1960s saw motivation as largely about satisfying the needs of people, needs only really ever satisfied through work. These 'needs deficiency' theories of motivation helped propagate a belief that if managers could identify the needs of employees, not only was it possible to control these needs, but managers could also shape or influence needs making it easier to motivate employees and improve employee performance.

The needs-based approach to motivation has left a profound legacy on management thinking and it has not been dispelled in many of the popular fads and fashions prevalent in the management market place, as evidenced in the 'buzz-words' described in Chapter 2, leadership theories in Chapter 5, and teams in Chapter 6. In this chapter we examine some of the more popular approaches to job redesign put forward since the time of Taylor and

Mayo and the motivation theories behind these approaches. Many approaches to job redesign have been premised on a homogeneous view of employees and their needs – usually male needs as already mentioned in Chapter 2. Motivation theories have dealt with a narrow range of needs and discussions about sense making, and meanings are only now gaining importance. This latter view of motivation suggests that needs emerge and are constituted in social activities and experiences that shape our identities or the social self – that needs are socially structured and negotiated within the context of different knowledge and power relations. Motivation means different things in different places or social contexts because, in this view, needs are no longer seen as necessarily pre-given, or as innate drives, uniformly fixed in everyone across all settings. A more critical view of motivation questions the idea that motivation is something easily controlled or engineered through such things as teamwork, culture or leadership. Instead, it deconstructs how strategies of job redesign reproduce certain motivational discourses that are embedded in power relations and particular disciplinary practices. Social contexts and relations in which people find themselves are critical to understanding the different perspectives people have of motivation.

Job redesign post-Taylor

Most early job redesign strategies were concerned with reversing the negative effects of Scientific Management, effects relating to rigid, over-specialized and inflexibly designed jobs, in order to find new ways of improving worker performance. Under Scientific Management and Fordism, many jobs were deskilled, reducing the value of labour, making labour less costly and easier to replace. Boring, repetitive and rigidly structured jobs produced inhumane working conditions in which workers suffered extensive psychological trauma and a poor quality of work life. Taylorism acknowledged the *messiness* of organizations and the factors that contribute to this messiness – individual characteristics, collective consciousness, uneven distribution of knowledge about tasks, and gender. The manager under Scientific Management needed to impose the principles that control and regulate such diversity. This regulation was an integral part of Taylor's work as a response to the persistence of the craft model in industry, which was rife with diversity along several dimensions, such as individual workers being responsible for setting their own work targets, patterns and hours, and often working with their own different sets of tools and producing varying outputs (see Chapter 6).

A key principle in Taylorism was the notion of *economic man* – a theory of motivation to cover all workers. Taylor, and many theorists after him, believed that the basic motivating principle for workers was money or wages. Men (workers) were assumed to be motivated by personal interest and gain, and capable of being satisfied principally by monetary rewards. Taylor saw this as a very rational type of behaviour supporting the principle of hard work or a Protestant work ethic. Taylor had been raised in a Quaker family and believed that everyone could succeed through hard work and enterprising values. He also believed that poor managers deprived workers of the opportunity to satisfy their economic needs and from reaching their highest possible rewards (Bendix 1956: 256–7).

In the 1960s and 1970s, high employment and tight labour markets in countries such as the USA, UK and Australia saw employers turn a critical eye to the effects of deskilling, especially in the wake of declining productivity, increased absenteeism, poor morale, rising rates of labour turnover and increased incidence of industrial sabotage and strikes (Child 1984: 31; Emery and Phillips 1976; Strauss 1976: 23). It is probably this last aspect of deskilling which has most concerned managers because of the obvious impact these problems can have on the overall performance of the organization. Job redesign became one solution for overcoming the problems caused by deskilling. Many job redesign strategies focused on improving the job satisfaction of employees (i.e. their motivation to work or their feelings about work), while also hoping to extract greater economic benefits for employers.

George Strauss (1976) suggests that the growing interest in job redesign in the 1970s also reflected concerns relating to managing and motivating a diverse workforce. He points out that the 'Baby Boomers' (the huge number of children born after the Second World War) entering the workforce were more resistant to, and challenging of, authority, and less afraid of economic insecurity. They were more inclined to value self-fulfilment, agreeable lifestyles, doing meaningful work and controlling their own destinies. Moreover, many women who were also entering the workforce at this period were less likely to measure success in terms of traditional economic goals. He points out that factors such as Women's Lib, civil rights agitation in the USA, and student activism of the 1960s were all affecting how satisfaction was being thought of in many quarters (1976: 21–4). These views are echoed by Kelly Goski and Mary Belfry (1991: 215–16) but who add that the next generation – the 'Baby Busters' – are even more focused on entitlements and less accepting of authority. This 'next generation' (based on US trends) is less committed to life-long employment with one firm (as their parents might have been) and is more prepared to take risks. They have also been brought up in more diverse ways (e.g. child care, single-parent families) than previous generations and 'motivating' them will entail different types of strategies than those upon which job redesign strategies are built.

Job enrichment and the needs hierarchy

Many job redesign strategies have their origins in the 1960s. Job enrichment theory has had a profound impact on job redesign and theories of motivation. The theoretical basis underpinning this job redesign strategy came from the school known as Neo-Human Relations. Elton Mayo's research (see Chapters 2 and 6) had encouraged a view which saw management's role include the development of 'good human relations' between itself and workers and between co-workers – a situation that was thought to motivate employees to work together productively, cooperatively and with economic, psychological and social satisfactions. Human Relations theory, however, stopped at the conditions under which the work was done and the relationships between people at work and thus never contradicted or challenged the assumptions of Tayloristic approaches to the organization of work and task specialization.

However, unlike Taylor, who saw workers as being rational and calculating individuals, Mayo did not believe this to be the case (see Chapters 2 and 6). On the contrary, he argued that people were motivated by personal sentiments and emotions and craved social routine. He believed that logical thinking only occurred when workers were pressed to solve problems. Logical thinking, and hence the pursuit of self-interest (i.e. 'economic man'), was something Mayo thought was a measure 'of the last resort' on the part of workers (Bendix

1956: 313–14). Mayo proposed instead a *social man* view of behaviour and motivation. He was concerned about the excessive emphasis placed on individualism and self-interest in society in general, and argued instead that people had a need for belonging to a community or having a sense of community. Small supportive work groups in organizations would fill the need of workers for an identity shaped and determined by social cohesiveness and social conformity. The forming of informal groups (i.e. the informal organization that Taylor rejected) was, he argued, natural to workers, but managers could gain control of employees by paying attention to their social needs and facilitating group cohesion (Bendix 1956: 316–17; Rose 1975: 120–1).

While not denying that this school was important, during the 1950s and 1960s researchers from the developing area of behavioural science began to extend the psychological dimension of human relations. Psychological well-being, it was argued, required not only good work conditions but also a meaningful job over which the individual worker had control. Abraham Maslow's (1943) hierarchy of human needs (see Chapter 2) provides the basis for this school. He developed a classification of human needs which he considered to be a logical sequential development from 'lower-order' to 'higher-order' needs. It is usually asserted that Maslow assumed that these needs applied universally to all individuals (see Chapter 2). The hierarchy is described below in Exhibit 7.1.

Self-actualization needs
(*Need to reach one's full potential*)
Self-esteem needs   **Higher-order needs**
(*Need for recognition and a belief in one's self*)
Social acceptance needs
(*Need to be able to form satisfactory and support relations*)

Safety and security needs
(*Need to feel safe, and free of fear*)   **Lower-order needs**
Basic physiological needs
(*Need for food, warmth, shelter, clothing*)

Exhibit 7.1   Maslow's hierarchy of needs

Since the physiological needs are classified as primary (or even primitive), they are given first priority. If a person is starving, only food occupies his or her mind. However, once this need is satisfied, the person becomes concerned with a need which was formerly of less significance, safety and security. According to Maslow, people are motivated by unsatisfied needs: a person is never completely satisfied on any need level, but a reasonable amount of gratification with basic needs must be felt before he or she proceeds up the hierarchy. Maslow's model has been used to argue that with growing economic security and affluence in society generally, and with educational levels rising, the workforce would increasingly be motivated only by the higher-order needs of self-esteem and self-actualization. This was not quite Maslow's analysis; Maslow in fact took the view that people were either self-actualizers or they were not, and society's problem was creating the conditions for those who were self-actualizers to self-actualize, rather than being reactive to circumstance. The 'economic man' needs of Taylor and the 'social man' needs of Mayo were thus given low priority in Maslow's 'complex man' approach – in fact, Maslow was concerned with those elite individuals he called self-actualizers, and in giving advice as to the sort of social and educational systems that should be developed for them. While he held onto a vision of a self-actualizing society, a less emphasized aspect of his theory was that not everyone was able to self-actualize because of their nature, and many people would remain caught at the lower motivational levels.

However, it should be noted that Maslow himself did not intend his model to be an all-embracing theory of motivation and was aware of its shortcomings (Aungles and Parker 1988: 13–17). In fact, he was critical of the fact that so many management theorists had adapted his work but no one had bothered to test it and develop it. This work was not done until the 1960s, after Maslow himself did his one and only piece of organizational investigation – an informal summer spent in a technology company in 1962 which he wrote up as a journal (Maslow 1965).

Frederick Herzberg (1966, 1987) could be said to have taken Maslow one step further by identifying the job or work itself as the substantive source of motivation. Herzberg denied that his theory was based on Maslow's work, but subsequent commentators have noted the similarities. Herzberg's theory grew out of research directed at ascertaining factors that lead to greater employee satisfaction. Studies undertaken prior to Herzberg's assessed employee satisfaction using a multiplicity of factors such as the work itself, pay, status, working conditions and so on. The underlying assumption was that there was a single continuum ranging from job satisfaction at one end to job dissatisfaction at the other. The Herzberg theory proposed that there were in fact two different continua, as follows:

- One class of factors, *hygiene factors*, makes up a continuum ranging from dissatisfaction to no dissatisfaction. Examples of these factors are pay, interpersonal relations, supervision, company policy, working conditions, job security, etc. Herzberg argued that these factors do not serve to promote job satisfaction. Their absence, however, can create job dissatisfaction. Their presence can only serve to eliminate dissatisfaction. These hygiene aspects were often referred to as the 'context of work'.

- The second class of factors, referred to as *motivation factors*, makes up a continuum leading from no satisfaction to satisfaction. Examples of motivators are the job itself being challenging, gaining recognition and scope for achievement, with the possibilities for growth, advancement and greater responsibility. If the worker is to be truly motivated, the job itself must be the source of that motivation (i.e. the 'job content'). All hygiene factors can do is eliminate dissatisfaction by cleaning up the environment (Herzberg 1966: 71–91).

Herzberg's approach to employee satisfaction rested on two assumptions about the nature of people: the need to avoid pain and the need to grow. Hygiene factors prevent dissatisfaction and pain by providing a good environment or work context. Motivation factors enable growth towards self-actualization. Herzberg arrived at these conclusions by surveying 200 engineers and accountants, but not operative-level workers. His methodology, that is, asking middle-class employees to report satisfaction or dissatisfaction with their job, and who were likely to attribute success to their own initiative (motivation factors), was also criticized (Fincham and Rhodes 1992: 112–13). However, given the two continua of hygiene and motivation needs found in the research, Herzberg argued that out of this we can discern two complementary continua based on, first, *mental health* and, second, *mental illness*.

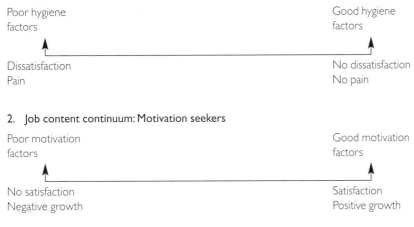

1. Job context continuum: Hygiene seekers

Poor hygiene
factors

Good hygiene
factors

Dissatisfaction
Pain

No dissatisfaction
No pain

2. Job content continuum: Motivation seekers

Poor motivation
factors

Good motivation
factors

No satisfaction
Negative growth

Satisfaction
Positive growth

Figure 7.1 Herzberg's needs typology

Source: Liz Fulop and Dennis Mortimer (1992) 'Job redesign strategies' in Fulop, L. with Frith, F. and Hayward, H. (eds),
Management for Australian Business: A Critical Text, *Melbourne: Macmillan, p. 83.*

There were four categories on the mentally healthy continuum, and three on the mentally ill
one (Herzberg 1966: 83-8).

In terms of a mentally healthy approach, Herzberg argued that self-fulfilment was found
in all personal growth experiences, including both work and non-work experiences. In
Herzberg's approach, a mentally healthy person was a motivation seeker who has a fixed set of
needs at the higher level of the hierarchy – this was unchangeable (Herzberg 1966: 81–91).
Herzberg argued that mental health requires a balance of both motivation and hygiene
factors. Hygiene seekers were put in the mental illness category because they could never
become motivation seekers, and vice versa. Figure 7.1 summarizes Herzberg's arguments.

Herzberg did not believe that all jobs were capable of being enriched – or for that matter
required enrichment. It was possible that hygiene seekers could be quite productive and satisfied in their jobs even if they were monotonous and deskilled ones (Herzberg 1987: 117).
However, in the case of motivation seekers, Herzberg believed that the principle of 'vertical
loading' (i.e. discretion) had to be an integral part of their job content. *Vertical (job) loading*
means designing jobs which increase motivation factors and allow for the psychological or
personal growth of the employee (i.e. achieve higher-order needs).

In order to develop the job content of motivation seekers, Herzberg proposed *job
enrichment,* which would increase basic skills on the horizontal level and autonomy and
responsibility on the vertical one. Job enrichment involves giving whole tasks to individuals
that require more complex skills and greater expertise. Through vertical job loading,
employees were given more responsibility, recognition, growth, achievement, challenge and
advancement. Herzberg was not particularly interested in looking at the effects of horizontal specialization, especially in relationship to unskilled work on assembly lines (Herzberg
1987: 114, 116). This is not surprising because he based his job enrichment theory on the
study of professional workers (i.e. engineers and accountants) who were not deskilled in
terms of horizontal specialization. The jobs Herzberg analyzed were highly amenable to
increases in discretion (i.e. problem solving or planning) (Child 1984: 36).

Herzberg's approach to job enrichment was improved upon and made popular by Richard Hackman, Greg Oldham and others, who developed the *job characteristics enrichment model* described in Figure 7.2 (hereafter called the *Hackman model*). In this model, needs are treated as a hierarchy and not two separate continua, as they were by Herzberg. The Hackman model suggests that in order to create job enrichment and job satisfaction, tasks have to be interesting and *meaningful*, entail *responsibility* for outcomes and provide *feedback* or *knowledge* about outcomes. These three components were the critical factors for high motivation, satisfaction and performance (Hackman and Oldham 1975: 162: see Figure 7.2). There are five *core dimensions of a job* and each of these impacts differently on job redesign. The first three, combining tasks, forming natural work units or teams and establishing client relations, make work meaningful, but not enriched. The remaining two, *vertical loading* (i.e. responsibility) and *feedback*, are the most important. Both of these relate to increasing discretion in a job and mean removing supervisory controls. The 'vertical loading' in Figure 7.2 is the core aspect of job enrichment. 'Personal and work outcomes' describe the expected benefits of job enrichment for the individual and the organization and satisfy growth needs.

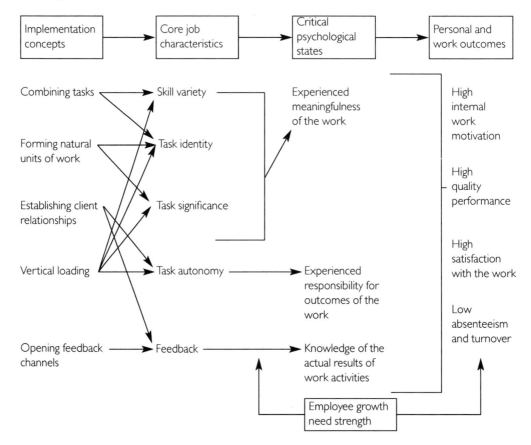

Figure 7.2 Job characteristics enrichment model

Source: From J. Richard Hackman, Greg Oldham, Robert Janson and Kenneth Purdy (1975), 'A new strategy for job enrichment', California Management Review *17(4) p. 58. Reprinted from* California Management Review *17.4 by permission of the Regents.*

Hackman and Oldham (1980: 82–8) state that individuals must have the knowledge and skills to perform their new tasks or jobs, otherwise frustration, stress and resentment will prevail. This might require training to allow success at an enriched job. According to the model, individuals whose jobs are to be enriched must have strong needs or desires for self-direction, learning and achievement or challenge. They must be intrinsically self-motivated. In Herzberg's term, they must be motivation seekers, but in Hackman and Oldham's, they must have high scores on *strength of growth needs,* a measure of commitment and the drive to succeed. According to the latter, studies show that high individual scores on the 'strength of growth needs' measure was strongly correlated with the attainment of job satisfaction from the enrichment of jobs, whereas low scores resulted in no satisfaction among workers even though their jobs had been enriched. Consistent with Herzberg and Maslow, Hackman's model of job enrichment suggests that lower-order needs (i.e. hygiene factors) must be satisfied if job enrichment is to be successful. However, the fact that the Hackman model introduced the notion of individual differences and needs put it into a slightly more acceptable form than Herzberg's original proposal, although those with high growth needs are still the only ones being targeted for enrichment (Child 1984: 36; Lansbury and Spillane 1983: 184). Moreover, in the model any failure to display the 'appropriate' need drives is an individual failure or weakness.

Job enrichment has been widely criticized for a number of reasons. First, the strategy seems more appropriate to professional jobs where limits on skill variety, task identity and task significance are more readily redressed. Second, it seems to be suited to individual tasks and not group ones. Third, it presumes universal, fixed needs for all workers and cannot explain or accommodate changing needs or wants, except as deviant behaviour or mental illness. Fourth, the approach fails to address the influence of contextual factors (e.g. unions, technology, wages, salaries and supervisory levels) in redesigning work; the moderators identified in Hackman's model relate to individual factors only. Fifth, the approach is managerialist since ideas for redesign are based on management's perceptions of the need for the strategies. Sixth, it presumes that motivation seekers will always need and welcome job enrichment, and thus assumes a continuous consensus between management and workers regarding job redesign. Last, the approach pays little attention to allowing worker participation in the job redesign strategy, and clearly rejects unions as a factor in improving job redesign (Buchanan 1979: 46–52; Fincham and Rhodes 1992: 126–30; Kelly 1982: 68–70; Strauss 1976).

A dynamic view of needs

David McClelland (1961) proposed a different view of motivation – one that included not only personality factors but social influences as well. Although this was not a theory of job redesign it offered a valuable corrective on the hierarchy of needs approach. McClelland did not subscribe to the view that people had a hierarchy of needs, but rather that needs varied based on the importance individuals attached to them. Needs can be significantly reordered in terms of priorities. McClelland (1961; McClelland and Burnham 1976) identified three basic needs of individuals: *need to achieve, need for power* and *need to affiliate.*

Need for achievement

The need to achieve is most closely related to business success. Persons with a high need to achieve react well to challenges while those with a low need to achieve are more likely to seek less stimulating and challenging work in order to avoid failure and risk taking. McClelland believed that the need for achievement, and the associated learning that supports this, is established early in life and is not easily changed. Ironically, McClelland noted that families who sought to instil self-control, high standards, individual initiative and independence were setting patterns for high need achievement. Yet in contrast, families who emphasized compliance, dependence, a collective orientation and getting on with others produced children with low need achievement (Fincham and Rhodes 1992: 73). Compliance, collective orientations and getting on with others (especially in team work) have often been cited as the basis of good management. McClelland believed that the need to achieve can be increased by training, which differs from Herzberg's view of fixed needs. The need to achieve is measured by a Thematic Apperception Test (TAT) (see below).

McClelland argued that high achievers set their own goals, are selective about the goals they pursue, tend to be independent in the choices they make and realistic about the likely success of these choices. High achievers seek immediate feedback. In McClelland's approach, people with high need achievement seek jobs that are already highly paid (thus not discrediting Herzberg) and offering them more pay has to be linked to some form of incentive for success by way of feedback.

The need to achieve seems to correlate positively with success among entrepreneurs, especially in small and medium-sized enterprises (SMEs). High achievers tend to seek careers in business and related areas, but do not necessarily make good managers because they tend to feel that they are the most competent person and will be reluctant to delegate (Fincham and Rhodes 1992: 83; Petzall, Selvarajah and Willis 1991: 62). One interesting aspect of McClelland's work was his attempt to show that the general level of achievement in individuals was linked with economic and technological growth in society (Fincham and Rhodes 1992: 73). Again, this emphasized a social dimension in explaining needs rather than seeing them as purely behavioural and innate.

Need for power

According to McClelland and David Burnham (1976), by including the dimensions of need for power and need for affiliation, it was possible to see how each of the three variables affected management's performance. McClelland and Richard Boyatzis (1982, cited in Fincham and Rhodes 1992: 83) found that effective or successful managers had a higher need for power than need for affinity. In short, they enjoy the exercise of power more than they enjoy being liked by colleagues or subordinates (Fincham and Rhodes 1992: 83). McClelland's concept of need for power also implied that there were two types of need for power. Negative power was used to dominate or exert undue influence over others and was the basis of corrupt and unsocialized forms of behaviour, such as using brute force to dominate subordinates. In contrast, positive or socialized use of power was associated with healthy competition, persuasion and interpersonal influence. The person who had a positive need for power was likely to excite and inspire followers to achieve higher goals and outcomes (Petzall *et al.* 1991: 62–3).

Need for affiliation

The need for affiliation is similar to the 'social man' theory of Mayo, and in McClelland's approach it is generally not associated with becoming a successful manager or with achieving high performance in the workplace. It is important, however, to balance the excessive need for power in its negative form. McClelland believed that there was only a moderate need for affiliation because of all the unpopular decisions a manager has to make. This might not hold true across all cultural groupings; for example Japanese managers have had strong need for affiliation encouraged in the workplace.

McClelland's work has been criticized on a number of counts, and was certainly not as popular as Herzberg's work. The method for establishing needs (i.e. the TAT test) is especially open to criticism. McClelland did not establish any sure way of measuring the needs he talks about. The TAT test is administered by an instructor and is based on subjects writing a story about a notional person seen in an image. Subjects usually project their own personalities and meanings onto the image or figure. Analyzing the 'stories' to select the various dimensions of needs was difficult to replicate. McClelland claimed needs, especially need for achievement, can be learnt but many others would reject this view, especially those psychoanalysts who believe that personality traits are established in youth and difficult to change (Petzall *et al.* 1991: 64). The theory is also presented as being culturally neutral and therefore hardly explains needs in different cultures despite the fact that McClelland conducted several cross-cultural studies. Nor does McClelland's theory recognize the importance of individual differences such as gender or age in defining various needs.

Nevertheless, researchers have used McClelland's ideas in trying to account for why women score lower on need achievement (using the TAT) than do men. One popular theory was that women who want to achieve also acquire a fear of success (Fincham and Rhodes 1992: 75, citing Horner 1972). The theory states that stress, anxiety and tension accompany this conflict in women with a high need for achievement and it can only be addressed by radical changes in the type of social learning that they are exposed to in early childhood. McClelland's theory at least supports early views that women's failure to achieve was at least as much explained by social factors as by individual predispositions (Wilson 1995: 297–301). However, McClelland gave only a crude indication of what constitutes factors important for high performance. Because his approach ignored a range of other factors that might also contribute to success and achievement in one's job, for example adequate resources to do the job or mentoring. Moreover, his focus was only on managers, as opposed to workers or other professionals, limiting his concept of 'needs' and thus exhibiting a bias similar to that found in Herzberg's work.

Motivation theory itself continued to produce other variants: *equity theory* (which proposed that individuals have an idea of what a 'fair' reward for their efforts is, and are affected adversely by either being paid too much or too little); *expectancy theory* (which argued that individuals are motivated according to whether they expect that they will be successful and whether the associated reward is valued); and various attempts to provide a motivational calculus to combine the two. However, we do not wish to dwell further on the specifics of motivation theory here, because our argument is that both job design and motivation have moved on under the influence of other disciplines such as systems theory, and the key current issues relating to both are now being addressed in literature, which does not always appear to be about either motivation or the technical specifics of job design. In the next section we look at a classic attempt to move beyond simple job design principles, sociotechnical systems, then we look at some more recent developments in the redesign of work, and follow that by looking at new ideas which relate to and, we argue, change considerably our understanding of motivational issues and issues beyond motivation.

Sociotechnical Systems (STS)

Some of the limitations of the job enrichment model(s) and needs theory were partially overcome in the emergence of the *sociotechnical systems (STS)* approach to job redesign. There are four critical factors in the STS approach:

1 analysis was switched from individuals to work groups;
2 small-group theory was integrated with systems theory, thus broadening the factors involved in redesign;
3 three systems were identified as being critical in job redesign (the technological, the social and the economic systems);
4 the creation of cohesive, self-regulating, autonomous work groups became the 'one best way' for redesigning jobs.

At its simplest level, the STS approach can be said to involve making a group autonomous and responsible for a whole task(s) in which the integration of technical and social aspects of work take precedence (Buchanan 1979: 98–114; Child 1984: 34–5; Dunphy 1981: 47–9, 163, 196–7; Dawson 1986: 67–9; Lansbury and Spillane 1983: 122–31). Attention to the group nature of work was the focus of the Tavistock Institute of Human Relations in London and of researchers such as Eric Trist and Kenneth Bamforth (1951), Fred Emery (1969), Eric Miller and Albert Rice (1967). Their work stated that organizations consisted of interdependent social and technical systems, operating in an economic environment. It was argued that managers had a degree of choice in the way they structured or designed work, and that the best design was the one which aimed for joint optimization of both social and technical systems (Lupton 1971: 66–70).

This approach was first developed in the context of a study of the effects of mechanization in British coal mining (Trist and Bamforth 1951: 3–38). The advent of coal-cutters and mechanical conveyors had made possible the working of a single long face in place of a series of short coal faces. In 'shortwall working', the focus was on a small group consisting of a skilled man and his mate, assisted by several labourers. The new 'longwall' method was organized around a coal face group of 40 to 50 men with task specialization according to shift, very specific job roles and different methods of payment per shift. It therefore took on the characteristics of a small factory system, which broke down the previous system of autonomous small groups. This breakdown led to manifestations of the miners' isolation and frustrations, such as different shifts blaming each other for failures, petty deceptions with regard to timekeeping and reporting for work, and informal cliques developing across small parts of the workplace, leaving some workers isolated. The reduced autonomy involved in the new process also made it virtually impossible for management to pinpoint the source of the problem.

Trist and Bamforth found that an alternative system, known as the 'composite longwall method', was possible within the same technological and economic constraints. This involved the reintroduction of work groups responsible for the whole task. Within each group, members allocated themselves to shifts and to jobs and were paid according to a group bonus. Instead of perpetuating blame across shifts, the new system led to situations where members of a group who finished their tasks early would stay on to undertake the next activity in the sequence to help group members on the next shift. This system was better geared to the workers' social needs and psychological needs for greater job autonomy and close working relationships, and therefore led to greater productivity, job satisfaction and reduced absenteeism (Pugh, Hickson and Hinings 1983: 84–6).

Trist and Bamforth's study showed the importance of the *semi-autonomous group* aspects of work, as well as viewing the role of work from the perspective of those actually undertaking it, rather than on the basis of an imposed perspective, such as that of Maslow and Herzberg. This study led Trist to the conclusion that working groups were neither technical nor social systems, but interdependent ones. The 'technical system' referred to equipment layout, workflows, interdependence of tasks and task uncertainty (i.e. whether a task is routine or not). The 'social system' referred to the social and psychological characteristics of workers. Later work by members of the Tavistock Institute, such as that of Miller and Rice (1967), however, became prescriptive in assuming workers' needs, especially affiliation and security needs (Buchanan 1979: 95, 109, 131; Honour and Mainwaring 1982: 82).

Even though the STS approach expanded the strategies for job redesign, its human relations origins made it compatible with job enrichment strategies. Thus many of its underlying assumptions, especially relating to the needs of workers, the role of management and external groups (i.e. unions) remained the same as in job enrichment (Honour and Mainwaring 1982: 82). However, STS departed from job enrichment in a number of ways: the level of worker participation in the design of tasks; the importance of group work or teams; incentive schemes (the 'economic man' concept); and the flexibility in setting standards. The STS approach principally departed from job enrichment principles because of the creation of semi-autonomous work groups or self-managing work teams as shown in Chapter 6 in NUMMI and Uddevalla.

Redefining motivation through TQM

During the 1980s the success of Japanese car manufacturers, especially in terms of quality and productivity, led to a new wave of interest in job redesign focused on quality principles and practices (Womack, Jones and Roos 1990). Just as Taylor before them, the new engineering gurus of total quality management (TQM), such as W. Edwards Deming (1986), Joseph Juran (1988, 1989) and Phillip Crosby (1979), set out to create a 'new mental revolution' in management. This new mental revolution was, in its most optimistic form, supposed to undo or reverse some of the most negative aspects of Taylorism, while at the same time incorporating the more progressive and humanistic elements of job enrichment and STS. Its underlying philosophy was *continuous improvement* as mentioned in Chapter 6.

As David Boje and Robert Winsor (1993) argue, TQM went far beyond other job redesign strategies because it sought to establish a carefully integrated programme of social and psychological engineering. Yet in the late 1980s and early 1990s, TQM was seen as one of the main vehicles for regaining the competitive advantage and restoring the pride and integrity of US manufacturing (Boje and Winsor 1993: 57–8). Of course TQM was not confined to manufacturing and in many Western countries was introduced into the public sector as well.

In both theory and practice, TQM sought to transform the entire work culture or ethic of Western business to reflect values, norms and attitudes (i.e. culture) to mirror Japanese workplaces, particularly trying to instil loyalty, trust and commitment by building a strong collective orientation to continuous improvement (see Chapter 6). The origins of TQM are disputed, but once taken out of the Japanese context, its ethos and implementation in Western businesses were problematical and achieved uneven success. As Boje and Winsor (1993) suggest, the view favoured in the USA was that TQM had been pioneered in Japanese business through the transfer of American management know-how, and that it was logical to attribute the success of Japanese manufacturing, at least in equal part, to American ingenuity.

However, many commentaries on TQM and Japanese management practices point out that even before Deming *et al.* arrived in Japan, lean production, using Fordist methods and Taylorism, had already been incorporated into Japanese manufacturing in firms such as Toyota. So too had the now well documented practices of life-time employment (supported by employee contributions to retirement accounts); apprenticeship training; company festivals and celebrations; school programmes emphasizing factory loyalty and the virtues of the efficiency of workers (i.e. the work ethic); company housing; company welfare and health services; and company funded education of the employee's children to adopt appropriate work attitudes and behaviour, such as emphasizing maths and science in curricula. Boje and Winsor (1993: 59), along with others, noted that the aforementioned factors were the pillars of building loyalty, commitment and a collective work ethic. They said these changes were entrenched by the 1920s in Japanese business and were reinforced by appeals to the Samurai tradition of constant learning and training to achieve perfection, along with other principles of mutual help and self-effacing contentment in helping others.

Later work practices, such as on the job training involving both reskilling (learning new work roles that are similar) and multiskilling (learning new and varied tasks and skills), job rotation, seniority-based wage and promotion systems, were also introduced. The seniority system meant that length of service, and hence loyalty to the organization, was valued and rewarded. Enterprise unions and bargaining (based and supported by the company) were also introduced. A relatively homogeneous and masculine workforce in the ranks of executives, engineers and supervisors in the large companies helped create an image of extreme industrial harmony, happiness and contentment of the workforce.

The concept of *Kaizen* or continuous improvement formed the guiding philosophy or framework for quality programmes such as TQM. *Kaizen* encompassed deeply entrenched norms and values aimed at building a strong culture of meticulous, detailed and incremental improvements. It also incorporated a set of tools and strategies used to reinforce quality practices. TQM led to the widespread use of statistical control methods and, in many respects, brought back to many workplaces the inflexibility and control elements so prevalent in Taylorism as evidenced in NUMMI (see Chapter 6). Although opinions vary, the core principles of TQM are described in Exhibit 7.3.

- Top management leadership of quality improvements, akin to heroic leadership or inspirational leadership.
- Customer focus (internal and external to organization) – driven by a service to the customer ethos.
- No tolerance for errors; prevention of anticipated problems or 'defects' to products or service.
- Fact-based decisions using a range of tools and techniques based on statistical quality control and a range of decision science techniques.
- Long-term planning and change with incremental improvements the norm.
- Teamwork using various types of teams to produce organization-wide quality practices.
- A culture of continuous improvement to help build trust and to eradicate the fear among employees of reporting errors, defects or mistakes in the work process or coming forward with suggestions for improvement – a direct legacy of Taylorism and the 'great mental divide' between managers and workers.

Exhibit 7.3   Principles of TQM

In terms of job redesign and motivation, TQM introduces a number of subtle changes in how job satisfaction is addressed, particularly in shifting the degree of accountability and control for outcomes back to the very group of workers who Taylor considered incapable of 'brain work' (see Chapter 6). It also deviates from the principles of specialization and division of labour as the keys to success and instead, focuses on new scientific tools and methods which, through training, are to be used by all employees to improve performance across all work processes. Building on STS theories, teams were to become the important units of production and no longer the isolated individual 'economic man' of Taylor's approach.

More importantly, proponents of TQM, as well as those of business re-engineering (e.g. Hammer and Champy 1993 below), believe that many Western organizations were dominated by specialists employed in narrow 'functional silos', such as marketing, accountancy and information systems, who looked inward to their departments and only cooperated when tasks straddled functional areas. In developing this cooperation they often created new layers of management to coordinate these tasks thereby creating more hierarchies in the organization. Both approaches argue that to redesign procedures or processes, which produce or supply something that customers value, means becoming outwardly focused. TQM is driven by the philosophy of service to customers, using new scientific methods, tools, rules and procedures to deliver value to customers. As Walter Balk (1995: 246) suggests, this brought accountability to external needs or constituents into the job redesign context.

An organization's structure does not necessarily change with TQM, but rather teams of various sorts replace individual approaches to work. Collective forms of problem solving and decision making become important. Delegation to teams for solving problems, creating continuous improvement projects, and building commitment to quality values are emphasized. Teams are encouraged to communicate up the hierarchy to improve processes and procedures. Self-regulation and self-control are devolved to teams (as discussed in Chapter 6). Steering committees, comprising top management, are still seen as 'the brain of TQM' (Cox 1995: 105), and these top management teams are meant to set goals and objectives to be achieved through TQM programmes and initiate TQM's introduction. Action teams, comprising lower-level participants and those who are volunteers, become the 'heart and soul' of TQM initiatives (Cox 1995: 106). Action teams can implement changes that they see as necessary without the authority of senior management (as described at NUMMI and Uddevalla in Chapter 6). Once TQM is implemented, action teams disappear and improvement teams are supposed to replace them. These teams can be either permanent or temporary, open to all, and focused on solving specific problems as an ongoing part of everyday work practices (Cox 1995: 106).

As already mentioned in Chapter 6, the team approach used in TQM is claimed to institutionalize the idea of collective control through teams as opposed to management control. A punitive form of peer assessment for errors or mistakes affecting a team's performance increases pressures for conformity and surveillance from within teams. These negative aspects of TQM have been particularly evident in Japanese 'transplant' companies where, for example, such things as flashing lights, buzzers and sirens are used regularly when a particular area of the production process is slowed down or an operator has difficulty keeping pace with production (Boje and Winsor 1993: 63).

As pointed out, at Uddevalla *Kaizen* methods were also introduced (see Chapter 6) but without the 'surveillance' regime of many Japanese transplant companies. The *Kaizen* philosophy was only one component of the approach used in Uddevalla to enhance performance and tap the different levels of knowledge needed to redesign jobs and enhance team-based learning. More importantly, the Uddevalla teams were not homogeneous, but rather accommodated diversity in the workplace and different forms of self-identity. TQM, viewed from a strictly Japanese transplant perspective, places little importance on managing diversity in teams and places enormous pressure on group conformity. Rigid training espoused by TQM proponents is also meant to ensure workers' conceptualize, interpret and frame quality problems in similar frameworks, and consensus decision making becomes the norm. There is little regard for the sense-making capacities of individuals and any view of them as active subjects with interpretive powers of their own (De Cock and Hipkin 1997: 670). As Christian De Cock and Ian Hipkin suggest (1997: 671, citing Spencer 1994) '…even though TQM…programmes may provide greater freedom of action than [more] mechanistic management practices, [they] actually may reduce freedom of choice by submitting employees to awareness training designed to create a common frame of reference and to skills training aimed at establishing preferred ways of solving problems and working in teams'. As such, TQM adopts a highly unitarist view (see Chapter 4).

Even though participation and empowerment are claimed to be the rewards for working in TQM teams, Balk argues that participation is not necessarily its own reward and after the first 'flush' of enthusiasm has dissipated, team members are likely to look for extrinsic and intrinsic rewards on an individual basis. Some small rewards have been offered under the 'suggestion' system, institutionalized through TQM, as a way of gathering up the knowledge of employees (also see Chapter 6 and the NUMMI example). As the following quote indicates:

> …a suggestion system implemented at Canon, Inc. yielded suggestions in 1983 alone worth a total of $100 million…In 1987, about 350 large Japanese companies saved approximately $2 billion from the implementation of employee suggestions… 'a small…token of recognition'…[T]he system used by Hewlett-Packard, where, to receive the *maximum* reward of $80 (which must be approved by the 'functional manager', which is three levels above the worker), employees are required to make a detailed suggestion which must be graded with perfect scores under five criteria and save the company at least $3,000 in the first year alone.

Then, in an annual 'award ceremony', a 'plaque' and a token of appreciation, such as a 'designer watch' are awarded to the *six best suggestions of the year*. In another example, a NUMMI worker's innovative and time-saving suggestion earned him '20 points' in the suggestion programme – equivalent to a bath towel or pair of socks…Overall, suggestion systems typically yield insignificant awards to the suggester…while resulting in immense savings to the company. Obviously there is little in these schemes which is of benefit to the employees, other than the increased workloads which frequently result (abbreviated from Boje and Winsor 1993).

As the above quote also demonstrates, TQM does not of itself reduce hierarchy and can increase it through the excessive formalization that the programme requires. As a job redesign strategy, TQM relies heavily on what Balk (1995: 246) terms 'analytical accountability'. The TQM approach assumes that team members will be motivated to continually monitor and improve their own performance using statistical and analytical techniques acquired through training. Balk points out that not everyone has the same interest or capacity to absorb such information (1995: 252). Others question if such training really leads to organizational learning and to promoting innovation and creativity. The training focus of TQM is claimed not to appeal to more educated and skilled workers who are apt to want more autonomy, creativity and control than TQM allows.

Perhaps one of the most subtle aspects of TQM has been the shift away from understanding employee needs and other motivational responses that were thought to enable management to control performance by manipulating worker satisfaction (Balk 1995: 246). At its extreme, TQM recasts the notion of employee satisfaction to one which depends on a complete subordination of the individual to the collective whole, be it the team, the organization or its culture. This 'subordination' is based on a form of corporate citizenship which demands considerable trust, loyalty and commitment on the part of organizational members. In Chapter 2 we raised concerns about the implications of the notion of a strong culture for managing diversity, change and organizational learning. We noted that in organizations where there are strong professional groupings, such as in hospitals and universities, it is difficult to create one all-embracing culture, whether it be based on quality or something else. In organizations that operate in a crisis mode, the same was evident.

As stated elsewhere (Halachami and Bouckaert 1995), there have been huge differences between the public and private sectors in respect of implementing TQM programmes. Some large organizations, such as Kodak-Eastman, boast great success with TQM as a change programme, while other companies who have tried it have subsequently abandoned TQM because it was either too costly, time consuming, bureaucratic or achieved few short-term gains. Other firms have expressed disappointment with results and the general lack of commitment by management to a 10–12 year programme of improvement, which is claimed to be the time frame for creating an organization-wide culture of improvement (see also De Cock and Hipkin 1997: 661).

Differences in markets, technology, 'culture', personnel and politics between organizations has meant that the principles of TQM have been introduced in many and varied ways, as indeed the NUMMI and Uddevalla cases demonstrate. This is also aptly illustrated by the case of Corning Inc. in the USA (see also Chapter 2), which embarked on a traditional quality programme as shown in Exhibit 7.4, but also sought to include issues relating to diversity.

The Policy

It is the policy of Corning to achieve total quality performance in meeting the requirements of external and internal customers. Total quality performance means understanding who the customers are, what the requirements are, and meeting those requirements, without error, on time, every time.

The Four Principles of the Total Quality Campaign

1. Meet the customer's requirements (definition of quality) – Quality is meeting the customer's requirements. The customer is everyone an employee deals with. It's absolutely vital that we understand and agree on requirements before starting an assignment.
2. Error-free work (standard of performance) – Errors are not acceptable.
3. Manage by prevention (method) – Quality must be built into the work.
4. Measure by the cost of quality (measure) – The cost of quality is made up of three parts: error cost, detection cost, and prevention cost. Often, as prevention cost rises, overall cost of quality falls.

Organizing for Quality

- The Quality Improvement Team
- Division Quality Executive
- The Management Committee
- The Corrective Action Team
- The Quality Council

Key Quality Events

1984   Quality Institute opened.
        Organization wide climate survey.
1985   Corporate statement of Corning values.
        James Houghton suggested, 'Decide on your top three vital issues. Pick one. Remove it. Permanently.'
1986   Goals set for 1991.
1987   National Quality Month chaired by James Houghton.
        The year of delighting the customer.
1988   Focus on total quality skills: benchmarking, process management approach, service quality, customer/supplier partnerships, union–management quality reviews, workplace partnerships, and using the criteria of the Baldrige award to judge quality.

Corporate Quality Goals Set in 1986 for 1991

1. To spend 5% of our time on education and training as a company.
2. To reduce by 90% the key errors in the company by using the *vital few concept* – picking the few most critical errors and solving them.
3. To introduce no new product that is not at least equal in quality to the product it is replacing or to the competition. You cannot ship your learning curve to the customer.

Exhibit 7.4   The TQM system at Corning

Source: Christopher Bartlett and Sumantra Ghoshal (1992), Transnational Management: Text, Cases and Readings in Cross-Border Management, *Homewood, Ill.: Irwin, p. 451.*

While Corning appears to have adopted a fairly conventional approach to TQM, it also appointed a quality-improvement team in 1986 to begin tackling the problem of how to retain and develop talented women and African-Americans. To improve quality, Corning considered it important to ensure that each employee had the opportunity '…to participate fully, to grow professionally, and to develop to his or her highest potential' (Hall and Parker 1993: 8). Listed below are the key initiatives that followed.

- Race and gender awareness training, in which aspects of corporate culture that inhibit flexibility are identified and addressed. For example, new employees are no longer encouraged to adopt the dress, style and social activities of the white male majority.
- Child-care services and expanded family-care leaves.
- Community-oriented projects that make the Corning geographical area more attractive to African-Americans.
- Career-planning systems for all, and more widely disseminated information about the processes for promotion.
- Incorporation of workplace flexibility into managerial performance ratings. Management performance in this area now affects raises and bonuses.
- Slow changes in the culture regarding the varied styles of different employees. Diverse styles are seen as a strength that helps the company relate to the varied styles of its customers.

Thus far, the changes seem to be working: the recruitment, retention, and advancement of women and African-Americans have all improved, and attention is now being directed to members of other racial groups (Hall and Parker 1993: 8). The question might be asked: why did Corning deviate from other TQM programmes? The criticisms of TQM outlined here, and elsewhere, repeatedly draw attention to the fact that the programme never works or follows the implementation strategies suggested by their proponents. Yet organizational members are always actively engaged in creating meanings and trying to interpret a whole array of management discourses – especially those of the gurus of management (see Chapter 1). When embarking on a TQM programme, managers have to appropriate language and the popular discourse of TQM into their own 'organizational' texts. They have to impose or introduce these texts into their own unique politicized contexts through discussions, meetings, negotiations, strategic planning days, and decision-making processes (see Chapters 8 and 11). The Corning example is a representation of Corning's TQM text, with its own meanings inscribed, from which other managers could learn but never recreate exactly the same programme in other situations. While other managers might try to reinterpret the Corning experience and fashion their own texts, they would still produce different outcomes and departures from the dominant discourse.

The 'failures' noted in the literature on TQM programmes, and the critique made of the approach, provide warnings to managers about confusing the TQM discourse with the texts of TQM that are peculiar to each organization. The TQM discourse privileges certain forms of knowledge (e.g. science based), is silent on other organizational issues such as politics and power, and marginalizes the positions of some groups in terms of their agency and identities, as shown in Chapter 6 at NUMMI. Yet the texts managers develop using TQM need not reproduce these privileging and marginalizing 'projects' as Corning shows.

Business re-engineering

The general disenchantment with TQM, or more particularly its focus on incremental or gradual process and systems improvements, led to the more radical job redesign strategy of *business re-engineering* (BR) and *business process re-engineering* (BPR). The most popular proponents of BR and BPR are Michael Hammer and James Champy (1993) and Thomas Davenport (1993). Unlike TQM, which focuses on continuous improvement, BR and BPR advocate radical improvements in costs, quality and service by starting from scratch or with a 'blank' or clean sheet of paper (Hammer and Champy 1993: 21, 134). Three key principles drive the BR and BPR processes – customers, competition and change. Inefficiencies of Scientific Management (fragmentation of tasks, many supervisory layers, bureaucracy) and other management methods have created what Hammer and Champy see as fragmented functional departments, narrowly focused over-manned organizations with many layers of management, and inflexible methods and systems. For Hammer and Champy, the focus of a business is its markets and a 'process' is anything the business produces that is of value to customers.

Under BR or BPR, to improve processes means looking at how things are done in an organization or asking why they are done at all rather than tinkering with existing processes. In Hammer and Champy's view, many processes exist because of historical precedent (i.e. 'the way we do it around here') or because of commonsense thinking rather than applying rational methods. BR and BPR depend on developing systems using information technology (IT), and using teams that mirror the processes that the business actually works around rather than the functions (e.g. marketing, finance) used to execute processes (De Cock and Hipkin 1997: 662).

Hammer, Champy and Davenport's ideas are IT driven (Oliver 1993), and they have built their BR and BPR approaches around an IT revolution occurring in organizations – in a sense similar to Taylor's version of a mental revolution led by the stopwatch! An example of an IT-driven BPR process would be Hewlett-Packard streamlining its purchasing functions by centrally developing block contracts for purchase of goods and using technology to develop a database to disseminate information to everyone in the organization relating to approved suppliers they can use. This achieves two of the early aims of BR and BPR – reducing staff levels and overhead costs (e.g. levels of inventory, telephone costs) (Hammer 1990, cited in De Cock and Hipkin 1997: 662).

Yet one major problem with BR and BPR is that the terms mean different things. Whereas BR suggests organization-wide change, BPR implies that only certain processes will be targeted for radical change or even elimination (Buchanan 1995: 5). According to David Buchanan, neither Hammer and Champy nor Davenport specify exactly what constitutes core processes. Those sympathetic to BR and BPR suggest this ambiguity is not a problem and is to be expected in a new approach. Others less sympathetic to the approach describe re-engineering as a consulting fad and a repacking of old ideas that are sold as a 'fresh start' approach implying all business activities can be up for review (Oliver 1993). The notion of being able to start afresh is questioned by many theorists.

Hammer and Champy stress that radical change or process re-engineering will not make people happy, will mean that some employees will lose their jobs and certainly will not advantage everyone. Even though they make it clear that they are not talking about restructuring or downsizing (which they say is doing less with less), but with doing more with less

(Hammer and Champy 1993: 48), a key characteristic of re-engineering is combining or eliminating jobs. For this reason, proponents of BR argue that the leaders of re-engineering have to be visionary, motivators (to build commitment) and 'leg breakers' (Stewart 1993), that is, to be able to inflict the hardship that BR implies for many employees. Hammer and Champy see the main drive and motivation for change coming from a senior executive who has the clout to turn the organization inside out and upside down (1993: 103).

The BR and BPR approaches espoused by Hammer, Champy and Davenport send confusing messages about job redesign and motivation. For example, cultures take a long time to change or establish; however, by contrast, BR and BPR suggest that radical change or creating a new dynamic culture is possible. Buchanan (1995: 5) argues that the re-engineering approach adopts a job enrichment approach, coupled with a 1970s view of cultural change in organizations (focusing on changing values, attitudes and beliefs) and empowerment, with its pluralist connotations (see Chapter 4). He says it is premised on the following prescriptions: multiskilled work (job enrichment), activity carried out in cross-functional teams (form of STS), flatter organizational structures and executives leading and not directing change (as under Taylorism) (Buchanan 1995: 4). Davenport also emphasizes the importance of cross-functional teams and organization culture – a culture that leads to empowerment, participation in decision making and open communication. Participative cultures become a prerequisite for higher productivity and employee satisfaction.

Hammer and Champy (1993: 71–2) believe that employees who are educated (i.e. knowledge workers) will form the core of future organizations thereby shifting the emphasis from training to education. These 'brain workers' constitute the 'right' type of employees for the challenges of re-engineering, that is, people who, using McClelland's term, have a high need for achievement. But Hammer and Champy insist that character is important for empowerment. People will be highly rewarded for individual achievements, for self-discipline and as long as they are self-starters and prepared to do everything to serve the customer. Presumably these people will be less in fear of losing their jobs, less inclined to want job security, less stressed by riveting change and be more individualistically oriented employees. As Hammer and Champy argue – old departments, divisions, titles and groups cease to matter. Psychological and political disruptions accompany these changes and without strong leadership the BR or BPR processes can be sabotaged (Hall, Rosenthal and Wade 1993: 119).

The most common examples of firms adopting BR and BPR given by Hammer and Champy and Davenport are those experiencing crises, struggles for survival or tough economic downturns. Claims of success for BR and BPR are as common as are the claims of failure. Claims of success for BPR comprise mainly case examples such as IBM Credit reducing the time to prepare a quote for buying or leasing a computer from seven days to four hours and increasing the number of deals a hundredfold (Hammer and Champy 1993: 38–9). Failures tend to focus on the inability of re-engineering programmes to meet performance targets, such as reducing costs, increasing profits or the value of shares (Mishra, Spreitzer and Mishra 1998: 84; Hall *et al.* 1993: 120). Stripping the organization of its knowledge repositories (see Chapter 8), and the people needed to undertake tasks when the organization 'turns around', are also seen as down sides of re-engineering.

De Cock and Hipkin (1997: 662–3) further suggest that studies of BPR show that the methods used to implement it are often simplistic and mechanistic, such as accountants determining the percentage reduction needed to improve 'bottom line' figures (e.g. profit, sales, turnover), and then BPR being used to legitimate drastic or radical cutbacks. Indeed, the authors quote studies that reveal BPR is not a single method, but many different approaches that do not in any way make it clear what the long-term successes are. Little is said about managing the human costs or the morale and motivation of those left behind or of the managers who have to carry out the downsizing exercises. A survey of employees in the USA found only 31 percent saying they still trusted their organizations after re-engineering. Survivors generally reduce their commitment if they consider the downsizing process was unfair. Managers who have to implement layoffs '…often become abrasive, narcissistic, withdrawn, alienated, apathetic, or depressed. Many blame themselves for the harm they have caused others' (Mishra *et al.* 1998: 84). The authors even suggest that contrary to the rhetoric of empowerment and being 'coaches' of change, many BPR programmes are extremely dictatorial and hierarchical, that is, determined and pushed through by senior management (De Cock and Hipkin 1997: 670; Mishra *et al.* 1998: 84).

The meaning of work

One of the factors affecting the success of job redesign strategies and other similar initiatives is the question of what work means to those who actually do it – a question largely ignored by job redesign strategies such as TQM and BPR. Studies on *orientations to work* have drawn a distinction between workers' needs and wants (Goldthorpe, Lockwood, Bechofer and Platt 1968). Instead of accepting that employees all have an inbuilt hierarchy of needs, the orientation to work approach (sometimes referred to as the *social action approach*) proposed that employee attitudes and behaviour should be understood in terms of the realities of a particular situation and based on the employees' own definitions of what work meant to them. Whereas self-actualizing theories of behaviour focused on the satisfaction of universal needs, the orientation to work approach claimed workers have variable wants that are not hierarchically arranged, but shift and change depending on the situation of the worker. Wants are not psychological constants as proposed in the hierarchy of needs; in other words, individuals order their priorities and act accordingly. Thus money and financial rewards may take precedence over career pathing and multiskilling if financial problems beset employees, who may change jobs in order to satisfy this want, even though they have, in Maslow's terms, reached the top of the self-actualizing hierarchy. The employee is not deviant or mentally ill, but rather making a rational choice or even an emotional one based on his or her assessment of priorities and preferences (Dawson 1986: 11–12; Lansbury and Spillane 1983: 139–40; Rose 1975: 23–42).

Some new directions in motivation theory have also linked the psychological treatment of motivation to the idea of the *meaning of work*, which has traditionally been a sociological question. Stephen Fineman (1983), through a study of unemployed executives, argues that studies of people in work can only provide a limited view of what is important to them, as much of what work provides is taken for granted or unconscious and until it is removed the individual is not aware of it. He argues that both our individual sense of what it means to be a person implicitly involves the idea of being a working person for many people. Similarly, our position in the social structure and among our circle of friends is affected. Think about what happens when one member of a working couple becomes unemployed, and is transformed from breadwinner or equal partner to dependent husband/wife or failed provider –

they experience a loss of identity. Work, he argues, is far more important to our late twentieth century psyche than most studies can acknowledge. The implications of this are that changes to the structure of work, increasingly part-time, flexible employment, inevitably affect our view of ourselves as persons – in other words they affect the structure of consciousness as well.

Burkard Sievers (1995), in a collection of studies originally written from 1985 onwards, argues that changes in the structure of work have deskilled many jobs and have made work more meaningless. Corporations, instead of recognizing this, have sought to place the blame on the individual and have treated it as a problem of motivation. They have addressed this through reward structures, but mainly through the development of strong collective corporate cultures and teams with which the individual can identify. This superficial sense of corporate community, he argues, is a mere distraction from the fact that the work remains intrinsically meaningless – motivation as a surrogate for meaning. Think about Disneyland or McDonald's he argues – behind the powerful family image of the company, both internally and externally, and the importance of team membership, are two highly Tayloristic organizations which studies have demonstrated depend on a high proportion of expendable part-time and contract labour and a punitive control system. George Ritzer (1990) makes similar arguments in a very provocative text on the influence of McDonald's and its processes on society at large. Ritzer argues that society is undergoing a process of 'McDonaldization' – that standardization and control are spreading on a global scale as large corporations acquire the power to dominate and homogenize their markets, which of course drives down the cost of sales. This is coupled with a push to drive down costs of production and disempower trade unions which leaves employees in a state of frequently oppressive exploitation, contradicting the image the company projects of wholesome family values and charitable corporate giving.

Howard Schwartz (1990) looks more deeply at this corporate 'meaning making' process. He demonstrates that when corporations attempt to make meaning – or at least this rather easy version of meaning – they are usurping what he calls the *ontological function* for individuals. In other words, we all need to ask, and to know, 'who am I?' When we enter the world the process of finding the answer is essential to our becoming fully developed individuals. Corporations with strong cultures, or who purport to have them, in effect say 'you do not need to ask, we'll tell you. Just do as we do, be one of us and the question is irrelevant.' As a result, Schwartz argues, something very dangerous happens. People stop asking important questions, and in significant ways stop thinking for themselves. His interest is in how supposedly excellent corporations can act in reckless and dangerous ways, with little regard for the safety of the rest of the world, while continuing to believe in their own righteousness. He discusses anti-social actions of committed organizational participants – in other words how large numbers of sane and well-meaning people can come to do things which actually or potentially damage the lives of even larger numbers of others. He uses the example of NASA and the Challenger disaster to illustrate this idea. Because of the way the NASA culture had developed, its members were unwilling to acknowledge that NASA could make mistakes and so denied or covered them up all along the line, while still believing they were right. Schwartz argues that the Challenger disaster (or some other one) had to happen sooner or later. The members of the organization were in effect addicted to their own organizational rhetoric – a condition which Schwartz calls *corporate narcissism* – which fed their fantasy of who they were, and they had to get more and more of it until reality, in the form of a disaster, rudely intervened (see Chapter 5).

Cross-cultural issues in motivation and job design

Another dimension that raises questions for the assumptions behind job design strategies is the issue of cultural relativity. As Geert Hofstede (1988: 119) points out, even without carrying out specific studies on motivation, theoretical knowledge of cultural orientations indicates a strong likelihood that existing motivational theories, dominated by a Western and indeed American sense of individuality, would not apply. Indeed, Hofstede argues that the USA has a combination of traits – low uncertainty avoidance (i.e. willingness to take risks), high masculinity (concern with performance, measurement, quantity), ultra-high individualism and moderate power distance (acceptance of authority) – that make it highly likely that human behaviour would be described or interpreted in terms of self-interest, and that needs-based theories like Maslow's hierarchy of needs and McClelland's approach are a natural consequence of such an orientation.

In looking at how other countries are grouped in terms of significant traits, Hofstede identifies three main groups: countries high in *achievement motivation* (performance and risk); countries high in *security motivation* (performance plus security); and countries high in *social motivation* (quality of life/security; but another variety can combine quality of life with risk). This last category may also be combined with collectivism, especially in Asia.

Hofstede notes that other countries high in achievement motivation scored high on McClelland's measure of achievement need, while countries in the other categories did not. Indeed, he argues that this type of motivation is found '… exclusively in countries in the Anglo-American group and some of their former colonies' (Hofstede 1988: 121). He also notes that the term 'achievement' is hardly capable of translation into other languages and could not be used in his cross-cultural research questionnaire.

Hofstede also notes, with importance for our consideration of job and work redesign, that the US approach has been predictably towards job enrichment and the restructuring of individual jobs. In contrast, Scandinavian countries have emphasized restructuring into group work. His explanation is that in the USA 'humanization' equates to 'masculinization' – greater opportunity to perform as an individual. In Scandinavia, this means greater 'feminization' – improving interpersonal relationships and reducing personal competitiveness. This reflection would seem to find some support in the differing circumstances of both NUMMI's 'learning bureaucracy' and Uddevalla's 'learning environment' (see Chapters 1 and 6).

Several studies have sought to test some of the classical theories in other cultures, as discussed extensively by Robert Westwood (1992) with regard to South East Asia (see Chapter 5). Westwood notes that the picture is confusing, but that studies have led to some significant modifications to theory in these different contexts, which we summarize in Exhibit 7.5.

1. McClelland's *need for achievement* (NAch) can be divided into two subtypes – *individual oriented* (IOAch) and *social oriented* (SOAch). This explains the high achievement scores of Chinese communities which are otherwise very different from Anglo-American cultures. Put simply, in these high collectivist cultures, achievement is for the family and not for oneself (Westwood 1992: 299; Yang 1982, 1986; Yu 1974).

2. Sociability, security and status needs are defined by Hsu (1971) as essentially *social* phenomena. Yang (1981) agrees that 'fitting in' to external social norms can be a strong motivator, with individuals acting to preserve face and avoid punishment, rejection, conflict, blame, embarrassment or ridicule. Bond and Hwang (1986) link this view to that of Snyder (1979) and *social facilitation* theory (Mitchell and Larson 1987), which argues that the mere presence of others is a motivating factor in social action. People perform for others, and in ways which recognize audience, appropriateness and acceptability, being aware that these performances, whether formal or informal, are being evaluated. We seek to look good and avoid looking bad. This aspect of motivation has been, with the possible exception of the work of Erving Goffman, neglected in Western motivation theory, but cross-cultural considerations should cause a reassessment of its importance (see 'Social view of motivation' below).

3. Yu (1991) found from tests of Herzberg's model, *three* factors rather than two. He discovered that rather than just *motivators* and *hygiene factors*, there were also clear *demotivators* (usually bipolar opposites of motivators).

4. Equity theory, which applies not so much to motivation but to reward, argues that people pay attention to the fairness or equity of the rewards they get for their efforts relative to others, whether overpaid or underpaid, and adjust the quality or quantity of their work accordingly. Most of the research supporting this has been via laboratory experiments, so its applicability to real situations is questionable. However, Yu (1991) noted that people will accept some differences in outcomes, and even inequity, before they feel that they have to make a response or protest (Westwood 1992: 307). Based on research in China he calls this the *equity difference threshold* – which determines whether a differential is important enough to merit a response. This concept is interesting as it can help to explain to Western managers in particular why feedback on changes in reward remuneration and recognition systems is not as readily forthcoming in Asian countries as it is in the West – and may appear to go smoothly for long periods until it suddenly goes awry (Linstead and Chan 1994).

Exhibit 7.5   Cross-cultural views of motivation

In summary, then, there is considerable, if mixed, evidence that motivation does take different forms in different cultures, even if some more general theories can be loosely applied cross-culturally. However, what is most significant is the potential for *defamiliarization* of cross-cultural studies – as the work of the Chinese researchers shows, theory needs modification when 'read back' into Western assumptions and raises some interesting questions about dimensions that may be neglected. In other words, Western individualism may not be a wholly accurate description even of Western human behaviour.

The social view of motivation

An alternative sociological view to motivation might overcome the problems identified in the more traditional approaches to motivation based on job redesign. One such approach is called the *social constructionist* view, which emphasizes the important role of meanings and interpretations in shaping people's motivations. Social constructionists emphasize the importance of interpretations – (how people understand and make sense of their organizational encounters – of events, situations, constraints, opportunities, moments of resistance and so on. Some would argue that: 'Social constructionism is a philosophy in its own right,

Table 7.1 Turner's model of interactional motivation

Theoretical perspective	Well-known theorists	Key concepts	Key 'motivational' assumptions
Exchange theory	George Homans (1961), Peter Blau (1996), Richard Emerson (1972)	Central motivational force is to maximize gratification, avoid deprivation or punishments in social interactions. Hierarchies of preferences and values, costs v. benefits, etc.	Key motivating force is *needs for power, prestige* and *approval* in social relations. Actors compete for both *material* and *symbolic* resources, and impression management is important (save face, etc.)
Social interactionism	Herbert Blumer (1969)	Behavioural capacities to sustain self (image) and cooperate with others. Individuals possess configurations of self-referencing attitudes, dispositions, feelings, definitions, meanings and they seek to reaffirm these configurations with others with whom they interact	Need to adjust, adapt and cooperate with others. Need for *sense of identity* (who am I?). Pressure to continually construct definitions of and orientations to situations. Need to sustain esteem and consistency in presenting the 'self' to others
Ethnomethodology	Harold Garfinkel (1967)	Actors are motivated to create a sense, even an illusionary sense, of sharing a common universe – to have a common reference point for belonging. Individuals create folk talk (or *ethnomethods*) to sustain or establish the presumption that they share a common world	*Need for a sense of facticity* – a presumption that individuals in social interactions share things in common. *Conversational exchanges* revolve around 'filling in', 'waiting for' or 'glossing over' information to create a common world; giving background information and dealing with unclear messages
Structuration theory	Anthony Giddens (1984)	Efforts to stabilize and/or establish routines and social integration. Reflexive monitoring by giving reasons for one's acts and others' and developing 'stock of knowledge' that help us move from one situation to the other – reduces anxiety and eases process of fitting in	Unconscious need to achieve *trust* and an unconscious need or drive to achieve *ontological security* – i.e. matters in the social world are as they appear, i.e. a sense of certainty
Interaction ritual chains	Randall Collins (1975, 1986)	Actors use resources to take advantage of a situation. Emotional energy (positive feelings and sentiments about oneself) and cultural capital (i.e. approval, prestige, group membership, control over materials/resources) are utilized in conversational exchanges. Actors monitor situations (work, ceremonial or social) to determine what levels of expenditure of emotional energy and cultural capital are needed	*Group membership* is the primary force behind expenditure of emotional energy and cultural capital. People seek a sense of group solidarity and have a desire to belong to groups. Extracting emotional and cultural 'profit' or benefits are the main motivations for social interaction

Source: Adapted from Jonathan Turner (1987), 'Toward a sociological theory of motivation', *American Sociological Review* 52, pp. 15–27.

and one which puts individuals at the centre of their own universe as architects, more or less, of their own world views and meaning systems' (Sims, Fineman and Gabriel 1993: 294–5, emphasis removed).

The social constructionists study motivation from an eclectic point of view and focus on accounts of motivation that are specifically learned, social, interpretative, cultural and context bound. Jonathan Turner's (1987) model of interactional motivation provides a useful example of the complexities that emerge when a social constructionist approach is used to study motivation, and an attempt made to link it to job redesign. Turner developed his model or approach by studying five main areas of sociological theory, and from these he distilled a number of key ideas relating to motivation. Table 7.1 outlines Turner's main findings in terms of key theories and concepts he used to develop a social interactionist theory of motivation. Turner's study was not exhaustive and excluded a number of areas such as political sociology and postmodernism. From his study, Turner concluded that there were seven fundamental states of being that people sought from their social interactions and three of these had primary motivational significance for how people thought and acted. The three were:

1 the need for a sense of *group inclusion*;
2 the need for a sense of *trust*;
3 the need for *ontological security*.

Referring to Table 7.1, the need for *group inclusion* derives from the interaction ritual chains approach, the notion of *trust* and *ontological security* from structuration theory. Turner argued that the need for inclusion, trust and security were very strong and the absence of these 'states' would lead to high anxiety. He also said that the need to maintain or have one's self-concept reaffirmed (e.g. one's sexual identity) also influenced how the needs for inclusion, trust and security were accomplished (Turner 1987: 24). Needs relating to *symbolic* and *material gratifications* (exchange theory) also influence or are related to how individuals manage their self-concept or how they develop ways of presenting the 'self' (see below). Similarly, symbolic/material gratifications also relate to achieving group inclusion and affect or influence negotiations and exchanges.

Turner believed his model revealed some of the more complex unconscious (i.e. anxiety-reducing) aspects of motivation. The key causes of anxiety were failure to achieve inclusion, trust and security. He also proposed that his model explained some of the more complex reasons why people cooperated (or failed to cooperate) than had previous theories of motivation. Turner's work reaffirmed the importance of sense making, understanding and language to motivational processes. He argued that people's *need for facticity*, or the presumption that they share with others an intersubjective world or have things in common, was directly influenced by the use of *ethnomethods* (see Table 7.1). Facticity was also influenced by or associated with anxieties (and deprivations) relating to (1) ontological security (a sense that things are as they appear), (2) trust (actions of others are predictable and reliable), (3) group inclusion (interactions are part of a common social process being shared by others), and (4) concept of 'self' (reactions of others to how you present yourself are sincere and genuine).

Turner suggested that when people use ethnomethods they employ conversational techniques to establish that their respective self-concepts have been sincerely, appropriately or adequately interpreted – that others know what you stand for and who you are. Ethnomethods are also used to establish ontological security – to establish that the situation one finds oneself in is how it appears, that there are no 'traps', 'surprises' or 'shocks' in store. Turner suggests that the successful or unsuccessful use of ethnomethods in negotiations and exchanges determines whether or not facticity is achieved (i.e. some sharing of and establishing common knowledge). Facticity influences how the self and ontological security are achieved and if ethnomethods fail to achieve facticity, then motivational dynamics or process become arrested (1987: 25). If Turner's last proposition is correct, then the whole idea of motivation and managing diversity takes on new challenges.

The importance of developing a common language and understanding among culturally diverse groups now becomes an important motivational issue (see previous discussion). The potentially negative motivational effects of not addressing identity issues (i.e. of the self) relating to gender and sexuality, for example, are also likely to affect the level of facticity (or shared meanings) that men and women can achieve. Turner was, however, cautious on this point, noting that while individuals strive to sustain group standards and affirm the self (or sexual identity) and cooperate with others (inclusion), these motivational forces need to be reconciled with each other, and indeed with other basic sex impulses, organic drives and various acquired needs (1987: 20). This reconciliation might prove impossible. But Turner still gave primacy to the learned, social and interpretive elements of motivation.

Emotions and motivation

Some aspects of Turner's model have gained increasing attention in the management and organizational discourse. Turner's work drew attention, although only in a limited way, to the role played in motivation by 'emotional capital' or feelings. Organizations (through their management systems) seek to remove unpredictable behaviour, which emanates from emotional states, to ensure rationality and order. Organizations or their managers often seek to deny emotional dimensions of behaviour. Emotion is usually treated as an abject phenomenon, denied, but ever present, yet never really dealt with except very superficially (Linstead 1997: 1142).

Stephen Fineman (1993: 14, citing Collins 1990) suggests that emotional energy is very important to creating a sense of belonging. He says feelings such as belonging, respect, diffidence, fear, awe, affection and even love help bind people to their 'organizational' worlds or roles. He contends that without '…socially connected emotions of embarrassment, shame and guilt' (1993: 17) order within organizations would be difficult to maintain. These emotions, he says, are the motivational springs to self-control and involve rejection, threats to how others see us (self), and how our performances are judged by others.

Fineman (1993, 1997, citing Hochschild 1983) (see also Chapter 3) also argues that organizations increasingly demand various forms of 'emotional labour', but this is not given recognition by the organization. 'Emotion management' is also built into the design of many jobs and job training. Not only do people have to deal with their own emotions in a motivational sense, but often prove their worth, loyalty and commitment to the organization by engaging continuously and 'successfully' in emotional performances. These performances amount to wearing the company-prescribed 'mask' in whatever form it takes and whatever situation arises, usually to satisfy customers or clients or respond to external accountability as shown in TQM (see the previous discussion). Fineman cites Arie

Hochschild's (1983) research on flight attendants and debt collectors that examines the types of emotional labour structured into these jobs – flight attendants smiling and being courteous under all circumstances and conditions; debt collectors being dominant in the situation and making the debtor feel guilty and unworthy. Emotional labour is increasingly built into many service-related jobs and becomes the 'feeling rules' that are associated with professional training and conduct, for example doctors being seen as 'caring', 'rational', 'scientific' and 'objective' (Fineman 1993: 86). However, emotional self-management can also extend to the self-identity of those with which the 'labourer' interacts, e.g. debt collectors have to move the person they are dealing with into thinking of themselves as someone who wants to and does pay their debts, through fear, guilt or other emotions, and doctors need to manage their patients' identities so that they will follow the prescribed treatment.

Emotional labour has its down side for those who cannot reconcile how they privately feel about the 'public performance' required of the organization, especially if they feel pressured or coerced into performing the 'act'. They might feel confused and uncomfortable about their self-identity or concept of the self that the performance violates (Fineman 1997: 18, citing Hochschild 1983). Fineman (1993: 21) suggests that ritualized expressions of emotions can also be invoked in situations that are seen as informal but operate through strong (unwritten) rules or obligations to participate. Some of these ritualized expressions include such things as drinking parties, pub crawls, sporting events and various 'bonding' sessions. Fineman (1993, citing Hochschild 1983) points out that while this emotional labour does not cause everyone to feel self-estranged it can do so for some people. A number of these rituals are, for example, gender based, and emotional labour carries high 'costs' for many women (and may be even for some men!) participating in more masculine forms of ritual expressions. Frequent participation can cause problems of self-estrangement, discomfort and loss of motivation. The same might apply for many men having to participate in what are seen as female forms of ritual expression. Nor is it entirely clear, according to Fineman, when an 'emotional performance' at work ceases or is carried on in the home or into other relationships.

Emotions are often left repressed or unspoken about in organizations, especially emotions that are seen as negative such as fear, envy or greed (Bedeian 1995). Greed and envy, for example, are often presented as a natural part of the personality, but social constructionists would explain it as part of the wider social influences in which society and its institutions reward certain forms of behaviour. Self-aggrandizement, individualism, opportunism and competitiveness are commonly rewarded in many Western businesses, but not in many Asian countries (see the previous discussion). Many people might not even be aware of why they are motivated to behave in these ways (i.e. as envious) in order to seek rewards and recognition and prove themselves 'worthy'. Depending on the social context or the culture, the notion of greed and envy might change or might not even exist (Burkitt 1991: 204, citing Lichtman 1982). Motivation is derived from both conscious and unconscious sources and these can be either resistant or malleable, recognized or unrecognized. A whole range of activities and forces shape motivation in particular social relations (Burkitt 1991: 205, citing Leontyev 1978, 1981).

Commitment and trust

Emotions, and emotional labour, play an important part in the type and level of commitment people make to others, to their work and their organizations. The management discourse is dominated by a number of themes, captured in the 'buzz-words' outlined in Chapter 1, such as: competition, organization learning, intellectual capital and knowledge (e.g. Sherman 1994; Stewart 1994; Ulrich 1998), flexibility in all processes, teamwork (virtual teams), diversity, empowerment, flat organizations and cross-boundary interorganizational relations (IORs). All of these depend on creating a more committed, motivated and diverse workforce. In motivational terms, commitment has been studied from two main perspectives: the attitudinal and behavioural.

From the *attitudinal* perspective, commitment is defined '...as the relative strength of an individual's identification with and involvement in a particular organization' (Oliver 1990: 19–20). The focus is on commitment to the organization, that is, beliefs in the goals of the organization are seen as a strong motivating force. Individual factors, such as personal characteristics, role-related features, work experience, nature of job and organizational structures (e.g. supervisory levels) are said to affect levels of commitment and these in turn affect outcomes such as turnover, productivity and compliance. Commitment is built around an exchange theory approach that sees commitment as being directly related to an exchange for rewards or anticipated rewards (Oliver 1990: 20). This approach has subsequently been defined as the *affective attachment* approach to commitment. The basic argument is that people with strong affective attachment stay in an organization because they want to (Allen and Meyer 1990: 2–3).

The *behavioural* perspective of commitment is concerned with how people develop commitment to their own actions rather than to the organization (Oliver 1990: 20). Two different approaches have emerged from within the behavioural school: side-bets and psychological ownership of actions.

Side-bets (theory proposed by Becker 1964) argues that concrete investments (time, resources, money) increase commitment by increasing the material cost of withdrawal from the organization (cost/benefit and exchange theory as mentioned by Turner in Table 7.1). The loss incurred in changing a course of action creates committing actions, even if the course of action chosen is a disastrous one (Oliver 1990: 21). This approach has been labelled by some as the *continuance approach* to commitment, which means people stay in their organizations because either they have invested too much to leave (e.g. in learning certain skills) or they see no alternatives to leaving, that is, the costs are too high or they have nowhere else to go (Allen and Meyer 1990: 3–4).

Natalie Allen and John Meyer (1990: 3) propose that a *normative approach* to commitment can also be discerned in the literature that focuses on *obligations* people feel to their organizations. Although a less common approach, it acknowledges the strong sense of responsibility some people feel toward their organizations. These people have '...totally internalized normative pressures' and therefore behave in certain ways that meet organizational goals or interest that they believe constitute the 'right' or 'moral' thing to do. Probably these people would be described as extremely loyal employees. Others label this as a *value commitment* which defines those people who have a strong identification with the organization and are therefore more likely to be cooperative, altruistic and engage in unrewarded spontaneous citizenship behaviour (Davis, Schooram and Donaldson 1997: 30).

Allen and Meyer do not see either of the three approaches as separate approaches to commitment, but rather as components of commitment that any one person could experience to some degree (Allen and Meyer 1990: 3–4). Others suggest that an *investment model* of commitment might be more appropriate, which views a person's commitment to his/her job as an '…additive function of satisfaction (conceived as the rewards the job offers less the cost it entails), investments in the job and alternatives to it' (Oliver 1990: 21). This approach combines elements of the attitudinal and side-bets views of commitment.

Psychological ownership of actions as proposed by Salancik (1977) argues that '…individuals become bound by actions and through these actions to beliefs that sustain them' (Salancik 1977: 62, cited in Oliver 1990: 20). In Salancik's view attitudes are malleable, messy, relatively private and not easily thought out. Behaviour or action is more public and irrevocable and once someone does something it is hard to undo it. If it becomes harder to change behaviour or undo one's actions (i.e. it has become irrevocable), then people will selectively mobilize to justify or rationalize the behaviour or actions they have taken and this alters their beliefs about commitment to an action (Weick 1995: 156).

Inconsistencies between attitudes and behaviour, that is, what one says or does, and between actions taken in a particular situation, are likely to cause people to seek reconciliation of these inconsistencies. Therefore, the context in which an action is taken becomes important. Four conditions in any context are thought to determine commitment to one's action: *explicitness* (how obvious is the action to others); *revocability* (how difficult is it to reverse the action); *publicity* (how many people know about the action); and *volition* (how voluntary is the action). These four states of being determine the level or extent of psychological investment in an action, and hence one's likely commitment to it (Oliver 1990; Weick 1995: 156–7).

Karl Weick believes commitment arises only if an action entails volition (or choice) and is done with few external demands or extrinsic reasons, such as threats, demands, sanctions or fear. It must also involve considerable effort or personal sacrifice. Without these further conditions, he believes people will not recognize or take responsibility for their actions, hence commitment is highly improbable (Weick 1995: 157). One of the main points of Weick's argument is that committed people see the world differently and behave differently. Organizations can alter contexts or situations to encourage commitment. He doubts, however, that organizations which are organized bureaucratically and encourage formalization and centralization (i.e. have high levels of control and limited power sharing) can foster commitment because they limit the exercise of choice, which he sees as a very important condition for making a commitment.

Psychological contracts

A third view of commitment argues that committing is an informal process that involves establishing psychological contracts, that is, an unwritten and often largely unverbalized set of expectations and assumptions about the obligations people ascribe to their organizations (Ring 1997: 137). According to several theorists (Herriot, Manning and Kidd 1997; Morrison and Robinson 1997), psychological contracts are becoming increasingly difficult to manage as restructuring, downsizing, forced redundancies, the increasing use of temporary workers, the increasing use of performance-based schemes, decreasing union power, diversity in the workplace, and foreign competition have altered the more traditional underpinnings of these 'contracts'. These underpinnings were job security, steady rewards for hard work and promotion opportunities from the organization, in exchange for loyalty, conformity and effort on the part of employees (Herriot *et al.* 1997: 152; Morrison and Robinson 1997: 226). Often these changes have occurred as executive salaries and conditions have been improving – frequently scandalously so in the case of many chief executives. For these reasons increasing attention is now being paid by researchers to the consequences of organizations breaching and violating their psychological contracts.

Traditional research on psychological contracts has focused on the nature of reciprocal obligations between employees and their organization, that is, the entitlements and benefits each party can expect to receive from the other, and what each is obliged to give the other in exchange for securing their contribution. Elizabeth Wolfe Morrison and Sandra Robinson (1997: 227–9) point out that employees' beliefs about these obligations are not always shared by the agents of the organization. Employees usually view the 'contract' as being between themselves and the organization, and not some third party individual such as a manager. Managers, accordingly, may see their role as rewriting this generic understanding in the light of everyday organizational operations and requirements. For such managers, psychological contracts are merely a form of 'motherhood' statement, relating to ideals and not realities. Generally speaking, in most of the research, psychological contracts are considered to be held by employees, not supervisors or other parties (Herriot *et al.* 1997: 151; Morrison and Robinson 1997: 228–9).

A further important distinction is drawn between psychological contracts that are largely *transactional* and those that are *relational*. One definition of the transactional contract says it is focused on monetarized values, such as employees taking on longer hours of work and additional roles in exchange for high performance–related pay, and job-related training and development. Relational contracts involve such socioemotional elements as loyalty, support, sacrifice and security (Herriot *et al.* 1997: 152; Morrison and Robinson 1997: 229, citing Rousseau and McLean Parks 1993). Morrison and Robinson suggest that employees can have both forms of psychological contract, but violations of each have different consequences for employees and their organizations. Peter Herriot, W.E.G. Manning and Jennifer Kidd (1997: 152–3) argue that because the psychological contract is based on reciprocity (see Chapter 4), it is more open to violation as well as generosity.

Herriot, *et al.* undertook research in the UK to ascertain what factors constitute the transactional and relational dimensions of a psychological contract. They selected two groups of 184 people, one comprising employees and the other representatives of organizations. These people were selected from a cross-section of industries, with men and women (though not ethnic or racial groups), different age groups, different lengths of service, public and private sectors and small, medium- and large-sized organizations all being represented. The organization group included supervisors, middle managers and executives while the employee group drew from a wide cross-section of occupations. Each person was asked to recall an incident where an employee and the organization had fallen short of or exceeded expectations of how they might reasonably have been expected to treat the other party – a form of 'critical incident' technique with broad similarities to that of Herzberg (Herriot *et al.* 1997: 254).

Table 7.2 shows the results of Herriot *et al.*'s findings in terms of what both employees and organizational representatives considered to be the *organization's obligations* to each party. Employees focused more on transactional relations or what seem to be Herzberg's

Table 7.2 *Frequency and percentage of incidents falling into 12 categories of organization obligation for both groups*

	Employee group		Organization group	
	Number	Percentage	Number	Percentage
Training – Providing adequate induction and training	**25**	9.62	**24**	8.36
Fairness – Ensuring fairness of selection, appraisal, promotion and redundancy procedures	**28**	10.8	**37**	12.9
Needs – Allowing time off to meet personal or family needs	15	5.77	14	4.88
Consult – Consulting and communicating with employees on matters which affect them	14	5.38	14	4.88
Discretion – Minimal interference with employees in terms of how they do their job	14	5.38	6	2.09
Humanity – To act in a personally and socially responsible and supportive way towards employees	19	7.31	**41**	14.3
Recognition – Recognition of or reward for special contribution or long service	11	4.23	**31**	10.8
Environment – Provision of a safe and congenial work environment	**39**	15.0	**25**	8.71
Justice – Fairness and consistency in the application of rules and disciplinary procedures	14	5.38	12	4.18
Pay – Equitable with respect to market values and consistently awarded across the organization	**31**	11.9	18	6.27
Benefits – Fairness and consistency in the administration of the benefit systems	**25**	9.62	**47**	16.4
Security – Organizations trying hard to provide what job security they can	**25**	9.62	18	6.27

Source: Peter Herriot, W.E.G. Manning and Jennifer M. Kidd (1997), 'The content of the psychological contract', *British Journal of Management* 8: 151–62.

hygiene factors, such as the work environment, pay, benefits and job security. Organizational representatives focused more on relational elements, most frequently nominating loyalty and good citizenship behaviour. Table 7.3 shows the expectations both groups had for *employee obligations*. The three most frequently cited obligations were hours, work and honesty. Organizational representatives also mentioned hours, work and honesty. They also mentioned loyalty and flexibility more often than did employees.

Herriot *et al.* suggest that the differences in these perceptions between the two groups can be explained by how each group deals with *reciprocity*. They argue that many organizations who have implemented the restructuring changes mentioned earlier, such as removing

Table 7.3 *Frequency and percentage of incidents falling into seven categories of employee obligation for both groups*

| | Employee group | | Organization group | |
	Number	Percentage	Number	Percentage
Hours	76	32.1	68	28.1
Work	46	19.4	54	22.3
Honesty	36	15.2	41	16.9
Loyalty	10	4.22	28	11.6
Property	20	8.44	9	3.72
Self-presentation	25	10.5	14	5.79
Flexibility	24	10.1	28	11.6

Source: Peter Herriot, W.E.G. Manning and Jennifer M. Kidd (1997), 'The content of the psychological contract', *British Journal of Management* 8: 151–62.

job security, have broken their side of the bargain and employees reciprocate accordingly by altering or lowering their commitment. What individuals see as being fair to expect from employees, which are principally transactional obligations, seems to enjoy greater consensus than do their views of the organization's obligations. Managers in the study mentioned intangibles such as humanity, recognition and benefits more than did the employee group. Morrison and Robinson (1997: 238) point out that balance (fairness) and repayment are important elements of fulfilling transactional agreements and are more easily monitored by employees. Herriot *et al.* (1997: 159–61) believe that it is their mistrust of management which probably accounts for employees preferring transactional relationships that highlight pay and security because the old relationally-based psychological contracts have either been, or are very likely to be, broken. They say that until organizations overcome this mistrust, the bases of commitment will be difficult to change, even though lean organizations require fewer people to do more and innovation and risk taking are still important in developing learning organizations (see also Ulrich 1998).

Morrison and Robinson (1997: 230–1) distinguish between contractual breaches and violations. They argue that a *breach* in a psychological contract is cognitive (i.e. involving a perceived breach or failure on the part of the organization to fulfil an obligation commensurate with one's contribution). A *violation* is the emotional or affective state or experience that can also accompany one's belief that there has been a failure by the organization to fulfil a psychological contract. Violation, they say, creates deep visceral feelings that, to quote:

> … involve(s) disappointment, frustration, and distress stemming from the perceived failure to receive something that is both expected and desired…In addition, central to the experience of violation are feelings of anger, resentment, bitterness, indignation, and even outrage that emanate from the perception that one has been betrayed or mistreated (Morrison and Robinson 1997: 231).

Violation, they suggest, decreases the trust employees have in their organization as well as the satisfaction they have with their jobs, with their organizations, the obligations they feel towards their organization, and their intention to leave. Some possible outcomes of violating a psychological contract are a reduced contribution from the person violated, unwillingness to take on extra roles (seen as citizenship behaviour) and, in the extreme, seeking retaliation, revenge, sabotage, theft or acts of aggressive behaviour (Morrison and Robinson 1997: 227).

The authors suggest that there is a whole range of complex reasons why organizations fail to fulfil a psychological contract and therefore renege on a perceived promise to an employee. These can include the inability of the organization to meet its obligations because its economic circumstances might have changed or the basis of making the promise (e.g. rapid promotion opportunities) might have been unrealistic. Sometimes the organization might be deliberately unwilling to fulfil an obligation because to do so might cost too much in the form of resources consumed (e.g., extra benefits for increased performance). It could also be because the employee has little bargaining power, such as expertise, and can be easily replaced. Sometimes employees' behaviour might not be considered appropriate or they may not come up to expectations and be perceived by the organization to have broken the contract, and the organization merely reciprocates (Morrison and Robinson 1997: 233–4).

Considerable sense making, interpretations and negotiations underlie the processes that eventually lead a person to feel that they have experienced a violation of a psychological contract and people will perceive and react differently. Cultural factors intervene as do others such as the viewed importance or salience of a violation. Feelings of violation, and the sense-making experiences that these entail, often involve employees having to come to terms with the outcomes of a breach (e.g. failing to get a promotion can also involve loss of status, loss of benefits, low self-esteem), or finding someone to whom to assign blame or responsibility for the breach; all of which can intensify feelings of anger and contempt for the organization. Morrison and Robinson argue that it is in the organization's interest to convince employees that the breach was beyond the organization's control or that it was not a purposeful act (even though it might have been). Employees who have high levels of trust in their organization are less likely to blame the organization for the breach and are likely to remain committed to some degree (Morrison and Robinson 1997: 244).

Reneging on a psychological contract in employment relationships that are transactional in nature (short term and motivated by self-interest) often carries fewer 'costs' to the organization than reneging on those that are relational (focused on building long-term commitment). Thus the nature of trust and commitment varies in each of these relationships as do the consequences of breaches or violations of a psychological contract. This attention to trust is not a recent development in organization theory, and was treated at length in Alan Fox's classic text, *Man Mismanagement* (Fox 1972). Fox argued that despite the arguments of Scientific Management it was impossible to specify the nature of a task – partly because of the nature of language, partly because of the nature of work – so tightly as to remove the need for an element of worker discretion, which entailed a degree of trust. Indeed, Taylor recognized this in his emphasis on the abilities and importance of the 'first class man'. Fox argues that the balance of trust and control should be, and needs to be, more even in workplace relations, and that this is in fact more efficient than excessive and ultimately costly control measures. He called for management to 'extend the hand of trust' to employees, rather than tighten regimes of control.

These sentiments were echoed by Richard Walton (1985), whose article, 'From control to commitment in the workplace', spelt out what he considered to be key job design strategies intrinsic to building a committed workforce. Some of the strategies he mentioned included equality of sacrifice, assurance of no job losses if employees take on more responsibilities, priority of training and retaining the existing workforce, flexible definition of duties, and a number of others. The aforementioned have been sacrificed in programs such as BR and BPR, and through a number of similar changes mentioned above. Other researchers suggest that commitment is contingent upon the organization broadening its perceptions of what employees want from their jobs to include more consideration of such things as family commitments (Ulrich 1998) and diversity issues (see Chapter 3).

'Extending the hand of trust' in today's work organizations is considered by some theorists to be at the very heart of creating a high-commitment management philosophy. It also entails recognizing that trust is associated with the willingness of a person to make themselves vulnerable and to take risks in the context of a particular relationship (Davis *et al.* 1997: 33; Mayer, Davis and Schooram 1995). This view of trust is somewhat different from Turner's conceptualization mentioned earlier and others found in the literature. Control-oriented systems, as described by Fox and Walton above, are designed to ensure that employees avoid risk, avoid making themselves vulnerable and therefore are unable to build very enduring trust-based relationships. Trust is established in all relationships whether between employees, agents of the organization or colleagues, and these relationships also involve power. Those who argue that organizations have to move away from control to commitment suggest that control systems create mainly transactionally based relationships which are based on hierarchical (or positional) power relations. Commitment-based control systems are likely to favour people using personal power and expert power as their main basis of influence in their relationship with others (Davis *et al.* 1997: 33–4; also see Chapter 5).

Transactional relationships create a type of trust that Peter Smith Ring (1997: 123–5) describes as *fragile trust*. This form of trust depends on a limited set of judgements made by individuals about others which predispose them to take some risks and trust the other party. This form of trust focuses on a person's *ability* and includes such things as: competence in one's job; business sense, good judgement, accessibility and interpersonal competence (Mayer *et al.* 1995; Ring 1997: 123–5). *Resilient trust,* by contrast, is the basis of developing the relational transactions that are important to building long-term commitments. The key element of this form of trust is a perception that the person trusted (i.e the trustor) will behave with *integrity* (which includes consistency in actions, communicating credibly about other people, being seen as having a strong sense of justice or being fair and showing discretion). The trustor also needs to be seen as a *benevolent* or caring person, being altruistic (doing good for others and being self-less), and showing loyalty, openness and consistency in their actions or behaviour.

Having read this one might ask: 'who can you trust?' Individuals can cooperate and even have confidence in someone without trusting them; for example cooperation can be induced through fear or threats. Confidence can come from being able to predict someone's behaviour, even if the behaviour is undesirable. Cooperating is not the same as making a commitment to something or someone (Mayer *et al.* 1995).

Conclusion

As we shall see in Chapter 11, trust and commitment are also central to the study of interorganizational relations (IORs). However, in nearly every area of management – leadership, teams, managing diversity, empowerment, culture – terms such as 'trust' and 'commitment' crop up. If we look at the elements of resilient trust, described above, it seems that many management practices are in fact focused on building fragile trust, and many job redesign strategies are extremely limited in the ways in which they develop the more enduring aspects of worker motivation, especially long-term commitment.

1 Why do people work?

Classical theories of motivation identify that we work because we have needs to satisfy – needs for the basic staples of life like food and shelter – and these are primarily obtained through the wage or salary. Beyond that, we may work to be regarded with affection by our colleagues, to be esteemed or, as Maslow puts it, for self-actualization, to realize our full potential. Of course, we may meet these needs equally well outside work. McClelland identified needs for power, achievement and affiliation as being socially significant, but more recent approaches to needs have taken even more account of the symbolic dimensions, or the ways in which people need to manage meaning. Turner identifies seven basic social needs of which three – group inclusion, trust and ontological security – are most important, and are particularly relevant to work.

2 Are people motivated in the same ways?

There are common features to motivation, but what motivates one person rather than another is subject to infinite variation. Life experience, age, physical and psychological make-up will be significant variables, but so also will gender, race and ethnicity – and people may be motivated differently at different times and in different contexts.

3 Is how we work affected by how we feel?

Emotion is an important and neglected part of work life, and theories of motivation have tended to view motivation as a sort of calculus rather than as a form of inspiration. Both approaches have something to offer, but the protracted neglect of the emotional impact on motivation means that we still have much to learn about it. Recent interest in the area of violation of psychological contracts suggests that emotions are an important part of understanding commitment and why people withdraw commitment or seem to lose motivation or interest in their work.

4 Can one person motivate another?

It is clear from the research that motivation is very complex, having material and deeper psychological and spiritual aspects. The old 'carrot-and-stick' model, which oscillated between bribery and bullying, has been superseded, and although simple linear relationships between what a manager does and how a worker responds have been discredited, there is still no shortage of effort to improve workplace motivation. These are perhaps better seen as attempts to influence the motivational context and process, so although one person may have an impact on another's motivation, it is rare that such motivation can be entirely attributed to that person's efforts.

5 Is the way a job is designed important for motivation?

Not exclusively, but research on job design does indicate that a well-designed job or group of jobs can have an influence. However, efforts which seek to motivate solely through good job design, neglecting other situational factors, such as organizational politics, are unlikely to be successful.

6 Does motivation vary from culture to culture?

Despite the fact that very few writers and managers have acknowledged it, the research evidence that it does is extensive. Discovering how it varies, and what impact these variations have in specific situations, will be an increasing challenge as world business globalizes further.

Returning to the case study:

1   Colin seems to think that commitment means commitment to a course of action, that is, meeting the targets laid down by the strategic plan for the business unit. Roger seems to regard commitment as an emotional thing which people express verbally from time to time. Eric seems to think that commitment means doing what he and the personnel director decide is best, and accepting disadvantage 'for the good of the team' in a mood of loyal self-sacrifice. Graham does not, he says, want to talk about commitment, but poaching of his staff. Graham's storyline reads very much like the emotional response, the deep visceral feelings described by Morrison and Robinson. Graham has failed to receive something he expected, felt he deserved and is being cheated from having.

It is unclear why the organization has reneged on its promise to Graham but, for him, talk of commitment is all empty rhetoric and hypocrisy. Doing what the company does, selling biscuits and crisps, is not something which is intrinsically motivating, and he questions the sanity of anyone who finds it so. He claims that the company's attempts to claim more and more of his time in the name of commitment, which is used merely as a mask for organizational politics, have gone too far. If that is what it takes, he declares, he is *not* committed.

2   How could Graham's real or apparent lack of commitment be handled? This is a difficult one. Clearly Graham's problem is not adequately expressed in the term 'lack of commitment'. Graham is annoyed that the company plays a political game, playing managers off against each other, forcing them to compete against each other to meet production targets. The competitive and divisive nature is masked by talk of 'commitment' to the team and the plan, when in fact the spirit is not collective but one of masculine aggression – note that the others try to 'cut him down to size'. What Graham is saying is that commitment here is empty, and it is just cut and thrust and power politics.

Graham does not like this, and finally he says so. The silence of the others indicates that he has struck a nerve. For a moment they wonder what would it be like if we really *were* a team? If we weren't constantly bickering but helped each other? And perhaps if we brought more of our family values into the workplace? They wonder what life would be like if work were perhaps more meaningful, more cooperative, based on trust rather than gamesmanship.

There is no way of dealing with Graham's lack of commitment at this level, because it would mean radical change. It would entail all the men in the room being able to set aside their political differences and open up about their misgivings about how they work together – and *committing* to change. In reality, they will stay silent for a while then change the subject; eventually Eric will talk 'man to man' with Graham and the incident will be forgotten. To really deal with the problem would require a different sort of commitment.

3 What precipitated the 'blow-up' was the political play which resulted in Graham losing his 'best man', which will affect his department's ability to meet its targets. However, it was also precipitated by the fact that everyone was drunk, and their night away seems as much an escape from the unpleasantness of the realities of work as it is a planning meeting. On this evidence, we might wonder whether any of them is really 'committed' – that is, believes in and values what the company is doing – beyond just working for long hours. Perhaps the problem is that Graham is struggling with the 'emotional performance' these events extract including the drinking and the 'rituals' of the annual event.

4 Would the meeting have been different if some of the managers were women? This is an interesting question, because the dynamics of this meeting are so masculine that it would almost certainly have to be. But the question underlying this is whether women and men are motivated differently, communicate differently, and have different values at work...

Consider, then what Eric might say to Graham after his outburst

(a) as a man

(b) if Graham was a woman

(c) if Eric was a woman, and Graham a man

(d) if the group were all women

References

Allen, N.J. and Meyer, J.P. (1990) 'The measurement and antecedents of affective, continuance and normative commitment to the organization', *Journal of Occupational Psychology* 63: 1–18.

Aungles, S.B. and Parker, S.R. (1988) *Work Organisation and Change*, Sydney: Allen & Unwin.

Balk, W.L. (1995) 'Is there life beyond TQM?', in Halachimi, A. and Bouckaert, G. (eds), *Public Productivity Through Quality and Strategic Management*, Amsterdam: IOS Press, and Brussels: International Institute of Administrative Sciences (IIAS).

Bartlett, C. and Ghoshal, S. (1992) *Transnational Management: Text, Cases and Readings in Cross-Border Management*, Homewood, Ill.: Irwin.

Becker, H.S. (1964) 'Personal change in adult life', *Sociometry* 27: 40–53.

Bedeian, A.G. (1995) 'Workplace envy', *Organizational Dynamics* 23(4): 49–56.

Bendix, R. (1956) *Work and Authority in Industry*, New York: Harper.

Blau, P.M. (1966) *Exchange and Power in Social Life*, New York: John Wiley.

Blumer, H. (1969) *Symbolic Interaction: Perspective and Method*, Englewood Cliffs, NJ: Prentice Hall.

Boje, D.M. and Winsor, R.D. (1993) 'The resurrection of Taylorism: Total quality management's hidden agenda', *Journal of Organizational Change Management* 6(4): 57–70.

Bond, M.H. and Hwang, K.K. (1986) 'The social psychology of Chinese people', in Bond, M.H. (ed.), *The Psychology of the Chinese People*, Hong Kong: Oxford University Press.

Buchanan, D.A. (1979) *The Development of Job Design Theories and Techniques*, UK: Saxon House.

Buchanan, D. (1995) 'The limitations and opportunities of business process re-engineering in a politicized organizational climate', Human Resource and Change Management Research Group, Loughborough University Business School, Leicestershire (Version: 31 January).

Burkitt, I. (1991) 'Social selves: Theories of the social formation of personality', *Current Sociology* 39(3): 1–217.

Child, J. (1984) *Organisation: A Guide to Problems and Practice*, London: Harper and Row.

Collins, R. (1975) *Conflict Sociology: Toward an Explanatory Science*, New York: Academic Press.

Collins, R. (1986) 'Interaction ritual chains, power and property', in Alexander, J., Giesen, B., Münch, R. and Smelser, N. (eds), *The Micro-Link*, Berkeley: University of California Press.

Collins, R. (1990) 'Stratification, emotional energy, and the transient emotions', in Kemper, T.D. (ed.), *Research Agendas in the Sociology of Emotions*, Albany: State University of New York Press.

Cox, R.W. (1995) 'Organization development and total quality management: Which is the chicken and which is the egg?', in Halachimi, A. and Bouckaert, G. (eds), *Public Productivity Through Quality and Strategic Management*, Amsterdam: IOS Press, and Brussels: International Institute of Administrative Sciences (IIAS).

Crosby, P. (1979) *Quality is Free*, New York: New American Library.

Davenport, T.H. (1993) *Process Innovation: Reengineering Work Through Information Technology*, Harvard: Harvard Business School Press.

Davis, J.H., Schooram, F.D. and Donaldson, L. (1997) 'Toward a stewardship theory of management', *Academy of Management Review* 22(1): 20–47.

Dawson, S. (1986) *Analysing Organisations*, London: Macmillan.

De Cock, C. and Hipkin, I. (1997) 'TQM and BPR: Beyond the myth', *Journal of Management Studies* 34(5): 659–75.

Deming, W.E. (1986) *Out of the Crisis: Quality Productivity and the Competitive Position*, Cambridge, Mass.: MIT Press.

Dunphy, D. (1981) *Organisational Change by Choice,* Sydney: McGraw-Hill.

Emerson, R. (1972) 'Exchange theory, Part II', in Berger, J., Zelditch, M. and Anderson, B. (eds), *Sociological Theories in Progress*, 2, Boston: Houghton-Mifflin.

Emery, F.E. (1969) *Systems Thinking: Selected Readings,* Harmondsworth, UK: Penguin.

Emery, F.E. and Phillips, C.R. (1976) *Living at Work,* Canberra: Australian Government Publishing Service.

Fincham, R. and Rhodes, P.S. (1992) *The Individual, Work and Organization: Behavioural Studies for Business and Management*, London: Weidenfeld and Nicolson.

Fineman, S. (1983) 'Work meanings, non-work and the Taken-for-Granted', *Journal of Management Studies* 20(2): 143–55.

Fineman, S. (1993) 'Organizations as emotional arenas', in Fineman, S. (ed.), *Emotion in Organizations*, London: Sage.

Fineman, S. (1997) 'Emotion and management learning', *Management Learning* 28(1): 13–25.

Fox, A. (1972) *Man Mismanagement*, Oxford: Oxford University Press.

Fulop, L. and Mortimer, D. (1992) 'Job redesign strategies' in Fulop, L. with Frith, F. and Hayward, H. (eds) *Management for Australian Business: A Critical Text*, Melbourne: Macmillan.

Garfinkel, H. (1967) *Studies in Ethnomethodology*, Englewood Cliffs, NJ: Prentice Hall.

Giddens, A. (1984) *The Constitution of Society: Outline of the Theory of Stratifications*, Berkeley: University of California Press.

Goldthorpe, J., Lockwood, D., Bechofer, F. and Platt, J. (1968) *The Affluent Worker,* Cambridge: Cambridge University Press.

Goski, K.L. and Belfry, M. (1991) 'Achieving competitive advantage through employee participation', *Employment Relations Today* Summer: 213–20.

Hackman, J.R. and Oldham, G. (1975) 'Development of the Job Diagnostic Survey', *Journal of Applied Psychology* 60(2): 159–70.

Hackman, J.R. and Oldham, G. (1980) *Work Redesign,* Reading, Mass.: Addison-Wesley.

Hackman, J.R., Oldham, G., Janson, R. and Purdy, K. (1975) 'A new strategy for job enrichment', *California Management Review* 17(4): 57–71.

Halachami, A. and Bouckaert, G. (eds) (1995) *Public Productivity Through Quality and Strategic Management*, Amsterdam: IOS Press, and Brussels: International Institute of Administrative Sciences (IIAS).

Hall, G., Rosenthal, J. and Wade, J. (1993) 'How to make reengineering really work', *Harvard Business Review* November–December: 119–131.

Hall, T.H. and Parker, V.A. (1993) 'The role of workplace flexibility in managing diversity', *Organizational Dynamics* 22(1): 8.

Hammer, M. (1990) 'Reeingineering work: Don't automate, obliterate', *Harvard Business Review* July–August: 104–12.

Hammer, M. and Champy, J. (1993) *Reengineering the Corporation: A Manifesto for Business Revolution,* New York: Harper Business.

Herriot, P., Manning, N.E.G. and Kidd, J.M. (1997) 'The content of the psychological contract', *British Journal of Management* 8: 151–62.

Herzberg, F. (1966) *Work and the Nature of Man,* London: Staples Press.

Herzberg, F. (1987) 'One more time: How do you motivate employees?', *Harvard Business Review* 46(1): 109–31.

Hochschild, A.R. (1983) *The Managed Heart*, Berkeley: University of California Press.

Hofstede, G. (1988) 'Motivation, leadership and organisation: Do American theories apply abroad?', *Organisation Dynamics* 9: 42–63, reproduced in Henry Lane and Joseph di Stefano, *International Management Behaviour: From Policy to Practice*, Scarborough, Ontario: Nelson Canada.

Homans, G.C. (1961) *Social Behavior: Its Elementary Forms*, New York: Harcourt.

Honour, T.F. and Mainwaring, R.M. (1982) *Business and Sociology*, London: Croom Helm.

Horner, M. (1972) 'Toward an understanding of achievement related conflicts in women', *Journal of Social Issues* 15: 157–75.

Hsu, F.L.K. (1971) 'Psychological homeostasis and jen: Conceptual tools of advancing psychological anthropology', *American Anthropologist* 73: 23–44.

Juran, J. (1988) *Juran on Planning for Quality*, New York: Collier Macmillan.

Juran, J. (1989) *Juran on Leadership for Quality*, New York: The Free Press.

Kelly, J.E. (1982) *Scientific Management, Job Redesign and Work Performance,* London: Academic Press.

Lansbury, R.D. and Spillane, R. (1983) *Organisational Behaviour in the Australian Context,* Melbourne: Longman Cheshire.

Leontyev, A.N. (1978) *Activity, Consciousness and Personality*, Englewood Cliffs, NJ: Prentice Hall.

Leontyev, A.N. (1981) *Problems of the Development of the Mind*, Moscow: Progress Publishers.

Lichtman, R. (1982) *The Production of Desire: The Integration of Psychoanalysis into Marxism,* New York: The Free Press.

Linstead, S. (1997) 'Abjection and organization: Men, violence and management', *Human Relations* 50(9): 1115–45.

Linstead, S. and Chan, A. (1994) 'The sting of organization: Command, reciprocity and change management' *Journal of Organization Change Management* 7(5): 4–19.

Lupton, T. (1971) *Management and the Social Sciences,* Harmondsworth, UK: Penguin.

McClelland, D. (1961) *The Achieving Society*, Princeton: Van Norstrand.

McClelland and Burnham, D.H. (1976) 'Power is the great motivator', *Harvard Business Review* 54: 100–10.

McClelland, D and Boyatzis, R.E. (1982) 'Leadership motive pattern and long–term success in management', *Journal of Applied Psychology* 67: 737–43.

Mangham, I.L. (1996) 'Beyond Goffman', in Jeffcutt, P., Grafton Small, R. and Linstead, S. (eds), *Organization and Theatre*, special issue of *Studies in Cultures, Organizations, and Societies* 2(1): 33–5.

Maslow, A.H. (1943) 'A theory of human motivation', *Psychological Review* 50(4): 370–96.

Maslow, A.H. (1965) *Motivation and Personality*, New York: Harper and Row

Mayer, R.C., Davis, J.H. and Schooram, D.F. (1995) 'An integration model of Organizational Trust', *Academy of Management Review* 20(3): 709–34.

Miller, E.J. and Rice, A.J. (1967) *Systems of Organisation: The Control of Tasks and Sentient Boundaries,* London: Tavistock.

Mishra, K.E., Spreitzer, G.M. and Mishra, A.K. (1998) 'Preserving employee morale during downsizing', *Sloan Management Review* Winter: 83–95.

Mitchell, T.R. and Larson, J.R., Jr (1987) *People in Organizations: An Introduction to Organizational Behavior* (third edition), New York: McGraw-Hill.

Morrison, W.E. and Robinson, S.L. (1997) 'When employees feel betrayed: A model of how psychological contract violation develops', *Academy of Management Review* 22(1): 226–56.

Oliver, J. (1993) 'Shocking to the core', *Management Today* August: 18–21.

Oliver, N. (1990) 'Rewards, investments, alternatives and organizational commitment: Empirical evidence and theoretical development', *Journal of Occupational Psychology* 63: 19–31.

Petzall, S.B., Selvarajah, C.T. and Willis, Q.F. (1991) *Management: A Behavioural Approach*, Melbourne: Longman Cheshire.

Pugh, D.S., Hickson, D.J. and Hinings, C.R. (1983) *Writers on Organizations*, Harmondsworth, UK: Penguin.

Rice, A.K. (1958) *Productivity and Social Organisation,* London: Tavistock.

Ring, P.S. (1997) 'Processes facilitating reliance on trust in inter-organizational networks', in Ebers, M. (ed.), *The Formation of Inter-Organizational Networks*, Oxford: Oxford University Press.

Ritzer, G. (1990) *The McDonaldization of Society*, Thousand Oaks: Pine Forge Press.

Rose, M. (1975) *Industrial Behaviour: Theoretical Development Since Taylor,* London: Allen Lane

Rousseau, D.H. and McLean Parks, J. (1993) 'The contracts of individuals and organizations', in Cummings, L.L. and Staw, B.M. (eds), *Research in Organizational Behavior*, 15: 1–47 (Greenwich, CT: JAI Press).

Salancik, G.R. (1977) 'Commitment and the control of organizational behaviour and belief', in Staw, B.M. and Salancik, G.R. (eds), *New Directions in Organizational Behaviour*, Chicago: St Clair Press.

Schwartz, H.S. (1990) *Narcissistic Process and Corporate Decay*, New York: New York University Press.

Sherman, S. (1994) 'Leaders learn to heed the voice within', *Fortune* August 22: 72–8.

Sievers, B. (1995) *Work, Death and Life Itself*, Berlin: Walter de Gruyter.

Sims, D., Fineman, S. and Gabriel, Y. (1993) *Organizing and Organizations: An Introduction*, London: Sage.

Snyder, M. (1979) 'Self–monitoring processes', in Berkowitz, L. (ed.), *Advances in Experimental Social Psychology* 12, New York: Academic Press.

Spencer, B.A. (1994) 'Models of organization and total quality management: A comparison and critical evaluation', *Academy of Management Review* 19(3): 446–71.

Stewart, T.A. (1994) 'Your company's most valuable asset: Intellectual capital', *Fortune* 3 October: 34–6, 40–2.

Strauss, G. (1976) 'Job satisfaction, motivation, and job redesign', in Strauss, G., Miles, R.E., Snow, C.C. and Tannenbaum, A.S. (eds), *Organizational Behavior: Research and Issues*, Belmont, CA: Wadsworth Publishing Company.

Trist, E.L. and Bamforth, K.W. (1951) 'Some social and psychological consequences of the long-wall method of coal-mining', *Human Relations* 4(1): 3–38.

Turner, J.H. (1987) 'Toward a sociological theory of motivation', *American Sociological Review* 52: 15–27.

Ulrich, D. (1998) 'Intellectual capital = competence × commitment', *Sloan Management Review* Winter: 15–26.

Walton, R.E. (1985) 'From control to commitment in the workplace', *Harvard Business Review* March–April: 76–84.

Weick, K.E. (1995) *Sensemaking in Organizations*, London: Sage.

Westwood, R. (1992) *Organizational Behaviour: South–East Asian Perspectives*, Hong Kong: Longman.

Wilson, F. (1995) *Organisational Behaviour and Gender,* London: McGraw-Hill.

Womack, J.P., Jones, D.T. and Roos, D. (1990) *The Massachusetts Institute of Technology 5 Million Dollar 5 Year Study on the Future of the Automobile Industry*, New York: Rawson Associates.

Yang, K.S. (1981) 'Social orientation and individual modernity amongst Chinese students in Taiwan', *Journal of Social Psychology* 113: 159–70.

Yang, K.S. (1982) 'The Sinicization of psychological research in a Chinese society: Directions and issues', in Yang, K.S. and Wen, C.I. (eds), *The Sinicization of Social and Behavioural Science Research in China*, Taipei: Institute of Ethnology, Academic Sinica.

Yang, K.S. (1986) 'Chinese personality and its change', in Bond, M.H. (ed.), *The Psychology of the Chinese People,* Hong Kong: Oxford University Press.

Yu, E.S.H. (1974) 'Achievement motive, familism, and Hsiao: A replication of McClelland-Winterbottom Studies', *Dissertation Abstracts International*, 35, 593A, University Microfilms, 74–14, 942.

Yu, W. (1991) 'Motivational and demotivational factors in enterprises', *Chinese Journal of Applied Psychology* 6(1): 5–14.

8
Decision making in organizations

Liz Fulop, Stephen Linstead and Rodney J. Clarke

Questions about decision making

1   What is a 'decision'?
2   Why is the decision-making process important in organizations?
3   What kind of choices do decision makers have?
4   How does the behaviour of organizational participants affect decision making?
5   How are knowledge, information and power related in decision making?

The moral maze of decision making

[The study of decision making] is complicated by the difficulties of assessing to what extent … rational devices actually are used in making decisions, particularly by higher-ups… The CEO of **Covenant Corporation** [pseudonym for a company in the US which is a large conglomerate], for instance, sold the sporting goods business from one of his operating companies to the president of that company and some associates in a leveraged buyout. The sale surprised many people since at the time the business was the only profitable operation in that particular operating company and there were strong expectations for its long-term growth. Most likely, according to some managers, the corporation was just not big enough to hold two egos as large and bruising as those of the president and the CEO. However, the official reason was that sporting goods, being a consumer business, did not fit the 'strategic profile' of the corporation as a whole. Similarly, Covenant's CEO sold large tracts of land with valuable minerals at dumbfoundingly low prices. The CEO and his aides said that Covenant simply did not have the experience to mine these minerals efficiently, a self-evident fact from the low profit rate of the business. In all likelihood, according to a manager close to the situation, the CEO, a man with a financial bent and a ready eye for the quick paper deal, felt so uncomfortable with the exigencies of mining these minerals that he ignored the fact that the prices the corporation was getting for the minerals had been negotiated 40 years earlier. Such impulsiveness and indeed, one might say from a certain perspective, irrationality, is of course always justified in rational and reasonable terms. It is so commonplace in the corporate world that many managers expect whatever ordered processes they do erect to be subverted or overturned by executive fiat, masquerading, of course, as an established bureaucratic procedure or considered judgement.

Looking up and around

Despite such capriciousness and the ambiguity it creates, many managerial decisions are routine ones based on well-established and generally agreed upon procedures. For the most part, these kinds of decisions do not pose problems for managers. But, whenever non-routine matters, or problems for which there are no specified procedures or questions that involve evaluative judgements are at issue, managers' behaviour and perspective change markedly. In such cases, managers' essential problem is how to make things turn out the way they are supposed to, that is, as defined or expected by their bosses.

A middle-level designer in **Weft Corporation**'s [pseudonym for a company in the USA] fashion business provides a rudimentary but instructive example of this dynamic at work. She says:

> You know that old saying: 'Success has many parents; failure is an orphan'? Well, that describes decision making. A lot of people don't want to make a commitment, at least publicly. This is a widespread problem. They can't make judgements. They stand around and wait for everybody else's reactions. Let me tell you a story which perfectly illustrates this. There was a [museum] collection coming, the [Arctic] collection, and there was a great deal of interest among designers in [Arctic] things. My own feeling was that it wouldn't sell but I also recognized that everybody wanted to do it. But in this case, [our] design department was spared the trouble. There was an independent designer who had access to our president and he showed him a collection of [Arctic] designs. There were two things wrong: (1) it was too early because the collection hadn't hit town yet; (2) more important, the designs themselves were horrible. Anyway, [the collection] was shown in a room with everything spread out on a large table. I was called down to this room which was crowded with about nine people from the company who had seen the designs. I looked at this display and instantly hated them. I was asked what I thought but before I could open my mouth, people were jumping up and down clapping the designer on the back and so on. They had already decided to do it because the president had loved it. Of course, the whole affair was a total failure. The point is that in making decisions, people look up and look around. They rely on others, not because of inexperience, but because of fear of failure. They look up and look to others before they take any plunges.

Gut decisions

Looking up and looking around becomes particularly crucial when managers face what they call 'gut decisions', that is, decisions that involve big money, public exposure or significant effects on one's organization. The term probably derives from the gut-wrenching anxiety that such troublesome decisions cause. At all but the highest levels of both Covenant Corporation and Weft Corporation, and frequently there as well, the actual rules for making gut decisions were quite different from managerial theories or rhetoric about decision making. An upper-middle level manager explains:

There's a tremendous emphasis put on decision making here and in business in general, but decision making is not an individual process. We have training programs to teach people how to manage, we have courses, and all the guys know the rhetoric and they know they have to repeat it. But all these things have no relationship to the way they actually manage or make decisions. The basic principles of decision making in this organization and probably any organization are: (1) avoid making any decision if at all possible; (2) if a decision has to be made, involve as many people as you can so that, if things go south, you're able to point in as many directions as possible.

Decision-making paralysis is, predictably enough, most common at the middle levels. A lawyer talks about the difficulty he has in extracting decisions from the managers he advises:

> It's tough for people to make decisions. Like today, I needed a decision from a business guy involving $200 000 and he just didn't want to make the decision. It involved a claim from another company. They claimed that a certain clause in the contract that we have with them is unfair to a partner of theirs and that it is costing them money and that to be equitable we owed them 200 grand [thousand dollars]. I reviewed the contract and checked with a couple of other lawyers and decided that we didn't owe them a dime. It was a pretty straightforward case in our view. But it's not our decision to make so we went to the proper business guy and he didn't want to decide. So we said we need a decision and we would have to go to the next highest guy, his boss, and get it. He said: 'No, no, don't do that, because he'll send it back to me.' And he wanted us to send it to some other guy, a counterpart of his in a business area that isn't even related. He felt uncomfortable about making the decision because of the amount of money involved. Also, he was afraid of making a mistake. And he was afraid of impacting on others in areas he couldn't even see. Now, clearly, he should have just taken the decision up to his boss. But people don't want to do that. People have a very hard time making decisions and there's no question that this guy had the authority to make this decision. You see this sort of thing all the time. If you just walk around and look at people's desks, you'll see them piled with paper and that's an indication of their paralysis.

Senior managers are generally better at making decisions precisely because their positions allow them to establish the evaluative frameworks against which their choices will be measured. But even they evince the same kind of paralysis if they sense trouble or if their purported autonomy is really a mirage. For example, a financial planning manager, in discussing one of the cycles of financial commitment making in **Alchemy Inc.** [a subsidiary of Covenant Corporation], describes how even very high-ranking managers look up and look around:

> People are fearful to make decisions on their own, and that goes all the way up to [the president, Smith]…People try to cover themselves. They avoid putting things clearly in writing. They try to make group decisions so that responsibility is not always clearly defined. This is obvious to me in the planning process; and all the plans end up on my desk…

> …'There's a lot of it [fear and anxiety]. To a large degree it's because people are more honest with themselves than you might believe. People know their own shortcomings. They know when they're in over their heads. A lot of people are sitting in

jobs that they know are bigger than they should be in. But they can't admit that in public and, at still another level, to themselves. The organizational push for advancement produces many people who get in over their heads and don't know what they are doing. And they are very fearful of making a mistake and this leads to all sorts of personal disloyalty. But people know their capabilities and know that they are on thin ice. And they know that if they make mistakes, it will cost them dearly. So there's no honesty in our daily interaction and there's doubt about our abilities. The two go together.'

Of course, one must never betray such uncertainty to others. Here the premium on self-control comes into play and many a manager's life becomes a struggle to keep one's nerve and appear calm and cool in the bargain. Making a decision, or standing by a decision once made, exposes carefully nurtured images of competence and know-how to the judgements of others, particularly of one's superiors. As a result, many managers become extremely adept at sidestepping decisions altogether and shrugging off responsibility, all the while projecting an air of command, authority and decisiveness, leaving those who actually do decide to carry the ball alone in the open field.

Source: Modified from Robert Jackall (1988), Moral Mazes: The World of Corporate Managers, *New York: Oxford University Press, pp. 76–80 (excerpts from Robert Jackall 1988).*

Questions about the case

1   What criteria do people apply when making decisions in the companies described?
2   Why are people afraid to make decisions?

Introduction

Decision making is generally considered by managers, and the academic discipline of management, to be central to organizational activity. There are several reasons why decision making is considered to be so crucial. There is the need to formalize and codify management work, to promote communication between managers and others in organizations, and to be able to justify a selected course of action from the range of likely or perceived options. There is also the very real disciplinary imperative to distinguish management work from other types of work in organizations. Describing management work as decision making seems so obvious and natural that it is hard to conceive of an alternative to it. In this chapter we will critically evaluate some of the assumptions behind traditional decision-making studies, including the notions of 'choice' and 'decision', drawing on traditions which normally lie outside the management discipline and its decision-making literature. We will then examine some major difficulties associated with these traditional management decision-making theories. In the last part of the chapter a postmodern, textual process model of organizations (Clarke 1991, 1992; Linstead 1985, 1999) is introduced which addresses some of the concerns raised in our evaluation of the traditional decision-making literature.

Despite the fact that managers are often expected to be and to appear 'decisive', and frequently report themselves to be 'decision makers', actually defining a 'decision' and identifying when it has been made is extremely difficult (Miller, Hickson and Wilson 1996). While our own experience of decision making in organizational contexts suggests that we can often predict the courses of action that will be decided upon, the process of decision making most often seems to resist reduction to discrete decisions taken, or choices avoided or suppressed. The Scientific Management approach, which we have discussed in previous chapters, even reduced the idea of the decision itself to the point of disappearance, implying that management was a process of applying and following abstract principles. Decision making was at best a matter which was tightly constrained by evidence gathered through scientific methods, on the best way of accomplishing a task.

It was Chester Barnard (1938), in *The Functions of the Executive,* who contested these assumptions and argued that managers have a range of possible actions over which they can exercise discretion and *choice.* Decision making for Barnard is rational, purposeful and intentional, and these characteristics have dominated subsequent approaches.

Many writers on decision making have emphasized the rational aspect of decision making, seeing causes and effects and assuming that all actions have clear and identifiable consequences. The theorists also tend to assume that decision makers are fully aware of what they are doing, and that they look for the best or optimum outcome in all circumstances. There is also a tendency to regard decisions as being made at specific moments in time, perhaps at meetings specially called for the purpose. Several pieces of research, which we will discuss later, have demonstrated that all of these assumptions can be questioned.

We will examine in more detail the following approaches to decision making: the rational model of decision making, the administrative or bureaucratic model (which questions whether managers are capable of making rational decisions), the garbage can model of decision making (which tries to introduce the idea that decisions are really problems looking for solutions, and the political model of decision making (which includes discussion of the role of very powerful groups in decision making called 'dominant coalitions' and why many decisions are really 'non-decisions'). Before we examine these models, we need to consider what might constitute a 'decision'.

What is a 'decision'?

We discuss the developments associated with later versions of the rational decision-making model further on in the chapter, but what concerns us now is how these assumptions have led people to define a 'decision' as a *product* of decision-making *processes.* In fact, the process of identifying a decision is often problematic, as Henry Mintzberg, James A. Waters, Andrew M. Pettigrew and Richard Butler (1990: 2) argue, because decisions are 'difficult to track down' and, as the cases above illustrate, managers often seek to avoid making decisions or obscure them. For Mintzberg *et al.*, because decisions may unfold rather than be explicitly made at one point in time, the important thing is *action* – once actions are observed, then patterns can be observed, and the role of the decision in determining these actions can be inferred by looking for a point where consensus emerges before the action. In effect, they say that 'decision' is too slippery a concept to work with and displace it in favour of action, although they infer that decision is a necessary prior condition for action.

Mintzberg *et al.* (1990) recognize that decisions are difficult to define, but still see them as products of action. An alternative approach sees decisions as occurring in a flow of smaller decisional acts. For example, when a manager chooses to pay attention to balance sheet figures rather than customer complaints, that is a kind of decision, but a very restricted one. This we can call a *decisional act.*

Think of a manager who at the beginning of the day sets priorities on several tasks, regarding some as more important, some less, and ordering them this way. Some tasks may not be very important themselves, such as putting more paper in the office printer, but may need to be done first, so the tasks need to be sequenced. Sometimes the tasks may be grouped or divided. Additionally, the manager will have to consider whose advice to take, or who to ignore, whose interests to respect and whose to take lightly, effectively placing some at the centre of the day and some at the margins. As events unfold, some commitments may need to be cancelled or erased, some 'pencilled in' for the future. Indeed, in ordering, sequencing, dividing up, centring, marginalizing, planning and erasing the day in this way, managers could be said to be 'writing' their world – because these are exactly the same things that we do when we write something.

Their little decisional acts pile up on each other, as managers and others are constantly making them, and form what can be called a *text*. We will discuss the nature of a text in more detail later in the chapter – but it is important to recognize that decisions may not be just the product of a process, but may be an inseparable part of the process itself. Decision processes produce not decisions as products, but texts – particular patterns of organizational experience that people come to accept as being relatively true or authoritative.

For example, consider the idea of a decision support system. The simplest of these is the coin – the old penny or dollar – which can be tossed in the air and determines, for example, which side bats first in a cricket match. However, the situation must already be carved up into a dualism, so that it can be expressed in the form 'heads is yes, tails is no' or something similar. So a range of alternatives is suppressed, condensed or discarded so that two relative dimensions can be carved out of the moment and a decision can be made. Of course, the captain of the cricket side might need to determine – or decide upon – a whole range of complex possibilities before they are able to decide whether, if they win the toss, they would like to bat or bowl, which would include the composition of their team and the other team, the weather conditions (and how the weather is predicted to develop), and the state of the pitch (and whether it is expected to deteriorate over the course of the game). How they condense these possibilities will depend on the procedures or *decision rules* they follow in order to try to influence the *outcomes* of the game through the *consequences* of the decision.

A slightly more elaborate device, which incorporates more variety and interactivity into the system, is the die, as exemplified in Luke Reinhardt's novel *The Dice-Man*. Here the hero, or anti-hero, develops a system for running his whole life, which eventually builds up into a cult following, based on the principle that all decisions (no matter how small or large, important or unimportant) can be divided into six optional courses of action, *one of which has to be unacceptable to the decision maker*. This element of challenge and risk adds excitement to the process – the possibility that the randomization of decision upon decision in this way as each day unfolds and presents its possibilities for action could lead to either a highly conservative outcome or a wildly unpredictable one. The decision maker never knows what is going to happen, and has only the responsibility of making the *range* of possible choices, never the choice itself, and feels a sense of being unburdened! The point here is that the die imposes a set of decision rules, which are appropriate to its technology (a six-sided cube), and also to its genre, or the style of its use, as in a game which one can win or lose, and the role of the Dice-Man is also clearly determined. Indeed, the rules of the decision system, especially with more complex systems, as they unfold create a pattern of inclusion and exclusion which we can regard as a *text*.

At the end of this chapter we will look more closely at what a *textual* approach to decision making looks like. However, we will now take a look at what traditional theories of decision making have to say about 'choice'.

Traditional decision-making theories and 'choice'

Decision making is a complex process which can be seen to involve many different stages or events before an actual decision is taken. Despite what we have just argued, managers do have to make decisions, and under varying circumstances, pressures and constraints. These have naturally led to competing explanations of decision making in organizations. There is strong evidence among traditional theories of a polarization between unitary and pluralist approaches to decision making. *Unitary approaches* to decision making posit a general agreement about goals and the best means to achieve them. *Pluralist approaches* to decision making emphasize conflict and power struggles between coalitions in organizations, although these occur in circumstances in which participants have substantial knowledge and information.

The basis of most of the traditional models of decision making, as we have observed, is choice. Decision making in this approach can be defined as *a response to a situation requiring a choice*. This is made after evaluation of alternatives on the basis of relevant choice criteria. Examples of such criteria could be 'maximum contribution to profitability', 'must complement existing product range' or 'must have an engine capacity of two litres'. In practice, however, as we have also noted, decision making is not always as objective and rational as this suggests. It may be influenced by values and institutional arrangements which bias data collection and evaluation, and affect the formulation of choice criteria. Parties to a decision may be unaware of the influence of these factors or may be outflanked because of their ignorance (see Chapter 4). If one accepts that organizational participants pursue objectives then the question of choice inevitably arises because there will not always be agreement about goals or the means to achieve them. Even if there is agreement on these things, the constrained nature of organizational resources is such that there will always be a weighing of pros and cons about particular courses of action. Decision situations in organizations range from relatively simple 'within policy' matters of staffing and operations to more open-ended concerns about goals, missions and strategic direction.

Some approaches to decision making focus on identifying the types of choices available to managers. These are: clear choice, competing choice, choice avoidance and choice suppression. An example of a relatively *clear choice* would be that between which of two new products to adopt, A or B. This type of choice is straightforward because the same decision-making methodologies can be applied to each alternative. If the choice criterion to be applied in this case is 'maximum contribution to profitability', it should be a relatively simple matter to estimate the expected returns for each alternative and calculate contribution to profitability. This example assumes that agreement has already been reached that there should be a new product, and that choice is limited to determining the best one financially. An example of a *competing choice* would be the alternatives of improving profitability by either launching a new product or upgrading computing facilities in order to improve bad debt collection. This type of choice is more open-ended than the previous example, and though it is still possible to evaluate each alternative in terms of profitability, it involves different assumptions and affects different interests within the organization. It might therefore be more problematical and conflict ridden. *Choice avoidance* occurs when issues arise requiring resolution but this does not occur. Non-action in this situation is itself a decision. *Choice suppression* is when information is distorted or suppressed in such a way that any decision made on an issue entails a predetermined outcome. This is a form of non-decision making (see Chapter 4).

Other approaches to decision making have sought to identify or categorize decisions into various types. One advantage of looking at decisions in this way is that it helps highlight the complexity of decision types that managers have to deal with. It also overcomes the tendency to simplify this aspect of decision making. Later when we examine various models of decision making, it will become apparent that many of these focus on certain types of decisions to the exclusion of others. In doing so, they tend to simplify the decision-making aspect of management.

Decision types

In the largest study of decisions to date (undertaken by David Hickson, Richard Butler, David Cray, Geoffrey Mallory and David Wilson 1986) the researchers found it necessary to describe the processes of decision making by categorizing decisions. The Bradford researchers (i.e. from Bradford University in the UK) argued that the categorization was related to the content of the decision. They identified three types of categorization for decisions: sporadic, fluid or constricted, and these are illustrated in Figure 8.1.

Sporadic decision processes are those which are informal, and will suffer from delays and impediments, being impeded by all sorts of things from waiting for information to overcoming resistance or opposition. There is often a variability in information because it is gathered from various sources of expertise, some better than others. As a result information sources are not usually regarded with confidence and more information may be requested. There will usually be scope for negotiation which takes place informally through personal contacts. The decision will take a long time to make and will eventually be made at the highest level. Political activity may well come to the fore in these decisions, and managers often find themselves involved in more than one of these processes, which may have a lifespan of between one and a half and three years, at any one time. An example may be a decision to purchase a stake in a supplier, where there is uncertainty about the future of the market – the kind of decision which does not happen on a routine basis – or what David Hickson *et al.* call weighty and controversial *vortex matters*.

Fluid processes are processes which flow, and are formally channelled, speedy and more predictable. Sources of information are fewer, familiar and reliable and there are fewer delays. There will be some but not much negotiation, more formal meetings and the decision will be made at the highest level. An example given by Hickson *et al.* (1986: 120–1) is the decision of a metropolitan authority to launch a lottery, which went through all the necessary committees very smoothly. This of course may well depend on the degree of political support the decision has and the majority of the dominant party in such a case – in other less formally political situations the known sponsorship of a dominant coalition can help to ensure that the process runs smoothly if all other things are equal. These decisions deal with unusual but non-controversial *tractable matters*. Hickson *et al.* (1986: 121) point out that

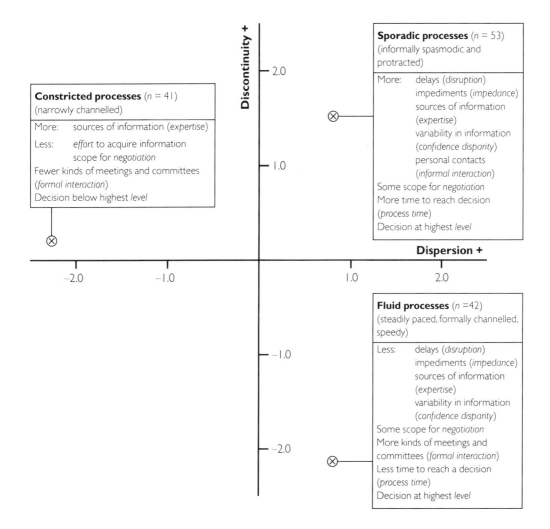

Figure 8.1 Three ways of making decisions (names of variables in italics)

Source: David J. Hickson, Richard J. Butler, David Cray, Geoffrey R. Mallory and David C. Wilson (1986), Top Decisions: Strategic Decision Making in Organizations, *San Francisco: Jossey-Bass, p. 117.*

the sporadic decisions are more political and the fluid decisions more rational. The first two types of decision correspond to what the administrative model of decision making calls non-programmed and programmed decisions (see p. 308) – although fluid decisions do usually have a greater element of uncertainty than this might imply.

Constricted processes are narrowly channelled. There is a need for more sources of information, but this is usually technical and there is less effort needed to acquire it as it is readily available. There is scope for negotiation but there are fewer meetings, and the decision can usually be made at the local level or a lower level than the top of the hierarchy. An example given by Hickson *et al.* is that of an insurance company which wanted to modernize its processes. These kind of decisions deal with *familiar matters.* Constricted processes are a variety of programmed decision.

The content of these modes of decision making are summarized in Figure 8.2.

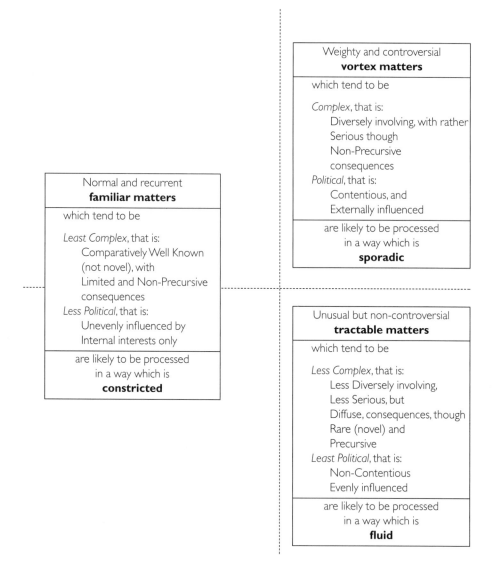

Figure 8.2   Three modes of decision making

Source: David J. Hickson, Richard J. Butler, David Cray, Geoffrey R. Mallory and David C. Wilson (1986), Top Decisions: Strategic Decision Making in Organizations, *San Francisco: Jossey-Bass, p. 175.*

The attempt to typologize decisions according to their characteristics by the Bradford Studies yielded some useful insights into the differences between decisions, and the conditions under which organizational politics was likely to have more impact. However, the Bradford Studies themselves were the result of a series of overlapping decisions over several years, including a variety of funding bodies and even, at one point, researchers who worked without pay, as Hickson notes in his introduction. The shaping processes that produced the investigations, and later the book, were influenced by the decisions that had to be made to keep the project going. These decisions sometimes blended and sometimes collided with the decisions being studied in the various organizations.

The next section of the chapter examines various models of decision making. Each of these makes different assumptions about various aspects of decision making such as: the preferences and goals of participants; the types of conditions with which different styles and processes of decision making are associated; the nature of power and authority implicit in them; expected results and outcomes; the nature of the technology employed; and the underlying values, beliefs and dominant rationale. Table 8.1 summarizes the key dimensions on which these approaches vary. Different types of choice criteria are implicit in each model. We also include in Table 8.1 what we have termed the *postmodern (textual)* approach to decision making, which was not originally mentioned by Jeffrey Pfeffer (1981), whose work forms the basis of Table 8.1.

The rational decision model

Under the rational model of decision making, the assumption is made that participants have agreed in advance that this is the right process to follow and that the rules and language of decision making are understood by all. The rational model aims at making optimal decisions on the basis of a careful evaluation of alternative courses of action. Depending on the complexity of the problem, computational or quantitative techniques may be used to assist this process. The model is claimed to be the basis of much decision making in private and commercial life and is effective under the conditions it assumes: a finite choice situation, relevant and unproblematic data, and clear and uncontroversial choice criteria. The model views the decision-making process as a sequential series of activities leading from an initial recognition of a problem, through the evaluation of alternative courses of action, and the selection of the preferred alternative, to the implementation of action (Dawson 1986: 182; Minkes 1987: 37–8). This sequential process is depicted in Figure 8.3 on p. 307.

Consider the decision processes involved in the choice about which of two new products should be launched. If the agreed objective was profitability, rationalists would say that it is a relatively straightforward procedure to estimate incomes and expenditures associated with both proposed products and to determine the preferred alternative. In these circumstances, decision making becomes largely a matter of technical expertise. Where there are adequate information, clear choice criteria and agreed goals, then the rational model is said to work well. However, not all decision situations are as clear cut as the example suggests, and the assumptions indicated above cannot always be presumed.

One major assumption is that the rational approach provides 'one best way' to reach decisions. However, the advocates of the rational approach pay little heed to the organizational context of decision making. As pointed out by Hickson *et al.* (1986), this context influences the way problems are defined, information gathered and choice criteria formulated. The use of logical frameworks and quantitative techniques do not of themselves make a decision rational. It would be better to regard such techniques as one input into a process which is influenced by the preferences and interests of key organizational participants (Pfeffer 1981: 31). For example, in the case of the product decision previously discussed, it would be illuminating to know how the organizational agenda was set to allow the emergence of the choice situation, that is, what events led to the decision to offer a new product. What profit-making alternatives were eliminated or overlooked in the process leading up to the choice situation (i.e. the competing choices)? Which organizational participants stand

Table 8.1 Overview of five organizational decision-making models

Dimension	Rational (unitary)	Bureaucratic (unitary)	Garbage can (pluralist)	Political power (pluralist)	Postmodern (textual)
Preferences and goals	Consistent among participants	Reasonably consistent	Unclear, ambiguous, may be constructed afterwards to legitimize actions	Inconsistent, diverse or conflicting goals and preferences	Goals and preferences become coherent according to the discourses which position them
Power and control	Focuses on hierarchical authority	Less centralized but still legitimate authority	Very decentralized, anarchic; power is also recognized	Shifting coalitions and interest groups who have power but not necessarily authority	Discourses and the institutions and practices which support them create compliant or oppositional 'social subjects' in decision making
Decision process	Orderly, rational	Procedural rationality embodied in programs and standard operating procedures	*Ad hoc*	Disorderly, characterized by push and pull of interest groups	Fragmented, networked, and shifts historically as discourse changes. Context and genre may produce unusual forms
Expected results and outcomes	Maximization and optimization	Follow from 'satisficing' mode	Unclear, ambiguous	Power and stabilization of demands	A simulation of order; a coherent 'text'
Information requirements	Extensive and systematic information gathering	Reduced by the use of rules and procedures	Haphazard collection and use of information	Information used and withheld strategically	Information flows and is held widely. Knowledge is distributed and needs to be shared; is often tacit and symbolic
Rationale	Efficiency and effectiveness in achieving agreed to performance criteria	Stability, fairness	Playfulness	Conflict and power struggles among relatively equal opponents	Speed of change; complexity of environment; diversity of representations of reality

Source: Modified from Jeffrey Pfeffer (1981), *Power in Organizations*, London: Pitman, p. 31.

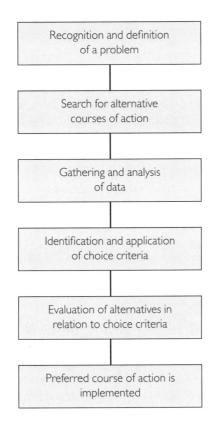

Figure 8.3 The Rational Decision Process

Source: Adapted from Anthony Hopwood (1974), Accounting and Human Behaviour, London: Accountancy Age Books, p. 124.

to gain or lose by the decision? Who supplied the information and to what extent have biases or values influenced the information-gathering process? What groups were not represented in the decision process (i.e. choice suppression)? Thus every organizational decision is influenced by a history, a social context and anticipated consequences for organizational participants.

The rational model has been greatly influenced by classical management and economic theory, especially the rational behaviour of individuals seeking the best rewards and using all available methods to achieve them, that is, profit maximization and choice optimization as per 'economic man'. Within the context of classical theory, decision making assumes a unitary frame of reference and a stable or predictable environment (Dessler 1976: 313–14). In fact, there is seldom agreement in organizations about goals and the means to achieve them. Moreover, environments are frequently characterized by uncertainty, time and cost frequently rule out the search for optimal solutions, and profit maximization is not the only criterion applied to choice situations (Hopwood 1974: 125).

The bureaucratic or administrative model of decision making

In reaction to the unrealistic assumptions of the rational model, Herbert Simon (1960) sought to develop a model of decision making based on the actual behaviour of decision makers. This approach has come to be known as the *bureaucratic* or *administrative model* (see Table 8.1). Simon recognized that in everyday life there are cognitive or mental limits to human rationality and that decision making is likely to be influenced by non-rational, emotional and unconscious elements in human thinking and behaviour, for example poor work habits, limited skills, pressure of time. Group pressures were also thought to limit the optimizing behaviour so central to the rational model of decision making. Furthermore, perfect information (on which to make decisions) is not always available, and there are time and cost considerations attached to information gathering and evaluation. The sheer amount of information to be processed and the necessity to meet deadlines frequently rules out optimal decisions. These limits or constraints on individuals mean that decision making is governed, according to Simon, by *bounded rationality* or sub-optimal efforts to reach decisions (Minkes 1987: 70–3; Mouzelis 1967: 124).

While ideally organizational arrangements should be set up to enhance decision making, which Simon sees as a primary management function, he nevertheless recognizes that in practice the conditions for perfect rational decisions will seldom be attained. Thus, in lieu of the optimizing 'economic man' of the rational model, Simon proposes an 'administrative man' who 'satisfices'. *Satisficing* is a term he coined to describe a 'best in the circumstances' decision. The metaphor suggested is that of 'looking for a needle in a haystack'. If one discovers a blunt or rusty needle that will more or less do the job required, it is unlikely one will keep searching until the perfect needle is discovered – and there may not even be one! Thus a satisficing decision is one which broadly satisfies the parameters of a problem. To continue to search for an ideal or optimal solution involves a cost which must be offset against the advantage of a quicker, near-enough or satisficing decision: hence the bounded rationality of decisions (Perrow 1972: 154–6; March and Simon 1958; Minkes 1987: 71–5).

In addressing the question of what needs to be done to enhance organizational decision making, Simon distinguishes between two types of decisions: programmed and non-programmed. *Programmed decisions* are not novel in nature and evolve from policies, precedents and guidelines. These decisions deal with repetitive and procedural events and could include such things as decisions about salary payments, customer orders, inventory restocking, etc. (i.e. they appear as clear choice criteria). In larger organizations, procedure manuals and precedents often set the direction for a programmed decision. This type of decision making is very amenable to bureaucratization ('red tape' and rules) and computerization (Weeks 1980). By contrast, a *non-programmed decision* involves finding solutions to problems which are novel or unstructured. Examples would be a decision to diversify, relocate, acquire a new business or initiate a range of staff redundancies for the first time. Usually there is little in the way of precedent or procedure to guide such decisions.

The distinction between the two types of decision making is important because they not only require different methods of problem solving but also involve different modes of managing and organizing. The implications and characteristics of the two decision-making modes are set out in Table 8.2. Programmable decisions lend themselves readily to operations research techniques and are compatible with mechanistic organizational structures. In a modernist view non-programmable decisions are best approached heuristically (i.e. using predictive models) and are compatible with more organic (i.e. non-bureaucratic or flexible) organizations. Simon believed that the decision-making activities of the middle and lower-level groups within an organization were more amenable to programmable decisions, while the upper levels were to deal more regularly with non-programmable decisions. Simon hoped that many decisions would become programmable and subject to more control and predictability.

In the postmodern context programmable decisions operate through various forms of self-discipline and control, as shown in Chapter 6 with teamwork, and culture in Chapter 3. Non-programmable decisions are associated with the virtual or teamnet-type organization discussed in Chapters 6 and 7. In these organizations, creating knowledge (intellectual capital) and learning are seen as critical to innovation and change (see Ulrich 1998). Simon did not include postmodern techniques of decision making in his typology, but these have been added to help draw comparisons between techniques of decision making.

Table 8.2 *Traditional, modern and postmodern techniques of decision making*

Types of decision	Traditional decision-making techniques	Modern decision-making techniques	Postmodern decision-making techniques
1. *Programmed* Routine, repetitive decisions; organization develops specific processes for handling them. Low uncertainty and ambiguity	(a) Habit (b) Clerical routine: standard operating procedures, policies and manuals (c) Organization structure: know your place (d) System of subgoals (e) Well-defined informational channels	(a) Operations research: mathematical analysis, models, computer simulations (b) Electronic data processing (c) Management information systems	(a) Decision devolved to 'empowered' teams *but* these teams are self-inspecting and policing (surveillance) (b) Manipulation of culture, myth and symbols to control decision outcomes and limit options (simulate contexts; simulacra)
2. *Non-programmed* One-shot, ill-structured novel policy decisions. Handled by general non-routine problem-solving processes. High uncertainty and ambiguity	(a) Judgement, intuition, and creativity (b) Rule of thumb (by top management)	Heuristic (problem-solving) techniques applied to: (a) constructing computer models (b) brainstorming (c) counter-planning (d) simulation	Risk-taking encouraged but within (a) the context of learning environments (b) fast flow of knowledge and information through virtual dissemination (c) flat flexible structures which can temporarily realign to support decision makers

Source: Modified from Herbert A. Simon (1984), 'Decision making and organizational design', in D.S. Pugh, (ed.), *Organization Theory: Selected Readings*, Harmondsworth, UK: Penguin, p. 208.

In terms of postmodern decision making two forms of knowledge have become particularly important for creating intellectual capital: *tacit knowledge* and *understanding* (Wikström *et al.* 1994: 10–12). Tacit knowledge is described by many theorists as being embedded in individuals as informal knowledge and embodying the skills and know-how of each unique individual. This form of knowledge is vital to organizations so that problems can be solved, questions answered about how things should or ought to be done, and decisions made based on lessons learnt from the past (Wikström *et al.* 1994: 11). Tacit knowledge has always been seen as important to efficiency and cooperation in workplaces (Manwaring and Wood 1985; Davenport, De Long and Beers 1998). As a source of intellectual capital, tacit knowledge is considered vital to gaining a competitive advantage by exploiting the brain power of individuals, and using the diversity of individual talent and know-how to create a winning edge. Tacit knowledge, as described here, draws on experience and skills *already* learnt in solving problems and getting the job done, and often by exceeding the demands of the job. Understanding, which is also embedded in individuals as informal knowledge, develops through interpretations of meanings, sense making (as discussed in Chapter 1) and, most importantly, reflection or self-reflexive practice (see Introduction).

Understanding builds from cognitive (judgements, intuition and awareness), emotional, spiritual and visceral (instinctive) experiences. The knowledge repositories from which people draw to develop understanding in organizations were described in Chapter 1 under the six different types of knowledge. Understanding leads to new insights, new frameworks of meaning, and new mental 'maps' through which people learn to be creative and innovative. Understanding allows people to identify or make new connections, come up with novel solutions to problems or discover new patterns of thought that are unique to them (Wikström *et al.* 1994: 12; Davenport *at el.* 1998: 43). Understanding, and its corollary learning, are hard to capture, measure, calculate or put a dollar value on both individually and organizationally (see Stewart 1994).

Nor is it is always easy or possible to draw a boundary around where skills and know-how end and understanding begins or how they can be separated in practice. Both forms of knowledge are enriched by particular contexts or situations in which they are acquired, so efforts to make this knowledge formal or explicit are fraught with problems and frustration. Knowledge management, as distinct from information management (see below), is primarily concerned with creating environments that induce people to create, reveal, share and use high-value knowledge to improve decision making and bring creativity and innovation into decision making (Davenport *et al.* 1998: 56). This high-value knowledge is thought important for creating breakthrough knowledge and thinking as distinct from incremental, trial and error learning noted in the modernist methods described in Table 8.2 (Prokesch 1997: 150, citing John Browne, chief executive officer (CEO) of British Petroleum). One way of achieving this is to create a fast flow of knowledge through virtual dissemination. In companies such as British Petroleum (BP), virtual teamnets use sophisticated computer networks linked to personal computers that have videoconferencing capabilities, electronic blackboards, individual home pages, scanners, faxes and group-ware that are meant to encourage the sharing of knowledge regardless of time, location, distance and organizational boundaries (Prokesch 1997: 152, citing John Browne, CEO of BP). BP's 'Virtual Teamwork' project was created to capture unstructured or tacit knowledge (carried in people's heads) by opening up opportunities to communicate and share this knowledge in various problem-solving situations. BP did not try to programme this knowledge or make it explicit (Ulrich

1998: 46). While BP is extending this concept, others believe that tacit knowledge, but probably more so understanding, seems to develop best in human networks, and in face to face exchanges, as opposed to electronic ones (Davenport *et al*. 1998: 56).

Knowledge also includes *information* and *explanatory knowledge*. Both forms of knowledge are public or *explicit knowledge* and are used to develop various knowledge repositories such as expert systems and, at the extreme, artificial intelligence (Davenport *et al*. 1998). Neither form of knowledge is the main source of competitive advantage in terms of building intellectual capital. Information and explanatory knowledge have been used extensively in organizations to aid decision making and problem solving as described in Table 8.2. Information is basically pieces of knowledge that have to be processed, organized or categorized to make them useful. Information can be used to develop skills and know-how as well as 'triggering' new forms of understanding. On its own though, information is not the source of innovation or learning, but is used by people to answer questions relating to the 'what', 'where', 'who', 'how' or 'when' of something that is of concern to them (Wikström *et al*. 1994: 11). Information is always public or explicit knowledge because it is able to be shared, can be bought or exchanged, has a definable value and is programmable as described by Simon. Virtual organizations or teamnets thrive on rapid and frequent exchanges of information in electronic forms, and in some situations this flow of information can radically alter how decisions are made and the structure of organizations in which they are made. For example, Thomas V. Malone (1997) has used the term 'cyber cowboys' to describe those people whose decision making will become increasingly autonomous (i.e. not referred back to a head office or does not go through a hierarchy), but is dependent on vast amounts of information accessed from remote sites through electronic means. This fast flow of information is what is commonly associated with the information revolution of the 1980s and 1990s, or the information age (Wikström *et al*. 1994: 13).

Explanatory knowledge is important to the development of tacit knowledge and understanding, but it is not the same as the former or the latter. Explanatory knowledge is usually equated with positivistic scientific knowledge used to solve problems and render solutions to processes or events that are predictable or potentially programmable. This knowledge was at one time person based or embedded in the individual, but has become public or explicit knowledge through dissemination (Wikström *et al*. 1994: 13). In other words, this form of knowledge has been documented, and while it might help develop individual understanding, and efforts are often made to document the understanding that has formed this knowledge, it is explicit or shared knowledge. Journals, conference papers, textbooks, manuals, reports, web sites and other electronic methods of information dissemination are commonly used to make this knowledge explicit and commodified in the sense that commercial values can be attached to it. Expert systems contain both information and explanatory knowledge, which are programmable and, from the viewpoint of theorists such as Simon, would increase the rationality of decision making in organizations. Explanatory knowledge tends to provide information that helps solve problems and can be highly valued or even overvalued by organizations because it is produced in a technical or scientific form (Wikström *et al*. 1994: 12–13). Other forms of explicit knowledge also exist, for example descriptive knowledge that comprises such things as organizational texts, stories, myths and metaphors, but this form of knowledge does not afford the same opportunities for becoming programmable and its relationship to problems solving is often more difficult to establish. Explanatory knowledge is easily transformed into information. In July 1997 BP boasted that its intranet sites (or home pages) contained approximately 40 000 pages of technical data, shared expert knowledge as well as other forms of 'how to' information. General managers of the 90 business units in BP (which employs 53 000 people worldwide) use their home pages to list projects and performance targets. BP is an extremely flat organization with few management layers between the CEO and the business units.

In fact organizations have a number of knowledge repositories that they develop but the greatest challenge remains accessing the tacit knowledge and understanding of people in the organization who usually have some control over how they use these forms of knowledge, although it is not clear that people can ever be fully aware of their knowledge repositories. While judgement, intuition and creativity were also acknowledged by Simon as traditional techniques of decision making (see Table 8.2), he said these were only applicable to situations of high uncertainty and ambiguity, and only applied to novel, one-off situations. For postmodernists many situations are novel and one-off and high uncertainty and ambiguity are the norm as organizations have to deal with diversity within the organization and with complex relationships in their environments. Simon's idea of programmable decisions was central to the information revolution, yet increasingly the area of non-programmable decision making is taking the centre stage in discussions about competitiveness, intellectual capital, knowledge management and decision making. Risk taking, innovation and learning have become synonymous with spreading non-programmable decision-making capacities across the whole organization. Simon's concerns about satisficing have been recast to concerns about maximizing the output in areas of non-programmable (virtual) decision making where there are many different forms of knowledge, and some we might never tap. Peter F. Drucker puts it another way: knowledge is taking the place of capital – the flow of things has been replaced by the flow of information – knowledge becomes power (Harris 1993: 120, citing P.F. Drucker). Simon was a unitarist and so he was silent on the issue of power and politics.

Disjointed incrementalism

Simon's approach to decision making was criticized for its neglect of the power or political dimensions of decision making (see below), for example for failing to take account of the diversity of interests in an organization and the role of powerful groups in shaping decision-making agendas (see Pettigrew 1972). Simon also failed to recognize that there might be advantages to using the satisficing approach in reaching decisions within political contexts. Simon's approach focused on the problems of decision making in businesses or commercial entities, but not in other organizations such as government institutions. A part of this was remedied in the work of Charles Lindblom, who also while seeking to highlight the limitations of the rational model of decision making introduced the concept of politics into decision making. Lindblom described decision making in public administration as being characterized by a process of 'muddling through' or *disjointed incrementalism*. He suggests that many policy decisions are so complex that they cannot be handled by the rational model of decision making, which he calls the 'root' method. Instead, Lindblom argues that policy decisions are made through the 'branch' method (Lindblom 1990: 278–82; Minkes 1987: 57–61). Policy decisions, such as where to locate new welfare housing or decrease unemployment benefits, are difficult if not impossible to deal with under any rational approach.

According to Lindblom, in incrementalism the decision maker does not attempt to root out all possible alternatives or objectives before tackling a problem, but rather places limits on the alternatives to be considered based on the current state of knowledge, and solves the problem through making small and gradual changes. Incrementalism reflects the troublesome character of decision-making processes arising from the competing interests and values that are brought into complex decision-making situations. Lindblom suggests that successful policy making proceeds by a process of 'mutual partisan adjustment', not some prior ordering of objectives and goals as advocated by the 'root' method. Decision makers simplify the choices between competing policies by identifying the margins by which circumstances or outcomes – if altered – will differ (Pugh and Hickson 1989: 130). Thus the only prior values that interest the policy maker are the increments by which two policies might differ. Lindblom argues that objectives can be fitted to policies and vice versa, since the process of decision making involves continual adjustments, modifications and reinterpretations of values and preferences. The 'science of muddling through' is a sophisticated problem-solving strategy which does not reject the rational approach but sees it as a form of 'simple-minded inadequacy'.

Lindblom is not, however, suggesting that policy makers simply make decisions on the basis of politics or intuition alone. Rather, he intends to expose the qualitative and politically motivated behaviours which lead to successful decision making in some situations. He does not support a 'one best way' approach to decision making, but he does subscribe to the concept of bounded rationality in terms of the limits on information search evident in the branch method. The model of disjointed incrementalism describes the type of decision making that is likely to occur in that 'grey area' between programmed and non-programmed decisions (Minkes 1987: 52). Moreover, because the choice criteria are marginal, the likelihood of conflict is considered to be minimal; changes are incremental and mutually adjusted. Logical incrementalism is moving closer to a pluralist view of decision making and thus avoids some of the obvious criticisms of the administrative model of decision making, which had little to say on politics and power.

The garbage can model of decision making

So far in this chapter several approaches to organizational decision making have been considered: the rational approach, which assumed that objectives and the means of achieving them could be clearly identified; the administrative one, proposing that organizational decision making is a product of bounded rationality; and incrementalism, introducing the notion of mutual adjustment and gradual change.

These approaches assume a clear linkage between goals, people and solutions. Michael Cohen, James March and Jon Olsen (1972) argue that this cannot always be assumed and that some organizations display characteristics of what they call 'organized anarchy'. The characteristics of organized anarchy are problematic goals, unclear technology (all sorts of methods are likely to be used to make decisions) and fluid (member) participation (see Table 8.1). Cohen *et al.* have noted that under such conditions, where clear criteria of choice are absent, extraneous matters tend to get lumped into the decision-making process, and solutions often bear little relation to problems. They have appropriately labelled this phenomenon 'the garbage can model of organization decision making'.

Under conditions of organized anarchy, it is not clear when an issue arises whether it is a problem or a solution to a problem. A collection of such issues is what Cohen *et al.* refer to as the 'garbage can'. Through a process of jumbled decision making, problems and solutions become linked together so that a problem in one area becomes a solution in another. For example, a university administration was moving to new premises elsewhere in the city and the question arose of what was to be done about the vacated premises. Ostensibly, this was a problem for the university. Elsewhere within the university there were moves to establish a new school of technology. One of the objections to this proposal had been the lack of suitable premises. After some discussion, it was decided that the new school would be established and that it would be located in the vacated premises.

While this decision seems, superficially, sensible, in the absence of clear choice criteria such as 'will it add to our surplus (profit)?', it was neither optimizing (as in the rational model) nor satisficing (as in the bureaucratic model). It was a reaction to circumstances by those who happened at that time to be on key committees (i.e. in fluid membership). No one asked critical questions, such as whether or not the new school was really required, whether the old premises were the best location for the proposed school, or what the effect would be on the budget.

These two issues, that is, the vacant premises and the proposed new school, were simultaneously problems and solutions. The decision was made by turning one of the issues into a solution. According to the garbage can theory of decision making, therefore, the factors that influence decision making in organizations are the range of issues *cum* solutions *cum* problems that happen to be in the garbage can at a particular time and the total demands upon the decision makers at that time. In comparison with the rational and administrative models of decision making, the garbage can model could be said to be based on 'circumstantial' rationality.

A noticeable difficulty with the model is its failure to account for the political activity of participants who encourage conditions of organized anarchy, or who exploit them for particular advantage. However, the approach does help us appreciate why decisions in organizations are not always 'rational' in an absolute or objective sense. In fact, Gunnar Westerlund and Sven-Erik Sjøstrand believe that the garbage can approach to decision making exposes one of the most popular myths in organizations, *the myth of the rational organization*. They suggest that the rational process of decision making (i.e. the step by step sequential process outlined in Figure 8.3) clouds the fact that the choice of problems and methods of handling them are largely influenced by the personal preferences, values and expectations of decision makers. What is often thought of as 'rational' simply depends on for whom it has to appear as being such (Westerlund and Sjøstrand 1979: 90–6).

The garbage can model also highlights *ritualistic decision-making* activities. For example, research has shown that not all problems lead to efforts to reach decisions that might solve them. Decision making often has to be forced on individuals who actively seek to avoid handling a problem as shown in the cases cited at the beginning of the chapter. Even though decisions are made, they may not be executed because someone may feel uncomfortable with the decision or it can be safely deferred (Westerlund and Sjøstrand 1979: 99). March (1984, 1988) has expanded on the ritualistic nature of decision making by proposing that much of what we observe about it is not so much concerned with how choices are made but how individuals interpret and justify their choices to others. He argues that most decision making is only incidentally about weighing up and evaluating choice criteria. Rather, decision-making sessions are often about how decision makers define the virtues and correctness of their choices, trying to make sense of what they have done and justifying future actions (see also Jackall 1988).

Decision-making events can also provide arenas for apportioning glory and blame. They create opportunities for reaffirming old alliances, friendships, antagonisms and power and status differences. March believes that these ritualistic aspects of decision making are useful for 'training' or 'educating' new recruits into the ways of the company. Furthermore, he says, decision-making processes can be a source of enjoyment and a way of having a good time while one learns the meanings of organizational life (March 1984: 96). However, choice avoidance is a common result of these processes.

There is another sense in which the garbage can approach has had a profound effect on the ways in which decision making is considered. March (1976) continued his criticisms of the rational model, but from a slightly different angle than is found in the garbage can approach. March entered a plea for incorporating what he calls 'playfulness' and *sensible* foolishness into decision-making processes. He wanted to see organizations encouraging untried or novel ideas and using intuition to address problems and make decisions (probably lateral thinking). These propositions were taken up by Tom Peters and Robert Waterman (1982/84) who argued that entrepreneurship and innovation could only occur on a grand scale if organizational leaders loosen up their control and coordination mechanisms, thereby encouraging experimentation and risk taking, that is, playfulness and foolishness (Peters and Waterman 1982/84: 29–54, 101). However, March, along with Peters and Waterman, recognized that more playful organizations were only feasible if widely held misconceptions or myths about rational decision making were tackled by senior managers.

The political model of decision making

In the discussion of the rational model, it was noted that there will not always be agreement between organizational participants over organizational goals and how they are to be achieved. Such disagreements may occur not because such participants are bloody-minded and/or 'difficult to get on with', but because of fundamental differences over values and preferences and the perceptions of various choice criteria. Disagreements may also occur because of the existence of such structural arrangements as divisions, departments or cost and profit centres, and the demands made by participants in these subunits on the scarce resources of the organization. The well-known tension that exists between the marketing and production functions in organizations may simply reflect that these groups have different roles to perform, which sometimes bring them into conflict; that is, marketing is concerned with adaptation and production with the maintenance of existing activities. However, it is also true that subunits in organizations may develop goals related to their activities that are important to the group and its priorities, but are hard to reconcile with the goals of other subunits or with the 'official' goals of the organization (i.e. competing choices) (Perrow 1972: 158).

The view that recognizes the role of conflict and conflict resolution in the decision-making process is, as we have described, the political model. This view was first proposed by Cyert and March (1963) who argued that organizations should be understood as consisting of shifting coalitions that form and reform around issues of concern to them. Coalition members will not all be drawn from the organization, and could include suppliers, customers, shareholders and external interest groups. Because of the shifting nature of coalitions it is difficult to draw strict boundaries around them, although fairly consistent alignments will emerge over some matters, for example during budget time department members will usually close ranks and support each other to get more resources.

By contrast with the unitary frame of the rational model, the political approach is pluralistic in nature, recognizing the role of stakeholders in affecting and shaping matters of significance to the organization. In this view, what are commonly referred to as the 'goals of the organization' are in fact the goals of coalitions (Lupton 1971: 119). Implicit in this is the possibility that these goals will be challenged by other coalitions, or that another dominant coalition may some day emerge. Decision making is thus about reconciling the interests of different stakeholders. Organizations are portrayed as a system adapting and learning to cope with a variety of internal and external constraints.

Once we accept the idea of coalitions, we are by definition recognizing that different groups have different goals and strategies for pursuing their interests (Weeks 1980: 196). Cyert and March are not unduly worried about the fact that coalitions may be chasing diverse or multiple goals. As long as an organization is not operating in a turbulent or hostile environment and has surplus resources, that is, slack, then conflict and power struggles will not be overly harmful. Moreover, they believe that organizations have mechanisms by which they can stabilize power struggles and conflicts. For example, when times are good and profits high, senior management may channel organizational slack (i.e. excess resources) into upgrading plant and equipment or embark on new acquisitions and takeovers. By directing resources into these sorts of ventures, the rising expectation of various coalitions may be tempered. Alternatively, when times are lean, senior management will continue to provide company cars and other fringe benefits to managers in order to maintain expectations and aspirations. A pool of surplus resources is maintained for these purposes. It would be a very unpopular company or organization which attempted to take away rewards such as company cars when times are lean and profits low. Slack, which underpins promises, deals and expectations, usually provides the basis for coalition formation, political activity and competition over resources.

Side-payments was a term used to describe the ways in which organizational slack is transformed into different forms of reward for coalition members. Side-payments can be such things as monetary rewards, preferential treatment, increased authority (status), or benefits from various policies. Cyert and March believe that side-payments of a monetary kind are not satisfactory methods of resolving conflict or buying loyalty from coalition members. Thus while side-payments of a monetary kind (overtime payments, leave loading, etc.) are considered important, side-payments which involve policy commitments to employees are thought to be more beneficial. These include employment contracts, retirement and superannuation schemes, workers' compensation arrangements, systems of annual review, promotional structures, or equal employment opportunity provisions. They are likely to minimize political activity and win the long-term support and loyalty of individual coalition members.

While side-payments tend to be associated with rewards to management, it has to be recognized that they need not be limited to this group alone: profit sharing can act to stall or neutralize conflict and political activity at all levels of an organization. Rewards such as bonuses for achieving or increasing targets for various managers and other personnel are an increasingly popular way of using the budgetary process to control the demands of coalition members while also ensuring that decisions are not being constantly challenged (see also Curwen 1963: 144).

Dominant coalitions and non-decision making

The pluralist view of decision making provides an important critique of the unitary perspective, particularly the rational model. However, the pluralist approach does not go far enough in mapping out or explaining how decisions can be made or avoided in organizations because of the influence or pressure of external groups who may form part of a dominant coalition. Furthermore, the pluralist approach presumes that conflict and power struggles occur under circumstances in which all participants have substantial knowledge and information about such things as organizational slack and have access to decision-making arenas.

Cyert and March's approach to decision making, for example, could not explain how very powerful individuals from a wide spectrum of interests (e.g. banking, media, legal, political) form coalitions which negotiate and bargain among themselves to influence and shape decisions not just in a single business but across whole sections of an economy or industry. The failure to account for the influence of these types of dominant coalitions was considered a serious flaw by John Child, who has been the major proponent of the strategic choice view of decision making (Child 1972: 1–11). He has sought to further explain decision-making processes by emphasizing the role dominant coalitions play in the choice of strategies made by organizations, choices which can impact on every individual and can dramatically affect such things as side-payments and slack.

According to Child, the *dominant coalition* does not necessarily refer only to formal authority holders (those with legitimate authority in an organization) but to a collection of individuals who hold power over a particular decision-making period and are in positions to have input into policy initiation and implementation. Coalition members can draw their support from a wide range of key or strategically placed individuals. Important strategic decisions (mergers, takeovers, moving off-shore, etc.) are often the result of negotiations and bargains between coalition members and not necessarily the result of some well-thought-out rational method of decision making. Decisions about such things as mergers, for example, are not necessarily made because there are laws, principles, facts or figures which support this strategy. A choice to merge may be made because a powerful person owes a favour, has cross-board membership, or is locked into a struggle to defeat a third party, etc. relating to Covenant Corporation.

Dominant coalitions can be so powerful that their members have opportunities to select the types of environments in which they will operate rather than passively responding to external threats and pressures. For example, some company leaders and their backers may simply choose to pull out of a particular strategy if it proves too hostile, or they may wait to enter a new market when conditions improve. However, the striking feature of dominant coalitions is that they can produce such awesome concentrations of power and influence that they can totally reshape the environment in which they are operating, and a few key decision makers can significantly alter the control and monopoly within and across a whole industry such as brewing, television, computer software, banking or the media. Dominant coalitions may face significant barriers in their environments, such as accusations of anti-competitive behaviour, but the point is that they do not treat the environment as passive (Robbins and Barnwell 1989: 159–60).

Child tends to counter the notion that all actors have the opportunity to engage in coalitions that will be of benefit to them. Dominant coalitions are not accessible to all because the nature of organizations is such that inequity and disadvantage are generic features: there are always the powerful and the powerless. Thus dominant coalitions are usually made up of managerial elites who are relatively unfettered in circumventing, breaking or modifying the bounds of decision making, and therefore determining what counts as a relevant decision topic for various groups (Wilson *et al.* 1986: 310, 328–9). This does not suggest that lower participants are entirely powerless in decision making (e.g. information filtering from members in various locations, such as sales staff, branch managers, etc.). However, Child points out that there is a sharp distinction between those who initiate a decision in regard to major organizational choices and those who are 'marginal' to these decision-making processes.

This last point leads into the second criticism of the pluralist approach. It would be misleading to believe that all organizational participants can form coalitions and act politically to influence major decisions affecting their rights and benefits. The pluralist view fails to account for the ways in which many important decisions are removed from decision-making processes or are suffocated and never become decision topics. Lukes uses the term *non-decision making* to describe how powerful individuals can use their authority and influence to ensure that sensitive or potentially harmful information can be neutralized, suppressed or hidden. Non-decision making involves considerable resources, effort and skill because certain individuals and groups have to be censured and kept in check or else they may force power holders to make revelations and be held accountable (see Chapter 4).

The essential feature of non-decision making is that it draws attention to the many ways in which powerful groups or individuals can structure organizational agendas to their advantage (Lukes 1974: 18–19). Once information is selectively filtered, suppressed or delayed from being made public, the outcome of certain decisions becomes a foregone conclusion, hence non-decision making. For many years the occupational health and safety of workers was an issue which was ignored and sensitive information was withheld at the cost of endangering the lives of workers. Often it was too costly to institute proper safety measures as well as maintaining profits, so safety issues were not incorporated into company policies or practices by key decision makers. The dangers of asbestos are a case in point. Its harmful effects have been known since about 1907, but many governments and businesses throughout the world mined the ore without providing proper protection for workers, thus causing many deaths and illnesses from asbestos-related cancers. Through non-decision making managers were able to control outcomes and suffocate opposition.

While Lukes is concerned with how potential issues are turned into non-decision events by the very powerful, in many large organizations the pressures and competition for scarce resources (salaries, etc.) and rewards (promotion, etc.) can encourage all sorts of individuals and groups to consciously and deliberately manipulate information, bend rules, policies and procedures in order to gain a distinct advantage or benefit from certain decisions. There are many instances of non-decision making in organizations. A quality control department which fails to implement proper tests and studies but lends support to the release of a new product without revealing the shortcomings of its findings is creating a non-decision-making situation. Perhaps because of pressures from other divisions and the need to be seen as efficient and competitive, some key staff in quality control may choose to allow others to make decisions about a product's safety while suppressing negative or unwelcomed results or, for that matter, concealing the fact that adequate testing was not undertaken. Many organizations become involved in costly litigation and bad media exposure because they are caught violating codes, standards and regulations applying to their industry. Often the decisions which lead to these situations can only be explained as outcomes of non-decision-making processes (Stephenson 1985: 153–4; Pfeffer 1981: 146–54).

The whole area of non-decision making raises many important issues about the ethical conduct of organizational participants and the exercise of power (see Chapter 9). Those who control major resources and activities are positioned more strategically to engage in effective non-decision making. In other words, it is easier to bend rules if you are in a position to make the rules or interpret them for others. Some recent decision theorists view non-decision making as being the most relevant of the traditional management decision-making models, especially in terms of describing the activities of powerful and dominant coalitions (see Chapter 4). Nonetheless, non-decision making is itself a problematic approach to decision making. Robert Chia (1996: 200–1), for example, proposes that 'obscured activity' better describes the processes of non-decision making, and that advocates of the model are oblivious to the 'formative nature' of the non-decision-making process. At the very heart of any non-decision making are 'decisional acts' of inclusion and exclusion, and such 'non-activity' is ultimately productive of social reality. This point is illustrated below.

Non-decisions

Decisions involving huge outlays of capital are almost always classic gut decisions; they involve risky, inherently ambiguous judgments between unclear alternatives. In mature industries, like textiles and chemicals, managers are regularly faced with troubling reinvestment decisions.

Alchemy Inc.'s* non-decision

Numerical measures and other seemingly sophisticated analytical tools can only be 'guideposts' in making such choices. Satisfactory rates of return are socially determined; they vary from industry to industry, indeed, from firm to firm, and involve complicated assessments of competitors' strategies, actual, possible, or pending regulation, possible alternative investments, and, most important, key managers' determinations of what levels of return are desirable, acceptable, and defensible. Since, as described earlier, credit flows up and details get pushed down in corporate hierarchies, managers at the middle and upper-middle levels are often left to sort out extremely complicated questions about technology, investment, and their bosses' desires and intentions.

Consider, for instance, the case of a large coking plant… Coke making requires a gigantic battery to cook the coke slowly and evenly for long periods; the battery is the most important piece of capital equipment in a coking plant. In 1975, the [Alchemy] plant's battery showed signs of weakening and certain managers at corporate headquarters had to decide whether to invest $[US]6 million to restore the battery to top form. Clearly, because of the amount of money involved, this was a gut decision.

No decision was made. The CEO had sent the word out to defer all unnecessary capital expenditures to give the corporation cash reserves for other investments. So the managers allocated small amounts of money to patch the battery up until 1979, when it collapsed entirely. This brought the company into a breach of contract with a steel producer and into violation of various Environmental Protection Agency (EPA) pollution regulations. The total bill, including lawsuits and now federally mandated repairs to the battery, exceeded $100 million. I have heard figures as high as $150 million, but because of 'creative accounting', no one is sure of the exact amount.

This simple but very typical example gets to the heart of how decision making is intertwined with a company's authority structure and advancement patterns. As Alchemy managers see it, the decisions facing them in 1975 and 1979 were crucially different. Had they acted decisively in 1975 – in hindsight, the only substantively rational course – they would have salvaged the battery and saved their corporation millions of dollars in the long run.

In the short run, however, since even seemingly rational decisions are subject to widely varying interpretations, particularly decisions that run counter to a CEO's stated objectives, they would have been taking serious personal risks in restoring the battery. What is more, their political networks might have unravelled, leaving them vulnerable to attack. They chose short-term safety over long-term gain.

… This goes to the heart of the problem. Managers think in the short run because they are evaluated by both their superiors and peers on their short-term results. Those who are not seen to be producing requisite short-run gains come to be thought of as embarrassing liabilities. Of course, past work gets downgraded in such a process. The old saw, still heard frequently today, 'I know what you did for me yesterday, but what have you done for me lately?' is more than a tired garment district salesman's joke. It accurately reflects the widespread amnesia among managers about others' past accomplishments, however notable, and points to the probationary crucibles at the core of managerial life. Managers feel that if they do not survive the short run, the long run hardly matters, and one can only buy time for the future by attending to short-term goals. As one manager says: 'Our horizon is today's lunch.'

Within such a context, managers know that even farsighted, correct decisions can shorten promising careers. A manager at **Weft Corporation** reflects:

> People are always calculating how others will see the decisions that they make. They are always asking: 'What are the consequences of this decision?' They know that they have to gauge not just the external…market consequences of a decision, but the internal political consequences. And sometimes you can make the right market decision, but it can be the wrong political decision…

> Decisions are made only when they are inevitable. To make a decision ahead of the time it has to be made risks political catastrophe. People can always interpret the decision as an unwise one even if it seems to be correct on other grounds.

When a decision is inevitable, managers say, 'The decision made itself.' Diffusion of responsibility, in the case of the coke battery by procrastinating until total crisis voided real choices, is intrinsic to organizational life because the real issue in most gut decisions is: Who is going to get blamed if things go wrong?

* Alchemy Inc. is a subsidiary of Covenant Corporation.

Source: Robert Jackall (1988), Moral Mazes: The World of Corporate Managers, New York: Oxford University Press, pp. 80–2, 84–5, with modifications.

The above case illustrates that although knowledge is extremely important in organizational decision making, organizational members will draw on a much wider variety of knowledge than decision theory is customarily able to recognize. Postmodern organization increasingly relies on the quality of its information for making critical decisions quickly, but as Robert Jackall (1988) notes these are often still 'gut decisions' rather than calculated ones. Put simply, this arises because all knowledge is about the past, and all decisions are about the future, so there is always an element of incommensurability to them – they do not quite fit together. Knowledge is often not shared between managers and groups of managers for political reasons despite the furious networking they may do *until* it looks as though their project may need some help to avoid failure. So knowledge in a real sense here is power, and is realized both through action and non-action, informed by information which ranges from, say, the president's body language to three feet of printout from scenario planning software.

Cross-cultural issues in decision making

Sue Miller, David Hickson and David Wilson (1996) note with alarm that virtually all the major studies of decision making have been American, British or Scandinavian. They note that the existing studies do display some evidence of differences between the different varieties of Western culture which are 'pluralistic, bluntly competitive and impersonal' (Miller *et al.* 1996: 308). Elsewhere in the world approaches may be more person centred, where loyalty is owed to the person not the job, higher authority may be greatly venerated, and harmony and consideration for others may offset the drive for achievement by the individual. As Miller *et al.* (1996: 309) suggest, these processes may not be adequately accounted for by such concepts as 'satisficing search, incrementalism, rationality and politicality, recycling, sporadic or fluid or constricted movement, or coinciding garbage'.

Decision making in the Arab Middle East tends to be centralized, with authority having high status, especially where it is family based. There is a certain *noblesse oblige* to consult subordinates, but this is not the Western sense of participation and has no impact on the decision-making process. In Latin America decision making is centralized and personal, and in Brazil in particular decisions are made almost hastily and informally. In Africa, decision making is likely to be more authoritarian and politicized. Such concepts as political sporadic processes, or the garbage can model, seem unlikely in these settings.

But of course what Miller *et al.* (1996) describe are the elements of different discourses which shape the decisional text, in regions where social subjectivity varies widely. Their puzzlement, which arises from an almost nostalgic feeling that earlier decision-making studies might have been engaging with a knowledge that was universal and not local, and that their own theories might have been caught up in that process, would not be perplexing when viewed from the textual approach which we outline later in this chapter. The first step for such research is to outline the elements of the intertext, or those other texts and influences which coincide in the situation under study. Difference here is not necessarily a problem – it is just difference. However, Miller *et al.* (1996) have moved a considerable distance from Anglo-American-centred universalistic discourse, and they cautiously argue for greater global research on decision-making processes, while observing that even in relatively open societies like the West managers do not readily open their doors to scrutiny of high-level decision making. In more authoritarian or familial cultures, these problems would become enormous – but it should still be noted that theories which depend on Anglo-American data neglect a huge proportion of humankind.

Critique of 'decision' and 'choice'

The management decision-making schools reviewed above develop their theories of decision making by making specific reference to the inherent capabilities of individual decision makers, especially their capabilities for rational thinking. They often also make assumptions that are essentialist in nature, that is, they assume decision makers have commonly held aspirations, goals or universal experiences. Historically, the use of 'choice' as an explanation for decision making has been crucial as a move away from the determinism of Management Science with its *normative* models of decision making. Peter Keen and Michael Scott Morton (1978: 62) point out that the emphasis had been '…on how managers *should* act rather than on observing how they actually behave'. Choice is such a compelling concept in decision-making theory that it has attained the status of 'commonsense' (Belsey 1980). Commonsense categories are rarely challenged, and as a consequence will tend to organize research directions, agendas and questions within a field. By recognizing that the idea of choice has become a commonsense category, our responsibility becomes one of questioning the prevailing assumptions implied by it. The commonsense category of choice, in the context of management decision making, organizes the field so as to view the function, status and value of management work in terms of purposefulness and reason (i.e. as rational).

There have been recent developments, as pointed out earlier, which recognize some of the limitations of traditional decision-making literature and have led to a shift away from 'decisions' to other concerns such as 'action' (Mintzberg *et al.* 1990); from 'choice' to that of 'change' in the context of decision making (Pettigrew 1990) or to the interpretation of 'action' (March 1988). These revisions acknowledge that the concept of a decision is problematic, and that managers are not always faced with clear-cut rational choices. March (1988) in fact argues that reality is messy, and that 'decision makers' often *value* ambiguity – it means that they do not have to commit themselves to potentially risky courses of action until it is absolutely necessary. It also means that they can see how events unfold and influence interpretations of them so that they can look good and avoid blame, as the managers in Covenant and Weft Corporations sought to do. However, in many respects 'actions', 'change' and 'interpretation' function simply as aliases for traditional categories. Underlying these new concepts are the same kind of assumptions concerning the individual, rationalist intentionality of management action, '…reinforced by a predisposition towards the use of linear causal thinking in the explanatory scheme of things and towards a subtle privileging of the conscious over the unconscious in accounting for decisional "events"' (Chia 1996: 193). A significant theoretical problem for most accounts of management decision making is the use of the psychological subject, that is the individual person, as the formative unit where groups are theorized as collections of individuals and group characteristics are the sum of individual characteristics. Group activities then are seen to be primarily shaped by psychological forces rather than, for example, social, anthropological, political or linguistic ones.

What these approaches fail to acknowledge is what we have termed, following Chia, the flow of *decisional acts* that contribute to the decision-making process. Managers in their everyday lives are ordering their world, constantly redrawing boundaries, and Mintzberg *et al.* and March are, at the level of theory, doing the same thing. Making a 'decision' is a matter of making distinctions between things, actions and events, which leads us to perceive the world in a particular way. To view 'decision' as choice, change, action or interpretation is to fail to pay attention to other alternatives, and also to see that this in itself is a decision. In fact, as Chia argues, making decisions, or decisional acts, is an inescapable condition of being human, not just a special activity undertaken by decision makers at specific decision-making events.

Mintzberg *et al.* (1990), Andrew Pettigrew (1972) and March (1988) do make some attempt to counteract the rationalist tendency in decision making and to produce a more fully *descriptive* and *analytical* rather than a *prescriptive* model of managerial decision making. However, they do not go far enough in addressing what such a model might require. We would suggest that its attributes would include:

- the replacement of the mentalist, rational concept of 'decision' with an explicitly social theory of *communicative action*;
- a social theory of *subjectivity* and *agency* to replace the individualism of rationalist models of management decision making;
- a *contextual approach* to decision making where context includes an account of both: (1) the broader disciplinary and institutional contexts, given that disciplines act to discipline and control their practitioners (Lenoir 1993: 70–102), and (2) the immediate situational contexts which inform specific decision-making occasions; and
- a *descriptive* and *textual* model based on a discursive (see definition below) theory of human communication, in order to describe under which organizational circumstances specific 'choices' become available or unavailable, permissible or not permissible, or thinkable or unthinkable for groups of managers.

Re-theorizing decision making

In light of the criticisms provided in the previous section, this chapter proposes a new model of decision making based on a *textual process model of organizations* (Clarke 1991, 1992). In order to build this model, we draw from theories of communication which have been developed in critical theory, communications and cultural studies, psychoanalysis, social semiotics and feminist studies. Much of this literature is generally unfamiliar to students of management, although you will find theory relating to its elements used in other chapters of this text (see, for example, the chapters concerning culture, gender and power). Re-theorizing decision making using a textual process model means in this instance that the analytical emphasis is placed on understanding communicative processes operating as organizational practices in specific organizational contexts. Elements of the model are described in turn (i.e. discourse, text, social subjectivity) in order to simplify the discussion and to introduce the necessary concepts.

Discourse

Knowledge is an important dimension of power as is recognized by most commentators on power, but especially by Michel Foucault (1972, 1980). Foucault was particularly aware of the importance of language for defining the way in which people view the world. This can mean that because the way we speak embodies particular ways of viewing the world, and because any way of viewing the world advantages the interests of certain groups rather than others, and entails certain actions or practices as a consequence of viewing the world in that way, *all language embodies power relationships*. Power for Foucault is inescapable and seeps through into the core of our being – we think in language so we think in terms of power, and when we act we act in terms of language and thus in terms of power, so power informs even our bodily movements. Foucault calls the complex nest of ideas, linguistic expressions, assumptions, justifications, defences, social institutions and practical actions that constitute a cohesive way of approaching the world a *discourse*. This idea is not the common understanding of discourse that we use in everyday life – it is much broader. It was originally introduced as a way of thinking about how ideology functions in culture, institutions and ourselves, although discourse has proved to be a much more flexible concept than the one it replaced (Holquist 1981: 426 and 428; Althusser 1971; Foucault 1972). A useful definition of discourse is provided below:

> Discourses are systematically-organised sets of statements which give expression to the meanings and values of an institution. Beyond that they define, describe and delimit what it is possible to say and not possible to say (and by extension – what it is possible to do or not to do) with respect to the area of concern of that institution, whether marginally or centrally. A discourse provides a set of possible statements about a given area, and organises and gives structure to the manner in which a particular topic, object, process is to be talked about. In that it provides descriptions, rules, permissions and prohibitions of social and individual actions (Kress 1985: 6–7).

Take a look below at an illustration of the discourse of 'enterprise' which has been common since the 1980s – 100 years ago the discourse of 'progress' might have performed the same role in mobilizing society. The important thing to remember here is that language and power are inseparably connected and have a much broader influence than simply the things we say.

Enterprise culture in the UK

During the 1980s, the Conservative Government of the UK led by Margaret Thatcher determined that it would change the social structures which had underpinned the Welfare State – regulation of business practices by the State, high levels of taxation, relatively militant trade unionism, high levels of welfare benefits paid. Along with this, they wanted to change the expectations of the people who, Thatcher believed, had become too dependent on the State and were insufficiently entrepreneurial, profit-orientated and business and competition minded.

> 'I used to have a nightmare for the first six years in office that, when I had got the finances right, when I had got the law right, the deregulation etc., that the British sense of enterprise and initiative would have been killed by socialism. I was really afraid that when I had got it all ready to spring back, it would no longer be there and it would not come back...' (Margaret Thatcher, *Sunday Times* 8 May 1988)

The project of economic reconstruction clearly went much further – 'Economics are the method. The object is to change the soul' (Thatcher, *Sunday Times* 7 May 1989);

'fighting and changing the culture and psychology of two generations…changing psychology to change the business culture' (Nigel Lawson, *The British Experiment* Fifth Mais Lecture, HM Treasury 1984). Although the overall project of Thatcherism was not completely cohesive, it involved the combined efforts of 'think-tanks' such as the Centre for Policy Studies, who produced papers on economic, political and legal issues associated with fiscal policy and deregulation; policy advisers such as Keith Josephs and Brian Griffiths who developed moral and ethical arguments; businessmen/politicians such as David Young who developed and applied the language of managerialism – competition, customers, enterprise, markets, niches, competitive advantage, distinctive competence, strategic positioning, quality, process control, cost, profit and loss etc – to all areas of the state including health and education; marketing specialists and advertising geniuses such as Saatchi and Saatchi who promoted and publicised the ideology; a minor military victory in the Falklands which provided the inspiration for the carefully orchestrated campaign against the 'enemy within' to break the power of the trade unions; support of the media, cemented by re-franchising the independent TV and radio stations and reforming the BBC; redrawing of electoral boundaries which reduced the impact of the opposition vote (i.e. the effective expression of dissension) in marginal seats; and of course the well-documented economic and legal strategies followed by the government. This complex web of speeches, books, articles, TV programmes, legislation, political stratagems and practical actions was designed to change not only the way people lived their lives but how they thought about themselves, and allowed room for no alternatives to the vision of personal independence, individual enterprise, and self-responsibility. The very meanings of such words as enterprise and quality were redefined in a way which fitted the political and ideological programme, and predisposed individuals and businesses to a certain type of action. This, in its entirety, was the **enterprise discourse**.

[See Russell Keat and Nicholas Abercrombie (1991), *Enterprise Culture*, London: Routledge, for an extensive treatment of how this discourse was constructed.]

To apply the concept of discourse to a management decision-making situation, consider the following hypothetical example: the strategic managers of an Australian corporatized public service company are faced with a continuing slump in profits due to the deregulation of the market in which they operate. The short-term decision-making prospects seem to be limited to a small range of 'tried and true' choices including management restructuring, corporate downsizing and outsourcing of 'non-core' activities. What dictates this particular set of options? In part, discourse theory suggests that the choices have already been preordained by what is currently considered to be efficient private sector best practice. As the current economic and management discourses dictate that public sector entities should operate in the same fashion as private sector entities, what chance is there that strategic managers might create atypical solutions, for example measures aimed at increasing the organizations' revenue? Probably the answer to this question is that the strategic managers will already be locked into specific courses of action which are already in part predetermined if these managers comply with discourses which assume the equivalence of public and private sector entities. In effect discourse theory says that these managers will already be actively involved in a kind of 'collective' and unacknowledged blindness to entire courses of action. This collective blindness is inscribed in the discourses which circulate within organizations predisposing, but in no way determining, what constitutes effective and efficient management decision making. It is important to note here that discourses never directly operate on managers or others. Discourses inform texts (see below) which in turn are 'read' by managers or others in specific organizational contexts – that is to say that discourses must have participants in order to function.

In an large number of modern 'scientific' disciplines, including modern management science, and its related disciplines of information systems and accounting, the psychological individual is viewed as the origin of meaning in social and cultural practices. In the previous section, we described decision-making theory as having attained the status of 'commonsense' (Belsey 1980; Garfinkel 1987). This is possible because particular types of discourse referred to as *liberal-humanist discourse* operate throughout Western culture. The effect of these types of discourse is to *naturalize*, that is, to allow to operate unchallenged, the view that individuals are single, unified, originators of meanings. In turn, liberal-humanist discourse has influenced academics and practitioners to reproduce uncritically these discourses as 'commonsense' when creating theories of decision making. As these traditional models pass into the literature and are adopted and enacted by practitioners, the 'commonsense' nature of the individual decision maker choosing from a range of unproblematic options becomes reproduced. Within the field of decision making, the literature simply assumes that managers are readily able to evaluate and select from a 'full range' of potential choices, directly selecting a clear choice, choosing from sets of competing choices, or by avoiding or suppressing choices altogether.

Furthermore, theorizing or presenting speakers (managers) as the originators of meanings (decisions) favours those who are allowed or authorized to speak in specific circumstances. Similarly, issues of power and control tend to be discussed from just such an individualist standpoint. Power in organizations is often treated as if it were a commodity: the possession of individuals. This individualism obscures the way organizations operate as a product of various influences, such as markets, technology, etc. and processes such as discrimination and exploitation. In this framework, even the discipline of organizational behaviour becomes reduced to a study of individuals compared to norms of behaviour against which dysfunctional characteristics can be treated and new functional behaviours reinforced.

Gender as a discourse

To illustrate our point about the importance of discourse, and of who is allowed to speak and in what way, let us take the example of gender. Men and women have never been viewed as or treated as equals in the workplace. Jobs have been differentiated and even whole occupations, especially those in service industries, have been designated 'women's work'. Fewer than 20 percent of all managerial posts are held by women, and at more senior levels this falls to 10 percent (see Chapter 2). Men are often seen to be rational, calculating and resilient whereas women are seen as being emotional, changeable and lacking resolution. This forms the background to what men and women do in any real organization, but the work of Deborah Tannen (1995) (also mentioned in Chapter 2) indicates that men and women actually *talk* differently and thus communicate different things when they speak. As Tannen argues, women tend to learn styles of speaking which make them appear less confident and self-assured than they really are, and as a result they lose out on those organizational issues – like promotion – that depend on appearing confident. They tend also to be called upon less to speak in decision-making processes, and if they are, are less likely to be regarded as being persuasive or credible.

In their study on the decision-making experiences of women and people of colour, Priscilla Elsass and Laura Graves (1997: 954–5) found evidence that confirmed women contribute to group tasks at the lower end, make fewer attempts to influence the group, are less often chosen as leaders, and are generally less committed to group outcomes. In terms of communication style, and echoing Tannen's comments in Chapter 2, Elsass and Graves noted that white male behaviour is typically the norm by which other groups are judged. In the context of decision making, the open-ended free-wheeling decision-making environment in many Western organizations is likely to intimidate those not comfortable with this style. In some cultures, speaking aggressively or interrupting others might also be seen as rude whether done by men or women.

In an interesting experiment Elizabeth Mapstone (cited in Powell 1998; also see Mapstone 1998) set up an experiment with 72 men and women, sorted into an equal number of pairs comprising man–man, man–woman, woman–woman. Each participant was given a detective story to read with a number of possible solutions. Once the story was read, each person was asked to discuss their decisions with their partners. While some men were able to convince their male partners to change their minds about the correct solution to the mystery, and the same occurred with women-only pairs, the men who had women partners were not influenced to change their minds. Mapstone concludes, as does Elsass and Graves, that there are so many stereotypes drawn upon when women seek to argue with or influence male colleagues that more often than not women's views are more easily discounted or not listened to. One corollary of this is that women often avoid arguing because of the negative stereotypes (hostile, aggressive, hysterical) and the discomfort this causes men around them. Mapstone's research was undertaken in the UK where she conducted 200 interviews, had diary records kept by 190 people, collected 200 questionnaires and conducted 200 formal interviews. The conclusion from these various studies suggests that powerful people, which usually means men, are more likely to reward and listen to people with similar language styles.

We also mentioned in Chapter 8 that language styles can affect the type and richness of information that we receive into the process. A restricted style can mean a restricted input of information, less fruitful discussion and a failure to achieve smooth implementation as not all the relevant dimensions of the problem were available for consideration. This must seriously impact on the quality of decision making under conditions of diversity. So what people say and how they say it can be different depending on their gender, and this may both open and close doors to them, and may enrich or impoverish the process of organizational decision making. An organization which only rewards one communicative style is losing its ability to hear a wide range of information and share knowledge and increase the flexibility of its actions.

Texts

Any utterance in a social setting, including discussions between managers involved in decision-making occasions, can be referred to as a *text*. The term 'text' is used to indicate that decision making involves language. According to this approach, language is patterned by genres which might include narrative or story genres. The spoken language of decision making also employs myths, signs and symbols (Linstead 1998). The plural form of the term is generally used simultaneously to signify two important aspects of the theory:

1   Decision making occasions, along with most other organizational practices, generally produce *more than one text*. If we were studying a specific decision-making occasion, we might use a tape recorder to make a record of what managers were saying (one text), which we might subsequently use to produce a transcript of what transpired during the meeting (another text), while also collecting associated written texts which would help understand what took place (agendas, minutes and attachments). All of these kinds of texts can be thought of as 'products', and
2   *Meaning-making occasions are 'processes'.* To consider a text as simply a document would be ignoring the fact that while a text can be defined as 'a structure of messages or messages traces which has a socially ascribed unity' (Hodge and Kress 1988: 6), its constituent messages, and consequently the text itself, can *never have a single, fixed meaning*.

This last point requires further consideration. Catherine Belsey (1980: 26) states that while language provides the possibility of meaning, any text exhibits multiple meanings because meanings never remain static. However, the most significant factor determining the plurality of meaning is that a text's possible set of meanings will vary according to the way discourses are recognized by readers. So it is possible to have a *single* position from which a text is intelligible, because, as Belsey (1980: 19–20) puts it, 'texts are rooted in specific discourses' – in other words, the people who produced the text already had a particular perspective on what the text meant or should mean. Meanings are subjective only to the extent that the contradictions and superimpositions of discourses construct different sets of meaning for each participant in a decision-making situation.

Genre

Apart from being simultaneously a product and a process, a text will also possess a specific staging, referred to as its *genre*. Knowing the purpose that a text serves in a particular social setting enables us to anticipate to a surprising degree of accuracy both the overall text structure and also its internal organization of messages. In a typical decision-making occasion, we would expect to be involved in a spoken text which conforms to the generic structure of a meeting, as opposed, for example, to a birthday party, a wedding or Holy Communion. If the meeting were preceded by the exchange of gifts, a request to all those who knew of any just cause or impediment why the meeting should not proceed or communal confession then we would be very puzzled indeed, just as we would be if asked to participate in a secret ballot on what games to play at a party, or to present a report on the previous year's birthday party. All of these situations would violate the conventions of the genre. A familiarity with the genres associated with a decision-making circumstance in a given organization helps managers 'understand' the meanings being negotiated with the text – for example, the weight to be given to the views of the chairperson, or the importance of 'looking good and avoiding blame' as a tactic to pursue in meetings. Participants understand texts in social contexts because they have prior experience of them and genres assist in making texts identifiable in specific social contexts. As a part of our lived experience within institutions (Martin 1992), we learn to ascribe certain kinds of meaning to certain kinds of texts.

Genres assist in constructing or reinforcing some of the meaning of the text – comic, tragic, epic, ironic – or how it is to be 'read', identifying the agent(s) of the text (the heroes and possibly villains) and specifying the audience. Belsey (1980: 26) points out that meanings in texts are conventional, requiring familiarity not intuition. How a text constructs meaning depends on how discourses are negotiated in the text by managers and others. Various discourses in a text need not necessarily be in harmony with each other. Indeed, it is the conflict and contradiction in a text which makes it possible for participants to read the text in different ways. It is also possible for the same participants to read off different meanings from the same text at different times and on different social occasions. In this way texts are '…implicated in social processes of development and change' and can be reconstructed and reinterpreted over time (Hodge and Kress 1988: 6).

Social subjectivity

Having defined the concept of discourse, and seen that managers and others in decision-making contexts negotiate specific sets of meanings (texts) on specific social occasions (genres), we turn our attention to the final major concept used in the textual process model of organizations. Managers and other participants in organizations are referred to by the term *social subject* (Clarke 1991). In society, at work, at home and at play, we are all social subjects. Following Julian Henriques *et al.* (1984), theories of the subject emphasize how the social domain constitutes 'subjectivity'. *Subjectivity* refers simultaneously to the condition of 'individuality' and self-awareness, which is continually formed and reformed under changing social, economic and historical circumstances. In the context of decision-making theory, using the social subjectivity concept to look at managers and others in organizations prevents us from adopting the rationalism identified in many of the traditional decision-making models reviewed in the first section of this chapter. It is often the case that readers encountering this concept for the first time recoil in horror at the thought that they are socially constituted and not individual free agents. This effect is discursively produced! It is the operation of liberal-humanist discourse that constructs the subject of psychology known as the 'individual'. As already noted, discourses never directly operate on managers or others (social subjects) but are 'read' by them in specific organizational contexts. Discourses must have social subjects in order to exist. Rather than being determined by mere discourses, we are social subjects *because of* them (Dore 1995: 151–76). Bound up with the concepts of discourse, text and social subjectivity is the concept of 'positioning'.

Social subjects are *positioned* (with respect to themselves and others) in relation to particular discourses and practices. Texts will usually appear coherent since parts of the text work together to shape the construction of its meaning. Texts will appear meaningful to a reader who adopts the particular configuration of discourses which is negotiated in and by the text. Texts address and position subjects by constructing what is referred to as a *reading position* (or discursive subject-position) which instructs the subject '…about who, what, and how to be in a given social situation, occasion, interaction…' (Kress 1985: 39; Linstead 1985). A reading position is the dominant position from which a specific text appears meaningful, and usually coherent. In adopting the reading position of the text, the subject agrees with the negotiation of discourses constructed in it. In adopting these discourses, a subject is referred to as a *compliant subject*. Reading positions and subject positions are interrelated by the operation of discourses (Kress 1985: 37). In adopting or 'occupying the reading position', the subject is defined and described by, and may identify with, the discourses of the text.

The idea of social subjects is based on Louis Althusser's (1971) idea of the *interpellated subject*, where subjects recognize themselves being called to or being subsumed by the text. Compliant subjects are actually positioned by the text so that they do not see any contradictions it may contain. Compliant subjects in organizations are sometimes socially rewarded so it becomes against their material interest to draw attention to any contradictions they might notice. When subjects resist the obvious reading position encoded in the text, or refuse to accept the role offered to them by the organization, they are referred to as a *resisting or oppositional subject* (Linstead 1985). Because subjects are socially and discursively formed, each will bring to the decision-making situations different sets of institutional and linguistic experiences (Kress 1988: 127). It is possible for those who share similar institutional experiences (for example, workplaces, schools, churches) and similar linguistic experiences (nationality, class and culture) to appear to comply quite naturally with specific discourses in decision-making contexts. However, as no two subjects will share absolutely identical discourses, it is unlikely that they will consistently share the same meanings, and people who agree may come to disagree in time without any obvious conflict.

Conclusion

As decision-making activities are often viewed as one of the distinguishing characteristics of management work, there has been sustained interest in theorizing and building models in order to understand it. Choice has proved to be a significant and enduring category in traditional decision-making theories and models. It is extremely difficult to presume that only unitary models of decision making (for example, rational and administrative approaches) accurately model decisions-making activities. In reaction to unitary models, other models of decision making have been developed including the garbage can, political, and dominant coalitions and non-decision-making models. These models at least critique the assumption that decisions are entirely predictable, neutral and objective, although these critiques often rest on dubious claims concerning the influence of 'subjective choices' and the 'preferences' of those participating in the decision making.

There have been developments which recognize the limitations of traditional decision-making literature. Alternatives proposed have included shifts to 'action' and 'choice'. However, these have been shown to function simply as aliases for traditional categories, while still relying upon the same kinds of assumptions concerning individual decision makers. In an attempt to re-theorize decision making in a way which does not reproduce these assumptions, this chapter has proposed a new model of decision making. This model, referred to as the textual process model of organizations, employs the concepts of discourse, text, genre and social subjectivity to place the analytical emphasis on understanding decision making as communicative processes operating in specific organizational contexts.

Case analysis

Let us now see how this analysis could be applied to the case study at the beginning of the chapter to illustrate the textual approach to decision making.

What criteria do people apply in making decisions in the companies described? First, in Covenant, they use rational vocabularies to disguise decisions which are essentially impulsive and irrational, made by those in power. In Weft Corporation, when non-routine decisions have to be made, they look up and around, to see what indications the powerful are giving about how they should act, and they do what they think is expected of them. When big decisions have to be made, they avoid them for as long as possible, then try to involve as many people as possible so that if the decision goes badly, they can pass or share the blame. They sidestep decisions where possible, and they try to avoid being seen to make a mistake.

Why are they afraid to make decisions? Partly because they know that any order they put in place could be swept away by the fiat of one of the senior managers and frequently is. This is partly because several of them have gone beyond their level of competence and are afraid of being found out. The culture of the company pushes them to grab for advancement, but they then doubt their abilities when they reach their limits and try at all costs not to let their uncertainties be exposed.

Looking at these companies as a text then, as they are so similar, what discourse can we see at work? First there is clearly a discourse of hierarchical, and probably patriarchal, power. This discourse indicates that the powerful can do whatever they like as long as they can make it look rational. The overt discourse here is one of rational management, but the subtext is clearly one of power. This entails a notion of careerism, because the higher you climb up the hierarchy, the less likely you are to be subverted or have your decisions overturned. However, the subtext here is to look competent because hierarchy also implies fitness for position, and ability. So the discourse operating is one of survival, by looking rational and competent, avoiding blame, mistakes and being found out.

The particular strategies which managers use in these companies – collective involvement, putting decisions off and avoiding them if possible – are all reported as part of the text. The behaviour at the unveiling of the designer collection indicated that there was more than one text in operation, but that most people were buying into the one which they thought the president supported. The very fact, however, that managers had to do a lot of collective interpretative work to 'define' the collection as a success indicates that even dominant texts do not have a fixed and final meaning, but they have to be sustained. In this case, the evidence of the awfulness of the collection was effectively denied, but only for so long…eventually the market redefined it as a failure. At that point, we would expect people to begin to rewrite history to try to distance themselves from the failure, saying, for example, that they had never liked it in the first place. Here it was the power element of the dominant discourse that had the managers acting, as they believed, to reflect the views of the powerful back to them, and thus reduce the risk of becoming unacceptable.

In terms of genre, the managers 'read' the viewing of the collection as though it were a public affirmation of the president's good taste and power, rather than a critical appraisal of the commercial potential of a set of designs. They viewed it, in short, as a ceremonial, a ritual, and not as a working meeting. This helped them all to act together in praising the collection, as they all understood what they thought was required of them. Cultures which set up ritual events may find that this produces solidarity as it did here, but it does not produce good decisions, as we also saw.

Where managers accept the need to preserve the appearance of being competent, to preserve the myth of the rational manager, they are acting as compliant subjects in the terms specified by the corporate discourse. Some of the managers who commented show signs of being resisting or oppositional subjects, but they appear relatively inactive rather than rebellious. So without accepting the imperatives of the corporation to be dishonest, they nevertheless are not fighting to overturn them. In this situation, then, decisions are not likely to be made on the evidence or treated according to their merits, but in a decisional flow which looks simultaneously forward to identify what action will gain merit, and backward to erase any mistakes or blemishes from the record. Whether this can be altered is largely dependent on the organization addressing these issues of hypocrisy for itself, learning to read its own 'text', developing greater language and analytic skills in its managers which, as far as possible within the power structure, would allow suppressed virtues to re-emerge and a new discourse – perhaps of a flat hierarchy where communication was open and managers supported and trusted rather than blamed each other – to develop and change the organization. Finally, our use of the text model illustrates how knowledge, information and power are closely connected through the concept of discourse.

Questions at the beginning of the chapter

Returning to the questions at the beginning of the chapter, a decision is not as straightforward to define as we might think, as the first part of the chapter explores. It can be regarded as a commitment to a course of action, but from that point views diverge. The decision process is important because the quality of decisions is important, and if irrational and whimsical actions are successfully presented as rational and ordered, then the organization ultimately suffers as the case study material illustrates. We looked at the issue of choice, and the ways decision-making behaviour can be said to be constrained by it, and indeed critiqued the concept of choice for preserving the 'mentalism' of the decision-making self, rather than seeing the actor acting within a field of influences and constraints. Decision making can be affected by the behaviour of the participants in many ways, as they may preserve defensive routines which delay a decision or stop it altogether, and cover up the inconsistencies in the organization's processes, or improve the process by reflexive critical engagement with it. The analysis of the case studies has explored the links between knowledge, information and power in decision making.

References

Althusser, L. (1971) *Lenin and Philosophy and Other Essays*, London: New Left Books.

Barnard, C.I. (1938) *The Functions of the Executive*, Cambridge, Mass.: Harvard University Press.

Belsey, C. (1980) *Critical Practice*, London: Methuen.

Chia, R. (1996) *Organizational Analysis as Deconstructive Practice*, Berlin: Walter de Gruyter.

Child, J. (1972) 'The role of strategic choice', *Sociology* 6: 1–22.

Clarke, R. J. (1991) 'Discourses in systems development failure', in Aungles, S. (ed.), *Information Technology in Australia: Transforming Organisational Structure and Culture*, Sydney: University of New South Wales Press.

Clarke, R. J. (1992) 'Some applications of social semiotics in information systems discipline and practice', in MacGregor, R., Clarke, R. J., Little, S., Gould, T. and Ang, A. (eds), *Information Systems as Organisational Processes – ISOP '92: Proceedings Third Australian Conference on Information Systems*, Department of Business Systems, University of Wollongong 5–8 October: 67–79.

Cohen, M.D., March, T.J. and Olsen, J.P. (1972) 'A garbage can model of organizational choice', *Administrative Science Quarterly* 17: 1–25.

Curwen, C.J. (1963) *Theory of the Firm*, London: Macmillan.

Cyert, R. and March, J.G. (1963) *A Behavioural Theory of the Firm*, Englewood Cliffs, NJ: Prentice Hall.

Davenport, T.H., De Long, D.W. and Beers, M.C. (1998) 'Successful knowledge management projects', *Sloan Management Review* Winter: 43–57.

Dawson, S. (1986) *Analysing Organisations*, London: Macmillan.

Dessler, G. (1976) *Organisation and Management: A Contingency Approach*, Englewood Cliffs, NJ: Prentice Hall.

Dore, J. (1995) 'The emergence of language from dialogue', in Mandelker, A. (ed.), *Bakhtin in Contexts: Across the Disciplines*, Evanston: Northwestern University Press.

Elsass, P.M. and Graves, L.A. (1997) 'Demographic diversity in decision-making groups: The experiences of women and people of color', *Academy of Management Review* 22(4): 946–73.

Foucault, M. (1972) *The Archaeology of Knowledge*, translated by Shendon Smith, A. M., London: Tavistock.

Foucault, M. (1980) *Power/Knowledge,* Brighton: Harvester.

Garfinkel, H. (1987) *Studies in Ethnomethodology*, Oxford: Polity Press.

Harris, G.T. (1993) 'The post-capitalist executive: An Interview with Peter F. Drucker', *Harvard Business Review* May–June: 115–22.

Henriques, J., Hollway, W., Urwin, C., Venn, C. and Walkerdine V. (1984) *Changing the Subject: Psychology, Social Regulation and Subjectivity*, London and New York: Methuen.

Hickson, D.J., Butler, R.J., Cray, D., Mallory, G.R. and Wilson, D.C. (1986) *Top Decisions: Strategic Decision Making in Organizations*, San Francisco: Jossey-Bass.

Hodge, R. and Kress, G. (1988) *Social Semiotics,* Oxford: Polity Press.

Holquist, M. (ed.) (1981) *The Dialogic Imagination: Four Essays by M. M. Bakhtin*, Austin: University of Texas.

Hopwood, A. (1974) *Accounting and Human Behaviour*, London: Accountancy Age Books.

Jackall, R. (1988) *Moral Mazes: The World of Corporate Managers*, New York: Oxford University Press.

Keat, R. and Abercrombie, N. (1991) *Enterprise Culture,* London: Routledge.

Keen, P.G. and Scott Morton, M.S. (1978) *Decision Support Systems: An Organizational Perspective*, Reading, Mass.: Addison-Wesley.

Kress, G. (1985) *Linguistic processes in sociocultural practice*, ECS806 Sociocultural aspects of language and education, Waurn Ponds, Victoria: Deakin University.

Lenoir, T. (1993) 'The discipline of nature and the nature of disciplines' in Messer-Davidow, E., Shumway, D.R. and Sylvan, D.J. (eds), *Knowledges: Historical and Critical Studies in Disciplinarity*, Charlottsville and London: University Press of Virginia.

Lindblom, C.E. (1990) 'The science of muddling through' in Pugh, D.S. (ed.), *Organization Theory, Selected Readings*, Harmondsworth, UK: Penguin.

Linstead, S.A. (1985) 'Organizational induction: The re-creation of order and the re-reading of discourse', *Personnel Review* 14(1) 8: 3–11.

Linstead, S.A. (1999) 'An introduction to the textuality of organization', in Linstead, S. (ed.), *The Textuality of Organizations*, special issue of *Studies in Cultures, Organizations and Societies* 5: 1–10.

Lukes, S. (1974) *Power: A Radical View*, London: Macmillan.

Lupton, T. (1971) *Management and the Social Sciences*, Harmondsworth, UK: Penguin.

Malone, T.W. (1997) 'Is empowerment just a fad? Control, decision making and IT', *Sloan Management Review* Winter: 23–35.

Manwaring, T. And Wood, S. (1985) 'The ghost in the labour process', in Knight, D., Willmott, H. and Collinson, D. (eds), *Job Redesign*, Aldershot, UK: Gower.

Mapstone, E. (1998) *War of Words: Women and Men Arguing*, London: Chatto & Windus.

March, J.G. (1976) 'The technology of foolishness', in March, J.G. and Olsen, J.P. (eds), *Ambiguity and Choice in Organizations*, Bergen, Norway: Univeritiets Forlaget.

March, J.G. (1984) 'Theories of choice and making decisions', in Paton, R. and Brown, S. (eds), *Organizations: Cases, Issues and Concepts*, London: Harper and Row in conjunction with Open University.

March, J.G. (1988) *Decisions and Organizations*, Oxford: Blackwell.

March, J.G. and Simon, H.A. (1958) *Organizations*, New York: John Wiley.

Martin, J.R. (1992) *English Text: System and Structure*, Philadelphia/Amsterdam: John Benjamins Publishing Company.

Miller, S.J, Hickson, D.J. and Wilson, D.C. (1996) 'Decision-making in organizations', in Clegg, S.R., Hardy, C. and Nord, W.R. (eds), *Handbook of Organizational Studies*, London: Sage.

Minkes, A.L. (1987) *The Entrepreneurial Manager: Decisions, Goals and Business Ideas*, Harmondsworth, UK: Penguin.

Mintzberg, H., Waters, J. Pettigrew, A.M. and Butler, R. (1990) 'Studying deciding: An exchange of views between Mintzberg and Waters, Pettigrew and Butler', *Organization Studies* 11(1): 1–16.

Mouzelis, N.P. (1967) *Organizations and Bureaucracy: An Analysis of Modern Theories*, London: Routledge and Kegan Paul.

Perrow, C. (1972) *Complex Organizations: A Critical Essay*, Glenview, Ill.: Scott, Foresman.

Peters, T.J. and Waterman, R.H. (1982/84) *In Search of Excellence*, New York: Harper and Row.

Pettigrew, A.M. (1972) *The Politics of Organizational Decision Making*, London: Tavistock.

Pettigrew, A.M. (1990) 'Studying deciding: an exchange of views between Mintzberg and Waters, Pettigrew and Butler', *Organization Studies* 11(1): 1–16.

Pfeffer, J. (1981) *Power in Organizations*, London: Pitman.

Powell, S. (1998) 'Nice girls do argue: Why do women almost never win arguments with men, even when they're right?' *The Australian* 4 May: 15.

Prokesch, S.E. (1997) 'Unleashing the power of learning: An interview with British Petroleum's John Browne', *Harvard Business Review* September–October: 147–68.

Pugh, D.S. and Hickson, J. (1989) *Writers on Organizations*, Harmondsworth, UK: Penguin.

Robbins, S.P. and Barnwell, N. (1989) *Organisation Theory in Australia*, Melbourne: Prentice-Hall.

Simon, H. (1960) *Administrative Behavior*, New York: Macmillan.

Simon, H. (1984) 'Decision-making and organizational design', in Pugh, D.S. (ed.), *Organization Theory: Selected Readings*, Harmondsworth, UK: Penguin.

Stephenson, T. (1985) *Management: A Political Activity*, London: Macmillan.

Stewart, T.A. (1994) 'Your company's most valuable asset: Intellectual capital', *Fortune* October (2): 34–6.

Tannen, D. (1995) 'The power of talk', *Harvard Business Review* September–October: 138–48.

Ulrich, D. (1998) 'Intellectual capital = competence × commitment', *Sloan Management Review* Winter: 15–26.

Weeks, D.K. (1980) 'Organizations and decision making', in Thompson, K. and Salaman, G. (eds), *Control and Ideology in Organizations*, Milton Keyness, UK: The Open University Press.

Westerlund, G. and Sjøstrand, S.E. (1979) *Organisational Myths,* London: Harper and Row.

Wikström, S., Normann, R., Anell, B., Ekvall, G., Forslin, J. and Skärvad, P.H. (1994) *Knowledge & Value: A New Perspective on Corporate Transformation*, London: Routledge.

Wilson, D.C., Butler, R.J., Cray, D., Hickson, D.J., Mallory, G.R. (1986) 'Breaking the bounds of organization in strategic decision making', *Human Relations* 39(4): 309–32.

9
Managing ethically

Robin Snell

Questions about business ethics

1   Does ethics have anything to do with business?
2   Should business decisions be governed by profitability alone?
3   Does there always have to be a conflict for business between serving the needs of staff members (i.e. personal gain) and pursuing corporate profitability (i.e. the interests of the shareholders)?
4   Should managers conform to local rules, customs and etiquette, or are there universal standards to follow?
5   What are the options for managers facing moral dilemmas?
6   What aspects of an organization's culture help managers to make ethical decisions?
7   How valuable are codes of ethical conduct in business?
8   To whom should managers look for moral leadership?
9   Is it possible to change a manager's ethical predisposition?

Consider this previously unpublished case reported to one of my colleagues in a recent research project (Snell, Chak and Taylor 1996). It concerned an ethical dilemma faced by 'Simon' (fictional name), a 35-year-old deputy accounting manager with eight years' service at 'Sunny', a Japanese-owned trading company with a branch in Hong Kong. Sunny is managed by expatriate Japanese, but employs mainly local Hong Kong Chinese staff – Simon is one of the latter. Simon's account of his ethical dilemma is given below:

Simon's Story

My boss regularly asks me to act as translator (English–Chinese) in meetings with other Chinese staff. He can speak only Japanese and English whereas the junior staff can only speak Cantonese. It was very difficult for me at one meeting, because my boss was going to dismiss a cleaning lady who had worked for the company for 20 years. I understood that the staff member was the bread winner of her family, and that such a decision would surely be a shock to the staff member. Therefore, during the translation, I changed the tone and the content of my boss's remarks a little bit. Instead of letting her

---

know that she was to be fired because of her age, I told her that the company wanted her to take her retirement a little earlier. [At this time there is no old age pension as such in Hong Kong, and many companies such as Sunny have no pension scheme of their own.] I also tried to add some further beautiful explanations. Despite my efforts, she felt very distressed and surprised at the management's decision. To behave professionally, I understood that my duty was to translate exactly what the boss told me. However, I could not do that as it would have hurt the staff member. In addition, I was myself ambivalent about the decision. In the company's interest, it was better to dismiss the staff member as she was quite old and she was not physically strong enough to complete all the cleaning jobs here. Therefore, in the end, I didn't discuss the decision with other staff. In fact, I was not sure whether that would secure any better arrangement for the dismissed staff member. However, I kept on thinking that this company does not care very much. She had worked so long for the company. However, I didn't take any action to voice my feelings and did not disclose the decision to others.

Questions about the case

Before proceeding with the rest of the chapter, ponder or ask yourself the following:

1   What else might Simon do, and why might or should he do it?
2   What would you, the reader, do in a similar situation?
3   What would your actions reveal about your ethical behaviour or predisposition?

Introduction

If Simon chooses to voice his feelings after all, an understanding of the various arguments and principles of ethics (such as *deontology* and *utilitarianism*) will enable him to put a stronger ethical case to his boss. Simon has mixed emotions. His sense of responsibility jars with feelings of subordination and powerlessness. To understand Simon's position better, some general behavioural options are introduced which might apply in cases where the 'underdog' or subordinate has or is trying to gain the high moral ground. Simon's motivations are also mixed: he is concerned for the feelings of the staff member, but he also wants to serve the 'company interest'. Therefore, it is important to explain how the various moral motivations of people may be ranked and prioritized. A useful way of doing this is to look at Kohlberg's stages of moral development.

Simon may conclude that he has a better solution than his boss to the ethical dilemma, but has absolutely no chance of applying it. Taking a moral stand may be much easier in some organizations than in others. To understand why this might be so requires a discussion of the influence of organizational culture and leadership, and the possible role of corporate codes of conduct, in shaping and supporting ethical behaviour.

Simon's case is a typical managerial dilemma which has no single, final right answer. Ethical managers nonetheless feel obliged to do their best in cases like this, and reflect on their actions afterwards, which ideally means continual self-improvement for them. Accordingly, besides suggesting how Simon might have responded on this one occasion, the chapter concludes by offering ideas for how he (and, or course, all managers) might draw upon everyday experience as a means of ethical development.

Objections to business ethics

There are four basic objections to business ethics and these can be represented as:

1 Psychological egotism
2 Machiavellian
3 Legal–Moral
4 Agency arguments

Psychological egotism

The first objection is that urging managers to take other people's best interests into account runs contrary to the spirit of human enterprise. The objection stems from the world-view of *psychological egotism*, which holds that people only ever follow their own immediate interest, looking out for 'number one' (Beauchamp 1988:16). This is referred to as 'self-interested, outcome-oriented individualism' (Mitchell and Scott 1990: 23). The work of Lawrence Kohlberg and other developmental psychologists (e.g. Kohlberg 1981, 1984, 1986; Kohlberg, Levine and Hewer 1983) suggests this might apply to a minority of adults who are retarded in their moral development.

There are two fundamental problems with the psychological egotism view of ethical behaviour. One of these is that it is refuted by any action of genuine altruism, benevolence, service or citizenship by a successful business person. The second one is more complex and even raises some concerns about the ideas of the developmental psychologists. Some theorists believe that certain strong feelings such as anger, fear, guilt or passion can, in particular contexts of situations, 'drive' a person to 'look out' only for 'number one' (Flam 1993: 59, citing Frank 1988: 53–4). Thus a person who is repeatedly overlooked for promotion for reasons that appear to be well founded on racist grounds might well decide that looking out for 'number one' is the best possible thing to do under the circumstances, until perhaps a new job is found.

Machiavellian

The second objection to business ethics is based on *Machiavellian* analyses of power, and claims that rising to the top of the organization necessitates games of manipulation, blaming and attacking rivals, controlling and massaging information, lobbying, image building, ingratiation, 'boot-licking', forming coalitions and allies, creating obligations and indebtedness among followers, gaining control of scarce resources and so on. It logically follows that attending to business ethics means surrendering these power tactics and resources and thereby condemning oneself to a 'loser's life' among the lower echelons of the organization. Another version of this argument is that business has its special brand of ethics, rather like those applying to the card game called poker (Carr 1993). This view is problematic. The office and the board room, unlike the poker table, are complex, interconnected sets of actions that have influence way beyond anything so fleeting as a card game. Employment consumes our most active years (Schor 1992). Industrial and commercial endeavour has a major impact on all other human (and animal) activity; how it is carried out is therefore a matter of wider ethical concern. To simply say that it is OK for businesses to develop their own brand of ethics – Machiavellian or otherwise – implies that business does not impact on wider society.

Legal–Moral

The third objection is that business ethics is unnecessary since 'if it's legal, then it's morally OK' (Bowie 1988). Much may go on in workplace relations that is unethical, such as unjustly reprimanding subordinates and 'padding' or 'fiddling' expense accounts, but it is not normally under legal scrutiny (Boatright 1993: 13–14). On wider social issues such as genetic engineering, equal opportunity and environmental protection, the enactment of law tends to lag behind the public interest. Indeed, in many countries, even 'democratic' ones, businesses may do their best to prevent the law being changed to accommodate fresh ethical considerations. They might do this by lobbying governments, secretly sponsoring political campaigns, playing the game of minimal conformity to legislation or the 'spirit' of the law, and hiring lawyers to fight their cause on technical grounds. Democratically derived law may not evolve perfectly or necessarily progressively, but broadly in line with the espoused underlying ethical principles of 'good faith', 'proper means' and the 'reasonable person'. Law in countries run by dictatorships is a different matter. Where the legal system is relatively undeveloped, and this is particularly evident in newly emerging economies such as China, what is legal or illegal may depend on the arbitrary decision of corrupt, dishonest or frightened bureaucrats or officials.

Agency arguments

The fourth objection is the *agency* argument of Milton Friedman (1970), who condemns what he calls 'the doctrine of social responsibility'. A corporate executive is legally the agent of the firm's owners or principals, and is thus contractually obliged to serve only their interests, while keeping within the law and avoiding deliberate deception. Friedman claims that using corporate resources for anything other than profit maximization is stealing from the principals. It would follow that managers should invest no more in serving the wider community interest than can be justified by the pay-offs in corporate image, consumer loyalty, less governmental interference and healthy share prices. Larue T. Hosmer (1987: 34–48) offers a succinct analysis of the microeconomic theory behind the agency argument. In an ideal state of affairs, goods and services are distributed so effectively by competitive markets that it would be impossible to make anyone better off without harming someone else. Hosmer exposes the flaws of this argument: the exclusion of segments of society (e.g. the poor and unskilled), its self-serving ideological nature and its low regard for the worth of human beings (Hosmer 1987: 51). When a company is sued for damages, or goes broke, shareholders stand to lose only the value of their shares because they enjoy the privilege of limited liability. Others affected may lose their livelihood, all their savings, even their lives. Thus business decisions can inflict massive harm or loss on individuals or communities which have no legal means of redress, other than claiming government compensation or benefits. It is therefore reasonable to expect managers to serve the interests of the wider community, not just the needs of the shareholders, although the law in many countries has not caught up with this point yet (see also Hosmer 1987: 51). Charles Handy (1995: 15) reminds us that Adam Smith, the founding father of free-market economic theory, argued in *A Theory of Moral Sentiments* that a stable society depends on everyone's moral duty to have regard and sympathy for fellow human beings. This principle is absent from microeconomic theory but without it, Smith's 'invisible hand', promoting the ends of society as a whole (Smith 1937: 423), cannot work to the benefit of all.

Modern business ethics

Having tried to defend business ethics against four 'attacks', this part of the chapter sketches out four bodies of thought which represent much, though not the entirety, of the substance of ethical thought and argument. These are: utilitarianism, deontology, justice and stakeholders.

Utilitarianism

Utilitarianism is based on the philosophy of Jeremy Bentham. According to Manuel Velasquez (1992), utilitarianism judges the moral worth of actions by the utility (surfeit or excess of benefits over costs) of their foreseeable consequences for each and every person affected by a certain set of actions. Actions leading to the greatest net benefits for the greatest number of people are favoured. Manufacturers of vacuum cleaners (helping to keep houses cleaner by their labour-saving devices) would probably do better in a moral assessment than manufacturers of landmines (still maiming and killing civilians in Cambodia long after hostilities have ceased). Velasquez goes on to refute a major criticism of utilitarianism – the claim that it values only that which can be measured precisely. He argues that it is possible to arrive at a mature moral assessment of the extent to which actions meet intrinsic human needs. Tobacco companies, with products which are not only allegedly damaging to health but which also cause much social nuisance, will come off poorly in such assessments. Velasquez warns, however, that utilitarianism (or any other system of thought) should not be used as the only source of moral standards. Utilitarianism examines what is achieved, produced, delivered or dumped, and weighs the consequences, but it neglects the processes through which all of this is done. It is therefore fortunate that there exists a contrasting but complementary school of thought in deontology.

Deontology

Deontology focuses on the processes, procedures and dynamics of our interactions with other individuals, groups, organizations and collectives. Deontology is based on the idea that we are morally obliged to follow fundamental rules of thumb or principles (Frankena 1963). Philosopher Immanuel Kant's 'categorical imperatives' belong here. There are two key principles of the 'categorical imperative' that have profound implications for how we act towards each other. First, act only on those principles that you would wish to be made a universal law for everybody and which represent how you want others to treat you (e.g. don't spy on your competitors, delay payment to your suppliers or deceive your customers). Second, never treat any single individual as merely a means to an end, but rather as an end in himself or herself (e.g. never conclude a deal or business transaction that you know runs against the interest of the other party). Principles such as these aim to defeat psychological egotism, and to protect the rights of everyone against exploitation, scapegoating or victimization by more powerful or privileged players.

Justice

Somewhere in between these two great schools is a body of thought on *justice*. Four kinds of justice can be identified: *compensatory*, to do with atoning for some prior harm or violation; *retributive*, concerning punishment for bad deeds; *procedural*, involving fair decision

procedures, practices or agreements; and *distributive*, concerning the handing out of benefits and burdens (De George 1995: 105). John Rawls (1971), focusing on the latter two
kinds of justice (i.e. procedural and distributive), argued that the architects of an imagined
society should, under the 'veil of ignorance', that is, not knowing what position they themselves would occupy in that society, resolve to establish basic equality of human rights,
opportunity and dignity. They should allow inequalities of wealth, income, influence and
prestige only if the least-advantaged group would ultimately become better off as a result,
and not be left impossibly far behind. In other words, if every manager took the view that
there is every chance that he or she could just as likely one day become the top manager or
be demoted to the lowest position in the organization, there might be more evidence of procedural and distributive justice in workplaces. Another interpretation (paraphrasing Rawls)
states that there should be 'a maximum degree of liberty compatible with a like liberty for
others' (Steidlmeir 1992: 68). This in turn implies that what people get should to a great
extent be based on their real needs; that rewards should also be based on equity – the effort
people put in and the merit of their contribution; and that rewards based on privilege
should be minimal (Steidlmeir 1992: 69–70). A fifth kind of justice was also identified:
interactional, regarding the quality of treatment received from a decision maker, and how far
the formal decision procedures are seen to be properly applied (Bies and Moag 1986).

Stakeholders

The notion of serving *stakeholders* goes against the notion of business as a 'game' (see Carr
1993), and against Friedman's maxim of responsibility to shareholders alone. Stakeholders
are defined as all those who affect or are affected by business decisions and actions (Weiss
1994: 9). Under this view corporations differ from individuals in that they depend on many
more stakeholders to achieve their goals. They must also evaluate the far-reaching economic, political, environmental and ethical consequences of their decisions for each of their
stakeholders. Who is a stakeholder? These can include individuals (e.g. employees, customers), groups (e.g. work groups, categories of staff), corporations (e.g. competitors and
suppliers), societal institutions (e.g. trade associations, regulatory bodies) and nations
(Weiss 1994). To these can be added communities near and far, future generations and
wider ecological systems.

Other views emphasize the importance of building trust and cooperation among all the
stakeholders, and claims that without this the company will become less competitive in traditional economic terms (Green 1994). Still others urge large corporations to conduct
'social audits' of their performance in relation to their various stakeholders on various
indices (Weiss 1994).

John Burgoyne (1994) warns, however, that understanding and resolving the contrasting motives, perceptions, feelings and values among different stakeholder groups is not a
straightforward matter of quantitative measurement, but requires critical political sensitivity. That would include not assuming that the most official and respectable-sounding voices
speak for anyone other than those with the most power. Hosmer (1991), recognizing the
difficulty and complexity of the stakeholder approach, optimistically predicted that by
1996 it would be given an emphasis in business education equal to that of other subjects
such as quantitative methods, information management and strategic planning. This
does not appear to have happened. While well-educated managers may thus still remain

conceptually ill-equipped to serve stakeholders, it is incumbent on them to try as best they can.

Global ethics or cultural relativism

A fifth objection to business ethics, which merits separate consideration, stems from the discovery that popular business customs and moral standards vary from culture to culture, as do feelings and perceptions about what is fair and just (Leung 1988). From a *cultural relativist* stance, such variations or differences are assumed to mean that there is no single set of universal or objective standards for judging moral conduct, and that a person's moral obligations stem from the customs, mores, laws and rules of a particular culture or society (Williams 1992: 14–16). It may thus be claimed that family upbringing and wider socialization through formal and informal education combine to form the moral principles which 'good citizens' within a particular culture share. It would follow that doing cross-cultural business is a matter of obeying the norms of the 'host' culture (e.g. in Australia 'mateship', in Malaysia deferring to superiors) even if this is sometimes unpalatable. Some may thus feel at liberty to discard the ideas of deontology, utilitarianism, justice and stakeholders, and simply go along with the expectations of those who 'own' the territory.

Cultural relativism is, however, a flawed concept (Wellman 1963). Norms and practices may indeed vary from society to society, but the prevailing norms and practices in one culture do not themselves determine what actions are ethically right or wrong. Even within a specific cultural context, that is a matter for critical analysis, judgement and debate. It is illogical to infer that because a certain state of affairs exists, it is necessarily right and good that things should remain that way. There is room for moral reform in most societies, especially those undergoing other kinds of change (e.g. social revolution). Official morality may primarily serve the interests of a ruling minority (for example, in classical Chinese ethics, the ritualistic principles of '*li*' justify the need for unquestioning loyalty to rulers and the unequal privileges afforded to these rulers). Particular business practices (e.g. paying commissions or bribes to intermediaries, child prostitution) may persist within a society even while deplored by a majority of its citizens. One danger of the cultural relativist position is that it may be used as an excuse by outsiders to cover up their levelling-down to, or acceptance of, such practices.

Perhaps the strongest argument against cultural relativism is that the teachings of every major religion (Buddhism, Christianity, Confucianism, Hinduism, Judaism and Islam) subscribe to the 'Golden Rule': do as you would be done by (see Allinson 1995: 30; Treviño and Nelson 1995: 277). Other analyses also run counter to ethical relativism (e.g. Singer 1991). The counter-argument suggests that the apparent collection of ethical philosophies from around the world, as pieces in a larger jigsaw puzzle, will one day provide a clear overall picture as schools of thought converge. In the international business community the idea of establishing, adopting and enforcing global business ethics standards has gained momentum, against those ready to 'level-down' for competitive advantage. One example is the set of Caux Round Table (CRT) principles, launched in 1986 in Switzerland by senior business leaders from Europe, Japan and North America (*Business Ethics Magazine* 1995). These are based on the Kantian notion of 'human dignity', that every individual has an unalienable right to be treated as an end, not as a means to some other end, and on the Japanese concept of *kyosei*, cooperation and fair competition for the sake of the common good. In practice, there is, however, a long way to go.

These broader ethical concerns can be examined in relation to particular ethical issues that are prevalent in business.

Bribes, commissions and gifts

A rough indicator of international moral agreement is the illegality of bribery in every part of the world (Alpern 1993: 57; Wambold 1977). It is universally illegitimate and if it exists attempts are made to conceal it (Transparency International 1996a). It is seen as interpersonally, procedurally (i.e. rules, policies) and distributively unjust. Nonetheless, it is widespread, particularly as nearly every country allows bribes to be paid out by its citizen businesspeople on foreign soil! In the 1970s Lockheed was discovered to have paid out around US$25 million in bribes in connection with sales of its Tristar L-1011 aircraft in Japan (Boulton 1978). The resulting outrage eventually led to the Foreign Corrupt Practices Act (FCPA) making the USA the only nation with a law prohibiting bribery abroad (Greanis and Windsor 1982). As summarized by Linda Treviño and Catherine Nelson (1995: 274), the FCPA prohibits the offering of bribes to politicians or government officials in order to sway their judgement and get or hold on to business. It allows 'grease payments' to persuade officials to do their job more swiftly or thoroughly, so long as the final outcome of such work is not distorted. Extortion payments, such as ransoms paid to free a hostage manager, are also allowed.

Other countries in the Organization for Economic Cooperation and Development (OECD) appear positively to encourage overseas bribery. An OECD study reported in *The European* (18 April 1996) revealed that in most constituent countries bribes paid out to foreign officials overseas are tax deductible. While there were complaints from business people from the USA that they suffer great disadvantage in developing international business (Pastin and Hooker 1980), the FCPA nevertheless survived the Reagan administration. Recent moves by the German federal government to adopt a similar bill provoked strong opposition from German business.

The Western business lobby has thus sought to maintain or restore overseas practices which have, during the 1990s, resulted in the fall of governments in Japan, India and Italy, and the prosecution of former political leaders in South Korea. From the standpoint of deontology, scrambling for distortions and loopholes in what would otherwise be universal law is indefensible. From the perspectives of utilitarianism and stakeholder analysis, the health of host economies and the welfare of the host communities must be considered, and colluding with bribery may do them little good. Transparency International (1996a) publishes a league table annually, based on assessments by the international business community. It turns out that the countries with the worst 'corruption index' ratings (the greatest perceived tendency to ask for and receive bribes), such as Indonesia, China, Pakistan, Venezuela, Brazil, the Philippines, India, Thailand, Mexico and Columbia, tend to have the lowest gross domestic products (GDPs). The correlation between corruption and poverty is no proof of causality, but the pitiful case of the Philippines, still crippled from the Marcos era, is a vivid illustration of how collusion between unscrupulous Western business people and corrupt officials and politicians can stunt the socioeconomic development of a host nation (Andrews 1988). Transparency International's idea of establishing a ranking of active bribery (readiness to offer and give bribes on foreign soil) is thus an important and useful means of exposing Western hypocrisy and opportunism (Transparency International 1996b).

This is not to deny the problems of doing business where corruption levels are high, but the narrow expediency of bribe giving is 'role distortion for the firm' (Waters 1988: 183), and thus subject to ethical challenge. Gift giving may go hand in hand with developing business relationships in places like China and South Korea and is often a sign of respect rather than personal advantage. However, companies without formal codes of practice requiring all gifts to be recorded invite a slide into abuse (Snell and Tseng 1996).

Ethics and managing the workforce

It is natural and understandable for employers to be concerned about the work ethics of current or potential employees (see, for example, Independent Commission Against Corruption (ICAC) (Hong Kong) 1996). Utilitarian principles suggest that in any industrial society employers have a right to expect that the workforce will meet basic standards of punctuality, accuracy and truth telling. It is reasonable that employers should have the right to dismiss employees who can be shown consistently to fail to meet these standards.

The corresponding duties and responsibilities of employers are more contentious. Laws may define the basic minimum standards for employers' conduct in human resource management, but they do not guarantee that even these bare standards are maintained. Using humiliation to discipline employees or intimidation to control them is unethical. It denies employees' basic justice and freedom, and treats them merely as a means to implement the boss's will. In May 1995, Albert Yeung, head of the Emperor group of companies (and owner of Hong Kong's most expensive car licence plate at approximately US$1.6 million), was tried in Hong Kong on two counts of false imprisonment and criminal intimidation towards former employee, Michael Lam. The *Eastern Express* (25 May 1995) reported how Mr Lam was alleged to have undergone a humiliating ordeal on the night of 9–10 December 1994 (after he had left the company and begun work for a possible competitor). This entailed being made to go down on his hands and knees to serve tea to another employee, being told by Yeung that the most junior employee would slap him in the face to make him smart, and being scolded by Yeung in front of other employees for about 15 minutes. Yeung also allegedly threatened to break Lam's left leg over a 'business dispute'. The *Sunday Hong Kong Standard* (28 May 1995) recorded that the magistrate said that he 'cannot declare justice has been done', on acquitting Yeung after five witnesses, including Lam, refused to give evidence and said that they could not recall what had happened. The newspaper described Yeung as 'a good friend of some of the most respected and well-known people in Hong Kong'.

This is, of course, an extreme case, but the ethical issue behind it is a more general one: the use of coercive power by employers to extract labour against employees' will. As one former personnel director from the UK put it: 'once management ever gets its act together, labour doesn't have a cat in hell's chance' (Snell 1993a: 136). Employers have no need to resort to physical coercion to assert their superior power when employees feel economically vulnerable (e.g. facing 'negative equity' on home mortgages), fear the loss of their jobs, and where unions are weak – they simply need to ask. In the West, job insecurity has grown among office staff as their working hours have lengthened. The 3000-hour year and the 60-hour week are now common (Handy 1995: 179), as it has been for some time in many industries in Hong Kong. In such work-dominated contexts, is it coercive for a boss, at 6.00 pm on Friday, to ask a subordinate, as a special favour, to complete a lengthy assignment by 9.00 am on Monday morning, or to greet and look after a client arriving at the local airport at 7.30 pm on the Saturday evening, or to collect a bag of golf clubs mistakenly left behind at one club house and take them to the client's preferred course on the Sunday morning? When a group of part-time MBA students at the City University of Hong Kong discussed how to be assertive with the boss, they concluded that there was no way for subordinates to decline requests of that nature, however great the sacrifice or inconvenience, without risking dismissal or 'career death'. An element of servitude is implied. Ethically, the boss has no claim over the subordinate's time if this is not part of the formal or implied contract. Employers thus have a moral duty to exercise restraint in the use of their inherently superior power over divided labour.

Ethics and 'green' concerns

There are a number of arguments for and against taking deliberate measures to protect our physical environment by restricting economic development (Donaldson and Werhane 1993: 379–80).

The arguments against are:

- economic growth enhances human life by providing us with more of what we want;
- Third World economies must be given room to develop, not held back;
- new technologies will inevitably be developed to repair earlier damage;
- if recycled products, national parks, a clean environment, etc. are such important preferences, then consumers will choose to pay for them directly.

Arguments in favour are:

- we otherwise face the disaster of wiping out our natural resources;
- future generations of human beings have the right to a livable environment;
- clean air, the preservation of rare animal species and virgin forests, etc. are valued by us as non-market resources despite their economic costs;
- the 'environment' itself has intrinsic moral standing as an inherent part of the natural order.

Such arguments, for and against, can be illustrated by the case of environmental pollution in Hong Kong, where the business community and the government, at least until recently, wholeheartedly adopted the 'against' position.

After the opening of Hong Kong's first container port at Kwai Chung in 1972, and the adoption of new economic policies in China in the late 1970s, a 'tidal wave' of steel flowed up from Kwai Chung towards the border with China. While most of the land was officially zoned for agricultural purposes, and the Hong Kong Government convicted a company called Melhado in 1982 for wrongful use of land, the owner, a local politician, won the appeal, sweeping aside the requirement for planning permission and precipitating a rush to industrialization that destroyed much of the area. Many farmers laid concrete over their fields and became millionaires by leasing the space for container storage, charging US$250 per container per day in early 1994. Some storage areas have held up to 800 containers, yielding US$200 000 per day. Other farmers used their land for scrapyards. New legislation followed, but between 1991 and 1993, out of 174 cases of unauthorized development of rural land, only 11 landlords and operators were convicted, with fines as low at US$1000.

The government blamed the illegal change of land use for causing traffic jams, and, more importantly, for widespread flooding during a typhoon in September 1993, which damaged one-third of the remaining farmland. In October 1993, Governor Chris Patten announced further legislation and the setting up of a special task force. The chairman of the Private Sector Committee on the Environment said that he spoke for '65% of the Hang Seng Index', in supporting these measures. Rural leaders, however, accused the government of stripping them of their right to use their own land. A government official who was leading the task force then admitted that since there was no statutory plan in the affected areas, the new legislation had no teeth – nothing would be achieved without cooperation with the landowners. Some local politicians reported that many appointed members of local governing boards had direct or indirect interests in the converted farmland, and had power and 'face' in the localities affected. A compromise solution was reached, under which operators would be issued with temporary licences for two to three years and required to plant trees around the land, pending the relocation of the container parks to designated areas. The understanding for the longer term appeared to be that former container parks would be used for housing rather than restored to farmland or open countryside. By the time of writing this chapter there had been, however, no discernible beautification of the areas or indeed any change in the status quo.

Source: Drawn from various items in the South China Morning Post *(13 October 1993, 26 October 1993, 25 November 1993, 28 April 1994, 12 July 1994, 18 October 1994) and from an article in* Window *(15 October 1993).*

Is the operator's role in the continued environmental despoliation morally justifiable? From a deontological point of view, the answer is a clear-cut 'no'. The integrity and dignity of the physical environment (of which we are all stewards) has a much stronger moral claim than serving the owners' rights. Applying utilitarianism and stakeholder analysis, the issues are more complex, but still broadly implicate the operators and owners.

One line of utilitarian argument supports their actions. Parks for empty containers play a necessary role within a successful wealth- and benefit-generating system. The growth in container traffic through Hong Kong reflects China's economic development and its increased involvement in international trade. Western consumers get more of what they want, Hong Kong trading companies thrive as 'go-betweens', and the access to overseas markets promises pathways out of grinding poverty for the emerging mainland Chinese manufacturing labour force. Just about everybody is happy with things as they are, and if finding alternative container park sites is too much of a problem then it is not the operators' fault.

On the other hand, it can be argued that the owners and operators should take account of the overall well-being of Hong Kong society, jeopardized by the insidious and irreversible loss of natural beauty and the extra inconvenience caused to travelling in the countryside (both non-market resources). While Hong Kongers show amazing resilience to stress, their physical environment may be approaching a point of deterioration that is intolerable and unsuitable for future generations. The owners and operators imply that the issue could be settled by market forces, putting the onus on those who feel the problem most acutely to buy their land and change its usage. That would set up an unfair and unjust 'bidding game', in which those relatively few Hong Kong citizens who actively recognize the value of natural beauty would be hopelessly pitted against a multitude of international consumers in the rest of the world each of whom ultimately pays an infinitesimal share of the rental charges for container storage, but may know nothing about the effects on the countryside. No group of citizens could afford to pay what would amount to a huge 'ransom' to keep containers off the land.

On top of the aesthetic decline, the operators' actions have resulted in loss of farmland. Consequently Hong Kong imports more food, mostly from China, where there are already concerns that there may soon be insufficient arable land to sustain the mainland population. It appears that no constructive attempt has been made to resolve the problems of container storage, scrap disposal and changed land use. Representatives of Hong Kong's big business community offered lip-service to the governor's plans, but seem to have given little else in return for their share of the benefits arising from the operation of the container system as a whole.

Ethical dilemmas and organizational dynamics

So far, in illustrating the conceptual application of business ethics principles, the chapter has analyzed a small selection of issues from an 'armchair critic' perspective. It is appropriate now to consider the practical challenges involved in facing organizational pressures and solving ethical dilemmas arising in day to day managerial work.

Ethical dilemmas and moral responsibility

Middle managers' everyday ethical dilemmas are typically much 'greyer' than the headline-grabbing issues discussed above (Toffler 1986). Patrick Maclagan (1995: 174) quotes from Chapter five of John Steinbeck's novel *The Grapes of Wrath* in which the spokesmen of a bank, which owned land, have the following dialogue with the tenant farmers whom they have been sent to evict:

'We're sorry. It's not us. It's the monster. The bank isn't like a man.'
'Yes, but the bank is only made of men.'
'No you're wrong there – quite wrong there. The bank is something else than men. It happens that every man in the bank hates what the bank does, and yet the bank does it. The

bank is something more than men. I tell you. It's the monster. Men made it, but they can't control it.'

Maclagan (1995: 174) goes on to ask:

Who is responsible? Can we identify individuals? Most importantly, can we criticize those sent to evict the farmers? Here we can recognize the conflict between … those who gave the orders to oust the tenants … and their spokesmen. But is the reaction of the latter based on reasoned thought, or is it emotive? Does it reflect a concern for justice, or a sympathetic reaction to the plight of particular people in a personal encounter?

These issues came to light in the Australian context, both relating to the effects of the droughts of 1994–95, and the alleged sale of inappropriate financial instruments (e.g. mortgages in foreign currencies) to the farmers which resulted in huge interest debts accumulating in short spaces of time as the money markets moved, with the banks being quick to repossess the farmers' land. One of the early cases, which cannot be quoted here, was settled by the bank out of court and the farmer was able to keep his land.

Barbara Toffler (1986), in her interview study of US managers' dilemmas, found that these were difficult to encapsulate, and involved many contrasting and possibly competing values, along with a variety of organizational pressures and demands. She found also that the managers usually wanted to do 'the right thing', but were uncertain of their responsibilities, unsure about what to do and often unable to put their preferred solutions into practice. Two-thirds of the dilemmas reported to Toffler related to the management of relationships. Another study found that 36 percent of dilemmas concerned line employees, and 6 percent concerned peers or superiors, while 22 percent involved customers and 19 percent suppliers (Waters, Bird and Chant 1986). Analyzing the source of 126 dilemmas reported by 39 managers in six Hong Kong companies, Snell *et al.* (1996) found that they typically stemmed from being asked to do something that was wrong or mistaken, or from noticing behaviour that was wrong or incompetent (see Table 9.1).

Table 9.1   Sources of dilemmas reported by interviewees

Sources of dilemma	% Incidence
Subordinates' perceived deceit, incompetence or disobedience	18
Policy, or request by superior, that is mistaken	25
Policy, or request by superior, that is ethically suspicious, exploitative or unfair	13
Improper, suspicious or unfair request from client, supplier or colleague	6
Conflicting instructions, decisions or directives from above	9
Caught in the middle in a direct conflict between other parties	5
Direct dispute with another party	6
Aware of other's misconduct, neglect or unfairness, but not directly responsible	8
Other	10

Source: Adapted from Robin Snell, Almaz Chak and Keith Taylor (1996) 'The impact of moral ethos on how ethical dilemmas are experienced and resolved in six Hong Kong companies', *Management Research News* 19 (9), p. 81.

Theoretical 'formulae', such as those introduced in the first half of this chapter, remain ideals only. Turning them into action tends to be the most difficult aspect of typical middle managerial dilemmas such as the one faced by Steinbeck's bank spokesmen, and by Simon in our opening case. There are 10 possible ways in which subordinate managers can respond to such situations where they observe or are involved in wrong-doing (Nielsen 1987):

1. Don't think about it.
2. Quietly, but knowingly, get on with it, conform.
3. Do it under protest, reluctantly comply.
4. Conscientiously object, refuse to play an active part, let others do it instead.
5. Quit the job.
6. Secretly (anonymously) blow the whistle (report it to the press, the police, etc.).
7. Publicly blow the whistle.
8. Secretly threaten to blow the whistle (e.g. anonymous letter to the CEO).
9. Sabotage (make the action impossible).
10. Negotiate and build consensus for change in the behaviour or policy.

Nielsen (1987) advises against option 6, because it may feel like betrayal and lead to distrust and suspicion. Regarding option 7, review of research on whistle-blowing supports the popular impression that such actions are likely to provoke dire retribution from employers, and may result in court cases, bankruptcy and possibly imprisonment (Vinten 1992). During the 1980s, whistle-blowing British civil servant Clive Ponting narrowly escaped gaol (Ponting 1986), but Sarah Tisdale (who tried option 6) was less fortunate.

While the moral progress of societies as a whole may depend on the radical courage of whistle-blowers, Nielsen recommends option 10, that is, negotiate and build consensus, wherever possible. How realistic is this for Simon in the Chinese context?

Dissenting options (Nielsen's 3, 4 and 10) may be most viable in countries where egalitarianism, flat hierarchies and individual human rights are widely aspired to (e.g. some Western democracies). Even so, Robert Jackall (1988) found, in three US companies, that disagreeing with the boss was said to be tantamount to 'putting your head between your legs and kissing your ass goodbye'. The prospect of dissent may be even more daunting in societies characterized by high *power distance* (see Hofstede 1980 and Chapter 3), where it is taken for granted that power is distributed and used unequally, and by high *collectivism*, where consensus is valued more than self-expression, and conformity provided in exchange for protection. In a special study of eight dilemmas reported by Hong Kong Chinese managers, arising from requests by a boss or supervisor to do something they knew to be wrong, the following four options were discovered (Snell 1996):

1 'Little potato' obedience (quiet, fearful, humble, deferential conformity).
2 Token obedience (following orders half-heartedly and semi-incompetently).
3 Undercover disobedience (only pretending to obey, and keeping disobedience hidden).
4 Open disobedience (conscientious objection).

In line with Jackall's finding, *open disobedience* was chosen only in the two cases where there was either an explicit and official right to dissent or where line authority was not direct, that is, the manager in question was not dissenting or disobeying an immediate 'supervisor'.

However, Janet Near and Marcia Miceli (1991) have seen the act of whistle-blowing as a practice that directly challenges managerial authority and power. A review of whistle-blower case studies (Near and Miceli 1987; Glazer and Glazer 1989; Near and Jensen 1983; Miceli and Near 1991; Perrucci, Anderson, Schendel, and Trachtman 1980) suggests that whistle-blowing and retaliation is not a discrete pair of stimulus–response events, but tends to involve a sequence of episodes triggered by an initial event. The triggering event is usually associated with an awareness of initial wrong-doing with regards to illegal, immoral or illegitimate organizational processes and practices. After pre-whistle-blowing decision-making processes have occurred, the actor reviews the choice of actions (or no action) available.

Generally, it can be shown that most whistle-blowers face some form of retaliation unless organizations who have suffered (loss of any kind), and have set in place internal mechanisms to take account of a whistle-blower's allegations, view a whistle-blower not as a dissident but as a reformer (Frith 1994).

Janet Near and Tamila Jensen (1983) also argue that a whistle-blower who stands alone without support is seen as powerless in the organization and can expect greater retaliation from the organization. This could be someone who has no or very few power resources, has strong power dependency relationships and can be easily replaced (Mechanic 1962; Kanter 1979; Luthans, Hodgetts and Rosenkrantz 1988; Conger and Kanungo 1988). These people might expect greater retaliation from the organization. Conversely, they argue, a whistle-blower who has many power resources, that is, is seen as irreplaceable, has others dependent on them, has influential networks, and has a strong case, namely the claims of wrong-doing (i.e. can generate public support), might be less vulnerable to retaliation from the organization. They go on to argue 'that there is a possibility that the organization's pattern of retaliation against whistle-blowers is simply random. In this case the organization may be reacting to a set of unique and unpredictable variables' (Near and Jensen 1983: 8). The following case study illustrates how whistle-blowing can surface in an organization and the type of retaliation that can ensue from a whistle-blowing event.

Edward Farkas was given the position of Acting Purchasing Officer for his company when Felix Shivers went on long service leave. One week into the job, Edward was surprised when one of the company's sub-contractors approached him about a forthcoming tender and intimated that he expected that it was 'business as usual'. Despite often being highest tender, the sub-contractor had been awarded a substantial number of contracts.

Edward was convinced that Felix had been accepting 'kickbacks' from this sub-contractor. He decided to take the issue up with his immediate superior, Nigel Walpole, Director of Finance. Nigel warned Edward that his allegations were very serious and that unless he had more conclusive evidence, he should drop the matter. Edward was dismayed by this response, and recommended that another contractor be awarded the tender. The sub-contractor in question was awarded the contract. Edward's work was now constantly criticised by Nigel. In retaliation, Edward went to Nigel and threatened to 'blow the whistle' on the tendering racket, having discovered yet another sub-contractor receiving preferential treatment.

Several weeks later, Edward was summoned to the CEO's office and told that several sub-contractors had alleged that he had asked for 'kickbacks' on tenders. Nigel accused Edward of having asked sub-contractors to deliberately inflate their tender prices to get their 'kickbacks'. Edward was summarily dismissed and escorted from the premises.

The organization in the case study has developed certain rituals of fear, intimidation and power to manage the wrong-doing and the retaliation is not random. To some extent the advice given to Edward by a senior manager to drop the matter raises a whole set of problems about moral responsibility, especially in regard to serious wrong-doings. As David Sims, Stephen Fineman and Yiannis Gabriel (1993: 59–60) argue, many organizations, indeed probably every organization, has a 'hidden economy' in which it is accepted that individuals can 'profit' and engage in some form of *fiddling* – bending rules, pilfering (e.g. taking extra pens, etc.), short-changing or overcharging, making unauthorized phone calls, etc. Fiddlers often see their fiddling as an added 'perk' or 'entitlement' of the job and something that others do as well. In effect, many organizations develop a 'zone of indifference' with regard to fiddling, and might even cost these 'activities' into their operational expenses. In other words, it becomes a part of embedded practice, is taken for granted and is usually more costly to police than to eradicate.

Unlike whistle-blowing, fiddling rarely upsets or brings into question the very issues that can precipitate whistle-blowing. In the case of whistle-blowing, the wrong-doing brings into stark relief and conflict for the whistle-blower the brand of morality practised in the organization, the public image the organization tries to present to the outside world, and the moral standards he or she tries to live by outside the organization (Sims *et al.* 1993: 60).

Moral reasoning and moral motivations

No account of business ethics is complete without discussing Kohlberg's stages of moral reasoning development. The model holds that in human sociomoral development, people pass through up to seven stages of ethical reasoning capacity. Kohlberg's final formulation of the model is summarized in Table 9.2.

At stages one and two, moral development is *preconventional*. Typically, the individual operates from pure self-interest and expediency, and is concerned only about personal gain or loss: 'What's in it for me? Why should I bother? Who's in charge?'. Social norms and conventions are obeyed only if there is a direct pay-off.

Stages three and four represent *conventional* morality, where conformity is valued for its own sake. At stage three, the concern is to please close friends, family and associates by meeting their expectations. At stage four, professional integrity and lawful pursuit of corporate-minded goals becomes an important end in itself.

Morality at stage five and beyond is *postconventional*. At this level, rules or goals are seen to be invalid unless founded on a concern for social justice and the benefits to others. Kohlberg's definitions of postconventional morality allow for mercy, compassion and empathy to be directed at strangers and do not undervalue caring, although some theorists claim that they do (e.g. Gilligan 1982). People who have attained stage five may seek new legislation which better protects human rights, or they may lead by altruism and moral example. In positions of leadership they may incline to value democratic decision making and defend the right for others to dissent from their proposals. Stage five is counter-culture in all societies. So it is, for example, in contemporary Russia, where Boris Yeltsin's rugged and ruthless approach to maintaining order is vastly more popular than the idealistic civil democracy practised by his predecessor, Mikhail Gorbachev. Fewer than one-fifth of adults may reach stage five (Hersh, Paolitto and Reimer 1979; Treviño 1986; Treviño and Youngblood 1990; Weber 1990) and stage six is rare (Colby, Kohlberg, Gibbs and

Table 9.2 Stages in Moral Development

Stage	Orientation	Moral motives	Principles of what is 'right'	Typical social concerns
Zero	Impulsive and amoral	None	Right is whatever I want at any time, regardless of the consequences	None at all
One	Obedient; punishment-avoiding	Irrational dread of punishment; fear of those in authority	People in authority, and the rules that they set, must be obeyed exactly, so that punishment or disaster is avoided	Self-preservation is all-important. One is preoccupied with what those in power want, and with how to avoid causing them anger
Two	Personal benefits and rewards; getting a good deal for oneself	How to get the most pleasure and gain for oneself; calculating the personal risks and pay-offs of an action	It is human nature to want to get the best for oneself, making deals with other people if necessary	Dealings are governed purely by self-interest. If cooperation with others is an absolute necessity, it is done through 'give and take' bargaining. If cooperation is not necessary, then other people's needs are ignored
Three	Conforming to social expectations; gaining approval	Avoiding disapproval by associates and close ones; wanting to be praised, liked and admired, rather than shamed	One must be nice to others and not hurt their feelings, be loyal to partners, and live up to others' expectations	The capacity for empathy with the feelings of those in one's immediate circle is developed. Approval and liking by others comes to be valued for its own sake, and affects self-image. Shared commitments come to be more important than narrow self-interest
Four	Protecting law and order; maintaining the existing system of official social arrangements	Performing formal duties and responsibilities. Meeting official standards, working for the best interests of an institution	One must perform one's duty to society by upholding its law and order, and by contributing to the good of the social institutions operating within it	Special effort is made to act consistently with official roles, duties and standards, and with properly laid down rules and procedures. One aims to serve the needs and goals of the institution as a whole
Five	Promoting justice and welfare within the wider community, as defined in open and reasonable debate	Following principles that serve the best interests of the great majority. Striving to be reasonable, just and purposeful in one's actions	For the betterment of society as a whole, the underlying spirit of basic democratic and contractual rights must be acknowledged and upheld, even if existing institutions do not protect them	Over and above institutional needs, concern develops for the 'greater good', the wider public interest. Principles of basic justice and human rights are followed, rather than only what is laid down by existing laws or by formal roles and rules
Six	Defending everyone's right to justice and welfare, universally applied	Applying well-thought-out principles, being ready to share and debate these openly and non-defensively with others	Everyone's basic human rights must be respected without exception; everyone has basic moral responsibilities from which no one is exempted	There is principled concern and respect for other persons because they are ends in themselves, and not mere instruments to meet others' purposes. One adopts a reflexive, self-critical approach in ethical decision making, so that the consistency of one's decisions is constantly under review
Seven	Respecting the cosmos as an integral whole, a oneness extending well beyond humanity	Respecting the intrinsic value of the cosmos, with its wider harmonies and paradoxes	Rights extend beyond what is immediately useful or interesting to humanity, e.g. to animal species and ecological systems regardless of their social utility	The integrity of 'the environment', and of other systems making up the universe, regardless of their immediate importance for *Homo sapiens*, is valued for its own sake

Model adapted from Lawrence Kohlberg (1981), *Essays on Moral Development, Volume One: The Philosophy of Moral Development*, San Francisco: Harper and Row, pp. 121–2, 128 and 409–12, and from Lawrence Kohlberg and Robert Ryncarz (1990), 'Beyond justice reasoning: Moral development and consideration of a seventh stage', in C.N. Alexander, and E.J. Langer, (eds), *Higher Stages of Human Development*, Oxford: Oxford University Press, pp. 193–5.

Lieberman 1983: 60). As pointed out earlier, Kohlberg *et al*.'s approach suffers from psychological determinism; that is, not giving enough weight to people's capacities to change their moral predispositions when faced with certain types of contexts and emotional threats.

Mapping ethical dilemmas

In another research study of 10 Hong Kong managers, Snell (1996) found that where moral reasoning capacity has extended to a particular stage (e.g. stage four), that stage is not necessarily used to make sense of and resolve everyday ethical dilemmas. This can be seen by examining once again the ethical reasoning used by Simon in the opening case.

Tables 9.3 and 9.4 shows Simon's dilemma split into two parts, and maps Simon's moral reasoning for or against a particular course of action. Simon's ethical reasoning capacity is probably no higher than stage four (he has little sympathy for the notion of the protection of the welfare of the least fortunate in society). While he employs stage four to consider whether or not to render an exact translation, he actually puts stage three into practice, resolving not to hurt the feelings of the colleague whom he has known for so long. He is confused about the second part of the dilemma (whether to disclose his own feelings about the dismissal). All his arguments are confined to stage three and he appears to conclude that saying anything will do no one any good. Surely, as an individual manager, he can do better? Surely also, if the company itself were different, he might find it easier to act as a moral manager?

Table 9.3 *Stage engagement maps for Simon's dilemma: Whether or not to translate exactly what his boss was saying*

Moral stage	Case for exact translation	Case against exact translation
3		Exact translation would hurt the staff member
4	Professionalism requires an exact translation of the boss's words	–
Decision		He changed the boss's tone and content a little bit. He also tried to add some beautiful explanation for the request

Table 9.4 *Stage engagement maps for Simon's dilemma: Whether (later) to disclose his own feelings about the decision*

Moral stage	Case for voicing feelings	Case against voicing feelings
3	The company does not care very much for staff, and she has worked so long for the company	(a) It may be in the company's interest to dismiss the staff member on the grounds of incapacity (b) Making the issue public may not result in a better settlement for the dismissed staff member
Decision		No disclosure or discussion

Corporate culture and moral ethos

Before discussing the possible merits and limitations of official, written company codes of conduct, it is necessary to examine the impact on moral reasoning of corporate culture or *moral ethos*: implicit, unwritten, informal codes of conduct within organizations.

Moral ethos may be defined as the force field of tacit norms, values, beliefs, expectations and prohibitions which influence ethical conduct in work settings. This set of pressures and inducements may differ from those in other walks of life. As Treviño (1992: 450) observed, 'individuals play highly differentiated roles that allow them to accept different values, norms and behaviours in different life domains (e.g. work and home)'. Some commentators believe that the typical moral ethos at work predisposes individuals to act amorally: 'There is no cause for optimism in the idea that a solitary individual may withstand the organization's blandishments and maintain a strong moral sense. For, while some rare individuals will do so, many will not' (Schwartz 1990: 44). Others warn also that 'Organization culture may influence perceptions of instrumentalities for motivation to engage in unethical behaviours' (Knouse and Giacalone 1992: 373). Other writers argue the contrary view that high standards of ethical management may develop as part of company tradition (Ryan 1994) and corporate culture (Schlegelmilch and Houston 1990), rather than as a result of formal, written codes.

One obvious explanation for such starkly opposed commentators' viewpoints is that moral ethos may vary dramatically from one company to another (and even between different parts of the same company). One moral ethos may emphasize principled high mindedness and community service, another self-centredness and profit maximization regardless of wider social responsibility. Accordingly, a number of theorists (Lavoie and Culbert 1978: Petrick and Wagley 1992; Snell 1993a) have speculated that a moral ethos can be located at one or other of the Kohlberg ethical reasoning stages, based, respectively, on:

- stage one: fear and coercion;
- stage two: greed, gain and manipulation;
- stage three: conformity to 'inner-circle' norms and prejudices;
- stage four: accountability to quasi-legal standards set by higher authority;
- stage five: democratically derived standards designed to meet wider societal needs;
- stage six: organizational integrity serving to balance competing moral principles.

The above ideas have been used to develop a moral ethos 'profile', within which the six Kohlberg stages receive varying degrees of emphasis (Snell *et al.* 1996). A questionnaire (reproduced in Snell, Taylor and Chak 1997) was developed with nine items covering: how information is used; how opinions are expressed; how performance is judged; how rewards are obtained; the relationships with customers; overall impact on employees' mindsets; the use of power; reasons for following rules; and how agreement is reached. Twenty-one Hong Kong-based companies were assessed anonymously by at least eight of their randomly selected employees, using the questionnaire. Moral ethos profiles have ranged from those emphasizing stages four, five and six, to those with most emphasis on stages one, two and three. Provisional findings suggest that companies perceived by employees to emphasize the 'higher' moral stages are also perceived by them to have higher levels of honesty, environmental awareness, accuracy of records, responsibility and fairness to customers.

While other findings from this current study suggest that the relationship between moral ethos and actual ethical conduct is by no means straightforward, in general Snell (and others) have found that moral ethos has a substantial impact on how employees, such as our Simon, experience their working environment and may affect how they construe and tackle the moral dilemmas arising there. Other factors, such as whether the organization structure is tall or flat, prevailing management styles and the character of one's immediate 'boss' might also affect ethical reasoning at work. If Simon is expected to defer to and obey his boss without question, his scope for moral action is limited.

Stephen Fineman (1997: 19) points out that ethical judgements also depend on a person's ability to feel emotions such as shame, guilt, embarrassment and fear. Emotions are socially defined (also see Chapter 7) and are important for exerting social control in society. Organizations mirror elements of wider forms of emotional control, but also have their own versions of 'working' moralities, defining for members what is 'right' and acceptable. More often than not, moral actions are dependent on what Fineman says are punitive emotions such as fear, humiliation and disloyalty. Moral behaviour can be motivated more by punitive emotions (e.g. fear of public censure in breaching environmental laws) than higher moral ideals or the social good. Thus it is not reasoning alone but also emotions that can affect ethical judgements, and might well explain lapses in moral behaviour.

Organization-based approaches to improving business ethics

Three possible means for improving ethical conduct within organizations have emerged in the literature: corporate codes of conduct, 'moral leadership' from the top and ethical democracy.

Corporate codes of conduct

These are written documents, ranging from a single paragraph to more than 50 pages, stating explicitly what is desired by a corporation regarding employee behaviour (Stevens 1994). The great majority of large US companies have such codes and their popularity has spread to Europe (Weaver 1993). In Hong Kong, within little more than one year of Governor Chris Patten lamenting that only 20 out of 182 listed companies had codes of conduct (ICAC 1994), a majority of companies had formally adopted their various versions (ICAC 1995). Early studies of typical themes in codes of conduct (Chatov 1980; Sanderson and Warner 1984; White and Montgomery 1980) identified the following common topics:

- dealing with extortion or kickbacks;
- conflicts of interest between employee and employer;
- the use of insider information by employees for personal advantage;
- the accuracy of accounting records;
- the misuse of company assets;
- moonlighting;
- fraud and deception.

This list has not changed significantly over the years, and critics have noted that the motivation behind the inclusion of such items appears to be mainly concerned with maintaining profits (Cressey and Moore 1983), and with protecting the company itself against legal liability (Stevens 1994; Warren 1993), rather than with the pursuit of wider social responsibilities and values. According to Simon Webley (1993), areas which codes have tended to neglect include the following:

- the needs and rights of suppliers;
- environmental protection and related 'green' issues;
- avoiding discrimination against and harassment of minority groups;
- duties to local communities;
- labour relations;
- safety for employees and customers;
- fair remuneration;
- due process in enforcing and monitoring the code itself.

There are many other criticisms of codes of conduct, yet some theorists (e.g. Donaldson 1989) condemn them for their failure to respect human beings and for not offering practical help. Codes may overlook the real concerns at the grass roots or in everyday practice. They may neglect the needs of the least powerful stakeholders. They may be 'conspiracies against the layman', smokescreens which boost the image of a profession, without actually improving its practices (Mitchell, Puxty, Sikka and Willmott 1994). Others criticize codes for coercing people into following imposed rules. A forbidding 'don't, don't, don't, must, must, must' style may foster preconventional, risk-aversive ethical reasoning (Warren 1993).

Not all codes are poor. Some, such as the one by NYNEX, have been praised by ethicists as more caring and practically helpful (Treviño and Nelson 1995: 248). The following has been suggested as a step by step procedure for preparing codes of ethical conduct (Collins and O'Rourke 1993):

1. Form small discussion groups based on common work tasks. Each group will then work independently through the next seven steps.
2. Identify and list the group's stakeholders.
3. Develop and list ideal standards for the group's own conduct, based, as far as possible, on creating the greatest good to the greatest number, and on maintaining respect for each and every stakeholder (i.e. balancing Kohlberg's postconventional stages five and six).
4. Reflect on and identify a truthful account of the group's actual, current relationships with each stakeholder.
5. Discuss and resolve what the group must do in order to close the gap between 'ideal' relationships (identified at step three) and 'actual' relationships (identified at step four).
6. Develop a formal policy statement setting down each ideal standard (from step three) and how each of these will be attained, monitored and rewarded (from step five).

7. Annually review the code (created at step six), paying special attention to its practicality and relevance, and to how new or ongoing problems may be resolved.
8. While keeping the ideal standards, make necessary modifications within the code as to how these will be attained, monitored and rewarded.

It is reasonable to expect that codes developed this way would be of direct practical use in guiding members' actual conduct, if they are based on members' genuine ideas and concerns, rather than on the imposition of rules from above. Unless, however, the reasoning of the groups is supported by training and development in ethical concepts, the codes generated may simply articulate Kohlberg's stage three, group-centred, morality (e.g. 'Motherhood' statements, be nice to people and don't upset them, don't do anything you wouldn't like your friends to know about, etc.) rather than radically addressing the needs of stakeholder groups, imaginatively defined. The process itself presupposes a democratic tradition within the corporation. It is unlikely that such bottom-up, developmental approaches would be tolerated in companies with a moral ethos oriented to the preconventional moral stages, and/or where cultural traditions allow only for authoritarian rule by 'sages' at the top and for its complement: unquestioning loyalty, deference, respect and obedience by subordinates.

The Business Roundtable (1988), a US-based association founded in 1972 to advise on corporate responsibility and ethics, prescribes a somewhat different code development procedure, still based on participative approaches, which ideally entails the following. Staff at all levels are interviewed by senior managers about ethical matters. Ethics programmes, reflecting top management commitment, then 'cascade' from the top. Related development programmes are run in order to build greater openness and trust. There is as much emphasis on education as on regulation. An ethics committee is set up, and compiles, clarifies, monitors, updates, disseminates and promulgates the corporate code of ethics, and investigates and mediates in ethical problem cases. There are confidential ethical dilemma telephone hotlines or counselling services, and specialist ethical ombudsperson posts. Such arrangements are fairly common in US corporations (Edwards 1995). Industrial chaplains have performed similar duties among paternalistic companies in the UK. Public sector organizations such as hospitals commonly have ethics committees.

All this must be congruent with other organizational change programmes and cultural values. There will be cynicism, anger and disillusionment, as well as social carnage, if other initiatives (for 're-engineering' read 'downsizing'?) with incompatible objectives are then introduced. It will collapse where people are unfamiliar with notions of clear accountability and where there is absolute rule by 'benevolent' despots, and if secrecy is common.

Moral leadership and democracy

Even if there is encouragement or pressure on a company, from governments or consumers, to 'clean up its act', moral leadership from within is necessary. Such leadership can take many forms. The 'philosopher ruler', who would grant employees the formal moral constitution, is ideal. The benevolent despot, laying down moral law unilaterally and idiosyncratically, is far from ideal. The philosopher would arrange open meetings to discuss moral issues of concern to the company, and strive for transparency in all decisions (Treviño and McCabe 1994). The despot would serve narrow, vested interests, would not 'move' a company's moral ethos away from preconventional moral stages and would not respect the ethical principles of other members.

Many moral leaders are somewhere in between the democratic and the despotic, in that they 'sell' ethical values persuasively, with vision and conviction, but are also prepared to respond to criticism. Also somewhere in between was the so-called Victorian 'British gentleman', who gained influence by demonstrating his trustworthiness and quiet altruism (Stewart and White 1995: 298). A study of some long-established British companies noted that moral traditions have grown from the non-conformist, religious convictions of the founding fathers (Ryan 1994).

Bob Haas, chairperson and CEO of Levi-Strauss, may not be a quantum leap away from the ideal. In 1987 he organized a retreat for the top management team and asked them: 'What do we want to be remembered for?' The resulting mission and aspiration statements expressed values with a strong ethical content. These 'corporate values', including honesty, promise keeping, fairness and integrity, have been reinforced by training programmes at all hierarchical levels, and are reflected in many of the human resource practices of the company (Yeung and Yeung 1995: 212–17).

The Body Shop's Anita Roddick is a charismatic, somewhat abrasive, liberal-minded role model (Roddick 1991). The extent to which her company practises the *deontological* principle of unexploitative sourcing and *justice* in trade and its basic honesty were questioned during 1994–95 by maverick critic and journalist John Entine, who claimed that the company's products and human resource policies were not all that they seemed. After some initial defensiveness, Roddick and The Body Shop responded positively by initiating a social, environmental and animal protection audit (The Body Shop 1996). Such openness helped the company to survive the attack.

Winston Lo, of the Hong Kong-based soya milk company Vitasoy, has a more conservative image and less direct appeal to youth, but radiates equally strong social commitment. Vitasoy's ethical claims are *utilitarian*, to 'produce and promote high-quality, nutritious and wholesome products that can be purchased anywhere, any time, and at a price that everyone can afford'. Lo adds, 'Vitasoy was founded by my father some 50 years ago … He saw the value of soya protein in order to alleviate the malnutrition among the locals during the war' (Kwong 1996). Lo weathered a crisis in confidence about the company's products (the sour-milk scandal) by a total product recall which cost the company approximately US$10million: 'at the peak of the crisis, we all shared and felt the pressure. We worked closely on the committee … we learnt a lot about ourselves and about each other.'

Leaders like Roddick and Lo are, in their own ways, charismatic rather than democratic. Adversity may strengthen their leadership. In inspiring conformity, trust and admiration (which related to Kohlberg's stage three morality), they do more for business ethics than leaders who appeal to calculative self-interest (stage two) or fearful obedience (stage one), while not approaching developmental or democratic ideals (Graham 1995).

We may rightly appreciate and respect moral leaders. For the most part, they make it easier for others to act ethically. We must not, however, depend on them. They are notoriously fallible. All managers are responsible for their own actions. They have a duty, regardless of formally assigned work roles, not to assume that all is as it should be, and an obligation to intervene in unethical practices wherever they occur.

Life-long learning and business ethics

Business ethics entails searching for continual moral self-improvement and is emphatically not about proving that you always get it right. Self-development strategies are given in more detail in Snell (1993a: 222–8). Here just two of these are identified: 'avoiding hubris' and 'holding onto the hot potato'.

Hubris, the fatal delusion that 'my way is always the only right way' may be reduced by inviting criticism, looking for disconfirmation, admitting when one's own plans are not working, respecting other points of view, entertaining possible futures rather than a single dream scenario and noticing when others do things well. It requires effort and self-discipline.

The 'hot potato' injunction was noted by Eric Berne (1975) as a vehicle for perpetuating domestic violence and alcoholism from one generation to the next. In time, the abused child becomes child abuser, and the adult child of alcoholics becomes an alcoholic parent. It is as if the victim must throw the hot potato to the next victim or remain forever burdened. Something analogous may happen between bosses and subordinates in the workplace (Snell 1993b). Every occasion on which, or situation within which, future managers perceive themselves to be on the receiving end of abuse, neglect, deceit or other forms of poor treatment can be an excuse, or even an unconscious imperative, for doing the same to their staff. The 'Golden Rule' in its negative, Confucian formulation (Allinson 1995: 30) reads, 'Do not impose on others what you yourself do not desire'. It is also an excellent starting point for learning, by triggering these questions:

- Why am I so upset, angry, aggrieved, etc.?
- What ethical principle has been violated?
- How can I follow, rather than breach, the principle that has been violated?
- Do I really want to follow the principle, or am I happy to break it too?
- How can I make sure that I remember this lesson?

Really doing this, rather than passing on the hot potato, is a test of self-reflexivity and character. Ethical management requires *critical self-management* rather than uncritical conformity to implicit social rules.

Conclusion

It is time to return to the introductory questions, along with the initial case about Simon's ethical dilemma.

1 Does ethics have anything to do with business?

Yes, of course. Simon is not the only manager to have faced an ethical dilemma. Such problems are an inherent aspect of business; lives are affected by managerial decisions and often livelihoods are at stake.

2 Should business decisions be governed by profitability alone?

No. It follows from the previous answer that managers should be sensitive to ethical considerations. In Simon's case, the dismissal of the cleaning woman breaches some key ethical principles. From a *utilitarian* perspective, the sacking brings little apparent benefit to anyone. Minutely small gains for the shareholders (if any) are outweighed by great misery for the woman and her dependents. Treating the woman as if she is merely an exhausted resource, to be discarded because she no longer serves the interests of 'the company', is also unacceptable from the point of view of *deontology*, which is founded upon respect for persons, their dignity and their human rights. Standards of procedural and interactional *justice* have not been met, for the decision is arbitrary and announced in high-handed fashion.

3 Is there a 'third way', between serving the needs of staff and corporate profitability?

Simon's boss could argue that replacing the woman with a younger, more vigorous cleaning worker may lead to a healthier working environment, better for the workforce, as well as using money more effectively. A genuine 'third way' would, however, involve doing a thorough *stakeholder* analysis, asking who is affected by the decision and what do they want and need? This may not have been done, for colleagues appear not to have been consulted, and the needs of the woman's dependents have been neglected. It is more than likely that there would be sympathy for the woman, and a desire to keep her on, employing an extra part timer to tackle the heavier tasks. The additional cost would be small, and may have a payback in better workplace morale and increased belongingness among colleagues.

4 Should managers conform to local rules, customs or etiquette, or are there universal ethical standards to follow?

The welfare of the cleaning woman is in jeopardy because of the relative absence of formal social security and benefits arrangements in Hong Kong, where employment law also makes it relatively easy to get rid of employees. These are, however, political and legal variables rather than ethical ones. Ensuring that employees' welfare is not jeopardized and that justice is done (regardless of whether or not the state does it or legislates for it) are universal ethical obligations.

5 What are the options for managers facing dilemmas?

Simon's actual conduct was a hybrid of *little potato obedience* and *undercover disobedience*. Simon can hardly *secretly threaten to blow the whistle*, for he would be too-readily identified. Whistle-blowing of any kind may be futile anyway, for the newspapers might not be interested in such a 'kitchen-sink' affair, and in Hong Kong whistle-blowers inevitably get fired. He might have tried *token obedience*, such as writing an extremely off-putting job advertisement and saying 'we have to go on employing her, for no one else will take up the job'. Examining the case in Kohlberg's terms, it would be better for Simon to make consistent use of the highest moral stage available to him (stage four). That would have entailed enacting stage four by offering an accurate translation of the boss's words, along with a message of personal sympathy: 'Mr X says that ..., but I personally feel ...'. Also from stage four, Simon might have tried suggesting to Mr X that it could be in the company's best interest to find some less physically demanding work for the woman to do, rather than dismissing her: 'This will improve morale by showing that the company cares about its staff' (*negotiating and building consensus for change*).

6 What aspects of an organization's culture help managers to make the best ethical decisions?

It would help Simon if his superiors were to assume that decisions did not have to be made unilaterally and that the questioning of managerial decisions was not mutiny. There is usually some room to manoeuvre, however unfavourable the circumstances.

7 How valuable are codes of ethical conduct in business?

Most codes of conduct are imposed top down and serve to protect the company, rather than offer security of employment. A formal code of conduct would, nonetheless, have clarified expectations and reduced the likelihood of Simon and the cleaning woman suffering sudden ethical shocks. Some codes are more helpful to moral decision making, but such codes would tend to arise in a higher-stage-oriented moral ethos.

8 To whom should managers look for moral leadership?

Not necessarily to their bosses! Simon would be advised to look to his inner conscience for self-guidance, and study the topic! Ethical dilemmas occur every day in the workplace.

9 Is it possible to change a manager's ethical predisposition?

Life-long learning is vital. Ethical principles are universal and thus unchanging. Rapid developments in the world economy and in organizational practices are likely, nonetheless, to present a persistent stream of new challenges to the *application* of these principles. Simon cannot assume that what was right yesterday will be right tomorrow.

References

Allinson, R.E. (1995) 'Ethical values as part of the concept of business enterprise', in Stewart, S. and Donleavy, G. (eds), *Whose Business Values? Some Asian and Cross-cultural Perspectives,* Hong Kong: Hong Kong University Press.

Alpern, K.D. (1993) 'Moral dimensions of the Foreign Corrupt Practices Act: Comments on Pastin and Hooker', in Donaldson, T. and Werhane, P.H. (eds), *Ethical Issues in Business: A Philosophical Approach* (fourth edition), Englewood Cliffs, NJ: Prentice Hall.

Andrews, J. (1988) 'Survey: The Philippines', *Economist* 7 May: S3–18.

Beauchamp, T.L. (1988) 'Ethical theory and its application to business', in Beauchamp, T.L and Bowie, N.E. (eds), *Ethical Theory and Business* (third edition), Englewood Cliffs, NJ: Prentice Hall.

Berne, E. (1975) *What Do You Say After You Say Hello?,* London: Corgi.

Bies, R.J. and Moag, J.S. (1986) 'Interactional justice: Communication criteria of fairness', in Lewicki, R.J., Sheppard, B.H. and Bazerman, M.H. (eds) *Research on Negotiation in Organizations,* Greenwich, CT: JAI Press.

Boatright, J.R. (1993) *Ethics and the Conduct of Business,* Englewood Cliffs, NJ: Prentice Hall.

Boulton, D. (1978) *The Grease Machine,* New York: Harper and Row.

Bowie, N.E. (1988) 'Fair Markets', *Journal of Business Ethics* 7(2): 89–98.

Burgoyne, J.G. (1994) 'Stakeholder analysis', in Cassell, C. and Symon, G. (eds), *Organizational Research: A Practical Guide,* London: Sage.

Business Ethics Magazine (1995) 'CAUX Roundtable Principles', Minneapolis, MN (also available in the Ethical Business directory on the Internet at http://www.bath.ac.uk/Centres/Ethical/Papers).

Carr, A.Z. (1993) 'Is business bluffing ethical?', in Donaldson, T. and Werhane, P.H. (eds), *Ethical Issues in Business: A Philosophical Approach* (fourth edition), Englewood Cliffs, NJ: Prentice Hall.

Chatov, R. (1980) 'What corporate ethics statements say', *California Management Review* 22(4): 20–9.

Colby, A., Kohlberg, L., Gibbs, J. and Lieberman, M. (1983) 'A longitudinal study of moral development', *Monographs of the Society for Research in Child Development, Series 200*, 48(1,2): 1–107.

Collins, D. and O'Rourke, T. (1993) *Ethical Dilemmas in Business*, Cincinnati, Ohio: South Western.

Conger, J.A. and Kanungo, R.N. (1988) 'The empowerment process: Integrating theory and practice', *Academy of Management Review* 13(3): 471–82.

Cressey, D. and Moore, C.A. (1983) 'Managerial values and corporate codes of ethics', *California Management Review* 25: 53–77.

De George, R.T. (1995) *Business Ethics* (fourth edition), Englewood Cliffs, NJ: Prentice Hall.

Donaldson, J. (1989) *Key Issues in Business Ethics*, London: Academic Press.

Donaldson, T. and Werhane, P.H. (eds) (1993) *Ethical Issues in Business: A Philosophical Approach* (fourth edition), Englewood Cliffs, NJ: Prentice Hall.

Edwards, G. (1995) 'Beyond the code: The implementation of corporate ethics', *Ethics in Practice 2*, Hong Kong: Ethics Development Centre.

Fineman, S. (1997) 'Emotion and management learning', *Management Learning* 28(1): 13–25.

Flam, H. (1993) 'Fear, loyalty and greedy organizations', in Fineman, S. (ed.), *Emotion in Organizations*, London: Sage.

Frank, R.H. (1988) *Passion with Reason: The Strategic Role of the Emotions*, New York: W.M. Norton.

Frankena, W.K. (ed.) (1963) *Ethics*, Englewood Cliffs, NJ: Prentice Hall.

Friedman, M. (1970) 'The social responsibility of business is to increase its profits', *New York Times Magazine* 13 September.

Frith, F. (1994) 'Crime and punishment: Whistleblowing and intimidation rituals', *Employment Relations: Theory and Practice* 3: 641–59.

Gilligan, C. (1982) *In a Different Voice: Psychological Theory and Women's Development*, Cambridge, Mass.: Harvard University Press.

Glazer, M.P. and Glazer, P.M. (1989), *The Whistle-Blowers: Exposing Corruption in Government and Industry*, New York: Basic Books.

Graham, J.W. (1995) 'Leadership, moral development, and citizenship behaviour', *Business Ethics Quarterly* 5(1): 43–54.

Greanis, G. and Windsor, D. (1982) *The Foreign Corrupt Practices Act: Anatomy of a Statute*, Lexington, Mass.: Lexington Books.

Green, R.M. (1994) *The Ethical Manager: A New Method For Business Ethics*, New York: Maxwell Macmillan.

Handy, C. (1995) *The Empty Raincoat: Making Sense of the Future*, London: Arrow.

Hersh, R.H., Paolitto, D.P. and Reimer, J. (1979) *Promoting Moral Growth, From Piaget to Kohlberg* (second edition), New York: Longman.

Hofstede, G. (1980) *Culture's Consequences: International Differences in Work Related Values*, Beverley Hills, Calif.: Sage.

Hosmer, L.T. (1987) *The Ethics of Management*, Boston, Mass.: Irwin.

Hosmer, L.T. (1991) *The Ethics of Management* (second edition), Boston, Mass.: Irwin.

Independent Commission Against Corruption (ICAC) (1994) *Conference on Business Ethics*, Hong Kong Convention Centre, 4 May.

Independent Commission Against Corruption (ICAC) (1995) *Conference on the Opening of the Business Ethics Resource Centre*, Hong Kong Convention Centre, 2 May.

Independent Commission Against Corruption (ICAC) (1996) *Report on a Survey of Young People's Attitude Towards Work Ethics*, Hong Kong: ICAC Community Relations Department.

Jackall, R. (1988) *Moral Mazes: The World of Corporate Managers*, Oxford: Oxford University Press.

Kanter, R.M. (1979) 'Power failure in management circuits', *Harvard Business Review* 57(4): 65–75.

Knouse, S.B. and Giacalone, R.A. (1992) 'Ethical decision-making in business: Behavioural issues and concerns', *Journal of Business Ethics* 11: 369–77.

Kohlberg, L. (1981) *Essays on Moral Development, Volume One: The Philosophy of Moral Development*, San Francisco: Harper and Row.

Kohlberg, L. (1984) *Essays in Moral Development, Volume Two: The Psychology of Moral Development*, New York: Harper and Row.

Kohlberg, L. (1986) 'A current statement on some theoretical issues', in Modgil, S. and Modgil, C. (eds), *Lawrence Kohlberg: Consensus and Controversy*, Lewes: The Falmer Press.

Kohlberg, L., Levine, C. and Hewer, A. (1983) *Moral Stages: A Current Formulation and a Response to Critics*, New York: Karger.

Kohlberg, L. and Ryncarz, R.A. (1990) 'Beyond justice reasoning: Moral development and consideration of a seventh stage', in Alexander, C.N. and Langer, E.J. (eds), *Higher Stages of Human Development*, Oxford: Oxford University Press.

Kwong, K. (1996) 'Purity over profit', *Sunday Morning Post, Agenda Section* 18 February: 2.

Lavoie, D. and Culbert, S.A. (1978) 'Stages of organization and development', *Human Relations* 31(5): 417–38.

Leung, K. (1988) 'Theoretical advances in justice behavior: Some cross-cultural inputs',. in Bond, M.H. (ed.), *The Cross-cultural Challenge to Social Psychology*, Newbury Park, CA: Sage.

Luthans, F., Hodgetts, R.M. and Rosenkrantz, S.A. (1988) *Real Managers*, Cambridge, Mass.: Ballinger.

Maclagan, P. (1995) 'Ethical thinking in organizations: Implications for management education', *Management Learning* 26(2): 159–77.

Mechanic, D. (1962) 'Sources of power of lower participants in complex organizations', *Administrative Science Quarterly* 7: 349–64.

Miceli, M.P. and Near, J.P. (1991) 'Whistleblowing as an organizational process', in Bacharach, S.B (ed.), *Research in the Sociology of Organizations* 9: 139–200 (Greenwich, C:T: JAI Press).

Mitchell, A., Puxty, T., Sikka, P. and Willmott, H. (1994) 'Ethical statements as smokescreens for sectional interests: The case of the UK accountancy profession', *Journal of Business Ethics* 13(1): 39–51.

Mitchell, T.R. and Scott, W.G. (1990) 'America's problems and needed reforms: Confronting the ethic of personal advantage', *Academy of Management Executive* 4(3): 23–35.

Near, J.P. and Jensen, T.C. (1983) 'The whistleblowing process: Retaliation and perceived effectiveness', *Work and Occupations* 10(1): 3–28.

Near, J.P. and Miceli, M.P. (1987) 'Whistleblowers in organizations: Dissidents or reformers?', in Staw, B.M. and Cummings, L.L. (eds), *Research in Organizational Behaviour* 9: 321–68 (Greenwich, C:T: JAI Press).

Nielsen, R.P. (1987) 'What can managers do about unethical management?', *Journal of Business Ethics* 6: 309–20.

Pastin, M. and Hooker, M. (1980) 'Ethics and the Foreign Corrupt Practices Act', *Business Horizons* December: 43–7.

Perrucci, R., Anderson, R.M., Schendel, D.E. and Trachtman, E. (1980) 'Whistleblowing: Professionals resistance to organizational authority', *Social Problems* 28: 149–64.

Petrick, J.A. and Wagley, R.A. (1992) 'Enhancing the responsible strategic management of organizations', *Journal of Management Development* 11(4): 57–72.

Ponting, C. (1986) *Whitehall: Tragedy and Farce*, London: Hamish Hamilton.

Rawls, J. (1971) *A Theory of Justice*, Cambridge, Mass.: Harvard University Press.

Roddick, A. (1991) *Body and Soul*, London: Vermillion.

Ryan, L.V. (1994) 'Ethics codes in British companies', *Business Ethics: A European Review* 3(1): 54–64.

Sanderson, R. and Warner, I.I. (1994) 'What's wrong with corporate codes of conduct?', *Management Accounting* 66: 28–35.

Schlegelmilch, B.B. and Houston, J.E. (1990) 'Corporate codes of ethics', *Management Decision* 28(7) 38–43.

Schor, J.B. (1992) *The Overworked American*, New York: Basic Books.

Schwartz, H. (1990) *Narcissistic Process and Corporate Decay*, New York: New York University Press.

Sims, D., Fineman, S. and Gabriel, Y. (1993) *Organizing and Organizations: An Introduction*, London: Sage Publications.

Singer, P. (ed.) (1991) *A Companion to Ethics*, Oxford: Blackwell.

Smith, A. (1937) *An Enquiry Into the Nature and Causes of the Wealth of Nations*, Cannan, E. (ed.), New York: Modern Library.

Snell, R.S. (1993a) *Developing Skills for Ethical Management*, London: Chapman and Hall.

Snell, R.S. (1993b) 'More than meets the eye: Adopting a management style through modelling', *Leadership and Organization Development Journal* 14(5): 3–11.

Snell, R.S. (1996) 'Complementing Kohlberg: Mapping the ethical reasoning used by managers for their own dilemma cases', *Human Relations* 49(1): 23–49.

Snell, R.S., Chak, A. M.K. and Taylor, K.F. (1996) 'The impact of moral ethos on how ethical dilemmas are experienced and resolved in six Hong Kong companies', *Management Research News* 19(9): 72–91.

Snell, R.S., Taylor, K.F. and Chak, A. M.K. (1997) 'Ethical dilemmas and ethical reasoning: A study', *Human Resource Management Journal* 7(3): 19–30.

Snell, R.S. and Tseng, C.S. (1996) 'Ethical dilemmas of doing business in china – are there any special problems?', paper presented at a conference entitled *Cross-Cultural Management in China*, 26–28 August, Baptist University, Hong Kong.

Steidlmeir, P. (1992) *People and Profits: The Ethics of Capitalism*, Englewood Cliffs, NJ: Prentice Hall.

Stevens, B. (1994) ' An analysis of corporate ethical code studies: "Where do we go from here?"', *Journal of Business Ethics* 13: 63–9.

Stewart, S. and White, W. (1995) 'Conclusion: Whose business values?', in Stewart, S. and Donleavy, G. (eds), *Whose Business Values? Some Asian and Cross-cultural Perspectives*, Hong Kong: Hong Kong University Press.

The Body Shop (1996) 'The Values Report 1995', on the internet at the University of Bristol http://bizednet.bris.ac.uk:8080/compfact/bodyshop/cs-eth.rtf

Toffler, B.L. (1986) *Tough Choices: Managers Talk Ethics*, Chichester: John Wiley.

Transparency International (1996a) 'Internet Corruption Ranking, 1996', on the Internet, http://www.GWDG.DE/~uwvw/rank-96.html

Transparency International (1996b) 'Transparency International Press Release', on the Internet, http://www.is.in-berlin.de/~ti/press_releases/poll_1996.html

Treviño, L.K. (1986) 'Ethical decision making in organizations: A person–situation interactionist model', *Academy of Management Review* 11(3): 601–17.

Treviño, L.K. (1992) 'Moral reasoning and business ethics: Implications for research, education and management', *Journal of Business Ethics* 11: 445–59.

Treviño, L.K. and McCabe, D. (1994) 'Meta-learning about business ethics: Building honorable business school communities', *Journal of Business Ethics* 13: 405–16.

Treviño, L.K. and Nelson, K.A. (1995) *Managing Business Ethics: Straight Talk About How to do it Right*, New York: John Wiley.

Treviño, L.K. and Youngblood, S.A. (1990) 'Bad apples in bad barrels: A causal analysis of ethical decision-making behavior', *Journal of Applied Psychology* 75(4): 378–85.

Velasquez, M.G. (1992) *Business Ethics: Concepts and Cases* (third edition), Englewood Cliffs, NJ: Prentice Hall.

Vinten, G. (1992) 'Whistle blowing: Corporate help or hindrance?', *Management Decision* 30(1): 44–8.

Wambold, J.J. (1977) 'Prohibiting foreign bribes: Criminal sanctions for corporate payments abroad', *Cornell International Law Journal* 10: 235–7.

Warren, R. (1993) 'Codes of ethics: Bricks without straw', *Business Ethics: A European Review* 2(4): 185–91.

Waters, J. (1998) 'Integrity management: Learning and implementing ethical principles in the workplace', in Srivasta, S. and associates (eds), *Executive Integrity: The Search for High Human Values in Organizational Life*, San Francisco: Jossey-Bass.

Waters, J., Bird, F. and Chant, P.D. (1986) 'Everyday moral issues experienced by managers', *Journal of Business Ethics* 5(5): 373–84.

Weaver, G.R. (1993) 'Corporate codes of ethics: Purpose, process and content issues', *Business and Society* 32(1): 44–58.

Weber, J. (1990) 'Managers' moral reasoning: Assessing their responses to three moral dilemmas', *Human Relations* 43(7): 687–702.

Webley, S. (1993) *Codes of Business Ethics – Why Companies Should Develop Them*, London: Institute of Business Ethics.

Weiss, J.W. (1994) *Business Ethics: A Managerial, Stakeholder Approach*, Belmont, CA.: Wadsworth.

Wellman, C. (1963) 'The ethical implications of cultural relativity', *Journal of Philosophy* 60(7): 169–84.

White, B.J. and Montgomery, R. (1980) 'Corporate codes of conduct', *California Management Review* 23(2): 80–7.

Williams, G.J. (1992) *Ethics in Modern Management*, New York: Quorum Books.

Yeung, A. and Yeung, J. (1995) 'Business values: A strategic imperative for the coming decades', in Stewart, S. and Donleavy, G. (eds), *Whose Business Values? Some Asian and Cross-cultural Perspectives*, Hong Kong: Hong Kong University Press.

10

Managing strategically

Michael Browne, Bobby Banerjee, Liz Fulop and Stephen Linstead

Questions about managing strategically

1 What is a strategy?
2 How are strategies formulated?
3 What is the value of strategic planning?
4 Why do some firms outperform others?
5 Do all organizations need a strategy?

The Sports Shoe Saga

Dick Foster was a worried man. As Vice President – Production of Image Inc., the sixth-largest sports shoe manufacturer in the world, his cup of sorrow (not water!) was over-flowing. His primary producing markets were in shambles. The Asian currency crisis had hit them hard, particularly in Indonesia, Malaysia, and Thailand. Their major sports endorsee, the first pick in last year's US National Basketball Association (NBA) draft, a rookie already of superstar status, died of a heroin overdose eight months after signing a $70 million endorsement deal with the company. They had signed him up for everything: running shoes, casual shoes, socks, shirts, shorts, wristbands, thighbands, earrings, nose-rings, watches, lotions, and whatever else their new product development people could think of. As Dan Flintstone, their R&D director frequently reminded his colleagues, 'we literally own his ass: he's got our logo tattooed right there, or so I've been told'. Labour costs all over were increasing and so was labour unrest: last month there were four demonstrations outside their Korean plant. The last one was particularly bad, one worker was killed by the police and several others injured. The local activist, Jae Sae Kim, a highly respected lawyer and a thorn in the side for transnational corporations, was jailed for her part in the demonstrations. Within hours, the international media had descended on the plains of Pusan. Both *48 hours* and *60 Minutes* did a story, and neither was remotely flattering to the company. After the story broke in the US and European markets, there was bad press everywhere. It was easing off a bit now, but for a while it had seemed like there was a reference to their company, mostly negative, every day. Wall St was jittery. Production was still suffering and there was talk of more trouble in the plant. The subcontractor threatened to shut down the plant if demonstrations continued. Their expansion plans in the Asia–Pacific region, a $3 billion investment, were put on hold by the executive board. The CEO had called the firm's directors from every region in the world for a series of strategy meetings over the next few days. And Dick Foster was going to be in the spotlight. They were his subcontractors, it was his region. With their annual shareholder meeting less than six weeks away, it wasn't going to be an easy time. Sighing resignedly, as he manoeuvred his car through the heavy midtown Manhattan traffic, Dick thought about the time when he was first put in charge of international production nearly twenty years ago. Could they have known this was going to happen? What was he going to recommend to his boss? Continue with their expansion plans in the region? Replace the subcontractors? Relocate? How could he ensure smooth production over the next few years? He needed to prepare a medium-term plan fairly quickly.

Jae Sae sat in her cell and contemplated her next move. The demonstration had gone off well, several of her colleagues were interviewed by both local and foreign media. Greenpeace announced its support for the Korean workers. In an interview with CNN some hours ago, the CEO of Image Inc. said he would be visiting Korean government officials and business people next week for talks on how to resolve the issue. She hoped they wouldn't be able to just shut down the plant. Things were bad enough as it was, and the last thing she wanted was to put people out of work in these hard times. The last few decades had seen phenomenal economic growth in the Asia–Pacific region with annual GNP growth of 8–10 percent. Rapid industrial development resulted in higher wages in South Korea and neighbouring countries, but was accompanied by social and environmental problems. Labour unrest became common in South Korea as the government's authoritarian control over the workplace diminished somewhat in the 1980s.

The global sports shoe market is a multibillion dollar industry employing over 100 000 people in the Asian region, with manufacturing operations in South Korea, Thailand, Malaysia, Vietnam, China, the Philippines, Taiwan and Indonesia. Reebok, Nike, Hi-Tec, Adidas and Puma are the market leaders, with Reebok having the highest sales value and Hi-Tec the highest volume sales. The biggest export market is the USA, accounting for 65 percent of the market by value, followed by Germany, the UK and France. Over 90 percent of branded athletic footwear production is located in Asia. In the late 1970s and early 1980s, Pusan, South Korea was the sneaker capital of the world. Cheap land, labour and raw materials were the chief sources of attraction for manufacturers of athletic footwear and low production costs more than offset the higher shipping costs. 'Manufacturers' is a misleading term: none of the major firms actually make their products. Instead, all production is subcontracted out to local contractors in the region. This practice, pioneered by Nike in the 1970s, was soon adopted by the other transnational corporations and is the norm in the industry. Competition over brand names became more fierce, with $250 million annual advertising budgets being common. After a period of extraordinary growth in the 1980s, the market unexpectedly began to stagnate. The attractiveness of South Korea and Taiwan as cheap labour markets declined as labour costs rose and competition became tougher and in the mid-1980s companies began to develop subcontractors in neighbouring regions especially in Indonesia, Thailand, China and Vietnam. Declining growth rates now threatened to diminish even more in the wake of the financial crisis sweeping over the region.

Footwear manufacturing is a labour-intensive process requiring little machinery but a large number of raw materials, especially volatile organic compounds. Strict environmental regulation covered the use and disposal of these materials in North America and Europe. Such is not the case in several Asian countries. Hourly wages of $9 and higher in North American and European markets could not compete with rates of 23 cents per hour and 37 cents per hour which were the norm in China and the Philippines. While it is difficult to calculate a precise break down of costs, estimates of labour costs range from 10–12 percent. Raw materials account for 70 percent of the cost. The labour component of a typical product with a retail price of $US60 at the store (including development, marketing and shipping costs, retailing costs, and profits) ranges from $0.46 to $1.50 per pair of shoes.

The major companies in the industry were mainly involved in design, distribution and marketing. Nike's pioneering 100 percent outsourcing strategy became a norm in the industry. Competition among subcontractors was fierce as a result of an industry strategy of pitting one subcontractor against another and awarding the cheapest subcontractor the largest share of production. It was not uncommon for one subcontractor to manufacture products for Nike, Reebok and Adidas, all made in the same plant. Most subcontractors were locally owned and controlled and regularly negotiated short-term production contracts with the transnational corporations.

Global branding was followed by all the major corporations. Richard Donahue, vice-chairman of Nike, described their strategy in the following terms: 'the commitment is to be a global company – one management, one theme, one value, one ethic throughout the world'. High advertising and promotion costs also characterized this market with huge sponsorship deals involving the world's top athletes. Many corporations shifted their subcontracting operations from South Korea and Taiwan to countries like Vietnam, Thailand and China to take advantage of cheaper labour costs. The low end of the market was crowded and Nike and Reebok were already looking to shift their focus to the higher end of the market with an emphasis on product innovation and quality.

News stories about labour practices in Asia highlighted many problems: forced overtime, minimum wages, hire and fire policies, the hiring of predominantly casual labour and refugees, discrimination against trade unions, inadequate safety standards, and in some cases, physical coercion and surveillance and the sexual harassment of women. In the *48 hours* news story, an employee of Image Inc.'s Thailand subcontractor was interviewed who claimed they were being paid half the normal rate and that she was fired when she complained. Her sister, who worked in the same plant, was fired after she became pregnant: over 85 percent of the subcontractor's workforce were female, the company hired single women only and no maternity benefits were provided. Subsequently, Dick Foster had met with the subcontractor and threatened to discontinue the relationship if work practices were not improved. The company was now working on a global code of conduct for subcontracting operations.

The companies' responses to these criticisms mainly revolved around issues of ownership. They claimed no local laws were broken and the minimum wage paid was in accordance with local customs. They had no financial or legal ties with the subcontractors and did not own the companies operating in Asia. As David Taylor of Reebok put it, 'we don't pay anybody at the factories and we don't set policy within the factories. It is their business to run'.

This case was developed by Bobby Banerjee. Image Inc. is a fictitious company. Figures cited and other material were gleaned from a variety of articles in the business press and a case study conducted by Bethan Brookes and Peter Madden from a research project commissioned by the Christian Aid Foundation.

Questions about the case

1 What is Image Inc.'s product?
2 How did the outsourcing strategy emerge?
3 What factors were considered in the decision to outsource?
4 Where is Image Inc.'s strategy headed?

Introduction

Planning was identified as a major function of top management long ago by the classical management theorists. Frederick Winslow Taylor argued that managers were to be the planners, to be forward looking, while the workers on the shopfloor were to be the 'doers' (see Chapter 6). Henri Fayol (1841–1925), one of the early classical management theorists, whose book *General and Industrial Management* was only translated into English in 1949, advocated that forecasting and planning were essential management functions in ensuring that an organization attained its objectives (Fayol 1949: 50). He also added control to the functions of management in order to ensure that plans were monitored and appropriate steps taken to correct performance. Modern strategic planning dates from the work of Igor Ansoff (1965) whose book *Corporate Strategy*, written in the USA, helped establish what became known as the *Planning School* approach to strategy. The central ideas of the Planning School were developed in the 1950s and 1960s, a period of steady economic growth and stability in world markets. Ironically, it was only in the 1970s, a period of unprecedented economic instability and stagnation, that the Planning School became popular.

Another influential approach to strategic planning, which emerged in the same period and in the same country, was the *Design School* with its focus on analyzing the strengths and weaknesses, opportunities and threats (SWOT) of organizations. SWOT analysis is still used by many managers in their planning processes. Both approaches placed great faith in the virtues of rational planning and the scientific rational approach to strategy formulation. The implicit assumption in these approaches was that the environments in which planners operated were sufficiently stable to allow for the development of strategies and the formulation and implementation of detailed plans often spanning 10 or 20 years.

In the 1980s strategy fell under the influence of the *Entrepreneurial School* and the *Positioning School*, again both originating in the USA. The former was associated with the works of Tom Peters and Robert Waterman (1982) and Terrence Deal and Allan Kennedy (1982) who were more cynical about the virtues of rational planning and more concerned with energizing and mobilizing planning efforts around turbulent environments using ideas such as corporate culture, vision, mission and transformational leadership. In the 1980s economics also began to exert a much stronger influence over the strategy field with the publication of two books by Michael Porter from the Harvard Business School (Porter 1980, 1985). The so-called Positioning School had its origins in his works with a noticeable shift to industry analysis as a key determinant of strategy. The *Extended Design School* also became popular in this period and its principles were, and are still, found in many texts throughout the world. Incorporating and refining the principles of rational decision making into the strategic process, and borrowing from the Entrepreneurial School, the Extended Design School model became the template for what was often described as strategic planning.

These approaches have had a profound influence over the strategy discourse, though none has been without its detractors. Formal planning has been widely promoted as the most rational approach to decision making. Through the application of formal planning principles and models, managers were supposed to achieve greater predictability, control and influence over the complex and increasingly uncertain environments in which they had to operate. The detractors and critics of formal planning suggested, however, that formal planning usually failed and nothing could stop the manager from 'surfing on the wave of events and decisions, without a real chance to control and to lead the development' (Westerlund and Sjøstrand 1979: 121). Some years later Henry Mintzberg (1994) was vociferous in criticizing strategic planning, devoting an entire book, *The Rise and Fall of Strategic Planning,* to the topic.

We will now offer a very brief description of the ten 'schools' of strategy formation to illustrate the variety of perspectives which exist in the strategy literature. We will then explore how a few of the more dominant of these schools have contributed to the emergence of the most popular prescriptive model of the *process* of strategy formulation, the Extended Design School model, which we here call the *Rational Model* (see Chapter 8). The Rational Model also includes the Positioning School, which draws on economic laws and principles to explain the notion of competitive advantage. This model is then criticized with reference to a range of dissenting views, again emphasizing the diversity of perspectives which fall under the umbrella of strategic management. This leads to a consideration of an alternative view of strategy formulation influenced by 'political' and 'learning' school perspectives, which we call the *Reconfiguration Approach*. Mintzberg is included in the Reconfiguration Approach, having described himself as belonging to the Configuration School (see below). We then consider how 'strategic thinking' has emerged as a key element in the Reconfiguration Approach.

Finally, a third approach has emerged recently which we call the *Postmodern Approach*. This approach treats strategy as a discourse, and principally as a textual flow of ideas, meanings and justifications (see also Chapter 8). The notions of *genre* and *social subjectivity* are reintroduced to render an account of how organizations develop their strategic *texts* or stories and how these texts become the 'official' strategy of the organization. This approach deconstructs how the 'official strategies' of managers and their organizations mirror dominant strategic discourses and the knowledge and power relations that are embedded in these discourses.

Dominant approaches to strategy

Table 10.1 describes the key differences between the three approaches to strategy discussed in the introduction to the chapter. The remainder of the chapter examines how these three approaches have emerged and what substantive claims they make about strategy.

Table 10.1   *Three approaches to strategy*

The Rationalist Model	The Reconfigurationist Model	The Postmodernist Approach
Mission and vision: a unitarist view of the organization	Multiple stakeholders: a pluralist view of the organization as consisting of different stakeholders with different interests. Objectives determined by *mutual partisan adjustment* (negotiation)	Objectives are written into the narratives of strategy. The players are encouraged/coerced to adopt suitable roles. Vision moves into three, four and five dimensions
Legitimate authority: managers have the power to command the activities of the enterprise	Multiple sources of power are distributed throughout organizations; the power of managers is limited	Power–knowledge relations are supported by the strategic narrative
Comprehensive rational analysis	Bounded rationality	Bounded emotionality, intuition, creativity
Evaluation of all possible alternatives	Limited, successive comparisons	Textual criticism; how the story is unfolding; subtexts and contexts
Explicit strategies and detailed plans	Strategies emerge over time, developing incrementally, 'grass roots' strategies	The story is told, retold and modified, contested and added to
Objectivity	Subjectivity and selectivity: different actors pay attention to different aspects of the organization and its environment leading to different interpretations of the situation	Intersubjectivity and intertextuality. There is more than one story and they all simultaneously compete and coexist

Strategic management, as a field of study, encompasses a very wide variety of perspectives and approaches, as illustrated by Mintzberg (1990). In a comprehensive review of the field to that date, Mintzberg catalogued no less than ten 'schools of thought' in strategy formulation. These ten schools of thought are described in Table 10.2. The first three he described as *prescriptive* schools of thought, that is, approaches which are primarily normative or focused on how the enterprise *should* approach strategy formation. These prescriptive approaches are based on applying rational models and theories to strategy. The remainder he described as *descriptive* schools of thought, less concerned with prescribing how strategy should be formulated than with the description and explanation of how enterprise strategies are actually formed in practice. Reconfigurationists are drawn principally from the descriptive approaches.

Mintzberg's catalogue of the field was impressive in its scope but his categories are not unproblematic. The twofold division into the three prescriptive schools on the one hand, and the seven descriptive schools on the other, is crude. It is as likely to mislead as to elucidate. Mintzberg's classification is narrowly focused on the process dimensions of strategy formulation with the result that with respect to some of the schools the classification must be forced. The Positioning School, for example, is almost silent on process issues; it is

Table 10.2 *Henry Mintzberg's ten schools of strategy formation*

The *prescriptive schools:* ideas about how strategy *should* be formulated	**The Design School** Strategy formulation is *a simple and informal conceptual process*, a process of designing a strategy that best matches the enterprise's capabilities to its opportunities. Seminal contribution: Edward Learned, Carl Roland Christensen, Kenneth Andrews and William Guth (1969) *Business Policy: Text and Cases* **The Planning School** Strategy formulation is *a formal process* that proceeds beyond conception to very detailed plans articulating specific and measurable goals, specific responsibilities and actions, and mechanisms for control and evaluation. Seminal contribution: Igor Ansoff (1965), *Corporate Strategy* **The Positioning School** Strategy formulation as *an analytical process* involving the analysis of the industry and market structures within which the enterprise operates, the analysis of their competitive dynamics, and the enterprise's current and potential competitive position in the industry. Seminal contribution: Michael Porter (1980), *Competitive Strategy*
The *descriptive schools:* explaining how strategies *are* formed	**The Cognitive School** Strategy formation as *a mental process*. Explores how strategies are formed in the minds of managers **The Entrepreneurial School** Strategy formation as *an expression of visionary and entrepreneurial leadership*. Explores the process by which managers elicit a sense of a common mission among members of an organization. Seminal contribution: Tom Peters and Robert Waterman (1982), *In Search of Excellence* **The Learning School** Strategy formation as a piece-meal, *incremental process* by which strategies emerge over time as the enterprise learns about its environment and its own capabilities. Seminal contribution: Ralph Stacey (1996), *Strategic Management and Organizational Dynamics* (second edition) **The Political School** Strategy formation is *a political process* of negotiation and compromise (and often of continuous renegotiation). Sees the enterprise as consisting of multiple stakeholders with different interests and among whom power is distributed. Seminal contribution: Andrew Pettigrew (1985), *The Awakening Giant – Continuity and Change in Imperial Chemical Industries* **The Cultural School** Sees enterprise strategies as *an ideological process* largely determined by the culture of the organization, its shared values and beliefs. Seminal contributions: Craig Hickman and Michael A. Silva (1984), *Creating Excellence: Managing Corporate Culture, Strategy and Change in the New Age;* Gerry Johnson (1987), *Strategic Change and the Management Process* **The Environmental School** Strategy is explained as *a passive process*, determined in response to the inexorable pressures of the enterprise's environment. Seminal contribution: Alfred Chandler (1962), *Strategy and Structure: Chapters in the History of Industrial Enterprise* **The Configurational School** Drawing on all of the above schools, the configurational school attempts a synthesis of them. Strategy formation is described as *an episodic process* to which each of the various perspectives may contribute explanations at one or more stages of the process. Seminal contribution: Henry Mintzberg (1987), 'Crafting strategy', *Harvard Business Review* July–August, pp. 67–81

Source: Modified from Henry Mintzberg (1990), 'Strategy formation: Schools of thought', in Frederickson, J.W. (ed.), *Perspectives on Strategic Management*, New York: Harper Business.

concerned primarily with the content of strategic decisions and its approach is better characterized as analytic rather than prescriptive. Many of the other classifications are open to debate as well. Some writers in the Entrepreneurial School, for example, could be regarded as being highly prescriptive rather than descriptive. It is also worth pointing out that Mintzberg's catalogue is becoming dated. In the last decade in particular the resource-based view has risen to prominence in the leading journals, reminding us that strategy is a continuously developing field of inquiry and debate. Other approaches, such as that of David Knights and Glenn Morgan (1991), offer a postmodern critique of strategic discourse.

Nevertheless, Mintzberg's typology is useful to the extent that it draws our attention to the variety of perspectives represented in the strategic management literature and the variety of meta-narratives within the strategy discourse. As for himself, as already mentioned, Mintzberg claims to be a member of the Configurational School. His approach is eclectic: each of the various schools provides some insight into strategic management but each is partial and incomplete.

The rational approaches have dominated the strategy discourse and from the Planning School, the Design School and the Extended Design School have emerged several key elements of what many managers would either identify or be taught to consider as universally applicable ways to go about formulating strategy. Three key elements are: the Hierarchy of Plans that has its origins in the Planning School; the SWOT analysis that derives from the Design School as mentioned above, and the Strategic Planning Model that has its origins in the Extended Design School model. We will now examine each of these.

The hierarchy of plans

A number of prominent writers on planning (e.g. Ackoff 1970; Ansoff 1979; Chandler 1977) started from the proposition that organizations needed a portfolio of plans. The portfolio or hierarchy of plans denotes the appropriate type of planning to be conducted at each level of the organization. A hierarchy of plans can be based on a range of criteria, for example which level of management is involved, the period of the plan and so on. Figure 10.1 describes a typical hierarchy of plans.

In an overview of the strategic management process, Charles Hofer and Dan Schendel (1978) proposed four hierarchical levels of strategy. These are: enterprise strategy at the top, followed by corporate, business and functional strategies. *Enterprise strategy* is the broadest level of strategy that integrates the total organization with its environment. Hofer and Schendel (1978) maintain that the focus of enterprise strategy is to examine the role the firm plays and should play in society. Firm governance, function and its form are areas that are addressed in enterprise strategy, questions that arise from a re-examination of the mission of the firm. Increasing shareholder value and providing customer satisfaction are examples of company mission – these are considered as acceptable goals for any business firm and a viable enterprise strategy is one way of conferring on firms their institutional legitimacy in society.

Corporate strategy involves identifying the kind of businesses that the firm should be in to meet its corporate and enterprise strategy goals. Integrating diverse businesses into a manageable portfolio is seen as an essential part of corporate strategy. Sociopolitical and cultural factors also are considered in this level of strategy, although at the corporate strategy level the

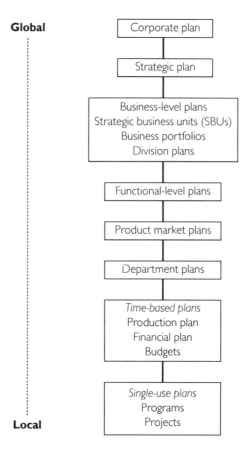

Global

Corporate plan

Strategic plan

Business-level plans
Strategic business units (SBUs)
Business portfolios
Division plans

Functional-level plans

Product market plans

Department plans

Time-based plans
Production plan
Financial plan
Budgets

Single-use plans
Programs
Projects

Local

Figure 10.1 Hierarchy of plans

focus is on the influence of these factors at the industry level rather than at the broader societal level. Product market decisions are meant to be made at this level of strategy, as are decisions on technology development and use.

A firm's *business strategy* is meant to involve the optimum allocation of its resources in order to achieve a competitive advantage. In addition, this level of strategy is said to focus on integrating the functional areas such as accounting and marketing into the business. *Functional strategy* integrates the subfunctional areas into the functional areas. Coordination is the key focus in a functional strategy: for example the advertising plan for a new product launch is coordinated with personal selling and sales promotions. Coordination is not limited to one department; in the above example the marketing activities must be coordinated with purchasing, accounting and production activities to implement a functional strategy successfully.

It is important to realize that these strategy levels are hierarchical and each level of strategy is constrained by the one above it. For instance, a functional strategy would be constrained by a firm's business strategy, which in turn is constrained by corporate and enterprise strategy. From this hierarchical structure, it follows that for a firm the enterprise strategy is the most important level of strategy that drives the other levels. However, it is also important to note that the strategy process is not unidirectional, despite the hierarchal structure that is advocated by the Planning School approach.

Lower levels of strategy can influence corporate strategy. For example, consider the increasing attention paid by many corporations to environmental issues. Think about a large multibusiness conglomerate (for example, a corporation involved in publishing, print, paper and paper packaging, dyes, inks and chemicals) that follows corporate strategies of cost leadership (producing products or services more efficiently than competitors) and differentiation (producing products or services that better serve the needs of customers). One of their operating businesses (let's say dye manufacture), however, is facing regulatory pressures to change its production process to a less polluting one. Suppose the senior managers of this business realize that a proactive approach to the natural environment will ensure the business's survival and long-term profitability, and decide to take appropriate action, and the change in process is not so costly as to require financial investment from corporate headquarters. In this case environmental issues have not been addressed from a higher enterprise level but have emerged from the business strategy level. Importantly, the positive consequences of such a strategy could have a feedback effect on the enterprise strategy of the firm, wherein the firm arrives at the realization that its survival and legitimacy in society may also depend on its level of environmentalism. Or the positive consequences could have an effect at the corporate strategy level by influencing product market decisions and the company could, on the strength of the success of its effort in the dye company and the processes it has developed, decide to diversify into the environmental protection business. Similarly, at a purely functional level, packaging modifications to include more recycled content can be the basis of a 'green' appeal in the firm's marketing strategy. The success of such a strategy can lead to the recognition of changing market needs which in turn can influence business, corporate or enterprise strategy, thus providing a feedback loop. In other words, whereas corporate environmentalism at the enterprise level will necessarily constrain strategic decision at lower levels, the converse may or may not be true. Two factors will be influential: first, whether the financial investment required is such as to necessitate corporate support, in which case the corporation may decide to close or sell the company if it is not prepared to invest; second, the degree to which the corporation is able to learn from its subunits, and share knowledge among them, so that successful ones can act as role models for the others.

What is clear is that many graphic descriptions of the planning process tend to give an impression of precision and simplicity (Westerlund and Sjøstrand 1979: 23). The neatness and tidiness implied is precisely what critics such as Mintzberg (1973) and John Kotter (1982) also questioned. Both were far from convinced that planning occurred in any ordered sequence or entailed a precise and predictable process as suggested by the hierarchy of plans approach. Strategic planning is usually represented as a unitary process in which conflict fades into the background, at least until various analytical tools and methods are adequately applied. The many models and techniques associated with strategic planning are concerned with describing the 'what', rather than the 'how' or 'who', of planning.

SWOT analysis

As mentioned earlier, the 'Design School' is the term that Mintzberg gave to the approach to strategy formulation pioneered by Professor Kenneth Andrews of the Harvard Business School in one of the first texts on strategic management (or business policy as the field was then known) called *Business Policy: Texts and Cases* (Learned *et al.* 1969). At the centre of

Andrews's approach to strategy formulation was a simple proposition: that strategy is concerned with identifying opportunities in the enterprise's external environment which it is better qualified to exploit than its competitors. From this simple proposition is derived the core prescription, that in formulating strategy managers should conduct an audit of their external environment to identify opportunities and threats; and conduct an audit of their internal environment to identify the strengths and weaknesses of the enterprise. This approach to strategy formulation is summarized in the acronym *SWOT* (strengths, weaknesses, opportunities and threats).

On face value, SWOT analysis seems to be a sensible and straightforward approach to strategy formulation. The typical way of going about it is to conduct a 'brainstorm'. Teams of managers pore over complex variables and compile lists – as comprehensive as possible – of the environment's opportunities and threats, and the strengths and weaknesses of the organization in relation to its competitors. But the results are often ambiguous: items listed as strengths, for example often appear also as weaknesses. Attempts to quantify the elements, scoring them as both strengths and weaknesses if necessary, more often lead to squabbles over technique than insights into competitive advantage. Often, in spite of the appeal (i.e. its lack of messiness) of the rational procedure (such as outlined in Chapter 8), the results are inconclusive. The progression from SWOT analysis to identifying an appropriate strategy in context is often unclear and ultimately unconvincing. Even when the opinions on strengths and weaknesses converge, often a consensus as to the strategy most appropriate in the circumstances fails to emerge. The process of text formation used in SWOT analysis acts to or strives to normalize and unify views, forcing diverse reality into two dimensions. It is not structured to accommodate contradiction or dissenting views. One reason why the procedure produces ambiguous and inconclusive results (although by no means the only reason) is that the process has been wrongly conceived.

The problem with SWOT analysis lies precisely in the questions: What constitutes a strength? What constitutes a weakness? On critical reflection it becomes apparent that strengths and weaknesses are *not* attributes of an enterprise. They are *judgements about* the attributes of an enterprise. Strengths and weaknesses do not exist in organizations, they exist only as constructions of reality by those doing the analysis. This raises a further question: if strengths and weaknesses are judgements about the attributes of an enterprise, on what basis do we make such judgements? With reference to what *criteria* are these judgements made? And on what basis can judgements that make sense in terms of the enterprise's strategy be made?

Essentially, SWOT analysis aims to identify actual and potential strengths and weaknesses, attempting to build on the former while minimizing the effect of the latter. One of the great difficulties with the internal audit (SW) is that management competencies are also meant to be subject to review and scrutiny. Often, because of subjective bias, lack of confidence and unwillingness to 'face reality', some important or hard issues are not confronted by managers. The development of an appropriate SWOT analysis depends on relatively objective and consistent criteria to overcome subjective bias and hence a reluctance to take on tough issues (Andrews 1988: 47). What seems to happen often is that managers rely on arbitrary, intuitive methods (e.g. rules of thumb, opinions, etc.) to identify organizational weaknesses, but are quite ready to use more 'objective', quantifiable and historically based data (e.g. budgets) to measure strengths. While there are tools or techniques developed for assessing strengths and weaknesses (e.g. a company capability profile, vulnerability analysis;

see Rowe, Mason, Dickel and Westcott 1987), the weighting of these measures is ultimately influenced by management's judgement, level of experience and political interests (Bowman and Asch 1987: 87).

The strategic planning model

Since Andrews's articulation of these simple propositions, the Design School has become arguably the dominant approach to strategy formulation. Over time, however, the model has been further elaborated – the prescriptions becoming more detailed as successive writers have sought to integrate other perspectives and approaches within the general framework of the Design School model. Of particular note have been the borrowing of ideas from the Entrepreneurial and Planning Schools of strategy formulation to develop what we have previously described as the Extended Design School model of strategy formulation. Figure 10.2 outlines the key elements of the Extended Design School model.

From the Entrepreneurial School was borrowed the prescription that enterprises should be infused with a sense of 'mission'. This is a singular and common sense of purpose, which is meant to provide a common source of motivation for all members of the enterprise and to which all the enterprise's decisions should be ultimately referenced. Often associated with this idea was also the idea of 'vision', that successful enterprises must be led by the 'vision' that the CEO conceives and articulates for the enterprise. In the development of the extended model of strategy formulation, 'vision' and 'mission' have been appended to the model as superordinate to the definition of more specific goals and objectives. Thus an enterprise might adopt a very general and even ambiguous statement of its mission (the almost ubiquitous 'mission statement') as the ultimate reference point for strategic decisions, but will also then articulate more specific objectives, and even very precise targets or goals as the focus of particular strategies.

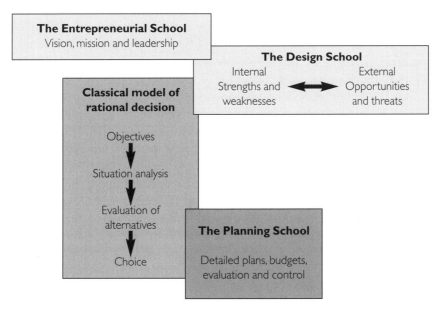

Figure 10.2 Components of the Extended Design School model

The Entrepreneurial School has a very optimistic view of the nature of management and the relationship between managers and their enterprises. As already mentioned, in the early 1980s, management writers Peters and Waterman (1982) and Deal and Kennedy (1982) popularized the view that the secrets to organizational success were a strong organizational culture, a set of strong common values and a common purpose (see Chapter 3). Their views were based on their observations of a number of very successful enterprises of the time. The prescription was simple – emulate these successful enterprises. If an enterprise was not infused with a common sense of purpose, a strong culture, the solution was leadership: the articulation by management of a 'vision' for the enterprise, a common destiny in which all the organization's members could share (see also Chapter 5). This is a 'unitarist' view of organizations – that the organization is viewed as a team unified by a common managerially defined purpose. Criticisms of this unifying push for managing diversity have been raised throughout other chapters in this book.

However, there is a very important difference between noticing that some successful companies exhibit a high degree of consensus and a strong sense of common purpose and deducing, without examining other possible explanations, that a sense of common purpose is the determining cause of the organization's success. It is a further quantum leap in logic to then offer the prescription that organizations without such characteristics could obtain them simply by the exercise of management leadership. Although these prescriptions were enthusiastically embraced by managers, the notion that an organization's culture was a variable amenable to management control is an ambitious assumption. Subsequent research has cast much doubt on the validity of this assumption (Furnham and Gunter 1993: 255; see also Chapter 3).

From the Planning School was borrowed an approach to the detailed articulation of strategies in specific action plans, budgets, etc. This strategic planning is predicated on prior determination of the organization's overall strategy and is concerned fundamentally with the details of planning, the allocation of responsibilities, tasks and resources necessary to operationalizing or implementing the strategy. The Planning School therefore provided the operating link between the formulation of strategy and its implementation. Detailed plans, however, are meant to have another role. Not only are they designed to govern the implementation of the strategy, but they are also designed to be used as a point of reference for evaluating and controlling the implementation of strategy.

As already mentioned, these four components of the Design School model are summarized in Figure 10.2 – SWOT, the classical model of rational decision making, the vision and mission of the Entrepreneurial School, and the operational detail provided by the Planning School – and together have forged what has become the textbook approach to strategy formulation: the Extended Design School model summarized in Figure 10.3.

The dominance of the Extended Design School model can probably be accounted for by its simplicity and practical appeal – for practising managers the Design School promises a systematic, comprehensive and ostensibly practical approach to formulating strategy. Ironically, however, the Extended Design School model is not derived from practical experience! Indeed, it is almost entirely a theoretical construct. At its core, the classical model of rational decision making relies not on experience but on purely abstract ideas as to what constitutes rationality. We specify our objectives, analyze the situation and evaluate all possible alternatives before making a decision, not because this has been the lesson of experience, but because we understand it is rational to do so (see Chapter 8). Similarly, the

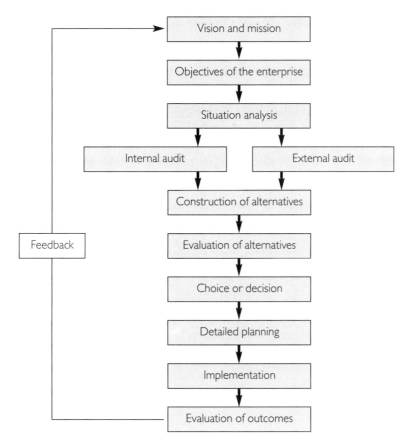

Figure 10.3 The Extended Design School Model

Source: John Forster and Michael Browne (1996), Principles of Strategic Management, *Melbourne: Macmillan, p. 168.*

proposition that success is to be achieved by exploiting opportunities in the external environment, for which the organization is better qualified by its strengths than its rivals has an intuitive appeal. But is this simple idea a sufficient basis on which to determine a strategy when the environment the organization faces is complex and uncertain? And how reliable in practice are the prescriptions that the Entrepreneurial and Planning Schools have lent to the model? Although the Extended Design School model has considerable appeal, as being both rational and practical, we need to look more closely at its underlying assumptions and the likely circumstances of its application in practice before we can be confident of its practicality.

The Extended Design School model prescribes, but often treats unproblematically, the analysis of the strategic circumstances of the organization. But the analysis of a strategic situation is by no means a simple and straightforward task; there are a number of considerations which may tend to make the task fraught with uncertainty and indeterminacy. Among these considerations are:

1   the diversity and complexity of both the internal and external environments;
2   the natural limits to the cognitive capacities of managers (bounded rationality); and, consequently,

3 the subjective bias or selectivity that these necessarily introduce into the exercise.

First are the issues of *diversity* and *complexity*. Strategic management is concerned with the management of organizations in the context of their economic relationships with customers and other organizations (as competitors, strategic allies, suppliers or joint ventures, etc.). It should be borne in mind that the phenomena with which strategy is concerned have been subject to extraordinary reinvention and change. Indeed, this has been the result of organizational strategies: economic relationships between organizations have been, and continue to be, the subject of deliberate strategies to re-engineer them in the interests of the various enterprises involved. Consequently, the external environments which face organizations are likely to be diverse, complex and dynamic. That is, they are subject to change and uncertainty.

Second, in the face of this diversity and complexity, managers are constrained by the natural limits of their cognitive ability. *Bounded rationality* as mentioned in Chapter 8 was the term coined by Herbert Simon (1976: 135; see also Simon 1979) to describe this natural condition of all decision makers. Taken together, the diversity and complexity of the environment, and the bounded rationality of decision makers imply that, except in very simple situations, managers are often unable to deal comprehensively and objectively with their external environments. Rather, they must deal *selectively* and *subjectively* with the external environment, paying attention only to those aspects of the environment which they judge to be crucial to the task of formulating strategy. This selectivity, inevitably, introduces a degree of subjective bias into the tasks of strategic analysis and strategy formulation. For not only must managers pay selective attention to aspects of their environment, different managers within the enterprise may pay selective attention to different aspects. Consider, for example, the problem of the specialist–generalist dimension or professional demarcations in organizations. Human resource specialists, marketing managers, and finance directors each pay attention to quite different aspects of the enterprise. Even where their interests do intersect they are likely to have quite different emphases and interpretations of the circumstances. Consequently, the specialist managers may reach quite varying conclusions about the situation at hand, the nature of the problem and the appropriate strategy to deal with the circumstances. This can be compounded if organizations have specialist professional groups such as those found in hospitals and universities (see Chapter 3).

These issues have significant implications for the application of the Extended Design School in practice. With subjectivity and selectivity, the possibility of a lack of consensus regarding the salience for strategy of various aspects of the environment, their implications and appropriate solutions, compounded by the possibilities of plural interests and the lack of a unifying common purpose, the purported rationality of the Extended Design School model (which was one of its primary intuitive appeals) starts to look shaky indeed.

Competitive strategy

As we have seen above, the Design School model provided the bare bones of an approach to strategy with SWOT analysis, the explicit attempt to search out those opportunities in the enterprise's environment for which the enterprise is better qualified by its capabilities (or strengths) to exploit than are its actual or potential rivals. Note how the analysis of the external environment, and the notion of rivalry or competition, is essential to this definition of strategy. Unfortunately, however, the Design School did not provide any more detailed framework for the analysis of the competitive environment. Michael Porter (1980) redressed this deficiency in his classic book *Competitive Strategy: Techniques for Analyzing Industries and Competitors*. His unique contribution was to translate, adapt and apply the theory and deductive logic of industrial economics, and its associated discourse, to problems of competitive strategy. Porter's contribution was to show how the ideas generated by industrial economists could be used to address the concerns of managers: how the structure of industries influence the competitive strategies of business enterprises (and vice versa) with a view to evaluating the impact of these structures and strategies, not on the welfare of society as a whole, but on the profitability of enterprises.

'Industry' as used here refers broadly to the system of production. Thus in describing an industry we can include the acquisition of raw materials and technology, the production of intermediate (component) and finished goods and services, their packaging, and wholesale and retail distribution systems. In this chain of production, from raw materials to final consumption, a very large number (and potentially thousands) of enterprises could be involved. But it is also possible for the entire system of industrial production to be managed within a single vertically integrated enterprise that controls all of the processes just mentioned. The term 'market' can be taken to refer to systems of competition and exchange: the points at which intermediate or finished goods are exchanged for money in the form of cash or credit.

The five forces

Central to Porter's approach to analyzing the strategic position of an enterprise within the context of its industry is the premise that an enterprise's profitability is determined by the bargaining power it enjoys in negotiating prices or the terms of exchange with its suppliers and its customers. Porter suggests that an enterprise in a strong bargaining position can negotiate low prices from its suppliers thus reducing the enterprise's costs. An enterprise in a strong bargaining position with respect to its customers can negotiate higher prices, higher revenues and consequently higher profits. Porter's contribution to strategic planning was to translate the theory of industry economics in such a way as to explain how elements of the economic structure of markets determine the bargaining power of enterprises. He also went on to explain how the strategies of enterprises could change the economic structure of markets with critical consequences for the prospective profitability of the enterprise. The determinants of the enterprise's profitability are summarized in Porter's *Five Forces Model* described in Figure 10.4. Key elements of the model are discussed below.

At the centre of Porter's model is his notion of *rivalry* – his synonym for competition – and it is indeed central to his analysis. As we have already seen, Porter's conception of the industry context is of the enterprise located at the intersection of several vertically related markets. Porter argues that in each of these markets the enterprise competes with other enterprises – whether for customers in downstream markets or for supplies (e.g. of labour, capital, fuel, finance) in upstream markets. In each of these markets, fundamental structural elements of competition will determine the bargaining power that the enterprise is able to enjoy. Whether one is analyzing upstream or downstream markets, the analytical principles are the same. It is from such circumstances that Porter derives three generic strategies:

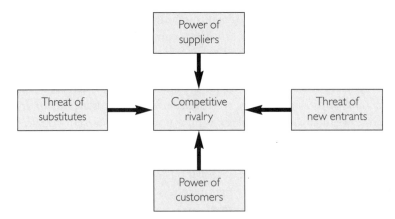

Figure 10.4 Elements of industry structure: Porter's Five Forces Model

Source: Adapted from Michael Porter (1980), Competitive Strategy, New York, The Free Press, p. 4.

1 *Cost leadership* If the enterprise is forced by competition to accept the market price, the only route to above-average profitability is to control cost.
2 *Differentiation* The provision of a range of differentiated products to meet the diverse needs of the market (and which are therefore not perfectly substitutable) provides an opportunity for the firm to rely less on competition on the basis of prices.
3 *Focus* A subset of differentiation whereby the enterprise focuses on supplying the needs of a particular market segment rather than producing a range of differentiated products and services for the various needs of different market segments.

The competitive conditions of each of the markets with which the enterprise engages in its industry (whether they be downstream markets in which they are a seller or upstream markets in which they are a buyer) are considered by Porter to determine the bargaining power of the enterprise with respect to prices and the terms of exchange. Porter believes that the competitive conditions in this constellation of markets determine the profitability and potential profitability of the enterprise. The inescapable conclusion for Porter is that those market structures which afford greater power to the enterprise to negotiate the terms of exchange, such as a monopoly of downstream markets and monopsony in upstream markets, will ensure the greatest profits.

Significantly, however, Porter emphasizes that the enterprise is not necessarily powerless in the face of given competitive conditions. Enterprises can and do adopt strategies which can change the competitive structures of the markets in which they are active. There are, according to Porter, two important constraints on the ability of enterprises to exploit relatively uncompetitive market situations, the *threat of entry* and *threat of substitution* (see Figure 10.4). In markets with high levels of concentration (that is, few competing firms), the behaviour of enterprises may nevertheless be constrained by the threat of new entrants. In contestable markets (those which do not have high barriers to entry) Porter believes cooperative strategies leading to higher prices and higher levels of profitability will only attract new entrants into the market. As a result, incumbent firms might adopt a strategy of 'limit pricing' where short-term profits are forgone in order to limit the attractiveness of the market to potential new competitors. High barriers of entry, on the other hand, shield incumbent firms from potential new entrants, thus increasing their power over prices.

The threat of substitution also impacts on the power of enterprises to determine the terms of exchange. Porter says a distinction needs to be made between rivalry and substitution, although the distinction is a matter of degree rather than essence. The term rivalry is normally used to describe competition between enterprises which are providing very similar, if not identical, goods and services in the market place. Thus the airlines British Airways and Virgin Atlantic are rivals on the north Atlantic air routes. Substitution, however, refers to products which are not in direct competition. Thus trans-Atlantic cruise ships may not be rivals for British Airways, Virgin Atlantic and other trans-Atlantic airlines, but for some customers they may be a substitute. The significance of substitution is that it qualifies the bargaining power of customers. Porter says the bargaining power of selling firms to set the terms of exchange, and in particular prices, will be limited by the extent to which customers have the power and the propensity to shift their purchasing decision to a substitute product.

To digress for a moment from Porter's work, parallel approach to strategy can be found in the works of Raymond Miles and Charles Snow (1978) and Snow and Donald Hambrick (1980), who identify four strategic postures for achieving competitive advantage. Their 'prospectors' are firms which pursue aggressive market tactics, while 'defenders' follow defensive tactics to protect their market share and limited resources. 'Analyzers' are essentially conservative, basing their strategic thrust on careful product/market analysis. Finally, 'reactors' are those firms which are obliged to pursue overtly competitive actions to recover lost competitive advantage and offset poor financial status.

Michael Goold and Andrew Campbell (1987) took a similar approach in trying to position strategic styles as the product of tensions between interacting forces. They identified five key tensions in operation:

1 *Multiple perspectives versus clear responsibility* Clearly defined jobs tend to produce efficiency, but restrict employees to those jobs and limit their discretion. This produces narrow thinking and inflexibility in the face of change, but if the organization moves towards multiple perspectives, loss of efficiency and even a loss of direction can ensue.
2 *Detailed planning reviews versus entrepreneurial decision making* Similarly, detailed planning and regular reviews produce greater efficiency and control, but narrow the focus of people and reduce their motivation, risking the loss of new opportunities.
3 *Strong leadership versus business autonomy* Strong control brings synergies, but local autonomy brings flexibility in the face of unexpected change.
4 *Long-term objectives versus short-term objectives* Short-term profitability is high when a company does not invest in facilities and research and development, but such a failure to invest reduces long-term profitability.
5 *Flexible strategies versus tight controls* In order to monitor performance, it is necessary to set out exactly what people have to do and attach targets to it. However, this removes autonomy and flexibility which may be necessary to deal with rapid change.

Goold and Campbell (1987) address these tensions by matching certain internal organizational factors – the nature of the business portfolio, the extent to which businesses overlap, the skills and personalities of key people in the business – with external factors such as the degree of uncertainty in the environment and the intensity of competition. Three dominant styles then emerge:

1   *The financial control style* Where organizations operate in highly stable market segments, a flat, decentralized structure can be adopted, focusing on short-term objectives – financial returns – and using quantitative systems for tight control. Any unforeseen change, strategic or long term, is dealt with by managers closest to the action, as long as targets are maintained, or by the acquisition strategy of senior management.

2   *The strategic planning style* Here complex, centralized structures are employed with top-down long-term planning. Emphasis is on long-term objectives and short-term failures may be tolerated. The objectives here are to gain overall balance in the portfolio and to have interconnections and synergies that will produce long-term competitive advantage, but all of this may take time. This approach is appropriate where there are turbulence and competition in the market, with rapidly changing customer requirements; or where businesses are interconnected with shared processes and technology or shared customers.

3   *The strategic control style* Here a balance between short- and long-term objectives is required, so short-term profit may be sacrificed, but only if there is a clear view of it leading to long-term profitability. Structures are usually simple, flat and decentralized, but some linking mechanisms may be in operation. Management is facilitative and negotiating, with planning being bottom up rather than top down. This style sacrifices some flexibility compared with the financial control style, but gains some synergies; however, though its synergies are not as great as the strategic planning style, it can respond more rapidly to change. It is suitable where change occurs rapidly but in markets which themselves are relatively well defined, and not subject to paradigm shifts (Goold and Quinn 1990; see also discussion in Stacey 1996: 188–9).

The value chain

Having captured the attention of both strategic management academics as well as practitioners with the publication of *Competitive Strategy* in 1980, Porter made a second major contribution in 1985 with the publication of *Competitive Advantage: Creating and Sustaining Superior Performance*. As we have seen, in his earlier work Porter focused on the strategic analysis of the external competitive conditions which firms faced in their industry. With *Competitive Advantage* his focus shifted to address the internal dimensions of strategy. At the centre of his analysis was the concept of the *value chain,* a description of the internal processes of production and/or service delivery within an enterprise. However, to realize the strategic importance of analyzing the internal value chain of the enterprise (i.e. as a technique for analyzing sources of competitive advantage) Porter argued that it was necessary to consider the broader *industry value chain* of which the enterprise forms a part.

In the earlier discussion of Porter's analysis of markets and industries, the industry was described as a system of production in which raw materials or resources are transformed into intermediate components and subsequently into final goods and services which are distributed for purchase and consumption by final consumers. This notion of an industry as a chain of production was described as the 'industry value chain'. By conceptualizing or describing this chain of production as a 'value chain', however, Porter draws attention to the way in which the successive processes involved in transforming raw materials into finished goods and services for final consumption can be represented as value-adding activities. The value to final customers of a finished good or service, a new car, for example, will be greater than the arithmetic sum of the costs of its raw material components. Porter argues that the ability of an enterprise to generate profits depends on its ability to realize added value in the form of revenues it is able to realize in its downstream markets in excess of the costs of production (Porter 1985: 38).

Porter's market-based approach to industrial organization presents an archetypal picture or symbol of an industry as a chain of successive value-adding processes coordinated through a set of vertically related markets – a rational, linear process. But how well does this archetype describe contemporary industry? If the market were the most efficient form of industrial coordination we would expect all industrial production to be coordinated in this form. Yet many successive processes of production are coordinated within enterprises by management, rather than between enterprises, by markets. Pre-eminent examples are the integrated steel mills of BHP at Port Kembla and Newcastle in Australia where successive stages in the production of steel products – the mining of iron ore and coal; the production of coking coal; transportation by rail and ship to the steel mills; the production of electricity for the plant; the smelting of iron; the production of steel and stainless steel; its rolling into plate and wire and a multitude of other forms; the production of finished products such as specially coated roofing materials and their transportation and distribution – are all coordinated internally within the corporation.

For this Australian example there are historical and political explanations (Blackmur 1997). But a general theoretical explanation for the emergence of organizational forms of coordination was provided by Ronald Coase (1937) who argued that markets are not necessarily the most efficient form of industrial coordination. In particular, he argued that market transactions are not costless. *Transaction costs* include the time and expense of market search and the negotiating, writing and enforcing of contracts as well as the risks of default and opportunistic behaviour on the part of suppliers (Oster 1994; Besanko, Danove and Shanley 1996: 93). Thus successive stages of industrial production may be coordinated within vertically integrated enterprises in circumstances where it is a more cost efficient form of coordination than the mediation of market-based transactions (see Chapter 11).

Porter's generic value chain of the enterprise is represented graphically in Figure 10.5. The figure describes the enterprise as a chain of production represented by the primary activities of inbound logistics, operations, outbound logistics, marketing and sales and service. Each of these primary activities is described in more detail in Exhibit 10.1. Also incorporated in Porter's generic value chain are a set of support activities: the infrastructure of the firm, the human resource management function, technology development and procurement. This representation is of course extremely general. For any particular enterprise a much more detailed and specific representation of the processes of production can be produced.

The purpose of this categorization is to draw attention to the specific activities of the enterprise so that they can be investigated for their actual or potential contribution to the competitive advantage of the enterprise as a whole. Porter's analysis of competitive advantage is referenced to the broader framework which he had already supplied in *Competitive Strategy*. That is, the sources of competitive advantage which are uncovered in an analysis of the enterprise's internal microsystem of production and value-adding are referenced to the generic strategies of cost leadership and differentiation. Notably, Porter believes, it is not sufficient that the enterprise's activities contribute added value (the difference between the

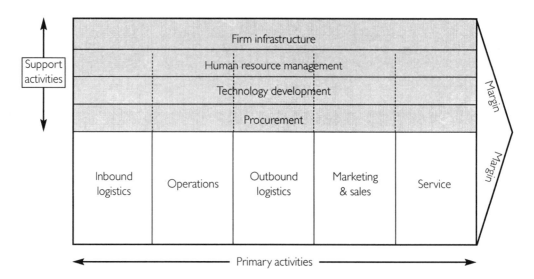

Figure 10.5 The generic (intra-firm) value chain

Source: Michael Porter (1985), Competitive Advantage: Creating and Sustaining Superior Performance, New York: The Free Press, p. 37.

costs of production and the revenues realized by sales in the market place). This may be achieved without achieving either a competitive advantage or superior performance. Rather, Porter says the route to superior performance requires the identification of actual or potential capabilities that constitute sources of advantage over the competition – the ability to produce comparable products more efficiently (cost leadership) or to produce products that better serve the needs of target customers (differentiation). Thus for Porter the strategic analysis of the enterprise's sources of competitive advantage demands external reference to both the enterprise's customers and to the enterprise's competitors.

- **Inbound logistics**   Activities associated with receiving, storing, and disseminating inputs to the product, such as materials handling, warehousing, inventory control, vehicle scheduling, and returns to suppliers.
- **Operations**   Activities associated with transforming inputs into the final product form, such as machining, packaging, assembly, equipment maintenance, testing, printing and facility operations.
- **Outbound logistics**   Activities associated with collecting, storing, and physically distributing the product to buyers, such as finished goods warehousing, material handling, delivery vehicle operation, order processing and scheduling.
- **Marketing and sales**   Activities associated with providing a means by which buyers can purchase the product and inducing them to do so, such as advertising, promotion, sales force, quoting, channel selection, channel relations and pricing.
- **Service**   Activities associated with providing services to enhance or maintain the value of the product, such as installation, repair, training, parts supply, and product adjustment.

Exhibit 10.1 Primary activities in Porter's generic value chain

Source: Excerpted from Michael Porter (1985), Competitive Advantage: Creating and Sustaining Superior Performance, New York: The Free Press, pp. 39–40.

The analysis of the enterprise value chain also raises issues regarding the set of activities of which it is composed, strategic decisions regarding the addition of new value-adding activities or the retirement of existing activities which no longer contribute to the enterprise's competitive advantage.

More recently, many large enterprises have reconsidered the relative economies of managerial and market forms of coordination. Whereas market forms of coordination may be associated with search and transaction costs and the risks of default in supply contracts or of access to essential supplies, management forms of coordination are not costless either. Indeed in industries characterized by rapid technological change or changes in market needs and expectations, investments in vertically integrated systems of production may leave the enterprise with a reduced ability to respond flexibly and efficiently. In recent years, many formerly highly vertically integrated enterprises have moved towards outsourcing those aspects of the production system which can be obtained at less cost or in higher quality from external suppliers than the enterprise is capable of producing itself. In strategic terms, such enterprises are focusing their energies on their core competencies: those activities in which they are able to maintain a distinctive competitive advantage against their competitors. But concomitant with outsourcing and concentration on core competencies comes the need to develop clear capabilities in negotiating and managing contractual relationships with suppliers. Of historical significance in this respect has been the influence of forms of industrial production that have emerged in Japan (see Chapter 11).

The resource-based view

As we have seen, in *Competitive Advantage* Porter shifted his focus from the external dimensions of enterprise strategy (the structural characteristics of the industry in which the enterprise competes) to the internal determinants of competitive advantage. Informed by the intellectual traditions of industrial and organizational economics, the two books share a common analytical perspective, and are therefore highly complementary. At about the same time as *Competitive Advantage* was published, however, other contributions began to emerge in the strategy literature which also redirected attention to the internal determinants of competitive advantage. With Birger Wernerfelt's (1984) article 'A resource-based view of the firm' the seeds were sown for what has since become one of the most active research agendas in the field, and one which, in the opinion of a number of commentators and contributors, shows promise of redefining the field (Mahoney and Pandian 1992; Foss 1997; Schendel 1994; Barney and Zajac 1994). Reflecting the influence of Wernerfelt's seminal article, this research agenda has adopted the collective term the 'resource-based view' or the 'resource-based perspective'.

In contrast to Porter's view that the profitability of enterprises is determined by the external industry-structural conditions within which they operate (i.e. the intensity of rivalry, the bargaining power of customers and suppliers, entry and substitution conditions), the resource-based view draws attention to the internal determinants of competitive advantage. The difference may be explained by use of an analogy. Consider an athlete competing in a middle-distance foot race. The athlete's success may be due in part to the strategies adopted on the day of the race – whether he or she chooses to lead from the start or stay with the pack and make a bid for the lead later in the race. However, the athlete's success or failure is more likely to be determined, not by the strategies adopted on the day of the race, but on the level of fitness the athlete has acquired through training (Forster and Browne 1996: 124). Similarly, an enterprise's performance (profitability) is likely to be determined not only by the external industry-structural conditions, but by internal capabilities which may be sources of competitive advantage.

The emerging resource-based view found its expression, as have most ideas in strategic management, in two different forums. The research agenda that it spawned has (like most research programmes) had a long and slow development and much research remains to be done. The hunger of practising managers for potential solutions to immediate strategic problems, however, has meant that the development of practical prescriptions has not waited on painstaking research; the ideas of 'core competencies', 'capabilities and sustainable competitive advantage' have quickly become part of the language of corporate management. C.K. Prahalad and Gary Hamel's (1990) article in the *Harvard Business Review*, 'The core competence of the corporation', was probably the vehicle for the popularization of the resource-based perspective.

The research program, as has been noted, has taken a more painstaking route. From its beginnings, the resource-based view has been bedevilled by problems of terminology. In 1980, R. T. Lenz complained that the terms used in investigating these issues were vague and ambiguous, and that there was great inconsistency in the frames of reference within which the terms were used. Eight years later, complaints about the 'welter of overlapping meanings of competitive advantage' (Day and Wensley 1988: 2) were still being voiced. And as recently as 1997, both Wernerfelt (1997: xvii) and Nicolai Foss (1997: 8) were still pointing to problems of terminology. Nevertheless, as Wernerfelt goes on to explain, 'the resource-based view is a puzzle under construction' and that in spite of differences in terminology a large degree of consensus has emerged that '(1) resources and fixed inputs and (2) sustainable competitive advantages are conferred by resources which are hard to imitate and scarce relative to their economic value' (Wernerfelt 1997: xvii).

The research agenda has focused in part on the issues raised by the resource-based view's challenge to Porter's industry-structural explanation of the enterprise's profitability. The problem raised by Porter's account is that if a firm's profitability or performance are determined solely by the structure and competitive dynamics of the industry within which it operates, then differences in enterprise performance should only be observed between enterprises operating in different industries and there should be no or little difference between firms within any one industry context. The prescriptive implication of Porter's framework is that the primary strategic question is the choice of industry(ies) in which the enterprise engages. The further implication is that once engaged in an industry, the enterprise's strategic choices are largely determined by the industry context (Schendel 1994: 1–2).

There have been a number of attempts to test the propositions of the resource-based view by measuring empirically the relative importance of external, industry-specific factors and internal, enterprise-specific factors for the performance (profitability) of the enterprise. These attempts, qualified of course by the problems of definition, conceptualization and operationalization of the research terms, the accessibility and reliability of data, and the specification of representative populations, have had mixed results. In one of the first empirical studies, Richard Schmalensee (1985) found that industry factors were strong compared to corporate and market share effects in explaining enterprise profitability. In contrast, a subsequent study reported by Gary Hansen and Wernerfelt concluded that:

…if our findings of the relative importance can be generalised, it would suggest that the critical issue in firm success and development is not primarily the selection of growth industries or product niches, but it is the building of an effective, directed, human organisation in the selected industries (Hansen and Wernerfelt 1989: 409).

Hansen and Wernerfelt's findings were supported by a later study in which Richard Rumelt (1991) found small stable industry effects and very large effects at the business unit level. These results implied, according to Rumelt, that the most important determinants of profitability were business-unit specific rather than industry specific (1991: 167).

For the purposes of providing early advice to practising managers, based on the emerging debate in the resource-based perspective, the inherent research problems have been put aside in an attempt to distil the perspective's essential implications. These are:

- that enterprise performance is not determined solely by the enterprise's external competitive strategy in the context of given industry-structural conditions;
- that differential performance between competing enterprises in the same industry may be explained by differential access to resources;
- that these resources may be financial, physical, human, organizational, and technological (Lenz 1980: 225; Grant 1991: 160);
- that the qualities of these resources are complex and diverse – they may be internally generated or externally acquired; they may be durable or consumed in production; they may tangible or intangible, they may transcend the borders of the enterprise to relationships with other enterprises through alliances or to customers in terms of reputation and loyalty (Forster and Browne 1996: 127);
- that groups of resources work together to create *capabilities* (Grant 1991: 158) and that such capabilities might also be represented as the core competence of the enterprise defined by Prahalad and Hamel as: 'the collective learning in the organization, especially how to coordinate diverse production skills and integrate multiple streams of technologies' (1990: 82);
- that for the enterprise's capabilities to constitute sources of *competitive advantage,* they must be considered in the context of: (i) the needs of customers, (ii) the capabilities of direct and indirect competitors, and (iii) the enterprise's vertical relationships within the industry value-chain (Forster and Browne 1996: 132);
- that to constitute sources of *sustainable* competitive advantage, the enterprise's resources and capabilities must satisfy the conditions that they are (i) scarce and therefore unavailable to competitors, (ii) unable to be imitated, (iii) unable to be substituted and (iv) imperfectly mobile, that is, relatively specific to the firm (see Foss 1997: 10).

Such is the potential of the resource-based view for integrating several themes in the strategy literature, which have hitherto been treated largely independently, that it can be read from a range of different points of view. One such view is that the emerging emphasis on core competencies arose from the reaction to the failure of strategies for growth based on acquisitions and diversification which were characteristic of the 1960s and 1970s (Sterne 1992). Many corporations had diversified to the point where their management capabilities were unequal to the tasks of coordination. Out of the experience of some notable failures arising from this strategy came a new maxim of 'sticking to the knitting' implying a more conservative approach to growth (Sterne 1992: 15).

A different reading of the importance of the resource-based view is provided by Dan Schendel who points out that for convenience much of the strategy literature had adopted arbitrary distinctions, such as those between the external and internal focii, between formulation and implementation, and between content and process. Ultimately, however, all of these facets of strategy are interdependent, he argues, and the resource-based view shows a potential for the integration of these various dimensions to strategic management (Schendel 1994: 1). Schendel also provides another suggestion, that the emergence of the resource-based view can be read as a reaction to the enormous success of Porter's *Competitive Strategy* and represents an attempt to redress the balance between the internal and external dimensions of strategy.

Reconfiguration approaches

The Positioning School is silent on the issue of implementing strategies. The Extended Design School model by contrast made the tacit assumption that senior managers, who have primary responsibility for the formulation of strategy, automatically enjoy the authority to command its implementation. The model, therefore, takes for granted a unitarist view of organizations, one which recognizes managerial authority as the only source of legitimate power to command the activities of the enterprise.

An alternative view, however, is that in practice managerial authority is not the only source of power in organizations, and indeed that both official and unofficial sources of power and influence are distributed throughout organizations (see Chapter 4). In these circumstances, it cannot be assumed that strategies formulated by senior managers will be implemented automatically and unchanged by organizational stakeholders and those responsible for their implementation. The relationship between formulation and implementation of strategies is not as unproblematic as the Extended Design School model might lead one to suppose.

In fact, the Extended Design School's work was supplemented in the 1980s with additions to the approach that focused on the implementation of strategy. Increasingly it became apparent that strategy had to include more devolved and participatory methods to ensure that all levels of the organization could contribute to the strategy process, identify with the plan or have a sense of ownership of it, and be committed to its implementation. This attention became focused on the constraints and opportunities impacting upon or affecting the implementation of strategy, that is, on the sorts of things that were likely to frustrate or impede the organization's capacity to carry out its strategies. Strategic change was recognized as involving the threat or real loss of power, influence and control over traditional resources and often placed new restrictions on people's ability to act independently. Resistance became identified as an inevitable consequence of implementing new plans. The organization's stakeholders were considered most likely to evaluate the costs and benefits of any proposed strategy with respect to their underlying assumptions, interests and values. In other words, the strategy had to be made to 'fit' the contours of these interests, as well as the resource and structural considerations of the organization vis à vis its competitive position. This contingency approach to strategy emphasized the importance of achieving *fit* between the company's structure, culture, strategy and environment. The better the fit, the smoother the implementation of any strategy, or so the argument went.

Stakeholders

Some theorists believe strategy, and its implementation, has less to do with rational behaviour and more to do with political negotiation and bargaining as discussed in Chapter 8. This was evident in the work of Charles Lindblom (1959) on *incrementalism* in decision making. Lindblom's ideas, derived from the public policy context, have nevertheless resonated with several writers in the field of private sector strategy formulation. For example, the conclusion that the processes of decision making in the organizational context are likely to be characterized by political rather than comprehensively rational processes is shared by a number of theorists (e.g. Brunnson 1982: 30; Narayanan and Fahey 1982; Jemison 1981: 604; Piercy 1989: 27). But Lindblom's ideas have been taken up most forcibly by James Brian Quinn (1980) who argued that 'logical incrementalism' is a more apt description for strategic decision making.

Logical incrementalism is a process for making decisions in the context of an uncertain environment. Arguably, most strategic decisions are indeed incremental as are their implementations. Take, for example, the marketing strategies an enterprise might employ. On relatively rare occasions – such as the launching of a new product – marketing strategy formulation may take the form of a marketing plan specified in detail prior to implementation. But this does not describe the vast majority of marketing decisions. Most decisions in marketing strategy are taken in the context where a strategy is already in place and a product is already active in the market. The decisions taken under these circumstances will be incremental – small piecemeal changes to the strategy already in place: a discount on prices, some further advertising, the negotiation of an extension to a distribution contract. These changes are taken in response to new opportunities. In the process the enterprise learns a great deal: how consumers respond to the enterprise's initiatives; the reaction of competitors; the reliability of the distribution system; the flexibility of the enterprise's own production team. Thus strategies do not derive from a rational planning process fully specified and ready for implementation. Rather strategies emerge incrementally over time and incrementalism is not 'muddling through' but '...is a purposeful, effective, proactive management technique for improving and integrating both the analytical and behavioural aspects of strategy formulation' (Quinn 1978: 8).

In reality the rational-consensus model of strategy implementation is distorted by conflicting goals, bargaining and negotiation of interests, leading to the creation of dominant/dependent coalitions within an organization's various domains of operation. In Quinn's terms, the whole strategy implementation process becomes fragmented and evolutionary, that is, it follows a path of 'logical incrementalism' (Quinn 1978). Decisions are taken incrementally and opportunistically as a result of communicating assumptions, integrating corporate and divisional plans and resolving political differences.

Each aspect of a strategy's implementation that involves the acquisition, reorganization and redistribution of scarce resources is contested by individual stakeholders when their expectations are threatened. The resolution of negotiations between stakeholders with differential bases of power produces a temporarily structured order within the company, so that, according to Anselm Strauss, strategic outcomes are the result of a process of 'negotiated order' (Strauss 1978), not the product of a rational-analytic planning process.

Organizational environments can be structured by the actions of key players operating in those arenas which provide them with the greatest strategic advantage (see Chapter 4). Strategic planners and managers will hold multiple roles within their organization, thereby enabling them to select the most propitious arenas in order to promote and pursue their agendas for strategic implementation. In this way strategy is continuously moulded and fashioned by the actions of key players. Strategy formulation is a political process involving various groups and individuals pursuing their interests using power and influence and various tactics to devise actions which can at times go against other major corporate players (Byrt 1973: 2). We have critiqued this view of action in Chapter 8.

The problem of strategic 'drift'

Not all commentators on strategy believe that it is possible to change an organization incrementally or otherwise, except in very specific circumstances, because human beings do not naturally work in that way. Mindsets, or cultures, only change slowly and often under extreme pressure, to the extent that some researchers question whether it is realistic to talk about changing the culture to facilitate a strategic change. Gerry Johnson (1992) argues, as does Peter Anthony (1994), that in the context of the organization or company it is the change of behaviour which matters most, and really the idea that managers can engineer change in belief systems is rather fanciful. Johnson suggests that the organization is embedded in a *cultural web* of stories and myths, rituals and routines, symbols, power structures, control systems, organizational structures, and all of these shape the *paradigm*. A paradigm is basically a formula for what the organization is and what it does and what the people in the organization think are the recipes for its success or otherwise. Figure 10.6 describes the key elements of such a cultural web. The paradigm is at the heart of the web, and is sustained by its other elements.

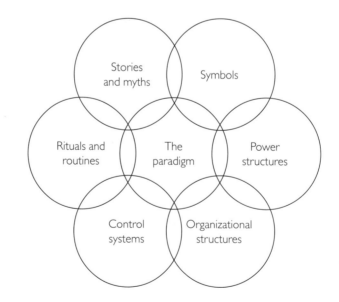

Figure 10.6   The 'cultural web' of an organization

Source: Gerry Johnson (1992), 'Managing strategic change – strategy, culture and action', Long Range Planning *25(1) p. 34.*

This paradigm can make the organization insensitive to change and produce the situation of *strategic drift* as described in Figure 10.7. Johnson gives several examples of this from manufacturing and service industries. The effect of strategic drift is that the organization (or its management) gets further and further out of step with its environment, while believing that it is doing everything possible to keep up. Incremental change is attenuated by the biased perception the organization has of its environment, and the modifications it makes are too little because of its cultural filter. When crisis approaches, the organization abandons its incremental progression and tries out a number of responses, but again none of them are radical enough by now and the organization is so confused that it often goes backwards and undoes some of the progress it has made. Eventually, radical change is necessary to enable the organization to survive, as in many of the corporate 'turnaround' stories of the 1980s. Johnson offers some advice on how to avoid strategic drift, which includes creating an open and communicative culture where challenge of the status quo is encouraged, frequent use of external consultants and outsider input to challenge established mindsets, and the constant deployment of symbols of change rather than tradition.

Mintzberg (1987: 71–3) also contended that many organizations are incapable of major shifts in strategic orientation. He maintained that organizations adopt different forms of strategic behaviour at different times. Strategic change often involves perfecting a given approach (e.g. retailing) and doing more of the same, but perhaps in a better way, for example pursuing continuous improvement in the firm's distinctive competencies. However, he noted that in pursuing this incremental approach, the environment of the business can change, even to the point of putting the organization's strategic orientation way

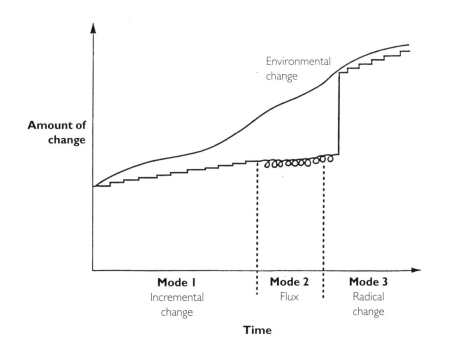

Figure 10.7   Strategic drift

Source: Gerry Johnson (1992), 'Managing strategic change – strategy, culture and action', Long Range Planning 25(1), p. 34.

out of synchronization with its environment. Mintzberg believed that a strategic revolution needs to take place to realign the organization and re-establish a 'fit' with its environment. In Johnson's terms, the paradigm has to be challenged and changed.

Mintzberg was optimistic about the potential for a radical turnaround of organizations in such turmoil. Organizations, he said, always have both deliberately planned and emergent strategies coexisting. He believed that many large-scale mass production organizations can be typified by incrementalism, but noted that some organizations are designed and operate to institutionalize change and encourage both emergent and deliberate strategies. For Mintzberg, managing incremental change is the predominant and normal strategic role for most managers, and those who are concerned with 'crafting strategy'.

Crafting strategy

Mintzberg drew a distinction between planning strategy and crafting strategy. He said:

> Imagine someone planning strategy. What most likely springs to mind is an image of orderly thinking: a senior manager or a group of them, sitting in an office formulating courses of action that everyone else will implement on schedule. The keynote is reason – rational control, the systematic analysis of competitors and markets, of company strengths and weaknesses, the combination of these analyses producing clear, explicit, full-blown strategies (Mintzberg 1987: 58).

Mintzberg has criticized the view that strategy making somehow reflects senior management's intentions alone. This view, espoused by many managers, creates an image of tidiness and purpose and conceals complexity and confusion – the many meetings, debates, dead ends and diverse ideas – that drive the organization forward (Mintzberg 1987: 67–8). He preferred instead to describe planning as crafting strategy and deliberately used the crafting metaphor to distance his concept of planning from the mechanistic or mechanical models of formal planning – to infuse it with the ideas of creativity, uncertainty, feeling involved and the fusion of design and implementation (1987: 66). Crafting strategy is more like a fluid learning process in which formulation and implementation merge to produce effective and creative strategies (Mintzberg 1987: 66). Not only did Mintzberg advocate that senior managers abandon top-down planning in favour of a more negotiated or interactive style, but he also argued that the concept of strategy had to incorporate emergent and more dynamic ways in which planning actually happens.

Crafting strategy involves managing the differences between *emergent* and *deliberate* (or intentional) *strategy* making. Mintzberg proposed that senior managers could develop an 'umbrella strategy' within their organizations, which would involve them only in setting broad guidelines or goals (e.g. to produce only high-margin products at the cutting edge of technology), leaving the specifics (e.g. the choice of products) to others in the organization. An umbrella strategy would allow scope for substrategy development within departments, units or divisions, that is, a portfolio of plans coordinated at the centre (Mintzberg 1987: 70–1). Mintzberg believed that the implementers of plans (the 'grass roots' people) had to become the formulators of plans as well or have a more significant role in devising strategies. He argued that senior managers should focus on strategy formation, rather than formulation, and involve the 'grass roots' of the organization, particularly middle managers (Mintzberg 1987: 70–1).

Crafting Strategy was considered especially important in adhocracies or in post-entrepreneurial organizations, which have been characterized by quite complex cross-functional relationships between departments, teams, divisions and suppliers and more turbulent environments (see Kanter 1989: 89–90). The focus on learning and strategy has become an important element in more contemporary views of strategy, particularly strategic thinking. Mintzberg's singular message in the use of the crafting metaphor was to argue that 'grass roots' strategies emerge or take root whenever people have the capacity or opportunity to learn. This opportunity to learn depends on a strategic framework or context that is deliberate, but not so inflexible that it leaves no room for experimentation, innovation or creativity (Mintzberg 1987: 69–71).

Strategic thinking

According to Lenz, 'most strategic planning processes do not facilitate the self-reflective learning that is necessary for organizations to adapt to changing competitive conditions' because of the 'paralysis of analysis' (1987: 34–9). Following this path avoids strategic thinking because it is crowded out by the mechanics of strategic planning (Rowe, Mason and Dickel 1986: 36). Rational thinking alone tends to preclude the use of dialogue, argument and debate, so that entrepreneurial creativity in strategic planning is stifled, and the process becomes mechanistic. Lenz suggests several steps to ensure a self-reflective strategic planning process and these essentially are:

- Make the job of the strategic planner concerned with facilitating organizational learning.
- Keep the process as simple as possible.
- Avoid routinized behaviour and processes.
- Emphasize logical arguments; use numbers as back-up material.
- Simplify planning reviews; focus on action, not theatricals.
- Stimulate thinking and action.
- Do not allow analytic techniques to oversimplify the situation: use them instead to illuminate problems.
- Strategic planning is good; strategic thinking is better.
- Base evaluation on insights provided, not techniques used.
- Manage the evolution of the planning process so it becomes self-learning
  (Lenz 1987: 39).

A similar sentiment is expressed by Kenichi Ohmae (1983), who also criticized strategy formulation for being too rational or formal and obsessed with facts and figures. Ohmae believed very firmly in the virtues of analysis, but not the sort of analysis that merely produces rational or predictable responses to problems. In a sense, much of what Porter describes as competitive advantage rests on the market's predictability and logic operating in certain industries, while Ohmae argues that strategic thinking requires going beyond the obvious, beyond appearances, beyond proven logic, to search out the truly novel sources of competitive advantage. For Ohmae, strategic thinking means seeking a clear understanding of the elements of a problem or situation and of the important underlying relationships, then restructuring or reconfiguring these relationships in the most advantageous way (1983:

12–15). Ohmae suggests that rational analysis has to be combined with imaginative reintegration if strategic thinking is to produce a competitive edge.

For Ohmae, the most important part of strategic thinking is the ability to identify critical issues and solutions – to abandon preconceived ideas and preconceptions. Ohmae suggests a number of steps managers can follow to develop their strategic thinking capabilities, as well as devising an issues diagram to identify issues and solutions-oriented questions. The issues diagram is similar to a decision tree, a rational method of decision making used to list a number of alternative possibilities to an issue, with 'yes' and 'no' alternatives identified to guide possible actions. Ohmae drew on his engineering background to develop the issue diagram by using value engineering and value analysis to determine or identify critical issues managers need to ask about their competing products (1983: 23). The former refers to quality and reliability issues relating to a product, the latter to the cost and price of products. Analysis for Ohmae, and the focus on quality, was deeply rooted in his Japanese origins (see Chapter 7).

Ohmae suggests that strategic thinking, and the development of an issues diagram, require four main processes:

1 identifying all the key factors in a business that put it at a disadvantage relative to its competitors;
2 grouping the factors based on some common denominator or principle;
3 evaluating each underlying relationship within the categories identified to try to find the critical issues; and
4 asking solution-oriented questions for each critical issue, with the ultimate aim being to prioritize actions.

As mentioned above, Ohmae draws concepts from engineering to identify critical issues. Ohmae's approach is less formula driven or based on a specific model. It is far more dependent on managers developing or mastering strategic thinking, which in the end means having the superior 'battle plan' (Ohmae 1983: 37–8, 240–1).

Strategic thinking has been considerably refined in the area of *scenario planning*, which is not focused on detailed predictions about the current environment of an organization but rather on learning and gaining insights through challenging assumptions and thinking creatively about the future of an industry. Scenario planning embraces the key elements of emergent and intended strategy, as described by Mintzberg in his crafting strategy metaphor, but also builds on the notion of strategy as learning – looking at or to the future and breaking paradigms (as per Johnson). It also goes much further than previous approaches by using narratives and stories as a way of breaking new ground in strategic thinking and questioning assumptions. In fact scenarios are treated as myths about the future (Schwartz 1996: 39). Scenario planning comes close to what might be described as a postmodern concept of strategy.

Scenario planning did not originate in the USA, nor is it derived from the corporate experience of that country. Rather, its key proponent, Peter Schwartz, learnt about scenario planning after joining the Royal Dutch Shell Company and working with some of the architects of the method, such as Pierre Wack (1985a, b). Wack was responsible for Shell being emotionally prepared for the 'oil crisis' of 1973. Shell emerged from this crisis to become a market leader and the most profitable oil company among its competitors. Wack had presented a scenario to Shell's directors of an impending oil crisis that meant they had to rethink their business dramatically (Schwartz 1996: 7–9).

Scenarios, as developed by Schwartz and his team at Global Business Networks (see Ogilvy 1998), are most typically developed by a multidisciplinary team comprising members from cross-functional areas or drawing people external to the organization. The senior management of an organization usually defines the strategic issue for which scenario planning is to be used, but in doing so they will not be in control of the outcomes – they direct them. Figure 10.8 presents key elements of a scenario planning process as developed by Global Business Networks (Ogilvy 1998; Schwartz 1996). Each step will be examined below.

1 *Focal issue* The first step in the scenario planning process requires the team to think about the issue for which they must develop sets of scenario logics. The team is confronted with the challenge of exploring the future of a particular issue for which a strategic choice needs to be made, for example should we enter a new market, should we broaden our product range, etc. There has to be *sufficient uncertainty about the future*, in particular the external environment, for scenario planning to be considered.

2 *Key factors* This step helps to identify the critical uncertainties that relate to the focal issue. Key factors tend to be issues over which the organization has some or would hope to have some future influence. Key factors usually relate to the industry(ies) within which the organization operates. These factors could be both internal and external factors, the key point being that the organization's management must believe they can influence these factors, for example size of market, competition, customer base, suppliers, employees, partners.

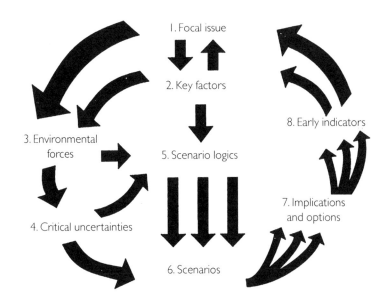

Figure 10.8   Developing scenarios

Source: Jay Ogilvy (1998) 'Learning scenario planning – an introduction to scenario thinking – a four day simulation course', 1–5 February, presented by Australian Business Network and Global Business Networks (Sydney).

Managing strategically

395

3   *Environmental Forces* This step relates to the previous one, whereby the team is looking to establish the critical uncertainties over which the organization has little or no influence. The team develops a list of key factors and environmental forces through a brainstorming process, for example social forces, technological changes, organizational competencies. These are not categorized as in a SWOT. This process is by no means highly structured nor does it result in an ordered set of factors.

In order to undertake steps 1, 2 and 3, additional research might be required. The team needs to have sufficient knowledge within the group to identify the issues exhaustively. As a result of steps 1, 2 and 3, the team might have a comprehensive list of the key factors and environmental forces that relate to the focal issue. There is a possibility that the focal issue might need to be reframed as a result of going through steps 1–3. For example, senior management might have seen the focal issue to be one of expanding the current business in expanded services offered by the organization. However, as a result of steps 1–3 the focal issue might change to examine the sustainability of core services rather than expansion. Alternatively, other focal issues might emerge after having gone through all eight steps.

4   *Critical uncertainties* In this step the team tries to identify what are both very critical and highly uncertain issues in relation to the focal issue. Issues need to be gradually eliminated so that the team arrives at the two most important and uncertain issues. This is best achieved by a stepped process of elimination (e.g. a voting system). In the process of elimination there is usually a strong element of distress in the team as issues, which were identified as important and/or uncertain, are eliminated by the voting process. This is referred to as 'the zone of terror'. The eliminated issues are in fact revisited in a later stage of the process. Issues have to be clustered in the elimination process and this in itself can cause distress. Scoring dictates the elimination of issues, whereby points or scores are allocated only on the most critical and uncertain issues.

In scenario planning a person called a 'lateral poppy' or 'remarkable person' (see Schwartz 1996) can be used to assist the team in breaking mental models or fixed frames of references (see Chapter 1). The remarkable person need not be a person who is an expert or familiar with the focal issue. These people challenge the assumptions made about the five or so clustered issues. The five issues are filtered down to the two most important and uncertain ones. The final choice of issues is a negotiated process.

The two issues selected are matrixed, one on a vertical axis and one on a horizontal axis. These are two bipolar axes that cannot be overly dependent on each other, for example you could not have the structure of the market on one axis and distribution channels on the other as these are dependent variables.

5   *Scenario Logics* At this stage the team now has a scenario matrix with four separate quadrants, each one representing what is best described as a version of the future. The purpose of this step is to create a meaning for each of the four quadrants. Each of the four quadrants requires that a theme or story be created around the four different quadrants, for example a healthy economy that is also outward looking is an environment for change and reinvention. Each quadrant should represent a theme and creative names are preferred to encourage frame breaking, but engaging themes that

are able to create new connections and new ways of seeing things are also encouraged. This stage is really where new understandings can begin to develop.

6 *Scenarios* This step involves developing the scenario logic into a story about the future. Any form of storyline would be helpful but some basic elements need to be captured in the story: it needs to be in line with the logic of the scenario, it needs to start today and move gradually to the end state (i.e. typically a 10 year time-line) and it should have a beginning, middle and end. As the team develops a story, it might be useful to discuss and capture what this scenario looks like two years from now (beginning), five years from now (middle) and 10 years from now (at the end). The purpose of this approach is to assist the audience (i.e. management group) who receive the scenarios and findings to be able to relate to the scenarios and be 'led' to the end state. Schwartz (1996: 136–55) actually describes the story as being somewhat akin to writing a movie script with plots that have storylines often around themes such as winners and losers, revolution, cycles or infinite possibilities. Stories should focus on the external environment of the organization, and should not describe the organization's strategies, activities or results. The story is outward looking and does not deal with how the organization would yet respond. This is explored under Step 7.

Once the four stories are developed for each scenario, it becomes important to identify which one of these scenarios the organization and its management believe best represents the organization's current environment and is supporting their current strategy. At this point in time this would be described as the organization's *official scenario*. The point of doing this is to provide some relevance or a frame of reference for managers to recognize where the current strategy fits among these various scenarios.

In making up the story for each scenario, the eliminated key issues are revisited and some are selectively woven into the text of the story. The story then might overcome some of the distress felt in 'the zone of terror' mentioned earlier.

7 *Implications and Options* After having constructed the four stories, the team then develops the implications for the industry and the organization of each scenario. Once the scenarios have been developed, then ideally implications of each scenario are further explored to develop strategic options for each scenario. So the team ends up with four sets of implications and strategic options. A number of different decision-making techniques can be used to order and prioritize options, for example identifying a robust scenario might mean eliminating 'no brainers' or those options within each scenario that are common to all four. Given the possible scenarios, senior management and/or the team can explore which options best suit the organization's future strategy orientation. Some of these are listed in Figure 10.9.

8 *Early indicators* The team has completed the scenario matrix and all the implications and options of each scenario. The purpose of this step is to identify early warning signs of change that support a particular scenario story. An example of this might be falling sales of McDonald's products in China as an early warning indicator of social dissatisfaction with Western capitalism or business methods.

Issues are likely to arise in the political environment of the organization when the team attempts to disseminate scenario outcomes. For a variety of reasons scenarios can be

**Given a set of alternative scenarios,
what are the possible strategic responses?**

Pick one
scenario and
bet the company

Hedge
across all
scenarios

Rank strategic
options by
risks and rewards

Modify
existing
strategy

?

Pursue
least regret
(Pascal's Wager)*

Reframe
the
industry

Become a
learning
organization

Identify
predetermined
elements

Look for
vulnerabilities
and bottlenecks

Figure 10.9   Strategic responses

(*Pascal's Wager refers to a seventeenth century French mathematician who developed a four-quadrant
matrix that identified the options available to a person trying to identify a limited number of choices)

*Source: Jay Ogilvy (1998), 'Learning scenario planning – an introduction to scenario thinking – a four day simulation course', 1–5
February, presented by Australian Business Network and Global Business Networks (Sydney).*

unacceptable to senior management; for example the results might not support the current strategy, and senior management are usually the dominant coalition in the organization and the defenders of the status quo. Scenarios have to be worked through the power structures at the top end of the organization to have any potential impact or acceptance. Unacceptable scenarios can even result in the dismissal or the disciplining of those who present unacceptable or unpopular scenarios. The team and its members can often be viewed as having a dissenting voice from the accepted strategy of the organization. A scenario might represent a major problem if it does not fit easily into the accepted discourse of strategy development that senior managers articulate for the organization. That is, it does not fit with the chosen storyline(s) of key strategists.

Although not exactly pushing a scenario planning approach, Hamel (1996) uses a similar approach to strategic thinking. Unlike Mintzberg, Hamel does not believe that incrementalism – whether it is in the form of re-engineering, continuous improvement programmes, looking at market share or following what competitors or the industry are doing – is a recipe for future strategic success in our rapidly changing world. *Strategizing*, he says, means adopting the posture of revolutionary change. He sets out 10 principles for developing revolutionary strategies and these are described in Exhibit 10.2. These 10 principles have a strong underlying message – that there are deeply entrenched political forces at the top of many organizations intent upon ensuring that 'official strategies' are not challenged and that incrementalism remains the norm.

1. **Strategic planning isn't strategic** Strategy making works from today forward, not from the future back, thus assuming that the future will be more or less the same as the present. Planning is elitist using a limited amount of the organization's creative capacity. Planning is the curse of incrementalism – strategizing is about discovery and a quest.

2. **Strategy making must be subversive** Creators of strategy must cast off industry conventions and look for new ways of thinking. Be rule breakers and try to redefine the industry rather than seeing it as a given.

3. **The bottleneck is at the top of the bottle** Senior managers are the most powerful defenders of orthodoxy – orthodoxy that protects their privileges and status. This group has the least diversity of views, invests heavily in the past and often represents industry dogma. Senior managers have to question their own limitations or capacities to change.

4. **Revolutionaries exist in every company** Most revolutionaries are in middle management but are constrained by orthodoxy. Senior managers have to look for 'revolutionaries' outside their own ranks.

5. **Change is not the problem; engagement is** Senior managers often assume people (especially middle managers) are against change and that only hero-led change (see Chapter 5) can force an organization forward. Senior managers adopt epic storylines to portray themselves as dragging their organizations into the future. Senior managers often talk of change as fear induced or as something nasty (e.g. downsizing). They often fail to give people responsibility for managing change and taking some control of their destinies. They do not create a dialogue about the future, but rather make directives and pronouncements.

6. **Strategy making must be democratic** Senior managers rely on others for operational improvements (e.g. continuous improvement programmes – see Chapter 6), but not for strategic improvements. Executives tend to want to 'learn' from each other, not recognizing that creativity is spread throughout an organization. The hierarchy of experience (position, status) must coexist with a hierarchy of imagination. Many potentially creative people (young people, new employees, employees in remote sites) are often automatically excluded from strategy making.

7. **Anyone can be a strategy activist** Senior managers are reluctant to give up their monopoly on strategy. Activists (revolutionaries) are needed because senior managers are often distracted or too busy protecting the past. Senior managers should see activists (challengers of the status quo) as good corporate citizens and not as anarchists.

8. **Perspective is worth 50 IQ points** Companies have to break their paradigms, reframe, invent new futures (as per scenario planning), identify and challenge unshakeable beliefs, search for discontinuities (e.g. in technology), develop deep understanding of core competencies and use all the company's knowledge to identify unconventional ideas.

9. **Top down and bottom up are not the alternatives** Strategy activists who fail to win the political support of top management achieve very little. Many senior managers still operate from the view that planners are at the top and doers at the bottom. Many people must endorse and be committed to a strategizing process to achieve diversity of input and unity of purpose (top management support).

10. **You can't see the end from the beginning** Strategizing can involve surprises (as we saw in scenario planning) and many senior managers are afraid of open-ended, inclusive processes. New voices and perspectives must come into the strategy-making process.

Exhibit 10.2   Hamel's 10 principles of revolutionary strategy

Source: Adapted from Gary Hamel (1996), 'Strategy as revolution', Harvard Business Review July–August, pp. 69–80.

Hamel's 10 principles, and the discussion on strategic thinking, move us into the last part of the chapter where we discuss how managers might consider strategy as a set of competing discourses. Viewing the various schools of thought as competing discourses opens up the opportunity for new discourses to emerge or at least challenge the dominant or popular ones. In many respects, Hamel (1996) and the scenario planning approach already hint at the need to consider alternative ways of looking at and practising strategy.

A postmodern approach to strategy

In the 1990s, and into the next millennium, it is claimed that strategic challenges will be different for organizations than they have been in the past. David Barry and Michael Elmes (1997: 442), for example, argue that the strategic needs of organizations are shifting because of accelerating changes in information technology, shifts in global politics and the rise in knowledge-based competition between and within organizations. The pace and rate of change are speeding up and, while opportunities for creating competitive advantage will be more fleeting, the opportunities will also multiply by virtue of the information revolution. Quick-thinking, knowledgeable employees who are capable of innovation and of working in paradoxical relationships, such as teamnets and virtual organizations, and through networks and interorganizational relations (IORs), will be more important for gaining strategic advantage than in the past. Barry and Elmes believe that the question of 'who knows what' or intellectual capital (see Chapter 8) will become a key part of strategy. The reliance on the printed word, on one strategic model or plan and familiar strategic discourses will simply have less advantage in a world where knowledge is rapidly changing and information is becoming more accessible to customers, clients and consumers. They believe diverse strategic narratives or texts are likely to proliferate in organizations, posing challenges as to how strategy is managed.

In Chapter 8 we introduced the notion of *discourse* – the complex nest of ideas, linguistic expressions, assumptions, justifications, defences, social institutions and practical actions that constitute a cohesive way of approaching the world. Postmodernism rejects modernistic representations of 'reality' through conventional scientific methods and focuses instead on the central role of language in constituting 'reality'. Consequently, if all knowledge is constituted by language, and (as we have seen in Chapter 8) knowledge is an important dimension of power, all language embodies power relationships. Barry and Elmes (1997) advocate looking at strategy as a type of narrative or story (or multiple narratives and many stories). One example of a broader strategic narrative, or meta-narrative (one which explains several more specific narratives, such as individual company strategies) is the narrative of 'globalization', popularly represented by the injunction to 'Think Global, Act Local'. Our case study at the beginning of this chapter illustrates this discourse.

Globalization is one of the 'buzz-words' of the 1990s: we live in a 'global' village, we consume 'global' brands, corporations have to be competitive in a 'global' market-place and governments have to be responsive to the needs of the 'global' economy. Companies are expected to achieve overall worldwide objectives by adapting to local conditions in several countries. In some cases this may mean tailoring products for national markets, in others paying exceptionally low rates for labour because it is the local norm. In the developed world executives and government officials often claim that globalization is responsible for the dismantling of social institutions, layoffs or plant closures. Globalization discourse is captivating. It can be used by its champions to promise a leaner, more efficient economy, one that will ensure growth and be beneficial to all the nations of the world.

When we begin to consider the research data available on globalization, it becomes evident that the 'benefits' of globalization are unevenly distributed, accruing primarily to large Western corporations (Renner 1997; Rodrik 1997). Indeed, globalization emerges as a strategic narrative, a gloss put on the explanation of a complex and disturbing reality which suppresses the consideration of some of its more perplexing aspects. In fact, many of the values, interests, ways of thinking, political, social and economic systems of the Western economies are often privileged in this narrative, while alternative perspectives and interests of marginalized cultures are ignored or suppressed.

Taking a view of strategy as narrative enables us to focus critically on the elements which any particular formulation of the strategic storyline may leave out. Elements of the globalization 'story' we have told above may serve to place the individual globalizing strategies of particular companies, or even countries, into a perspective that is quite different from how they are more commonly portrayed and is one that, we would argue, needs to be taken fully into account in strategic analysis.

A number of the theories discussed in this chapter are embedded in what some writers call the 'modernist' project (Parker 1992). The core of modernity is rationalism – the belief that science and reason can enable humans to understand nature and things 'out there' and that our capacity to generate knowledge about the world we live in, especially laws and principles, is related to achieving progress. Dominant theories of strategy are embedded in this context and 'accurate' representations of the business environment overwhelmingly use 'rational' criteria like sales, market share, return on assets and profitability. The narrative of modernism is a belief in science as progress and this world view, that assumes its own validity, is called a 'meta-narrative' (Kilduff and Mehra 1997; Lyotard 1984; Rosenau 1992). As we have seen in Chapter 8, looking at strategy as sets of discourses helps the manager focus on paradox and a critique of the underlying assumptions of all theoretical perspectives.

Traditional views of strategy do not explicitly address the role of language in strategy development. A narrative view of strategy would focus on how language (rather than unexamined notions of, for example globalization, 'fitting into external environments') is used to construct meaning and how this meaning (which is not 'truth') then creates a discourse that positions people in an organization. This fictional view of strategy can be applied to all schools of strategy; and, as Barry and Elmes (1997: 432–3) point out, emergent strategies are also fictional in the sense that future stories are constructed (organization actions are labelled as 'strategic') and the past is interpreted as other stories. The strength of the story is manifested by its degree of acceptance by readers and the extent to which organization members take on the roles of the characters in the story. In other words, the effectiveness of a strategy is less to do with its inherent 'truth' and more to do with its acceptance and approval by organization members and the extent of their participation in the story, as we saw in scenario planning.

Taking this approach highlights the importance of language in the strategy discourse and allows the questioning of constructs like 'market' or 'competition', which go unchallenged in traditional approaches to strategy. Barry and Elmes (1997) argue that a narrative approach to strategy is more effective in revealing the politics of strategy because of the type of questions that can be asked: who gets to write and read strategy? How are reading and writing linked to power? Who is marginalized in the writing/reading process? (Barry and Elmes 1997: 430).

The notion of *genre*, which we have discussed in Chapter 8, is also useful in postmodern analysis. All texts are developed in a specific setting and narratives of strategy are no exception. The genres of strategy assist in constructing and reinforcing the meanings of narratives, including who reads them, how they should be read and who are the 'heroes' and 'villains'. Mintzberg's schools of strategy are all genres containing narratives with specific structures and content. For instance, Barry and Elmes (1997) described how Mintzberg's Design School is an 'epic genre', where organizations following a SWOT model 'become epic journeyers', systematically navigating towards opportunities and success. This 'epic' genre faded away after producing an initial burst of narratives as managers identified several problems with the model (e.g. How are strengths and weaknesses identified? How are they evaluated? Who evaluates them?).

Epic genres are constituted by appealing to the familiar: we all know stories of the handsome stranger (inevitably white, male and heterosexual) who gets rid of the bad guys and cleans up the town. The hero fights his enemies and wins. This genre can be seen in some strategy narratives: if we employ the right 'weapons' (e.g. SWOT) we can win the war. Thus the manager fighting a battle in the market becomes a hero when the enemy is defeated (a book detailing the Coke–Pepsi 'wars' is entitled *The Other Guy Blinked*).

Barry and Elmes (1997: 437–8) also describe how a plot could be romantic. Companies facing hard times and engaging in significant downsizing as a result often follow a romantic plot. ('We need to do some soul searching about who we really are and where we want to go. Then we will return to our position as market leader.') The company's stakeholders are implicated in this romantic revival: shareholders must make do with less return, employees with fewer rewards, although this rarely means that CEOs will do with less (a point also raised by Hamel 1996).

Another characteristic of the narrative process is defamiliarization (Barry and Elmes 1997: 439). Defamiliarization refers to the novelty of a narrative and how new ways of looking at things make the story more effective. Maintaining novelty over a period of time is not easy, as the initial excitement wanes and we become familiar with the story. Barry and Elmes argue that different strategic frameworks were developed precisely because the novelty of each preceding one wore off and people were ready for a new method. Thus different schools of strategy emerged, each within its own genre. For instance, Barry and Elmes (1997: 440) describe the emergence and wide acceptance of the 'purist genre' as exemplified by the works of Miles and Snow (1978) and Porter (1980). It provided distinct identities and categories ('cost leadership' or 'differentiation' or 'defenders') and showed how companies could 'succeed' in competitive markets. Heavily character based, the purist genre appealed to managers by reframing market and organizational conditions as personalities – 'leaders', 'defenders', 'prospectors', 'differentiators', 'focusers', 'reactors' or 'muddlers'). The novelty of this narrative, however, appears to be waning as managers found the typologies difficult to operationalize and other frameworks emerged (Barry and Elmes 1997).

Looking at strategy as discourse uncovers new dimensions of power relationships that remain hidden in the meta-narratives of 'efficiency'. Narratives of strategy arose not from a meta-narrative of scientific progress but from a peculiar set of local conditions in postwar North America. These include changes in corporate ownership relations and changes in international market conditions after the Second World War (Knights 1992; Knights and

Morgan 1991). 'True' representations of markets and environments, and effects of strategies on markets and environments, were constructed within the dominant science of the day, that is, rational economic models, without widespread questioning of the assumptions behind these theories. Concepts like 'strategy', 'cost leadership', 'flexible specialization', or 'niche marketing' emerged not through a scientific ordered progression of thoughts and ideas but as products of power relations between corporations, governments and educational institutions (Knights 1992). Strategy is not therefore simply a body of knowledge but a mechanism of power. These power effects have important consequences: as David Knights and Glenn Morgan point out, they 'provide managers in organizations with a rationalization of their successes and failures, while generating a sense of personal and organizational security for managers' (1991: 262).

In Chapter 8 we also introduced the notion of *social subjectivity*, as the sense of individuality and socially positioned self-awareness, which is continually formed and reformed under changing social, economic and historical conditions. By engaging in strategic discourse in an organization, by using the language of markets and competition, by using the methodological tools of the particular discourse, organizational members constitute their sense of reality in organizational practice. This process allows the emergence of selected 'experts' within and outside the organization who continue to engage in the strategy discourse and continue to construct representations of the different realities their organization must face while attempting to bring under control the complex relations between a firm and its environment through a 'rational' process. Thus the discourse presents to the outside world and to itself 'rational' managerial actions without a representation of the power relations underlying the discourse and thereby facilitating and legitimizing the exercise of power (Knights and Morgan 1991).

Challenging dominant forms of representation in the strategy discourse makes explicit embedded power relations. Conceptions of rationality that have dominated the strategy discourse are based on a primarily masculine model – control (of the external environment), assertiveness and aggressiveness are typically 'masculine' traits (Knights and Morgan 1991). Conventional strategy discourse fits in conveniently with other masculine identities of managers, aggressive salesmen and the like (for instance, organizations need to 'penetrate' markets) and tends to promote masculinist conceptions of power (Knights and Morgan 1991).

The rationale behind strategic planning is based on the assumptions of rationality in neo-classical economics and strategy. Historical analysis of the use of the term 'strategy' in language indicates that its origins were located in descriptions of eighteenth century battles (Knights and Morgan 1991; Whipp 1996). The transition from military battles to competitive battles in the market place is still transparent in some of the business jargon we use today: 'rival firm', 'winning or losing (market share)', 'offensive and defensive strategies', 'attacking' a competitor's market or 'defending' one's market share, 'surrendering' market position, 'leader' or 'follower', or 'first mover advantage' strategies. The market place is the modern battlefield, the managers the generals. The battle and war metaphors pervade the language of strategy across many cultures (see below).

Using a postmodern framework to analyze Porter's model of strategy, Knights (1992) shows how the rules of formation of strategy are linked to power and knowledge. He describes how notions of 'cost leadership' and 'differentiation' are constructed by Porter without any attempt to problematize them in terms of power. Instead, the dominant scientific method of the day – neoclassical economics – is used to construct these categories and establish relationships between them. Assumptions underlying positive models of science do not take into account the behaviour of individual organizational members in the process of achieving competitive advantage. Rather, the language of strategy transforms the individuals into subjects who constitute their sense of reality and individuality through the discourse by making sense of the representations. Managers in an organization will engage in practices that support notions of competitive advantage, cost leadership and niche marketing.

Through this process, the status of 'expert' knowledge is not questioned, rather subjectivity is constituted to meet the needs of the knowledge produced. This does not mean that all members behave the same way or follow similar strategies to 'get there'. As the descriptive school of strategy suggests, managers do not automatically follow a strategy prescribed by top management – internal politics could result in a wide range of behaviours. However, as Knights (1992) points out, the diversity of behaviours is still enclosed within the representation of 'official strategy'. This is an example of the power effects of strategy discourse (Knights and Morgan 1991). Strategy is used to rationalize 'success' and 'failures' – in Porter's model, companies that are neither 'cost leaders' nor 'niche players' are doomed to fail – a self-fulfilling prophecy that is determined by the conditions of the production of these categories in the first place. Thus the 'truth effects' of Porter's model remain entrenched regardless of whether organizations are able to apply these strategies successfully or not. The fact that the knowledge produced by Porter is unreliable can only be exposed through an analysis of the discourse of knowledge production with a particular emphasis on subjectivity (or in this case, how knowledge production ignores subjectivity).

A postmodern approach would take into account and make explicit the conditions that made it possible for such knowledge to develop, thus exposing its fragile nature. By confronting the power–knowledge relationship, a postmodern approach to strategy does not produce truths; rather it perceives truth as an effect of these relations (Knights 1992). It attempts to disrupt universal knowledge by exposing the subjective conditions in which such knowledge, deemed rational or 'objective', and whose underlying assumptions remain unchallenged, is produced.

A postmodern approach to strategy, then, reminds us that the categories which other perspectives on strategy treat as unproblematic – competence, the environment, competitiveness, rationality – are all themselves constructs, not things in themselves. The meaning of these constructs shifts according to the ways in which they are positioned in strategic narratives, relative to each other. These meanings are always affected by the interconnections of knowledge and power from which they arise. The idea of strategy itself, not just of which strategies emerge under what conditions, is always under critical scrutiny from a postmodern perspective, Importantly, from taking such a perspective we become acutely aware of the deeper influences of culture on strategy, and it is these we will consider in the next section.

A cross-cultural view of strategy

Strategy will have different meanings for different national and cultural groups, and our discussions of the cultural relativity of basic theories such as leadership (which underpins strategic implementation) in other chapters reinforce this. During the 1980s, however, there was considerable interest in cultural difference in strategy formulation and implementation. This was closely related to the intense interest in Japanese economic success, and focused on two ancient books which were widely held to be the foundational texts for Japanese business strategists – *The Book of Five Rings* by the Samurai Miyamoto Musashi, and *The Art of War* by the Chinese military genius Sun Tzu. Rosalie Tung (1994) summarizes these books and two others – *The Three Kingdoms* by fourteenth century author Lo Kuan-Chung (which is issued to all Sony executives on promotion to senior management), and *Lure the Tiger out of the Mountains* by Gao Yuan, which is based on the *I Ching*, or the *Book of Changes*, and the *Thirty Six Stratagems*. Tung identifies 12 themes or principles running through these texts as shown in Exhibit 10.3.

- The importance of strategies
- Transforming an enemy's strength into weakness
- Engaging in deception to gain a strategic advantage
- Understanding contradictions and using them to gain an advantage
- Compromising
- Striving for total victory
- Taking advantage of an adversary's or competitor's misfortune
- Flexibility
- Gathering intelligence and information
- Grasping the interdependent relationship of situations
- Patience
- Avoiding strong emotions

Exhibit 10.3 Strategy and culture

Source: Rosalie Tung (1994), 'Strategic management thought in East Asia', Organizational Dynamics Spring, pp. 58–9.

The importance of strategies, the first point, emphasizes strategy as a means of avoiding perhaps costly and damaging warfare – on the principle that the supreme victory is to subdue the enemy without fighting. To this end, Tung notes, East Asians tend to play mind games, trying to find hidden meanings and strategies behind communications. Game playing here is considered an asset, not a distraction as in the West. Turning the opponent's strength into a weakness (or its converse, your weakness into a strength) teaches that it is unwise to be complacent because fortunes and misfortunes are reversible, times and situations change in cycles – and preparation should be made for these changes. Deception, which might be considered immoral or amoral in other cultures, is a way of life in East Asia, where it is important to look as prosperous as possible even in hard times, and weakness is conversely often feigned to make the opponent complacent. This adds a cautionary note to the later point about taking advantage of an adversary's misfortune – it may not always be easy to tell when misfortune is genuine or not. A useful point to remember is that it is necessary to think like the other thinks in order to understand them, and not to operate out of one's own cultural suppositions.

Understanding contradictions means to see every situation in terms of its light and dark aspects, positive and negative sides, and exploit it accordingly. Compromise implies an ongoing relationship, and may involve sacrifice, bribery, gift giving and lavish entertainment in order to secure greater rewards later in the piece. Striving for total victory emphasizes again the need not to be complacent even when winning as long as there is opposition able to act – if there is an opponent then their next move must be anticipated. Taking advantage of an adversary's misfortune may seem to be unsporting to Westerners, but it is an entirely pragmatic issue to the East Asians. If the opponent is down, then they are there to be eliminated. Where the Japanese are taught that it is courageous to face death, the Chinese believe it is better to run away and live to fight another day, and as a result may be harder to eliminate in the long term. Flexibility is a related principle – there are times when it is advisable to attack, and others when it is advisable to flee.

Gathering intelligence and information, or using spies, is a normal part of business life in East Asia, and includes the spreading of misinformation. This issue is of particular consequence in relation to global partnerships and alliances, where partners who are expected to share information often do not, but steal the partner's know-how only to set up independently in competition. East Asian businesses spend a long time developing relationships and gathering information to prevent such problems occurring in a world where competition and cooperation may be part of the same relationship. Indeed, grasping the interdependence of relationships, taking a holistic view, is important enough in its own right, as in the long term things that seem to be unrelated may indeed be related. Patience and the avoidance of strong emotions are similar aspects of the need to take a very long term view and not to let one's perspective become distorted by powerful feelings or passions.

Tung argues that these cultural dimensions are important shapers of the ways in which East Asians develop strategies, yet commentators such as Richard Whitley (1992) and Monir Tayeb (1988) have argued that cultural dimensions of strategy are not as important as the social, political and economic institutions which constrain and enable business relationships such as the *chaebol* in Korea to exist. They argue that it is Japanese financial organizations and the Ministry of International Trade and Industry (MITI) which have engineered Japanese economic success more than the Japanese character. As Tayeb states:

> The term 'culture' is very narrow in scope and it should give way to 'nation'. We perhaps should be talking about cross-national as opposed to cross-cultural studies of organisations. Organisations are influenced by other national institutions besides culture (understood as a set of learned, shared values and ideas). The term 'nation' not only refers to culture but also to other societal, economic and political institutions which have bearings on the nature of organisations located in particular countries (Tayeb 1988: 154).

Barry Wilkinson (1996) takes a slightly different view, arguing for the relevance of culture but noting that both cultural and institutional theorists tend to overstate their position. Wilkinson argues for an approach which focuses more on the specific contextual factors that affect particular groups of actors, saying, in effect, that strategy formation needs to be studied as the product of the actions of identifiable groups of actors embedded in identifiable social, institutional, political and economic contexts, and needs to be researched in an appropriate way.

Although strategy has its effects across cultures, causing companies to operate in and withdraw from markets and producing areas, it is also itself a cultural construct. As Tung points out, Western strategists would not think in the same ways as Asian ones, and would therefore be unlikely to produce the same decisions consistently. However, one of the problems with the cultural approach she exemplifies is that it tends to draw on literature which is about personal or organized combat, usually in a medieval setting. This is too removed from contemporary business and can therefore only apply metaphorically. Precisely how particular cultural assumptions work in reality (rather than hypothetically) to give rise to the specific decision-patterns of actual decision makers and strategies of real businesses is not clear. Yet it is a factor that cannot be dismissed.

Conclusion

Let us take a look at the questions with which we began the chapter. Remember there are no absolutely right answers and you may have different views of your own – the important thing is to know why views differ and what to do about this difference, which is also a challenge for strategic thinking itself.

1 What is a strategy?

As we have seen, there are many possible answers to this question. A strategy is a general view of what sort of 'business' the enterprise is or should be in, and entails some planned and systematic consideration of how to remain or become successful in that business, addressing factors internal to the organization, such as its structure and people, and external factors, such as its customers and competitors. It may well operate through a hierarchy of plans, but arguably it is just as likely to have elements which emerge through the action of people involved in making decisions and carrying them out, as Mintzberg suggests. An alternative view of strategy is that it is a story, or narrative, which attempts to 'write' or account for a whole series of disconnected and emergent elements as though they were a unified whole – but more than one such story is possible. These stories then act as guides to action.

2 How are strategies formulated?

Strategies may be formulated in a variety of ways, from the simple and rule-of-thumb approach to SWOT (which may become more complex in itself), through fairly disciplined and calculated planning approaches, to the blue-sky anticipatory exercises involved in scenario planning. Yet the influence of cultural and cross-cultural elements should not be discounted even in the most calculative of formative processes.

3 What is the value of strategic planning?

Strategic planning helps the organization to place its resources where they are likely to be of most benefit, to identify and remedy what appears to be weaknesses in its resourcing, skills, product offering, service support, etc., especially relative to its competitors. It also enables a big picture to be identified, so that focused operational developments can maximize their coordinated contribution to the long-term development and success of the enterprise. It enables the organization to anticipate the actions of its competitors and to be proactive rather than responding to the initiatives of others. This of course entails a calculated risk, but if the risk is controlled and properly attenuated it can be fully exploited if it pays off.

4 Why do some firms outperform others?

There is no answer to this question which is good for all situations at all times – sometimes the answer is good luck, or being in the right place at the right time, and political, social and economic positioning often limits the effects even of the best managerial practices. But firms which acquire and create knowledge, and are able through critical self-reflection and analysis of their relationships with different parts of their environment, and investment in their own development, to strengthen and change these relationships, are more likely to be able to convert this into sustainable competitive advantage over the long term. In other words, they will develop and implement strategies to become learning organizations.

5 Do all organizations need a strategy?

Strategy, like structure and culture, is something which happens as a result of processes which will emerge whether managers like them or not. Although structures, cultures and strategies may be more or less formal and visible, they will always be present, always in change and flux. The question therefore is not whether organizations need a strategy, as they will have one whether they like it or not, but whether the strategy they have – the strategic story they are implicitly or explicitly acting out – is the one they really want. This can only be determined by the sort of critical self-reflection we have been arguing for throughout this book.

Case analysis

The case can be analyzed at different levels with differing results and outcomes. For instance if we take the *rationalist approach*, we can understand how the outsourcing strategy emerged. In a highly competitive market, with high advertising and promotion costs and a constant emphasis on product innovation, companies can secure a competitive advantage through product differentiation or cost leadership. The market leaders did differentiate their products from their competitors through strong branding strategies. However, the battle of market shares at the top end of the market meant that firms needed to be more competitive. The major players in the market all offered premium products; competitive advantage in this part of the market meant lower costs. The strategy these firms developed was to lower production costs, the rationale being that in a consumer market marketing costs could not be reduced. Thus the 'rational' strategy was to reduce production costs in an attempt to be more competitive in the market.

Image Inc. followed this strategy, looking at the success of outsourcing strategies developed by Nike and Reebok. Reducing production costs meant finding cheaper sources of labour and cheaper raw materials. Obviously European and North American labour costs were many times higher than the labour costs in developing countries. In fact, the cost differentials more than made up for the higher shipping costs. It can be argued that the labour component of sports shoe manufacturing is not significantly high (10–12 percent), so why should the companies concentrate so much on finding sources of cheap labour? There could be several reasons why outsourcing remains such a popular option. First, even if the labour component is not significantly high, wage rates are still considerably higher in European and North American markets. One could argue that the reason why the labour component is small is because of the low wage rates in the developing countries. Second, other production costs were also significantly lower in developing countries which provided cheap raw materials. Companies did not face strict regulation relating to the disposal of chemicals in developing countries and as a result found it easier and cheaper to produce in these regions. Third, the outsourcing strategy meant that very few resources needed to be deployed by companies. Here the discourse of globalization we mentioned earlier was useful to managers, who could present their actions as being necessitated by global business logics, and distance themselves from the less admirable consequences of their actions – sweatshop conditions, health and safety violations, subsistence wages, discrimination and failure to feed back any profit into the community.

Thus the rational strategy for Image Inc. is to continue to focus on reducing costs in order to stay competitive. The other option is to enhance its presence at the high end of the market and focus on producing premium products. These strategies would lead to different outcomes: in the first instance, the company's efforts would be directed at developing new production centres and regions that offer cheaper labour and raw materials. A premium product strategy would focus on innovation and design (differentiation) and, while production costs are important, they would not drive the strategy.

A *reconfigurationalist approach* in this case implies that the company should acknowledge the needs of multiple stakeholders. Image Inc.'s argument that it is not 'their business' how factories are run is questionable if we take a stakeholder approach: the labour force may be employed by subcontractors, however, they are stakeholders of the company as well because the company's action has a direct impact on the lives of these people. Different stakeholders have different interests and the task of the company is to balance these interests and develop objectives that would meet the needs of all stakeholders. Is it possible for a company to do this? Stakeholders in this case could include subcontractors, factory workers, labour activists, environmental agencies, governments and neighbouring communities apart from the company's employees, customers and shareholders. How can Image Inc. accommodate everyone's interest? Whose interest should be given first priority? Who will argue for the legitimacy of stakeholders who do not command sufficient resources to be heard? Fear of public boycotts and a negative company image might compel Image Inc. to take a broader perspective of the situation. Developing a universal code of conduct that all subcontractors must follow is one way by which Image Inc. can address stakeholder interests. However, labour reform by subcontractors could mean higher costs for the company which means it could lose its competitive position, especially if their competitors do not change their practices and continue to enjoy cheap wage rates. Unless all players in the industry are compelled to change labour practices, it is not in the financial interest of Image Inc. to do so. Of course, public boycotts and a negative image can harm the company's financial position, and provides a rationale for changing current practices.

While such a pluralist view of the organization might address these issues, it is important to realize that the process by which these issues are resolved remains embedded in the power relations between different stakeholders. The process of negotiating stakeholder relations operates within the economic paradigm of markets, profits and cost leadership and these criteria continue to direct the rationale behind strategies. A postmodern approach to the case can highlight the power relations that drive the negotiation process in an emergent strategy.

For instance, if we look at *strategy as a narrative* we can see how the narrative supports power–knowledge relations. In this case, the strategy narrative is one that frames market share and profitability as its objectives. Within this framework, different actors in the organization take on (either by encouragement or coercion) different roles and perform actions that the script allows. Dick Foster is worried because his performance will not look good if labour unrest continues or customers boycott his company's products. The story of his company's strategy is the story of leveraging a dominant position in the market. As this story unfolds in different locations, other stories are created and more characters emerge and are manipulated within the text. Dick Foster's role is *interpellated* in this strategic text; his role as Vice President of production is positioned in the narrative and the narrative also specifies the range of possible actions he can take. In other words, the text constructs Dick Foster's reading position and he can make sense of the situation by being a part of the discourse – in this case by solving the company's current production problems – or reject it by refusing to be read in this way by resigning.

Even the stakeholder approach is part of the discourse of strategy. The overall objective in this case of acquiring a competitive position in the market, thus enhancing profitability and shareholder value, seems to have an undesirable consequence: abusive labour practices are apparently giving the company its advantage. A traditional strategy discourse would frame stakeholder interests within the dominant market discourse without interrogating power–knowledge relations. The narrative supports the kind of knowledge that supports the dominance of the organization or industry. Thus, Dick Foster would have to show that he is an 'international production expert' by solving the company's problems. Concepts such as 'flexible specialization' or 'relationship building' are constructed and deployed within the strategy narratives of market share and profitability. Other narratives like the abuse of workers in the factories are positioned as 'problems' that need to be solved, often problems created by 'them' and not 'us' and part of going global. Obviously, strategy gets written by 'us', those of us employed in organizations; the extent of the influence of other stakeholders emerges only in situations of conflict such as the one in which Image Inc. finds itself.

The situation described in the case could have several outcomes: the company could change the subcontractors' labour policies, the foreign governments could pass new labour and environmental laws, the subcontractors could relocate to other 'less problematic' regions, media interest could wane and the subcontractors could return to their old ways of doing things. A postmodern view would be less concerned about the 'truth' of the different actions; rather it would reveal how these truths were arrived at.

The answer to a question we asked at the end of the case, 'what is Image Inc.'s product?', is less obvious than it appears. After all, what *is* their product? Sports shoes? What about their other lines: clothing, perfume, soft drinks, health care products? Or do we consider Image Inc. to be a consumer products company? What is becoming more apparent in this industry is the power of the brand. One could argue that Nike's product is the 'swoosh' which now adorns shoes, T shirts, socks, wrist bands, watches, personal care products (and even the Australian cricketer Shane Warne's ears). Image Inc.'s product is really its brand – in the postmodern world we live in, the brand has become the product and the product has become the brand, regardless of whether the product is a shoe or clothing item or a piece of jewellery.

References

Ackoff, R.L. (1970) *A Concept of Corporate Planning*, New York: Wiley Interscience.

Andrews, K.R. (1988) 'The concept of corporate strategy', in Quinn, J.B., Mintzberg, H. and James, R.M. (eds), *The Strategy Process: Concepts Contexts, Cases*, Englewood Cliffs, NJ: Prentice Hall.

Ansoff, H.I. (1965) *Corporate Strategy* (revised edition 1987), London: Penguin.

Ansoff, H.I. (1979) *Strategic Management*, London: Macmillan.

Anthony, P. (1994) *Managing Culture*, Buckingham: Open University Press.

Barney, J.B. and Zajac, E.J. (1994) 'Competitive organisational behaviour: Toward an organisationally-based theory of competitive advantage', *Strategic Management Journal* 15: 5–9.

Barry, D. and Elmes, M. (1997) 'Strategy retold: Toward a narrative view of strategic discourse', *Academy of Management Review* 22(2): 429–52.

Besanko, D., Danove, D. and Shanley, M. (1996) *The Economics of Strategy*, New York: John Wiley.

Blackmur, D. (1997) 'Determinants of organisational size: BHP and vertical integration', *Journal of the Australian and New Zealand Academy of Management (JANZAM)* 3(1): 15–29.

Bowman, C. and Asch, D. (1987) *Strategic Management*, London: Macmillan.

Brunnson, N. (1982) 'The irrationality of action and action rationality: Decisions, ideologies and organisational actions', *Journal of Management Studies* 19(1): 29–44.

Byrt, W.J. (1973) *Theories of Organisation*, Sydney: McGraw-Hill.

Chandler, A.D., Jr (1962) *Strategy and Structure: Chapters in the History of Industrial Enterprise*, Cambridge, Mass.: MIT Press.

Chandler, A. D., Jr (1977) *The Visible Hand – The Managerial Revolution in American Business*, Cambridge, Mass.: The Belknap Press of Harvard University Press.

Coase, R. (1937) 'The nature of the firm', *Economica* 4: 386–405.

Day, G.S. and Wensley, R. (1988) 'Assessing advantage: A framework for diagnosing competitive superiority', *Journal of Marketing* 52 (April): 1–20.

Deal, T.W. and Kennedy, A.A. (1982) *Corporate Cultures*, Reading, Mass.: Addison-Wesley.

Fayol, H. (1949) *General and Industrial Management*, London: Pitman.

Forster, J. and Browne, M. (1996) *Principles of Strategic Management*, Melbourne: Macmillan.

Foss, N.J. (ed.) (1997) *Resource, Firms and Industries: A Reader in the Resource-Based Perspective*, New York: Oxford University Press.

Furnham, A. and Gunter, B. (1993) 'Corporate culture: Definition, diagnosis and change', in Cooper, C. L. and Robertson, I. T. (eds), *International Review of Industrial and Organisational Psychology 1993*, 8, 233–261, London: John Wiley.

Goold, M. and Campbell, A. (1987) *Strategies and Styles*, Oxford: Blackwell.

Goold, M. and Quinn, J.J. (1990) *Strategic Control: Milestones for Long Term Performance*, London: Hutchinson.

Grant, R.M. (1991) 'Analyzing resources and capabilities', extract from Grant, R.M., *Contemporary Strategic Analysis: Concepts, Techniques and Applications*, Cambridge, Mass.: Blackwell, reprinted in Lewis, G., Morkel, A. and Hubbard, G. (1993), *Australian Strategic Management: Concepts, Contexts and Cases*, Sydney: Prentice Hall.

Hamel, C. (1996) 'Strategy as revolution', *Harvard Business Review* July–August: 69–80.

Hansen, G.S. and Wernerfelt, B. (1989) 'Determinants of firm performance: The relative importance of economic and organisational factors', *Strategic Management Journal* 10: 399–411.

Hickman, G.R. and Silva, M.A. (1984) *Creating Excellence: Managing Corporate Culture, Strategy and Change in the New Age*, London: Allen & Unwin.

Hofer, C.W. and Schendel, D.E. (1978) *Strategy Formulation: Analytical Concepts*, St Paul, Minn.: West Publishing.

Jemison, D.B. (1981) 'The importance of an integrative approach to strategic management research', *Academy of Management Review* 6(4): 601–8.

Johnson, G. (1987) *Strategic Change and the Management Process*, Oxford: Blackwell.

Johnson, G. (1992) 'Managing strategic change – strategy, culture and action', *Long Range Planning* 25(1): 28–36.

Kanter, R.M. (1989) 'The new managerial work', *Harvard Business Review* November–December: 85–92.

Kilduff, M. and Mehra, A. (1997) 'Postmodernism and organizational research', *Academy of Management Review* 22(2): 453–81.

Knights, D. (1992) 'Changing spaces: The disruptive impact of a new epistemological location for the study of management', *Academy of Management Review* 17(3): 514–36.

Knights, D. and Morgan, G. (1991) 'Strategic discourse and subjectivity: Towards a critical analysis of corporate strategy in organizations', *Organization Studies* 12(2): 251–73.

Kotter, J. (1982) *The General Manager*, New York: The Free Press.

Learned, E.P., Christensen, C.R., Andrews, K.R. and Guth, W.D. (1969) *Business Policy: Text and Cases* (revised edition), Homewood, Ill.: Irwin.

Lenz, R.T. (1980) 'Strategic capabilities: A concept and framework for analysis', *Academy of Management Review* 5(2): 225–34.

Lenz, R.T. (1987) 'Managing the evolution of the strategic planning process', *Business Horizons*, January–February: 34–9.

Lindblom, C. (1959) 'The science of "Muddling Through"', *Public Administration Review* 19(2): 79–88.

Lyotard, J.F. (1984) *The Post-Modern Condition: A Report on Knowledge*, Minneapolis: University of Minnesota Press.

Mahoney, J.T. and Pandian, J.R. (1992) 'The resource-based view within the conversation of strategic management', *Strategic Management Journal* 13: 363–80.

Miles, R.E. and Snow, C.C. (1978) *Organizational Strategy, Structure and Process*, New York: McGraw-Hill.

Mintzberg, H. (1973) *The Nature of Managerial Work*, New York: Harper and Row.

Mintzberg, H. (1987) 'Crafting strategy', *Harvard Business Review* July–August: 67–81.

Mintzberg, H. (1990) 'Strategy formation: Schools of thought', in Frederickson, J.W. (ed.), *Perspective on Strategic Management*, New York: Harper Business.

Mintzberg, H. (1994) *The Rise and Fall of Strategic Planning*, Hemel Hempstead: Prentice Hall International.

Narayanan, V.K. and Fahey, L. (1982) 'The micro-politics of strategy formulation', *Academy of Management Review* 7(1): 25–34.

Ogilvy, J. (1998) 'Learning scenario planning – an introduction to scenario thinking – a four day simulation course', 1–5 February presented by Australian Business Network and Global Business Networks (Sydney).

Ohmae, K. (1983) *The Mind of the Strategist: Business Planning for Competitive Advantage*, New York: Penguin.

Oster, S. (1994) *Modern Competitive Analysis*, New York: Oxford University Press.

Parker, M. (1992) 'Post-modern organizations or postmodern organization theory', *Organization Studies* 13(1): 1–17.

Peters, T. and Waterman, R. (1982) *In Search of Excellence*, New York: Addison-Wesley.

Pettigrew, A.M. (1985) *The Awakening Giant: Continuity and Change in Imperial Chemical Industries*, Oxford: Blackwell.

Piercy, N. (1989) 'Marketing concepts and actions: Implementing marketing-led strategic change', *European Journal of Marketing* 24(2): 24–42.

Porter, M.E. (1980) *Competitive Strategy: Techniques for Analyzing Industries and Competitors*, New York: The Free Press.

Porter, M. (1985) *Competitive Advantage: Creating and Sustaining Superior Performance*, New York: The Free Press.

Prahalad, C.K. and Hamel, G. (1990) 'The core competence of the corporation', *Harvard Business Review* May–June: 79–91.

Quinn, J.B. (1978) 'Strategic change: "Logical Incrementalism"', *Sloan Management Review* Fall: 1–21.

Quinn, J.B. (1980) *Strategies for Change: Logical Incrementalism*, Homewood, Ill.: Irwin.

Renner, M. (1997) *Fighting for Survival: Environmental Decline, Social Conflict and the New Age of Insecurity*, London: Earthscan.

Rodrik, D. (1997) 'Has globalization gone too far?', *California Management Review* 39(3): 29–53.

Rosenau, P.M. (1992) *Post-Modernism and the Social Sciences: Insights, Inroads, and Intrusions*, Princeton, NJ: Princeton University Press.

Rowe, A.J., Mason, R.O. and Dickel, K.E. (1986) *Strategic Management: A Methodological Approach*, Reading, Mass.: Addison-Wesley.

Rowe, A.J., Mason, R.O., Dickel, K.E. and Westcott, P.A. (1987) *Computer Models for Strategic Management*, Reading, Mass.: Addison-Wesley.

Rumelt, R.P. (1991) 'How much does industry matter', *Strategic Management Journal* 12: 167–85.

Schendel, D. (1994) 'Competitive organisational behaviour: Toward an organisationally-based theory of competitive advantage', *Strategic Management Journal* 15: 1–5.

Schmalensee, R. (1985) 'Do markets differ much?', *American Economic Review* 75 (June): 341–51.

Schwartz, P. (1996) *The Art of the Long View*, NSW: Australian Business Network (originally published in 1991, New York: Currency/Doubleday).

Simon, H.A. (1976) 'From substantive to procedural rationality', in Latsis, S.J. (ed.), *Method and Appraisal in Economics*, Cambridge: Cambridge University Press.

Simon, H.A. (1979) 'Rational decision making in business organisations', *American Economic Review* 69 (September): 493–512.

Snow, C.C. and Hambrick, D.C. (1980) 'Measuring organisational strategies: Some theoretical and methodological problems', *Academy of Management Review* 5(4): 527–38.

Stacey, R.D. (1996) *Strategic Management and Organizational Dynamics* (second edition), London: Pitman.

Sterne, D. (1992) 'Core competencies: The key to corporate advantage', *Multinational Business* 3 (Summer): 13–20.

Strauss, A. (1978) *Negotiations: Varieties, Contexts, Processes and Social Order*, London: Jossey-Bass.

Tayeb, M.H. (1988) *Organisations and National Culture*, London: Sage.

Tung, R.L. (1994) 'Strategic management thought in East Asia', *Organizational Dynamics* Spring: 55–65.

Wack, P. (1985a) 'The gentle art of reperceiving', *Harvard Business Review* September–October: 73–89 (part 1).

Wack, P. (1985b) 'Scenarios – shooting up the rapids', *Harvard Business Review* November–December: 139–50 (part 2).

Wernerfelt, B. (1984) 'A resource-based view of the firm', *Strategic Management Journal* 5(2): 171–80.

Wernerfelt, B. (1997) Foreword to Foss, N.J. (ed.) (1997) *Resource, Firms and Industries: A Reader in the Resource-Based Perspective*, New York: Oxford University Press.

Westerlund, G. and Sjøstrand, S.E. (1979) *Organisational Myths*, London: Harper and Row.

Whipp, R. (1996) 'Creative deconstruction: Strategy and organizations', in Clegg, S.R., Hardy, C. and Nord, W.R. (eds), *Handbook of Organization Studies,* London: Sage.

Whitley, R. (1992) *Business Systems in East Asia: Firms, Markets and Societies*, London: Sage.

Wilkinson, B. (1996) 'Culture, institutions and business in East Asia', *Organization Studies* 17(3): 421–47.

11
Networks and interorganizational relations

Ewa Buttery, Liz Fulop and Alan Buttery

Questions about networks

1   What does the term 'network' mean?
2   Why do organizations form networks or interorganizational relations?
3   What types of cooperation and/or collaboration are possible in networks?
4   What common problems face organizations wanting to cooperate or collaborate?
5   What problems are associated with networking across cultures?

Evans Co. looks for partners

Evans Co. is a manufacturer of circuit boards for specialized hospital equipment. Evans is not an industry leader as its current technology is considered dated and it is under threat of losing its market share to more technically advanced competitors. Formax is a producer of component parts and is a supplier to Evans. Both companies are SMEs*. The component parts supplied by Formax are also used by Evans's competitors. While Formax has been Evans's chief component supplier for many years, Evans has recently developed new technology which requires component parts that they know are produced by Zercon Pty Ltd at a comparable cost to Formax, but of higher quality. Zercon is a direct competitor of Formax. The new technology Evans has produced will be 'state-of-the-art' and place the company in a strong competitive advantage compared to its main rivals and position it to enter overseas markets. The initial start-up costs will be high and Evans is thinking of entering into an arrangement with Zercon and also Tran Holdings, who can produce essential castings. To date, Zercon has had no dealings with Evans and to enter the business arrangement, Evans would have to reveal its new state-of-the-art technology to Zercon's management. Evans is aware that Zercon has a good reputation for quality and service in the industry, but recently Zercon has employed a new CEO who is a close friend of Formax's CEO.

To produce the new technology will also require new casings for the equipment and Evans wants to invite Tran Holdings, which is a large company (employing over 1000 people), to join the network. Tran Holdings is a leader in the production of the casings Evans wants to use. Tran Holdings is based in Singapore and has several offices in major cities throughout the world. Evans has had no prior dealings with Tran Holdings and is aware that Tran Holdings supplies to a number of Evans's competitors, and one of its subsidiaries competes directly with Zercon. Tran Holdings has had dealings with Formax, and Formax's management has experienced no major problems with the company, except that they have a high turnover of senior management. Tran Holdings' global senior management is not usually drawn from local managers, that is, they employ mainly Singaporeans (expatriates) to fill these positions.

Evans's management wants to begin exporting its new state-of-the-art technology to Singapore and Asia and considers the inclusion of Tran Holdings a key part of their strategy to enter these markets.

Tran Holdings has formed partnerships with a number of large firms to develop new product lines and enter new markets. Only one of these firms has been from outside Asia. Two of the alliances have proved successful business ventures while at least two others have failed. Tran Holdings has not been involved previously in a partnership with SMEs and has always preferred to be the lead company in its other partnerships.

* Definitions of small to medium-sized businesses (SMEs) vary across countries and industry sectors, for example in Australia 100 employees or less is considered small to medium in manufacturing, while in the UK this would be 200 employees and in Europe 500 (Fulop 1992: 326). A micro-firm is a business employing one or two people.

Questions about the case

1   What would you do in the place of Evans's management?
2   What would you do in the place of Zercon's management?
3   How might Tran Holdings's management react to an offer from Evans to cooperate?

Introduction

The generic term 'interorganizational network' or 'network' refers to a whole host of different forms of cooperation and collaboration among organizations. Some of these include the following: 'strategic alliances', 'business networks', 'clusters', 'strategic partnering' and 'linkages'. 'Interorganizational' means activities that go on *between* organizations, as opposed to *within* them. Indeed, organizations can enter into networks for many different reasons, and have done so for years. These can range from very simple forms of cooperation to more sophisticated levels of collaboration. For example, cooperation might be for the purpose of sharing information, premises or some equipment that is useful to both parties, but does not threaten either's competitive position. Collaboration, on the other hand, refers to the sharing of a significant aspect of each partner's core competence. As we shall discuss, the sharing of a core competency might not be how a network begins, but over time collaboration might emerge. A number of theorists have claimed that what is really new is the rapid growth and development of collaborative arrangements among both large and small enterprises, and across both the private and public sectors.

A key challenge for managers is to examine why organizations enter networks or interorganizational relations (IORs) and what choices managers have in this regard. To do this they will have to consider what it means to move beyond purely competitive arrangements (as discussed in Chapter 10) to seeking *collaborative advantage* (see Huxham 1993, 1996; Kanter 1994). Managers will also need to understand what collaborative advantage actually means, and how it can be fostered across different industries, organizations and cultures where issues of diversity become paramount. Some argue that the growth in the sheer number and types of networks is part of a large-scale social experiment occurring between organizations, industries and governments to find the appropriate design and operation of businesses into the twenty-first century (James 1994: 56, citing Mitroff and Linstone 1993).

This chapter explores why networks are on the rise and the pressures that account for these developments. We examine the different ways theorists have sought to explain how networks operate and what distinguishes them from other forms of organizing. We will describe some of the prevalent types of networks and the problems associated with establishing and managing them. Key *relational* issues in managing networks will be considered, particularly the problems associated with *trust, commitment* and *power*. The cross-cultural dimensions of networks or networking will also be considered.

In this chapter we adopt a very broad definition of 'networks', which includes cooperative and/or collaborative efforts among businesses, public sector organizations, non-government organizations (voluntary sector organizations such as neighbourhood centres, refuges, major aid organizations and charities, etc.) and persons or entities that are interconnected in various ways (Ring 1997a: 115). Within this broad definition are a number of distinctions that can be made to identify what constitutes networking and what other types of activities or relationships fail to qualify as such. However, the focus of this chapter is on *business networks* or predominantly networks in the private sector. Networking is an issue in the public sector as well as in non-government organizations and there are networks that bridge both the private and public sectors (Huxham 1996; Alter and Hage 1993).

Rise of networks

It is clear from the global interest in networks in recent years, and the different types being identified in the literature, that interorganizational cooperation and collaboration will question the ways in which organizations compete, conduct their business, and are managed. Ewa and Alan Buttery (1995) carried out a literature search and identified a number of key internal and external triggers accounting for why many businesses form networks. The main reasons are summarized in Exhibit 11.1.

Internal triggers to network
- ensure the survival of the firm
- increased profitability potential
- lack of resources for marketing products and services to best advantage
- limited essential expertise and knowledge in foreign markets and cultures
- realisation that market opportunities cannot be exploited solo
- limited finance for development
- limited technological know how
- realisation that partner can produce a good more efficiently
- limited management expertise/desire to buy in management talent

- finding a means to replace the market mechanism (i.e., rather than trading in a market setting, the firm enters into a longer term networking arrangement which effectively supersedes the market)
- collecting information about a competitor.

External triggers

- government encouragement, e.g. grants, allowances
- regional policy to lift the game of a depressed region
- taking advantage of a naturally occurring phenomenon, for example the opportunity to regenerate an area or region following fire, flood, etc.
- overcoming prejudice in the market by joining with an indigenous partner
- spreading business risk by diversifying out of a single economy
- overcoming pressure generated by customers in the market place
- generating national or global flexibility by being able to join and leave networks.

Exhibit 11.1   Triggers for networking

Source: Ewa and Alan Buttery (1995), The Dynamics of the Network Situation, Canberra: AusIndustry Business Networks Program, pp. 16–18.

To a great extent this list provides the motivation for networking. It represents what an organization's management might be seeking from networking and also contributes to a climate that is conducive to networking. A number of key developments seem to explain best why organizations in many parts of the world are accelerating and experimenting with different types of networks. These can be summarized under a number of key interrelated developments:

- Technology in the past
- Rise of marketing
- Information technology and knowledge
- Globalization

Technology in the past

Technology has been important to organizations since the industrial revolution. The post-industrial revolution saw a clamber towards using standardization of products, combined with specialization of processes, to generate economies of scale as evidenced by Taylorism and Fordism (see Chapter 6). Such combinations were seen in the automation that occurred during the mid-twentieth century. It was automation, and the incessant pursuit of economies of scale in production, that led to larger and larger organizations, often based on vertical integration. Industrialists, such as Henry Ford and Alfred P. Sloan Jr (from GM), believed that vertical integration could guarantee sources of supply and also allow the larger firm to 'squeeze' their suppliers. In the USA the three big auto manufacturers (Ford, GM and Chrysler) at one time vertically integrated into coal, iron ore, steel plants, glass and rubber factories to gain competitive advantage (Slocum, McGill and Lei 1994: 36). Indeed, John Kenneth Galbraith (1974) gave a name to such giants, and it was the term 'technostructure'. Others called these large organizations 'hierarchies' or the 'integrated firm' and these are the terms that will be used in this chapter. An example of what Galbraith meant by a technostructure would have been a firm such as Ford, GM or Chrysler.

Rise of marketing

One thing that could be relied on in the integrated firm was the total focus on economies of scale and it was up to the marketing departments of such organizations to 'sell' what was produced. By the time we reached the 1960s marketing departments were claiming a customer focus, but it was a cynical focus aimed at finding out what could most easily be sold to the often uniformed customer and how the product could be augmented by intangibles, for example, better after-sales service or improved packaging. It was against this background that the worst excesses of such organizations were challenged by the 'consumerism' movement led by activists such as Vance Packard and Ralph Nader in the USA. Nader, for example, led a relentless campaign against the defects and safety problems in the manufacture of automobiles (Alter and Hage 1993: 18). To most people in the Western world it was going just too far when firms were building into their products planned obsolescence and deliberate defects. One impetus for organizations moving away from the integrated firm, and its mass-marketing approach, was the increasing level of education in Western societies and the pressure among more educated groups to question the environmental impact of products and services (Alter and Hage 1993: 18–19). There was also increasing consumer demand for higher quality and customerized (boutique) products and services (Piore and Sabel 1984).

It was the same clamber for growth, driven by mass-marketing strategies, that inspired the growth of the multinational enterprise (MNE), which sought cheap raw materials or human resource inputs in the newly emerging economies in areas such as South East Asia and Latin America. Alternatively, the MNEs aimed to exploit new markets for products already at the end of their life cycle in countries such as the USA, an example being the 'trickle-down' effect in agricultural machinery and the selling of outdated models in Asian markets. In the early 1970s organizations were particularly bent on gaining size through using all possible means of expansion. This included *market penetration,* which was reflected as keen competition between organizations to obtain increased market share along with the considerable use of intensive advertising to increase the 'size of the cake'. *Market development* was also used as a means of expansion reflecting the need to discover new market segments or entirely new markets at home and overseas. This led to exporting and direct foreign investment and contributed to the spread of the MNE.

Product development added to the size of the organization by using Research and Development (R&D) to generate new products. Merger and acquisitions were also seen as a means of obtaining new products and ideas for products. Finally, *diversification* opened up brand new opportunities for developing new products for new markets, and *concentric diversification* enabled organizations, particularly with competence in strategic management, to acquire the potential to develop products on the basis of complementary strengths between the acquiring firm and the acquired firm; for example, the combination of laser technology and computers spawned new developments in non-invasive surgery.

All these methods of growth were generally driven by either internal R&D developments in production and marketing or acquiring new products or markets through merger and acquisition. This led to the worldwide merger mania of the early 1970s, and produced mammoth organizations capable of considerable cost benefits through economies of scale and scope (i.e. developing more differentiated products). Sometimes the mergers were between firms at the same point in the value-adding chain, for example the merger between two competitors. Several successive mergers in the UK brewery industry left 80 percent of output concentrated in the hands of only six mega-brewers by the mid-1980s. Other mergers were based on acquisitions of organizations that were sequential in the value-adding chain where, for example, a producer took over a supplier. Sometimes vertical or horizontal integration generated new organizations with diversified products. The MNE 'Tootal' in the UK started out as a thread manufacturer, and through merger and acquisition moved into textiles, and eventually into the production of material used in space programmes. Horizontal and vertical integration always led to larger firm size and introduced the possibilities of economies of scale. Often integration strategies were motivated by the urge to own or dominate a market or segment through increasing a firm's scope of offerings.

During the late 1980s and into the 1990s, downsizing of vertically integrated firms became a feature across a number of industry sectors, such as automotives, engineering and other heavy industries. What this revealed was that the vertically integrated firm was not always the most competitive way of organizing a business. In the USA alone around 800 of the *Forbes* 500 companies (ranked in terms of sales, profits, assets or market value) had decreased the number of persons employed by 2-4 million between 1976–86 (Johnston and Lawrence 1988: 99). Moreover the manufacturing practices of Japanese companies (see Womack, Jones and Roos 1990) revealed that they did not internalize, as did integrated firms, all their activities but instead had become proficient at outsourcing or contracting out many parts of their production systems. Thus by 1988 Toyota was producing only 20 percent of the value of its cars while GM, Ford and Chrysler in the USA were producing 70 percent, 50 percent and 30 percent respectively (Buttery and Buttery 1994: 17).

Information technology and knowledge

It was later on, towards the 1990s, that information technology became sufficiently advanced enough for firms to combine it with new organizational forms to achieve all the benefits of vertical and horizontal integration, without the inflexibility of internalizing all operations within one massive organization.

As we approached the 1990s the development of computer technology and telecommunications had the effect of 'shrinking the world' and making information from all corners of the world quickly available. This seemed to be the last barrier to more global development as it gave the MNEs the ability to control production on a world scale. It was not uncommon for the parts of a car, for example, to have visited numerous different countries before the car was finally assembled near major markets. Operations were planned on a global basis, firms owned and controlled assets in getting on for 100 different countries and the international finance system was geared up to finance these unwieldy giants. The problem with this method of organizing was that it needed vast markets to gain economies of scale from standardization and specialization.

Another leap in technology, robotics, coupled with computer-aided design (CAD) and production, however, injected a new potential flexibility into the production arena. Long production runs brought about by the need to re-tool were no longer the deciding factor in production. Robotics took over; even the workforce changed from being semi-skilled to being dominated by technicians and scientists and fewer of them were required. It was soon recognized that getting to market quickly was a real distinctive competence and so in addition to CAD/computer-aided manufacturing (CAM) and robotics, we witnessed the development of concurrent design and engineering and Just-In-Time (JIT) production systems (see Chapter 6).

While information technology facilitated the network form, the combination of growth in knowledge, hastened by rapid technological change and growth in R&D expenditure and fuelled also by shortening of product life cycles and demand for customization, stimulated and necessitated the development of networking (Alter and Hage 1993: 21). One study in 1988, for example, found that of 829 international cooperative or collaborative agreements, two-thirds were for the purpose of product development (Hergert and Morris 1988, quoted in Alter and Hage 1993: 20). Some writers suggest that the major benefits of networks are derived from sharing information and expertise and sharing of risk, including the risk of failure in the joint product development process.

Data from the USA have revealed that firms in certain industry sectors have accelerated the rate at which they have been forging strategic alliances with overseas firms, with about 12000 of them formed in the 1980s (Alter and Hage 1993: 4, citing Work 1988). Peter Smith Ring noted that the number of strategic alliances in the USA had reached record levels by 1993 (Ring 1997a: 113). Catherine Alter and Jerald Hage observed that alliances had been formed predominantly in areas where the cost of product development has been high or the speed of product development was rapid. They also noted (citing Pollack 1992) that there were discernible industry trends, with bio-tech firms, for example, leading the field in the rate at which they were forming overseas or cross-border alliances. Similar trends were noted in other industries in the USA such as information technology, new materials manufacture (especially in the steel industry), chemicals, aviation and automotives (Alter and Hage 1993: 4–5; also Buttery and Buttery 1994).

Globalization

The flexibility in production, coupled with vast leaps in the development of information technology, completely freed up the world to globally managed production and challenged managers to seek new organizational forms to manage this situation. It was not long before some managers realized that they did not need to invest in production facilities if they could find other people, perhaps in other parts of the world, to take the risk. It was far more important to develop and own brands and be able to manage marketing than production. An example would be Reebok sports shoes that are sought after in many countries by customers who pay for the name. The shoes themselves are made in Asia, but do the customers know in which country, or do they care?

This has led us now to a world where production can be separated from marketing, marketing can be described as global, that is, managed on a global basis, but it recognizes local requirements and cultures (see Chapter 10). Brand names exchange for billions of dollars and managers are willing to look around the world to see where it is best (and cheapest) to produce various parts of the product, how to market on a global basis and how to finance the deals globally. Such arrangements have ensured that in many cases MNEs have become very powerful networks providing the nucleus of a 'locomotive firm' which attracts other firms into its net and often rewards them handsomely or exploits them mercilessly, in the new game called 'networking'. Beyond the integrated or hierarchical ways of organizing, networking means being able to build connections to get things done without necessarily investing oneself in everything required for the future (Kanter 1989).

SMEs and their opportunity to network

Even small organizations (i.e. SMEs and microfirms) often try to tap into networks by becoming suppliers to larger firms. When a single SME joins such a network a potential niche is left in the market for another SME. Sometimes even the niches are too large and so small firms combine, again as networks, to supply such niches, for example local management consultants joining together to support a government feasibility study. The experience of networking can lead to other networking opportunities. These opportunities can be related to such things as creating economies of scale – the sharing of technology so that new technologies can be adopted, the combining of distinctive competencies to develop new products and services or the combining of resources to conquer new markets, and having clout and influence with suppliers and customers. The name of the game these days is to cooperate or collaborate at one level and to compete at a higher level. All these developments have given rise to a new, more flexible approach to organizing called the 'business network'.

Theories of networks

The study of networks has been dominated by two competing views, to which we could add a number of other theoretical perspectives of lesser influence (Grandori and Soda 1995; Johannisson and Mønsted 1996). One view, championed by theorists such as Walter W. Powell (1990), has sought to establish that the network form is a distinct organizational type very different from other forms of organization based on traditional markets and hierarchies (or the integrated firm). Networks are claimed to have distinct characteristics or 'traits' and thus represent a unique way of doing business based on '...peer group joint decision-making, reciprocal, preferential, mutually supportive actions, trust and informal, extra-contractual agreements' (Ebers and Grandori 1997: 266).

A second view, championed by Oliver Williamson (1985), and drawing heavily on *transaction cost economics*, treats networks as an intermediate or hybrid organizational form in which one is likely to find elements of both markets and hierarchies. From this perspective, many forms of cooperation can be included under the term 'network' (Ebers and Grandori 1997: 266).

Network as a new organization

Powell (1990) is one of the best-known proponents of the view that the network should be treated as a unique organizational form. Powell basically asked the question: if firms were exchanging things such as 'know-how', and were pooling strategically important resources, and their relations were long term and recurrent, did it still make sense to speak of these entities as separate organizations operating competitively and opportunistically, as the market generally dictates (1990: 301)? Moreover, if these entities were 'held together' by other dynamics, such as obligation, indebtedness, reputation and trust, and their interdependence or reliance on each was so embedded, could these entities still be treated the same as organizations that were under one common ownership (e.g. the single firm) or legal agreement? Powell argued that the term 'network' was a more appropriate concept for describing relationships that were not merely the old forms of cooperation, such as many joint ventures, but represented new forms of collaboration (1990: 301). Powell was keen to show that the network was a new type of organization with its own form of governance.

In developing the network concept, Powell sought to differentiate it from markets and hierarchies. While he actually never believed there was such a thing as a pure or perfect market or hierarchy, he believed that the activities in networks were sufficiently unique to differentiate them from more traditional forms of business operation. Table 11.1 provides an adapted version of Powell's now famous distinctions between *market, hierarchy* and *network*.

The market

Powell (1990: 302) depicted the market as a place where opportunistic behaviour and self-interest are the norm, and while this form of behaviour is a key to success in the market, it would not work the same way in networks. In fact, he asserted that those who prosper in markets might well be seen as 'untrustworthy shysters' in the network context. Powell considered the market as a distinct form of business transaction and therefore network relations were unlikely to emerge from market-based relations. In markets, the preferred strategy is to drive a hard bargain, the benefits of the transaction are clear, no trust is required and the

Table 11.1 *Powell's comparison of forms of economic organization*

| | Forms | | |
Key Features	Market	Hierarchy (vertically integrated firm)	Network
Normative basis	Drive the hardest bargain Contracts – classical and spot Property rights Legal sanctions	Employment relationship One's position in the hierarchy matters most Career mobility Personal advancement	Synergistic strengths Relational contract
Means of communication	Formal, limited within context of exchange	Routines/Policies Procedures	Open, relational Communication within the parameters of the network
Methods of conflict resolution	Haggling – resort to courts for enforcement	Administrative – resort to procedures for solution	Norm of reciprocity – Reputational concerns
Degree of flexibility	High – anyone can enter or leave at will	Low, very rigid structure	Medium
Amount of commitment among the parties	Low, individual self-interest, non-cooperative, opportunism	Medium to high	Medium to high
Tone or climate	Precision and/or suspicion	Formal, bureaucratic	Open-ended, mutual benefits
Actor preferences or choices	Independent (arm's length)	Dependent	Interdependent

Source: Adapted from Walter W. Powell (1990), 'Neither market nor hierarchy: Network forms of organization', *Research in Organizational Behavior* (by JAI Press Inc.), 12, p. 300. (All rights of reproduction in any form reserved.)

bargain is supported by legal sanctions (Powell 1990: 302). Market transactions are depicted as entailing very limited personal commitment. While the market is open to any play, there are no future attachments necessary, there are no bonds, just choice, opportunity and flexibility. Communication is simple, price alone decides production and exchange (Powell 1990: 302). In the market situation, Powell said that managers or owners of firms exercise choice as to when they enter or leave the market, they enjoy the flexibility to run their businesses how they see fit, and they are not dependent on others in developing their strategies.

In markets, the classical and spot contracts (as shown in Table 11.1) represent a longer-term agreement that determines the actions of both parties as events unfold. These contracts are legally binding and often follow a period of intense negotiation. Typical classical contracts include leasing agreements, works contracts and bank finance agreements. Spot contracts represent the vast majority of contracts engaged in in the business world; they take place at market prices, are based on standard terms and do not require protracted negotiation. However, firms also engage in spot contracts for their least important expenditure, for example the purchase of stationery. There are numerous situations, however, where the spot contract is not appropriate, and where in its place long-term relationships are obligatory, as Powell suggests.

The hierarchy

Hierarchies, on the other hand, emerge when the firm stretches its boundaries and internalizes transactions hitherto conducted in the market place, for example canners taking over farming organizations. As Powell puts it, '… the visible hand of management supplants the invisible hand of the market' (1990: 303). In the hierarchy (or integrated firm) the employment contract becomes the basis of stability in relations and so careers are important. Relationships are shaped by previous interactions between players. Interorganizational communication is conducted between players, familiar with the firm and each other; the parties become dependent on each other. The main characteristics of hierarchical relations, as described by Powell, are shown in Table 11.1. One of the key characteristics of the hierarchy is that people relate to each other in terms of their status and roles or in terms of their positions in the hierarchy. Rewards in this organization flow from the ability to act in predictable and routine ways.

Powell argued, as have many other theorists, that the hierarchical organization was well suited to the demands of mass production and mass distribution, where high volume, standardization and price were critical to economic success (see Chapter 6). Large, vertically integrated firms, that were created to control their markets both to obtain resources and distribution, depended on the hierarchical form. It was and is also a highly impersonal form of organization that is dominated by rules, regulations and policies.

Inflexibility was and is one of the key features of hierarchies. Most importantly though, this system of administration is seen to be efficient because it is designed to measure and monitor how resources are consumed through the development of controls using complex and detailed systems of reporting and accountability. What is evident from this description is that the hierarchical form of organization (in terms of the integrated firm) is not well suited to conditions of rapid change or sharp fluctuations in markets (Powell 1990: 303). This image of the hierarchical organization, and the one presented in the transaction cost approach discussed below, fails to acknowledge the political and power (see Chapter 4) dimensions present in *all* organizations. Mark Granovetter (1985: 504), for example, suggests that the personal desire of CEOs for self-aggrandizement might just as much motivate the acquisition of another firm (i.e. a takeover or merger) in a hierarchy, while 'efficiency' is merely the language used to justify such actions.

The network

Powell argued that the network involved people looking outside their organization, beyond its boundaries, to form new relationships with other firms to secure critical resources. Many traditional theories of the firm (and strategy) had developed from the view that the prime unit of economic activity was the stand-alone firm, organized in particular ways (e.g. monopoly, oligopoly) to dominate its markets. In the network situation, by contrast, standard behaviour is to create long-term obligations through *relational contracts.* Relational contracts are '…tacit agreements between the parties which are enforced not through legal processes, but through the shared needs of the parties to go on doing business with each other.' (Kay 1993: 55). The parties agree to forgo the right to pursue their own interest at the expense of the other partner. Powell said it takes time to establish and sustain networks, and as time goes on knowledge about the partner assists problem solving, while benefits and encumbrances are shared. In short, the 'entangling strings' of reputation, friendship, interdependence and altruism become integral parts of the relationship (Powell 1990: 304, citing Macneil 1985). But if ever problems do occur, the strategy is to apply normative rather than legal sanctions, for example, threatening to reveal the dishonest behaviour of a partner rather than resorting to legal actions. Ultimately the best insurance against opportunism, however, is the belief that both parties need a long-term perspective in their relationship and must keep doing business with each other.

Networks, Powell claimed, involve '…reciprocal, preferential, mutually supportive actions' (Powell 1990: 304). Powell argued that in network relations, *dependency* was high on the list of resources of another organization or person, but the advantages of pooling resources were equally high. Once this form of interdependence develops, which occurs over a period of time, parties are unable to act on the basis of self-interest alone or opportunistically. Interdependence also means that they no longer control their own destinies as a stand-alone firm might. Powell believed that firms having complementary needs (as opposed to being competitors) was one of the building blocks of successful production networks (see below).

Networks were also considered to provide unique opportunities to be competitive because, according to Powell (1990), they were more flexible and much more effective in the exchange of 'commodities' whose values are difficult to measure, such as know-how, enhancing technological capabilities or transfer, in fostering innovation or experimentation, and sharing valuable information that is not traded readily in the markets or is difficult to extract in hierarchies. He said that networks are best suited to transmitting and learning new knowledge and skills. Powell (1990: 304) suggested that the type of information that is most valued for transmitting and learning new knowledge is more easily accomplished in networks, where personal relations are important.

Intermediate or hybrid form of the network

Transaction cost theory has been applied to explain the behaviour of a wide range of organizational activities including bureaucracy (Williamson 1979), vertical integration of production (Williamson 1991; Klein, Crawford and Alchian 1978), clan-like relations among firms (Ouchi 1980), organizational culture, as well as networks. Transaction costs are associated with an economic exchange, such as costs of monitoring and enforcing contractual agreements. These 'costs' have been termed *transaction costs* by Oliver Williamson (1985). They arise from the fear of opportunism that results when firms specialize to capitalize on what they do best in order to enhance their performance. Three key terms are used by transaction cost theorists:

1   asset specificity;
2   governance structure; and
3   efficiency.

Asset specificity
Transaction cost theorists argue that the fundamentals of economic exchange are built around the costs and benefits that accrue to the owner of a specialized resource. In theory, the benefit to an owner of any specialized resource derives from the fact that they should be able to charge more for its use than for a less specialized resource, and this is what leads firms to pursue specialization. However, the more specialized a resource becomes (i.e. the greater *asset specificity* it has), the fewer alternative uses it generally has. Asset specificity refers to such things as investment in dedicated equipment or a specialized labour force. Thus the buyer of the specialist resource has a degree of 'hold' over the owner or seller of the specialist resource who cannot easily change its use or application, for example, IBM have computer chips produced in the Philippines, but the only customer for such specialized chips is IBM. The Philippine workforce, and the equipment to produce those chips, are totally specialized. The fear of opportunism becomes the cost of such a transaction, which, if uncontrolled, can be destabilizing for the owner of specialized assets. Therefore transaction cost theorists argue that some form of control is called for to provide, at a minimum cost, the mechanisms necessary for parties to believe that engaging or doing business with others in an exchange relationship will make them better off (Williamson 1985).

Governance
In terms of these exchanges, market exchanges can be considered at one end of a continuum, while transaction costs within hierarchies can be considered at the other end of the continuum. According to transaction cost theorists, exchanges that are easy, straightforward or non-repetitive, and require no transaction-specific investments, are likely to take place in markets (e.g. leasing agreements, work contracts, finance agreements). This requires hardly any relationships at all according to transaction cost theorists, only very clearly defined, detailed contracts that reduce the flexibility of each party so that they cannot 'cheat' on each other. Transactions that are repetitive, involve uncertainty and are complex, thus requiring transaction-specific investments, are internalized, for example, power station design and building. This type of relationship requires the kind of administrative relationships that exist in hierarchical organizations. As the features which favour internalization build up, there is a movement away from markets to internalization within a hierarchy.

According to transaction cost theory, when asset specificity is low, then market governance through spot and classical contracts is judged to be the most efficient means of conducting business. The sale of general stationery is conducted via a spot contract, and setting up a loan with a bank is conducted by classical contact. In these cases, buyers and sellers have alternative options. Conversely, when asset specificity and environmental uncertainty are deemed to be high, firms ideally organize through the hierarchy (e.g. a unique, but critical input to a specialized machine, using outsourcing arrangements, however well protected contractually, may still represent a risk the firm is unable to take). Networks fall somewhere in between. Therefore what theorists such as Williamson are saying is that as asset specificity makes a firm more productive, but the fear of exploitation and opportunism, that is, the transaction cost, makes it important for firms to find the right governance structure, that is, between markets and hierarchies. Therefore, the degree of asset specificity and levels of uncertainty will determine what the most efficient governance structure is.

Efficiency

The key to efficiency in the transaction cost approach is to match a governance structure with the level of asset specificity and uncertainty. If a firm fails to do this it can be costly (Hennart 1988). Examples of costs are loss of market discipline where a firm pays over the odds for a component, or being cheated because the firm has not contractually safeguarded its transaction. Transaction cost theory is built around the assumption that competitive economic behaviour is based on the pursuit of self-interest, but also opportunism, guile and deceit. Individuals are portrayed as subtle and devious creatures operating in predictable, socialized ways. Malfeasance is the norm in the market place (Granovetter 1985: 487–489). Indeed, one of the principles of transaction cost discourse is that decision makers have limited information (bounded rationality) and might pursue their self-interest with incomplete or misleading information disclosure (i.e. engage in opportunism) (see also Chapter 8).

Transaction cost theorists view hierarchies as an efficient, impersonal means by which to curb malfeasance and opportunism beyond market transactions. Hierarchies are deemed efficient in curbing opportunism because management is in control of all decision making. They see no significant role for personal or social relations either in helping to build trust or curbing malfeasance and opportunism, even in networks (Granovetter 1985: 490–1). While Williamson has acknowledged that trustworthy behaviour can extend into market relations, and such things as a firm's reputation for fairness might be an important asset, he maintains that transactions based on personal relations are the exception and not the rule in the way business is or ought to be conducted.

Transaction cost theory has been heavily criticized for presenting the behaviour of markets and hierarchies as though social dimensions and contexts have no part to play in explaining business and organizational practices. Personal relations are seen as irrational forms of behaviour, while self-interest and opportunism are 'plainly' more sensible and likely (Granovetter 1985: 506). The transaction cost approach ignores the *embeddedness* of these forms of economic activity in social and cultural forces (Granovetter 1985: 490; Grabher 1993; Powell 1990: 299). Thus a transaction cost approach would argue that one incentive in the market place for not cheating is the cost of damage this might cause one's reputation. The embeddedness approach suggests that we establish the reputation of a person or business not just on the bases of some general economic motive (a firm not cheating because it will damage its reputation), but also through either what some trusted informant might have to say about their experiences with the person or firm in question, or preferably, our past dealings with the said person or firm. In other words, social relations create strong expectations about trust and the absence of opportunism in dealings with others (Granovetter 1985: 490–1). Granovetter, a staunch critic of the transaction cost approach, argues, however, that the social or more personal nature of trust-based relations also creates opportunities for malfeasance, such as cheating, confidence rackets, fraud, kick-backs and so on (Granovetter 1985: 493). However, unlike transaction cost theory, the embeddedness approach does not suggest that malfeasance is the norm – context and social relations play an important part in explaining all transactions (see Introduction).

Legacies of network theories

A number of legacies remain from these early conceptualizations of network theory. The study of networking has been dominated by efforts to:

- classify network types;
- identify the 'costs' and 'benefits' of networking and the impediments to networking;
- explain the competitive advantages firms derive from networking; and
- develop theories of trust in cooperation and collaboration.

More recently, and associated with these trends, has been a focus on organizational learning, or how firms extract new forms of knowledge from network arrangements that enhance their core competence (Lei 1997; Lütz 1997; Dyer and Singh 1996; Levinson and Asahi 1995; Hamel 1991; Parkhe 1991; Doz, Hamel and Prahalad 1989). We actually introduce the concept of the 'learning network' (see below) to describe those networks in which knowledge that affects at least one of the partners' core competences is traded or exchanged.

The cross-cultural aspects of networking have also received attention in the literature with the growth of international or cross-boarder alliances and globalization during the 1990s (De Laat 1997: 147–8).

Classification of networks

As networks became more prominent strategies, scholars began to classify them. From the literature, we can distil a hierarchy of network classifications. We have included in this clas-sification more conventional forms of cooperation such as licensing and franchising and joint ventures. This is done because these forms of cooperation have often been the bases for more novel forms of cooperation and collaboration that we have identified at the beginning of the chapter as falling under the network 'umbrella'. As already mentioned, we also intro-duce the concept of a *learning network* and restrict this to those networks that involve the exchange or sharing of resources or activities affecting members' core competence (Lei 1997; Lütz 1997). Broadly speaking, many networks involve different forms of learning (see Levinson and Asahi 1995), but the focus on the learning network is on the trading of tacit knowledge (also see Chapter 8).

A number of different classification systems have emerged in the network literature and some of the more common ones are listed in Exhibit 11.2 and will be covered in this part of the chapter.

- Vertical and horizontal networks
- Pooled and complementary networks
- Product and service networks
- Number of firms in the network
- Strategic focus
- Learning networks
- Power relations

Exhibit 11.2 Classification of network types

Vertical and horizontal networks

At the broadest level, networks are classified according to whether they are *vertical* systems that extend along the value-adding chain (see Chapter 10), for example buyer and supplier relationships (e.g. the Toyota network of component suppliers) and franchises, or whether they are *horizontal* systems or arrangements that continue at the same stage of the value-adding chain, for example a group of oyster growers forming a network to market their products nationally and internationally.

Pooled and complementary networks

If a network fits into the *horizontal classification*, two further subdimensions apply, pooled and complementary alliances. This second-level classification is based on the work of Bryan Borys and David Jemison (1989) and relates to the idea of *competitive domain overlap*. If network partners compete head on and share common opportunities and threats, if they belong to the same strategic group because they share a similar past, and are from the same industry sector, the resulting arrangement may be referred to as a *pooled* network, for example the Airbus programme which was formed from a consortium of French, Dutch, German, Spanish, British and Italian aerospace manufacturers to develop, manufacture and market the A300 and A310 aircraft.

Competitors tend to join forces because projects are outside the financial reach of a single company, examples being in such industries as telecommunications, aerospace or pharmaceutical sectors. Sometimes competitors combine to deal with major environmental threats, as was the case in selected horticultural sectors in Australia where agents exploited the fragmented industry structure. Economies of scale and scope are also powerful motivators in forging pooled networks. There is evidence that the 'collisions' between competitors in the pooled network tend to be short lived and fail to achieve their strategic and financial goals: 'Most collisions between competitors end in dissolution, acquisition by the other partner or a merger' (Bleeke and Ernst 1995: 101). When direct competitors commence a network, conflict tends to be widespread, involving disagreements regarding target customers, product selection and whose factory to choose for the joint operations. In order to resolve the problems, the partners tend to have to move closer towards integration, that is, they need to merge or alternatively dissolve the alliance.

Alternatively, if partners do not compete, perhaps even come from differing industries, the resulting network may be termed a *complementary* network, in which case the participants may seek to combine differing strengths, for example the complementary alliance set up between Lipton Tea and Pepsico to market iced tea in cans. Complementary networks stand a much better chance of survival, especially if the network involves two strong partners who maintain their strengths during the course of the relationship. These mutually beneficial networks are likely to enjoy longevity beyond seven years.

Complementary networks are strongest when they combine resources or capabilities that are unique and therefore difficult to imitate within a single firm because of the scarcity of the collectively owned resource, or when the combined resources or capabilities are idiosyncratic (hard to imitate) and indivisible (cannot be obtained from a partner outside the alliance) (Dyer and Singh 1996: 19).

Production, service and learning networks

The third level relates to the *tangibility of the cooperative benefit* and draws on the work of Joe Burke (1990). One subclassification measures if all partners are involved in operating together on one or more projects to create a tangible product; if this is the case, the *production* network emerges. If partners simply jointly buy or provide a service (e.g. marketing) that does not result in the joint ownership of anything, the *service* network emerges. A competitive advantage may be derived from a third type of collaboration, the *learning* network, where firms seek out national and international partners who provide leading-edge expertise in areas of core competence. We will have more to say about the learning network below. Of all the network types, this probably represents the greatest opportunities and threats to network members.

Figure 11.1 illustrates the various types of networks considered so far. Exhibit 11.3 provides examples of the network types shown in Figure 11.1.

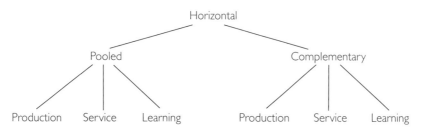

Figure 11.1   Hierarchy of networks classification of horizontal relations

- **Pooled production network** a group of growers who set up a joint sorting and packing operation.
- **Complementary production network** Kentucky Fried Chicken (KFC) combining its operational skills and store format with Mitsubishi's site selection skills in Japan to establish a KFC chain in Japan.
- **Pooled service network** a number of hotels pooling advertising dollars to promote the region's tourist attractions.
- **Complementary service network** a selection of enterprises in education, manufacturing or tourism pooling advertising dollars to promote an entire region.
- **Complementary learning alliance** the forging of an alliance between Siemens with its strength in global telecommunications and cable manufacturing technology and Corning with its technological expertise in optical fibres and glass to create leading-edge technology in fibre optics.
- **Pooled learning alliance** a number of dental laboratories combining to develop state-of-the-art dental implant technology.

Exhibit 11.3   Examples of different types of horizontal networks

Number of firms in network

Alter and Hage (1993: 23) introduce another important distinction based on the *number of firms* in a network. They argue that the term 'interorganizational relations' (IORs) refers principally to dyadic relations, where only two parties (organizations) are involved. They would cite many joint ventures as examples of IORs. They would reserve the term 'network' for *multiple* relationships involving at least three or more parties or partners, sometimes even competitors (see also Fulop with Kelly 1995; 1997a: iii). In fact, they argue that when the relationships between multiple partners are aggregated, then a *network* emerges (Alter and Hage 1993: 23). Alter and Hage believe these *multiorganizational networks* are the really interesting new developments in cooperation and collaboration.

They argue that networks with many members find it harder to cooperate or collaborate than do IORs with dyadic or triadic membership (three organizations). In the networking situation one often hears that the ideal size of the group is four to six members. Once a group gets too large for an individual to weigh up trust and the aims and preferences of colleagues, and cope with different personalities, the group can become less cohesive and more prone to opportunistic behaviour. For some theorists the very notion of social exchange implies a limited number of partners to ensure better communication and coordination so that there is stability of membership and a more focused use of resources (Ring 1997a: 115). But more importantly, many theories of trust have been based on studies of the dyadic relationship, that is, how trust develops between two people on a personal level and not among a group of people, and particularly people who are strangers and might even be competitors.

For the purposes of this chapter, we intend to address both IORs and networks. We also intend to distinguish networks from other forms of 'cooperation', for example mergers, takeovers and acquisitions, that are forms of vertical integration, on the basis that a network arrangement only exists while the majority of participating members or organizations remain *separate entities*. One of the reasons why organizations enter into network arrangements is to avoid the problems, particularly the power struggles, legal battles, bad publicity, etc., that often come with takeovers and mergers.

Strategic focus

Both vertical and horizontal networks, and the various subclassifications under them (see Figure 11.1), can be further categorized. To gain a competitive edge, organizations may consider five broad categories of cooperative and collaborative arrangements, and each of these is described in more detail below:

1 Licensing and franchising
2 Supplier – buyer relationships
3 Joint ventures
4 Consortia
5 Supplier alliances along entire value-added chain

Licensing and franchising

An unsophisticated, yet potent form of cooperation, especially in the service sector, is represented by licensing, which involves the purchase of the right to use an asset for a particular time, and offers rapid access to new products, technologies or innovations (Borys and

Jemison 1989). The pursuit of a licensing strategy permits a firm to control product image and quality while requiring little financial investment. Licensors must, however, secure substantial training, set adequate standards of performance, and define compensation; their lack can represent a serious threat to the licensing arrangements. The major benefits of licensing include the ability to reach large, often unexploited markets quickly, and permit expansion where local laws hinder direct foreign investment. Also, in the manufacturing context, the strategy can be gainful when resources are limited and would otherwise hinder the speedy, global diffusion of technology.

Licensing has been of benefit to Sun Microsystems, who developed their innovation by using Philips' production and distribution expertise. Sun Microsystems expects that its chips will be utilized in other Philips' consumer electronic products while simultaneously gaining access to the European market. Licensing arrangements, as a rule, are enforceable by contract, but the strategy is not without risks, and the risks are magnified if the licensor transfers core competence technology, or if the transfer occurs across frontiers where licensing arrangements are sometimes hard to enforce. RCA licensed its colour technology to the Japanese only to find that the Japanese competitors were beating RCA in developing related technologies. We will have more to say about this aspect of franchising when we consider learning networks.

Franchising too improves control without takeover or merger. Here trademarks, management assistance and know-how are granted in return for lump-sum payments, royalties and compliance with the rules and procedures of the franchisor. The concept of franchising is widespread and in the USA around 2000 companies in 50 industries have marketed their product through franchising (David 1993). Part of the reason for its success is the speed at which expansion can take place owing to the spread of costs and opportunities among many individuals. Readers will be well aware of the many global franchise arrangements which include KFC, McDonald's, Century 21, Coca Cola, Avis, Singer and Yoplait.

Supplier–buyer relationships

Supplier–buyer relationships, also referred to as sequential or vertical alliances, are based on contracts where one firm's output is purchased by another. Under a supplier–buyer arrangement, buyers must ensure that suppliers' transformation processes, capacity and inputs meet their quantitative and qualitative requirements in a timely manner, while the supplier designs a product that meets the appropriate technical standards and delivery schedules of the purchaser. The vertical alliance may start its life cycle as a contractual arrangement between the buyer and the supplier (i.e. market transaction). As the relationship proves beneficial, it is likely to be converted into a single sourcing arrangement, and ultimately the supplier becomes an important part of the buyer's product and marketing process. Close relationships have been forged between the Italian giant Bennetton and the British retailer Marks and Spencer and their corresponding suppliers.

Chrysler's stunning revival has been attributed to the company's rethink regarding supplier relationships (Dyer 1996). As was the case with many Western car manufacturers, Chrysler's relationship with its suppliers was one of distrust and suspicion. Suppliers were chosen on the lowest cost per component, ignored when they had cost-saving ideas and not consulted on design. Today, suppliers come in at the early stages of the car concept development stage, the company and its suppliers work side by side to develop components, management solicit cost-saving ideas and share any savings. Jeffrey Dyer (1996) reports that the company enjoyed savings of $1.7 billion per annum from these relationships, proving that highly productive partnerships are the wave of the future.

Nevertheless, the supplier–buyer network can be considered a double-edged sword, leading to long term collaboration that brings about less monitoring and fewer defects and increased quality, or alternatively moving to an arm's length relationship emphasizing curtailed costs, diminished trade union power and employment opportunities (Macneil 1978). The dependence means that firms must have a close interest in the health of the supplying firm, while at the same time seeking out low-cost components.

Joint ventures

A joint venture refers to two or more organizations forming a separate enterprise for cooperative purposes. When it comprises only two partners it is an IOR. Within the new business, partners of the joint venture decide strategy and make decisions. Joint ventures are often formed to gain economies of scale, especially in mature industries such as steel production and car manufacture or for R&D purposes. USX, for example, has formed a joint venture with Pohang Iron and Steel in South Korea in a 50–50 venture.

Organizations team up to gain economies of scope, for example to develop full production lines as was the case for the joint venture between Nestlé and General Food, or to improve related skills so as to strengthen an already existing competence. General Motors and Toyota desired to enhance their similar substantial expertise in their field by joining a partner who already was an expert. IORs of compatible but complementary equals have enjoyed great success by combining their strengths to create value. Pepsico's expertise in marketing canned drinks combined with Lipton's considerable image as a major tea brand to sell jointly iced tea in cans would be an example.

More often though, joint ventures are struck to learn new technological, production or marketing skills (through R&D and new product or process developments). Asian companies as a rule have benefited more from such joint ventures in the past, often because the Asian partner assists the market entry into the Asian market, while the Western company provides technical expertise. The former is frequently founded in personal relationships between the Asian firm and the Asian market, and therefore cannot be transferred, while the technical expertise once transferred, can be enjoyed by the Asian firm. Indeed, GE and Samsung are now competing head on in kitchen appliances following an alliance in the field of microwave ovens. Joint ventures between Western companies can be very successful, for example, as the marriage of Ericsson's technological strength in telecommunication with Hewlett-Packard's computer and software expertise to market network management systems proves.

A joint venture may also represent an alternative strategy to putting a business up for sale because it does not suffer from plummeting morale of employees, and prospective buyers are able to assess the true value of intangible assets. According to Ashish Nanda and Peter Williamson (1995), the proof is the successful joint venture between Whirlpool and Philips and the poor result of the Maytag purchase of Chicago Pacific. Philips and Whirlpool had used the joint venture option in the late 1980s as a restructuring tool: by 1991 Philips managed to receive a substantially higher price than it would have gained through a direct sale, while Whirlpool had established a strong European presence. In contrast, Maytag chose to enter the European white goods market by buying Chicago

Pacific. The lack of a transition period during which management could acquire a thorough understanding of the European market proved costly, with Maytag booking a $130 million loss in the process.

While the management burden of restructuring joint ventures can be heavy to avoid, the benefits can more than outstrip the efforts. According to Joel Bleeke and David Ernst (1995), disguised sales partnerships, such as mergers, rarely last more than five years.

Consortia

Consortia involve a number of firms pooling their resources into an integrated organization, leading to economies of scale and the efficient use of specialist equipment and resources. Often, the consortium represents the only means of avoiding duplication of projects within a national economy or developing large, complex projects.

Within the European Community, consortia were being set up to increase the competitiveness of high-tech industries such as micro electronics and semi-conductors. A very successful program is the Airbus arrangement, which requires cooperation between partners from different European nationalities. In the USA, consortia became legal in 1984 when Congress passed the Cooperative Research Act. Since then numerous consortia have sprung up in biotechnology, energy, telecommunications and car manufacturing.

In some instances, consortia prospered through the support of regional governments, often also tied to broad industry sectors; examples are the consortia representing the silk industry around Lyon in France, the garment and fashion industry around Milan, Italy and Baden Württemberg, Germany, and the diamond trade in Holland. In every instance, the driving force of the consortium is bringing about critical mass in R&D technology and marketing. Associated with this feature is cost reduction for individual firms, risk diversification and increased economies of scale and scope, often underpinned by close supplier–buyer relationships. For the government, increasing the competitiveness of a region and avoiding unnecessary duplication of R&D and increased specialization are the pay-off.

Asia too boasts its consortia. In Korea, the *chaebol,* translated as 'financial clique', is used to describe a large business group created by an entrepreneur and spread over many diversified areas. The *chaebol* is a creation of the Korean Government, which identified talented individuals in the 1960s and systematically sponsored them by granting preferential import licences, credit and tax and afforded them domestic protection. Among the *Fortune 500* companies, 12 Korean *chaebols* rival Western business. The largest, Samsung, taps into nationalism, reflected in its motto 'we do business for the sake of nation building'. Consisting of 25 enterprises, the *chaebol* manufactures everything from VCRs, aircraft, hydraulics, consumer appliances, chemicals, commercial vehicles and computer chips. In their effort to become leading global organizations, many *chaebols* have entered in to a series of cooperative ventures with overseas companies.

In Japan, the concept of cooperation or long-term obligational ties and implicit contracts (Scher 1997: 3) is part of the national culture. Most Japanese describe themselves in terms of their place in a network of relationships rather than as individuals. The Japanese firm also defines its role and status through its relationship with other firms rather than as a stand-alone organization (Lasserre and Schuette 1995). The Japanese consortium, the *keiretsu*, combines 25 to 50 companies of the same industry as vertically affiliated members owned by a bank or trading company. Along side the *keiretsu*, which is based on feudal and asymmetrical power relations, is the clan form, or *kigyo shudan*, which comprises firms no longer owned by a holding company and in which relations are based on a system of colle-gial, non-competitive behaviour. Mitsubishi, for example, now comprises a number of firms on an equal footing, but the *kigyo shudan* still depends on the group's trading company to help develop joint ventures (Scher 1997: 9–10). Apart from these vertically and horizontally organized groups, which rotate staff and share a belief in *kaisha*, the dogma of long-term growth rather than short-term profitability, vertical agglomerations of a large number of SMEs under the umbrella of a major manufacturer are commonplace through the *keiretsu* (Scher 1997: 10). The Toyota production system linking 10000 subcontractors is the most famous example.

Strategic alliances along the entire value-added chain

We have already looked at vertical networks that link buyers and suppliers. The link can be made even more powerful if it extends the complete length of the value-added chain (see Chapter 10). The vertical *keiretsu* discussed above is well known for buying and selling goods at every step of the value-added chain in a global market environment. Alliances along the value-added chain involve a '…set of independent companies that work closely together to manage the flow of goods and services along the entire value-added chain' (Johnston and Lawrence 1988: 94). A typical manufactured product would display a value-added chain (see Chapter 10) such as the one shown below:

Farmer–agent–processor–distributor–retailer–end consumer

The value-added chain is concerned with showing how value is added at each stage of producing and distributing a product. In the case shown above, the crops (the farmer's products) are grown by the farmer and it costs money to make sure that a seed turns into a suitable crop. It takes fertilizers and a combination of labour, technology and time to ensure the product is suitable for the market. The value added by the farmer is costed in this way. Of course the farmer is not an agent and the agent adds more value by taking over the product and undertaking the distribution to an organization which processes the raw product, perhaps packaging it or putting it in tins. This adds even more value to that added by the farmer and the agent. So it goes on throughout the chain perhaps through a retailer and then to the final customer. The chain is therefore concerned with identifying what value is added at each stage.

A Western example is provided by the McKesson Corporation who have built a network of distributors, manufacturers, retailers, consumers and medical insurance companies through facilitating technology. Its success, however, is also derived from instilling a whole value-added chain culture that supports the realization of all players in the chain that they need to contribute to the success of the whole chain.

The learning network

In this section of the chapter we examine three key concepts:

1 Core competence
2 Tacit and explicit knowledge
3 Credible commitments

Core competence

In Chapter 10 we introduced the 'resource-based view' of strategy. Its proponents generally argue that in order to maintain competitive advantage, different types of firm-specific resources, such as skills and capabilities, particularly know-how, can be enhanced through cooperation and collaboration (Lei 1997: 209). In the case of SMEs and microfirms, knowledge acquisition and transfer, which is often taken for granted in many large firms, is only possible through cooperation and collaboration, and the network becomes a rare source of knowledge diffusion for these firms (Reve 1995: 10). David Lei (citing Prahalad and Hamel 1990) suggests that all firms can build or enhance their core competence by working across the boundaries of their organization. In very simple terms, core competences are '...a bundle of firm-specific knowledge, skills, technological capabilities and an organization that form the basis of the firm's ability to create value in ways that other competitors cannot do so easily' (Lei 1997: 211). As Lei points out, core competences are dependent on different types and forms of knowledge being learnt by people over many years as they enhance their skills, adapt to change, experiment with new technologies and applications or gather information and organizational intelligence. Core competencies are interwoven into the 'social fabric' of the organization, where they are largely 'invisible' and 'embedded' in the daily routines and practices of the organization and in the complex social relations of people who work in it (Lei 1997: 211). In effect, a firm's core competence is *context specific* and is therefore hard to imitate or even fully fathom.

Core competences can be both the source of advantage over competitors and a disadvantage to the organization. Lei (1997: 211–12) says that because knowledge accumulation occurs over long periods of time a firm's capabilities, and hence its future directions, are constrained by what it has done and learnt in the past. It is limited by the types of information and knowledge it has invested in over the years, including the people it has employed, to create its core competence. Each firm or organization also develops a unique core competence, whether this turns out to be adequate or inadequate to sustain a competitive advantage. In effect, core competences are *idiosyncratic* because they are built through unique organizational relations, practices, routines and discourses. In this sense, every organization has to live with its own history, culture, politics, past decisions and circumstances, which collectively 'act' as an 'irreversible' investment in the future. No organization can totally reinvent itself or start over again from scratch.

In developing their core competences, firms and organizations can gain advantage from 'lock in', which means they have learnt skills and knowledge that are usually highly specialized, likely to be sustainable for a while and are also untradable. Something that is untradable is hard to value in dollar terms, difficult to sell and often indecipherable to outsiders. The intellectual capital of an organization comprises what many would describe as an untradable 'asset'. To understand what constitutes another organization's core competence, an outsider would have to understand fully, and have 'access' to, the whole repertoire of skills and knowledge embedded in an organization's dynamic routines, practices, politics, culture and the multiple and complex relations that bind people to the organization (Lei 1997: 212; Levinson and Asahi 1995). Without the capacity to learn and change, an organization and its people are unable to get ahead of competitors or even keep up with them and thus become incapable of influencing the environment in which they have to compete or operate (Lei 1997: 212). 'Lock in' gives a firm or an organization the advantage of being able to search out and find new ways of building or redefining its competencies and knowledge base.

However, the downside of developing a firm's core competence is that it also creates the potential danger of 'lock out'. Lei argues that this happens when a firm or organization is unable to change and/or build new competences because it has become so dependent on what it has done in the past, usually very successfully, and has invested heavily in certain resources, routines and practices that lock it into a hopeless future. An organization and its management can become incapable of redeploying or reacquiring highly specialized and non-tradable 'assets'. Lei gives the example of the US consumer electronics industry in the 1970s which failed to invest in new skills and technologies, such as miniaturization and automated production (e.g. CAD/CAM and robotics) that became the bases of the next generation of televisions, VCRs, multimedia equipment and compact disc technologies (Lei 1997: 213).

Firms therefore need to develop both a firm-specific core competence (i.e. they need to 'lock in') as well as ensuring that they avoid the traps of being 'locked out' to such an extent that they lose all their capacity to assimilate new technologies, knowledge and skills in their field. One way of trying to protect against 'lock out' is to enter into cooperative and collaborative arrangements with other organizations through a process of *interorganizational learning*. While firms can invest in their own R&D and undertake a whole range of activities, such as continuous improvement, poaching employees from competitors and developing new products and processes, the evidence from the literature suggests that most innovations in products, processes and technology emerge from sources external to the organization. Through copying or importing ideas and practices learnt from suppliers, competitors and customers, for example, many organizations are able to innovate in their own right (Dyer and Singh 1996: 9; Lei 1997). However, networking is a way of trying to develop superior inter-firm knowledge-sharing routines and practices that can help accelerate the innovation process, reduce costs and speed up the commercialization of products (Dyer and Singh 1996: 10; De Laat 1997; Lei 1997: 215).

Tacit and explicit knowledge

Networking involves two key strategies that can enhance a firm or organization's core competence in the context of interorganizational learning, and this occurs principally through knowledge sharing and building up complementary resource endowments, as already described above in the discussion of complementary networks (Dyer and Singh 1996). As we mentioned in Chapter 8, there are two kinds of knowledge that are seen as having strategic importance in organizations: *tacit knowledge* and *explicit knowledge*, and the knowledge firms are most reluctant to trade or exchange is tacit knowledge. Despite evidence indicating that most innovations come from external influences (see above), and not from internal R&D, for example, the fact remains that firms or organizations are reluctant to cooperate or collaborate in areas that are strategically important to them in developing what they define as their core competence and their distinct competitive advantage (Lütz 1997: 222). Those that do, qualify as learning networks.

For firms or organizations that operate under conditions of uncertainty (e.g. rapidly changing markets, technology or customer demand) and have complex, knowledge-intensive products (e.g. large numbers of interdependent components, functions or processes), there is high value and urgency associated with 'non-contractible' activities such as innovation, flexibility, responsiveness and knowledge sharing. These firms or organizations in particular have to find ways of sharing and acquiring knowledge through relational exchanges (Dyer and Singh 1996: 30–1; see also Powell 1990).

Exhibit 11.4 describes the types of knowledge that are considered to fall into the tacit and explicit categories.

Tacit knowledge

- Unwritten know-how
- Ways of solving problems
- Imagination, creativity
- Craftsmanship
- Artisan-like skills
- Metaphors
- Myths and stories
- Symbols
- Discourses

Explicit knowledge

- Blueprints for design
- All forms of formulae
- Technical specifications
- Training manuals
- Circuit patterns
- Steps in a manufacturing process
- Specifications
- Best practice benchmarks
- Industry standards

Exhibit 11.4   Tacit and explicit knowledge

Source: Adapted and modified from David Lei (1997), 'Competence-building, technology fusion and competitive advantage: The key roles of organizational learning and strategic alliances', International Journal of Technology Management 14 (2/3/4), p. 213 and Chapter 8.

As already mentioned in Chapter 8, tacit knowledge refers to know-how, while explicit knowledge is said to embody information that is written down, encoded, explained and understandable by any one with some expertise in a specific field. Tacit knowledge, by contrast, is 'sticky', complex and difficult to codify, interpret and understand (see Lei 1997: 213–14; Dyer and Singh 1996: 10–11). Moreover, tacit knowledge is context specific or embedded in organizational routines, practices and relationships, and is part of sense making that draws on various forms of knowledge and experiences (see Chapters 1 and 8). When Apple Computers, for example, was designing the Macintosh computer, one of the metaphors that drove the design team was that the computer was to make people feel 'warm and fuzzy'. The Macintosh design team flew the 'Jolly Roger' (pirate) flag over its building to symbolize that they were the 'bad kids' of the company who were allowed to break rules. They were also incredibly selective in who they allowed into the team.

Tacit knowledge is embodied or captured in organizational discourses and, as we described in Chapter 8, these provide the descriptions, rules, permissions and limits of actions of groups, such as a project team, and of individuals (see Chapter 8, pp. 310–12). In other words, discourses give expression and meaning to power in particular contexts and actions. It is no surprise then that there is considerable debate in the management literature as to whether or not tacit knowledge is something organizations can 'manage', control or direct in any purposeful way. Knowledge, whether described as tacit or explicit, is not neutral and is influenced by power, and what becomes defined as tradable or revealable, or even valued as knowledge, depends on how particular discourses operate across different organizations.

Tacit knowledge is so context specific and comprises different texts and genres (see Chapter 8), and is therefore difficult to learn, copy or imitate in arm's length relationships. So firms or organizations look to networks and strategic alliances to achieve these ends. Lei maintains that core competencies rest on firms developing both forms of knowledge, but it is tacit knowledge which gives an organization its dynamic routines and practices, both of which are so important to innovation and change. Indeed, he says firms or managers who build their core competence on explicit knowledge, which is usually product or process embedded, are not building a sustainable core competence (Lei 1997: 215; see also Chapter 8). Irrespective of patents, almost everything involving explicit knowledge can be copied.

Networks and alliances that are formed principally to trade in explicit knowledge do not often require close interaction and are largely based on contractual relations, which are also more likely to encourage opportunism (Lei 1997: 215; also see De Laat 1997). In joint ventures, in particular, the trading or sharing of explicit knowledge often means that another firm with a strong intent to learn, and having a comparable knowledge base, is able to acquire this knowledge, whether it is technological, marketing or production related, and eventually decode the knowledge and recombine it into their own core competence. Disloyal partners can start competing with their alliance partner and make the partner dependent on them for future components, and even the next generation of new products. Alternatively, they can 'go it alone' and become direct competitors of the joint venture or alliance partner (Lei 1997: 215; De Laat 1997: 150). As we already mentioned, this was particularly evident in strategic alliances formed between Japanese and US and European companies with the Japanese partner often becoming a competitor against its alliance partner or the joint venture firm (Lei 1997: 215). For this reason the cooperation of these networks is usually very limited and remains largely based on contractual arrangements that are often detailed and highly codified. This form of contract encourages limited commitment and so will usually invite the risk of opportunism, such as cheating, stealing secrets, partners meeting only minimal obligations, starving the alliance of resources, and not committing the best people to the venture (De Laat 1997: 149–56; Ring 1997a: 120).

When it comes to sharing tacit knowledge in network relations, organizations cannot hope to achieve this in an arm's length relationship, but must enter into an 'apprenticeship' relationship or some form of relationship that involves '…long term, dense social interactions' (Dyer and Singh 1996: 11; Lei 1997: 216). Staff will have to be exchanged, premises opened up or even combined and secrets shared. As already mentioned in Chapter 8, knowhow is typically transferred or learnt in direct, intimate relationships and with extensive face to face exposure. Individuals or small groups sharing know-how have to develop their own unique language and discourse to transmit complex forms of 'sticky' knowledge (Dyer and Singh 1996: 12, citing Kogurt and Zander 1988: 389).

However, one of the great risks of sharing tacit knowledge is, as Paul De Laat notes (as do others), the problem of inequity. Rarely are partners on equal terms and the stronger partner can, if they are technologically superior, 'outlearn' the other partner (De Laat 1997: 167). Lei also suggests that differential learning rates (or the absorptive capacity of organizations) will significantly affect the bargaining power of alliance partners. He says that '…disparities in organizational receptivity to learning, knowledge embeddedness and strategic intent will work to favour one partner's "outlearning" the other in absorbing and internalizing the skills over time' (Lei 1997: 216). In a similar vein, others argue that the ability to learn in the interorganizational context is related to the 'absorptive capacity' of an organization or its managers and this means having the ability to unpackage, assimilate and act upon new knowledge and know-how. It also means being able to create, for example, the necessary dialogue, communication and language to achieve this, or, in other words, a new network discourse (Dyer and Singh 1996: 13–14; Levinson and Asahi 1995: 58–60). This capacity is not equally distributed in many networks, and often learning networks are used as races to 'outlearn' a partner or become a 'competition for competence' (Lei 1997: 216).

Credible commitments

De Laat (1997: 167) also warns that inequity in resources, for example the superior market or financial position of one partner over another, is also an incentive for organizations to 'run off' with jointly developed projects or results. The incentives for knowledge sharing (transferring) and knowledge acquisition (receiving) are inherently unequal in many instances and mutual benefits are difficult to achieve (see discussion below on power). De Laat (1997: 151) suggests that this is why, in the case of R&D, separate research companies or consortia are favoured over joint ventures. In the consortia or separate companies, cooperation or collaboration is non-competitive and the hazards of knowledge abuse are greatly reduced because results are incorporated into a differentiated product from those of the alliance partners or destined for different markets. For example, the alliance between Philips and Siemens in the 1980s to develop integrated circuits saw Philips focus on SRAMs and Siemens on DRAMs. The memory chips were for different applications in different markets: SRAMs in telecommunication equipment in professional markets and DRAMs for the upgrade of electronic products for consumers. In this arrangement both parties had agreed to exchange all relevant knowledge (De Laat 1997: 151).

De Laat describes a number of elaborate forms of *credible commitments* that organizations use on their own or along with other forms of contracts to make it possible to share know-how. Commitment represents an explicit or implicit pledge of relational continuity between partners (Dwyer, Schurr and Oh 1987). These include such agreements as 'phased commitments' or partners agreeing to share knowledge as the alliance unfolds and not upfront. Another is 'mutual commitments' where partners agree to suspend or limit their own independent research while participating in the alliance. De Laat says that when firms are willing to negotiate credible commitments they actually provide tangible proof or watertight guarantees that they will faithfully execute the agreement (1997: 156–60). He also suggests that as credible commitments are built up and executed, trust of a very resilient kind emerges (De Laat 1997: 163–5). Learning networks would have to be more dependent on credible commitments than classical contracts alone in order to facilitate the sharing of tacit knowledge.

To illustrate how a learning network might emerge, with the sharing of tacit knowledge and credible commitments, the following case study, entitled 'A learning network', adapted from research by Susanne Lütz (1997), is included. This is a very interesting case because it shows how a third-party or intermediary, in this case, a number of research institutes, helped to create collaboration. The role of third parties in network formation has not been well researched (see Fulop with Kelly 1997b: 82–8).

A learning network

The case study refers to a multilateral research collaboration, conducted as part of the German government programme on production technologies, sponsored by the Federal Ministry for Research and Technology. The project, 'Adhesion as a Production Technology', represents an example of a quite demanding and, at the same time, successful, multilateral network, both in terms of innovation and its level of collaboration. Technologically, the research group was able to prove that an alternative manufacturing technology, that is adhesive bonding, could be employed in those areas of industrial production where, historically, welding technology had previously dominated. A lack of basic knowledge concerning a scientifically sound understanding of adhesion, as well as general construction rules, but also uncertainty with respect to the application in repetitive processes of mass production, characterized the research at the onset of the project. Multilateral research successfully demonstrated the technical feasibility of adhesion as a mass production technology, established a sound body of chemical and physical knowledge and substantiated pilot applications under actual working conditions.

In terms of cooperation, a network evolved [of partners] who had never collaborated before: the research group consisted of 20 participants, among them scientific institutes Fraunhofer-Institut fur Angewandte Materialforschung (IFaM) and Laboratorium fur Werkstoff- und Fugetech- nik (LWF) at Paderborn University doing basic research and providing testing facilities. Two steel producers (Hoesch and Thyssen) provided the materials to be connected, and eight adhesive producers individually developed a great number of adhesives. A user's perspective was introduced by two automobile producers (Volkswagen (VW) and Audi), who first specified their requirements regarding the adhesive products, and finally tested them.

It should be stressed that this kind of network was genuinely new because different types of interdependency were connected for the first time: horizontally, a large group of adhesive competitors worked together, primarily adhesive producers, but also steel suppliers. Vertically, adhesive and steel suppliers collaborated with customers from the automobile industry. Scientific institutes, however, played a crucial role in this setting of actors: since they conducted tests on the products of each participating firm, they were linked to each industrial partner. One particular consequence of this was that scientific partners acted as brokers between competing adhesive producers.

Although each of the adhesive competitors developed an adhesive of their own, they were nevertheless linked to each other via the scientific intermediaries: the institutes tested the adhesives and gave accounts of their specific properties to each project member. By informing each competing producer about the 'state of the art' of adhesive technology among the group of rivals, institutes created a state of almost complete information – each competitor came to know about his rival's capacities to fulfil the requirements of the users from the automobile industry [thus creating credible commitments]. The special intermediary role scientific partners played within the group was one of the main factors which made the process of network formation successful in the end.

Linked by scientific intermediaries, a research group evolved, transcending well beyond the scope of conventional R&D projects. For the first time, this network allowed the combination of different types of know-how, which, by being synthesized [created new tacit knowledge]: fundamental knowledge concerning the principles of adhesion could be combined with applied know-how about the use of adhesives in actual production processes. At the same time, knowledge from several disciplines, such as chemical and engineering know-how, was linked. Forms of collaboration included a common definition of goals and plans of work, a jointly agreed division of labour, a joint use of testing facilities and an interactive evaluation of necessary adaptations in the research process. Although R&D was mainly conducted in separate company labs, there was a high degree of joint decision making.

Prior to this, the relations between the adhesive producers was characterized by secrecy and distrust. As suppliers of the car industry, they were predominantly competing for the orders of their customers; this lack of communication within the adhesive supplier group was the reason why the client (i.e. the car producers) was able to put them under competitive pressure – since each supplier was eager to strengthen his relation with the customer, it was mostly the user's needs that governed the research activities of their suppliers. In this way, not only secrecy and distrust, but also a feeling of inequality characterized the informal relationship between members of the adhesive sector.

Symptomatic of this competitive orientation were several efforts to prevent competing adhesive producers from collaborating closely with the car producer. In the early phase of the project, for instance, one of those adhesive producers, who was already a supplier of Audi, was eager to establish a closed-shop type of project together with his customers, one of the steel suppliers (Hoesch), and one of the research institutes (LWF).

As competition was still the rule governing the suppliers' relationships, their expectations towards each other were based on incomplete information about knowledge base and learning capacities. Given this lack of solidarity within the supplier group, the position of the car industry as an influential user of adhesives was strengthened. The general reason for car manufacturers to participate in the network was that they were interested in solving a demanding technological problem, which was of potential relevance for the whole car industry. Since the customers (car manufacturers) were able to control the information flows within the group of competing firms, they could use the suppliers' state of incomplete information about the individual performance of each competitor in order to put each of them under pressure to optimize his products.

By the scientific partners informing each partner about the testing results, a rather unexpected definition of the situation emerged; none of the (adhesive) firms taking part in the project provided a product even approximately fulfilling the specifications of the car industry. For the adhesive producers in particular, this information altered their situation fundamentally. Competing for the orders of the manufacturer was no longer the dominating rule of the game. If no one was able to fulfil the user's requirements by now, it was no use hoping to gain competitive advantages and to maximize the individual gain within a perceived zero-sum game. Given the fact that all participants in the project were collectively worse off than expected, the relative benefits of possible gains from cooperation increased. Each adhesive producer, knowing that neither they nor one of the other suppliers was able to fulfil the users' requirements by now, was facing the very likely perspective of being excluded from further collaboration. Based on the common perception that no one in the suppliers' group was able to gain a competitive advantage, the supplier representatives could practise collective resistance more easily.

For the first time, adhesive suppliers were the winners in a power struggle with their customers (car manufacturers). This interaction effect could only evolve owing to a state of complete information within the group of adhesive competitors. Since the users (the car manufacturers) no longer possessed advanced information about the suppliers' performances, they could not put them under competitive pressure. Furthermore, a coalition of producers now replaced several atomized firms, thereby simply reducing the number of the users' alternatives.

Not surprisingly, then, this conflict caused the car producers to revise their definition of interest towards collaboration. Rather than insisting on products developed to fulfil their actual needs, the customers now attempted to use the research project to work on technical problems of common interest and of an uncertain nature.

For the first time in the adhesive sector, technicians belonging to different disciplines were discussing problems of adhesive bonding; chemists from the supplier firms and chemical research institutes on the one hand and engineers from the car and steel manufacturers as well as from the engineering research institutes on the other hand were thus able to synthesize complementary knowledge in order to solve their demanding technological problem. This shared professional identity enabled the group members to develop a 'common language'. Each actor was now willing to share their knowledge because they could be sure of receiving novel information in the future. Within this sequence of mutually beneficial transactions, the collaboration partners developed a relationship of [resilient] trust, allowing them to discuss technical problems without giving the whole show away.

Source: Adapted and abridged from Susanne Lütz (1997), 'Learning through intermediaries: The Case of inter-firm research collaboration', in M. Ebers (ed.), The Formation of Inter-Organizational Networks, New York: Oxford University Press, pp. 224–232. Comments in square brackets have been added by the author of this part of the chapter.

Power dimensions of networks

No organization is able to generate internally all the resources and functions required by itself. Managers must find the best ways to compete for resources. Resource acquisition is usually problematic and involves uncertainty. Each actor is involved in the dynamic process of actions and reactions of getting resources that are subjected to variation in control and discretion of each party. Beyond the normal interdependencies because of interorganizational division of labour and specialization of functions, some interdependencies are sought (or avoided) on account of the power and control possibilities inherent in the development of dependence. Networking is no exception.

Powell (1990) also noted that networks involve tensions and conflicts and power struggles as well because of the nature of *dependency* among network members as seen above in the case study. Networks can formulate quite inclusive rules of membership (or exclusion of others) and place different values on knowledge and expertise and resources being contributed by members. Networks need a degree of interdependence to ensure successful cooperation or collaboration, thus reducing the opportunities for one-way influence (see Anderson and Narus 1990; Buttery and Buttery 1994; Harrigan 1985; Kanter 1989). Nonetheless, there is ample evidence in the network literature to suggest that weaker partners (e.g. firms smaller in size, capital or share in network) can be exploited by stronger partners who deliberately set out to dominate the relationship. De Laat notes that certain large firms in the UK deliberately draw small firms into R&D alliances so that they can behave in a '…predatory manner' (De Laat 1997: 168). In regard to the network form and power, the International Labour Organization (ILO) appraised two types they termed 'kingdom' and 'republic' networks (see Sengenberger, Loveman and Piore 1990).

Kingdom network

A kingdom network ties small suppliers to a large corporate customer in a vertical supplier chain, under the strategic direction of the large company, often called a 'lead company'. The best-known example is the Toyota production system involving in excess of 10000 supplier–buyer relationships. As a rule, the smaller firm depends almost entirely on 'big brother' (the *keiretsu*) who in turn prioritizes connections with those that show most long term commitment. The system fosters information exchange, joint product development and simplified and fast delivery procedures based on low transaction costs. The kingdom relationships are long term but are dictated by short-term contracts which often require price reductions for renewal. At least two suppliers are pitted against each other for every component and are expected to absorb additional costs of production (Scher 1997:10–11). However, Robert Howard (1990) determined that 68 percent of Japanese subcontractors had never changed their 'king' and 53 percent had operated under the same kingdom network for 15 years or more.

Benefits aside, a study by the Massachusetts Institute of Technology (MIT), featured in Howard (1990: 94–6), shows that 'kings' tend to take advantage of their 'subjects'. Remuneration in the lower echelons of the pyramid are frequently one-quarter lower than payment received by employees of the lead company while job security is also more guaranteed at that level. Moreover, lead companies insist on simultaneous increase of higher quality and lower prices, and are known to punish suppliers who fail to comply with the demands by swapping their business in favour of a more compliant competitor.

Republic network

This refers to horizontal or vertical links between highly specialized homogeneous producers in circumstances where no one organization dominates. The benefit of the republic-type network has been clearly demonstrated in the Italian region of Emilia Romagna where a combination of horizontal and vertical links have lifted the game of an entire industry in the region. Once the fourth poorest region of Italy, through the employment of networks to cope with fast-changing technology and markets and through joint R&D, design and planning, the region is now Italy's second richest.

There is evidence elsewhere of the republic-type network's popularity. In France, a number of small milk packaging companies have used the injection of technology to reduce dependence on the 'king' or large firm by forming a republic and by extending their business through packaging of wine and fruit juice as well as milk (Pache 1990). Similarly, in Tokyo's famous Ota-ku district, where 95 percent of firms employ less than 30 staff, the previous exclusive bond to the 'king', or Toyota, is being severed. The recent past has seen the advent of the horizontally linked cooperative in such districts.

Alliance of giants

A further phenomenon is the collaboration of giants in capital- and research-intensive industries. The alliance of giants recognizes that even the largest global competitors in an industry often cannot muster the resources necessary to compete in the future in their industry. Shortened product life cycles, combined with increased research and product development costs, have forced these giants into a strategy where they must cooperate to compete. Swedish giants such as Ericsson, Volvo, Saab-Scania and Fairchild have been involved in projects in aerospace, engineering, mining and metallurgy. The global car industry is well known for its extensive links between various players as are pharmaceuticals and telecommunication enterprises. AT&T in the USA has links with Sun Microsystems, Ricoh, Lucy Goldstar, Philips and Olivetti. Through Olivetti they are connected with Toshiba, Intel and Mitsui, who in turn link AT&T indirectly to Nippon Electric company and Hitachi.

The hybrid network

Howard suggested that '…new hybrids are growing that explode the distinction between kingdom and republics altogether' (1990: 100). Small companies, for example, are forging strong republic-type links with traditional 'king' organizations. He notes, Weitck, employing less that 250 employees, considered small under the US definition of business, collaborated with Hewlett-Packard, a large manufacturer of computer systems. In no way, however, was Hewlett-Packard the umbrella or parent organization in this instance (Howard 1990: 100).

Mark Ebers and Anna Grandori (1997: 273, 274) believe that research on networks has generally focused on the benefits of these forms of cooperation and collaboration to the individual firm to the exclusion of considering undesirable 'costs'. They believe that joint ventures, consortia, franchizing, and a range of other forms of association can create negative effects for firms excluded from the networks. Entry barriers based on reciprocal cooperation are often used to exclude competitors. Ebers and Grandori (1997) cite a study of coalitions of construction and engineering firms forming joint ventures or consortia to bid for job assignments. These firms sign contracts among themselves and only include firms that have close informal links and have cooperated in the past. These potential negative costs of networks warrant attention because they reveal how various forms of cooperation and collaboration can stifle competitions and act as 'costs' to a whole range of excluded groups. Consumers, for example, often find their choices limited, prices fixed and efficiency not guaranteed once these exclusionary consortia or joint venture arrangements come into play.

Costs and benefits of networking

As a result of the influence of transaction cost economics on network theories, the costs and benefits of networking have been generally defined in terms of economic exchange and therefore other costs or benefits of networking that are not purely economic have been excluded. Negative or destructive 'costs' of networks are also often overlooked as many authors present the network as a panacea or 'one best way' to organize (Ebers and Grandori 1997: 273). While there is sufficient evidence to suggest that networking is on the rise (see earlier discussion), there is also ample evidence to suggest that many who enter networks report lack of success or that their expectations were not met by the network experience.

De Laat (1997: 147–8) reminds us that networks are fraught with risk, particularly in joint ventures, and that many attempts to set up networks actually fail. Moreover, he cites research showing that once an alliance or network is formed only 30 percent (based on a sample of 92) thrive in the long run, while other studies report up to 45 percent success rate (based on a sample of 895 alliances, and mainly joint ventures). The authors of this chapter between them have surveyed 50 networks and over 200 firms in Australia covering a range of network types, mainly among microfirms and SMEs. They found that only about 20 percent of these networks were successful measured across a range of indicators, including evaluations made by network members. Of those that have been successful, complementary operations networks dominate with a small sample of pooled operations networks also succeeding. The pooled operations networks (of competitors) have either succeeded because of a major crisis in the industry making the network a viable option for dealing with the crisis, the network has sought new markets and products that have not threatened existing markets or products, or alternatively they have set up a separate company. The greatest frustrations, disappointments and failures have been found in service networks. Networking is not easy and sometimes the costs far outweigh the benefits.

Some of the common costs and benefits associated with networking are described in Table 11.2, which is based on research by Alter and Hage (1993: 35–8) who drew on an extensive list of authors to identify what they considered to be the 'calculus of interorganizational collaboration'. They did not suggest that their list of costs and benefits was exhaustive, however, they do note that costs and benefits cover a wide range of motivations and perceptions relating to the risks associated with cooperation and collaboration. Benefits are usually associated with opportunities to gain access to information, know-how and expertise or create new niche markets in areas that require a great number of specializations, especially where product development is both costly and lengthy. Minimizing risk and uncertainty are two prime benefits of cooperation. Alter and Hage also noted that risk and uncertainty rise dramatically when firms try to enter foreign markets, and cooperation and collaboration are often sought with foreign partners in order to reduce this risk and uncertainty. Sometimes governments, such as in the People's Republic of China, require that firms develop a cooperative venture of some sort in order to enter the country in the first instance (Alter and Hage 1993: 37–8). The 'calculus of interorganizational collaboration' has to be read as every cost also being a potential benefit, and vice versa.

Issues in networking

A study by the Butterys (1995), also based on an extensive literature review and follow-up research, identified 19 key issues likely to affect or be of concern to network members. These issues are listed in Figure 11.2. Also shown in Figure 11.2 are issues that were subsequently identified by Liz Fulop (Fulop with Kelly 1997a, b; also Fulop with Kelly 1995). Her research on networks has focused on networks formed through government-sponsored programmes. The issues mentioned in Figure 11.2 represent areas that firms will need to address somewhere in the process of forming or developing their networks. Few studies actually include longitudinal or long-term studies of how network relationships develop and change over time (for exceptions see Lütz 1997; Ring 1997b). Buttery and Buttery and Fulop, and indeed many other researchers studying networks, have mainly studied the problems of firms forming networks rather than how network relationships are sustained over time. Nonetheless inappropriately formed networks have little chance of success.

The authors can offer a few summary observations about some of the points raised in Figure 11.2, but to cover all of them would be beyond the scope of this chapter. We have found, for example, that trust tends to be a serious concern of new networks, especially where members have had no prior associations or do not know each other well and the

Table 11.2 *Calculus of interorganizational collaboration*

Costs	Benefits
Loss of technological superiority; risk of losing competitive position	Opportunities to learn and to adapt, develop competencies or jointly develop new products
Loss of resources – time, money, information, raw materials, legitimacy, status, etc.	Gain of resources – time, money, information, raw material, legitimacy, status, etc.; utilization of unused plant capacity
Being linked with failure; sharing the costs of failing such as loss of reputation, status, and financial position	Sharing the cost of product development and associated risks (such as failure to develop new products quickly enough and with enough quality), risks associated with commercial acceptance, and risks associated with size of market share
Loss of autonomy and ability to unilaterally control outcomes; goal displacement; loss of control	Gain of influence over domain; ability to penetrate new markets; competitive positioning and access to foreign markets; need for global products
Loss of stability, certainty, and known time-tested technology; feelings of dislocation	Ability to manage uncertainty, solve invisible and complex problems, ability to specialize or diversify; ability to fend off competitors
Delays in solutions due to problems in coordination	Rapid responses to changing market demands; less delay in use of new technologies
Government intrusion, regulation, and so on	Gaining acceptance from foreign governments for participation in the country

Source: Modified from Catherine Alter and Herald Hage (1993), *Organizations Working Together*, Newbury Park, CA: Sage, pp. 36–7.

network is large, but trust seems less of an issue as firms engage in projects and actually start succeeding (Fulop 1998: 46–7). Creating shared goals presents major problems when firms joining a network do not have anything to offer other members or have no domain overlap. In fact, selecting network partners whose goals are likely to be congruent with other firms in the network, at least to start with, is very important. Difficulties arise in this regard when firms who are not growth oriented join a network. It is almost a recognized 'rule' that firms with no real growth opportunities make poor network partners. We have also found that firms joining networks often place little strategic importance on the network and, if there are a sufficient number of firms in this position, the network is doomed.

Firms or their managers often join networks thinking it will be easy to be a member only to find that it takes up a lot of time and consumes more resources than was first thought. Those who stay in networks and try to make them work attest to the fact that it is an extremely time consuming way to do business, but is also rewarding. One very serious issue for networks is that firms often do not contribute or cannot contribute the same amounts of resources and money and this inequity can create tensions, especially where lead firms or large organizations are more able to finance and resource the network (see discussion above). Many network members resent the role these lead firms play in their networks and often develop rules or protocols to prevent them dominating the network. We have also found

Buttery (1995)	**Fulop with Kelly (1997a)**
Trust	Trust
Creating shared goals	Creating shared goals
Strategic importance to firm of network	Strategic importance to firm of network
Level of support provided by firm	Level of support provided by firm
Stake in project of network	Stake in project of network
Exit barriers – how to get out	
Satisfactory performance/mutual benefit	Satisfaction with performance/mutual benefit
Degree of interdependence or power relations	Degree of dependence and power relations
Time relationship existed prior to alliance being formed	
Communication/information	Communication/information
Social bonding	
Organization culture similarities	
Environmental factors/transaction costs	Main business environment of firms
Expectations	Expectations/reasons for joining
Cognitive dissonance (frustration, fears and anxieties about decision to join)	Concerns about the network
Perceived competencies of other members	
Incidence of planning	Incidence of planning
Adaptation	How to make networks succeed
Commitment	Commitment

Figure 11.2   Issues in networking

Sources: Adapted from Liz Fulop with Jo Kelly (1997a), A Study of Business Networks in Australia – An Indepth Investigation: Summary Report, *Sydney: Australian Business Chamber, p. 28.*

that in many networks the benefits from projects are not equally shared. This can be a cause of dissension and resentment, although there are firms in networks who expect very little and this is often not a plus for the network. Firms that expect little usually contribute little.

In our studies satisfaction with the performance of the network was often affected by how long the network had been in existence and what had already been contributed by member firms. We found that many members were unhappy with what they had received from their network and this was most pronounced in service networks. We found that few networks were able to give equal benefit to member firms and many sought unequal contributions. Firms fear forming dependencies on other firms and the only networks in which we have seen strong dependency relations forming have been in the complementary production networks. Power relations and politics are an issue in some networks, especially competitor-based ones, such as the pooled operations network, but are less evident in complementary networks. Networks that have strong leaders and executive committees are more prone to be seen as dominated by politics than where a leadership team exists, as was common in the complementary operations networks studied.

To bond effectively, members of a network need time. Bonding cannot be effective early in the networking process. Members of the network need time to perform tasks together and build respect and shared meanings. When bonding creates a pleasant experience with positive outcomes, it leads to a quality and caring relationship. This, in turn, would stimulate members of a network to consider other networking opportunities. Commitment has been a factor considered by every writer we reviewed for our networking research. Indeed, we identified that asymmetry of effort and commitment dooms relationships, and can lead the network towards a failure trajectory. We found that increased commitment is fostered by an increased stake in the network, so simultaneously exit barriers increase as members have committed to irretrievable investments which cannot be recovered if the relationship ends.

We found that the way members perceived each others' competencies was important to a network's survival. Mutual respect, we suggest, is paramount for cooperative ventures. A further important issue related to communication and information. Failure to communicate freely and in a timely fashion between partner firms, even a hint of withholding information, can be devastating to a network's operation. As with all organizations, network partners that planned their collaborative venture and its ongoing implementation improved the chances of success.

The costs and benefits described above, together with the essential issues confronting those who intend to form networks, reveal the complexity of the networking phenomenon. As the network trajectory develops, these facets of networking change according to context, and may have a varying, but nevertheless important impact over the life of the network.

Trust

If we examine the issues affecting networking and the literature on networks, one aspect that has attracted enormous attention has been the issue of trust. Partners in networking need to rely on each other in a number of different ways. The ideal basis of the relationship offering maximum flexibility is trust, although to the extent that complete trust is not present networking members always have the option of partially substituting complete trust with contracts or with what De Laat (1997) has termed 'credible commitments' (see above). According to Powell (1990, 1996), *reciprocity* and *trust* in conducting business define networks as distinct forms of organizing (Powell 1990: 304). Reciprocity involves notions of indebtedness and obligation and Powell drew on the work of Marcel Mauss (1967/1925; also see Chapter 4) on 'gift giving' to explain how reciprocity helps create long-term commitments in network relations. The obligations to give, to receive and to return are important in creating a sense of mutual interest, and setting standards of behaviour that disavow self-interest or opportunism. Long-term commitments, he said, help bring a sense of security and stability into relations that will facilitate the sharing of information and learning, and from this flows trust. Powell believed that in other more instrumental or calculating relations, such as those found in markets and hierarchies, reciprocity is based on obligations that involve rough equivalents or notions of *equivalent exchange* – '...returning ill for ill and good for good' (Powell 1990: 304) – and making sure that one's self-interest is protected. In establishing notions of reciprocity in networks, the idea of fair dealings or some idea of mutual benefit is essential. Equity, which is the key to fair dealings in networks, implies that inputs or outcomes are never going to be equally divided at any given time (Ring and Van de Ven 1994: 94).

It is interesting to consider what firms in networks believe constitutes trust. In a pilot study by Fulop (1998) of four networks in a government business network programme in Australia, network members were asked what they believed constituted the basis of trust in their network. The four networks, which comprised 19 firms, were chosen because they were considered by the sponsoring department to be examples of successful networking. Three of them were complementary production networks while the other one was a pooled network that had been set up as a separate company. Table 11. 3 shows a sample of their responses.

Elements of reputation, prior association, reciprocity, disclosure and fair dealings seem to underpin what members described as the basis of trust (also see Ring and Van de Ven 1994). When members were asked to rank the level of trust they had in each partner in the network, the responses were nearly evenly divided between 'total trust' and 'slightly less than total trust'. But when asked what type(s) of commercial or financial information they would withhold from the network, there was quite an extensive list of items that members did not consider appropriate to share, for example income, business plan, profit–loss information, pricing and client base. No one mentioned an unwillingness to share-know how and other forms of technical knowledge.

Powell's position, and those of many network theorists, is that without trust you cannot have an effective network (Noorderhaven 1992; Ring and Van de Ven 1992, 1994; Vangen and Huxham 1995: 4; Johannisson and Mønsted 1996). In trying to theorize what trust

Table 11.3 *Basis of trust in network*

	Category
The togetherness of all firms	(Bonding)
Open partnership	(Disclosure)
Informing each other of potential opportunities, everything put to Board and network decides on this. We can then offer a business opportunity to other firms privately or go elsewhere	(Disclosure)
Despite politics fair amount of trust; must trust those who negotiate contracts for the network	(Fair dealings)
Quite heavy as other members have opportunity to win business in their own right if they wanted to	(Fair dealings)
High level, no formal agreements.	(Fair dealings)
We are like-minded people and get on well – not competitors, so no fear that they will run away with each others' customers	(Fair dealings)
Very high mostly due to personality and openness of individuals. Got rid of unethical person early	(Fair dealings) (Disclosure)
Already knowing people concerned, having certain trust in people in general	(Prior association)
Regularly communicating on a personal level	(Prior association)
High degree of peer support. Development of strong friendships and mutual respect	(Prior association) (Reputation)
Absolute trust and faith in each other's ability to perform at crisis level	(Reputation)
We are all willing to work as hard as the next person	(Reputation)
Members have been in the industry for many years (reputation, etc.)	(Reputation)
We have worked together for many years now and know each other quite well. There are no hangers on	(Reputation)
Mutual respect and regard is very high	(Reputation)

Source: Adapted from Liz Fulop (1998), *Networks: The Next Generation,* report prepared for AusIndustry Business Networks Program, Canberra, full report unpublished.

means in the network context, the influence of transaction cost theory is evident. The theories of trust tend to follow the distinction between networks and other forms of exchange, so we end up with two key concepts: *fragile trust* and *resilient trust*, as already described in Chapter 7. Both concepts of trust are associated with the willingness to take risks and make oneself vulnerable in a relationship, with resilient trust encouraging the most risk taking. This perspective of trust is also based on the notion of a dyadic relationship, or a relationship between two people, and strongly supports the view that trust can only emerge in personal relationships and not on the basis of some abstract idea of trustworthiness of a firm, as was suggested by theorists such as Williamson (see earlier discussion).

Fragile trust

Ring, who coined the terms 'fragile' and 'resilient' trust, maintains that fragile trust can operate in networks, especially in their early stages, and has done so in more traditional forms of cooperation, such as in joint ventures. Fragile trust still involves the underlying assumption that people will act opportunistically and in self-interested ways (Ring 1997a: 120; also De Laat 1997). However, it does not preclude people moving on from relationships based solely on fragile trust to those based on resilient trust. Nor does it exclude the fact that fragile trust can invite political behaviour and power plays because opportunism and struggles to control or limit dependency remain important. In fact, one of the problems with any notion of trust that does not draw these distinctions is that it will fail to account for when people take a risk because of trust or, alternatively, when they feel they have no choice but to do so because of unequal dependency relations or power (Hardy, Phillips and Lawrence 1996: 4–5). As we said in Chapter 7, cooperation does not necessarily signal that someone trusts another party. In fact there is a great difference between '…cooperation achieved through power differentials that render some partners *unable* to engage in opportunistic behaviour, and a willingness to *voluntarily sacrifice* the benefits of opportunistic behaviour in order to cooperate with a trusted partner' (Hardy *et al.* 1996: 6).

Fragile trust typically relies on contractual agreements, hedging bets with guarantees and safeguards, including courts, mediators and arbitrators. Ring argues that economic actors rely on more than one form of trust. Reputations of individuals based on their personal competence (see Chapter 7) can also nurture fragile trust, but this will not encourage network members to commit in any significant way to a network, except contractually.

Ring says that economic exchanges are usually imbued with elements of fragile trust, while social exchanges, which are important in networks, depend more on resilient trust. De Laat also maintains the distinction between fragile and resilient trust and suggests that when organizations conduct their network business on the basis of classical contracts they are really signalling distrust that can end up spiralling into greater distrust. Organizations that enter into classical contractual agreements do so to specify in minute detail all the conditions of the exchange, with the aim of trying to control completely the partner or partners. He says this usually encourages partners to find 'loop holes' or breach the contract any way because it is so restrictive that its terms and conditions are hard to meet (De Laat 1997: 163–4). So while these forms of classical contracts signal some form of trust they are inherently biased towards creating distrust.

Resilient Trust

Resilient trust, as defined by Ring (1997a: 121–2), is based on the assumption that goodwill or the moral integrity of others count when greater risks and sacrifices are being sought in a network. For Ring, the notion of resilient trust is not based on one's reputation as a person to be trusted, but rather the experiences a person has of having successfully completed transactions in the past with others, and how successful these were in establishing norms of equity and reciprocity (1997a: 128). Equity or fairness in this context means cooperating or collaborating on the basis that some time in the future one will receive proportional benefits from the exchange. Reciprocity, in the context of resilient trust, means that there is an accepted and demonstrated moral obligation on the part of those involved in a network to give back to all members some fair return for the investment they have made in the network.

De Laat (1997: 164) points out that in making credible commitments, therefore, and showing more resilient trust, network members actually signal a willingness to take risks. In effect, over time the reliance on fragile trust can also transform into resilient trust and this is when a network proper emerges. However, De Laat makes it clear that networks are likely to use both classical contracts and contracts entailing credible commitments, but neither is a substitute for the other – they imply different types of trust (De Laat 1997: 164). A contract between two network members might, in fact, be necessary to satisfy the demands of the network's customers. It is therefore unlikely, especially in the short term, that the contract is replaced by resilient trust. On the other hand, the existence of a contract in different circumstances might do nothing to build trust with network partners.

Ring (1997b) also states that the dominance of the transaction cost approach to networks has meant that the more affective and emotional aspects of networking have been played down or underemphasized, yet these also help to create trusting relations. For example, he says that the sheer fact that people actually come to like, or even love, each other, and care for others in a network relationship can go a long way in building deeper commitments than those based on credible commitments (Ring 1997b: 9). He also says that this strong emotional connection is likely to lead to very different types of learning occurring than is traditionally discussed in network theory. It is likely to be based on greater empathy for others and developing a better understanding of oneself as well as the values, ideas, fears and concerns of others. In Chapter 1 we associated this type of learning with reflexive practice. Ring gives an example of a joint venture between NASA in the USA and 3M, both of whom had had no prior business involvements but built their IORs on the emotional bonds between people rather than trust as a prerequisite. The project was focused on the commercial use of outer space. It was the genuine liking and bonding between two of the key players from the respective organizations that eventually pushed the project, and the joint venture ahead, even when there was opposition to it in both organizations at the very highest levels.

Trust as sense making

Personal trust and emotional bonds are often claimed to be the foundations of networks. But the reality of many networks, especially those involving multiorganizational arrangements, as opposed to IORs, is that trust is very difficult to create. Often networks involve people from different backgrounds and cultures who have no history of positive interactions (Hardy *et al.* 1996: 9). Moreover, the length of time involved in establishing networks also means that different people can be involved at different stages of development. In networks that have few partners (i.e. are dyadic or triadic) this might not be a problem, but in consortia, for example, relying on personal bases for trust is not likely to be possible. Even the use of credible commitments will not eliminate all elements of opportunism.

Hardy *et al.* (1996: 10) argue that trust is really based on developing shared meanings between partners about what trust stands for. In other words, it is largely irrelevant, for example, what reputation means or even goodwill in another organization or culture unless the symbols used to signal these elements of trust have meaning for all those involved. They say meanings are established in language, and the conversation and talk between different actors provide the ritual context for developing shared understandings and a common language to make sense of ideas such as trust. This view is supported by Ring who also argues that the need for facticity, or the need to create a world in which one feels connected and one shares common meanings and understandings with others, motivates people to construct shared meanings (Ring 1997a: 137; see also Chapter 7). He also says that sense making is really related to people's need to clarify or create an identity for themselves in a social relationship, such as in a network (1997a: 134–5).

Hardy *et al.* (1996: 10) also believe that trust arises through people trying to invoke a sense of a common or shared reality. Trust, they say, is like any other story or myth created by people to signify some common understandings about membership of a group, and the protocols and practices acceptable to that group. The myth of trust only applies to those who accept or share the meanings of the group. They say networking symbolizes the common actions taken on the basis of shared meanings and understandings attached to the myth of trust. This myth facilitates the sharing of information, informal interactions and other forms of action that are then labelled as trust based, as the examples in Table 11.4 illustrate. Trust did not mean the same thing to all network members, as their responses reveal, but there was sufficient commonality of meanings to signal trust. The understandings that develop through negotiating credible commitments, which are more personalized, or through bonding, might serve to strengthen the myth of trust. Other forms of understanding, developed through, say, interpreting and negotiating contracts might make it more difficult for people to create the myth of trust (Ring 1997a: 136).

Creating common myths or identities is complicated when symbolic meanings (or symbols used to signal trust) are not shared or trust itself has no significant meaning to a group. As we shall discuss below, the notion of trust actually has no real symbolic meaning in Japanese business practices (Scher 1997: 12). And there is no guarantee that when actors try to create common meanings that this process will not be dominated or 'hijacked' by those who can manipulate meanings for their own vested interests, with the intention of consolidating the power of one person or group over another (Hardy *et al.* 1996: 13). This comes back to Granovetter's earlier point that the belief in trust opens up enormous opportunities for people to manipulate it for their own ends. Indeed, in our own studies we have identified instances where apparent trust-based relationships, rather than being enhanced over time, have eroded, only to be replaced by abuse of power and intense distrust. The recognition of this 'Janus' or two-sided nature of trust probably accounts for why it receives so much attention in network theory and why it is one of the greatest concerns of firms who enter into network arrangements.

Network theory has adopted a less masculinist language than found in many areas of management, particularly in strategic management, where war metaphors are frequently adopted (e.g. 'defensive move', 'fighting for market share', 'market penetration'). In the relational view of networking, words such as 'sharing', 'trust', 'loyalty', 'benevolence', 'altruism', 'fair dealings' and 'equity' are common. In the affective view proposed by Ring (1997b), words such as 'love' and 'caring' are also being used. The content and meanings of these words, including trust, are established in discourses or the discursive practices of managers. Yet networking discourses exist alongside others in organizations, such as the competitive strategy discourse described in Chapter 10 and above. In many organizations, the underlying frameworks of meanings are so deeply rooted in various ideas of competitiveness, control, and self-interest that notions of trust, even in the network discourse, will rarely carry substantially new or different meanings. So, the practices of networking will remain inherently the same as other practices in the organization.

Cross-cultural dimensions

Empirical evidence on international networks shows that cultural problems are at the heart of numerous conflicts and problems within partnerships (Harrigan 1985; Lasserre and Boisot 1980). Cooperative ventures are inevitably affected by differing societal, political and economic systems, by geography, language and climate, religions and philosophies, all of which shape the way people do business with each other. Although over the years no monolithic business culture has emerged from the West or from Asia, if there is anything that Asians have in common that differs from the West, it is the high degree of importance attached to personal relationships in preference to contractual ones (Lasserre and Schuette 1995: 187). A contractual approach to business can be frowned upon in Asia. As a result, Western and Asian firms have different attitudes to cooperation and collaboration, and given the importance of the relational dimension in networks, and the rise of cross-border networking, it is important to consider some of the tensions caused by cultural differences. However, we reiterate that national cultures are not immutable or unchangeable; organizations have within them an array of different types of cultures such as professional cultures (see Chapter 3), and people themselves are continually adapting and changing (Levinson and Asahi 1995: 53).

As late as the mid-1970s, Lee Iacocca, CEO of General Motors, refused to deal with Honda, responding with a quote from Ford, 'No car with my name on the hood is going to have a Jap engine inside'. Western firms, particularly American firms, tended to stay away from strategic alliances because of the lack of complete control over the venture, which does not suit the American corporate personality – sharing goes against the competitive spirit. The entire tradition of strategic management thinking in the USA has been dominated by competitive strategies that were based on arm's length relationships (see Michael Porter's work cited in Chapter 10). Eventually, when US firms did consider cooperative ventures, they did so assuming that the foreign firm represented the student, while the US firm played teacher. Their attitude was confirmed by surveys, for example by Modic (1988), showing that US CEOs in the 1980s were positively claustrophobic about networks; for example, only 17 percent of American, compared to 75 percent Japanese, CEOs considered networks in a favourable light.

The gulf in cultures has a direct effect on how networking partners deal with managerial issues that need careful consideration and agreement prior to joint venture commencement.

Joint operations with Korean firms, for example, need to take on board the social and nationalistic role firms play compared to the Western purpose of business that tends to be related to shareholder satisfaction (see Introduction). Japanese firms, due to the political system in Japan, are able to take a long-term perspective in strategy making while Western firms must often consider the short-term planning horizon. As Western firms are in business to satisfy shareholders, profit needs to be, at least in part, shared by the payment of dividends to shareholders. In contrast, a Japanese or Korean firm is able to reinvest profits. In many South East Asian cultures, firms are over-reliant on higher echelons of management, while the Western firm tends to emphasize a managerial culture. Performance as it emanates from the individual is valued in the West, while group performance tends to be the norm in most of Asia. These are some of the more pertinent cultural differences; clearly each and every one has the potential to bring down the network.

Relationship building is at the heart of networks; however, relationships are valued differently in different cultures. Cooperation between Western organizations is not as common as competition. Indeed, the Protestant work ethic drives the business system in the USA and many Western countries. It has at its heart the need to work and succeed, and competition between organizations and individuals in organizations for promotion has been commonplace in the past.

In contrast, in the Asia-Pacific region, building and cultivating relationships is crucial to business development. Cultivating relationships with suppliers, customers, partners and government officials is standard practice. In Japan, a number of complex factors have helped forge a system in which it is expected that the individual works for the improvement of the group. The notion of what a business relationship means is very different in Japan and, as Mark Scher (1997: 11–12) suggests, many Western commentators fail to appreciate the very limited or non-existent meaning trust has in Japanese business. He says the word 'relationship' in Japan comes from two words: *kan*, meaning barrier or gate, and *kei*, meaning duty to the familial or clan group. Access, he says, in Japanese business is not about opening doors, but of controlling entry and determining who is allowed past the barrier gates. He cites examples of the Japanese exclusionary system of *dango*, which entails a collusive, rigged bidding or tendering system that has roots in the guild system. *Dango* is used to afford access to a chosen group of contractors, no matter what. Scher says that long-term relationships among Japanese businesses are often portrayed as being based on trust, but this is not a word commonly used by the Japanese to describe their transactions. The right of 'access' provided by *keiretsu* relationships is seen as a franchise or license to do business, while trust refers to credit, credit associations, trust companies, trust funds and trust agreements and the like (Scher 1997: 12). It is not that trust is absent in Japanese culture, but rather it is not translated into the business context to mean loyalty, obligation, integrity, etc. In Japanese businesses transactions are based on the 'insider–outsider' status.

In the People's Republic of China, *Guanxi*, or mutual obligation that derives from being connected to someone through a third party, is a precursor for business deals, and it could be argued that relationships are valued much more highly than contracts or money. The quality of the relationship is, however, much more important than the number of relationships. *Guanxi* is an interesting concept in Chinese business behaviour because it is a long-established and well-advanced form of business networking, although it extends much further than just to the business situation. It forms the basis of virtually all important interactions in Chinese society. Networks are also prevalent in non-Chinese societies, in Korea, Indonesia, the Philippines, Japan or Thailand.

It is not surprising that business people from the USA trust in written contracts and the stability of money as a means of exchange. The legal system in the USA is uniform and well established and the breaking of a contract leads to sometimes expensive and protracted court cases. Individuals and organizations alike believe that once established a contract is sacrosanct. In China the contract, far from being immutable, is considered only the start of negotiations and the partner in the contract is expected to be flexible and continue negotiations after the contract has been signed. An example is provided by the *South China Morning Post* on 12 January 1994 which states: 'Major changes to the terms of Sino-foreign joint ventures are being thrashed out following the recent unification of yuan exchange rates. Mr Chan said adoption of a unified exchange rate of about 8.7 yuan to the US dollar had materially altered the contracts signed between foreign investors and mainland partners, but which were yet to be implemented … But Mr Chan added that how the deals were negotiated really depended on the sincerity of both partners' (Buttery and Leung 1998: 386). It is not entirely surprising that one would expect a member of one's *Guanxi* circle to understand such problems and therefore be willing to be flexible even though a contract has been signed. It seems that Mr Chan was suggesting that the relationship is more important than money or contracts and in China this is often the case. It arises from a consideration of China's history.

The Chinese population, at about 1.2 billion, is vast and holding the whole economy together is just about as much as the Chinese Government can manage. In the past there have been shortages of everyday necessities in some regions, communication systems have been primitive, and local bureaucracy has prevailed. It is not surprising that the value of money has not been consistent and that legal systems that have existed have tended not to be entirely uniform throughout the People's Republic of China. Therefore *Guanxi* acted as the currency to perform practical roles. The right *Guanxi* can bring cheap and reliable supplies of goods and services, tax concessions, approval to sell goods at home or overseas and provide all kinds of help and assistance when problems in business arise. There is no point in foreigners trying to force this system into their mould. It might lead to misunderstandings, conflicts and different perceptions if one enters a network arrangement with a Chinese partner who believes that relationships follow the rules of *Guanxi*.

Sufficient has been said about the contrast between doing business in the West and in China. However, one could equally expect different understandings of relationships and doing business in other cultures too. In this regard, the work of Hofstede (1991) is important as a means of understanding culture. Hofstede brings to our attention five important dimensions to understanding culture and these have been discussed in various chapters (Chapters 3, 5, 6, 7, 8) and include power distance, collectivism, femininity v. masculinity, uncertainty avoidance and long-term orientation. In cross-border networks each of these five dimensions must be considered; if they are not, an inappropriate approach in a particular cultural context can at best cause offence and at worst, prevent sufficient progress being made to make the network viable. As we have discussed above, the notion of collectivism or how relationships are built and maintained can be completely misunderstood in the West when Western concepts such as trust are used to try to understand how the Japanese do business and create some form of collective orientation. In the USA business people are brought up in the belief in the Protestant work ethic and so individuality and competition is a more natural approach than cooperation. In Japan, however, cooperation and putting the group above the individual has become the favoured discourse of networking. *Guanxi* is just one form of sense making and nothing happens in business until *Guanxi* has been built sufficiently for the Chinese to trust its foreign partner.

Hofstede's dimensions play a role in trying to explain how relationships develop, but again the meanings of his dimensions are limited because, as we have already argued in Chapter 10, many differences we observe in business practices across borders are also based on institutional practices, such as have built up in the *keiretsu,* which is an extremely complex system based on general expectations that decisions will be made (even though they might not be commercially sound), and discretion used to service long-term relationships (Scher 1997: 15). This form of reliance is not built on personal trust or the type of bonding we favour in the West, but rather on uncodified ground rules of behaviour. These are deeply embedded in traditional power relations of inclusion and exclusion that are known, accepted and codified by the group (Scher 1997: 16).

It can be appreciated, therefore, that some adaptation or abandonment of ideas, objectives and behaviour must be considered if an organization enters a cross-cultural relationship. A knowledge of the similarities and differences in cultures, as expressed by Hofstede's five dimensions, is of considerable importance to understanding cross-cultural networking. However, these dimensions can be added to and recast to illuminate the more subtle and deeper meanings that attach to the relational dimensions of cross-border networks, such as Ring points out, the affective and emotional dimensions of networking.

Conclusion

A consideration of networking was kept until Chapter 11 as it adds new dimensions to the challenge of management and, in fact, generates an organizational form that is a decidedly new way of considering organizations. It is a form which can serve the global aspirations of the largest MNEs as well as opening up new opportunities for networks of small local firms. It even provides the bridge between locomotive organizations and small independent firms who are encouraged to share in the business opportunities of the giants.

We have shown that currently the global business environment is conducive to the formation of networks. This has arisen, in no small measure, because of new technologies, new communication and marketing opportunities. We have traced the key characteristics of organizations that have directly led to networking. These have been traced from the industrial revolution to postmodern society, from standardization and automation, to flexibility in production and communications, and from a business environment geared to competition to one seeking the advantages of cooperation and collaboration to meet the demands of society from the local to the 'global village'.

The added complexities of networking reflect a rich pastiche of technology, people and resources capable of delivering all sorts of benefits, though also entailing numerous costs and heartaches. Indeed, networking seems at times to fly in the face of extant management theory and practice, in focusing on the relational dimensions of interorganizational relations, which suggests why it is a developing organizational form in the postmodern world. Sufficient work has been carried out in the area to reflect what works well for networks and what may lead to their demise. Challenges remain, though, in exploring how networks can enhance interorganizational learning and the sharing of tacit knowledge. This might in fact be the biggest challenge of all to network theorists and practitioners.

In the postmodernist vein we would ask our readers to keep an open mind about the potential for networking opportunities and to try not to be surprised how this way of organizing will tackle the problems of the world in future. In a more traditional vein, we have tried to capture what the current thinking is about networks. To do this we have classified networks and compared and contrasted networking according to these classifications. We have identified issues facing networks and how these represent ongoing concerns in the networking situation.

Throughout the analysis we have recognized that it is people and their relationships who stand at the centre of networks. Society, culture, economics, politics, aspirations and greed are all reflected in our attempt at explaining what networking is about.

Finally, we have used many small vignettes and examples to bring our story of networking alive. They have been drawn from MNEs and SMEs from around the world, which in itself helps to demonstrate the ubiquity of networking in the global economy of today.

In explaining network relationships, a number of themes dominate and these relate principally to trust, commitment, power, mutual benefit and learning. We believe these themes will continue to challenge all managers into the next century, as managers will increasingly experiment with new organizational forms. We believe all these elements combine to create collaborative advantage.

Questions at the beginning of the chapter

1 What does the term 'network' mean?

Very broadly, 'networking' means groups of people coming together either to cooperate or collaborate, without losing their own legal status. It describes relationships between firms or organizations and not within organizations. People often refer to networks as 'cross-boundary relations' or 'interorganizational'. Most importantly, the term 'network' is meant to describe a form or way of organizing that is different from conventional forms such as markets or hierarchies. For some it connotes the organization of the future.

2 Why should organizations form networks?

Generally, organizations form networks to benefit from such things as economies of scale and scope, to facilitate market entry, particularly into foreign markets, to improve their learning capabilities, and to secure their future in a more globally oriented world. However, some organizations form networks to exploit others, dominate their markets or industry and to generally create entry barriers to competitors. Some organizations are more prone or pressured into networking because their environments are volatile and their technologies change rapidly, as do their customers' demands. Some networks arise because they are the only mechanisms available to enter foreign markets.

Networking holds out the promise of all sorts of expediencies through relationship building. Through sharing, networks are also able to reduce many costs and create more flexibility in their operations and transactions. Sharing, however, can carry enormous risks and uncertainty, especially when strategically important knowledge is at stake.

3 What types of cooperation and/or collaboration are possible in networks?

One of the real challenges of either studying or trying to form networks (or IORs) is the enormous variety and complexity of network types, and the types of cooperation and/or collaboration found among them. We have noted, for example, that networks comprising large firms and SMEs, for example, can follow the pattern of a kingdom network, or large firms the alliance of giants. These represent different concentrations of power and/or dependency and interdependency.

Networks can be formed for a number of reasons and we described six different types of networks using labels such as 'pooled', 'complementary', 'production', 'service' and 'learning'. We noted that the most successful of these seem to be complementary production networks or complementary learning networks. Pooled networks that bring together competitors are usually fraught with problems.

Networks or IORs can have different strategic foci, with licensing and franchising involving the least commitment to developing strong relational ties. Joint ventures seem to carry high risks when R&D or the sharing of tacit knowledge is involved. Consortia or separate companies offer more protection and less scope for opportunism when tacit knowledge sharing is an issue for network partners.

Learning networks present the greatest opportunities for firms or organizations to enhance their core competence, but the risks are also the greatest. The learning network depends on building credible commitments and the language and dialogue to create an environment of trust where sharing know-how is possible. The whole area of interorganizational learning requires much more research, both to appreciate the limits and boundaries of relational dimensions of networking.

Most importantly, we have tried to show that networking is multidimensional, involving varying levels and degrees of commitment and diverse strategic orientations. Networks are dynamic phenomena that can be configured in many different ways.

4 What common problems face organizations wanting to compete and collaborate?

Networking entails fairly well documented costs and benefits. Major benefits include: gaining access to new information, know-how and expertise, product development opportunities and access to new markets, especially foreign ones. However major 'costs' or the negatives of networking include: loss of control or autonomy, having other firms steal secrets, having to contribute resources that could have been better deployed elsewhere and, perhaps more successfully, and ultimately receiving no mutual benefit.

We have identified a range of issues that networks have to confront, including the major one of trying to develop trust among members. It has also been pointed out that the success rate among networks varies, and failures are more common than are successes.

We have identified how difficult it is to develop trust among network members and indeed proposed that trust is a myth that is created by network members to sustain their relationships. However, networks often 'hang together' not because of trust but, rather, because of power.

5 What problems are associated with networking across cultures?

Networking has been principally described as involving relational exchanges and, more recently, even affective or emotional 'exchanges'. Cultural problems, as well as institutional factors, play a large part in explaining the numerous conflicts and tensions that arise in cross-border networks. Clashes occur at the basic cultural level in terms of what cooperation and collaboration constitute in different settings. We gave the example of US firms expecting to dominate their foreign alliance partners. We noted that taken-for-granted assumptions, even about what trust means from one culture to another, are dangerous.

Relationships are differentially valued across cultures and embedded in very different forms of institutions, for example, in Japan it is more 'access' that defines the boundaries of interorganizational arrangements than the Western concepts of 'trust' or even contract. Similarly, in the People's Republic of China, being connected through third parties 'oils' relationships, and written contracts mean very little.

We have suggested that Hofstede's five cross-cultural dimensions are useful for trying to understand culture at the national level, but we warned that there are enormous subtleties that are played out in the institutional context and at other more personal and individual levels. It is in these more dense levels that the discourse of networking is worked at and the game of networking is played in earnest.

Case study analysis

As the core of this case study is the question of trust, and what will prompt Evans to share its know how, it might well be the case that Evans should not enter into a network.

With regard to *question 1*, Evans's management need good-quality components and castings and they need help to enter the Singapore and Asian markets. They know they must share their knowledge of the new product with whichever component manufacturer they select.

The ideal partners would have the following characteristics:

1   The component supplier should supply good-quality parts and be trustworthy. They will have knowledge of the new product technology.
2   The partner in Singapore/Asia should be in a position to help with market entry, especially to the main customers of Evans, who are likely to be hospitals or hospital equipment suppliers.
3   The producer of castings should produce good-quality castings and be reliable suppliers.

For characteristic 1, Zercon has the quality component reputation but is not known to Evans. Evans knows Formax, but the quality of their components is lower than Zercon's, and they supply Evans's competitors.

With regard to characteristic 2, Tran Holdings are a large firm in Singapore and probably have some influence in that country with perhaps less influence throughout Asia. However, they are unlikely to have influence in the specific hospital and hospital supply sectors. There are likely to be better partners around, more suited to help Evans's market entry.

For, characteristic 3, good castings are required and it would help in Singapore, but not necessarily elsewhere in Asia, if a Singapore firm had a significant input to the product. However, any good supplier will do and perhaps being close to the manufacturer is important too.

Considering these characteristics, Evans may be concerned about the need to protect their technology from competitors. Evans therefore needs to gather information on component suppliers including Formax and Zercon. Chapter 11 of the book will help you to consider the characteristics of a good partner, but trust to maintain confidentiality about the new technology would certainly be high on the list as this technology represents tacit knowledge for Evans.

It is likely that there are organizations in Singapore and Asia that are more directly able to help Evans's market entry than Tran Holdings. You should consider the ideal characteristics of the organization Evans needs to network with, and also consider how that firm would need to become a good network member.

The castings can be obtained from any casting firm. The only advantage of Tran Holdings is the fact that it is a large Singaporean firm. However, this reputation might or might not hold sway in the rest of Asia that is included in the target market of Evans.

Evans's management must consider how important the protection of the technology is to them. If it is very important, then perhaps a joint venture or IOR with possibly a component manufacturer may be the answer, especially if both firms have a considerable investment and both share in the benefits of the sales of the new product, that is there are mutual benefits.

If Evans is less concerned about protecting the technology, then a network with three or more partners is possible and, if so, then the question is 'Are the currently identified partners likely to be the best ones?'.

If the technology is easily copied, but it is a product that is useful to the rest of Asia, perhaps the rest of the world, then Evans needs to recoup its investment and generate profits as quickly as possible. Under these circumstances, perhaps licensing might be the best course of action. This represents a low-cost strategy for Evans who, while not being able to receive their full economic benefit from their invention, could yield good profits and enhance their reputation.

With regard to *question 2*, if Zercon was approached to become a member of the network they should be pleased because they have an input into a product which is state of the art and this means they are likely to enjoy a steady, indirect demand for their components into the future. They will learn about a new technology and from their point of view it is ideal to have a buyer dependent on the one keeping the secret. The power balance is the right way round for Zercon. They could even 'outlearn' Evans.

Zercon may be concerned about the size and reputation of Tran Holdings, but they might intend to persuade Evans to seek another partner, especially as Tran Holdings is not entirely suitable for Evans's requirements (see Question 1). Zercon is likely to do everything possible to encourage Evans to pursue this venture, but hopefully with a different Asian partner. Zercon is likely to try and persuade Evans to minimize any penalties related to patent protection unless the arrangement was a joint venture or IOR, and they might be prepared to consider making some credible commitments to secure Evans's trust. Probably Zercon would prefer a consortia or separate company to a joint venture as the returns are likely to be similar, but the risk to them is much less.

With regard to *question 3*, Tran Holdings would have little risk if they became involved in the venture because if it is successful their casting sales would grow, and if it failed they would not suffer any real consequences.

Tran Holdings would like the idea of controlling the Asian market entry. Evans would be dependent on them and this is a good balance in the relationship for Tran Holdings.

They would try to persuade Evans to use Formax rather than Zercon as:

- they know Formax well and can work with them;
- they also know that Formax is an SME and is therefore potentially easily influenced by Tran Holdings;
- Zercon might be seen as an unwelcome competitor.

Perhaps Tran Holdings may not plan to act opportunistically, but if they did then controlling the market and being able to influence Formax, which is a small company, seems to be a good idea and has all the potential of creating a kingdom network. Tran Holdings has a reputation as operating as a lead firm. Tran Holdings might not feel it has to consider making credible commitments with SMEs unless it sees significant long-term benefits from the network. Tran Holdings is likely to limit its commitment to contractual guarantees.

The case study illustrates the complexities of networking, and also that practice not informed by theory can be very dangerous, as we showed in Chapter 1, and throughout the book.

References

Alter, C. and Hage, G. (1993) *Organizations Working Together*, Newbury Park, CA.: Sage.

Anderson, J. and Narus, J. (1990) 'Model of distributor firm and manufacturer working partnership', *Journal of Marketing* January: 42–58.

Bleeke, J. and Ernst, D. (1995) 'Is your strategic alliance really a sale?', *Harvard Business Review* January–February: 97–105.

Borys, B. and Jemison, D. (1989) 'Hybrid arrangements as strategic alliances: Theoretical issues in organizational combinations', *Academy of Management Review* 14(2): 234–49.

Burke, J. (1990) *Networking*, a discussion paper for the Australian Manufacturing Council, March.

Buttery, A. and Leung, T. (1998) 'The difference between Chinese and Western negotiations', *European Journal of Marketing* 32(3/4): 374–389.

Buttery, E. and A. (1995) *The Dynamics of the Network Situation*, Canberra AusIndustry Business Networks Program.

Buttery, E. and Buttery, A. (1994) *Business Networks*, Melbourne: Longman Business & Professional.

David, F.R. (1993) *Concepts of Strategic Management* (fourth edition), New York: Macmillan.

De Laat, P. (1997) 'Research and development alliances: Ensuring trust by mutual commitments', in Ebers, M. (ed.), *The Formation of Inter-Organizational Networks*, New York: Oxford University Press.

Doz, Y., Hamel, G. and Prahalad, C. (1989) ' Collaborate with your competitors and win', *Harvard Business Review* January–February: 133–9.

Dwyer, R., Schurr, P. and Oh, S. (1987) 'Developing buyer-seller relationships', *Journal of Marketing* 51: 11–27.

Dyer, J.H. (1996) 'Does governance matter? Keiretsu alliances and asset specificity as sources of Japanese competitive advantage', *Organizational Science* 7(6): 649–66.

Dyer, J.H. and Singh, H. (1996) 'The relational view: Relational rents and sources of interorganizational competitive advantage', paper presented at Academy of Management Meeting, Cincinatti, May: 1–28.

Ebers, M. (1997) *The Formation of Inter-Organizational Networks*, New York: Oxford University Press.

Ebers, M. and Grandori, A. (1997) 'The forms, costs and development dynamics of inter-organizational networking', in Ebers, M. (ed.), *The Formation of Inter-Organizational Networks*, New York: Oxford University Press.

Fulop, L. (1992) 'Small enterprises in Australia', in Fulop, L. with Frith, F. and Hayward, H., *Management for Australian Business: A Critical Text*, Melbourne: Macmillan.

Fulop, L. (1998) *Networks: The Next Generation*, a report prepared for AusIndustry Business Networks Program, Canberra, (full report unpublished).

Fulop, L. with Kelly, J. (1995) *A Survey of Industry Network Initiatives in NSW – Final Report*, A Strengthening Local Economic Capacity Project (SLEC), A Commonwealth Department of Housing and Regional Development Initiative, Canberra.

Fulop, L. with Kelly, J. (1997a) *Study of Business Networks in Australia – An Indepth Investigation: Summary Report*, Sydney: Australian Business Chamber.

Fulop, L. with Kelly, J. (1997b) *A Study of Business Networks in Australia – An Indepth Investigation: Main Report*, Sydney: Australian Business Chamber.

Galbraith, J.K. (1974) *The New Industrial State*, Boston: Houghton-Mifflin.

Grabher, G. (1993) 'Rediscovering the social in the economics of interfirm relations', in Grabher, g. (ed.), *The Embedded Firm: On the Socioeconomics of Industrial Networks,* London and New York: Routledge.

Grandori, A. and Soda, G. (1995) 'Inter-firm networks: Antecedents, mechanisms and forms', *Organization Studies* 16(2): 183–214.

Granovetter, M. (1985) 'Economic action and social structure: The problem of embeddedness', *American Journal of Sociology* 91(3): 481–510.

Hamel, G. (1991) 'Competition for competence and life-partner learning within international strategic alliances', *Strategic Management Journal* 12: 83–103.

Hardy, C., Phillips, N. and Lawrence, T. (1996) 'Forms and façades of trust: Distinguishing trust and power in interorganisational relations', paper presented at 'Diversity & Change: Challenges for Management into the 21st Century', Australian and New Zealand Academy of Management (ANZAM) Conference, December, Wollongong, NSW, 4–7 December.

Harrigan, K. (1985) *Strategies for Joint Ventures*, Lexington, Mass: Lexington Books.

Hennart, J. (1988) 'A transaction cost theory of equity joint ventures', *Strategic Management Journal* 9: 361–374.

Hergert, M. and Morris, D. (1988) 'Trends in international collaborative agreements', in Contractor, F. and Lorange, P. (eds), *Cooperative Strategies in International Business*, Lexington, Mass.: Lexington Books.

Hofstede, G. (1991) *Cultures and Organisations: Software of the Mind*, London: McGraw-Hill.

Howard, R. (1990) 'Can small business help countries compete?', *Harvard Business Review* November–December: 88–103.

Huxham, C. (1993) 'Collaborative capability: An intra-organizational perspective on collaborative advantage', *Public Money and Management* July–September: 21–28.

Huxham, C. (1996) *Creating Collaborative Advantage*, London: Sage.

James, D. (1994) 'The struggle to make sense of a world beyond ideology', *Business Review Weekly* 31 January: 57–8.

Johannisson, B. and Mønsted, M. (1996) 'Networking in context – SMEs and networks in Scandinavia', Plenary Presentation of the 9th Nordic Small Business Conference, Lillehamer, Norway, 29–31 May.

Johnston, R. and Lawrence, P. (1988) 'Beyond vertical integration: The rise of the value-adding partnership', *Harvard Business Review* July–August: 94–101.

Kanter, R.M. (1989) *When Giants Learn to Dance*, New York: Simon and Schuster.

Kanter, R.M. (1994) 'Collaborative advantage: The art of alliances', *Harvard Business Review* July–August: 96–112.

Kay, J.A. (1993) *Foundations of Corporate Success: How Business Strategies Add Value*, Oxford. Oxford University Press.

Klein, B., Crawford, R.G. and Alchian, A.A. (1978) 'Vertical integration, appropriate rents and the competitive contracting process', *Journal of Law and Economics* 21: 297–325.

Kogurt, B. and Zander, U. (1988) 'Knowledge of the firm, combinative capabilities, and the replication of technology', *Organization Science* 3(3): 383–97.

Lasserre, P. and Boisot, M. (1980) 'Transfer of technology from Europe to Asean enterprises: Strategies and practices in the chemical and pharmaceutical sector', *Euro Asian Research Paper* 2, Fountainbleau, France.

Lasserre, P. and Schuette, H. (1995) *Strategies for Asia Pacific,* Melbourne: Macmillan Business.

Lei, D.T. (1997) 'Competence-building, technology fusion and competitive advantage: The key roles of organizational learning and strategic alliances', *International Journal of Technology Management* 14(2/3/4): 208–37.

Levinson, N. and Asahi, M. (1995) 'Cross national alliances and interorganisational learning', *Organizational Dynamics* Autumn: 50–63.

Lütz, S. (1997) 'Learning through intermediaries: The case of inter-firm research collaboration', in Ebers, M. (ed.), *The Formation of Inter-Organizational Networks*, New York: Oxford University Press.

Macneil, I.R. (1978) 'Contracts: Adjustment of long-term economic relations under classical, neoclassical and relational contract law', *Northwestern University Law Review* 72(6): 854–905.

Management: A Critical Text

Macneil, I.R. (1985) 'Relational contracts: What we do and do not know', *Wisconsin Law Review* 3: 483–526.

Mauss, M. (1967/1925) *The Gift*, New York: Norton.

Mitroff, I. and Linstone, H.A. (1993) *The Unbounded Mind: Breaking the Chains of Traditional Business Thinking*, New York: Oxford University Press.

Modic, S. (1988) 'Strategic alliances – a global economy demands global partnerships', *Industry Week* 3 October: 46–52.

Nanda, A. and Williamson, P. (1995) 'Using joint ventures to ease the pain of restructuring', *Harvard Business Review* November–December: 119–28.

Noorderhaven, N.G. (1992) 'The problem of contract enforcement in economic organization theory', *Organization Studies* 13(2): 229–43.

Nuevo, P. and Oosterveld, J. (1988) 'Managing technology alliances', *Long Range Planning* 21(31): 11–17.

Ouchi, W. (1980) 'Markets, bureaucracies and clans', *Administrative Science Quarterly* 20: 129–41.

Pache (1990) Abstract only sighted, reference unknown.

Parkhe, A. (1991) 'Interfirm diversity, organization learning and longevity in strategic alliances', *Journal of International Business Studies* 22(4): 579–601.

Piore, M.J. and Sabel, C.F. (1984) *The Second Industrial Divide: Possibilities for Prosperity*, New York: Basic Books.

Pollack, A. (1992) 'Technology without borders raises big questions for U.S.', *The New York Times* 1 January: 1.

Powell, W.W. (1990) 'Neither market nor hierarchy: Network forms of organization', *Research in Organisational Behaviour* 12: 295–336, Greenwich, CT: JAI Press.

Powell, W.W. (1996) 'Trust-based forms of governance', in Kramer, R. and Tyler, T. (eds), *Trust in Organizations*, Thousand Oaks, CA: Sage.

Prahalad, C.K. and Hamel, G. (1990) 'The core competence of the corporation', *Harvard Business Review* 68(3): 79–93.

Reve, T. (1995) 'Networks – the Norwegian way: An evaluation of the Norwegian Business Network Program', *Network News*, Issue 3 (December): 10–12 (Canberra: AusIndustry Business Network Program).

Ring, P.S. (1997a) 'Process facilitating reliance in trust in inter-organizational networks', in Ebers, M. (ed.), *The Formation of Inter-Organizational Networks*, New York: Oxford University Press.

Ring, P.S. (1997b) 'Transacting in the state of exchange governed by convergent interests', *Journal of Management Studies* 34(1): 1–25.

Ring, P.S. and Van de Ven, A.H. (1992) 'Structuring cooperative relationships between organizations', *Strategic Management Journal* 13: 483–98.

Ring, P.S. and Van de Ven, A.H. (1994) 'Developmental processes of cooperative interorganizational relationships', *Academy of Management Review* 19(1): 90–118.

Saxenian, A. (1990) 'Regional networks and the resurgence of Silicon Valley', *California Management Review* Fall: 89–112.

Scher, M.J. (1997) 'The limitations of 'trust-based' theories in Japan's interorganizational networks in the era of globalization', paper presented at 13th EGOS Colloquium: *Sub-Theme 2; Interorganizational Networks and Radical Environmental Change*, Budapest, July: 1–18.

Sengenberger, W., Loveman, G. and Piore, M. (1990) 'The re-emergence of small enterprise: Industrial restructuring', in *Industrialised Economies*, Geneva: International Labour Organisation (ILO).

Slocum, J.W., Jr, McGill, M. and Lei, D.T. (1994) 'The new learning strategy: Anytime, anything, anywhere', *Organizational Dynamics* Autumn: 33–47.

Vangen, S. and Huxham, C. (1995) 'Theory based approach for translating collaborative insight into practice' (Draft), *Second International Workshop on Multi-organisational Partnerships: Working Together Across Organisational Boundaries*, Glasgow, June: 4.

Williamson, O. (1979) 'Transaction cost economics: The governance of contractual relations', *Journal of Law and Economics* 22: 233–61.

Williamson, O. (1985) *The Economic Institutions of Capitalism: Firms, Markets and Relational Contracting*, New York: The Free Press.

Williamson, O. (1991) 'Strategizing, economizing and economic organization', *Strategic Management Journal* 2: 75–94.

Womack, J.P., Jones, D.T. and Roos, D. (1990) *The Massachusetts Institute of Technology 5 Million Dollar 5 Year Study on the Future of the Automobile Industry*, New York: Rawson Associates.

Work, C. (1988) 'Business without borders', *U.S. News and World Report* 20 June: 48.

Name index

Subject index